Inside
LANtastic 6.0

Kevin Stoltz

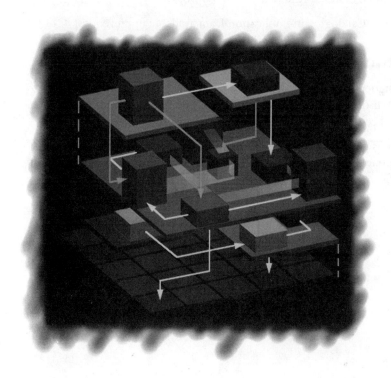

NEW RIDERS
PUBLISHING

New Riders Publishing, Indianapolis, Indiana

Inside LANtastic 6.0

By Kevin Stoltz

Published by:
New Riders Publishing
201 West 103rd Street
Indianapolis, IN 46290 USA

Printed in the United States of America   2 3 4 5 6 7 8 9 0

Library of Congress Cataloging-in-Publication Data available upon request

Warning and Disclaimer

This book is designed to provide information about the LANtastic computer program from Artisoft, Inc. Every effort has been made to make this book as complete and as accurate as possible, but no warranty or fitness is implied.

The information is provided on an "as is" basis. The author and New Riders Publishing shall have neither liability nor responsibility to any person or entity with respect to any loss or damages arising from the information contained in this book or from the use of the disks or programs that may accompany it.

Publisher
Lloyd J. Short

Associate Publisher
Tim Huddleston

Managing Editor
Matthew Morrill

Product Development Manager
Rob Tidrow

Marketing Manager
Ray Robinson

Director of Special Products
Cheri Robinson

Product Director
Emmett Dulaney
Drew Heywood

Acquisitions Editor
Alicia Krakovitz

Production Editor/Team Leader
Rob Lawson

Editors
Sarah Kearns
Cliff Shubs
Suzanne Snyder

Technical Editor
Robert Waring

Acquisitions Coordinator
Stacey Beheler

Editorial Assistant
Karen Opal

Publisher's Assistant
Melissa Lynch

Production Imprint Manager
Juli Cook

Cover Designer
Jay Corpus

Book Designer
Roger Morgan

Production Imprint Team Leader
Katy Bodenmiller

Proofreading Coordinator
Joelynn Gifford

Indexing Coordinator
Johnna VanHoose

Production Analysts
Mary Beth Wakefield
Dennis Clay Hager

Production Team

Carol Bowers	Elaine Brush
Ayrika Bryant	Kim Cofer
Lisa Daugherty	Steph Davis
Kimberly K. Hannel	Greg Kemp
Debbie Kincaid	Stephanie McComb
Jamie Milazzo	Casey Price
Ryan Rader	Kim Scott
Susan Shepard	Tonya R. Simpson
SA Springer	Dennis Wesner

Indexer
Greg Eldred

About the Author

Kevin Stoltz is an independent consultant specializing in LANtastic networks and system integration services for small businesses. He has been installing LANtastic networks for more than five years and is an Artisoft 5 Star dealer. He is also the leader of the Seattle area LANtastic User Group. He authored *Inside LANtastic 5.0*, co-authored *The Modem Coach*, and contributed to *Ultimate Windows 3.1*, and *Inside Lotus 1-2-3 for Windows 4.0*, all from New Riders Publishing.

Born and raised in Spokane, Washington, Kevin attended the University of Washington at Seattle where he received a degree in Aeronautical Engineering. He worked for the Boeing Company for more than six years as an engineer and systems analyst. He and his wife started CompuPlus, which now operates a VAR specializing in networking and system integration for small businesses.

Kevin lives with his wife, son, and daughter in Mukilteo, Washington.

Trademarks

All terms mentioned in this book that are known to be trademarks or service marks have been appropriately capitalized. New Riders Publishing cannot attest to the accuracy of this information. Use of a term in this book should not be regarded as affecting the validity of any trademark or service mark. LANtastic is a trademark of Artisoft, Inc.

Dedication

To my wife, Dana, for putting up with my "piles" and for remaining cheerful and supportive during this project. And to my children, Zak and Katie, for sacrificing having a father during the many weeks and long hours required to produce this book.

Acknowledgments

A special thanks to the many people whose hard work, dedication, and sacrifices made this book possible:

- ✔ Alicia Krakovitz, NRP Aquisitions Editor, for keeping the book on schedule and for constructive advice when unexpected circumstances occurred.

- ✔ Drew Heywood, Product Development Specialist, for initial development and suggestions for organization and content.

- ✔ Emmett Dulaney, Product Development Specialist, for the overall development and valuable contributions to this project.

- ✔ Rob Lawson, Team Leader and Production Editor, for managing the editorial flow and pre-production preparation of text in addition to his valuable suggestions which contributed to the success of this book.

- ✔ Sarah Kearns, Cliff Shubs, and Suzanne Snyder, NRP Copy Editors, for taking the time to "get it right." Thank you for helping to ensure this book's quality.

- ✔ The entire production staff of Macmillan Computer Publishing, whose hard work and long hours are appreciated.

- ✔ The many people at Artisoft, Inc., for their support and assistance to make this book possible. Special thanks to Joe Stunkard, Becky McKee, Claude Haynes, the technical support staff, and the engineering staff.

Contents at a Glance

Table of Contents

INTRODUCTION

I n the late 1970s and early 1980s, the introduction of the personal computer heralded major changes in the computer industry and in the way businesses operated. Until that time, many businesses relied on huge mainframe computers to perform all their computing needs. Although very powerful, mainframes were not friendly to the non-computer-literate user who needed to obtain information from the computer. Users often found that it was extremely time-consuming to get any computed results.

You might remember the process, or at least have heard about it. First, you keypunched your data onto cards, and then you handed over your input cards to a person in the computer room. This person loaded and ran your data at some point in the future, depending on the backlog, and you were assigned a time to pick up your reports. At the appointed hour, you rushed to get your printouts and cards, hoping that a message did not appear in red on your printout sheets, such as a "data error in line 48." If you were lucky, you got a usable report. If not, you had to figure out where your data went wrong before you could resubmit the corrected cards. The process was very frustrating.

Over time, users demanded better and easier access to data. They were provided with *terminals* (screens with attached keyboards connected by cable to the mainframe), at which they could enter their data directly into the computer. Each user attached to the mainframe had to wait for the central processing unit (CPU) to phase them in (wait for a free cycle of the CPU) before it accepted their input for processing; therefore, some delay still existed in obtaining output.

Getting the output became easier when printers were located near the user's terminal or centrally located in a room where users could pick up their printouts as the computer generated them. You might find it hard to imagine doing business this way now, but a few years ago this setup was considered "high-tech."

IBM gave personal computing a kick start with the introduction of the IBM PC in 1981. *End users* (the individual workers who needed computed information) suddenly found that they had access to vast computing power right on their desktops—the business world was changed forever.

By the mid-1980s, individuals were conceiving all kinds of uses for their new powerhouses. Development of more sophisticated software applications, such as spreadsheet and database-management programs, set loose a firestorm of user demand for data and processing power. Everyone, it seemed, was "crunching numbers."

Software companies sprang up and began to develop new and more powerful software to meet the growing user demand. The battle for software market control was on, and a giant industry was born.

By the end of the 1980s, the emphasis within the business and computer world had forever shifted to the individual worker's desktop, thus relegating the once-dominant mainframes to a position of lesser importance. The rapidity of these changes was breathtaking. New developments seemed to emerge weekly—sometimes daily—and keeping abreast of the latest innovations became an enormous chore in itself. This phenomenon still continues today.

After individual workers were able to take on and solve enormous computing problems themselves, they began to want to exchange ideas and information with co-workers. Carrying a disk from one computer to another or exchanging paper printouts was too cumbersome and risky. Workers wanted to send notes to each other, to share files electronically, and to share the expensive laser printers and other peripheral equipment available to them.

A new term emerged to describe these capabilities: connectivity. The solution to the connectivity issue was the *local area network* (LAN). The designers of LANs borrowed from the ideas of their mainframe counterparts to link together physically separated PCs by using cables and software applications. The LAN era was born.

A LAN consists of two or more computers that are connected by a high-speed communication medium, usually a cable. In addition to the software that normally runs on a workstation (DOS, applications, and so on), a LAN includes a *network operating system* (NOS) that enables the computers on the LAN to share files, printers, and other resources. The network operating system also can provide security, electronic mail, and other services.

Many NOSs are big and expensive, and they require you to dedicate a PC to function as the network file server. You cannot use this PC as a workstation. The most popular NOS is Novell NetWare, which supports the needs of the most demanding network users. In many cases, however, the cost of a high-end NOS and a dedicated server is difficult to justify. If you do not need all the features and power of a high-end network operating system, you probably should not pay the price.

Artisoft's LANtastic NOS is the leader in providing the most important network services inexpensively. Although LANtastic costs only a fraction of the price of a "high-end" NOS, LANtastic is a robust, full-featured NOS offering most of the features found in the more expensive NOSs, and then some.

What Is LANtastic?

In 1987, Artisoft released its first version of LANtastic. LANtastic is a DOS-based NOS that enables connected computers to communicate in a peer-to-peer network configuration. *Peer-to-peer* means that each computer on the network is of equal status and can share its resources with all other computers on the network and vice versa. Since its release, LANtastic has won awards for technical excellence and simplicity. It is a very sophisticated and powerful package implemented in a deceivingly simple manner.

You usually purchase LANtastic in a complete "starter kit" that includes the network software, interface cards to go in your computers, and cabling to connect them together. Chapter 4, "Artisoft Network Products," provides a detailed description of the Artisoft network products available.

Who Should Read This Book?

Inside LANtastic 6.0 gives the reader with little or no networking background a strong working knowledge of LANtastic. It provides a good foundation of the networking concepts and terms required without getting too heavy into the details and technical jargon. The intent is to provide the foundation necessary to understand and accomplish the tasks required to successfully plan and implement your LANtastic network.

Inside LANtastic 6.0 is written in an organized and easy to understand format that takes you from learning what a network is, through the planning and implementation of a LANtastic network. After your LANtastic network is up and operational, this book will serve as a valuable reference, providing the LANtastic commands as well as tips and techniques for maintaining the network and troubleshooting any problems you may encounter.

Inside LANtastic 6.0 also is an excellent reference for anyone already familiar with LANtastic. There are separate sections for the LANtastic command reference and the LANtastic products available. The well-organized and indexed chapters also make it easy to find the tips and techniques that may be required when upgrading or maintaining your LANtastic network.

In addition, *Inside LANtastic 6.0* includes complete coverage of both the DOS and Windows implementations of LANtastic. The DOS and Windows coverage is divided into separate sections in each chapter, which are independent of each other so the readers can read the appropriate section for their situation.

This book assumes the reader has a good working knowledge of DOS. Because LANtastic is a DOS-based network operating system, it uses DOS-like commands for network functions. Understanding the DOS directory structure and the common DOS commands used to manipulate files and directories is essential to truly understanding LANtastic.

How This Book Is Organized

Inside LANtastic 6.0 is designed for use as a tutorial and as a reference guide to augment the Artisoft manuals that come with the software and network adapter cards. Each chapter in this book covers a specific topic, progressing from introductory ideas to the more complex issues associated with network use and management.

Chapter 1, "Quick Start," is a step-by-step checklist that enables you to set up a basic two-computer LANtastic network in under an hour. By following the steps outlined in this chapter, you can accomplish a successful LANtastic installation without reading a great deal of technical documentation. Thorough instructions guide you through each step, with tips on how to best configure the setup.

Chapter 2, "Learning the Basics," gives you the basic information you need to understand what networks are and how they work. The information contained in this chapter serves as the foundation on which additional network knowledge is built.

Chapter 3, "Planning Your LANtastic Network," gets you started on the right foot. This chapter covers all the considerations and preliminary planning required to ensure that your final LANtastic installation is everything you envisioned it to be.

Chapter 4, "Artisoft Network Products," reviews the various hardware and software LANtastic products available from Artisoft.

Chapter 5, "Installing a LANtastic Network," covers the installation of your LANtastic network hardware and the LANtastic for DOS and LANtastic for Windows software.

Chapter 6, "Setting Up User Accounts and Shared Resources in DOS," shows you how to add users to the network and how to enable users to share network resources using the DOS LANtastic Network Manager Program. It also covers how to set up and configure resources to be shared with other computers.

Chapter 7, "Setting Up User Accounts and Shared Resources in Windows," covers the same information as Chapter 6, using the Windows LANtastic Network Manager program.

Chapter 8, "Using Disk Drives and Printers," explains what to do now that the network is running. You learn the basics of accessing and using network resources, such as disk drives and printers.

Chapter 9, "Using LANtastic to Communicate with Others and Manage Your Account," explains how to use the communication productivity tools, such as electronic mail and CHAT.

Chapter 10, "Printing with LANtastic," picks up where Chapter 8 left off in the discussion of LANtastic printing. This chapter provides a detailed look at the process of network printing and the options available.

Chapter 11, "Managing Your Network Using the LANtastic Network Manager," examines network administration in detail. The basic server configuration is sufficient in many situations, but you might need to know more to enhance security, improve performance features, or enable some applications you might use on the network.

Chapter 12, "Installing and Configuring LANtastic with Windows," discusses how to install Windows after you have installed LANtastic. This chapter also shows you how to configure LANtastic and Microsoft Windows to work best together. Although LANtastic and Windows work nicely together, you should know a few things before you jump in.

Chapter 13, "Using Artisoft Exchange," shows you how to use the new sophisticated Exchange Mail and Scheduler programs to maximize your productivity with LANtastic.

Chapter 14, "Using NET Command Line Commands," explains the 37 NET commands and shows you how to perform many LANtastic network functions from the command line. You can put these commands into batch files to automate operations that are often repeated.

Chapter 15, "Getting the Most out of LANtastic," shows you how to use some of the special features provided with LANtastic, and discusses how LANtastic and other hardware and software can work together to increase your productivity. Network optimization and a special section on tips and tricks will allow you to obtain even greater performance and flexibility from your LANtastic network.

Chapter 16, "Troubleshooting Your Network," gives you a plan for dealing with network failures. Network troubles are inevitable; however, by using the right approach, you can usually restore your network's health quickly.

Appendix A, "Network Adapter Configuration," discusses the hardware interrupt (IRQ) and I/O address requirements for your network adapters. Configuring the Artisoft NodeRunner adapters using the NRSETUP program is also covered.

Appendix B, "Glossary," defines a number of terms you need to know as you work with your LANtastic network.

Conventions Used in This Book

Throughout this book, certain conventions help you distinguish the various elements of LANtastic and DOS. Before you begin reading, take a few moments now to examine these conventions:

- ✔ Information that you type is in **boldface**. This convention applies to individual letters and numbers, as well as text strings. This convention, however, does not apply to special keys, such as Enter, Esc, and Ctrl.

- ✔ New terms appear in *italic*.

- ✔ Text that is displayed on-screen, such as prompts and messages, appears in a special typeface.

New Riders Publishing

The staff of New Riders Publishing is committed to bringing you the very best in computer reference material. Each New Riders book is the result of months of work by authors and staff, who research and refine the information contained within its covers.

As part of this commitment to you, the NRP reader, New Riders invites your input. Please let us know if you enjoy this bcok, if you have trouble with the information and examples presented, or if you have a suggestion for the next edition.

Please note, however, that the New Riders staff cannot serve as a technical resource for LANtastic application-related questions, including hardware- or software-related problems. Refer to the documentation that accompanies your LANtastic application package for help with specific problems.

If you have a question or comment about any New Riders book, please write to NRP at the following address. We will respond to as many readers as we can. Your name, address, or phone number will never become part of a mailing list or be used for any other purpose than to help us continue to bring you the best books possible.

New Riders Publishing
Attn: Associate Publisher
201 W. 103rd Street
Indianapolis, IN 46290

If you prefer, you can FAX New Riders Publishing at the following number:

(317) 571-4670

You can send electronic mail to New Riders from a variety of sources. NRP maintains several mailboxes organized by topic area. Mail in these mailboxes will be forwarded to the staff member who is best able to address your concerns. Substitute the appropriate mailbox name from the list below when addressing your e-mail. The mailboxes are as follows:

ADMIN	Comments and complaints for NRP's Publisher
APPS	Word, Excel, WordPerfect, other office applications
ACQ	Book proposals inquiries by potential authors
CAD	AutoCAD, 3D Studio, AutoSketch and CAD products
DATABASE	Access, dBASE, Paradox and other database products
GRAPHICS	CorelDRAW!, Photoshop, and other graphics products
INTERNET	Internet
NETWORK	NetWare, LANtastic, and other network-related topics
OS	MS-DOS, OS/2, all OS except Unix and Windows
UNIX	Unix
WINDOWS	Microsoft Windows (all versions)
OTHER	Anything that doesn't fit the above categories

If you use an MHS e-mail system that routes through CompuServe, send your messages to:

    mailbox @ NEWRIDER

To send NRP mail from CompuServe, use the following to address:

    MHS: *mailbox* @ NEWRIDER

We also welecome your electronic mail to our CompuServe ID:

    74507,3713

To send mail from the Internet, use the following address format:

    mailbox@newrider.mhs.compuserve.com

NRP is an imprint of Macmillan Computer Publishing. To obtain a catalog or information, or to purchase any Macmillan Computer Publishing book, call (800)428-5331.

Thank you for selecting *Inside LANtastic 6.0*!

Chapter Snapshot

This chapter is for individuals who must get their LANtastic network up and running immediately. Discussion is limited to the bare essentials, and the general format is that of a numbered checklist. You learn about the following in this chapter:

✔ Installing the Network Cards

✔ Installing the Network Cable

✔ Installing LANtastic in DOS

✔ Installing LANtastic in Windows

✔ Running LANcheck

By following these steps, you should be able to complete a basic two-computer LANtastic installation in less than an hour.

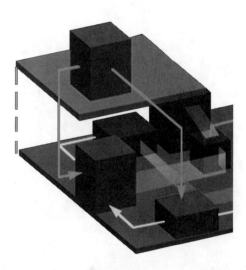

CHAPTER

Quick Start

The LANtastic version 6.0 installation program may be installed either from DOS or in Windows. If installed from DOS, the installation program will search your path for Windows; if Windows resides on your machine, it will run the LANtastic Windows installation program. This chapter includes directions for installing either LANtastic from DOS or LANtastic in Windows.

Prior to LANtastic version 5.0, you always installed LANtastic for DOS. LANtastic for Windows was a separate utility program that was installed within Windows. Although LANtastic for Windows was not required for LANtastic network functions to work with Windows, it did provide a flexible and easy-to-use interface for LANtastic network functions.

Beginning with LANtastic version 5.0, you could purchase either LANtastic for Windows or LANtastic for DOS. The LANtastic for DOS installation didn't change. LANtastic for Windows, however, was installed entirely from within Windows and included everything that came with LANtastic for DOS.

LANtastic 6.0 includes both the DOS and Windows versions of LANtastic. The installation program automatically detects whether or not Windows is installed and installs LANtastic accordingly. As with LANtastic 5.0, if LANtastic is installed for Windows, all the LANtastic DOS programs and functions are installed and available from DOS.

To set up your LANtastic network quickly, the following items must be true:

✔ You purchased a LANtastic 6.0 network starter kit (which includes NodeRunner/SI 2000/C network adapters) for DOS, a LANtastic for Windows NodeRunner 2000/C Starter Kit, or an AE-2 Starter Kit.

✔ You are connecting two computers located within one room and not more than 25 feet apart. (If computers are located in separate rooms, more time will be required to run the cable through the ceiling or the wall.)

✔ You are installing the LANtastic network interface adapter cards and software in 80286-, 80386-, or 80486-based computers with at least 640 KB of RAM.

✔ No conflicts exist with any of the adapter's default settings. (80286-, 80386-, and 80486-based computers provide additional memory interrupts [IRQs] 10 and 15—Artisoft now uses IRQ 15 as its default for its adapters.)

If your computer does not meet these basic requirements, you cannot use the Quick Start checklist. If your system differs from this setup, see Chapter 5, "Installing a LANtastic Network," for detailed instructions to help you install LANtastic for your configuration.

Quick Start Checklist

The following sections provide you with step-by-step instructions for setting up a basic LANtastic installation. You learn to install the network cards, cable, and the LANtastic software.

Installing the Network Cards

To set up your LANtastic network, you must first install your network interface cards (NICs) in each computer. To install the cards, follow these steps:

1. Check the two interface adapter cards (one for each computer) to ensure that you have two BNC terminator plugs and one BNC T connector for each adapter card.

2. Remove the T connector from each of the adapter cards (Artisoft ships the interface cards with the T connectors already installed), and set them aside.

3. Turn off your computer and remove the case.

4. Locate an available bus expansion slot (look for a long 16-bit expansion slot) and remove the rear cover plate for that expansion slot.

5. Ground yourself to drain off any static electricity by touching the power supply case inside the computer. The power supply case is the big silver box usually located in the back-right corner of your computer.

6. Carefully grasp the interface card by the upper edge near each end, place it in the bus expansion slot, and press down firmly to ensure that it sits fully in the slot. Fasten the card's rear-mounting bracket to the rear cover of the computer with the screw you removed from the rear slot cover in step 4.

7. Reinstall the computer's case, and plug in the power cord.

8. Repeat steps 3 through 7 to install the other interface adapter card in the second computer.

Installing the Network Cable

After you successfully install the network cards, you can install the cabling that you will use. Follow these steps to install the cable:

1. Reinstall the BNC T connectors to the BNC connector on the back of the two network interface adapter cards (see fig. 1.1).

Figure 1.1
Location of BNC
connector on a
NodeRunner/
SI 2000/C
Ethernet card.

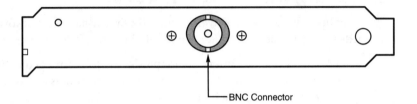
BNC Connector

2. Uncoil the coaxial cable that came with your starter kit.

3. Stretch the cable out behind the tables or desks on which you want to install the computers. Make sure that the cable contains no kinks.

4. Connect the BNC connector on one end of the cable to one side of the T connector on the back of the first computer's network interface card.

5. Place a terminator plug on the other end of the T connector.

Always use the BNC T connectors, even though the cable will connect directly to the back of the network interface card. Your LANtastic network will not operate properly without the use of the BNC T connectors and the associated terminator plugs.

6. Connect the other end of the cable to one end of the T connector on the second computer, and install the second terminator plug to the open end of the second computer's T connector.

Installing LANtastic in DOS

You are now ready to install the LANtastic software. This section describes the installation of LANtastic in DOS. If you have Microsoft Windows on your computer, refer to the next section, "Installing LANtastic in Windows," for installation instructions.

When installing LANtastic in DOS, if the LANtastic installation program finds Windows on your computer, it will start Windows and run the LANtastic Windows installation program, regardless of the fact that you were attempting to do so in DOS.

The LANtastic software must be installed on each computer. To complete the installation, follow these steps:

1. Use the DOS DISKCOPY command to make a working copy of the LANtastic NOS disks. Place the original disks in a safe place.

2. Place the LANtastic NOS disk 1 working copy in drive A of the computer. Type from the C:> prompt **A:INSTALL**, and then press Enter.

 The LANtastic 6.0 installation program will search for Microsoft Windows in your path and, if found, will automatically run the LANtastic Windows installation program.

3. After the LANtastic version 6.0 installation screen appears, press any key. The installation process begins.

   The installation program prompts you to enter information in each of several screens. Each installation screen explains what information is to be entered. Where applicable, the installation program lists a default value. The default value listed is appropriate for most systems, but this default value may be changed if desired.

4. Type the name of the computer on which you are working and press Enter at the Enter computer name field (see fig. 1.2).

   The name you give your computer is the name it will be known as in the network and may contain up to 15 characters. DOS delimiter characters such as commas, colons, semicolons, and spaces are not allowed. 386-25, ZAK, STATION1, and KATIES-PC are examples of names that may be given to your computer.

5. At the next screen, select the drive onto which you want LANtastic installed. Select drive C: and press Enter.

6. Next, you are prompted for the directory in which the LANtastic files will be installed. Accept the default \LANTASTI directory and press Enter.

```
              LANtastic  Version 6.00  INSTALLATION

       Each computer in the LANtastic network requires a
       name.  No two names in one network should be the same.
       Usually, people use some variation of their own name
       for their computer.  Or computers could be named by
       location (e.g. UPSTAIRS) or function (e.g. GAMES).
       Please name your computer now with a word containing
       up to fifteen letters with no spaces.


          ═══════════Enter computer name═══════════
          │ ZAK                                    │
```

7. You are then asked if you want to share your disk drives or printers with others. Accept the Share my computer's drives or printers option and press Enter.

When you choose to share your computer's disk drives or printers with others in the network, you are configuring your computer as a server. If you choose not to share your computer's disk drives or printers with others in the network, you are configuring your computer as a workstation. A workstation can only use the resources on other LANtastic servers; it is not capable of sharing its own resources with other users.

Unless your computer does not have a hard disk, you will generally want to configure it as a server so it can share its resources with others.

8. In the next screen, you are asked for the maximum number of computers that will be permitted to connect to your computer at once. Accept the default Keep maximum connected computers at 10 option and press Enter.

9. The last of the installation screens enables you to select additional LANtastic features that connect you to servers in other networks, including Novell NetWare, Windows NT, LAN Manager, and others. In addition, an option called Load files to enable "Install Services," once loaded, permits other network users to connect to your computer to run the LANtastic installation program. Select the Load files to enable "Install Services" option by highlighting it using your arrow keys, and then selecting it by pressing the spacebar. Press Enter to continue.

Artisoft Exchange is Artisoft's sophisticated mail and scheduling program that runs in Microsoft Windows. Although you cannot run Exchange in DOS, a computer not running Windows may be used as a post office for Artisoft Exchange mail. Select the Artisoft Exchange - Mail Post Office option to use this computer as a post office for Artisoft Exchange.

10. A screen appears, showing your selections (see fig 1.3). Select OK to continue with installation and press Enter.

Figure 1.3
Summary of installation options already selected.

11. Next, you are prompted to select the network adapter installed. Accept the default LANtastic NodeRunner 2000 Series Ethernet Adapter option and press Enter.

12. The next screen asks if you want to set up drive or printer connections. Accept the Set up permanent drive or printer connections option and press Enter.

13. Now you are asked to enter the name of the other computer that has the disk drive to which you want to connect. Enter the network name of the other computer and press Enter. In this example, assume KATIE is the name of the other computer.

14. You are now prompted to enter the name of the drive resource on the computer to which you want to connect. Accept the default C-drive drive name and press Enter.

15. Next, you are asked to enter the drive letter you will use to connect to the C-DRIVE resource on computer KATIE. Accept the default D-drive letter and press Enter.

In choosing a disk drive letter to use when accessing the shared disk drives on another computer, choose a letter not assigned to a physical drive already existing on your computer.

16. You are now prompted to enter the name of another computer with a drive you want to use. Press Enter to continue without establishing a connection to another computer's drive.

When default disk drive or printer connections are selected as described, a line is inserted in the STARTNET.BAT file created in the LANTASTI directory to make the connection when the network is started. You can change the STARTNET.BAT file at any time to add, remove, or change the default printer or disk drive connections.

17. The next screen prompts you to enter the name of the computer that has the printer you want to use. Enter the name and press Enter. In this example, assume KATIE is the name of the computer.

18. Next, you are prompted to enter the name of the printer on KATIE to which you want to connect. Accept the default @PRINTER name and press Enter.

19. You are then asked to enter the printer port on your computer that you will connect to the @PRINTER resource on KATIE. Type **LPT2** and press Enter.

20. A summary screen is now shown listing the selections you have made so far (see fig 1.4). Press Enter to continue.

21. The next screen explains that your CONFIG.SYS and AUTOEXEC.BAT files will be changed. Also listed is the name to which your previous CONFIG.SYS and AUTOEXEC.BAT files will be changed. Press any key to perform the installation.

    The files display on-screen as they are loaded onto your computer's hard disk. You are prompted, when necessary, to enter the next disk.

22. When the installation finishes, LANtastic displays a summary screen stating that the installation is complete, and prompts you to press any key to continue.

23. Finally, a screen appears stating that your computer will be rebooted. Press any key and your computer will be rebooted. LANtastic will be started when your computer boots.

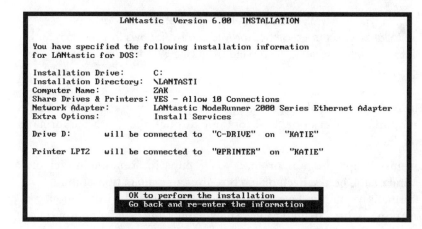

Figure 1.4
Summary of installation options.

You have completed the installation of LANtastic on your computer. The LANtastic installation program has created a batch file located in the LANTASTI directory called STARTNET.BAT, which contains the commands necessary to load the LANtastic software and establish the desired default printer and disk drive connections. The installation program has also changed your CONFIG.SYS file and added the following line to your AUTOEXEC.BAT file so LANtastic will automatically start each time your computer is booted:

```
call C:\LANTASTI\STARTNET.BAT
```

Installing LANtastic in Windows

You now are ready to install the LANtastic software. The LANtastic software must be installed on each computer. Installing LANtastic in Windows installs the LANtastic DOS software in addition to the LANtastic Windows software. To complete the installation, follow these steps:

1. Use the DOS DISKCOPY command to make a working copy of the LANtastic NOS disks. Place the original disks in a safe place.

2. Place the LANtastic NOS disk 1 working copy in your computer's drive A.

From Windows Program Manager, select **F**ile, then **R**un; type **A:INSTALL** in the Run dialog box, and select OK. Alternatively, type **A:INSTALL** at the C:> DOS prompt.

When typing **A:INSTALL** at the DOS prompt, the LANtastic 6.0 installation program searches for Microsoft Windows in your path and, if found, will automatically run the LANtastic Windows installation program.

3. The Artisoft Install Message dialog box appears, congratulating you on your purchase. Click on OK to continue through the first two informa-tion dialog boxes.

   The installation program prompts you to enter information in each of several dialog boxes. Each dialog box gives an explanation of the information that is to be entered. When applicable, the installation program will list a default value. The default value listed is appropriate for most systems, but this default value may be changed if desired.

4. The Enter computer name dialog box appears. Enter the network name you want to give to your computer, then click on OK or press Enter (see fig 1.5).

   The name you choose to give your computer is the name it will be known as in the network and may contain up to 15 characters. DOS delimiter characters such as commas, colons, semicolons, and spaces are not allowed. 386-25, ZAK, STATION1, and KATIES-PC are ex-amples of names that may be given to your computer.

Figure 1.5
Entering the network name of your computer.

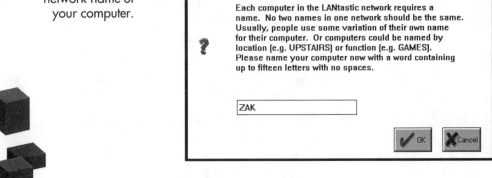

5. The Enter target drive dialog box appears, displaying the drives available on your computer. Accept the default drive C: option and click on OK or press Enter to continue.

6. Next, the Enter directory dialog box appears, showing the \LANTASTI directory as the location to install the LANtastic files. Accept this and click on OK or press Enter to continue.

7. The Share drives and printers dialog box appears, asking whether you want to share your computer's disk drives or printers with others in the network. Accept the default Share my computer's drives or printers option, and click on OK or press Enter.

> When you choose to share your computer's disk drives or printers with others in the network, you are configuring your computer as a server. If you choose not to share your computer's disk drives or printers with others in the network, you are configuring your computer as a workstation. A workstation can use only the resources on other LANtastic servers; it is not capable of sharing its own resources with other users.
>
> Unless your computer does not have a hard disk, you will generally want to configure it as a server so it can share its resources with others.

8. The next dialog box asks for the maximum number of computers that will be allowed to connect to your computer at one time. Accept the default Keep maximum connected computers at 10 option, and click on OK or press Enter.

9. The Select all that apply dialog box enables you to select additional LANtastic features that include permitting you to connect to servers in other networks including Novell NetWare, Windows NT, LAN Manager, and others. Select the Artisoft Exchange—Mail and Scheduler, and the Load files to enable "Install Services" options by clicking on each one. Click on OK or press Enter to continue.

10. The Select Artisoft Exchange Mail option dialog box appears. Accept the default Artisoft Exchange—Mail Client option and click on OK or press Enter.

If using the Artisoft Exchange Mail or Schedule programs, one computer in your network will need to be set up as a post office. If the computer at which you are sitting will be the post office, select the Artisoft Exchange—Mail Post Office option instead of the Artisoft Exchange—Mail Client option.

11. Next, the Enter name of computer that has post office dialog box appears. Enter the network name of the computer that you have chosen to have the post office, and click on OK or press Enter. For this example, assume that computer 386-25 will have the post office.

12. The LANtastic Information Check dialog box appears, showing the information you have specified so far (see fig. 1.6). Accept the default OK to continue with the installation option, and click on OK or press Enter to continue.

Figure 1.6
Summary of installation options already selected.

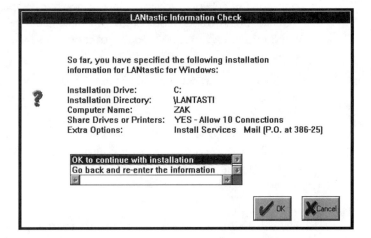

13. The Select network adapter dialog box appears, listing the available network adapters. Accept the default LANtastic NodeRunner 2000 Series Ethernet Adapter option and click on OK or press Enter.

14. The Set up drive or printer connections dialog box appears, enabling you to specify whether or not you want to set up permanent drive or printer connections. Accept the default Set up permanent drive or printer connections, and click on OK or press Enter.

15. In the Enter computer name dialog box, enter the name of the other computer possessing the drive you want to use. In this example, assume KATIE is the name of the other computer. Click on OK or press Enter to continue.

16. Now the Please enter drive name dialog box appears, asking for the name of the drive on KATIE you want to use. Accept the default C-drive name and click on OK or press Enter.

17. In the Enter drive letter dialog box, enter the drive letter you will use to connect to the C-DRIVE resource on computer KATIE. Accept the default D-drive letter and click on OK or press Enter.

In choosing a disk drive letter to use when accessing the disk drives on another computer, choose a letter that is not assigned to a physical drive that already exists on your computer.

18. Now the Enter computer name dialog box appears, asking for the name of another computer with a drive you want to use. This time, do not enter anything. Click on OK or press Enter to continue.

When default disk drive or printer connections are selected as described, a line is inserted in the STARTNET.BAT file created in the LANTASTI directory to make the connection when the network is started. You can change the STARTNET.BAT file at any time to add, remove, or change the default printer or disk drive connections.

19. The Enter computer name dialog box appears, asking the name of the computer with the printer attached that you want to use. Enter the name, then click on OK or press Enter. In this example, assume KATIE is the name of the computer.

20. In the Enter printer name dialog box, enter the name of the printer you want to use. Accept the default @PRINTER name and click on OK or press Enter.

21. In the Enter printer port dialog box, enter the printer port that you will connect to the @PRINTER resource on KATIE. Type **LPT2** and click on OK or press Enter.

22. The LANtastic Final Information Check dialog box appears, listing all the installation information you have specified (see fig 1.7). Accept the default OK to perform the installation option, and click on OK or press Enter to continue.

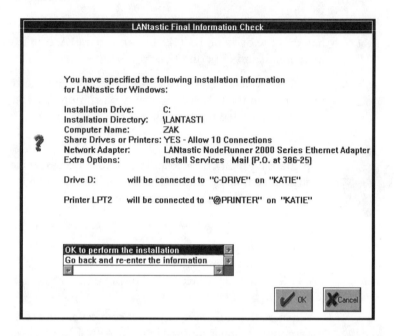

Figure 1.7
The LANtastic
Final Information
Check dialog
box.

23. The Artisoft Install Message dialog box appears, explaining that several of your system files will be changed and the names of the old files renamed. Click on OK or press Enter to perform the installation.

    The LANtastic files are now loaded on your computer's hard disk. You are prompted, when necessary, to enter the next disk.

24. When the installation finishes, the Artisoft Install Message dialog box appears, indicating the installation is complete. Click on OK or press Enter to continue.

25. Finally, the Artisoft Install Message dialog box appears, indicating that Install will shut down Windows and reboot your computer. Click on OK or press Enter to reboot your computer. LANtastic starts when your computer boots.

You have completed the installation of LANtastic on your computer. The LANtastic Windows installation program has created a batch file located in the LANTASTI directory called STARTNET.BAT, which contains the commands necessary to load the LANtastic software and establish the desired default printer and disk drive connections. The installation program has also changed your CONFIG.SYS file and added the following line to your AUTOEXEC.BAT file so LANtastic will automatically start each time your computer is booted:

```
call C:\LANTASTI\STARTNET.BAT
```

Up and Running

You now have completed your LANtastic installation. When you start each computer in your LANtastic network, the STARTNET.BAT file will be called from your AUTOEXEC.BAT file. STARTNET.BAT contains the commands necessary first to load your LANtastic network software and then to establish any default disk drive and printer connections you have specified.

For a detailed discussion of the commands in the STARTNET.BAT file and their purpose, refer to Chapter 5, "Installing a LANtastic Network."

When your computer starts, you will observe more information scrolling up your screen (see fig. 1.8). The information is displayed as the LANtastic network software is loaded.

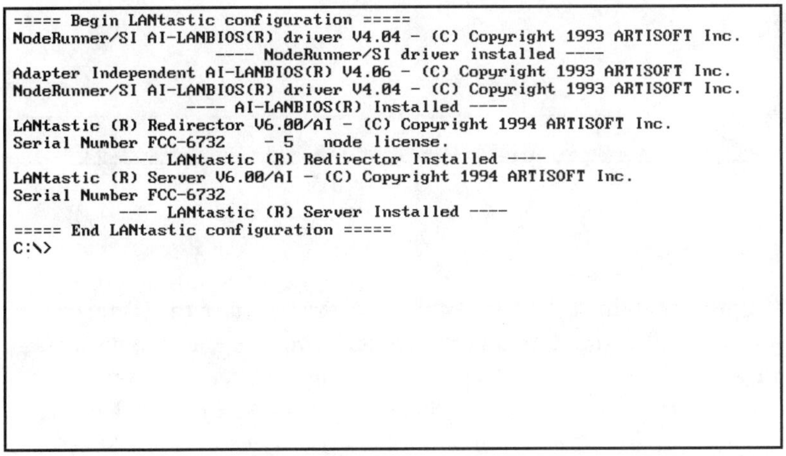

```
===== Begin LANtastic configuration =====
NodeRunner/SI AI-LANBIOS(R) driver V4.04 - (C) Copyright 1993 ARTISOFT Inc.
               ---- NodeRunner/SI driver installed ----
Adapter Independent AI-LANBIOS(R) V4.06 - (C) Copyright 1993 ARTISOFT Inc.
NodeRunner/SI AI-LANBIOS(R) driver V4.04 - (C) Copyright 1993 ARTISOFT Inc.
               ---- AI-LANBIOS(R) Installed ----
LANtastic (R) Redirector V6.00/AI - (C) Copyright 1994 ARTISOFT Inc.
Serial Number FCC-6732     - 5   node license.
          ---- LANtastic (R) Redirector Installed ----
LANtastic (R) Server V6.00/AI - (C) Copyright 1994 ARTISOFT Inc.
Serial Number FCC-6732
          ---- LANtastic (R) Server Installed ----
===== End LANtastic configuration =====
C:\>
```

Figure 1.8
The LANtastic network software loading.

Running LANcheck

After your computer has started and the LANtastic network software is running, you should perform one final, quick test to make sure that your network adapter cards are communicating properly across the network.

Included with LANtastic is a DOS-based program called LANcheck. LANcheck displays the network adapter status and an error index to help you determine if your network adapter cards are communicating properly. LANcheck should be run on each computer concurrently. To run LANcheck, type **LANCHECK** at the DOS prompt.

Figure 1.9 shows the main LANcheck information screen. Each computer that is running LANcheck should be displayed on the screen. The Status column for each computer should say either local or active. The Error-Index column should be either zero or close to zero.

Figure 1.9
The LANcheck
main screen.

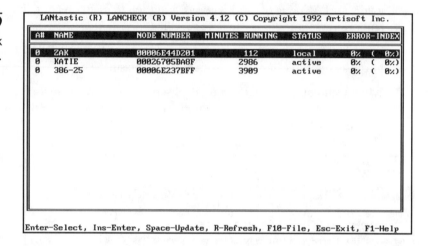

```
LANtastic (R) LANCHECK (R) Version 4.12 (C) Copyright 1992 Artisoft Inc.

A#  NAME          NODE NUMBER   MINUTES RUNNING   STATUS      ERROR-INDEX

0   ZAK           00006E44D201            112     local      0%  (  0%)
0   KATIE         00026705BA8F           2986     active     0%  (  0%)
0   386-25        00006E237BFF           3909     active     0%  (  0%)



Enter-Select, Ins-Enter, Space-Update, R-Refresh, F10-File, Esc-Exit, F1-Help
```

Summary

You now have completed the installation of the network interface cards, the coaxial cable that connects your computers, and the LANtastic software. Your network is complete and ready to use. Refer to Chapter 6, "Setting Up User Accounts and Shared Resources in DOS," or Chapter 7, "Setting Up User Accounts and Shared Resources in Windows," for information on setting up user accounts and shared resources. Enjoy the productivity gains of your new LANtastic network!

Chapter Snapshot

This chapter helps you learn network fundamentals and terminology so you can follow the installation and configuration steps in later chapters with ease. You will learn the methods used to enable different computers to share resources, such as disk drives and printers, with other computers on the network. You learn about the following in this chapter:

✔ Understanding what a network is

✔ Understanding why you would want a network and what it can do for you

✔ Understanding the way networks operate

✔ Exploring network components

✔ Examining the advantages and disadvantages of networking

✔ Exposing potential problems

After reading this chapter, you will have a good understanding of what a network is, how a network allows you to communicate with other computers, and how you can increase your productivity by implementing a network.

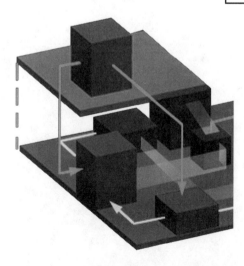

Learning the Basics

Imagine yourself in the following predicament. You have just come out of a
meeting in which your boss nominated you to install a new LANtastic network
system. He nominated you because he knows that you use a computer to get
your work done, but he doesn't know that you don't know anything about networks. So what do you do now?

Relax. This chapter familiarizes you with the capability and functionality of networks. The network fundamentals and terminology you learn in this chapter
enable you to follow the installation and configuration steps in later chapters with
ease. You discover what a network is and the way it works. You learn the fundamentals of accessing hard drives and printers connected to other computers. In
addition, you learn what the pieces of a network are and, toward the end of the
chapter, discover some of the advantages of a network and some of the trade-offs
in using one. Finally, you are presented with some thoughts about potential
problems that might occur when employing a network in your daily routine. By the
end of this chapter, you will have gained sufficient knowledge and confidence to
successfully complete the installation of your new LANtastic network.

Introducing the Network Concept

A *network* is basically two or more computers interconnected by a communications medium to enable data and other resources to be shared.

Although many types of networks exist, PC networks fall into two general types: local area networks (LANs) and wide area networks (WANs). As the name implies, LANtastic fits into the LAN group. The type of network is fairly well described by its title, but you need more information to adequately understand the differences.

LANs are used to connect microcomputers or PCs in close proximity (local) to each other. LANs can include PCs in the same room, PCs in several rooms on the same floor of a building, PCs in several rooms on multiple floors of a building, or PCs in several rooms on multiple floors of more than one building.

The key feature that differentiates LANs from WANs is the use of dedicated communication mediums to connect the network elements. The communication medium serves no other purpose than to provide data transfer between the elements. PCs (or elements) connected by the LAN are commonly referred to as *nodes* or *workstations.*

WANs are similar to LANs, but they use a combination of dedicated and nondedicated communication mediums to connect the elements. *Nondedicated mediums* are anything available, such as a telephone line or a microwave relay. Nondedicated mediums are not reserved solely for the network transmissions, hence the name.

WANs are not geographically limited in size. You can use them to connect LANs in different offices in the same city or to interconnect offices in different cities. Given the sophisticated satellite, infrared, microwave, and fiber-optic communication links available today, WANs easily can become global area networks. WANs, by sheer size and complexity, pose significant technological challenges for users, but the resulting business control and efficiency can be considerable.

WANs can use specialized hardware and software to include minicomputers and mainframe computers as elements on the network, in addition to the microcomputers of the LANs. As a result, WANs can have extremely powerful overall computational capability.

This book focuses on the LANtastic implementation of local area networking. A basic understanding of WANs can prepare you for which direction to head if your LANtastic network increases in size and you find it necessary to connect your LANtastic network to a WAN.

Understanding the Purpose of a LAN

A LAN enables previously separate computers to share disk drives, printers, and peripherals, which enables you to do the following:

✔ Store programs and data in a common location available to other users

✔ Have more than one person use the same program and associated data at a time

✔ Access and use printers connected to other computers

✔ Use electronic mail to communicate with others

✔ Transfer data between different computers and types of disk drives

By sharing disk drives and associated directories, you can choose a central location to store program and data files. A LAN also enables you to use a printer that is connected to a different computer. Not only is flexibility provided by the number and types of printers available to each computer, but it saves money by not requiring a printer for every computer.

CD-ROM drives are a popular means of accessing large amounts of data. If you have one CD-ROM drive on a LAN, you can access it from any other computer in the network.

Accounting is a good example of the way storing programs and data in one location for many users to access can be beneficial. By using the network version of a particular accounting software package, multiple users can access the accounting program and the data. This enables two people, for example, to enter invoices while a third person enters accounts receivable information. When the users print invoices, both of them can print to the same printer.

Another popular use of LANs is database management. Many companies maintain lists of clients or prospective clients in a database. A telemarketing team can call clients and notify them of a new product offering or a special that your company is running. Because the database is stored in a common location, every user on the LAN has access to the database and can modify information in the database concurrently.

Electronic mail enables messages and files to be sent to users connected to the network. Scheduling meetings and appointments also is greatly improved with a

LAN. Because the team can access the same database, duplication of effort is eliminated; as one record is updated, the changes are immediately available to other users on the network.

If you need to read data from a 3 1/2-inch floppy disk and you only have a 5 1/4-inch floppy drive on your computer, a LAN enables you to access the 3 1/2-inch drive on another computer to read the data into your computer.

Finally, one of the most beneficial uses of a LAN is to exchange information. You can prepare a report that needs to incorporate information being prepared by a co-worker. Rather than transfer the information from one computer to another by using a floppy disk (often referred to as *sneaker-net*), you can access the file by using the network without getting up from your desk.

Understanding the Way Networks Operate

In your PC, all computer functions are controlled by the disk operating system (DOS). DOS enables each hardware component in the PC to recognize and talk to the other components. The components include (but are not limited to) the disk drives, monitor, interface cards, keyboard, and printers. DOS coordinates the functions of the components by interpreting the instructions given by the software applications and directing the components of the computer to carry out the instructions. Without DOS, your computer can't do its intended functions.

DOS, or more specifically MS-DOS (Microsoft DOS), is the most popular operating system for PC's. Other popular operating systems include OS/2, Windows NT, and Novell DOS.

Operating Systems

A *network* is two or more computers connected by a communication medium. Communication mediums have strict rules, known as *protocols*, for all data sent over the medium. Each type of medium has a distinct set of protocols. The proper protocol is implemented by the network adapter cards in each computer and in the network driver software that controls the operation of the adapter.

The network operating system, or NOS, combines with and augments the functions of DOS to provide additional instructions to enable pieces of data to be sent across the media to another computer. Although DOS controls the internal functions of the computer, the NOS manages the preparation, transmission, and receipt of data between computers on the network. Some manufacturers put specialized software in a chip on their proprietary interface boards. This specialized software is stored in what is called *ROM*, or *read-only memory*, and performs the NOS's physical link management functions. The NOS is then free to perform its other work more efficiently, resulting in faster data transmission across the network.

Some network operating systems actually replace DOS and incorporate the features normally found in DOS into the Network Operating System (NOS).

Understanding Servers and Workstations

The computers connected to a LAN are configured as servers or workstations. A *server* is a computer that can share its resources with other computers in the network. Resources include, but are not limited to, hard drives, floppy drives, CD-ROM drives, and printers. A *workstation* is a computer that can access and use the shared resources on other servers but cannot share its own resources with other computers in the network.

Servers can be dedicated or nondedicated. A *dedicated server* shares its resources with other network computers—it cannot be used for performing local tasks. You can't sit at a dedicated server, for example, and use a spreadsheet program. A dedicated server typically has a special program running that displays information about the network operations being performed by the server (such as the resources being accessed by other nodes). Because a dedicated server only performs network related functions and nothing else, a dedicated server usually offers the best network performance.

A *nondedicated server* can share resources with other computers, and can be used for other local operations, such as word processing or running a spreadsheet program. A nondedicated server shares its resources and performs its network operations in the background so you can continue using your computer while it serves the requests of other network nodes (computers).

Different networks implement the usage of workstations and servers differently. Some networks have only one server in a network and all other computers configured as workstations. Other networks allow the use of more than one server, but the servers have to be dedicated servers.

LANtastic offers the most flexibility when you set up your network. Unlike many other networks, LANtastic enables you to configure your computers in any combination of nondedicated servers, dedicated servers, and workstations.

Understanding the Types of LANs

LANs generally are classified into one of two categories: server-based (sometimes referred to as client-server) or peer-to-peer. A *server-based* LAN typically consists of a single server with all the other computers configured as workstations. Because the server is the only computer that shares its resources with others, workstations can access and use the shared resources on the server but not resources on other workstations.

A *peer-to-peer* LAN enables each computer in the network to be configured as a nondedicated server so every computer can share its resources with every other computer in the network, while at the same time every computer is available for local operations. A peer-to-peer LAN offers much more flexibility for sharing resources than a server-based LAN because any resource on any computer can be shared. Managing the shared resources in a peer-to-peer LAN can be more confusing than a server-based LAN because you have to keep track of and control the various resources on every computer in the network rather than the resources on a single server (or just a few servers).

Figure 2.1 illustrates a comparison of a server-based network with a peer-to-peer network. In a server-based network, you can only access the shared resources (disk drives, printers, and so forth) on the server. In general, you cannot use a printer connected to another computer. If you want to transfer a file to another workstation in a server-based network, you have to copy the file from your workstation to the server, and then go to the workstation where you want the file to end up, and copy it from the server to the workstation. In a peer-to-peer network, you can access and use the shared resources on any other computer (nondedicated server) in the network. You can use the printer on any other computer or transfer files directly from or to another computer.

LANtastic is a peer-to-peer LAN and includes all the features necessary to share resources among every computer in the network. You also can configure LANtastic as a server-based LAN. In addition, LANtastic includes the software necessary to set up a dedicated server if you need the best possible network performance.

LANtastic 6.0 provides the capability for a computer running LANtastic to act as a client (or access the shared resources) to servers running non-LANtastic network operating systems including Novell NetWare, IBM LAN Server, LAN Manager, Windows for Workgroups, and Windows NT.

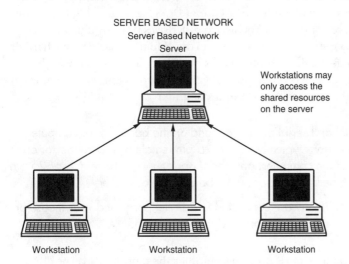

SERVER BASED NETWORK

Server Based Network
Server

Workstations may only access the shared resources on the server

Workstation   Workstation   Workstation

Figure 2.1
Comparison of a server-based network with a peer-to-peer network.

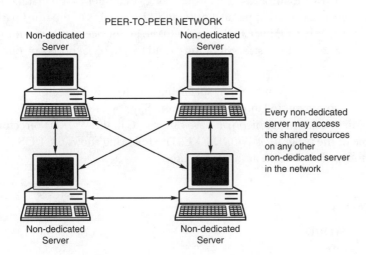

PEER-TO-PEER NETWORK

Non-dedicated Server   Non-dedicated Server

Every non-dedicated server may access the shared resources on any other non-dedicated server in the network

Non-dedicated Server   Non-dedicated Server

Accessing Network Resources

Accessing the shared resources on other computers is very similar to the way you currently access the resources (disk drives/directories, printers) on your computer.

Because this is a book on LANtastic, this discussion focuses on the way network resources are accessed and used with LANtastic, although the basic principles apply to all LANs.

On your stand-alone computer, you access resources (disk drives/directories, printers) by specifying a name (such as C) that DOS has assigned to that resource (disk drive/directory or device). You access disk drives by using a drive letter followed by a colon, such as A:, B:, C:, and so on. When you access your hard drive, for example, you use C:. If you want to look at a directory listing on your hard drive, you specify the DOS command DIR C:. DOS also assigns device names to the parallel and serial ports that exist on your computer.

Parallel and serial ports are found on the back of your computer. *Parallel ports* typically have a 25-pin female type D connector on the back of the computer, and *serial ports* typically have a 9- or 25-pin male type D connector on the back of the computer.

Printers usually are connected to parallel ports, and your mouse or an external modem is connected to a serial port.

DOS assigns any parallel ports on your computer the names LPT1: (or PRN:), LPT2:, and LPT3:. LPT1: and PRN: are device names that refer to the first parallel port. LPT2: refers to the second parallel port, and LPT3: refers to the third parallel port. Similarly, COM1:, COM2:, COM3:, and COM4: are device names given to serial ports, and refer to the first, second, third, and fourth serial ports on your computer.

When you run a program, you begin by specifying the drive and directory and then the appropriate command to launch the program. Suppose, for example, that you want to run Microsoft Word, which you have on drive C in the WORD5 directory. The file name of the program is WORD.EXE. The following shows the DOS commands to type if you begin at the A:\> prompt:

A:\>**C:**

C:\>**CD \WORD5**

C:\WORD5>**WORD**

Your prompt displays the current drive and directory, as shown in the preceding example if the following command is included in your AUTOEXEC.BAT file or typed at the DOS prompt:

PROMPT=PG

To open the file in Word, you specify the drive and directory name of the file (such as C:\WORDDOCS) and select the name of the file on which you want to work (such as MEMO.DOC). If you print your document, specify where to send the document (such as LPT1: to print to the printer connected to your LPT1: parallel port).

A LAN enables you to access and use drives/directories and printers on other computers (servers) similar to the way you currently use them on your own computer. By using a LAN, you can create a logical drive (such as K) on your computer that, when accessed, is actually accessing a shared drive/directory on another computer. To view a directory listing of the hard drive on the other computer, for example, you can issue the DOS command DIR K:. Because your logical K drive actually points to the hard drive on a different computer, you view the directory of the hard drive on the other computer. Similarly, you can copy files from and to the other computer by specifying the K drive (such as COPY C:\INFO.TXT K:). Because you have access to the hard drive on another computer by using the K drive, you also can run a program from the other computer's hard drive on your computer.

 A *logical drive* is a drive that does not really exist on your computer. It is used to access a resource that exists somewhere else. A logical drive also is referred to as a *redirected drive*. A *physical drive* is a drive that actually exists on your computer.

To better understand the way to access the shared network resources of other computers from your computer, you need to learn a little more about the way shared resources are created.

Just as you access individual drives and printers on your computer with DOS and other application programs by specifying a name (such as C for your hard drive or LPT1: for your printer), the different computers in your network are given a name. The network name given to each computer cannot be used by other computers in the network. You use the network name to identify the computer to which you want to connect when you establish a network connection.

Figure 2.2 illustrates the basic network fundamental of sharing resources between computers. The example shows three different computers, each with a network name (DANA, ZAK, and KATIE). You can name your computers after people, locations, functions, or any other scheme. Just as you distinguish between different computers in your network by specifying a network name, you also can specify the available resources on each computer that you will connect.

Figure 2.2
Illustrating
sharing and
accessing
shared
resources.

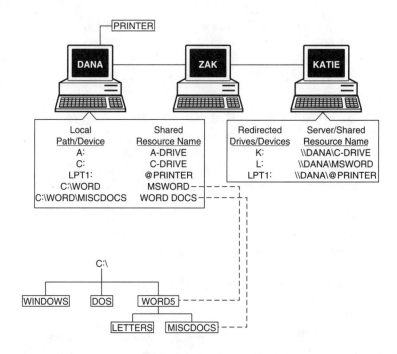

To share disk drives, directories, and printers with other users in a network, give each shared resource a name. In LANtastic, a shared resource name may contain up to eight characters followed by an optional period, and then up to an additional three characters (such as C-DRIVE or MYDRIVE.C), just like a DOS file name. The names for shared printer resources must begin with the @ character in LANtastic. @PRINTER and @LASER.HP are examples of shared printer resource names.

Figure 2.2 illustrates the way shared resources work. The example shows three computers—DANA, ZAK, and KATIE—as part of a LANtastic network; each computer is configured as a nondedicated server so it can share its resources with others. A printer is connected to server DANA.

To make shared resources on a server available to others, specify on every server a shared resource name and the local path/device on the server to which the shared resource name actually points. In this example, you are setting up shared resources on server DANA. As shown in figure 2.2, you create shared resource names that point to a local path (drive\directory) or device (LPT1:) that physically exists on server DANA. This representation is shown as follows:

A-DRIVE   =>   A:

C-DRIVE   =>   C:

```
@PRINTER   =>      LPT1:

MSWORD     =>      C:\WORD5

WORDDOCS=>         C:\WORD5\MISCDOCS
```

The shared resource named A-DRIVE on server DANA points to the physical A floppy drive on this server. The shared resource C-DRIVE points to the physical C hard drive. @PRINTER is the name of the shared printer resource that points to the LPT1: port to which the printer is connected.

> When LANtastic is installed, a default resource list is created. Use LANtastic's NET_MGR program to define additional shared resources for each computer.

The next two shared resource names actually point to directories on the hard drive, as illustrated by the directory tree in figure 2.2. The MSWORD resource points to the C:\WORD5 directory, and the WORDDOCS resource points to the C:\WORD5\MISCDOCS directory. With LANtastic, you can specify which users (or accounts) can use each resource. You might want to share the documents in your C:\WORD5\MISCDOCS directory with everyone in the network, for example. You give all accounts access to your WORDDOCS resource. On the other hand, you probably don't want everybody to be able to access your C drive. Restrict access to the C-DRIVE resource so only the users you specify can access this resource.

> In LANtastic, if a user accesses a server's shared drive/directory resource, the user has access to the drive/directory defined in the resource name and any directories below it. In figure 2.2, for example, if a network user accesses the C-DRIVE resource, he has access to the root directory and all directories below it, including WINDOWS, DOS, WORD5, WORD5\LETTERS, and WORD5\MISCDOCS. If a user accesses the MSWORD shared resource, he has access to the directories WORD5, WORD5\LETTERS, and WORD5\MISCDOCS. He doesn't have access to any directories above WORD5, which include DOS, WINDOWS, and the root directory.

Now that the shared resources on server DANA are defined, see what happens when you access and use shared resources from another computer.

Suppose that you are sitting at server KATIE and you want to run Microsoft Word. You don't have Microsoft Word on your computer, but it is on server DANA. You can run Microsoft Word by accessing the program from the hard drive on server DANA. First, establish a network connection to the shared resource you want to access on server DANA. Choose a logical drive letter on your computer to establish a network connection to a shared resource on server DANA. For this example, you can access the C-DRIVE resource on server DANA by redirecting your K drive (on server KATIE) to point to the shared resource C-DRIVE (see fig 2.2). Now when you access drive K, you are accessing drive C on server DANA. If WORD.EXE is the name of the MS Word program file, type the following commands at the C:\> prompt to run MS Word from drive K:

C:\>**K:**

K:\>**CD\WORD5**

K:\WORD5>**WORD**

If you run a program from another computer on the network, the program files actually are transferred from the server's hard drive to your computer, where they are processed or run. You use the hard drive on the other computer, not the processor.

If you redirect a logical drive letter on your computer to point to a shared drive/directory resource on another computer, you can think of it as having another hard drive installed in your computer that you can access with the chosen drive letter.

Now take this example one step further. When you redirect drive K to access the C-DRIVE shared resource on server DANA, you have access to the entire C drive on server DANA; not just the WORD5 directory. For security reasons, you might not want other users to access the C-DRIVE resource on server DANA. You might, however, want others to be able to run MS Word from server DANA. For this reason, the shared resource MSWORD is created on server DANA.

Suppose that you are sitting at server KATIE and you establish a network connection to the MSWORD shared resource on server DANA by redirecting the drive L on your computer. To run MS Word as you did before, type the following at your DOS prompt:

C:\>**L:**

L:\>**WORD**

This time you did not have to change to the WORD5 directory, as you did when you used your K drive in the previous example, because you redirected your L

drive to the MSWORD resource on server DANA, which actually points to the
C:\WORD5 directory. When you access your L drive, you are accessing the
C:\WORD5 directory on server DANA. The following table shows what your DOS
prompt looks like if you access the MSWORD resource with your L drive and what
directories you are actually in on server DANA:

Local DOS Prompt	Directory on Server DANA
L:\>	C:\WORD5
L:\LETTERS>	C:\WORD5\LETTERS
L:\MISCDOCS>	C:\WORD5\MISCDOCS

To connect to the shared printer resource @PRINTER on server DANA, redirect
one of your printer devices (such as LPT1) to point to the shared printer resource
@PRINTER on server DANA.

Network connections are established with the LANtastic NET program
or by using NET commands from a DOS prompt or in a DOS batch
file.

You now have a good understanding of the way networks share and access shared
resources. The knowledge in this section serves as the building blocks for your
future LANtastic accomplishments. As you continue to learn about LANtastic and
networking in general, consider reading this section again to help you understand
the basics that the LANtastic or networking principles are built on.

Implementation Methods

Artisoft produces two major LANtastic NOS implementations. The standard
implementation supports Artisoft Ethernet and 2 Mbps network adapters, as well as
network adapters from other manufacturers which may include Ethernet, ARCnet,
Token Ring, and other network protocols. The second implementation, called
LANtastic Z, provides for a two-station network using a modem, standard parallel,
or serial ports.

Prior to LANtastic 6.0, Artisoft offered four LANtastic NOS implementations. They offered their original proprietary 2 Mbps implementation, an Ethernet implementation used with Artisoft Ethernet adapters, an adapter-independent implementation (LANtastic/AI) used with network adapters from other manufacturers, and an implementation called LANtastic Z, which provides for a two-station network using a modem, standard parallel, or serial ports.

2 Mbps refers to the network's capability of transmitting two million bits-per-second over the medium. This type of implementation is adequate if you have older PCs to connect.

Ethernet is more sophisticated and is capable of up to 10 million bits-per-second data transmission speed. Ethernet is the most common implementation for newer computers that have 80286-, 80386-, or 80486-based central processing units (CPU).

LANtastic Z is designed to be used by two computers using standard serial ports, parallel ports, or modems in place of a traditional network adapter card. You can use LANtastic Z to connect two computers that are geographically separated by using modems and standard telephone lines. A laptop computer is connected to another computer by a serial or parallel cable that is plugged into the serial or parallel port on each computer being connected.

Chapter 4, "Artisoft Network Products," includes additional information about Artisoft LANtastic products.

Your LANtastic starter kit package is shipped from Artisoft with the proper cable, network interface cards, and NOS software. Chapter 3, "Planning Your LANtastic Network," has information to help you determine the best LANtastic implementation and cable for your situation.

The LANtastic NOS prepares data for transmission by dividing it into manageable pieces of predetermined sizes. You might think of the pieces of data as individual letters, each letter containing a set amount of information in the format prescribed by the NOS. These "letters" are called *packets*.

Each packet is sent in its own envelope. The envelope has a mailing address (the destination computer address), a return address (of the computer that sent it), and a special block of information that indicates the sequence of the packet in relation to any others being sent. A single file transmitted over the network can be made up of hundreds—even thousands—of packets.

Before transmitting a file, the originating computer listens to the network to ensure that no other transmissions are already on the network. If no other traffic is present, the originator sends the file. If more than one computer sends a file simultaneously, the NOS senses the collision of data, and causes the originators to resend their data. The NOS assigns senders a different random wait period before allowing them to retransmit to lessen the chance of another collision happening immediately. This media access control (MAC) standard is known as *carrier sense multiple access with collision detection* (CSMA/CD) and is used by LANtastic.

The receiving computer identifies each packet by its sequence number and reconstructs the full file from the pieces. If a piece is discovered missing or is determined to be unreadable, the NOS forces the originator to resend the packet.

Now that you have a feel for what a network is and the way it works, take a look at what physically comprises a network.

Exploring Network Components

From the previous discussions, you see that the pieces of a network are:

- ✔ Hardware
- ✔ NOS software
- ✔ Communication medium over which the data is transmitted

Hardware includes microcomputers, printers, modems, network interface cards installed in each computer, and connectors that attach the cable to the interface cards. Communication media (network cabling) are sometimes included in this group; for the purposes of this book, however, media is considered separately.

The software portion consists of the NOS and the network adapter drivers discussed earlier. The NOS is the key element of network functionality. Without the NOS, the computers on the network cannot send or receive data. For that matter, they cannot even recognize that other computers are connected without the NOS to provide the link.

The communication medium is the physical link connecting the nodes of the network. Usually this link is a cable, but some networks use laser, infrared, and radio (wireless) transmitters to perform the physical connection function. This discussion is limited to cable-type media, which is the only type of media used in most LANtastic installations.

If you implement an Ethernet LANtastic network, you can use one of three types of cabling: Ethernet (thick) coaxial cable, Ethernet Thinnet coaxial cable, or unshielded twisted-pair (UTP) cable.

Standard Ethernet coaxial cable is fairly thick and lacks flexibility. As a result, it can be hard to install in your office environment and is rarely used in new installations. The Thinnet version is easier to work with and provides a greater degree of installation flexibility. Unshielded twisted-pair cable is similar to the cable used for telephone installation and thus provides the greatest freedom during installation.

The physical shape of the network (the way the nodes are connected to each other) is determined by the network adapter cards. The following three types of physical layouts, or topologies, are typically used in LANs:

✔ Star

✔ Token ring

✔ Bus

In the star arrangement, the nodes of the network are arranged around a central hub (also called a concentrator) and are connected in a way that forms a shape like a star (see fig. 2.3).

The 10BASE-T Ethernet standard that uses UTP cable is arranged in a star configuration. 10BASE-T is a relatively new Ethernet standard and is rapidly becoming the Ethernet standard of choice because of its flexibility and use of common UTP cable. 10BASE-T eases cabling installation and later troubleshooting because the concentrator can be located in a wiring closet from which the network cable is run to each individual computer.

The next topology addressed is token ring. In this configuration, all nodes are connected to a central cable system laid out as a circle or ring (refer to fig. 2.4). The actual physical installation of a token ring network often resembles a star topology, where each computer is connected to a central device (called an MAV) with two cables: one for sending data and the other for receiving data.

IBM developed the Token Ring network system standard to take advantage of this topology. This type of network uses a series of empty packets, called tokens, that circulate on the network at all times. An originating station simply picks a token off the network, examines it for content, and, if empty, puts in the data that it needs to transmit. If the first token is full, the NOS puts it back on the network and selects another.

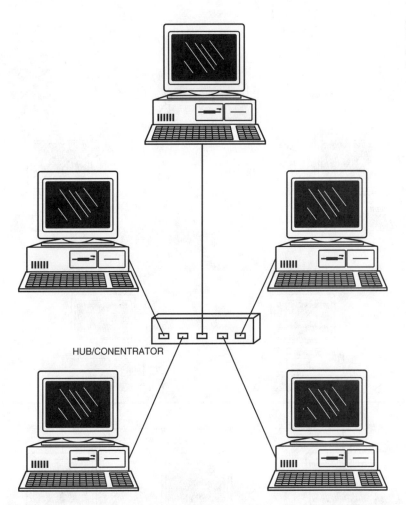

Figure 2.3
An example of
star topology.

HUB/CONENTRATOR

The destination address and the packet identifying sequence are attached to the token before it passes back to the network for delivery. The advantage of this system is that data collision is eliminated and the transmission speed is very high, even in a heavily used network. However, the cost of the cable and interface cards for token ring topologies is high. For this reason, token rings usually are found only in heavily used networks in which the cost is justified. LANtastic supports several network adapter cards that support token ring topology.

Figure 2.4
An example of
token ring
topology.

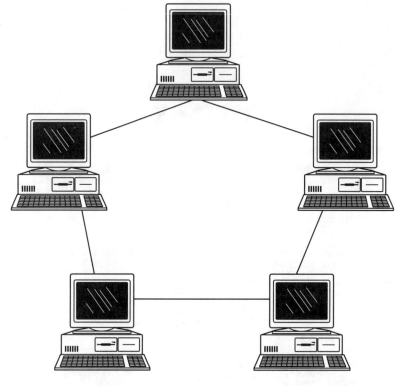

Figure 2.5
An example of
bus topology.

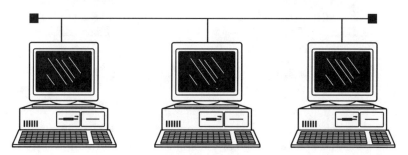

Bus topology is used by thin Ethernet (coax), thick Ethernet, and the LANtastic 2 Mbps adapters. This topology consists of a central cable, or bus, with terminator plugs connected at each end (see fig. 2.5). The network nodes are attached to the cable along the length of the bus. Thin Ethernet uses T connectors to connect each node to the network cable. LANtastic 2 Mbps adapters have an internal T connector built in, and are connected in what appears to be a daisy chain (in and out of each computer), but is actually a bus topology because of the internal T connector.

Bus topology networks are very popular with LANs because they are easy to install and expand. They also operate very well in all but the most demanding situations. The length of the network can be extended by installing repeater amplifiers in line. Repeaters take the signal being transmitted and boost it for retransmission further down the bus cable.

When you buy Artisoft's LANtastic starter kit, you get a complete package, cables, cards, software, and connectors, all optimized to run the LANtastic networking system. You can't go wrong with this choice—all of your potential problems are eliminated and the prices are very reasonable.

Understanding the basics of networking can go a long way toward easing any anxiety you might have about installing your LANtastic network. Knowing about your potential gains, what you might have to give up, and what could go wrong provides further insight before you begin your installation.

Network Components for Connecting Networks

As your LANtastic network grows, you may find that you need additional hardware and software components to connect your networks together. Some of the more popular network expansion components are described below:

✔ **Repeater.** A Repeater is a device which takes the network signal and amplifies it so you can extend your network cable length. For example, normally when using Thinnet Ethernet cable, you are limited to a network cable length of 607 ft. You can use a Repeater to connect two 607 ft. network cable segments for a total network cable length of 1214 ft.

A network cable segment is the network cable length without any connection or amplification devices. Placing a repeater in a network, for example, would break a single network segment into two segments. Also, in an Ethernet 10BASE-T network, each cable from the concentrator the computer is considered a network segment.

✔ **Bridge.** Bridges enable you to connect similar networks together. For example, you could connect a LANtastic network that uses Artisoft's 2Mbps network adapter cards with a network using Ethernet adapter cards by putting one of each type of network card in a computer, and then using LANtastic Interchange bridging software to bridge the two networks so they operate as one.

✔ **Routers.** Routers enable you to connect networks using different topologies such as Ethernet and token ring. Routers are more sophisticated than bridges—they include features that enable them to examine the network packets and determine if the information needs to be transmitted through the router, or if the information is for a network node on the same network segment. Routers or bridges with routing features are often
used to control network traffic congestion by filtering out packets that don't need to be transferred to the other network segment.

✔ **Gateways.** Gateways enable you to connect your network to a different type of network, such as connecting a LANtastic network to an Apple Macintosh network. The Gateway translates between the different networks. Gateways are also used to enable your network to communicate with different devices, such a fax gateway, to let you send information to a fax machine.

Examining the Advantages of Networking

The most popular reason for installing a network is to share resources over the network. These resources might include files, expensive printers or high-density storage devices (disk drives or tape units), or software applications. The idea is to maximize the use of available resources and reduce the cost.

Another popular reason is the need for more effective communication. A network with an electronic mail system can virtually eliminate the old pink phone message slips and missed calls. Not only can you send and receive messages, you can send whole files back and forth, or attach extracts from files to your notes. Think how much more efficient you can be.

A popular outgrowth of networking is the formation of work groups. These groups share everything electronically, giving immediate access to needed data and collaborating on changes without interrupting individual work schedules. The application of networking technology is limited only by your imagination.

Considering the Disadvantages of a Network

Probably the biggest thing you sacrifice when you install a network is individual user independence. New network users tend to forget they cannot always do what they want when they want to with their machines. If they are logged in to a network, they must consider that someone else might be using their resources and that if they turn off the computer or somehow cause it to freeze, a fellow worker can suffer a work setback or lose data. Common sense and consideration for others goes a long way in avoiding co-worker disputes and frayed nerves. Fortunately, it does not take long for people to get used to the idea of being part of a network, and after they do, they usually love it.

Network software uses some of the conventional memory that may be required by other application programs. This can be a disadvantage on systems in which you can't make use of upper memory to load DOS or the network software into upper memory, thereby freeing up some conventional memory.

In addition, some application programs do not operate properly when paired with the network. Often the result of a conflict between an application program and the network is a network crash (the network becomes inoperable until you reboot your computer). Most application programs operate properly with networks, but many games and some older application programs can cause problems.

Exposing Potential Problems

With very few exceptions, the software applications you use now operate fine in your LANtastic network. On rare occasions, you may discover an application program that does not operate properly. After a network is installed, most of the problems you encounter with improperly operating software are caused by the software improperly implementing the standard DOS conventions that DOS and the network use. Usually the software vendor will have an updated version of the program that addresses any problems you might encounter. Artisoft also has excellent technical support and service.

Because a network shares resources, most of the problems you face are related to conflicts in requests for those resources. Your existing software applications are most likely the single-user versions: only one person can use the program at a time. If more than one person will be accessing a program at the same time, you need to purchase the network version of that program. A mistake many make is to think that installing a network automatically enables several users to use the programs on one computer concurrently.

Each software manufacturer has its own licensing agreements. If you run software in a network environment, check with the manufacturer of your software application to determine the licensing requirements.

Summary

This chapter provides an overview of networking basics. You learned what a network is and the different kinds of networks available. The fundamentals of sharing resources and using shared resources were covered in detail. In addition, you also learned the different network topologies used.

You now have a good understanding of network basics and are ready to proceed to Chapter 3, "Planning Your LANtastic Network."

Chapter Snapshot

This chapter introduces you to the planning steps necessary to obtain all the information required to set up your network. This critical first step determines the ease or difficulty of your installation experience. You learn about the following in this chapter:

✔ Determining the purpose of your network

✔ Understanding the duties of a network manager

✔ Identifying network equipment

✔ Identifying network users

✔ Locating the pieces of the network

✔ What type of network interface cards do I need?

✔ Determining cable type

When you finish this chapter, you will be ready to install your LANtastic network, having determined the placement and type of network equipment required as well as the general network software configuration.

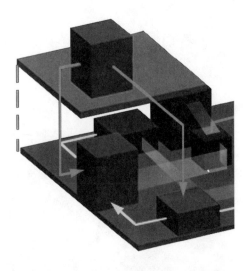

Planning Your LANtastic Network

The previous chapters presented an overview of networks. You learned what they are, what they are comprised of, and the way they work. Now you are ready to begin the process that leads to the installation of your LANtastic network. The first step is to plan your network.

This chapter provides sample charts to help you organize information about your network (see figs. 3.1 and 3.2). Copy these figures freely and fill them in as part of your planning process before you begin installing. You can add other information to the charts as needed by using the blank spaces provided or by writing your own information on the back of the copied form. After you fill in the charts, keep them handy as you install LANtastic. Refer to them for important information required by LANtastic to set up your network.

Figure 3.1

A sample Network Hardware Inventory Card.

Network Hardware Inventory Card

Description of computer:_____

CPU type and speed (Ex. 80486-33):_____

Monitor type (Mono, VGA, etc.):_____

RAM Installed:_____

Hard drive size:_____ Type:_____ Access time (if known):_____

Drive letter:_____ Partition size:_____

Drive letter:_____ Partition size:_____

DOS Version:_____

Floppy drive A type/capacity _____

Floppy drive B type/capacity:_____

Tape backup type/capacity:_____

Other drives(CD-ROM/Worm/etc.): _____   Drive letter:_____

Serial ports - COM1(Y/N):_____   COM2(Y/N):_____

Modem(Y/N): _____ COM Port (1/2/3/4): _____

Parallel ports -   LPT1(Y/N):_____ LPT2(Y/N):_____ LPT3(Y/N):_____

Printer attached:_____   Port:_____

Printer attached:_____   Port:_____

Software applications installed (Accounting, Spreadsheet, Word Processing, TSRs, Memory managers, Windows, utilities, etc.):

_____

Network Name of computer _____   Configured as: ___ Server   ___Workstation

Drives/Directories to share (if configured as a Server)

Local drive/directory:_____   Network Resource Name:_____

Local drive/directory: _____   Network Resource Name:_____

Local drive/directory: _____   Network Resource Name:_____

Local drive/directory: _____   Network Resource Name:_____

Local drive/directory: _____   Network Resource Name:_____

Local drive/directory: _____   Network Resource Name:_____

Printers to share (if configured as a Server)

Local Device (LPT1:,LPT2:,etc.): _____   Network Resource Name:_____

Local Device (LPT1:,LPT2:,etc.): _____   Network Resource Name:_____

Network Account Card

Individual User Account Name/Wildcard Account Name:_____

Password:_____

Description:_____

Category (room/floor/department/etc.):_____

Date account established:_____

Primary tasks:_____

_____

_____

Primary software used:_____

_____

ACL Groups:_____

_____

Privileges(Y/N):   ___A - Super ACL

                      ___Q - Super Queue

                      ___M - Super Mail

                      ___U - User Auditing

                      ___S - System Manager

                      ___O - Operator

                      ___D - Despooler

                      ___N - Network Manager

Comments:_____

_____

_____

_____

Figure 3.2
A sample
Network
Account Card.

Determining the Purpose of Your Network

You need to decide your purpose for installing the LANtastic network. Keep this purpose in mind throughout the installation process. If you encounter a situation that conflicts with your goal, seek further guidance before continuing.

The previous chapter showed you the way networks operate, and the way LANtastic networks can help you obtain network goals. Hopefully you thought of some additional ideas that you can implement in your LANtastic network to increase your productivity.

If your goal is simply to increase the productive use of available computing resources, you can easily set up your LANtastic network with a general configuration to satisfy that objective.

If you want to use your network for tasks, such as a network accounting system, that require network access to shared resources for some users while restricting the access for others, you need to set up a user account structure that enables you to distinguish between authorized users and unauthorized users. You also need to specify which users have access to the shared resource that contains the accounting information, and which users you want to restrict or deny access to those resources.

If you just want to share disk drives and printers, and security is not an issue, you can set up LANtastic quickly by avoiding individual user accounts.

When first learning LANtastic, it is much easier to avoid setting up individual user accounts. After you and your users are comfortable with LANtastic, you can then set up a more elaborate user account structure if necessary.

If you have a clear understanding of what you want your LANtastic network to do, the installation and use of LANtastic is much easier. If you don't have a clear understanding of what you want your LANtastic network to do, now is a good time to take a few minutes and write down what you want from your LANtastic network and any network security concerns that might apply to your installation.

If you have not purchased LANtastic, you have several options. You can buy LANtastic directly from Artisoft at full price, from a full-service dealer at a discount, or by mail order at a significant discount. The advantage of buying from a dealer is that the user has two lines of support: the dealer and Artisoft. Buying through mail order is sometimes significantly cheaper, but the user rarely has technical support available from the mail-order company.

Understanding the Duties of a Network Manager

All new network managers—or network administrators, as they are sometimes called—experience anxiety about what is required of them. The network manager usually is responsible for physically installing the hardware and software needed to make LANtastic work. The network manager also sets up shared resources and user accounts, and configures individual computers to operate efficiently in a network environment. Other duties include teaching fellow workers to use the network, maintaining the network after installation, and troubleshooting user problems. By using LANtastic, a network manager's responsibilities are not as difficult or time-consuming as they may seem.

Administering the network is not more difficult than administering other processes. You gather information about the computer equipment you have, what printers and other peripherals you have on hand, who uses the equipment, and the ways they use it.

Before you begin gathering the information, you may want to get a few useful tools. A large three-ring binder and some blank paper is helpful to keep the information organized. Your binder is the definitive record of your new network; everything that pertains to your network is referenced in it, so if you are sick or on vacation, a designated person can look through the binder and easily figure out what the network is all about, how it is put together, and ways to make changes if necessary.

This notebook is for only you to use and not available for general use, especially if you implement password usage and keep the master password list in the binder. You might want to keep the binder in a locked drawer or file cabinet.

You also might want to appoint an alternate network manager to serve in your stead when you are not available. Make sure that the alternate network administrator knows where the notebook is and has access to it.

As the network administrator, you want to be prepared to write a policy and procedures guide for your network. This document is for your network users. Thinking about this guide as part of your planning makes your transition to full operation easier. It also forces you to consider many things that can cause problems later. Considering the worst case scenario beforehand and planning accordingly is much easier than reacting to a situation after the fact.

The following is a list of suggested topics to include in your network administration guide; feel free to add or delete as you see fit:

- ✔ Statement of purpose for the network implementation
- ✔ Statement of policy regarding software installation (who is authorized, what is authorized, and so on)
- ✔ Statement of policy regarding hardware maintenance and tampering
- ✔ A LAN layout diagram that shows all stations and peripheral locations

✔ A network user list

✔ Some common network courtesy hints

✔ Generic network login procedures

✔ Password rules (if you decide to implement them)

✔ Software availability list that names the software and the computer on which it is installed

✔ Generic guide to using network resources (peripherals and software applications)

✔ Procedures for reporting problems with the network

✔ Procedures for seeking help about the network or one of the applications on the network

✔ Generic network logout procedures

As the network administrator, you must set the policy for using and maintaining your network. Users look to you for guidance and assistance. You can modify the list depending on the size of your network and the amount of control you want to implement. You can modify the list even after you have been up and running for a time. Periodic reviews of the network should become part of your routine.

Identifying Network Equipment

You need to meet with the managers who are responsible for any computer equipment and who have users connected to the network. Your objective is to identify all the equipment they want connected to the network and build a detailed inventory list of existing equipment. Record this information in your network binder.

If you haven't made enough copies of the Network Hardware Inventory Card (shown in figure 3.1) to have one for every computer connected to your LANtastic network, do so now. To fill out each card, identify and record the physical configuration of every computer and determine the network name of the computer and what, if any, resources, such as disk drives and printers, you want to share with other users on the network.

Identifying the Physical Configuration of Each Computer

The first step to identifying your network equipment and the way each computer is used is to find out how your computer is equipped. After you know what you have, you can determine the way the computer is used in the network.

Identifying the physical configuration of each computer is made much easier if you use a software utility, such as CheckIt by TouchStone Software Corporation, QAPlus by DiagSoft, PCTools by Central Point Software, or The Norton Utilities by Symantec.

Included with Windows 3.1 and MS-DOS 6.0 and higher is the MSD (Microsoft Diagnostics) program, which provides you with system configuration information similar to what a software utility provides.

To help you fill out your Network Hardware Inventory Card, use the utility that you selected to list the configuration of each computer on the network. Figures 3.3 and 3.4 show examples of the information that these utilities provide. The report function of these utilities enables you to print the information about each computer. Then you can put it in your network binder.

Don't worry about filling in all the information for every computer on the Network Hardware Inventory Card. Fill in what you can. As you continue planning, you realize the additional information necessary for each computer according to its purpose in the network.

If you do not have one of the preceding utilities, you can manually construct a reasonable equipment configuration list. It just takes a little longer. Look on the back of each computer, monitor, and printer. Record the make and model on your charts. If a printer is attached to a computer, record the port number. If only one connection for a printer exists, you can assume that it is port LPT1. Also look for a modem connection or a serial printer connection. Record the port number(s) of any that you find. If the ports are not labeled, you usually can determine the numbers from their physical layout (see fig. 3.5).

Read the owner's manual for each computer and try to ascertain the amount of memory installed, the size of the hard drive, the default switch settings, and optional equipment you can install. During initial setup, many dealers and users record the optional equipment and switch settings in the owner's manual for future reference. A look at the front of each computer tells you the number of floppy disk drives that are installed.

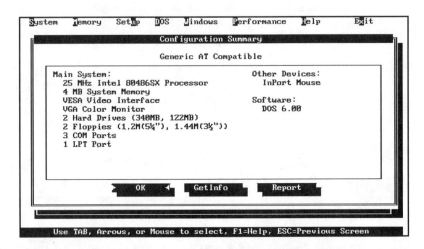

Figure 3.3
CheckIt's Configuration Summary screen.

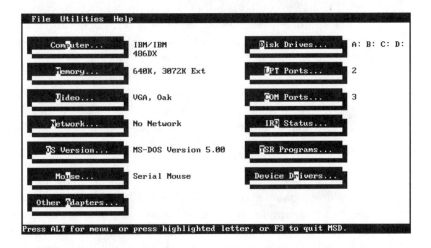

Figure 3.4
The MSD main menu/information screen.

If you use MicroSoft DOS 5.0 or higher, MEM/C|MORE enables you to see the contents of the base and upper memory areas and to see whether DOS is using the high memory area. In addition, the mem command will tell you the total amount of conventional, extended, and expanded memory you have in your computer.

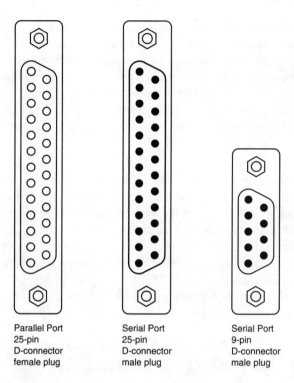

Figure 3.5
Parallel and
serial printer
port D
connectors.

Parallel Port
25-pin
D-connector
female plug

Serial Port
25-pin
D-connector
male plug

Serial Port
9-pin
D-connector
male plug

If the owner's manual doesn't tell you what size hard disk you have, or the amount of memory that is installed, DOS can help you. At the root directory prompt (the DOS prompt), type **CHKDSK**, and press Enter. A list similar to the following appears:

```
C:\>CHKDSK
Volume Serial Number is 2517-12FC

127490048 bytes total disk space
  8099840 bytes in 20 hidden files
   233472 bytes in 99 directories
 47835136 bytes in 2057 user files
 71321600 bytes available on disk

     2048 bytes in each allocation unit
    62251 total allocation units on disk
    34825 available allocation units on disk

   655360 total bytes memory
   607200 bytes free

C:\>
```

This list tells you the total amount of conventional memory, but does not tell you the amount of expanded or extended memory. It does provide some basic information about the configuration and usage of the space on your hard drive. If you don't have DOS 5.0 or higher (MEM command), you can see the amount of RAM that is installed by watching the memory test when you first turn on the computer. The first 640 KB is always conventional memory. Memory above 1024 KB is usually extended memory. Record all of this information on your network configuration inventory sheets that you keep in the binder.

Conventional memory is the memory from 0 to 640 KB addresses. *Extended memory* is 1 MB to the total amount of RAM installed. *Expanded memory* exists in the memory banks on an add-in card with a built-in memory manager (usually found in older 8088, 8086, and 80286 computers). 80386 and higher computers emulate expanded memory by using a portion of extended memory with memory manager software, such as EMM386.EXE included with DOS 5.0 and higher. *High memory* is the first 64 KB of extended memory. *Upper memory* is the memory between conventional and extended memory.

Determining the Network Capability of Each Station

LANtastic is a very powerful and flexible network operating system that enables you to configure almost any computer any way you want. You cannot share resources you do not have, of course, such as a hard drive on a diskless workstation, but in many respects LANtastic gives you the flexibility to do almost anything you want.

Just as a more powerful computer is better suited for graphics-intensive applications, such as CAD (Computer Aided Design), certain parameters make one computer better suited for certain network functions than another. The following is a list of general guidelines that help you determine the types of network functions you want to permit, based on the configuration of each computer recorded on your Network Hardware Inventory Card:

✔ 286-based or lower computers that run applications that require a large amount of available conventional RAM (512 KB or more) should be configured as workstations (not servers).

✔ 386-based or higher computers that run applications that require a large amount of available conventional RAM (512 KB or more) should have at least 1 MB of memory with 384 KB configured as extended and DOS 5.0

or above (enabling you to load DOS and the network drivers in upper memory, freeing up the required conventional memory).

✔ Servers with hard drives that are heavily accessed by other users benefit by having at least 4 MB and a fast processor (such as a 486-33). A server that holds a network accounting program and data or a relatively large database application is an example.

✔ Printers do not need to be connected to a high performance computer (such as a 486-33), but they require at least 5 MB of available storage space on the hard drive to hold print jobs sent (spooled) over the network.

The more powerful the stand-alone computer, the faster it performs in a network environment.

Determining the Function of Each Station

After you identify the configuration of each computer in your LANtastic network, you can decide which resources you want to share with other network users. You can use the lower portion of your Network Hardware Inventory Card to list the network name of the computer, determine whether to configure it as a server or workstation, and decide upon the drives/directories and printers you want to share with other network users.

You can configure each computer in your LANtastic network as a server or a workstation. A server can share its resources (such as disk drives and printers) with other users on the network. A server also can use the shared resources of other computers. A workstation can only use the resources on other LANtastic Servers; it cannot share its resources with other users.

Unless your computer does not have a hard disk, it should be configured as a server so that you can share its resources with others on the network.

Every computer in your network needs a unique network name. The *network name* is the name used to identify each computer. If the computer is configured as a server, the network name is part of the description when a user accesses a resource (disk drive or printer) on the server. If, for example, a computer has the network name ZAKS-486, and drive C on that server has the resource name C-DRIVE, the network path name used to establish a network connection to the C-DRIVE resource on server ZAKS-486 is, therefore, \\ZAKS-486\C-DRIVE.

In deciding network names for the computers, try to establish naming conventions that make it easy for you and your users to identify the computer being used. The best naming convention is often one that identifies the network name of each computer with the name of the individual who uses the computer. Examples of network names that use this naming convention are ZAK, KATIE, DANAS-PC, and so on. If the person for whom the computer is named moves to a different office or leaves the company, the network name needs to be changed to match the user who takes over the computer (assuming that you want to keep the network name associated with the name of the individual who uses the computer). Sometimes the naming convention identifies the location of the computer, such as ROOM11 or OFFICE3. You might want to identify your computers by department, such as SALES01 or ACCTG10. One final naming scheme distinguishes servers from workstations, such as SERVER1, SERVER2, STA-10, STA-35. The examples here are only suggestions. You are free to choose a naming convention described here, or you can make up your own.

Next, you need to determine whether your computer is to be configured as a server or a workstation. In general, it is advisable to configure all your computers as servers. Computers should only be configured as workstations under one or more of the following conditions:

- ✔ No hard disk
- ✔ No chance of sharing resources with other users on the network for any reason
- ✔ You need to maximize the available amount of conventional memory (not configuring as a server saves about 46 KB of memory)

Configuring a computer as a server does not necessarily mean a compromise of network security. If you set up your shared network resources on each computer, you can specify which users can and cannot access those resources.

If you decide to configure your computer as a server, the next step in the planning process is to determine which resources you want to share with other users on the network.

When you install LANtastic 6.0, the LANtastic installation program automatically installs several resources, including the following disk drive and printer resources:

A-DRIVE	The A floppy drive on the server
B-DRIVE	The B floppy drive on the server
C-DRIVE	The C hard drive on the server
@PRINTER	The printer attached to the parallel port LPT1: on the server

If you do not want other network users to use the resources on your server, you can restrict access to the resources or delete the shared resource using the LANtastic Network Manager program later. One good reason to keep the default resources, even if you do not share your disk drives or printers with other network users, is that you can give yourself access to your own computer so that you can access it from another computer.

To define drive/directories and printers to share, specify a drive letter/directory or a printer device name. Then choose a network resource name that other network users use to connect to the shared resource on your computer. If you have a laser printer connected to the LPT1: port on your computer, for example, the Local Device is LPT1: and you might choose a Network Printer Resource Name of @LASER.

Resource names can have up to eight characters with a three-character extension (such as @HPLASER.NEW, or @LASER). Printer resource names must begin with the @ character.

Perhaps there are only certain directories on your hard drive that you want to share. You might have a directory on your computer named \GENERAL, for example, that contains general information that you typically share. Even though you may not want to give other users access to all of your C drive (by means of the C-DRIVE resource), you might want to make your \GENERAL directory available to others. You can choose a Network Resource Name of GEN-DATA, for example, with a Local drive/directory of C:\GENERAL. You can specify to share the GEN-DATA network resource with all users while keeping access to your C-DRIVE resource restricted to authorized users, such as yourself and the network manager. Suppose that you have a CD-ROM drive on your computer that you access by means of drive D. If you want to share your CD-ROM drive with other users on the network, you can set up a resource name of CD-ROM1, for example, that has a Local drive/directory of D.

Identifying Network Users

After you identify the computers and the resources on each shared computer, you need to determine which users get access to the shared resources. Initially, you do not have to be very detailed. Use the Network Account Card shown in figure 3.2 to help you identify the users/accounts that have access to network resources. Begin by filling out only the information with which you are comfortable. As you learn more about network accounts, you can complete the card. Depending on what kind of security and access measures you choose, you might not have the Network Account Cards filled out until after you learn the information contained in Chapter 6, "Setting Up User Accounts and Shared Resources in DOS" and in Chapter 7, "Setting Up User Accounts and Shared Resources in Windows."

After you identify your network users, you can list each individual user, list accounts by groups such as department or job function, and use a general wild-card account for all or any combination of users. After you install LANtastic, you can specify for LANtastic to set up the wild-card account * . A server that has the * account does not require separate accounts for individual users; the * applies to everyone and automatically logs in anyone who tries to access a shared resource on a server.

Before you begin filling out your Network Account Cards, you need to determine the type of accounts you want to use. If all users have the same level of access to the various shared resources, a single * wild-card account on each server suffices, greatly simplifying network configuration.

If users are permitted different types of access to the various shared resources on the network, you probably want to set up an account for each user. If you set up individual accounts, you can specify by user which network resources any particular user has access to. This method is the most time-consuming, but also offers the greatest amount of security.

Another option that still maintains a level of network security is to set up wild-card accounts. You can specify the type of access each group possesses to selected shared network resources. You might have, for example, a wild-card account by the name of SALES*. The SALES* account has a password associated with it so that anyone who knows the appropriate password can log in to a server by using this account.

It often makes sense to use a combination of account types. For example, you might have several users you want to use shared network printers and some shared drive/directories. You can configure the basic shared resources to be accessed by means of the * wild-card account. Basic network users don't have to have accounts to use the basic shared resources. You give some users a much higher level of access. For these users, you can set up an individual account (or a group wild-card account). Users who log in to a server by means of this account have access to more shared resources than users who use the * wild-card account.

Now that you have an understanding of the types of accounts you can set up, you can begin filling in your Network Account Cards accordingly.

Locating the Pieces of the Network

The next step in your network planning process is to determine where you want the pieces of the network to go. Sketch out the office spaces for the network. If you are not artistically inclined, you can probably get a copy of the floor plan from your building management office. Make several copies of your diagram or floor plan before you mark locations for the equipment.

Record the exact position of each existing computer, printer, and any other peripherals. If the network's installation necessitates moving a piece of equipment, show its new location. You will need this information when you define your cable needs.

At each computer location on the floor plan or diagram, mark the user's name and the type of equipment. You can use this information to assign names for each station. Verify the information you record by consulting the manager responsible for each area. If a conflict arises between your needs for the network and a manager's idea of the situation, sit down and discuss the situation and work out a compromise if necessary.

Anticipating Problems

The ability to anticipate potential problems before they occur enables you to take precautionary measures to either prevent the problem from occurring in the first place or have the proper response when the problem does occur.

Look at the floor plan or diagram and identify structural features that might prevent you from connecting a computer to the network. Are the computers on the same floor? Is a computer located in a room that has no access to the rest of the office spaces? Do you need to drill any holes in walls or floors? If so, do you need the building management's approval? Can you do this type of work? Can you run the cable through the ceiling space? Can you attach it to walls using cable channels? Do fire codes allow you to install any type of cable, or do you need to buy special cable or follow special procedures?

Before you begin any kind of work effort, you must resolve these questions. In addition, before you can calculate the exact amount of cable you need, you will require this information. If your computers are located within a few feet of each other and are in the same room, you do not have to deal with these issues.

If you follow this chapter's advice, your problems should be minimal. Occasionally, however, you may encounter a small hitch that aggravates you, such as the following:

✔ **You incorrectly measured the lengths of your cable runs.**

Try to move the computers closer together. If this is not possible, see if you can exchange a cable from a different location. If all else fails, remeasure and order the proper length. Save the original cable for use elsewhere, or use it as spare cable.

You may find it helpful to consult a cable installer to ensure that your installation is laid out with the appropriate cable type and length.

✔ **You omitted a computer or a peripheral from your inventory and location survey.**

Simply add the information to your charts and order the connectors and software to connect them. LANtastic enables you to add or delete workstations easily. (You can connect up to 500 computers by using LANtastic and the appropriate hardware.)

✔ **A piece of equipment refuses to function on the network or the entire network does not function properly.**

This problem is probably the most serious that you encounter. This subject is discussed in Chapter 16, "Troubleshooting Your Network."

What Type of Network Interface Cards Do I Need?

You should base the specific interface cards for your LANtastic installation on the optimal use of existing computers and on potential plans for expansion. This section discusses the selection of network adapter cards for your network and the type of cable that each adapter uses. Cable types are discussed in more detail in the next section.

If your building is already wired for a network, make sure that the installed cable is the proper one for the type of network you are planning.

The first step in the selection process is to determine the type of LANtastic network you are installing. Your two choices are Artisoft's proprietary 2 Mbps adapters or Ethernet. Ethernet is an industry standard and transmits data over the network at a speed of 10 Mbps (10 million bits per second). In general, an Ethernet implementation is the best choice. Ethernet is an industry standard; therefore, equipment is available from several manufacturers. Ethernet is faster than the 2 Mbps and offers greater potential for future expansion. Some situations, however, favor implementing a 2 Mbps network. If your network consists of PC- or XT-type computers (8088), 2 Mbps adapters are fast and require less conventional memory. The 2 Mbps adapters handle some of the network processing tasks using a built-in microprocessor. This feature reduces the CPU's network processing tasks. The following table lists advantages and disadvantages of Artisoft's 2 Mbps adapters, as compared to Ethernet adapters:

Table 2.1
Artisoft 2 Mbps Adapters

Advantages
Uses less conventional memory than Ethernet implementations
Microprocessor on network handles some of the network overhead

Disadvantages
Slower than Ethernet
Not an industry standard, so you are locked in to purchasing hardware provided by the manufacturer

If you select Ethernet network adapters, you must choose whether to use Thin Ethernet (coax) or UTP (Unshielded Twisted Pair).

Artisoft manufactures adapters that support Thin Ethernet (10BASE2), Thick Ethernet (10BASE5), and UTP (10BASE-T). Thin Ethernet and UTP are the most common Ethernet cable types used today. The Ethernet adapter you use has to support the type of cable you are using. Thin Ethernet and UTP both have advantages and disadvantages (see the following list).

✔ Thin Ethernet is less expensive to implement than UTP because a hub (concentrator) is not required.

✔ A single break in a Thin Ethernet cable disables the entire network. A single break in a UTP cable only disables the computer on the other end of the break.

✔ Thin Ethernet is connected in a Bus topology (computer to computer) whereas UTP is connected in a star topology. A *star topology* enables you to run the cable for each computer from the computer to a common location where the concentrator is located.

The following is a list of the LANtastic Ethernet adapters that support Thin Ethernet (10BASE2) cabling:

✔ **NodeRunner 2000/C.** A new software-configurable 16-bit Ethernet adapter

✔ **NodeRunner 2000M/TC.** A new software-configurable 16-bit Ethernet adapter for computers based on the MicroChannel bus

✔ **NodeRunner 2000/A.** A new software-configurable 16-bit Ethernet adapter that supports thick, thin, and UTP Ethernet cabling

The NodeRunner Ethernet adapters are now available in the NodeRunner/SI configurations. Although less expensive than the preceding NodeRunner adapters, these adapters cannot be used with the LANtastic 5.0 and earlier Ethernet software. (These adapters do work with LANtastic/AI 5.0 and earlier.)

Chapter 4, "Artisoft Network Products," describes in detail the differences between the NodeRunner and NodeRunner/SI Ethernet adapters and explains each adapter's application.

✔ **AE2.** A 16-bit Ethernet adapter that supports both thick (10BASE5) and thin (10BASE2) Ethernet cabling (discontinued 3/94)

✔ **AE3.** A 16-bit Ethernet adapter that supports thick, thin, and UTP Ethernet cabling (discontinued 3/94)

The following is a list of the LANtastic Ethernet adapters that support UTP (10BASE-T) cabling:

- ✔ **NodeRunner 2000/T.** A new software-configurable 16-bit Ethernet adapter

- ✔ **NodeRunner 2000M/TC.** A new software-configurable 16-bit Ethernet adapter for computers based on the MicroChannel bus

- ✔ **NodeRunner 2000/A.** A new software-configurable 16-bit Ethernet adapter that supports thick, thin, and UTP Ethernet cabling

- ✔ **AE1/T.** An 8-bit Ethernet adapter (discontinued)

- ✔ **AE2/T.** A 16-bit Ethernet adapter that supports both thick and UTP Ethernet cabling (discontinued 3/94)

- ✔ **AE3.** A 16-bit Ethernet adapter that supports thick, thin, and UTP Ethernet cabling (discontinued 3/94)

Some adapters use the same adapter card to support both Thin Ethernet and UTP. Although adapters that support more than one type of cabling tend to be more expensive, it is advantageous to have the flexibility to buy one adapter for either Ethernet implementation method.

These interface cards support the higher data throughput of 10 Mbps. You can use these cards in older 8088 or 8086 machines without concern, but they're not as fast as 80286 and higher CPUs, and are not recommended for use as network servers.

A LANtastic network that uses Artisoft's 2 Mbps adapters is typically cabled computer to computer (a *bus topology*). Artisoft's HUB enables you to configure a 2 Mbps network in a star or tree topology.

If you have only 8088 or 8086 machines, consider using the 2 Mbps interface cards and software for your implementation. This speed of interface card is the best for these machines, based on the capability of the internal bus to compute and share resources.

If you expand your network and add faster machines at a later date, you still can use slower machines effectively. Set up the slower computers on a 2 Mbps network leg and attach them to a faster server. A fast server can support both the 2 Mbps leg and a faster 10 Mbps network leg simultaneously. This is accomplished by putting both a 2 Mbps interface card and one of the faster 10 Mbps interface cards in the same server. The only drawback is that the machines on the 2 Mbps leg cannot communicate directly with the machines on the 10 Mbps leg. The slower machines still can exchange information with the faster machines by placing files on the common server for the faster machines to access.

Artisoft has introduced a product called LANtastic Interchange that will allow both the 2 MBPS and the 10 MBPS networks to communicate as if they were a single network. (LANtastic Interchange is known as a *software bridge*, which can connect LANtastic networks that use different topologies.)

Determining Cable Type

The type of cable you choose for your LANtastic network is influenced by a number of factors. If you are installing LANtastic 2 Mbps adapters, your cable choices are different than if you are installing Ethernet adapters. Different Ethernet adapters, moreover, require different types of cabling. If you have already chosen the type of network adapter you want, you probably already know the type of cable you must use. This section describes different types of cabling in detail.

Examining Cabling Options

As LANs increase in popularity, more cabling options become available. Today you can choose twisted-pair, coaxial, or fiber-optic cable. Fiber-optic cable is not discussed here because Artisoft does not support this type of installation with its existing network adapters.

The following list gives cable specifications for different cable types used with LANtastic network adapters. Included in this list are the cable names, the part numbers from various manufacturers, and the maximum cable lengths.

> ✔ **2 Mbps Adapters:**
>
>   Artisoft dual twisted-pair cable - 1,500 feet maximum cable length
>
>   Beldon 9729, 89729 - 1,000 feet maximum cable length
>
>   Phone grade DTP, 24 gauge, 100 ohm - 300 feet maximum cable length

> ✔ **Thin Ethernet (10BASE2) - 607 feet maximum cable length per segment:**
>
>   Artisoft RG58A/U coax
>
>   Beldon 9907 or 89907 (plenum) RG58A/U coax

Any IEEE 802.3 compliant RG58A/U or RG58C/U coax

✔ **UTP (10BASE-T) - 328 feet maximum cable length per segment (1 node):**

Artisoft UTP

AT&T 104, 315, 205

Beldon 1227A

Twisted-Pair Cable

This cable, also used in telephone systems, consists of two or more pairs of plastic-coated copper wire twisted in a precise pattern and wrapped in a protective outer covering. The way the wire pairs are twisted increases the cable's capability to transmit data over long distances. Flat untwisted wiring cannot match the performance capabilities of twisted-pair cable. Twisted-pair cable is round and is available in the following configurations.

Shielded Twisted-Pair Cable

This cable uses a special aluminum-impregnated mylar wrap inside the external cover. This shield protects data that is transmitted over the cable from external electromagnetic interference (see fig. 3.6).

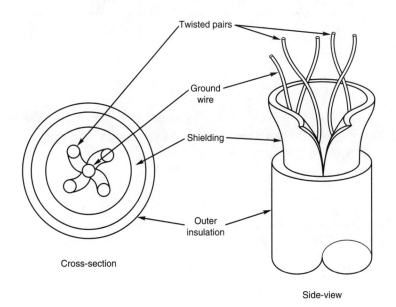

Figure 3.6
An example of shielded twisted-pair cable.

Shielded twisted-pair cable is suitable for installations near potential sources of interference from high-power electrical motors, electrical transformers, or strong radio frequency sources.

You can use shielded twisted-pair cable with LANtastic. Keep in mind, however, that the RJ45 connectors that connect the cable to the interface boards, are not protected against electrical interference.

Unshielded Twisted-Pair (UTP) Cable

This type of cable is used by phone companies and installed inside the walls of homes and office buildings. Unshielded twisted-pair (UTP) cable is smaller in diameter than shielded cable and is vulnerable to external interference (see fig. 3.7).

Figure 3.7
An example of unshielded twisted-pair cable.

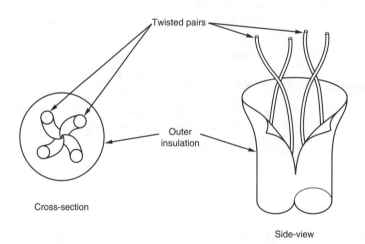

Unshielded twisted-pair cable works well for office networks because these environments usually do not have major sources of electrical interference. This type of cable is the cheapest and is available from many sources. Level 3 cable is rated for up to 10 Mbps, whereas Level 5 is rated for up to 100 Mbps.

Do not use the flat telephone-type cord for LANtastic connections because it is not suitable for network data transmission loads.

Some people use existing telephone wiring successfully in their office LANS. If you decide to use existing wiring, first test the cable for integrity and interference, such as "cross-talk" (other conversations heard in the background). Interference is disastrous to computer data because data can get scrambled and mixed with other data. You also need to diagram the exact location of all the wiring you use so that you can trace a problem.

Coaxial Cable

If you have cable TV in your home, you are familiar with coaxial cable. This type of cable is available in multiple sizes and varieties and the thickness depends on the diameter of the cable's copper wire core.

Coax, as it commonly is called, has a single copper wire core surrounded by an inner insulating material. A special shielding (also used in shielded twisted-pair cable) covers the insulating material, and a wire mesh is wrapped around this shielding. A final outer cover seals and protects the cable (see fig. 3.8).

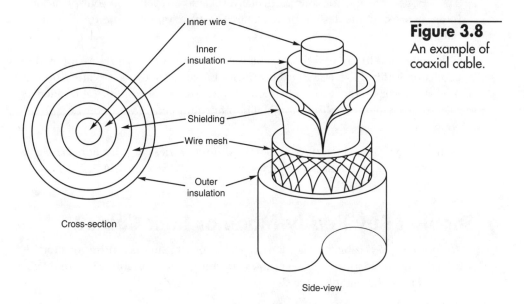

Figure 3.8
An example of coaxial cable.

The outer coating of coax can be made of PVC, Teflon, or another waterproof material. PVC is a durable plastic coating, but because it burns easily and gives off toxic fumes, it is prohibited in many commercial installations. Teflon is a coating that resists high temperatures in a fire and is called for by many fire codes. Teflon coaxial cable often is referred to as plenum cable.

Older Ethernet installations and high-power networks use thick cabling. This variety is yellow, fairly stiff, and does not install easily. This type of cable is not normally used for LANtastic networks, but if you need to use it, hire a professional installer.

The most common type of coax found in Ethernet installations (and the kind that LANtastic includes in its starter kits) is similar to the type of coax used for cable TV. Thin coax is flexible enough to install yourself, and it provides excellent data protection and performance.

Thin coax has become the most popular cable for network use because of its capability to support fairly powerful network throughput loads and its ease of installation. If you use this cable initially in your LANtastic network, it can expand without restriction for a long time.

Which Cable Is the Best for My Network?

The best type of cable for your particular installation depends on your plans for future expansion, the desired network flexibility you want to achieve, and your budget.

If flexibility and future network capability are your major concerns, as opposed to cost, choose 10BASE-T (UTP) cable for your LANtastic network. Because 10BASE-T is used in a star topology, you will need to purchase a concentrator (also called a *hub*) to which all the cables from the different computers in your network will be connected.

Many concentrators, including Artisoft's T-Runner series concentrators, have a BNC connector on the back so that you can mix 10BASE2 and 10BASE-T networks.

Should I Buy Ready-Made or Bulk Cable?

Ready-made cable is cable that is cut to a specific length, and has end connectors already installed. Normally, these cables are checked for continuity before they are shipped from the manufacturer.

Artisoft packages 25-foot lengths of thin coax with each Ethernet starter kit. Artisoft also sells 25-foot, 50-foot, and 100-foot lengths of ready-made cable to fit your potential needs. You can buy additional cable and network interface cards to add new stations to your network as you need them.

Thin coax cable is preferred because of its flexibility and expansion capability. Unless you have a need for unusually long runs of cable (in excess of 100 feet), the starter kits and additional ready-made cable from Artisoft eliminate guesswork and ensure that you get matched cable and interface cards. These kits also are the easiest and quickest way to set up and run your network.

If you need to install cable runs longer than 100 feet, or connect workstations on different floors, you may want to buy bulk cable and make your own cable lengths. If you buy several hundred feet of cable, do not be afraid to ask for a discount (you can buy partial spools).

If you buy bulk cable, you also need to purchase BNC end connectors, BNC T-connectors, BNC terminator plugs, a special coaxial cable stripper, and a crimper to install the connectors. The stripper and crimper should cost less than $75. The connectors vary in price from approximately $2.45 for each end connector to $5.50 for each T-connector. The terminator plugs should cost around $7. Ask your local dealers for exact pricing.

Stripping the cable ends and installing the connectors is not difficult. Just follow the instructions packaged with the crimper and make sure that you get a good crimp on the connectors. You will need to adjust your cable stripper until the cable is stripped properly without partially cutting into the conductors. It's important to use the right tools for the job, especially for cabling. It's also important to make sure the crimper is matched for the type of connectors you are using; otherwise, your connection may be faulty even though you may think that it is correct. Most network-related problems are due either to the wrong cable or to faulty network cable connections.

Summary

By now, most of your fears and concerns should be alleviated. You have completed the critical planning phase and are ready to begin the actual installation of your network. Before you begin, however, put together a small toolkit that includes several sizes of straight-bladed screwdrivers, Phillips-head screwdrivers, and a pair of needle-nosed pliers. Make sure that you also have a small screwdriver. If you are installing or configuring your own cable, having the proper tools for the job is critical to your success.

Chapter Snapshot

This chapter provides a list of the various products now produced by Artisoft, and gives a brief description of each. The application of the different products and how they relate to each other is also covered. You learn about the following in this chapter:

✔ Network Operating System (NOS)

✔ Artisoft network adapters

✔ LANtastic starter kits

✔ LANtastic add-on kits

✔ Connectivity products

✔ Concentrators

✔ Utility software

✔ Other Artisoft products

After reading this chapter, you will understand the Artisoft products available and which products apply in your situation.

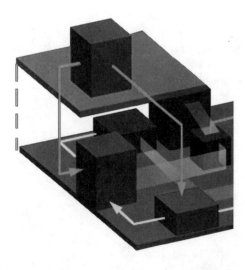

Artisoft Network Products

S ince its founding in 1982, Artisoft has been producing exceptional peer-to-peer networking products. Dedication to the improvement of network technology has won Artisoft award after award over the years. Artisoft produces network hardware and software products, including network adapters, the LANtastic Network Operating System (NOS), and several other products to enhance network functionality and capability. In addition to this NOS, Artisoft also produces an entry-level NOS, called Simply LANtastic, for small businesses and home offices.

Network Operating System (NOS)

LANtastic, first released in 1987, was developed to be a powerful yet easy-to-use network operating system for the small to medium-sized business. It is relatively inexpensive to implement, doesn't require a significant amount of memory (LANtastic's "Tiny RAM"), and works with your existing computers; dedicated servers or expensive hardware upgrades are not required. As a peer-to-peer network, LANtastic enables every computer in the network to share its resources (such as disk drives and printers) with other users in the network. In addition, any user can access and use the shared resources on other computers. Today, LANtastic is the leading peer-to-peer network operating system offering easy installation and use without sacrificing features and performance.

As LANtastic evolved, users demanded more features and power—and Artisoft delivered. After LANtastic 5.0 was introduced, Artisoft realized that LANtastic had grown so powerful, with so many features and flexibility, it was no longer considered an entry-level network operating system for the small business and home user.

LANtastic 6.0 is an extremely powerful network operating system offering flexible configuration options and supporting a host of add-on options for a variety of tasks.

LANtastic 6.0

Introduced in 1994, LANtastic 6.0 is a high-end network operating system offering a broad range of features, high performance, and the flexibility required by today's businesses. LANtastic 6.0 features relatively small RAM usage, multiple levels of security, extensive electronic mail and scheduling capabilities, Windows compatibility, and audit-trail generation. Resources can be available from any station on the network, and LANtastic provides full support for CD-ROM and other types of drives.

LANtastic 6.0 enables you to configure your network as peer-to-peer, dedicated server, or a combination of both. LANtastic allows your computers to connect with servers using NetWare Core Protocol (NCP) and Server Message Block (SMB) protocol, permitting your LANtastic nodes to access servers running network operating systems from Novell, Microsoft, and IBM.

A computer configured as a LANtastic server uses a total of 89 KB of memory (RAM) in the default configuration using the Artisoft Ethernet adapters. Configured as a workstation, the same computer uses 46 KB less for a total of 43 KB. LANtastic 6.0 enables you to change the features and performance of a LANtastic server, thus using more or less memory than the default configuration.

LANtastic 6.0 supports all the Artisoft network adapters as well as many adapters from other manufacturers. With the NDIS support included with LANtastic 6.0, you can use virtually any network adapter so long as the manufacturer provides an NDIS driver for it.

Prior to LANtastic 6.0, several different implementations of LANtastic were available. The primary difference between the different implementations of LANtastic was the network adapters that each supported. In addition, each implementation (with the exception of LANtastic Z) was packaged as a DOS or Windows version. The DOS version supported Windows but did not include the Windows versions of the LANtastic programs such as NET and NET_MGR. The Windows version included the Windows LANtastic programs as well as the DOS programs. The different implementations are as follows:

LANtastic 5.0 (Ethernet) (DOS/WIN). This implementation of LANtastic supported Artisoft Ethernet adapters including NodeRunner Series, AE Series, and NE Series. This was licensed per network, meaning a single copy supported up to 500 network nodes. This implementation is still available, although the pricing discourages the purchase of LANtastic 5.0 in favor of LANtastic 6.0.

LANtastic 5.0 (2 Mbps) (DOS/WIN). This implementation of LANtastic supported all the proprietary Artisoft 2 Mbps adapters. Licensed per network, a single copy supported up to 500 network nodes.

LANtastic/AI 5.0 (DOS/WIN). This is the Adapter Independent (AI) implementation of LANtastic that supported non-Artisoft network adapters manufactured by other companies. LANtastic/AI was licensed per node, meaning one licensed copy of the software was required for each computer in the network.

LANtastic Z 5.0 (DOS). This implementation supported connecting two computers together using parallel ports, serial ports, or a modem. A single licensed copy of LANtastic Z was required for the two computers being connected. This is the current implementation for LANtastic Z. (LANtastic Z is not available in a LANtastic 6.0 implementation.)

LANtastic 6.0 is licensed on a per node basis. The LANtastic 6.0 software is available in a 1-, 5-, 10-, 25-, 50-, and 100-user license. Also, a LANtastic 6.0 starter kit and two LANtastic 6.0 add-on kits are available.

Following are some of the major features and benefits of the LANtastic 6.0 network operating system (NOS):

✔ **Shares files, printers, hard drives, and CD-ROM drives.** LANtastic enables you to use the shared resources on any other computer and enables other users to use the shared resources on your computer.

✔ **Faster than previous versions.** LANtastic includes efficient internal file and record locking. The DOS Share command is no longer required for file and record locking.

✔ **Communicates and interoperates with Novell NetWare 2.x, 3.x, and 4.x servers using NCP.** If you have a Novell server, any LANtastic node can access and use the resources on your Novell server.

✔ **Communicates and interoperates with LAN Server, LAN Manager, Windows for Workgroups, and Windows NT servers using SMB protocol.** Any LANtastic node can access and use the shared resources on servers running LAN Server, LAN Manager, Windows for Workgroups, or Windows NT network operating systems.

✔ **Supports connections to OS/2, WORM (Write Once Read Many), and other non-DOS drives.** Drives previously only available to the computer on which they are physically installed may be available to other users in the network.

✔ **Any computer can be configured as a dedicated server, workstation, or nondedicated server/workstation.** LANtastic gives you the greatest amount of flexibility to configure your network as you require.

✔ **Compatible with LANtastic 5.0 and Simply LANtastic network stations.** You do not have to upgrade your entire network to LANtastic 6.0; you can mix computers running LANtastic 6.0 with those running LANtastic 5.0 and Simply LANtastic, and they will still be able to "talk" with each other.

✔ **Full compatibility with Windows 3.1.** Also supports network DDE with Linkbook feature. LANtastic enhances Windows 3.1 features and even supports network Dynamic Data Exchange (DDE).

✔ **Supports NDIS-compliant network adapter drivers supplied by many manufacturers.** Since almost all network adapter manufacturers ship their adapters with NDIS adapter drivers, LANtastic 6.0 will work with virtually all network adapters manufactured today.

✔ **Extensive network management services.** This feature includes performance monitoring, import and export of user accounts, network configuration from a single computer, audit trails to track network activity, remote server shutdown, and UPS support.

✔ **Unloadable from memory without rebooting.** You can remove LANtastic from memory when not needed to make more conventional memory available for other programs.

✔ **Extensive security features with 30 levels of protection for everything from individual files to entire drives.** Security for individual users or groups of users. You can specify exactly which users can have access to which resources and the level of access they may have.

✔ **Supports wildcard user names and groups.** You can specify accounts for individual users or groups of users, or even an account that enables everyone to log in to a server without specifying a username or password.

✔ **Automatically reconnects to server if connection has been broken.** If for some reason a computer is rebooted, the network will automatically re-establish the connection.

✔ **Includes Artisoft Exchange Mail and Scheduling program with fax and pager capability.** The sophisticated e-mail and scheduling package runs in Microsoft Windows.

✔ **Easy to install and use.** The installation program will set up a wild-card account and shared resources, so no additional setup is required to use a fully functional LANtastic network.

✔ **Increases network performance with LANCACHE.** This feature improves network speed by caching disk drive reads and writes.

✔ **Implements resource caching to improve network performance even more.** Resource information can be accessed from RAM instead of from the hard drive.

✔ **Network commands may be issued in a variety of ways.** You can use easy-to-use menus, batch files, command lines, and the Windows interface.

✔ **Low memory (RAM) requirements.** NOS can be loaded into upper memory using memory manager programs such as EMM386, included in DOS 5.0 and higher.

✔ **Remote Accounts.** LANtastic enables you to set up user accounts on a single server that can be accessed by all other servers in the network.

✔ **Global Resources.** You can set up a resource on a server that actually points to a resource that exists on a different server. When the global resource is accessed, a direct link is established between the server with the resource and the machine accessing the resource so performance doesn't suffer.

✔ **Deferred NET LOGIN and NET USE Commands.** You can defer the actual connection to a server until the resource actually is used.

✔ **Remote Despooling.** Any computer in the network can despool print jobs from a server. Multiple computers can despool the same print queue.

LANtastic Z

LANtastic Z uses your computer's serial or parallel port or a modem to make the physical link between two computers, instead of using the standard network adapters commonly used. Because it does not require adapters, LANtastic Z is a good alternative for portable and laptop computer users who must connect to their home office servers by means of modem. In the office, you can connect two computers together by using serial or parallel port connections and have a fully functioning LANtastic network on the two computers. LANtastic Z also allows two computers to be connected using modems.

Although LANtastic Z enables you to have a fully functional two-station LANtastic network without the use of network adapters, the downside is that network performance is relatively poor since performance is limited by the speed limitation of the parallel port, serial port, or modem used.

Currently, LANtastic Z implements LANtastic 5.0 and only the DOS version. (It does have Windows support, but does not include the LANtastic for Windows programs.)

Simply LANtastic

Simply LANtastic is Artisoft's entry-level network for small businesses and home offices. It was designed to be easy to install and use while maintaining compatibility with LANtastic 5.0 and 6.0. Simply LANtastic is available in a starter kit, an add-on kit, and a software kit.

The Simply LANtastic software kit includes the software for one PC in a Simply LANtastic network and a 25-foot cable. You have to supply your own network adapter. Simply LANtastic supports Artisoft Simply LANtastic adapters, Artisoft Ethernet adapters, and any other adapter that comes with an NDIS network adapter driver.

Following are some of the features and benefits of Simply LANtastic:

✔ **Quick and easy installation and setup.** Your Simply LANtastic network will be up and operational in a matter of minutes.

✔ **True peer-to-peer operation.** This feature allows any computer to share disk drives and printers with any other computer.

✔ **Easily shares resources.** These resources include printers, disk drives, files, programs, and even CD-ROM drives.

✔ **Works easily in DOS and Windows environments.** You can have any mixture of computers running DOS and Windows without limitations on your network functionality.

✔ **No special PC hardware requirements.** Simply LANtastic runs on anything from an older XT type computer to a 486 or Pentium computer.

✔ **Security features.** These possibilities include setting no access, read only access, or full access for network resources shared with others.

✔ **Includes electronic mail.** E-mail can be used for sending messages and files to other users.

✔ **Compatible and upgradable.** Simply LANtastic can work with the LANtastic network operating system.

Artisoft Network Adapters

Artisoft manufactures a variety of network adapters. The following is a list of the adapters currently available as well as those which have recently been discontinued.

NodeRunner Series Adapters

The NodeRunner series of Ethernet network adapters (see fig. 4.1) incorporate Artisoft's ALICE Ethernet controller chip. They include 32 KB of on-board buffer RAM (compared to 16 KB on the AE series adapters) and are 16-bit adapters. The adapters are software configurable, meaning no jumper settings need to be set on the adapter itself. The adapters automatically adjust to 8- or 16-bit expansion slots. The adapters support remote booting (except for the 2000M/TC) with Programmable Erasable Read Only Memory (PEROM) for diskless workstations. The data transfer rate is 10 Mbps.

There are two families of NodeRunner adapters: the NodeRunner series and the NodeRunner/SI series. The NodeRunner series Ethernet adapters enable you to purchase the adapter without additional LANtastic software to add stations to your network running LANtastic Ethernet software prior to 6.0. The NodeRunner/SI series Ethernet adapters are system independent (SI) and were developed to be used with other network operating systems.

 Although the NodeRunner Ethernet adapters also emulate the Novell NE2000 Ethernet adapters and therefore work with other network operating systems, they are more expensive than the NodeRunner/SI adapters.

Although the NodeRunner adapters do not require you to purchase additional LANtastic software, the NodeRunner/SI adapters require a copy of LANtastic/AI for each computer prior to LANtastic 6.0.

LANtastic 6.0 is now licensed per network node so the NodeRunner/SI series network adapters are the appropriate choice. In fact, it is less expensive to purchase a NodeRunner/SI series adapter and LANtastic 6.0 software than to purchase just a NodeRunner series adapter to be used with a version of LANtastic prior to 6.0.

 Prior to LANtastic 6.0, a single copy of LANtastic could be purchased and used for up to 500 computers in a network, provided you purchased Artisoft network adapters. The Artisoft adapters were more expensive than many competing products, but because you didn't have to purchase additional network software, it was less expensive to buy an Artisoft adapter than to buy a non-Artisoft adapter with the required LANtastic/AI software for each adapter.

As prices of network adapters continued to erode, the spread between the price of Artisoft adapters and adapters with the same specifications from other manufacturers became larger. In response to this price erosion, Artisoft developed the NodeRunner/SI series of Ethernet adapters to compete. The NodeRunner/SI adapters required the purchase of LANtastic/AI for each computer and would not work with the standard LANtastic Ethernet software for Artisoft Ethernet adapters.

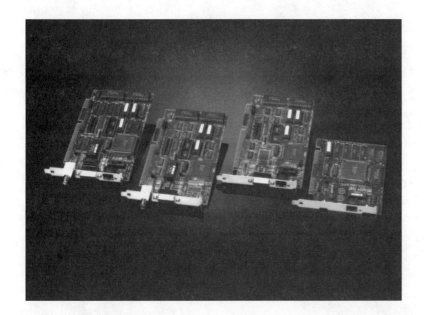

Figure 4.1
The LANtastic 2000/C, 2000/A, 2000/T, and 2000M/TC NodeRunner adapters.

The following lists each NodeRunner adapter available and the type of cable and interface each adapter supports:

NodeRunner 2000/C and NodeRunner/SI 2000/C. Supports thin Ethernet cable (Thinnet coax) and standard Industry Standard Architecture (ISA) bus.

NodeRunner 2000/T and NodeRunner/SI 2000/T. Supports unshielded twisted-pair cable (10BASE-T) and standard ISA (Industry Standard Architecture) bus.

NodeRunner 2000/A and NodeRunner/SI 2000/A. Supports thin Ethernet cable (Thinnet coax), thick Ethernet cable, and unshielded twisted-pair (10BASE-T) cable. Supports standard ISA bus.

NodeRunner 2000M/TC and NodeRunner 2000M/TC. Supports thin Ethernet cable (Thinnet coax) and unshielded twisted-pair (10BASE-T) cable. Supports Micro Channel bus.

AE Series Ethernet Adapters (Discontinued)

The Artisoft AE series Ethernet adapters have been replaced by the newer NodeRunner series Ethernet adapters. The AE series Ethernet adapters were very popular and widely used in LANtastic networks. The AE series Ethernet adapters were configured using jumpers on the adapter and were not software configurable as the NodeRunner adapters are.

Following is a list of the AE series Ethernet adapters:

AE-1/T Ethernet Adapter. An 8-bit Ethernet adapter. Supports unshielded twisted-pair cable (10BASE-T) and standard ISA bus. This adapter was designed to be a low-cost network solution and was actually introduced after the AE-2 series 16-bit Ethernet adapters.

AE-2 Ethernet Adapter. A 16-bit Ethernet adapter. Supports thin Ethernet cable (Thinnet coax), and thick Ethernet cable. Supports standard ISA bus.

AE-2/T Ethernet Adapter. A 16-bit Ethernet adapter. Supports unshielded twisted-pair cable (10BASE-T) and thick Ethernet cable. Supports standard ISA bus.

AE-3 Ethernet Adapter. A 16-bit Ethernet adapter. Supports thin Ethernet cable (Thinnet coax), unshielded twisted-pair cable (10BASE-T), and thick Ethernet cable. Supports standard ISA bus.

2 Mbps Adapters

LANtastic was originally available only for Artisoft's 2 Mbps (2 million bits per second) proprietary adapter. Because Ethernet is the widely accepted standard of choice, the 2 Mbps adapter is usually not a first choice for new network installations. The latest version of this adapter is called the A2 Mbps and comes in both standard ISA bus and Micro Channel bus compatible versions. Each adapter includes a 10 MHz coprocessor and 32 KB of on-board RAM. Artisoft's NetBIOS implementation is loaded and executed within the adapter's RAM, and all network processing is performed by the adapter. Off-loading the network processing to the adapter keeps the overhead RAM requirement to 2 KB for the host computer. For this reason, these adapters work well with older PCs. These adapters can support cable lengths of up to 1,500 feet using Artisoft's dual twisted-pair cable, or up to 300 feet using AT&T telephone-grade cable. A 32-node maximum is allowed per 2 Mbps network segment. Data transfer rate is 2 Mbps.

Simply LANtastic Adapters

The Simply LANtastic adapters are an 8 bit 10 Mbps (10 million bits per second) adapter. The technology used for the adapter is the same as the NodeRunner Ethernet adapters, although the cabling used to connect the adapters is not a standard Ethernet implementation. Each adapter has two 3.5mm phono plugs. The nodes are connected in a daisy chain arrangement with thin RG174 coax cable available from Artisoft in 10-, 25-, and 50-foot lengths. The total network cable length may not exceed 200 feet and no more than 20 computers may be connected with Simply LANtastic adapters. A Simply LANtastic cable segment may be connected to a thin Ethernet (thin coax, RG58A/U) segment with a BNC adapter available from Artisoft, although the total network segment length of 607 feet available with thin coax is reduced when adding a Simply LANtastic cable segment.

LANtastic Starter Kits

Artisoft packages both LANtastic and Simply LANtastic in starter kits containing every element needed to make installation worry-free. Each kit contains the necessary software, network-interface adapters, and cable to connect two computers in a fully functioning peer-to-peer network. The available kits are described in the following paragraphs.

LANtastic 6.0 Starter Kit

The LANtastic 6.0 network starter kit includes everything necessary to install a LANtastic 6.0 network on two computers, using thin coax (10BASE2 Ethernet) cabling. The LANtastic 6.0 NodeRunner/SI 2000/C network starter kit (see fig. 4.2) contains two NodeRunner/SI 2000/C Ethernet network adapter cards, the LANtastic 6.0 network operating system for two computers, two BNC T-connectors, two terminator plugs, documentation, and a 25-foot thin coax cable.

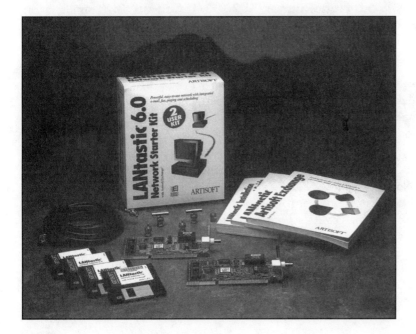

Figure 4.2
The LANtastic 6.0 NodeRunner/SI Network Starter Kit.

Simply LANtastic Starter Kit

The Simply LANtastic starter kit contains everything necessary to install a Simply LANtastic network on two computers. Included are two Simply LANtastic network adapters, the Simply LANtastic network operating system software for two computers, documentation, and a 25-foot Simply LANtastic network cable.

LANtastic Add-on Kits

The LANtastic add-on kits include the network hardware and software necessary to add a station to your existing LANtastic or Simply LANtastic network. Instead of having to purchase the network adapter and then the appropriate LANtastic software, the add-on kit bundles the two together.

LANtastic 6.0 Add-on Kits

Two LANtastic 6.0 add-on kits are available to enable you to add a LANtastic 6.0 network node to your existing LANtastic 6.0 thin coax or UTP (10BASE-T) Ethernet networks. The LANtastic 6.0 add-on kits include a network adapter and the LANtastic 6.0 software with documentation, but do not include the cable necessary to add your additional LANtastic 6.0 network node—make sure you purchase the appropriate thin coax or UTP cable in addition to the add-on kit.

LANtastic 6.0 NodeRunner/SI 2000/C Add-on Kit. This kit includes a NodeRunner/SI 2000/C Ethernet adapter for use on a thin coax network, the LANtastic 6.0 software for one network node, and documentation.

LANtastic 6.0 NodeRunner/SI 2000/T Add-on Kit. This kit includes a NodeRunner/SI 2000/T Ethernet adapter for use on a UTP (10BASE-T) network, the LANtastic 6.0 software for one network node, and documentation.

LANtastic 5.0 add-on kits are still available for the LANtastic NodeRunner (not NodeRunner/SI) adapters. They include the NodeRunner adapter (NodeRunner 2000/C, NodeRunner 2000/T, NodeRunner 2000/A, or NodeRunner 2000M/TC) and a license for the additional network node. The pricing of the LANtastic 5.0 add-on kits discourage their purchase in favor of either a LANtastic 6.0 add-on kit or the purchase of a NodeRunner/SI Ethernet adapter and the LANtastic 6.0 network operating system.

Simply LANtastic Add-on Kit

The Simply LANtastic add-on kit enables you to easily add a Simply LANtastic network node to your Simply LANtastic network. Included is a Simply LANtastic adapter, the Simply LANtastic network operating system software and documentation for one computer, and a 25-foot Simply LANtastic cable.

Connectivity Products

The Artisoft connectivity products are products that may be added to your LANtastic network to enable computers in this network to connect to and communicate with remote computers or in other types of networks.

LANtastic for TCP/IP

LANtastic for TCP/IP enables users in your LANtastic network to connect to computing platforms that use Transmission Control Protocol/Internet Protocol (TCP/IP). This permits any PC in your LANtastic network to access data and resources on UNIX, VMS, and IBM TCP/IP hosts, including computers such as DEC/VAX, HP, SUN, NCR, and AT&T mini-computers, IBM mainframes, and other PCs running SCO UNIX. LANtastic for TCP/IP enables a user on a LANtastic network to share the host computer's printers, disk space, data files, and applications.

LANtastic for TCP/IP is implemented by first installing the LANtastic for TCP/IP management software on a single LANtastic server (called the LANtastic TCP/IP server). From the LANtastic TCP/IP server, an installation is performed on the LANtastic network nodes (called LANtastic TCP/IP workstations) that will be accessing a TCP/IP host computer. The LANtastic TCP/IP server stores the TCP/IP software, which is run on the LANtastic TCP/IP workstations. In addition, the LANtastic TCP/IP server takes care of all the management services required when communicating with other computers using TCP/IP. Once LANtastic for TCP/IP is installed and configured, any LANtastic for TCP/IP workstation can access a TCP/IP host computer. LANtastic for TCP/IP is available in 1-, 5-, 10-, and 100-user licenses. The LANtastic for TCP/IP server keeps track of the number of TCP/IP workstations accessing it and, as soon as the license count is reached, prevents additional workstations from performing any TCP/IP-related operations.

LANtastic for TCP/IP comes as software only; the PCs in your LANtastic network are connected to the same physical Ethernet cable as the other TCP/IP hosts they will be accessing. Applications supported by LANtastic for TCP/IP include

TELNET (terminal emulation), FTP (file transfer protocol), LPR (printing utilities), FTPD, TFTP, RCP, RLOGIN, RSH, NFS (client), and MAILX (send only). In addition, Windows applications include TELNET, FTP, and LPR.

LANtastic for Macintosh

LANtastic for Macintosh enables you to use a PC as a gateway server to connect your LANtastic network with a Macintosh network. Files stored on the gateway computer are visible from both the PCs in the LANtastic network and the Macs in the Macintosh network. Macintosh computers can access files on any LANtastic server, and PCs are able to access Macintosh files that have been saved on the gateway server. In addition, Macintosh computers may access PostScript printers on any LANtastic server.

The gateway server requires two network adapter cards to be installed; one is connected to the LANtastic network, and the other is connected to the Macintosh network. LANtastic for Macintosh supports LocalTalk, EtherTalk, and TokenTalk Macintosh networks.

The following three packages are available for LANtastic for Macintosh:

LANtastic for Macintosh Windows Gateway. This package runs on a dedicated or non-dedicated gateway PC running Microsoft Windows. The gateway program runs as a background Windows task, while in the foreground other Windows applications may be run. When used in a Macintosh Ethertalk network, the LANtastic for Macintosh Windows Gateway supports NodeRunner adapters or other NE2000 compatible adapters.

LANtastic for Macintosh software-only kit. This package runs on a dedicated gateway PC. The dedicated PC should be a 286-based computer or better with a minimum of 640 KB RAM, DOS 3.3 or higher, and a hard drive. The network adapter connecting to the Macintosh network must be a compatible LocalTalk, EtherTalk (3COM 3C503), or TokenTalk adapter.

LANtastic for Macintosh hardware/software kit. This package includes an adapter to connect the gateway PC to a Macintosh AppleTalk network, in addition to the LANtastic for Macintosh software described previously.

LANtastic Interchange

LANtastic Interchange is a software product that enables you to bridge two dissimilar LANtastic networks, permitting the two LANtastic networks to communicate with each other. LANtastic supports multiple network adapters in a single PC. Without LANtastic Interchange, two dissimilar LANtastic networks could share a common PC if you put a network adapter for each network in a single PC. Each network would be connected to the appropriate network adapter. LANtastic Interchange bridges the two networks and allows the networks to operate as a single LANtastic network. In addition, LANtastic Interchange provides routing capability so the network traffic not destined for the other network segment doesn't cross to the other side, thereby preventing unnecessary network congestion.

LANtastic Interchange may be used in conjunction with LANtastic Z and modems to connect two physically separate LANtastic networks, creating a low-cost (and admittedly low-performance) Wide Area Network (WAN).

Another beneficial use for LANtastic Interchange is to connect a LANtastic network using 2 Mbps adapters with a LANtastic network using Ethernet adapters. This can be very common in situations in which a company originally started with 2 Mbps adapters and, as computers are later acquired, purchases Ethernet adapters with the systems. LANtastic Interchange enables the two types of LANtastic networks to appear and operate as one.

 LANtastic Interchange uses 80 KB RAM and requires a 386SX or better computer with 1 MB RAM.

Central Station II

The Artisoft Central Station II (see fig. 4.3) is a device that acts as a network station by enabling you to connect printers, modems, and other devices to your network. The Central Station II includes software, called StationWare, which allows the Central Station II to act as an external Ethernet adapter, enabling you to connect a PC or laptop computer to the network using the parallel port on the computer. In addition, StationWare is included to allow Central Station II to act as a print server, relieving a server in your network from that task. Up to five printers (three serial and two parallel) may be attached to Central Station II concurrently. With the supplied Dial-Up Connection StationWare, computers located remotely may dial in to and become part of your LANtastic network with the use of high-speed modems. StationWare is also available to provide the same features in a Novell NetWare network.

Figure 4.3
The Artisoft
Central Station II
Connectivity
Processor.

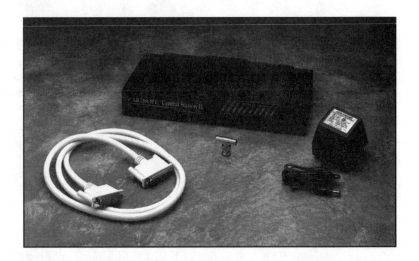

Central Station II includes a BNC connector for thin coax and a RJ-45 connector for 10BASE-T to connect your Central Station II to your network. Other ports on the Central Station II include a parallel port, a PC port, two serial ports (DB9 connectors), and an AUX serial port (DB9 connector). The parallel port may be used to connect a parallel printer to your LANtastic network. The PC port enables you to connect a PC or laptop computer to your LANtastic network using the parallel port on the computer. The PC port may also double as a parallel port, used to connect an additional parallel printer to your network. The serial ports may be employed to connect serial printers or external modems for dial-in network connections. The AUX serial port may be used to connect a serial printer to the network. Central Station II supports simultaneous use of its ports, so any combination of the preceding uses may be used concurrently.

The Central Station II has its own on-board processor and 128 KB of RAM, which may be upgraded to 256 KB or 640 KB. The serial ports support baud rates up to 57,600. LEDs provide constant monitoring of the station's connections and ports.

Concentrators

Artisoft manufactures two types of concentrators that may be used with your 10BASE-T network: the internal Peer-Hub, and the external T-Runner 800/TC and T-Runner 1200/TC (see fig. 4.4).

Figure 4.4
The Artisoft Peer-Hub, T-Runner 800/TC, and T-Runner 1200/TC Concentrators.

Peer-Hub

The Peer-Hub is an intelligent internal hub that includes 5 RJ-45 ports for 10BASE-T connections. It is an 8-bit card that installs inside a PC and includes internal connectors to allow up to 5 Peer-Hubs in a single PC. An AUI kit is also available to assist you in linking your UTP (10BASE-T) network and your thin coax Ethernet network with the use of an Artisoft AE-3 network adapter (now discontinued).

Software is included for monitoring and controlling the ports. Peer-Hub's software enables the host computer to observe the status of the ports and to enable or disable each individually. The on-board memory stores your network configuration, enabling you to restore your network quickly in the event of a power outage.

T-Runner (8 and 12 Port)

The T-Runner 800/TC and T-Runner 1200/TC are 8- and 12-port concentrators/hubs for use in connecting your 10BASE-T network nodes. In addition to the RJ-45 ports for 10BASE-T connections, the T-Runner also contains a BNC connector that enables you to connect up to 30 concentrators (per network segment) or to bridge your 10BASE-T network to thin Ethernet (coax) segments. Each port has two LEDs to confirm the link integrity and to show port activity as data is displayed.

Utility Software

Artisoft has several additional software packages that help to enhance the capability of your LANtastic network. The following packages enable you to share modems across the network, back up and manage the data on your LANtastic network, and remotely control or view other nodes on your LANtastic network.

Articom (Modem/COM Sharing)

Articom is a software package that allows a modem in any PC on the network to be shared with other users in the network. Articom also allows any bi-directional serial device, such as a plotter, to be shared on the network. Articom includes terminal emulation software, which contains a dialing directory and multiple file transfer protocols for uploading and downloading files. Any other communications software package that has INT 14 support may be used to access the serial devices shared with Articom. When you need to use a modem, the modem pooling feature allows Articom to search for an available modem in your network and establish the connection.

Additional software enables you to configure the serial ports to be shared with others. Connections to shared COM ports on other computers may be established using the ACOM utility or from the DOS command line.

Supported terminal emulations include DOS, ANSI BBS, DEC VT-100, DEC VT-52, DEC VT-320, and TTY. Articom supports baud rates from 110 to 115200; parity of None, Odd, Even, Mark, and Space; stop bits of 1, 1.5, and 2; and flow control using XON/XOFF, hardware, or none.

Artisave (Tape B/U)

Artisave is a sophisticated tape backup program specifically designed to back up computers in a LANtastic network. While most tape backup software allows a fair amount of flexibility when it comes to what to back up, very few provide any features to help you manage your backups. Artisave allows complete, differential, incremental, and selective backups, while also providing several features to help you manage the backup data by tracking the computers from which the backups were made as well as the data backed up. The Librarian tracks every file that has been backed up, and which disk, directory, and computer it came from. The Librarian also tells you which tape contains the file you are looking for and the last time it was backed up. If you lose a hard drive, the Rescue feature enables you to reconstruct the data that was on the drive at the time of the last backup, based on the previous backups that were performed on that drive. You can use the

Scheduler feature to specify the computers and types of backups to perform automatically at pre-specified times.

Artisave is a Windows-based application and supports SCSI tape drives with a backup rate of 10 MB per minute. Artisave is also available with the Mountain SideCar II, which plugs into a parallel port and provides backup rates of up to 2 MB per minute.

Network Eye

The Network Eye is a remote control program that enables you to view and control the screen on another computer. You can view and control multiple computers at once, with the screen from each computer appearing in a separate window on your computer. Up to 32 screens may be viewed at once. The ability to view the screens and control other computers from a single computer is especially useful for network managers and other personnel who are responsible for helping and troubleshooting problems encountered by other users. The Network Eye also enables the screen on a single PC to be transmitted to and viewed by other computers. This feature is especially valuable in a training environment in which the instructor can demonstrate a procedure on his own PC and have his screen appear on the students' screens.

The Network Eye only supports character-based application viewing, which means graphical-based programs such as Windows are not able to be viewed or controlled with the Network Eye.

Other Artisoft Products

In addition to the products already described, Artisoft manufactures two additional products: the Sounding Board, which incorporates voice and sound in LANtastic networks, and Artiscribe, which incorporates the Sounding Board in a network document and dictation system.

Sounding Board

The Artisoft Sounding Board is a hardware/software combination that brings the excitement of voice and sound to your network. The package includes one 8-bit Sounding Board adapter, one telephone handset, documentation, and the utility software. The package's software digitizes your voice and stores it on your server's hard disk just like electronic mail. Users can record and play back messages with amazing clarity. The board also has audio input and output jacks for connecting to stereo equipment and speakers. Using the Sounding Board and its supporting software, you can include recorded sounds in any application that supports the Windows Object Linking and Embedding (OLE) capabilities. This function is useful for creating multimedia presentations. Two workstations equipped with the Sounding Board and software can carry on direct communication by using the chat function of the network, similar to a telephone conversation. In addition, the Sounding Board on a LANtastic network enables regular e-mail to become voice mail—you can leave voice messages for others and listen to voice messages left by others for you. The application of this award-winning product is limited only by your imagination.

Artiscribe

Artiscribe works with the Sounding Board and your network operating system to bring digital-dictation capabilities to your users. By using this software, you can record notes in a file and later play back the message by using voice commands. Start your word processing package, pop up the Artiscribe utility, select the message or file to be transcribed, and return to your word processor. The voice dictation continues. You can type the information as you control the playback with voice commands—such as start, stop, go back, rewind, and fast forward—similar to working a dictation machine, but by speaking commands. You also can integrate voice, text, and graphics into a single file and publish it for access by any network user. Best of all, there are no tapes to worry about.

Summary

Artisoft continues to push the limits of technology with its innovative products. This chapter focused on Artisoft's network operating systems, network adapters, and starter kits, as well as products to expand and enhance your network. Artisoft's product line continues to expand, providing even more capabilities for its already powerful LANtastic network operating system. Look for more to come in the future from this creative company.

Chapter Snapshot

In this chapter, you install the necessary hardware and software to create a fully operational LANtastic network. This chapter discusses the following topics:

✔ Installing the network cable for your LANtastic network

✔ Installing the network interface cards in your computer

✔ Installing the LANtastic Network Operating System (NOS) in DOS

✔ Installing the LANtastic Network Operating System in Windows

✔ Installing LANtastic 6.0 over a previous version of LANtastic

✔ Automating LANtastic installations

✔ Checking the operation of your LANtastic network

When you finish this chapter, your LANtastic network will be fully functional, and you can begin using your LANtastic network immediately. You can also choose to customize your network by performing tasks such as setting up user account or additional shared resources.

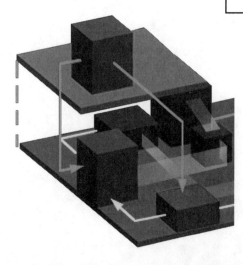

CHAPTER

Installing a LANtastic Network

I n Chapter 3, you read about planning for the installation of your LANtastic network. Chapter 4 described the Artisoft products available to implement a LANtastic network. If you were unable to use Chapter 1, "Quick Start," or prefer a more detailed installation guide, you are now ready to perform the installation of the network hardware and software that comprise your LANtastic network.

Testing the Network Cable

In Chapter 3, you determined the type of network cable to use and how much you need. Cable in hand, you now are ready to begin installation.

How Do I Know the Cable Will Work?

This is an important step in your installation. If you neglect to test network cable before you install it, you can double your work effort if you need to remove a bad cable after installation.

 Make sure that you test all ready-made cable lengths, in addition to those you fabricate.

If you are using Thin coax (Thin Ethernet) as your cable type, you can easily test the cable for continuity prior to installation by using the following method.

If your cable type is UTP (10BASE-T) or you are installing 2 Mbps adapters, the easiest way to test the cable prior to installation is to connect the cable between two computers with network adapters installed and LANtastic running. Then run LANcheck to verify proper network communication. To set up this test configuration, install your network adapters in two computers that are near each other and install the LANtastic software, as explained in the following sections. With this test configuration, you can test each cable for proper operation before permanently installing the cable.

 If you use UTP (10BASE-T) cable, you need to connect the two computers to the hub (concentrator). Connect one UTP cable between the first computer and the hub; then connect another UTP cable between the second computer and the hub.

If you use 2 Mbps adapters, connect the cable between the two computers and plug the terminator plugs into the open DB9 connector on each network adapter card.

 To test a Thin coax cable, follow these steps:

1. Place a terminator plug on one end of a BNC T-connector that came with one of your network adapter cards.

2. Connect one end of the cable to the open side of the BNC T-connector.

3. Using an ohmmeter, measure the resistance by placing one lead on the center wire core and the other on the BNC connector on the open end of the cable. You should have continuity, and the ohmmeter should measure 50 ohms resistance.

If you follow these steps correctly, you should get a good continuity check, indicating that the BNC connectors are installed properly and that the cable is fault-free.

If you do not get a good reading, follow these steps:

1. Carefully check the BNC connector installations for any problems.

2. Fix any visible problems and recheck the continuity.

3. If the test is still bad, determine the bad component by first testing the terminator plug by itself, then the BNC connector with the terminator plug installed, and then the original configuration.

    If the test succeeds until you attach the cable, the cable is defective.

Most of the time, problems with continuity checks are due to bad connector installations; replacing them usually fixes the problem. After you check the cable lengths for continuity, you are ready to install them in their permanent positions.

Laying Out the Network Cable

As part of your planning, you diagrammed your network layout. Check your diagram to see if computers are in more than one room or on more than one floor. If either is shown in your diagram, you need to check a few things before you decide how to install your network cable. If all the computers are in one room, you have four basic choices for installing cable:

✔ Connect the cables to the computers and lay the loose cable on the floor behind the desks and along the wall. This installation is fine if the cable does not stretch across a door opening or across an open stretch of floor where someone can trip on it. (If someone trips on the cable, the cable or interface cards can be damaged.)

✔ Install plastic channel (*cable raceways*) along the baseboards and run the cable inside the channel (see fig. 5.1). The raceways have snap covers to enclose the cable for protection and visual appeal.

✔ If your office has a suspended ceiling, connect the cable to the interface cards and run the cable up the wall into the space above the suspended ceiling. Cable is exposed as it runs up the wall, which can look very unattractive. String the cable through the overhead space to a point directly above the other computer(s) and drop it back down along the wall near the second computer. Leave a little slack in the cable (about five feet) in both the overhead space and behind the computer to allow for minor position adjustments of the computer.

Figure 5.1
An example of plastic cable raceway components and an installed raceway.

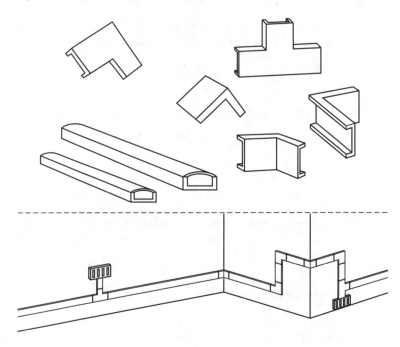

✔ If the second computer is located in the middle of the room, you can drop the cable straight down from the ceiling. Again, your cable is fully exposed. If you do not like the appearance of free hanging cable, buy a service pole from an office furniture store to hide it. A service pole attaches to the ceiling tile suspension grate and stands on the floor.

✔ Use a combination of the preceding second and third options to make your installation easy and flexible. Following these guidelines will protect the cable from potential damage and wear, and presents a less cluttered appearance in the workspace.

To run cable through a suspended ceiling, use a short stepladder and a tennis ball with a string attached to it.

With a partner, open two ceiling panels and throw the ball from one panel to the other. After you run the string where you want the cable, attach the ball end of the string to the cable with masking tape and pull the string (and the cable) back through the ceiling space. Have your partner feed the cable to avoid kinks or severe twists. You may find that the space in the ceiling overhead is limited, but you can pitch the ball farther than you can reach with your arm.

The connectors on the end of the cable used for Artisoft's 2 Mbps adapters are a 9-pin D-style connector (DB-9). One end of the cable is a male type connector and the other end is a female type connector. When you route your cable, keep in mind that the end of one cable connected to the card must have a male connector, and the other cable end must have a female connector; otherwise, you won't be able to plug the cables into your network adapter card, which has one DB-9 female connector and one DB-9 male connector on it.

To prevent possible interference or heat damage to the cable, make sure that it does not touch any lighting fixtures or electrical junction boxes. In addition, to ensure that the cable does not become twisted or bent, you might want to hook the cable onto the wire that holds the ceiling tile supports in place. Usually a few inches of excess wire is at the ends. This is one way to keep the cable from resting on the light fixtures.

If your LANtastic network spans several rooms, you have the following installation options:

✔ Use a combination of the third and fourth options from the preceding example.

✔ Run the cable inside the walls and up through the overhead space.

✔ If the computers you want to connect are in adjoining rooms, run the cable directly through the wall into the next room.

To run the cable inside your walls, you need a sturdy stepladder (a six-foot stepladder is fine), a drill, a small weight (a lead sinker is good), and some string. Perform the following steps to hide cable:

1. Remove the ceiling panels above the position of the first computer and nearest to the wall.

2. Drill a hole in the top wall stringer (in commercial construction, the wall stringers are metal) and enlarge the hole with a sturdy

screwdriver. The finished hole should be about 3/4-inch to 1 1/2-inches in diameter depending on the type of network cable being used and whether or not the connectors are preinstalled.

3. Try to eliminate sharp corners of tags that jut out in this hole and use a flashlight to see if any insulation is installed inside the wall.

If you install cable in a wall, do not use existing holes that have electrical wiring running through them if possible. They are a potential source of interference.

4. If no insulation is inside the wall, make a mark directly below this hole (you can use the string and weight to determine the spot).

5. Use the drill, then a small knife or saw, to cut a hole about 1 1/2-by-2-inches wide and about a foot off the floor.

6. Attach the weight to the string, feed the string through the hole in the top of the wall stringer, and look for the weight to appear in the hole you cut in the wall nearest you (you need a partner).

7. Capture the weight and pull it through the hole. Disconnect the weight and use masking tape to attach the string to your cable. Do not use a lot of masking tape because the hole at the top of the wall is fairly small.

8. Pull the string and the cable back through the hole into the ceiling space.

9. After you pull the cable into the ceiling space, string the cable through the ceiling space. (See preceding Tip.)

After you get to the opposite wall through which you want to pull the cable, reverse the first part of this example by pulling the string and cable through the wall and out the hole (instead of in the wall and up the hole). You can now connect the computers at both ends.

If insulation is in the wall, you can abandon this method in favor of raceways and service poles, or use a metal fish wire, available at hardware stores, to feed through the wall to the lower hole.

Unless you use UTP (10BASE-T), you have two cables routed to each computer, except for the computers located at both ends. Keep this in mind when you route your cables; it's easier to route two cables in a wall at the same time than to try to route them separately.

Although you use the same process for multiroom, multifloor installations as you did in the preceding example, you may have difficulty installing cable between floors. Look for an existing air shaft, plumbing shaft, or wire shaft that goes between floors, and feed the cable through the shaft. Make sure that you avoid contact with other wires or cable whenever possible. Now is one time you want the protection of coax cable. If no opening exists, ask your building management to help you run cable. Expect to spend some money for their assistance.

To run cable directly through the wall from one room to the next, cut a 1 1/2-by-2-inch hole in the wall close to the nearest computer. Then reach through the hole you just cut and use a screwdriver to punch a small pilot hole through the other wall. Go into the other room, find the pilot hole, and cut a matching 1 1/2-by-2-inch hole in the other wall. You can install wall plates to cover the holes or leave them open if they are not conspicuous. Pull the cable through and connect the computers to the ends.

Installing Network Adapters

You are now ready to install the network adapter cards in each computer that is part of your network. After an adapter is installed in each computer, connect the cable—you are ready to install the LANtastic software.

Installing Network Adapter Cards

Network adapter cards are relatively easy to install in your computer:

1. Disconnect your computer from the electrical outlet, and then disconnect all cabling and connectors that can interfere from the back of the computer. (Make a list of what is attached so you can reinstall everything as you found it.)

2. Set aside the monitor and clear some space so you can work.

3. Turn the computer around and remove the screws from the back that hold the case in place (see fig. 5.2). Now remove the case to expose the inside of the computer.

Figure 5.2
An example of
removing a
case.

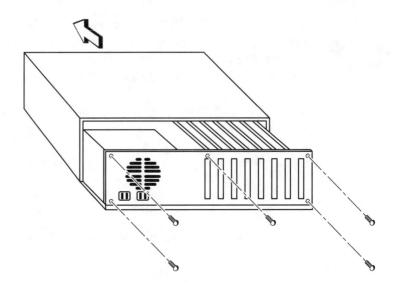

4. Look for a free expansion slot on the motherboard. If your machine is an 80286, 80386, or 80486, you may have both short and long expansion slots on the motherboard.

5. Locate an empty long slot (a 16-bit bus expansion slot). If no 16-bit slots are available, see if an 8-bit card that you can move is installed in a 16-bit slot. If not, locate an empty short (8-bit) slot (see fig. 5.3).

If you cannot use a 16-bit slot, you cannot use IRQ interrupts 10 and 15 with an 80286 or better machine.

If you have a 16-bit network adapter card (such as the NodeRunner/SI 2000/C card) and you install it in an 8-bit slot, network performance for this computer and other computers accessing it is not as good as if the adapter were installed in a 16-bit expansion slot.

6. Remove the rear case slot cover for the selected expansion slot. Make sure that you ground yourself before proceeding to the next step.

You can ground yourself by touching the power supply. The power supply is the rectangular silver box usually located in the back corner of the case.

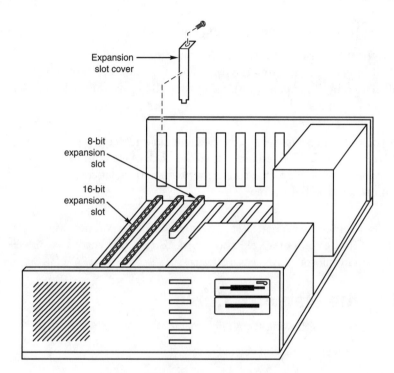

Figure 5.3
An example of internal computer bus expansion slots.

Expansion slot cover

8-bit expansion slot

16-bit expansion slot

7. Place a towel or soft cloth on the desk. Carefully unwrap the LANtastic interface adapter card. Place the plastic anti-static wrap on the towel or cloth on the desk in front of you and lay the adapter card on the plastic wrap.

8. If you are not using the NodeRunner series network adapter cards, you must now set the jumper settings on the card. Open the Artisoft manual that came with the adapter card and set the switches and jumpers as instructed. (Artisoft's manuals contain extensive information on setting up the interface adapter cards.)

The default jumper settings work fine in most situations. You still want to verify that your card is actually set to the default settings by comparing the jumper settings on the card with those in the manual.

The NodeRunner Ethernet adapters do not have any jumpers to change on the board. The configuration information for the card is changed after the card is installed in the computer by a software configuration program that comes with the adapter. Consult your adapter installation guide for more information.

Appendix A contains additional information for configuring Artisoft network adapters.

You now are ready to install the card in the computer.

9. Hold the adapter card by its top edge and insert it into the bus expansion slot. Press firmly along the top edge of the adapter card until it is fully seated in the expansion slot. Reinstall the screw that held the slot protector in place.

If you have an adapter that supports thin Ethernet (coax), you will have to remove the BNC T-connector from the back of the card to fit it into the computer. Reinstall the connector after the adapter card is in place and secured with the screw.

Reinstall the case and fastener screws. Reconnect all the cables you removed in the first step and plug in the computer's electrical cord. You now are ready to connect the LAN cable and install your LANtastic software.

Connecting the Network Cable

Your cable has one of the following types of connectors:

✔ BNC T-connector (for thin coaxial cable)

✔ 9-pin D-connector (for 2 Mbps networks)

✔ RJ45 modular type connector (for 10BASE-T networks)

✔ 15-pin D-connector (for thick net Ethernet drop cables)

Locate the appropriate jack on the back of the adapter-interface card and attach the cable connector.

If you are using thin Ethernet (coax) cable, the BNC connector requires a slight push and twist to seat it on the card connector. You have network cable connected to both sides of the T-connector, unless the computer you are connecting is at the end of the network cable segment. If your computer is at the end of the network cable segment, one side of the BNC T-connector is connected to a cable and a terminator plug is connected to the other end.

If your network uses Artisoft's 2 Mbps adapters, you have two cables with DB-9 connectors that you plug directly into the back of the network adapter card, unless the computer you are connecting is at either end of the network cable segment. If your computer is at the end of the network cable segment, the cable is connected to one connector on the card and a terminator is connected to the other.

If you use a 10BASE-T (UTP) cable, simply plug the RJ45 plug into the receptacle at the back of your network adapter card. The opposite end of each cable is plugged into the hub (concentrator).

This completes the hardware portion of your network installation. With the network hardware installed, you are now ready to begin your LANtastic software installation.

Installing LANtastic

You are ready to load the LANtastic software on your computers. Before you work with the software, make a working copy of the LANtastic NOS disks using the DOS DISKCOPY command. Put the original disks back in their original envelope for safekeeping. Make sure that you have the *LANtastic Installation and Management Guide* and your Network Hardware Inventory Cards available for reference as you perform the installation.

The LANtastic software must be installed on each computer. When you type INSTALL from the DOS prompt, the LANtastic installation program will search your path for Microsoft Windows and, if found, start the LANtastic Windows installation program. Otherwise the LANtastic DOS installation will be performed.

LANtastic 6.0 may be installed either in DOS or in Windows. Following are the instructions for installing LANtastic in DOS or LANtastic in Windows.

Prior to LANtastic 5.0, you always installed LANtastic for DOS. If you had LANtastic for Windows, it was installed separately from within Windows. LANtastic for Windows was a separate utility program that was not necessary if you wanted to use LANtastic with Windows, but it made using LANtastic much easier when in Windows.

Beginning with LANtastic 5.0, you could purchase LANtastic for Windows or LANtastic for DOS. LANtastic for DOS was installed the same as it was prior to version 5.0. LANtastic for Windows, however, was installed entirely from within Windows. In addition to the Windows version of LANtastic, LANtastic for Windows included everything found in LANtastic for DOS.

LANtastic 6.0 includes both the DOS and Windows versions of LANtastic. The installation program will automatically detect whether or not Windows is installed and install LANtastic accordingly. As with LANtastic 5.0, if LANtastic is installed for Windows, all the LANtastic DOS programs and functions are installed and available from DOS.

Installing LANtastic in DOS

You are now ready to install the LANtastic software. This section describes the installation of LANtastic in DOS. If you have Microsoft Windows on your computer, refer to the next section, "Installing LANtastic in Windows," for installation instructions.

When installing LANtastic in DOS, if the LANtastic installation program finds Windows in your path, it will start Windows and run the Windows LANtastic installation program.

Switches may be used on the INSTALL command line to force desired operation of the installation program. The use of command line switches with the installation program is covered later in this chapter.

To install LANtastic in DOS, place the LANtastic working copy NOS disk 1 in drive A or B. Type **A:Install** (or **B:Install**) and press Enter.

After the LANtastic Version 6.0 Installation screen appears, press any key. The installation process begins.

The DOS LANtastic 6.0 installation program requires that you have at least 510 KB of available conventional memory. If you don't have 510 KB available, the installation program will respond with an error. If this occurs, you will need to temporarily remove any resident programs from loading in your CONFIG.SYS and AUTOEXEC.BAT files to free up additional memory.

The installation program will prompt you to enter information in each of several screens. Each installation screen gives an explanation of the information that is to be entered. Where applicable, the installation program will list a default value. The default value listed is appropriate for most system configurations, although this default value may be changed if desired.

LANtastic 6.0 enables you to automate your installation by creating a file called INSTALL.INF and including it on your first installation disk. INSTALL.INF contains the configuration information normally entered during installation.

Using INSTALL.INF to automate the installation process is covered later in this chapter.

After you press any key, the screen changes and prompts you to enter your computer name. Type the name of the computer on which you are working and press Enter at the Enter computer name prompt (see fig. 5.4). In the example shown, ZAK is the name given to this computer. The name you choose to give your computer is the name it will be known by in the network. ZAK, 386-25, STATION1, and KATIES-PC are examples of names which may be given to your computer.

```
              LANtastic  Version 6.00  INSTALLATION

  Each computer in the LANtastic network requires a
  name.  No two names in one network should be the same.
  Usually, people use some variation of their own name
  for their computer.  Or computers could be named by
  location (e.g. UPSTAIRS) or function (e.g. GAMES).
  Please name your computer now with a word containing
  up to fifteen letters with no spaces.



        ═══Enter computer name═══
   ZAK
```

Figure 5.4
Entering the network name of your computer.

After entering the name of your computer, the next screen appears, prompting you to select the drive on which you want LANtastic installed (see fig. 5.5). The default selection is Drive C: and if you have additional hard drives, such as Drive D: and Drive E:, those drives will also appear as selections. In the example shown, the only hard drive on the computer is Drive C:. After selecting the drive, press Enter and the next screen appears, prompting you to enter the directory in which you want the LANtastic files installed (see fig. 5.6). The default directory is \LANTASTI. Accept the \LANTASTI directory or type in a different one and press Enter to continue.

The next screen asks if you want to share your disk drives or printers with others (see fig. 5.7). The selections available are Share my computer's drives or printers, or Do not share my computer's drives and printers. The default Share my computer's drives or printers option enables others on the network to use the drives and printers on your computer. The alternative is that you may use the shared drives and printers on other computers, but not share your computer's drives and printers with others. Select the option you prefer and press Enter.

Figure 5.5
Entering the drive on which to install LANtastic.

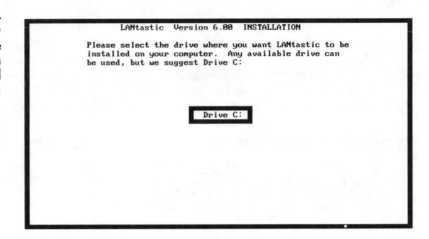

```
         LANtastic  Version 6.00  INSTALLATION
  Please select the drive where you want LANtastic to be
  installed on your computer.  Any available drive can
  be used, but we suggest Drive C:




                    ┌──────────┐
                    │ Drive C: │
                    └──────────┘
```

Figure 5.6
Entering the directory for the LANtastic files.

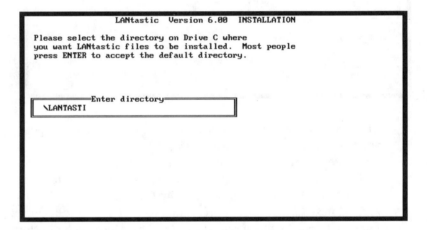

```
         LANtastic  Version 6.00  INSTALLATION
  Please select the directory on Drive C where
  you want LANtastic files to be installed.  Most people
  press ENTER to accept the default directory.


        ┌════════════Enter directory════════════┐
        │ \LANTASTI                              │
        └────────────────────────────────────────┘
```

When you choose to share your computer's disk drives or printers with others in the network, you are configuring your computer as a server. If you choose not to share your computer's disk drives or printers with others in the network, you are configuring your computer as a workstation. A workstation can use only the resources on other servers; it is not capable of sharing its own resources with other users.

Unless your computer does not have a hard disk, you will generally want to configure it as a server so it can share its resources with others. You can set up security features later to allow access only to the shared resources you choose. In addition, you may change your computer from a server to a workstation by disabling the LANtastic server program.

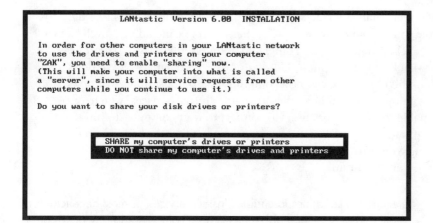

Figure 5.7
Choosing to share drives and printers with others.

The next screen asks the maximum number of computers that will be allowed to connect to your computer at once (see fig. 5.8). Unless you have more than 10 computers that will be using the shared resources on your computer simultaneously, accept the default Keep maximum connected computers at 10 option and press Enter.

If you later need to change the maximum number of computers that will be allowed to connect to your computer, you may change this number from the LANtastic NET_MGR configuration program, on the SERVER command line in the STARTNET.BAT file, or in the @STARTNET.CFG switch file.

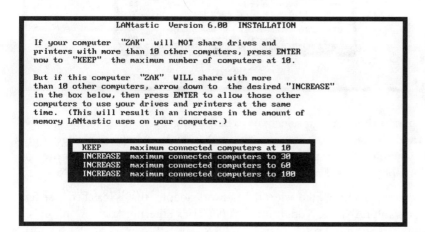

Figure 5.8
Selecting the maximum number of computers that may access your computer.

The next screen enables you to select additional LANtastic features (see fig. 5.9) that enable you to connect to servers in other networks, including Novell Network, Windows NT, LAN manager, and others. In addition, there is an Artisoft Exchange—Mail Post Office option. Although Artisoft Exchange is a Windows application, the Post Office can be a computer that is not running Windows. Also available is an option called Load files to enable "Install Services" which, once loaded, enables other network users to connect to your computer to run the LANtastic installation program. Select the desired options by highlighting each option using your arrow keys, and then selecting the option by pressing the space-bar. Press Enter to continue.

Selecting the Load files to enable "Install Services" is most beneficial for installing a new version of LANtastic on a computer already active on the network. This option will not be useful for a first time installation—the computer must be able to access the server that has the LANtastic installation files installed to actually launch the LANtastic install program.

Figure 5.9
Selecting additional LANtastic features.

```
                LANtastic  Version 6.00   INSTALLATION

Select one or more (or none) of the following additional
LANtastic features listed below if you need them.  (Any features
you select will be added to your current installation.)

      >> Use the SPACE bar to toggle the selections below   <<
      >> Press ENTER to accept the selections you have made <<


         Artisoft Exchange - Mail Post Office      NO
         Client to Novell   3.11 File Server       NO
         Client to Novell   4.01 File Server       NO
         Client to Windows(tm) for Workgroups      NO
         Client to Microsoft  LAN Manager          NO
         Load files to enable "Install Services"   YES
```

A screen appears showing your selections so far (see fig. 5.10). Review your selections and choose OK to continue with installation. If you want to change your selections, you may do so at this point by selecting the Go back and re-enter the information option. Press Enter to continue.

The next screen prompts you to select the network adapter that is installed (see fig. 5.11). The default LANtastic NodeRunner 2000 Series Ethernet Adapter option is the appropriate selection if you purchased a LANtastic 6.0 Network Starter Kit and are using LANtastic NodeRunner 2000 Ethernet adapters. Several other adapter options including NDIS support are available. Select the appropriate adapter for your installation and press Enter to continue.

Figure 5.10
Summary of installation options selected so far.

Most network adapters are now shipped with NDIS (Network Driver Interface Specification) drivers. You can purchase nearly any network adapter from any manufacturer as long as it has an NDIS driver supplied with it and will work with LANtastic.

Figure 5.11
Selecting the network adapter installed.

The next screen asks if you want to set up drive or printer connections (see fig. 5.12). If you want to establish a default connection to shared drives or a printer, accept the Set up permanent drive or printer connections option. Otherwise select the Do not set up any drive or printer connections option. Press Enter to continue.

After default drive or printer connections are selected, a line is inserted in the STARTNET.BAT file that was created in the LANTASTI directory to make the connection when the network is launched. You can modify the STARTNET.BAT file to add, remove, or change the default drive or printer connections.

Figure 5.12
Choosing to set up permanent drive or printer connections.

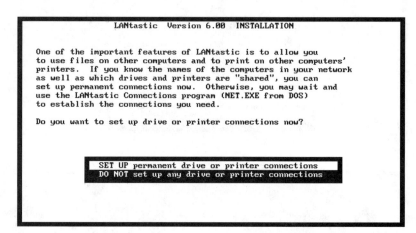

```
          LANtastic   Version 6.00   INSTALLATION

One of the important features of LANtastic is to allow you
to use files on other computers and to print on other computers'
printers.  If you know the names of the computers in your network
as well as which drives and printers are "shared", you can
set up permanent connections now.  Otherwise, you may wait and
use the LANtastic Connections program (NET.EXE from DOS)
to establish the connections you need.

Do you want to set up drive or printer connections now?



        SET UP permanent drive or printer connections
        DO NOT set up any drive or printer connections
```

If you choose to set up permanent drive or printer connections, the next screen will ask for the name of the other computer that has the disk drive to which you want to connect (see fig. 5.13). Enter the network name of the other computer and press Enter. Press Enter without entering a name to skip to the printer connection setup. In this example, assume KATIE is the name of the other computer. You are now prompted to enter the name of the drive resource on the computer to which you want to connect (see fig. 5.14). The default C-DRIVE drive resource name is listed. Accept the default C-DRIVE name or enter another and press Enter to continue.

If you choose to share your disk drives and printers with others, the LANtastic installation program automatically creates the C-DRIVE resource. If you choose a different drive resource name to connect to when LANtastic is started, you must create that resource name later using the LANtastic NET_MGR configuration program.

Finally, the next screen prompts you to enter the drive letter you will use on your computer to connect to the shared drive resource specified on the other computer (see fig. 5.15). Accept the default drive letter D or type in a different letter and press Enter to continue.

When you choose a disk drive letter to access the disk drives on another computer, choose a letter that is not already assigned to a physical drive on your computer. For example, if you redirect your C drive to point to a drive on another computer, you no longer can access the physical C drive on your computer.

```
          LANtastic  Version 6.00  INSTALLATION
OTHER COMPUTER with a DRIVE you want to USE...
_____

Please type the name of the other computer that has
the drive you want to connect to and use.

Or just press ENTER to continue, skipping  drive setup.

If you skip permanent drive setup, you will have an extra
step to perform every time you turn on your computer.

>>> You can do this before the other computer is set up.<<<

       ═Enter computer name═
      │ KATIE                                          │
      │                                                │
```

Figure 5.13
Entering the name of the other computer to connect to.

```
          LANtastic  Version 6.00  INSTALLATION
NAME of DRIVE you want to USE on KATIE...
_____

Please enter the name of the drive on  "KATIE"
that you want to connect to and use.  This will most likely
be the computer's hard disk named "C-DRIVE".  But you can
instead choose another hard drive if  "KATIE"  has one, or
choose a floppy drive named "A-DRIVE" or "B-DRIVE".
(Drive names can be up to 8 letters.)



       ═Please enter drive name═
      │ C-DRIVE                                        │
      │                                                │
```

Figure 5.14
Entering the drive resource name to connect to.

You are now prompted to enter the name of another computer with a drive you want to use. If you want to set up another permanent drive connection, type in the name of the computer that has the drive to which you want to connect, and you will again be prompted to enter the name of the drive resource and the drive letter on your computer you want to use for the connection. If you don't want to set up another permanent drive connection, leave the Enter computer name field blank and press Enter to continue.

Figure 5.15

Entering the local drive letter to use for the connection.

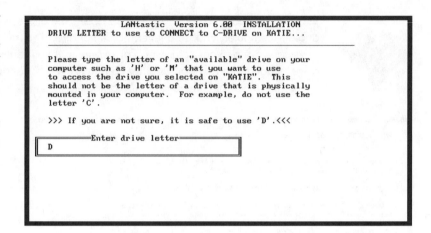

```
                LANtastic  Version 6.00  INSTALLATION
       DRIVE LETTER to use to CONNECT to C-DRIVE on KATIE...

       Please type the letter of an "available" drive on your
       computer such as 'H' or 'M' that you want to use
       to access the drive you selected on "KATIE".  This
       should not be the letter of a drive that is physically
       mounted in your computer.  For example, do not use the
       letter 'C'.

       >>> If you are not sure, it is safe to use 'D'.<<<

       ┌──────────────Enter drive letter──────────────────┐
       │ D                                                 │
       └───────────────────────────────────────────────────┘
```

The next screen prompts you to enter the name of the computer that has the printer you want to use (see fig. 5.16). Enter the name and press Enter. If you do not want to set up a connection to a printer at this time, leave the name blank and press Enter. In this example, assume Katie is the name of the computer that has the printer attached.

Figure 5.16

Entering the name of the computer with a printer attached.

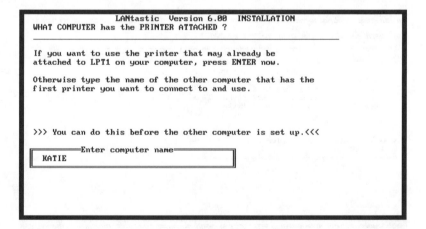

```
                LANtastic  Version 6.00  INSTALLATION
       WHAT COMPUTER has the PRINTER ATTACHED ?

       If you want to use the printer that may already be
       attached to LPT1 on your computer, press ENTER now.

       Otherwise type the name of the other computer that has the
       first printer you want to connect to and use.



       >>> You can do this before the other computer is set up.<<<

       ┌──────────────Enter computer name──────────────────┐
       │ KATIE                                              │
       └────────────────────────────────────────────────────┘
```

The LANtastic installation program allows only one printer connection. This is a limitation of the installation program only. LANtastic allows connections to printers using ports LPT1, LPT2, LPT3, LPT4, COM1, COM2, COM3, and COM4. You may establish additional permanent printer connections later by adding the appropriate commands to the STARTNET.BAT file in the LANTASTI directory.

If you share your printer with other network users, always specify a connection to your own printer.

If a network user uses your printer and you have not established a network connection to it, you can't access your printer until you do.

If you entered a name of a computer with a printer attached, the next screen prompts you to enter the name of the printer on KATIE to which you want to connect (see fig. 5.17). Accept the default @PRINTER name and press Enter. Finally, you are asked to enter the printer port on your computer which you will connect to the @PRINTER resource on KATIE. Accept the default LPT1 or type in another printer port and press Enter. In the example shown, LPT2 is chosen (see fig 5.18).

If you specify default connections, make sure that the server and resource name you specify exist. Otherwise, when you launch LANtastic, it doesn't establish the connection you specified and displays an error message, such as Cannot Locate Server Name.

```
              LANtastic   Version 6.00   INSTALLATION
NAME of PRINTER you want to USE...
─────────────────────────────────────────────────────────

Please enter the name of the printer on "KATIE"
that you want to connect to and use.  This will most
likely be the default name "@PRINTER".  However, you
can delete "@PRINTER" and type in another name such as
"@LASER".  (Printer names always begin with "@".)


        ┌─Enter printer name─────────────────┐
        │ @PRINTER                            │
        └─────────────────────────────────────┘
```

Figure 5.17
Entering the printer resource name to use.

The next screen shows the installation options you have specified (see fig. 5.19). Accept the OK to perform installation option and press Enter to continue. To change any of your selections, select the Go back and re-enter the information option and press Enter. You can change any option and then are returned to this same screen (fig. 5.19).

Figure 5.18
Entering the
printer port to
use for the
connection.

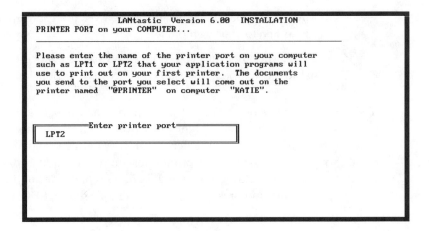

```
                    LANtastic  Version 6.00  INSTALLATION
  PRINTER PORT on your COMPUTER...
  ────────────────────────────────────────────────────────────

  Please enter the name of the printer port on your computer
  such as LPT1 or LPT2 that your application programs will
  use to print out on your first printer.  The documents
  you send to the port you select will come out on the
  printer named  "@PRINTER"  on computer  "KATIE".



       ╔════════════Enter printer port════════════════╗
       ║ LPT2                                          ║
       ╚═══════════════════════════════════════════════╝
```

Figure 5.19
Summary of
installation
options
specified.

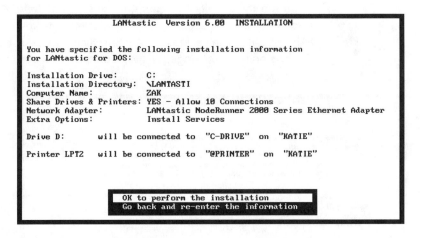

```
                    LANtastic  Version 6.00  INSTALLATION


  You have specified the following installation information
  for LANtastic for DOS:

  Installation Drive:       C:
  Installation Directory:   \LANTASTI
  Computer Name:            ZAK
  Share Drives & Printers:  YES - Allow 10 Connections
  Network Adapter:          LANtastic NodeRunner 2000 Series Ethernet Adapter
  Extra Options:            Install Services

  Drive D:        will be connected to  "C-DRIVE"  on  "KATIE"

  Printer LPT2    will be connected to  "@PRINTER"  on  "KATIE"



              ┌──────────────────────────────────────────┐
              │ OK to perform the installation           │
              │ Go back and re-enter the information     │
              └──────────────────────────────────────────┘
```

The next screen explains that your CONFIG.SYS and AUTOEXEC.BAT files will be changed (see fig. 5.20). Also listed is the name that your previous CONFIG.SYS and AUTOEXEC.BAT files will be changed to. Press any key to perform the installation.

The files display on-screen as they are loaded onto your computer's hard disk. You are prompted when necessary to enter the next disk. When the installation finishes, the LANtastic installation program displays a summary screen stating that the installation is complete (see fig. 5.21). Press any key to continue.

Finally, a screen appears, stating that your computer will be rebooted. Press any key and your computer will be rebooted. LANtastic will be started when your computer boots. Pressing ESC will exit the installation program without rebooting.

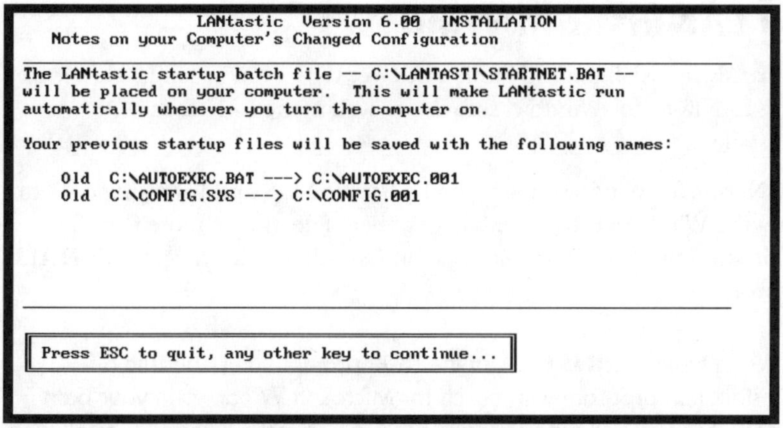

```
          LANtastic  Version 6.00  INSTALLATION
    Notes on your Computer's Changed Configuration
--------------------------------------------------------------
The LANtastic startup batch file -- C:\LANTASTI\STARTNET.BAT --
will be placed on your computer.  This will make LANtastic run
automatically whenever you turn the computer on.

Your previous startup files will be saved with the following names:

    Old  C:\AUTOEXEC.BAT ---> C:\AUTOEXEC.001
    Old  C:\CONFIG.SYS ---> C:\CONFIG.001



--------------------------------------------------------------

  Press ESC to quit, any other key to continue...
```

Figure 5.20
Notes on changed computer configuration.

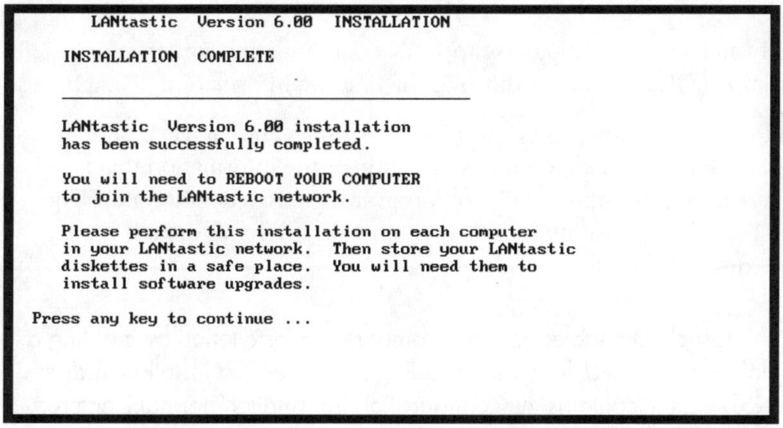

```
      LANtastic  Version 6.00  INSTALLATION

  INSTALLATION  COMPLETE
  _____

  LANtastic  Version 6.00 installation
  has been successfully completed.

  You will need to REBOOT YOUR COMPUTER
  to join the LANtastic network.

  Please perform this installation on each computer
  in your LANtastic network.  Then store your LANtastic
  diskettes in a safe place.  You will need them to
  install software upgrades.

  Press any key to continue ...
```

Figure 5.21
LANtastic installation complete.

You have completed the installation of LANtastic on your computer. The LANtastic installation program has created a batch file, located in the LANTASTI directory, called STARTNET.BAT, which contains the commands necessary to load the LANtastic software and establish the desired default printer and disk drive connections. The installation program has also changed your CONFIG.SYS file and added the following line to your AUTOEXEC.BAT file, so LANtastic will automatically start each time your computer is booted:

```
call C:\LANTASTI\STARTNET.BAT
```

You have completed the installation of LANtastic on your computer.

Installing LANtastic in Windows

You are now ready to install the LANtastic software. When you install LANtastic in Windows, the LANtastic for Windows software as well as the LANtastic DOS software is installed.

To install LANtastic for Windows, place the LANtastic NOS disk 1 working copy in drive A. From the Windows Program Manager select **F**ile, then choose **R**un. Type **A:INSTALL** in the Run dialog box and click on OK. Alternatively, type **A:INSTALL** at the DOS prompt.

When typing **A:INSTALL** at the DOS prompt, the LANtastic 6.0 installation program will search for Microsoft Windows in your path and, if found, will automatically run the LANtastic Windows installation program.

The Artisoft Install Message dialog box appears, congratulating you on your purchase. Click on OK to continue through the first two information dialog boxes.

The installation program will prompt you to enter information in each of several dialog boxes. Each dialog box gives an explanation of the information that is to be entered. Where applicable, the installation program will list a default value. The default value listed is appropriate for most systems, although this default value may be changed if desired.

LANtastic 6.0 enables you to automate your installation by creating a file called INSTALL.INF and including it on your first installation disk. INSTALL.INF contains the configuration information normally entered during installation.

Using INSTALL.INF to automate the installation process is covered later in this chapter.

The Enter computer name dialog box appears (see fig. 5.22). Type the name of the computer on which you are working and click on OK or press Enter. In the example shown, ZAK is the name given to this computer. The name you choose to give your computer is the name it will be known by in the network. ZAK, 386-25, STATION1, and KATIES-PC are examples of names which may be given to your computer.

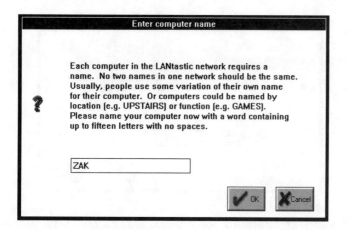

Figure 5.22
Entering the network name of your computer.

The Enter target drive dialog box appears, showing the drives available on your computer (see fig. 5.23). The default selection is Drive C: and if you have additional hard drives, such as Drive D: and Drive E:, those drives will also appear as selections. In the example shown (fig. 5.23), the only hard drive on the computer is Drive C:. After selecting the drive, click on OK or press Enter to continue.

Next, the Enter directory dialog box appears, showing the \LANTASTI directory as the location to install the LANtastic files (see fig. 5.24). Accept the \LANTASTI directory or type in a different one and click on OK or press Enter to continue.

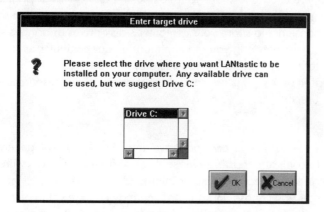

Figure 5.23
Entering the drive on which to install LANtastic.

Figure 5.24
Entering the directory for the LANtastic files.

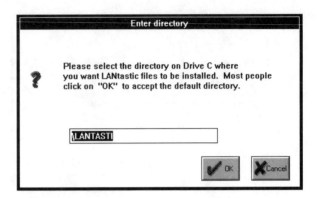

The Share drives and printers dialog box appears, asking whether you want to share your computers disk drives or printers with others in the network (see fig. 5.25). The selections available are Share my computer's drives or printers, or, Do not share my computer's drives and printers. The default Share my computer's drives or printers option will enable others on the network to use the drives and printers on your computer. The alternative is that you may use the shared drives and printers on other computers, but not share your computer's drives and printers with others. Accept the default Share my computer's drives or printers option and click on OK or press Enter.

When you choose to share your computer's disk drives or printers with others in the network, you are configuring your computer as a server. If you choose not to share your computer's disk drives or printers with others in the network, you are configuring your computer as a workstation. A workstation can use only the resources on other LANtastic servers; it is not capable of sharing its own resources with other users.

Unless your computer does not have a hard disk, you will generally want to configure it as a server so it can share its resources with others. You can set up security features later to allow access only to the shared resources you choose. In addition, you may change your computer from a server to a workstation by disabling the LANtastic server program.

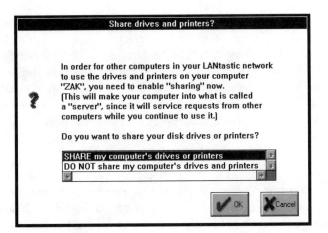

Figure 5.25
Choosing to
share drives and
printers with
others.

The next dialog box asks for the maximum number of computers that will be
allowed to connect to your computer at once (see fig. 5.26). You may select
predefined increments from the list. Unless you have more than 10 computers that
will be using the shared resources on your computer at once, accept the default
Keep maximum connected computers at 10 option and click on OK or press
Enter.

If you later need to change the maximum number of computers that will
be allowed to connect to your computer, you may change this number
from the LANtastic NET_MGR configuration program, on the SERVER
command line in the STARTNET.BAT file, or in the @STARTNET.CFG
switch file.

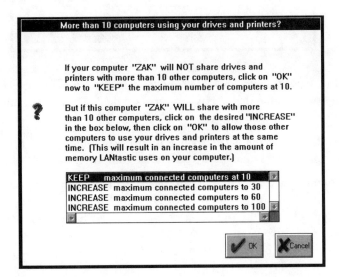

Figure 5.26
Selecting the
maximum
number of
computers that
may access your
computer.

The Select all that apply dialog box enables you to select additional LANtastic features, which include enabling you to connect to servers in other networks including Novell Networks, Windows NT, LAN manager, and others (see fig. 5.27). Also available are the options to install the Artisoft Exchange—Mail and Scheduler programs. The last item listed is an option called Load files to enable "Install Services" which, once loaded, enables other network users to connect to your computer to run the LANtastic installation program. Select the options you want to install by clicking on them. Click on OK or press Enter to continue.

Selecting the Load files to enable "Install Services" is most beneficial for installing a new version of LANtastic on a computer already active on the network. This option will not be useful for a first time installation—the computer must be able to access the server that has the LANtastic installation files installed to actually launch the LANtastic install program.

Figure 5.27
Selecting additional LANtastic features.

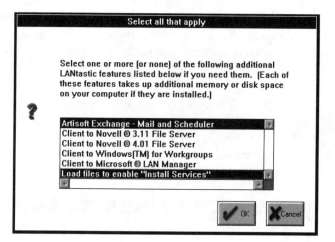

If you selected the Artisoft Exchange—Mail and Scheduler option, the Select Artisoft Exchange Mail option dialog box appears (see fig. 5.28). Below is an explanation of the three options listed:

✔ This option installs the necessary files on your computer's hard drive to enable you to access mail on the post office computer.

✔ This option allows your computer to access mail on the post office computer by running the appropriate software from the post office computer. Selecting this option saves space on your hard drive at the cost of slower performance since the software is being run from another computer instead of off your own hard drive.

✔ One of the computers in your network must be set up as a post office to use Artisoft Exchange. Select this option to set up the computer at which you are sitting as the Artisoft Exchange Mail Post Office.

Click on the option you want to install and click on OK or press Enter to continue.

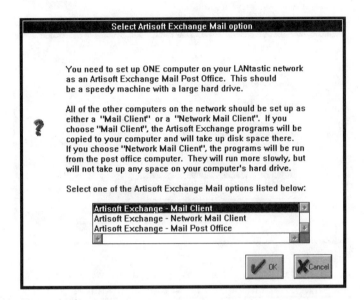

Figure 5.28
Selecting the Artisoft Exchange Mail option.

If you selected the Artisoft Exchange—Mail Client or Network Mail Client, the Enter name of computer that has post office dialog box appears (see fig. 5.29). Enter the network name of the computer that you have chosen to support the post office and click on OK or press Enter. For this example, assume that computer 386-25 will have the post office.

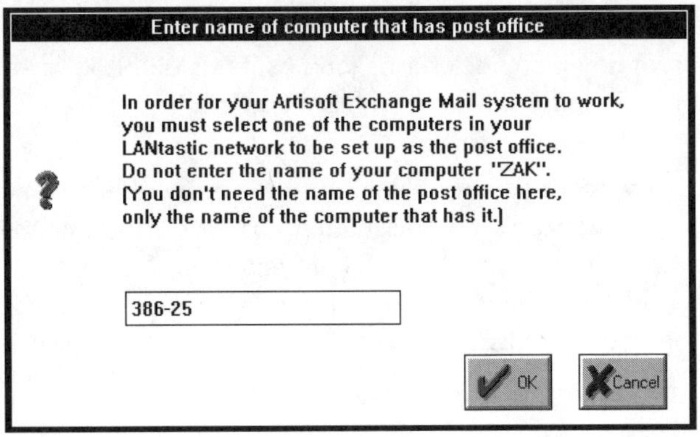

Figure 5.29
Specifying the network name of the computer with the Artisoft Exchange Post Office.

The LANtastic Information Check dialog box appears, showing the information you have specified so far (see fig. 5.30). Review your selections and choose OK to continue with installation. If you want to change your selections, you may do so at this point by selecting the Go back and re-enter the information option. Click on OK or press Enter to continue.

Figure 5.30
Summary of installation options so far.

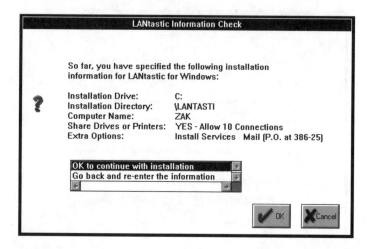

The Select network adapter dialog box appears, listing the network adapter options available (see fig. 5.31). The default LANtastic NodeRunner 2000 Series Ethernet Adapter option is the appropriate selection if you purchased a LANtastic 6.0 Network Starter Kit and are using LANtastic NodeRunner 2000 Ethernet adapters. Several other adapter options including NDIS support are available. Select the appropriate adapter for your installation by clicking on it; then click on OK or press Enter to continue.

Most network adapters are now shipped with NDIS (Network Driver Interface Specification) drivers. You can purchase nearly any network adapter from any manufacturer as long as it has an NDIS driver supplied with it and it will work with LANtastic.

The Set up drive or printer connections dialog box appears, enabling you to specify whether or not you want to set up permanent drive or printer connections (see fig. 5.32). If you want to establish a default connection to shared drives or a printer, accept the Set up permanent drive or printer connections option. Otherwise, select the Do not set up any drive or printer connections option. Click on OK or press Enter.

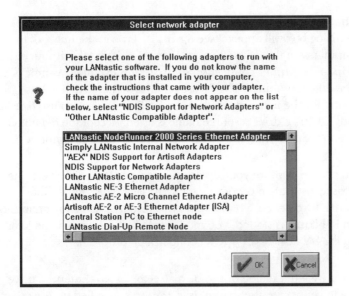

Figure 5.31
Selecting the network adapter installed.

After default drive or printer connections are selected, a line is inserted in the STARTNET.BAT file that was created in the LANTASTI directory to make the connection when the network is launched. You can modify the STARTNET.BAT file to add, remove, or change the default drive or printer connections.

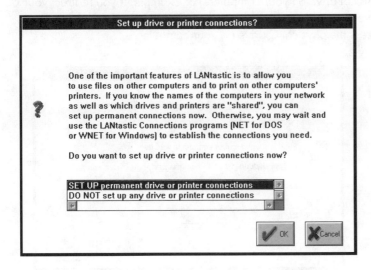

Figure 5.32
Choosing to set up permanent drive or printer connections.

If you selected the Set up permanent drive or printer connection option, the Enter computer name dialog box will appear (see fig. 5.33). Type in the network name of the other computer with the drive you want to use. Click on OK without entering a name to skip to the printer connection setup. In this example, assume KATIE is the name of the other computer. The Please enter drive name dialog box appears next, asking for the name of the drive on KATIE you want to use (see fig. 5.34). The default C-DRIVE drive resource name is listed. Accept the default C-DRIVE name or enter another, then click on OK or press Enter to continue.

If you choose to share your disk drives and printers with others, the LANtastic installation program automatically creates the C-DRIVE resource. If you choose a different drive resource name to connect to when LANtastic is started, you must create that resource name later using the LANtastic NET_MGR configuration program.

Finally, the Enter drive letter dialog box appears (see fig. 5.35). Enter the drive letter you will use to connect to the shared drive resource specified on the other computer. Accept the default drive letter D or type in a different letter, then click on OK or press Enter to continue.

When you choose a disk drive letter to access the disk drives on another computer, choose a letter that is not already assigned to a physical drive on your computer. For example, if you redirect your C drive to point to a drive on another computer, you no longer can access the physical C drive on your computer.

Figure 5.33
Entering the name of the other computer to connect to.

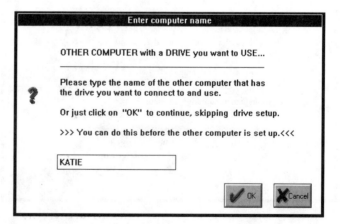

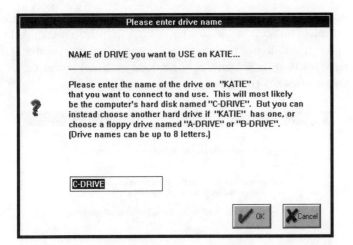

Figure 5.34
Entering the drive resource name to connect to.

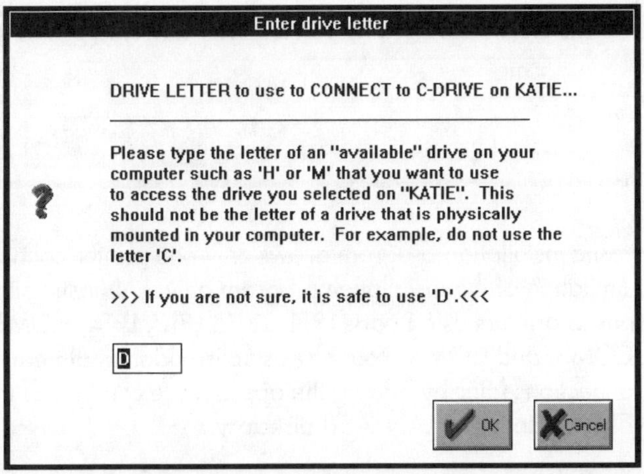

Figure 5.35
Entering the local drive letter to use for the connection.

Now the Enter computer name dialog box appears, asking for the name of another computer with a drive you want to use. If you want to set up another permanent drive connection, type in the name of the computer that has the drive to which you want to connect, and you will again be prompted to enter the name of the drive resource and the drive letter on your computer you want to use for the connection. If you don't want to set up another permanent drive connection, do not enter anything. Click on OK or press Enter to continue.

The Enter computer name dialog box appears, asking for the name of the computer having the printer you want to use (see fig. 5.36). Enter the name and click on OK or press Enter. If you do not want to set up a connection to a printer at this time, leave the name blank and click on OK or press Enter. In this example, assume Katie is the name of the computer.

Figure 5.36
Entering the
name of the
computer with a
printer attached.

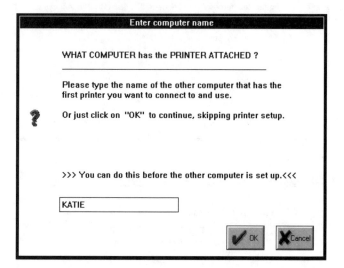

Enter computer name

WHAT COMPUTER has the PRINTER ATTACHED ?

Please type the name of the other computer that has the first printer you want to connect to and use.

Or just click on "OK" to continue, skipping printer setup.

>>> You can do this before the other computer is set up.<<<

KATIE

OK   Cancel

The LANtastic installation program allows only one printer connection. This is a limitation of the installation program only. LANtastic allows connections to printers using ports LPT1, LPT2, LPT3, LPT4, COM1, COM2, COM3, and COM4. You may establish additional permanent printer connections later by adding the appropriate commands to the STARTNET.BAT file in the LANTASTI directory.

If you share your printer with other network users, always specify a connection to your own printer.

If a network user uses your printer and you have not established a network connection to it, you can't access your printer until you do.

If you entered a name of a computer with a printer attached, the Enter printer name dialog box appears (see fig. 5.37). Enter the name of the printer you want to use. Accept the default @PRINTER name and click on OK or press Enter. Finally, in the Enter printer port dialog box, enter the printer port on your computer which you will connect to the @PRINTER resource on KATIE. Accept the default

LPT1 or type in another printer port and click on OK or press Enter. In the example shown, LPT2 is chosen (see fig. 5.38).

If you specify default connections, make sure that the server and resource name you specify exist. Otherwise, when you launch LANtastic, it doesn't establish the connection you specified and displays an error message, such as Cannot Locate Server Name.

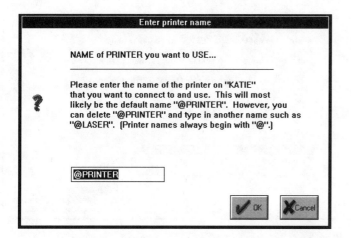

Figure 5.37
Entering the printer resource name to use.

Figure 5.38
Entering the printer port to use for the connection.

The LANtastic Final Information Check dialog box appears, listing all the installation information you have specified (see fig. 5.39). Accept the default OK to perform the installation option and click on OK or press Enter to continue. To change any of your selection, select the Go back and re-enter the information option and click on OK or press Enter. You can change any option, and then are returned to this same screen.

Figure 5.39
Summary of
installation
options
specified.

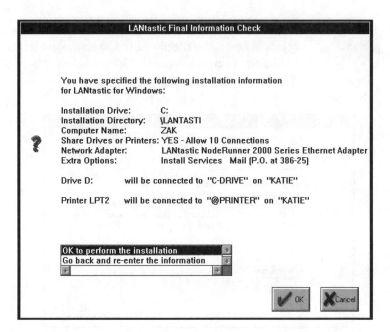

The Artisoft Install Message dialog box appears, explaining that several of your system files will be changed and the names of the old files will be renamed (see fig. 5.40). Click on OK or press Enter to perform the installation.

Figure 5.40
Notes on
changed
computer
configuration.

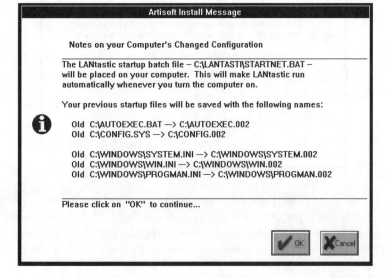

The LANtastic files are now loaded onto your computer's hard disk. You are prompted when necessary to enter the next disk. When the installation finishes, the Artisoft Install Message dialog box appears, indicating the installation is complete. Click on OK or press Enter to continue.

Finally, the Artisoft Install Message dialog box appears, indicating that Install will shut down Windows and reboot your computer. Click on OK or press Enter to reboot your computer. LANtastic will be started when your computer boots. Click on Cancel or press ESC to exit the installation program without re-booting.

You now have completed your LANtastic installation for this computer. The LANtastic installation program has changed your WIN.INI, SYSTEM.INI Windows files, changed your CONFIG.SYS file, and created a batch file in the LANTASTI directory, called STARTNET.BAT, which contains the commands necessary to load the LANtastic software and establish the default printer and disk drive connections. The LANtastic installation program also has added the following command to your AUTOEXEC.BAT file that causes LANtastic to launch if you turn on your computer.

      call C:\LANTASTI\STARTNET.BAT

The LANtastic 6.0 Windows installation has also created the LANtastic program group, which contains several LANtastic for Windows programs (see fig. 5.41).

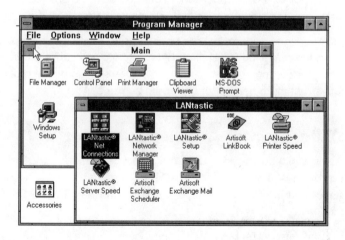

Figure 5.41
The LANtastic program group.

Upgrading a Previous Version of LANtastic

If you are currently running a LANtastic network, the LANtastic 6.0 installation program includes some additional features to make the upgrade process easier. When installing LANtastic 6.0, you have the option of keeping your existing

LANtastic configuration (CONFIG.SYS, AUTOEXEC.BAT, STARTNET.BAT) or replacing it with new settings. In addition, the LANtastic 6.0 installation program can create an install resource from which you may run the LANtastic 6.0 installation program from a network drive instead of from floppy disks.

Installing "Install Services" on a Server

If you want to install LANtastic 6.0 by accessing the installation files on a server instead of from floppy disks, you must first perform a normal installation on the server on which you want to have the LANtastic 6.0 installation files.

Perform the installation as described previously; however, when you get to the section in the installation program that enables you to specify additional features, select the Load files to enable "Install Services" option. Figure 5.9 shows this option in the DOS installation, and figure 5.27 shows this option in the Windows installation. Selecting the Load files to enable "Install Services" option will create a resource named INSTALL on the server which points to the directory containing the installation files necessary to run the LANtastic 6.0 installation program. When you finish the installation, LANtastic 6.0 will be installed on your computer, as well as the LANtastic 6.0 installation files.

If you will be upgrading your other computers from a version of LANtastic prior to 5.0, *do not* reboot your computer before you have performed the upgrade on the other computers in your network.

LANtastic versions prior to 5.0 are not compatible with LANtastic 6.0. Rebooting the server after installing LANtastic 6.0 will cause LANtastic 6.0 to be loaded, making that computer inaccessible to all the other computers running a version of LANtastic before 5.0.

Upgrading LANtastic from Another Computer

To upgrade to LANtastic 6.0 by accessing the LANtastic 6.0 installation files on another computer, you must first redirect a drive letter to point to the INSTALL resource on the server that has the LANtastic 6.0 installation files. At the DOS prompt, type the following:

```
NET USE I: \\Server\INSTALL
```

where I: is the drive letter you want to use to access the LANtastic 6.0 installation program, and Server is the name of the server that has the LANtastic 6.0 installation files loaded and an INSTALL resource name created which points to those files.

To start the installation program, from the DOS prompt type the following:

    `I:INSTALL`

The LANtastic installation searches your path for Windows and, if found, loads the LANtastic Windows installation program. Otherwise, the LANtastic DOS installation program is run.

> You can also upgrade from within Windows by using the LANtastic for Windows NET utility to redirect a drive to the INSTALL resource on the server that contains the LANtastic 6.0 installation files. With the drive redirected, from the Program Manager, select **F**ile, then **R**un; type **I:INSTALL** in the Run dialog box, and select OK. The LANtastic 6.0 Windows installation will begin.

If the LANtastic 6.0 installation program detects a previous version of LANtastic installed on your computer, it will notify you that it has detected a previous version of LANtastic and enable you to specify whether you want to Keep your current LANtastic settings or Replace them with new settings generated by the LANtastic 6.0 installation program. Figure 5.42 shows the Keep or replace current LANtastic settings dialog box displayed by the LANtastic 6.0 Windows installation program. The LANtastic 6.0 DOS installation program displays a similar screen.

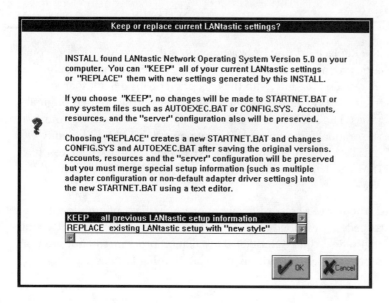

Figure 5.42
The Keep or replace current LANtastic settings dialog box.

If you choose the Keep all previous LANtastic setup information option, LANtastic 6.0 will be installed, but will not change any of your system files including CONFIG.SYS, AUTOEXEC.BAT, and STARTNET.BAT. All the user accounts, shared resources, and server configuration information will remain the same. The LANtastic 6.0 installation program will create several system files (CONFIG.NEW, AUTOEXEC.NEW, STARTNET.NEW, WIN.NEW, AND SYSTEM.NEW) which you may need to incorporate into your existing system files using an editor such as DOS EDIT or Windows Notepad. The following table shows the files created by the LANtastic 6.0 installation program, as well as the associated system file:

Created by LANtastic 6.0 Install	System File Name
CONFIG.NEW	CONFIG.SYS
AUTOEXEC.NEW	AUTOEXEC.BAT
STARTNET.NEW	STARTNET.BAT

If you have Microsoft Windows, the following files are also created:

Created by LANtastic 6.0 Install	System File Name
WIN.NEW	WIN.INI
SYSTEM.NEW	SYSTEM.INI

If you choose the Replace existing LANtastic setup with "new style" option, your existing LANtastic user accounts, shared resources, and server configuration information will remain the same, with the exception of any default shared resources such as C-DRIVE and @PRINTER which will be reset to their original installation settings. The LANtastic 6.0 installation program will modify your system files and save the original files under a different name. INSTALL will modify CONFIG.SYS, AUTOEXEC.BAT, and STARTNET.BAT. If you have Microsoft Windows, INSTALL will also modify the WIN.INI and SYSTEM.INI Windows system files.

After choosing whether to Keep or Replace your LANtastic configuration, the installation proceeds as described previously. If you choose to Keep your existing LANtastic configuration, the LANtastic 6.0 installation program will not prompt you to enter information already specified in your existing LANtastic configuration.

LANtastic Installation Switches

When you run the LANtastic installation program, it assumes certain things about your system. For example, if you are running the LANtastic 6.0 installation program from the DOS command line, and you have Windows installed on your computer, the installation program assumes you want to run the LANtastic 6.0 Windows installation program and not the DOS installation program. Installation switches placed on the command line after INSTALL enable you to specify special installation parameters which override the default installation parameters. For example, to run only the LANtastic 6.0 DOS installation (even if Windows was installed on your system) you would type the following at the DOS prompt:

    INSTALL/DOS

The following are the INSTALL command line switches and the function each switch performs:

/HELP	Lists a screen showing the available switches and the function of each. The /? switch also performs the same function.
/INF	Lists information about the commands and syntax for the INSTALL.INF file which contains commands to automate the LANtastic installation process.
/BW	Runs the installation program using only black-and-white.
/MONO	Runs the installation program on Monochrome (MDA) monitors.
/DOS	Forces the installation program to run the DOS installation even if Windows is present on the system. The LANtastic for Windows programs will not be installed and Windows will not be configured for use with LANtastic.
/WIN	Forces the installation of LANtastic for Windows programs and configures Windows for use with LANtastic. When combined with the /DOS switch, enables you to run the LANtastic DOS installation program to install all the Windows features including Artisoft Exchange.
/FLOPPY	Installs a minimum LANtastic configuration on a floppy disk used to start LANtastic on computers without a hard disk. The installation program will automatically create the CONFIG.SYS and AUTOEXEC.BAT files if they don't already exist. Also, if you plan on booting your computer from this disk, make the disk bootable before installing LANtastic on it.

The LANtastic files require a minimum of 391112 bytes of storage space so you cannot install LANtastic on a 360K floppy disk. After LANtastic is installed however, you can delete some unnecessary files so you can copy the required files to a 360K floppy disk.

/REMOTE   Performs a partial LANtastic installation to a network drive.

/EXTRACT   Enables you to remove specific groups of files from the installation diskettes which are in a compressed format.

Automating the LANtastic Installation Program

If you have several computers on which to install LANtastic 6.0, you can significantly reduce the time expended installing LANtastic with the use of an installation script, containing answers to questions asked during installation. If the LANtastic 6.0 installation program encounters a file named INSTALL.INF on the installation disk (whether it be a floppy disk or the INSTALL resource on a server), it will use the options specified in INSTALL.INF to perform the installation.

When LANtastic 6.0 is first installed, it creates a file called SAMPLE.INF in the LANtastic directory; it may be easily modified with a text editor, such as DOS EDIT or Windows Notepad, to contain installation instructions specific to your requirements. If you save the modified sample file as INSTALL.INF and place the file on your first installation disk (or in the INSTALL resource on a server), when the LANtastic 6.0 installation program is run, it will use the parameters you have specified.

Figure 5.43 shows the SAMPLE.INF file created when the LANtastic 6.0 Windows installation was run for computer ZAK. The SAMPLE.INF file contains a [LANTASTIC] header. The INSTALL.INF you create may contain several different headers to be used for different users or types of installations. If you leave the ComputerName options in the INSTALL.INF file blank, the LANtastic 6.0 installation program will prompt you for a username and then access the installation parameters specified for that user. Chapter 3 of *The LANtastic Installation and Management Guide* contains a list of the INSTALL.INF commands and their functions.

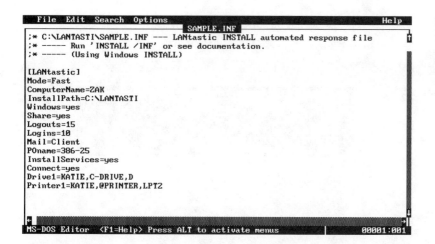

Figure 5.43
The SAMPLE.INF file created during LANtastic 6.0 Windows installation for computer ZAK.

Changing Your LANtastic Setup

When you install LANtastic 6.0, the installation program includes a program called LANSETUP.EXE in the LANTASTI directory. If you installed LANtastic for Windows, there is a LANtastic Setup icon in the LANtastic program group which will run LANSETUP. Figure 5.44 shows the Windows LANtastic Setup program menu and figure 5.45 shows the DOS LANtastic Setup program menu. The same options are available whether you are in Windows or in DOS. The LANtastic setup program enables you to perform tasks such as disabling LANtastic when your computer is booted, or just disabling the LANtastic Server program, which allows your computer to share it's resources with others. You can also add default LANtastic resources and view online LANtastic documentation or system information about your computer.

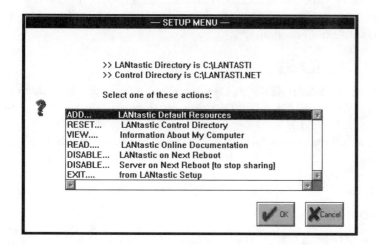

Figure 5.44
The Windows LANtastic Setup program main menu.

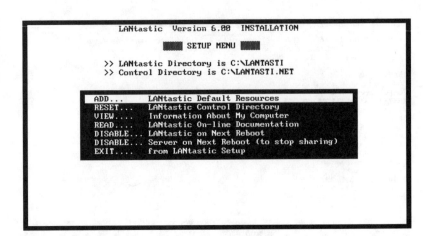

Figure 5.45
The DOS
LANtastic Setup
program main
menu.

```
         LANtastic  Version 6.00   INSTALLATION

                ▓▓ SETUP MENU ▓▓

        >> LANtastic Directory is C:\LANTASTI
        >> Control Directory is C:\LANTASTI.NET

     ADD...      LANtastic Default Resources
     RESET...    LANtastic Control Directory
     VIEW....    Information About My Computer
     READ....    LANtastic On-line Documentation
     DISABLE...  LANtastic on Next Reboot
     DISABLE...  Server on Next Reboot (to stop sharing)
     EXIT....    from LANtastic Setup
```

Examining CONFIG.SYS, AUTOEXEC.BAT, and STARTNET.BAT

After your computer is turned on and performs its initial tests, it looks for two system files in the root directory of your hard drive and executes the commands contained within them. The first file your system looks for is CONFIG.SYS. This file usually contains general system operating parameters, such as hardware device drivers and the number of files you can open at one time. The next file your system looks for is AUTOEXEC.BAT, which contains other commands to load programs (such as the SMARTDRIVE or LANCACHE disk cache programs) and other device drivers (such as the driver for your mouse). When you install LANtastic, changes are made to both the CONFIG.SYS and the AUTOEXEC.BAT files. The LANtastic 6.0 installation program also creates a DOS batch file, located in the LANTASTI directory (unless you specified a different directory during installation), with the name STARTNET.BAT—this file contains the commands to actually launch your LANtastic network.

Examining CONFIG.SYS

When you install LANtastic, the INSTALL program adds or modifies several lines in your CONFIG.SYS file. In a standard LANtastic installation where you configure your computer as a server, the following lines are added (or modified if they already exist with different values specified) with the values shown as follows:

FILES=100

BUFFERS=30

LASTDRIVE=Z

If your computer is configured as a workstation, the lines have the following form:

FILES=60

BUFFERS=30

LASTDRIVE=Z

> If you choose the additional LANtastic feature for your computer to be a client to a non-LANtastic server, there may also be network device drivers added to your CONFIG.SYS file.
>
> In addition to the preceding statements, the LANtastic 5.0 installation included the FCBS=16,8 statement.

The FILES statement needs to have a high value. FILES=100 is the minimum recommended value for a server. If you have application programs that open a large number of files concurrently, such as a database or an accounting program, you may need to increase this value.

The BUFFERS statement primarily affects performance. It specifies the number of buffers used for transferring data between the hard drive and memory. If you have a disk-caching program installed, such as SMARTDRIVE or LANCACHE, setting this value to 8 usually results in the best performance.

The LASTDRIVE statement specifies the last drive letter DOS enables you to use. Setting LASTDRIVE=Z enables you to redirect drive letters A through Z to access shared network resources.

Examining AUTOEXEC.BAT

When you turn on your computer, you typically want LANtastic loaded and operational immediately. By including the line

    call C:\LANTASTI\STARTNET.BAT

in your AUTOEXEC.BAT file, your LANtastic network software loads and runs when this statement is encountered. CALL causes the system to branch to the batch file STARTNET.BAT, execute the commands contained within it, and then return and continue processing the rest of the commands in AUTOEXEC.BAT.

> Instead of specifying the STARTNET.BAT file to launch your network, you can include the same statements in your AUTOEXEC.BAT file. Although this approach is not wrong, if you have a choice it's easier to call the STARTNET.BAT file.

Examining STARTNET.BAT

The STARTNET.BAT file is created by the LANtastic installation program and includes all the commands necessary to launch your LANtastic software and establish any default drive and printer connections specified during installation. Figure 5.46 shows a typical STARTNET.BAT file for a computer with a NodeRunner Ethernet adapter installed.

Figure 5.46

A typical STARTNET.BAT file for a system with a NodeRunner Ethernet adapter installed.

```
@echo off
rem LANtastic  Version 6.00  installed 94/02/21 04:53:49
rem (for Windows)

C:
cd C:\LANTASTI

SET LAN_CFG=C:\LANTASTI

rem If LANtastic is disabled, skip everything.
IF EXIST DISABLED GOTO :STARTNET_DONE

@echo ===== Begin LANtastic configuration =====

PATH C:\LANTASTI;C:\LANTASTI\NW;%PATH%
SET LAN_DIR=C:\LANTASTI.NET
SET NWDBPATH=C:\LANTASTI\NW

LOADHIGH NR
AILANBIO @STARTNET.CFG

REDIR ZAK @STARTNET.CFG

IF EXIST NOSHARE GOTO :NOSHARE
SERVER C:\LANTASTI.NET @STARTNET.CFG
NET LOGIN \\ZAK
GOTO :CONTINUE

:NOSHARE
@echo LANtastic server was installed but turned off.

:CONTINUE

rem If CONNECT.BAT exists, run it to set up connections.
IF EXIST CONNECT.BAT GOTO :CONNECT

rem Otherwise set up connections specified during install.
NET LOGIN/wait \\KATIE
NET USE D: \\KATIE\C-DRIVE
NET USE LPT2: \\KATIE\@PRINTER
NET LPT TIMEOUT 10
GOTO :CONNECT_DONE

:CONNECT
@echo Setting up LANtastic connections from CONNECT.BAT
rem Build CONNECT.BAT like this: "NET SHOW/BATCH > C:\LANTASTI\CON
NECT.BAT"
rem   (or run the batch file SETNET.BAT)
call CONNECT.BAT

:CONNECT_DONE
NET POSTBOX

@echo ===== End LANtastic configuration =====

:STARTNET_DONE
cd \
```

The STARTNET.BAT file contains a number of configuration items, including statements that will cause parts of the batch file to be skipped if certain conditions are met. The primary commands are described as follows:

The PATH statement causes your C:\LANTASTI directory to be included in the DOS path, so you can issue NET commands and similar functions in any other directory.

Prior to LANtastic 6.0, the DOS SHARE command was included in the STARTNET.BAT file.

The DOS SHARE command provides file and record-locking features that are used by most multiuser applications to prevent users from accessing the same files or records at the same time.

LANtastic 6.0 now has the features of the DOS SHARE command built into the NOS; the DOS SHARE command is thus no longer necessary.

NR is the network adapter device driver. This driver is required in order for your network adapter to communicate with the NETBIOS.

AILANBIO is Artisoft's NETBIOS program. It is the basic communication standard used for network communication.

Command line options may be included after LANtastic commands, or you may include the options in a switch file. The @STARTNET.CFG option listed after AILANBIO, for example, instructs the AILANBIO program to use the options specified in the STARTNET.CFG switch file.

Figure 5.47 shows the associated STARTNET.CFG switch file for the STARTNET.BAT file shown in figure 5.46. When a switch file is used, the command uses the switches listed under the appropriate heading in the switch file. For example, because @STARTNET.CFG is listed after AILANBIO, AILANBIO uses the switches listed after the [AILANBIO] heading in the STARTNET.CFG switch file.

REDIR is the LANtastic Redirector program. It enables you to redirect your drives and printer device names to access the shared resources on other servers. The network name of your computer is specified on the same line as REDIR. In this example, ZAK is the network name of the computer. The LOGINS statement under the [REDIR] heading in the STARTNET.CFG file specifies the number of servers you can be logged in to at one time.

Figure 5.47
The
STARTNET.CFG
switch file.

```
;STARTNET.CFG - LANtastic switch settings
[AILANBIO]
   MAX_NCBS=44
   NCBS=44
   MAX_SESSIONS=38
   SESSIONS=38

[REDIR]
   LOGINS=15

[SERVER]
```

The LOGINS switch used with the REDIR command should be set to at least as many servers as are on your network. If you have five servers in your network and your LOGINS switch only specifies three (LOGINS=3), only three servers appear on your servers list in the LANtastic NET program.

SERVER is the LANtastic server program. It enables your computer to share its resources with other users. If your computer is configured as a workstation, your STARTNET.BAT file does not include the SERVER program statement.

The NET LOGIN and NET USE statements are the result of the default drive and printer connections you specified when you installed LANtastic. You can change these lines at any time to add or remove default network connections as your requirements change. The following is a description of every NET command in the STARTNET.BAT file:

✔ This command logs you in to the server named KATIE. NET LOGIN is the LANtastic command used to log you in to a server. /WAIT is a switch that instructs LANtastic to continue login attempts until the requested server responds. \\ is a LANtastic command-line separator, and a server name must be proceeded by it in the command statement. KATIE is the name of the server to be logged in to.

Because the installation program automatically installed the wildcard account *, you can log in without specifying a username or password.

✔ This command logs you in to server ZAK so you can use the resources on ZAK. Since ZAK is the computer with this command, you are logging in to yourself with this command.

✔ This command redirects your drive letter D to the C-DRIVE resource on the server named KATIE.

✔ This command redirects your printer port LPT2 to point to the @PRINTER resource on the server named KATIE.

✔ This command searches the servers you are logged in to for mail.

✔ This command specifies that if more than 10 seconds elapse before information from an application program is received by the LANtastic spooler, the print job is to close and spool to the printer.

If, instead of the NodeRunner adapter, you had the Artisoft AE2 or AE3 network adapters, the only difference in your STARTNET.BAT file would be that the NR adapter driver in the STARTNET.BAT file would be replaced with an AEX adapter driver. If you had the Artisoft A2MBPS network adapter, the NR and AILANBIO command lines would be replaced with a single LANBIOS3 command. This is because LANBIOS3 includes both the network adapter device driver and the NETBIOS.

When you start your computer, as the LANtastic software is loaded, you will notice much more information scrolling up your screen indicating that LANtastic is being loaded.

Running LANcheck

After your computer is launched and the LANtastic network software is running, one final test remains to make sure that your network adapter cards are communicating properly across the network.

Included with LANtastic is a program called LANcheck. LANcheck displays the network adapter status and an error index to help you determine if your network adapter cards are communicating properly. Run LANcheck on each computer concurrently. To run LANcheck, type **LANCHECK** at the DOS prompt.

Figure 5.48 shows the main LANcheck information screen. Each computer running LANcheck is displayed on-screen. The Status column for each computer says local or active. The Error-Index column should be zero or very close to zero.

Figure 5.48
The LANcheck
main screen.

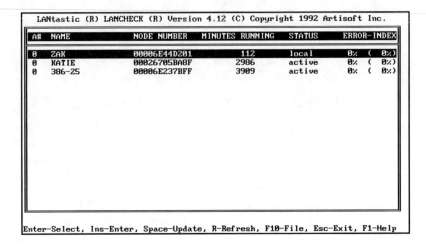

```
LANtastic (R) LANCHECK (R) Version 4.12 (C) Copyright 1992 Artisoft Inc.
 A#   NAME             NODE NUMBER    MINUTES RUNNING    STATUS      ERROR-INDEX
 0    ZAK              00006E44D201          112         local      0%  ( 0%)
 0    KATIE            00026705BA8F         2986         active     0%  ( 0%)
 0    386-25           00006E237BFF         3909         active     0%  ( 0%)


Enter-Select, Ins-Enter, Space-Update, R-Refresh, F10-File, Esc-Exit, F1-Help
```

Summary

This chapter covered the installation process for your LANtastic network. You
learned how to install your network cable and the network adapter cards in each
computer. You also learned the way to install the LANtastic software on your
computer. You examined the changes that the install program made to your
system files, and you learned about the commands in the STARTNET.BAT file.
Finally, you discovered the way to do a quick test to confirm that your network
adapters are communicating properly.

The next next two chapters discuss how to set up user accounts and shared
resources in DOS and Windows.

Chapter Snapshot

This chapter discusses ways to set up and configure user accounts and shared resources using LANtastic in DOS. This same information as it applies in Windows is covered in Chapter 7, "Setting Up User Accounts and Shared Resources in Windows." The following topics are included:

✔ Determining your server's function and the resources you want to share with other users

✔ Understanding the different types of accounts and Access Control List (ACL) groups

✔ Setting up individual and wildcard accounts using the LANtastic NET_MGR program in DOS

✔ Setting up ACL groups and shared resources using the LANtastic NET_MGR program in DOS

After you finish reading this chapter, you will be fully prepared to set up and configure shared resources on your LANtastic network.

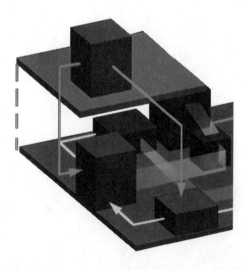

CHAPTER

Setting Up User Accounts and Shared Resources in DOS

I n the preceding chapters, you learned the procedure you must follow to install your network. You also learned the fundamentals of LANtastic, as well as ways to plan your installation, set up your hardware, and install the LANtastic software. By the time you finished Chapter 5, you had performed all the required steps to set up a complete, functioning network.

To use and manage your network effectively, however, you need to learn more about what the LANtastic software can do. You need to know how to set up user accounts and shared resources, how to manage the network, and how to make it work best for your installation.

This chapter discusses how to set up user accounts and shared resources in DOS using the DOS LANtastic Network Manager program. If you prefer to use Windows, the same information is covered in Chapter 7. It doesn't matter whether you use the DOS or the Windows LANtastic Network Manager program to set up the accounts and shared resources; these are available to you in both the DOS and Windows environments.

Determining Your Server's Function

In Chapter 3, "Planning Your LANtastic Network," you decided which computers would share their resources with others, which resources would be shared, and which users would have access to those resources.

This section concentrates on the specific functions that you want your server(s) to perform for you. You first must determine the type of information necessary to complete the setup of the network user accounts and shared resources.

Refer to the configuration inventory sheets that you completed. Specifically, remember where the printers and software applications are physically located. You now will use that information to set up the user accounts and shared resources.

Do not use your existing single-user applications in a multiuser setup without obtaining a legal multiuser copy or license. Although some software companies sell applications as single-user applications, the software may support more than one user at a time. By law, you are obligated to purchase the multiuser version or obtain a license from the manufacturer to use it in a multiuser environment.

You can place those applications that do not support multiple users on the network if only one person at a time uses them. This distinction is much like the copyright laws for books. You cannot make copies of a book without permission from the publisher, but you can let another person read the book. If only one user at a time can access the application, you are usually not violating the copyright.

You must decide whether you want to set up a dedicated server, a single non-dedicated server, or multiple servers that also act as workstations. Most people find that it is more convenient to install multiple servers so that users can access the software applications and printer resources from multiple computers. If your installation is small, you probably do not want to forfeit the use of one of the computers to use it as a dedicated server. You can assume, therefore, that you will have multiple servers that share their resources with all other users on the network.

The next phase in configuring your network is to set up the controls for the access and use of the resources. The following sections discuss setting up user accounts, passwords and access control lists, and shared resources that LANtastic will recognize and monitor for you.

Understanding Accounts and ACL Groups

User accounts are one of your most valuable tools for maintaining control of your network. Because of the shared nature of resources on a network, you do not want one user to disrupt the work of another user. You can control and restrict access to specific network resources by setting up a user account and assigning a password and access controls for each user.

LANtastic enables you to set up two different types of user accounts: individual accounts and wildcard accounts. These accounts are set up on each server using the LANtastic network manager program.

Figure 6.1 shows the DOS LANtastic Network Manager (NET_MGR) program main menu. The first two selections, Individual Account Management and Wildcard Account Management, enable you to set up user accounts for individuals or for wildcard groups.

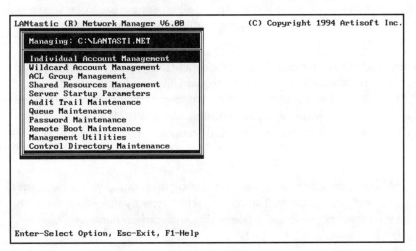

```
LANtastic (R) Network Manager V6.00        (C) Copyright 1994 Artisoft Inc.

  Managing: C:\LANTASTI.NET
 ┌──────────────────────────────────┐
 │ Individual Account Management     │
 │ Wildcard Account Management       │
 │ ACL Group Management              │
 │ Shared Resources Management       │
 │ Server Startup Parameters         │
 │ Audit Trail Maintenance           │
 │ Queue Maintenance                 │
 │ Password Maintenance              │
 │ Remote Boot Maintenance           │
 │ Management Utilities              │
 │ Control Directory Maintenance     │
 └──────────────────────────────────┘




 Enter-Select Option, Esc-Exit, F1-Help
```

Figure 6.1
The NET_MGR program main menu.

A *wildcard account* has a name that ends with the wildcard character *. The wildcard works the same way it does with DOS file names. The wildcard account name SALES-*, for example, would enable a user to log in using any name or group of characters in place of the *. SALES-JOHN, SALES-JAN, SALES-KYLE, and so on would all be valid user names for the SALES-* wildcard account.

When LANtastic is installed, a default wildcard account is created. With this wildcard account, LANtastic does not require a user name and password when logging in to a server; it automatically logs you in (assuming the wildcard account exists on the server you are trying to log in to).

Many LANtastic networks are set up using only the default wildcard account on each server, and without setting up any accounts for individual users. If you do not have specific network user security requirements, using the wildcard account will greatly simplify your LANtastic configuration.

Individual accounts are set up for each person who is allowed access to a particular server. Setting up each person with his or her own account offers the greatest security. Individual accounts enable users to change their own passwords, and network usage auditing may be traced to individuals rather than a group of individuals—a possibility with wildcard accounts.

Wildcard accounts make more sense if many users will be using a particular server. You can create wildcard accounts that represent departments in your business or a particular location.

Your business might have an engineering department, a shipping department, and an accounting department. You can, therefore, have all your engineering data on one computer and all your accounting data on another. Setting up different wildcard accounts for appropriate departments enables you to allow access only to authorized users, while eliminating the need to set up specific accounts for each user.

LANtastic enables you to have any combination of individual accounts and wildcard accounts. You can, therefore, specify individual accounts for certain key personnel while having wildcard accounts available for use by others.

ACL (Access Control List) Groups allow the grouping of individual or wildcard accounts according to the type of access they have to the resources on the server. When you set up shared resources on a server, you can specify each resource name that can access the resource and the level of access the user can have.

Suppose that you have a resource named C-DRIVE on your server, and you do not want anyone to be able to access it except the users with names NETMAN, KEVIN, and DANA. LANtastic enables you to specify those users' names in an Access Control List for that resource. Better yet, you can create an ACL group comprised of users NETMAN, KEVIN, and DANA. If you call this ACL group POWER, you can specify the POWER ACL Group instead of each user's individual name in the C-DRIVE resource Access Control List.

An added benefit of using ACL groups occurs if you later decide to add additional users who would have the same access privileges as those in the POWER ACL Group. At the time the new users are added, you can specify the ACL groups to which they belong. You do not have to go into each resource and add the new accounts to the ACL because the new users will already be part of the ACL group that is listed for that resource.

Make sure that you set up matching accounts for each user on every server on the network. Doing so enables users to log in to any server without remembering different user names and passwords for each server.

Using LANtastic, you can copy the accounts and ACL groups created on one server to any other server in the network. This powerful feature enables you to set up your users and their access rights at the same time; as soon as you have the setup just the way you want it, you can copy it to every other server. You do not have to set up each server separately.

After a person logs in to a server and requests the use of an application or device resource, LANtastic checks its user account tables to see if the user has approved access to the requested resource. If the user has approval, access is granted. If the user does not have the appropriate level of access, LANtastic displays a warning message and denies access.

When used together, individual accounts, wildcard accounts, and ACL groups can create a powerful and flexible network security structure.

Setting Up Individual Accounts

Suppose that you want to set up two user accounts, one for you as the network administrator and one for another user. For this example, the administrator is called NETMAN (network manager). You first will set up your account using NETMAN as the name. The second account name can be one of your choice. Try to keep all user names as short as possible because users must type their name each time they log in.

Begin by rebooting both computers. Rebooting ensures that any changes that may have been made to the CONFIG.SYS or AUTOEXEC.BAT files during the installation process are properly loaded at boot time. Watch the screen on each computer to make sure the LANtastic software is being loaded.

If you did not notice the LANtastic programs loading after you rebooted your computer(s), then your AUTOEXEC.BAT file may not be executing the LANtastic STARTNET.BAT file. Check your AUTOEXEC.BAT file to make sure it includes the following line:

```
CALL C:\LANTASTI\STARTNET.BAT
```

If your AUTOEXEC.BAT file does contain the preceding line, then look at the statements before CALL C:\LANTASTI\STARTNET.BAT to make sure another program (such as a menu program) isn't causing AUTOEXEC.BAT to be terminated before the network is started.

At the DOS prompt, type **NET SHOW** and press Enter. Your screen should display information similar to that shown in figure 6.2. The LANtastic NET SHOW command displays information about the current state of the network, including other servers to which you are not currently logged on, and the resources to which you are connected on those servers.

Because you are setting up user accounts and network resources, you must load the LANtastic Network Manager program NET_MGR. This utility program enables you to create user accounts and to determine security and access controls. Type **NET_MGR** and press Enter. The NET_MGR main menu appears, as shown in figure 6.3.

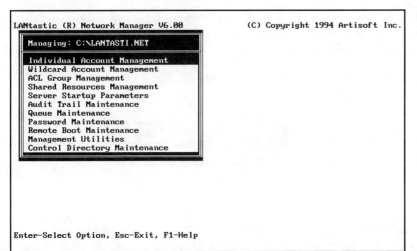

```
C:\>NET SHOW
LANtastic (R) Connection Manager V6.00 - (C) Copyright 1994 ARTISOFT Inc.
Machine KSOFFICE is being used as a Redirector and a Server
File and record locking is currently ENABLED
Unsolicited messages will BEEP, POP-UP and SPEAK
LPT notification is DISABLED
LPT timeout in seconds: 10
Autologin is ENABLED with username KSOFFICE
Logged into \\KSOFFICE as KSOFFICE on adapter 0
Disk K: is connected to \\KSOFFICE\C-DRIVE


C:\>
```

Figure 6.2
An example
NET SHOW
results screen.

```
LANtastic (R) Network Manager V6.00          (C) Copyright 1994 Artisoft Inc.

  Managing: C:\LANTASTI.NET

  Individual Account Management
  Wildcard Account Management
  ACL Group Management
  Shared Resources Management
  Server Startup Parameters
  Audit Trail Maintenance
  Queue Maintenance
  Password Maintenance
  Remote Boot Maintenance
  Management Utilities
  Control Directory Maintenance




Enter-Select Option, Esc-Exit, F1-Help
```

Figure 6.3
The NET_MGR
main menu
screen.

NET_MGR has several menu selections. At this time, however, you will set only some of the items. The remaining menu selections are discussed in Chapter 11, "Managing Your Network Using the LANtastic Network Manager." Highlight the first choice on the menu, Individual Account Management, and press Enter. The Individual Accounts list appears (see fig. 6.4). Press Ins, and another dialog box opens, enabling you to enter an account name. For this example, type the name **NETMAN** in the box, and press Enter (see fig. 6.5).

Figure 6.4
The Individual
Accounts list.

Figure 6.5
Entering an
account name.

NET_MGR displays another dialog box and asks you to enter a password for this user (see fig. 6.6). Because this is the network manager's file, you must enter a password for the account so that no other user can have access to it.

Make sure that you write down this password and store it in a secure place. Press Enter after you type your password selection.

Figure 6.6
Entering a
password for
the NETMAN
account.

The next dialog box prompts you for a description of this account. This dialog box is an optional entry field; you can leave this entry blank if you want or fill in information that serves as a reminder to you (see fig. 6.7). The description can contain any text up to a maximum of 32 characters. LANtastic makes no use of this information; it is strictly to help you remember information about an account. Press Enter after you type the description. If you choose to leave the description blank, press Enter to return to the NET_MGR menu.

Figure 6.7
Entering the
account
description.

The next screen asks you to identify the number of concurrent logins to this server for the account (see fig. 6.8). You specify the number of logins that may be made to the server using this account. In other words, if you specify two concurrent logins, you may log in to this server using this account name from no more than two computers. Press Enter after you type the concurrent login number.

Figure 6.8
Entering the number of concurrent logins.

The screen returns to the Individual Accounts list and shows the name of the user you have just entered (see fig. 6.9). Place the highlight bar on NETMAN and press Enter to display the information screen about this Individual Account (see fig. 6.10).

Figure 6.9
The Individual Accounts list showing NETMAN added.

The Account Information screen contains the following menu options:

- ✔ **Name.** This field contains the network login name for the account (16 characters maximum). In this chapter's example, the field contains the name NETMAN for the network manager account.

- ✔ **Description.** This 32-character text field is used to describe this account. You may want to place the user's real name or position title in this field.

- ✔ **Account Modifications.** This field may be toggled between Allowed and Disallowed by pressing Enter. If Account Modifications are Allowed, users are able to change the password and disable the account after they log in.

Figure 6.10
The Account
Information
screen.

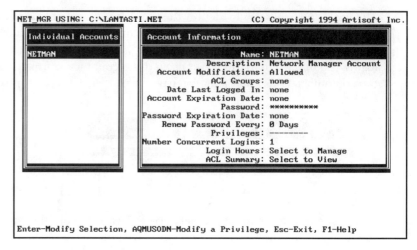

```
NET_MGR USING: C:\LANTASTI.NET          (C) Copyright 1994 Artisoft Inc.
┌─Individual Accounts─┐  ┌─Account Information──────────────────────────┐
│ NETMAN              │  │                      Name: NETMAN            │
│                     │  │               Description: Network Manager Account │
│                     │  │       Account Modifications: Allowed         │
│                     │  │                ACL Groups: none              │
│                     │  │         Date Last Logged In: none            │
│                     │  │     Account Expiration Date: none            │
│                     │  │                  Password: **********        │
│                     │  │    Password Expiration Date: none            │
│                     │  │        Renew Password Every: 0 Days          │
│                     │  │                 Privileges: --------         │
│                     │  │     Number Concurrent Logins: 1              │
│                     │  │               Login Hours: Select to Manage  │
│                     │  │               ACL Summary: Select to View    │
│                     │  │                                              │
└─────────────────────┘  └──────────────────────────────────────────────┘
 Enter-Modify Selection, AQMUSODN-Modify a Privilege, Esc-Exit, F1-Help
```

The default setting for the Account Modifications field is Allowed for
Individual Accounts and Disallowed for Wildcard Accounts. These
default settings make sense—you normally want to enable users to
change their password or disable their account, but you do not want to
enable an individual using a wildcard account to have this privilege
because it would then prevent others from using the same wildcard
account.

✔ **ACL Groups.** This selection enables you to select and modify the Access
Control List groups to which this account belongs. An account does not
have to belong to any ACL groups.

✔ **Date Last Logged In.** LANtastic updates this each time a user logs in
to the network. You cannot change the data in this field. This field
currently displays "none" because this is a new account that has not been
used yet.

✔ **Account Expiration Date.** You can set a date on which this account
will no longer be available for use. This field is convenient to use if you
need an account for a short time. Suppose, for example, that you have an
employee who is visiting from another branch office for a short period of
time. You can set up an account for a specific amount of time. After the
account expires, no user can access and use the account. This security
practice prevents unauthorized network access.

✔ **Password.** This field is updated when a user changes his password. The network administrator can force a password change at any time by modifying this field. The actual content of the field is hidden; only a string of asterisks displays to prevent the password from being compromised.

✔ **Password Expiration Date.** Placing an entry in this field causes the password to expire on a specific date. An attempt to log in after the expiration date will be refused, except as described in the following Renew Password Every description.

✔ **Renew Password Every.** This field contains the interval, in days, that the account password must be changed. As the end of the cycle approaches, LANtastic presents a warning to the user that his or her password needs to be changed. If the current date is later than the Password Expiration Date, the user will be allowed to log in once and change his password. After an interval has been entered in this field, the Password Expiration Date will automatically be updated.

✔ **Privileges.** This field holds the special access privileges for this account. An entry in this field overrides any resource access controls that have been set. To assign a privilege, highlight the field and type the letter(s) corresponding to the privilege(s) you want to select.

These privileges are for special types of access; therefore, you should consider carefully before assigning any of these privileges to an account. An account does not have to have any assigned account privileges in order to access and use shared resources on the network.

✔ **Number Concurrent Logins.** This field enables you to set the number of concurrent logins that a user account can make to the server. If, for example, you set the number of concurrent logins to 3, there can be three different computers at a time logged in to the server using this account name. If you log in to the server you are sitting at with this account name, it would count as one of the three logins allowed. Several concurrent logins may be useful if you have a single account that multiple users will be using (such as a GUEST account), or if you will be logged in to the server from more than one computer at the same time.

Tip   To disable an account, set the Number Concurrent Logins to 0.

✔ **Login Hours.** This option defines when the user can log in to this server. You can set specific limits on the days and times during those days that a user can log in to the server.

✔ **ACL Summary.** Selecting this item displays a summary of the Access Control List (ACL) for this account as determined by the ACL for each shared resource on this computer. This summary is extremely useful for verifying that the ACLs have been set up the way you want them for each resource. For each shared resource listed on the ACL Summary list, there are three columns of information; ACLs, Accounts, and Groups. The ACLs column is the sum of the Accounts column and the Groups column, and represents all the ACL rights for this account. The Accounts column shows the ACL rights for this specific account. The Groups column shows the ACL rights for the group or groups for which this account is a member.

Figure 6.11
The ACL summary list for an account.

Resource Name	ACLs	=	Account	+	Groups
.	R---L---E---		R---L---E---		R---L---E---
LANTASTI.SHR	RWC-L---E---		RWC-L---E---		RWC-L---E---
A-DRIVE	RWCMLDKNEA--		RWCMLDKNEA--		RWCMLDKNEA--
C-DRIVE	RWCMLDKNEA--		RWCMLDKNEA--		RWCMLDKNEA--
@MAIL	RWC-L-------		RWC-L-------		RWC-L-------
@PRINTER	RWC-L-------		RWC-L-------		RWC-L-------
@SCREEN	R---L-------		R---L-------		R---L-------
@SCREEN.BIN	R---L-------		R---L-------		R---L-------
@KEYBD	RWC-L-------		RWC-L-------		RWC-L-------

The following sections walk you through the ACL Groups, Account Expiration Date, Password Expiration Date, Privileges, and Login Hours fields. Although these features add flexibility and control to your LANtastic network, remember that you do not have to change any of the settings from their default values unless security concerns require it.

Selecting ACL Groups

The ACL Groups field enables you to select and modify the ACL groups to which this account belongs. To select the ACL groups for your account, highlight the ACL Groups field and press Enter (see fig. 6.12). The ACL Groups dialog box appears showing the ACL groups to which this account currently belongs. In this example, you have not selected any ACL groups for this account, so the dialog box is empty.

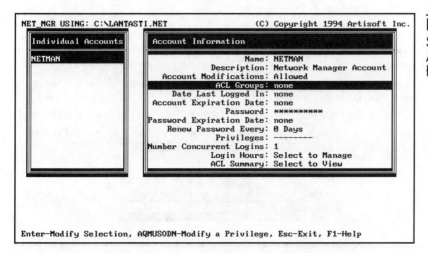

Figure 6.12
Selecting the ACL Groups field for an account.

To select the ACL groups for the NETMAN account, press Ins. The next dialog box shows the defined ACL groups and the number of accounts that are currently members of the ACL group (see fig. 6.13). In this example, four ACL groups already have been defined. You want the NETMAN account to belong to the previously defined ADMIN ACL Group, so highlight ADMIN and press Enter. A check mark appears next to the ACL groups you have selected, and the groups appear in the ACL Groups dialog box (see fig. 6.14).

Figure 6.13
Selecting ACL groups for an account.

Figure 6.14
Selected ACL groups for the NETMAN account.

Now, to go one step further, suppose you want this account to belong to an ACL group that has not yet been defined. Instead of exiting this selection and creating a new ACL group, you can define a new ACL group name by pressing Ins. Type **THE-BOSS** as your new ACL group name in the name for the ACL Group dialog box (see fig. 6.15). Type **Executives** as the description for this ACL group (see fig. 6.16). Now press Enter; the ACL group you have just defined has been created and is selected in the ACL Groups dialog box for your account (see fig. 6.17). Pressing Esc twice will return you to the Account Information screen.

Figure 6.15
Entering a new ACL group name.

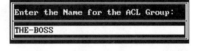

Figure 6.16
Entering a description for the new ACL group.

Figure 6.17
Selected ACL groups for the NETMAN account.

The preceding example showed how to create new ACL groups while selecting ACL groups for an account. If you create ACL groups in this manner, the account automatically becomes a member of the new ACL group. If you create ACL groups from the ACL Group Management main menu selection in NET_MGR, you can select the accounts that will be members of the ACL group.

Setting the Account Expiration Date and the Password Expiration Date

To change the account expiration date, highlight Account Expiration Date from the Account Information screen and press Enter. A dialog box appears that enables you to change the expiration date (see fig. 6.18). To move between the month, day, and year fields, use the left and right arrow keys. To change the value for the month, day, and year, use the up and down arrow keys. Press Enter when finished.

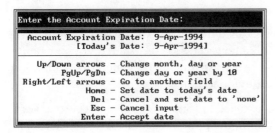

Figure 6.18

Entering a new account expiration date.

To change the password expiration date, highlight Password Expiration Date from the Account Information screen and press Enter. The date is changed in exactly the same way you changed the account expiration date in the previous section.

Selecting Privileges

To select privileges for an account, highlight Privileges from the Account Information screen and type **AQMUSODN** (see fig. 6.19). As you type each letter, the privilege turns on or off.

In this example, you are setting up the network administrator's account. You would not set these privileges for all users. You may want to consider giving one or two specific users the Q privilege to help manage the print queue for you.

Figure 6.19
The Account
Information
screen showing
privileges
AQMUSODN
entered.

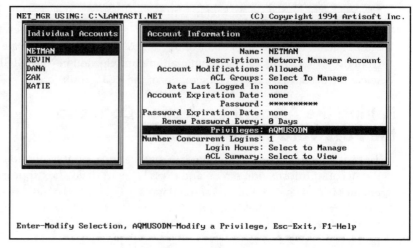

```
NET_MGR USING: C:\LANTASTI.NET                    (C) Copyright 1994 Artisoft Inc.
┌─Individual Accounts─┐  ┌─Account Information──────────────────────────────────┐
│ NETMAN              │  │                    Name: NETMAN                       │
│ KEVIN               │  │             Description: Network Manager Account      │
│ DANA                │  │    Account Modifications: Allowed                     │
│ ZAK                 │  │              ACL Groups: Select To Manage             │
│ KATIE               │  │      Date Last Logged In: none                        │
│                     │  │    Account Expiration Date: none                      │
│                     │  │                Password: **********                   │
│                     │  │ Password Expiration Date: none                        │
│                     │  │    Renew Password Every: 0 Days                       │
│                     │  │              Privileges: AQMUSODN                     │
│                     │  │ Number Concurrent Logins: 1                           │
│                     │  │             Login Hours: Select to Manage             │
│                     │  │             ACL Summary: Select to View               │
└─────────────────────┘  └───────────────────────────────────────────────────────┘

   Enter-Modify Selection, AQMUSODN-Modify a Privilege, Esc-Exit, F1-Help
```

The choices for setting account privileges are as follows:

✔ **A.** This privilege, called the Super ACL (Access Control List) privilege, gives the user unlimited access to every shared resource on this server. You should reserve this assignment to the network administrator and alternate administrator accounts.

✔ **Q.** This privilege, called the Super Queue privilege, enables the user to exercise control over the print queue. The user can view all print jobs in the queue, start and stop selected jobs, delete selected jobs, and start and stop the print spooler. Do not grant this privilege to all users; reserve it for those users who need to control the print-queue functions. Without this privilege, you can only view and control your own print jobs in the print queue.

✔ **M.** This privilege, called the Super Mail privilege, functions in a similar manner to the Super Queue privilege except that it relates to the electronic mail functions of LANtastic. With the privilege enabled, a user can control all mail in the mail queue; without it, a user can only view and control his own mail.

✔ **U.** This privilege, called the User Auditing privilege, works in conjunction with the audit trail function of LANtastic. If you enable the audit trail function, this privilege allows a user to issue NET AUDIT commands and to record entries in the server's audit log. Although this capability may be useful in some instances, its importance is left to the network manager. This privilege is not normally assigned to every user account.

✔ **S.** This privilege, called the System Manager privilege, should be assigned only to the network administrator and the alternate administrator. This privilege enables the user to perform the special network manager functions that control the network. By using the privilege, the user can execute the commands to shut down the network remotely, or log out users from the server(s).

✔ **O.** This privilege, called the Operator Notification privilege, provides the user with messages that would require operator intervention, such as a message from a printer indicating it is out of paper.

✔ **D.** This privilege, called the Remote Despooler privilege, allows the remote despooling program to despool jobs from the server's print queue to a local printer.

✔ **N.** This privilege, called the Network Manager privilege, allows the user to gather statistics kept by the server.

Selecting Login Hours

The last option on the Account Information screen is the Login Hours option. With this option, you can control the specific time frames that a user can log in to the network. Highlight the option and press Enter (see fig. 6.20). The diamonds indicate the half-hour blocks of time when the user can log in; the dots (.) indicate the times when the user cannot log in.

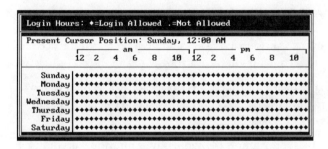

Figure 6.20
Setting the Login Hours for the account.

Each diamond or dot on the screen represents a half-hour interval. To disallow the account to log in at a particular time, move the cursor to the desired time using the arrow keys and press the Del key. Similarly, to allow the account to log in at a particular time, perform the same action and press the Ins key. You can select a block of time by moving the cursor to a start time using your arrow keys, pressing B (to select a block of time), and highlighting a block using your arrow keys. With a block selected, pressing the Ins or Del key, as previously described, enables you to allow or disallow logins for the account. Pressing the spacebar will toggle the setting from its previous value.

For now, leave the screen unchanged and press Enter. Press Enter again to return to the Individual Accounts screen.

You now have completed the setup for the NETMAN account. Repeat the preceding steps for each new user account that you want to establish. Omit the Privileges setup unless you want to grant a user some specific controls over one of LANtastic's functions. After you finish installing all the user accounts, your current Individual Accounts list might look something like the one shown in figure 6.21.

Figure 6.21
The Individual
Accounts list.

Setting Up Wildcard Accounts

Wildcard accounts are accounts that can be used by more than one person at a time to access the server. Although individual accounts also can be used by more than one person, wildcard accounts enable you to set up a prefix for the account name; then the account will accept any characters for the rest of the account NAME.

When LANtastic is installed it normally sets up a wildcard account called *. This account does not require the user to enter a user name when logging in to a server; he or she is logged in automatically.

Wildcard accounts are set up almost the same way as individual accounts. To set up wildcard accounts, first start the NET_MGR program by typing **NET_MGR** at the DOS prompt and pressing Enter. At the NET_MGR main menu, select Wildcard Account Management and press Enter (see fig. 6.22).

Figure 6.22
Selecting
Wildcard
Account
Management
from the
NET_MGR main
menu.

The Wildcard Accounts dialog box appears showing a single account * that was
created by LANtastic during installation (see fig. 6.23).

Figure 6.23
The Wildcard
Accounts dialog
box showing the
* account
created during
installation.

For this example, you will be creating a wildcard account called KS*. First, assume
that you do not want the general wildcard account *. To delete an account,
highlight the account name and press the Del key. Press Enter to confirm, and the
wildcard account * is deleted.

To add the new wildcard account KS*, press the Ins key. In the dialog box that
appears, enter KS as the account name (see fig. 6.24). Enter a password, a description, and the number of concurrent logins as you did when you set up your
individual accounts, and the new wildcard account KS* is created (see fig. 6.25).

Figure 6.24
Creating the
new wildcard
account KS*.

When creating new wildcard account names, you do not have to include the * as part of the name. LANtastic will automatically append it to the end of the name for you.

Also, the number of concurrent logins defaults to 255 for wildcard accounts in order to allow multiple users to login using the same wildcard account.

Figure 6.25
The Wildcard Accounts dialog box showing the newly created KS* account.

With this account, a user could log in to this server using any name that started with KS. The following would be valid account names for this example: KS, KS123, KS-MIKE, KSMONICA, and so on.

When a user logs in to a server, LANtastic first searches the Individual Accounts list and then the Wildcard Accounts list for a match.

If you have defined multiple wildcard accounts with similar prefixes, the first match found will be the wildcard account used. If you have two wildcard accounts with names SALE* and SALES* listed in order, and the user enters SALES-KEVIN, the wildcard account SALE* will be used.

When entering new accounts, the new account will be inserted above the current highlighted account. This allows you to control the listing order of your accounts. For example, if you had the SALES1*, SALES*, ENGR* wildcard accounts listed, and you want to insert the wildcard account SALES2* just before the SALES* account, highlight SALES* and press the Ins key to add a new account. SALES2* will be placed just before SALES*.

To change the account information for a wildcard account, highlight the account name, press Enter, and follow the same process as that used for individual accounts. The process is identical for wildcard accounts.

The default setting for the Account Modifications field is Disallowed for Wildcard Accounts. Normally individuals should not be allowed to change their passwords or disable wildcard accounts, because that would prevent others from accessing the accounts unless they were notified of the changes.

After you have set up all your wildcard accounts, your Wildcard Accounts list may look similar to the one in figure 6.26.

Figure 6.26
A completed Wildcard Accounts list.

Setting Up ACL Groups

ACL groups are a powerful feature of LANtastic, enabling you to group different accounts according to the type or level of access they have to your shared network resources. Using ACL groups also saves time when setting up new user accounts, because you can define the new user as belonging to an ACL group that already exists. You do not have to add this new user to each shared resource ACL, because the ACL group that the user belongs to already will be listed on the shared resource ACL.

To create an ACL group, select ACL Group Management from the NET_MGR main menu and press Enter (see fig. 6.27). A dialog box appears that lists the defined groups and the number of accounts that currently are members of each group. In this example, you have not defined any ACL groups yet, so the list is empty (see fig. 6.28).

Figure 6.27
Selecting ACL
Group
Management
from the
NET_MGR main
menu.

Figure 6.28
The ACL
Group list.

To create a new ACL group, press the Ins key. A dialog box appears asking for the ACL Group name. In this example, type the name **GENERAL**, and press Enter (see fig. 6.29). Type **General ACL Group** for the description, and press Enter (see fig. 6.30). GENERAL now appears as an ACL group with 0 members (see fig. 6.31).

Figure 6.29
Entering an ACL
group name.

Figure 6.30
Entering the
description for
an ACL group.

Figure 6.31
The ACL Group list showing GENERAL as an ACL group.

With the ACL group created, you can add members to the ACL group in two ways. The first method is to select the ACL group when entering new or modifying existing account information. This method is described in the previous sections.

The other method to add members to an ACL group (used in this example) enables you to choose the members from a list of existing accounts. Highlight the GENERAL ACL Group and press Enter. The ACL Group Information dialog box appears (see fig. 6.32). Press the Ins key to add members to the ACL group, and a list of defined accounts appears (see fig. 6.33).

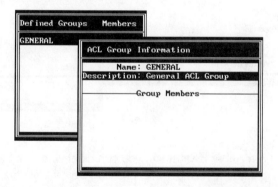

Figure 6.32
The ACL Group Information dialog box.

To add members, highlight the account and press Enter. A check mark appears next to the account, and the account is displayed as a group member in the ACL Group Information dialog box. In this example, select all the defined accounts as members of the GENERAL ACL Group (see fig. 6.34). Press the Esc key until you get back to the main menu.

Figure 6.33
The Defined Accounts dialog box.

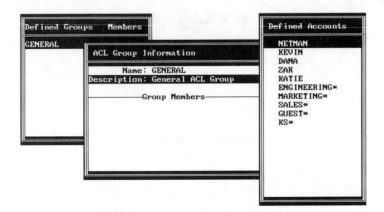

Figure 6.34
Selecting members for the GENERAL ACL Group.

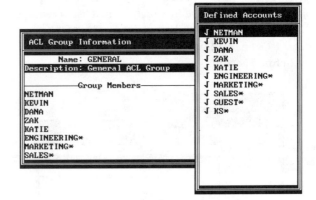

If you select a member by mistake, you can delete the member from the list by highlighting the member and pressing Del while in the ACL Group Information dialog box.

You can continue adding as many ACL groups as you like. Members can be added to or deleted from the groups at any time, and the groups can be added or deleted at any time. Figure 6.35 shows an ACL Group list with several groups added.

Figure 6.35
A completed ACL Group list showing the number of accounts that are members of each group.

Setting Up Shared Resources

This section discusses the way to set up shared resources for use by all users on the network. A *resource* can be a device, such as a printer, disk drive, or application program; or a resource can be a capability, such as the capability to create and send mail messages to other network users. A shared resource is available to more than one user at a time.

From the NET_MGR main menu screen, scroll and highlight the Shared Resources Management option, and press Enter. Your screen shows the default resources list that LANtastic created during the installation process (see fig. 6.36). This list varies depending on the physical configuration of your computer(s).

Figure 6.36
A default resources listing.

The . resource represents the control directory for LANtastic that you specified during the installation process. The @MAIL, @PRINTER, @SCREEN, @SCREEN.BIN, @KEYBD, @KEYBD.BIN resources also were added by LANtastic during the installation process. Leave these resources as they appear for now.

You can add and delete resources as you want. If you do not want to share your local floppy disk drives, you can delete them from the resource list. Highlight the selection and press Del. Press Enter to confirm the deletion. Deleting these resources from the resource list does not actually remove them from your system; they are removed from the access list that other computers can use.

Press Ins to insert a new resource. In this example, you will add a new resource called D-DRIVE. The D-DRIVE resource actually points to the physical D drive on the server. Type **D-DRIVE** as the name of the new resource in the Enter resource name dialog box that appears and press Enter (see fig. 6.37). Type the physical drive that this resource name points to on the local computer when the Enter server's true path for this resource dialog box appears. For this example, type **D:** (see fig. 6.38). You now see the resource list that shows the new resource you have just added (see fig. 6.39).

Do not use the @ character as the first character in a drive resource name. This character is used when defining resources such as printers and mail. If you use the @ character as the first character in your resource name, LANtastic will assume it is a printer resource, and you will not be able to select a physical drive/directory path for the resource.

Figure 6.37
Entering the D-DRIVE resource name.

```
Enter the Resource Name:
D-DRIVE
```

Figure 6.38
Entering the server's true path for this resource.

```
Enter the Server's True Path for This Resource:
D:
```

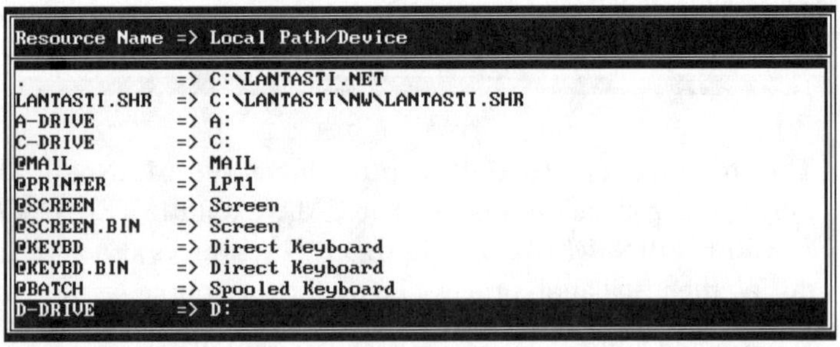

Figure 6.39
Resource list showing the new D-DRIVE resource added.

```
Resource Name => Local Path/Device
.                => C:\LANTASTI.NET
LANTASTI.SHR     => C:\LANTASTI\NW\LANTASTI.SHR
A-DRIVE          => A:
C-DRIVE          => C:
@MAIL            => MAIL
@PRINTER         => LPT1
@SCREEN          => Screen
@SCREEN.BIN      => Screen
@KEYBD           => Direct Keyboard
@KEYBD.BIN       => Direct Keyboard
@BATCH           => Spooled Keyboard
D-DRIVE          => D:
```

Scroll down and highlight the new resource, then press Enter to see a screen of detailed information about the resource (see fig. 6.40). You can modify any of these items by highlighting them and changing the information.

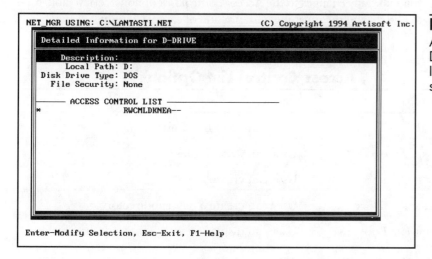

```
NET_MGR USING: C:\LANTASTI.NET              (C) Copyright 1994 Artisoft Inc.
┌─────────────────────────────────────────────────────────────────┐
│  Detailed Information for D-DRIVE                                 │
│                                                                   │
│      Description:                                                 │
│        Local Path: D:                                             │
│   Disk Drive Type: DOS                                            │
│     File Security: None                                           │
│                                                                   │
│  ──── ACCESS CONTROL LIST ─────────────────────────               │
│  *              RWCMLDKNEA--                                       │
│                                                                   │
│                                                                   │
│                                                                   │
│                                                                   │
│                                                                   │
│                                                                   │
│                                                                   │
└─────────────────────────────────────────────────────────────────┘
Enter-Modify Selection, Esc-Exit, F1-Help
```

Figure 6.40

A resource Detailed Information screen.

The Detailed Information screen for drive resources contains the following information:

✔ **Description.** This is the description of the resource. It may be up to 64 characters long. The description is not required, but it helps give additional information when connecting to the resource using the NET program.

✔ **Local Path.** This is the full path name of the resource as it is referenced locally from the server. The local path includes the drive letter and subdirectory (if applicable).

✔ **Disk Drive Type.** This option is normally set to DOS. LANtastic also supports CD-ROM, WORM (Write Once Read Many), and other types of drives. Pressing Enter while in this field displays a list of drive types that you can select. The following drive types are listed: DOS, CD-ROM, WORM, NetWare, OS/2, and Other.

✔ **File Security.** This option allows you to enable file-level security. By defining file templates, such as *.EXE, and associating them with access control lists, you can limit the access of an account to a resource at the file level.

✔ **Access Control List.** The Access Control List (ACL) determines the access that an account has to a shared resource. The ACL includes the account, ACL group names, or both, and their associated rights. Before you make any changes to the Access Control List options, review table 6.1 to understand the meaning and function of each ACL right.

Table 6.1
Access Control List Options

Option	Function
R-Read Access	User can open files for reading
W-Write Access	User can write to files
C-Create File	User can create files
M-Make Directory	User can create a new subdirectory
L-Allow File Lookups	User can display or search through directories or subdirectories
D-Delete Files	User can delete files
K-Delete Directories	User can delete subdirectories
N-Rename Files	User can rename files
E-Execute Programs	User can execute programs
A-Change File Attributes	User can change the attributes of files in a shared directory
I-Indirect Files	User can create and use indirect files within this shared directory
P-Physical Access	User can use a special subdirectory to connect directly to DOS devices without having to go through the server's spooler. Use this option with care because it can cause some delay in printer availability to network users

The Local Path can be the drive letter on the server that you want to assign to the resource name, or it can be a combination drive letter/directory. When you assign a drive letter for the local path of a resource name and users access that resource, they are accessing the entire drive associated with the drive letter you assigned. The Access Control List and File Security sections for the resource establish the access limitations a user may have.

> When creating a shared resource for a directory, a user will be able to access the shared directory and any subdirectories below it. The user will not be able to access any higher-level directories, such as the root directory.
>
> Suppose that you create a shared resource called MYDOS, which has a local path of C:\DOS. If users connect to the MYDOS resource using the drive letter K, for example, they will see the files in the C:\DOS directory of the server when they do a DIR of the K drive. Users cannot access the root directory on the server. From the users' standpoint, when they are at the K:\ prompt on their computer, they actually are at a root directory, even though they are at the C:\DOS directory on the server.

The Disk Drive Type you select will be DOS when sharing the standard hard drives or floppy drives on your computer (see fig. 6.41). If you have a CD-ROM drive you want to share, select CD-ROM as the disk drive type. Be sure to specify the same drive letter for the local path that you use to access your CD-ROM drive from the local computer.

> CD-ROM drives include device drivers and extension software (such as Microsoft's MSCDEX.EXE). The extension software assigns a DOS drive letter to access the CD-ROM drive. The CD-ROM extension software must be loaded after LANtastic's REDIR program but before LANtastic's SERVER program, as shown in the following example:

```
REDIR OFFICE1
MSCDEX.EXE /D:MSCD004 /L:D
SERVER
```

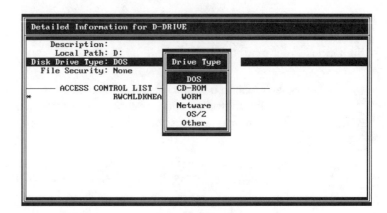

If you have a WORM drive, a device driver will have been loaded that assigns a drive letter to your WORM drive. Selecting WORM from the Disk Drive Type selection dialog box and choosing the appropriate local path drive letter enables you to share your WORM drive with the rest of the network.

The Other selection can be used to set up a drive resource that actually exists on another server. Suppose that the drive letter K on your computer is actually redirected to the C-DRIVE resource on another server. You could create a shared drive resource on the server at which you are sitting that has a local path of K:. When users access this newly created drive resource on your computer, LANtastic will see that they really are accessing drive K, which is actually a shared resource on a different computer.

The technique described above is an excellent way to give a computer access to a drive it normally would not be able to access; such is the case when connecting a laptop computer to a computer on the network using LANtastic Z. Although you may have several computers in your network, LANtastic Z permits only the laptop computer to communicate with the computer to which it is physically connected. If, however, you set up a shared drive resource of the Other type that points to the drive letter being used to access the laptop computer from the computer to which it is physically connected, other computers in the network may then access that resource to use the shared drive on the laptop computer.

This technique can be especially useful for backing up the laptop computer when the tape drive is located in a computer that is not physically connected to the laptop computer.

The Access Control List section enables you to list any combination of accounts or ACL groups and the type of access each can have. When a resource is created, LANtastic gives full access to every account. The * listed under the Access Control List section means every account has the full access rights listed to the shared resource (see fig. 6.42).

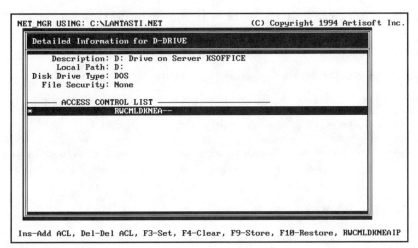

Figure 6.42
The default Access Control List created by LANtastic for a resource.

Figure 6.43 illustrates what could be a typical Access Control List. This example shows the GENERAL account as having full access to the resource. Someone who logs in using the GUEST account would have only read access to the files. Everyone else (*) would have no access to the resource.

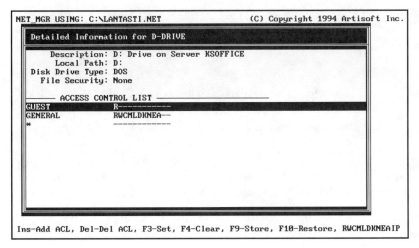

Figure 6.43
A typical Access Control List.

To change or add accounts or ACL groups to the Access Control List, scroll down and highlight the desired entry in the ACL section. To turn a specific access type on or off, highlight the appropriate account or ACL group, and press the letter you want to turn on or off.

The following keys enable you to add, modify, and delete ACL entries:

✔ **Ins.** Adds a new account name or ACL group to the list. The new entry is added just above the current cursor location. Type the account or ACL group for the ACL in the dialog box that pops up, and press Enter.

✔ **Del.** Deletes the highlighted entry from the list.

✔ **F4.** Clears all access types for the highlighted account or ACL group.

✔ **F3.** Sets all access types for the highlighted account or ACL group.

The list order of the accounts/ACL groups is important because LANtastic starts at the top of the list and goes down to determine access rights for a particular user. Consider the following two accounts that could be listed in the Access Control List:

ACCT-DANA   RWCMLDKNEA-

ACCT-*   RWCML-NEA-

These entries allow the user ACCT-DANA to delete files and directories, but do not allow the rest of the users with the ACCT- prefix to do so. If ACCT-* had been listed before ACCT-DANA, then when a user logs in using the ACCT-DANA account, LANtastic would see ACCT-* as the first match and would not allow files and directories to be deleted.

Wildcards also may be used when specifying entries. ACCT-* could be a wildcard account, or the * could represent any other characters appended to ACCT-. The account or ACL group does not have to be defined already.

The * account cannot be deleted from the Access Control List. If you do not want to allow all accounts access to this resource, clear all access rights for the * entry by highlighting it and pressing the F4 key.

The File Security selection enables you to specify templates and associated ACLs to limit access to selected files or subdirectories or both.

To specify file-level security, highlight the File Security field and press Enter. A File Templates dialog box appears. In this dialog box, you can enter a template for files or subdirectories. \DOS*.EXE would be a valid template for specifying all files in the DOS directory with an EXE extension. For this example, you will restrict access to some specific subdirectories, so type **\ACCTG** and press Enter (see fig. 6.44). Now you see a File Templates and an ACL Template dialog box (see fig. 6.45).

When specifying file templates, the local path of the resource determines the actual location of the files. In this example, in which D: is the local path, a file template of \DOS*.EXE affects the files in D:\DOS*.EXE.

If the local path was D:\DOS, then to affect the same files, you would specify *.EXE as the file template. Putting the two together gives you D:\DOS*.EXE, which is what you want. If you specified \DOS*.EXE for the file template, you would be affecting the files in D:\DOS\DOS*.EXE, which probably does not exist.

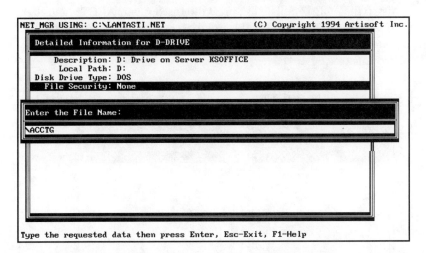

Figure 6.44
Entering a file template.

In this example, you want to restrict access to the ACCTG directory, except for members of the accounting department (wildcard accounts ACCT*) and the network administrator (NETMAN account). First, press the Tab key to move to the ACL Template dialog box. With the * highlighted, press the F4 key to clear the access rights for all accounts (see fig. 6.46).

Figure 6.45
File Templates
and ACL
Template dialog
boxes.

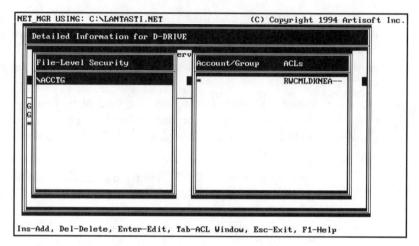

To add accounts to the ACL Template list, press the Ins key, type **ACCT***, and then press Enter. Press Ins again, type **NETMAN**, and then press Enter. Now you have an ACL Template list that gives full access to ACCT* and NETMAN, and no access to the other accounts (see fig. 6.47).

Figure 6.46
Clearing the
access rights for
all accounts.

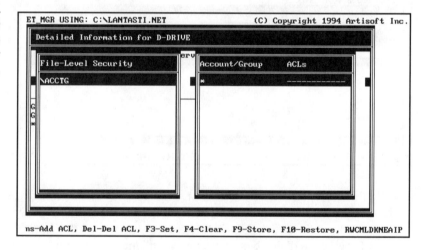

The keystroke commands for entering information in the ACL Template list are the same as those used when entering information in the Access Control List.

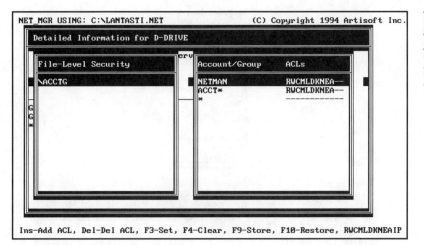

```
NET_MGR USING: C:\LANTASTI.NET              (C) Copyright 1994 Artisoft Inc.

 Detailed Information for D-DRIVE

                          erv
   File-Level Security          Account/Group    ACLs

  \ACCTG                        NETMAN           RWCMLDKNEA--
                                ACCT*            RWCMLDKNEA--
 G                              *                -----------
 G
 *




 Ins-Add ACL, Del-Del ACL, F3-Set, F4-Clear, F9-Store, F10-Restore, RWCMLDKNEAIP
```

Figure 6.47
The ACL Template list for the \ACCTG directory.

As you add additional file template entries, you may enter an ACL template list for each entry. As you scroll through your file template list, the ACL Template list changes to show the ACL entries for the highlighted entry.

Setting Up Shared Printer Resources

Shared printer resources are set up in much the same way as other shared re-sources. One obvious difference is that the names for printer resources begin with the @ character. This character tells LANtastic that this resource has a local path that is different from the drive letter/directory used for other drive resources.

In this example, you will set up a printer resource called @LASER, which points to an HP laser printer connected to port LPT1 on your computer. To set up a printer resource, press the Ins key from the resource list just as you would to set up a drive resource. In the Enter resource name dialog box, type **@LASER** and press Enter (see fig. 6.48). Select the device your printer is connected to from the Output Device dialog box and press Enter. For this example select LPT1 and press Enter (see fig. 6.49). The @LASER resource now appears on the resource list (see fig. 6.50).

```
 Enter the Resource Name:

 @LASER
```

Figure 6.48
Entering a printer resource.

Figure 6.49
Selecting the
output device to
which the printer
is connected.

```
Output Device
Global
----Spooled----
LPT1
LPT2
LPT3
COM1
COM2
COM3
COM4
Remote
Keyboard
----Direct----
Screen
Keyboard
```

Figure 6.50
Printer resource
@LASER shown
on the resource
list.

```
Resource Name => Local Path/Device

.                 => C:\LANTASTI.NET
LANTASTI.SHR      => C:\LANTASTI\NW\LANTASTI.SHR
A-DRIVE           => A:
C-DRIVE           => C:
D-DRIVE           => D:
@MAIL             => MAIL
@PRINTER          => LPT1
@SCREEN           => Screen
@SCREEN.BIN       => Screen
@KEYBD            => Direct Keyboard
@KEYBD.BIN        => Direct Keyboard
@BATCH            => Spooled Keyboard
@LASER            => LPT1
```

With the new printer resource highlighted, you can press Enter to change the detailed information for the printer. For further configuration information for printer resources, see Chapter 10, "Printing with LANtastic."

Summary

This chapter led you through a detailed tour of the setup and configuration of individual accounts, wildcard accounts, ACL groups, and shared resources using the DOS NET_MGR program. You now have a strong working knowledge of how accounts and shared resources are set up and configured with LANtastic.

The next chapter discusses the same information as this chapter did, using the Windows LANtastic Network Manager instead of the DOS LANtastic Network Manager (NET_MGR) program. Chapter 8, "Using Disk Drives and Printers," familiarizes you with the procedures and commands you must know to connect to and use disk drives and printers in your LANtastic network.

Chapter Snapshot

This chapter discusses ways to set up and configure
user accounts and shared resources using LANtastic in
Windows. This same information—as it applies in
DOS—is covered in Chapter 6, "Setting Up User
Accounts and Shared Resources in DOS." The follow-
ing topics are included:

✔ Determining your server's function and the
   resources you want to share with other users

✔ Understanding the different types of user accounts
   and Access Control List (ACL) groups

✔ Setting up individual and wildcard accounts using
   the LANtastic Network Manager program

✔ Setting up ACL groups using the LANtastic
   Network Manager program

✔ Setting up shared resources using the LANtastic
   Network Manager program

After you finish reading this chapter, you will be fully
prepared to set up and configure shared resources on
your LANtastic network.

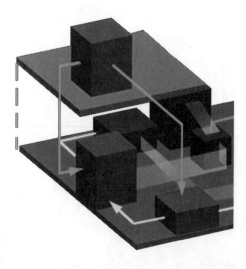

7

CHAPTER

Setting Up User Accounts and Shared Resources in Windows

The following sections describe setting up accounts, ACL groups, and shared resources in Windows using the Windows LANtastic Network Manager program.

Setting Up Individual Accounts

Suppose that you want to set up two user accounts, one for you as the network administrator and one for another user. For this example, the administrator is called NETMAN (network manager). First, set up your account using the account name NETMAN. The second account name can be one of your choice. Try to keep all user names as short as possible because users must type their name each time they log in.

Begin by rebooting both computers. Rebooting ensures that any changes that may have been made to the CONFIG.SYS or AUTOEXEC.BAT files during the installation process up to this point are properly loaded at boot time. Watch the screen on each computer to make sure the LANtastic software is being loaded.

If you did not notice the LANtastic programs loading after you rebooted your computer(s), then your AUTOEXEC.BAT file may not be executing the LANtastic STARTNET.BAT file. Check your AUTOEXEC.BAT file to make sure it includes the following line:

```
CALL C:\LANTASTI\STARTNET.BAT
```

If your AUTOEXEC.BAT file does contain the preceding line, then look at the statements before CALL C:\LANTASTI\STARTNET.BAT to make sure another program (such as a menu program) isn't causing AUTOEXEC.BAT to be terminated before the network is started.

The LANtastic Network Manager program located in the LANtastic program group (see fig. 7.1) is used to set up user accounts and network resources. This utility program enables you to create user accounts and to determine security and access controls. Select the LANtastic Network Manager icon by clicking on it and start the program by selecting **F**ile and then **O**pen from the Program Manager main menu. The LANtastic Network Manager program starts and displays several selections (see fig. 7.2). At this time, however, you will use only some of the items. The remaining menu selections are discussed in Chapter 11, "Managing Your Network using the LANtastic Network Manager."

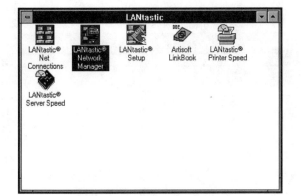

Figure 7.1
The LANtastic
program group.

Figure 7.2
The LANtastic
Network
Manager
program.

Click on the **A**ccounts option or select **M**anage and then **A**ccounts from the
LANtastic Network Manager main menu. The Accounts dialog box appears (see
fig. 7.3) with a choice of Individual Accounts and Wildcard Accounts. To add a
new account, select Individual Accounts by clicking on it and pressing Ins or
selecting **A**dd from the **E**dit menu. The New Individual Account dialog box
appears (see fig. 7.4).

Enter **NETMAN** in the Name field followed by a description, if desired, in the
Description field. The description is optional; you can leave it blank or fill in
information that serves as a reminder to you. Because this is the account for the
Network Manager, you want to require a password so click on the Set Password
option in the Password field and type the password. The Account field enables you
to specify whether the account is enabled or not and the number of concurrent
logins that may be made to the server using this account. In other words, if you
specify two concurrent logins, you may log in to this server using this account name
from no more than two computers.

Figure 7.3
The Accounts
dialog box.

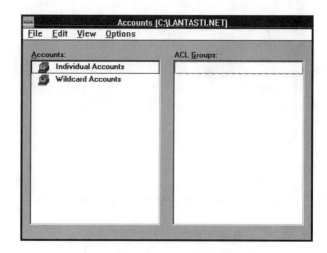

Figure 7.4
The New
Individual
Account dialog
box.

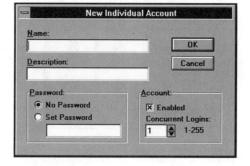

Figure 7.5 shows the New Individual Account dialog box with all the information filled in for the NETMAN account. Click on OK to accept the information for the NETMAN account.

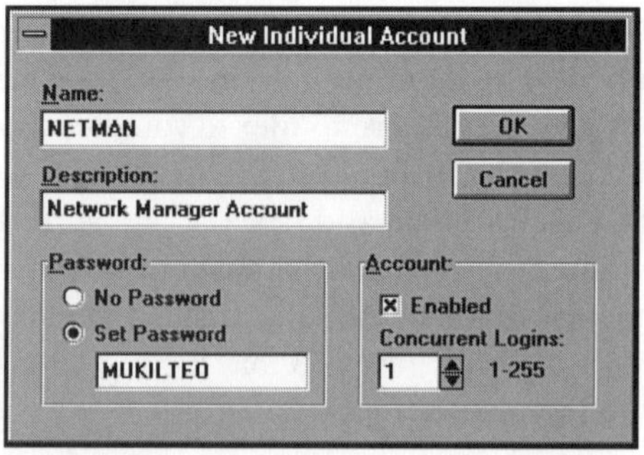

Figure 7.5
The New
Individual
Account dialog
box with the
NETMAN
account
information
entered.

After clicking on OK, you return to the Accounts dialog box. Expand the Individual Accounts directory by double-clicking on Individual Accounts or by selecting it and pressing Enter. Under the Individual Accounts heading the newly added NETMAN account appears (see fig. 7.6).

 Accounts listed under Individual Accounts are sorted alphabetically by name.

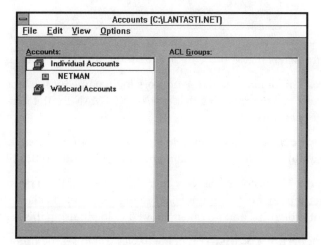

Figure 7.6
The NETMAN account listed under the Individual Accounts directory.

Highlight the NETMAN account by clicking on it and select the **M**odify option from the **E**dit menu. The Account Parameters dialog box appears showing the current settings for the account (see fig. 7.7).

 By selecting the Modify on Double-click option from the **O**ptions menu, you can go directly into Modify mode by double-clicking on the desired account or by pressing Enter with the desired account selected.

Figure 7.7
The Account
Parameters
dialog box.

The Account Parameters dialog box contains the following menu options:

✔ **Name.** This field contains the network login name for the account (16 characters maximum). This chapter uses NETMAN for the network manager account.

✔ **Description.** A 32-character field is used to describe each account. You may want to place the user's real name or position title in this field.

✔ **Account.** The account may be either enabled or disabled depending on whether the Enabled option is checked or not. If not checked, the account is disabled and no one is allowed to log in using this account.

Concurrent Logins. This field enables you to set the number of concurrent logins that a user account can make to the server. If, for example, you set the number of concurrent logins to 3, there can be three different computers at a time logged in to the server using this account name. If you log in to the server you are sitting at with this account name, it would count as one of the three logins allowed. Several concurrent logins may be useful if you have a single account that multiple users will be using (such as a GUEST account), or if you will be logged in to the server from more than one computer at the same time.

✔ **Account Expiration.** You can set a date when this account will no longer be available for use. This field is convenient to use if you need an account for a short time. Suppose, for example, that you have an employee who is visiting temporarily from another branch office. You can set up an account for a specific amount of time. After the account expires, no user can access and use the account. This security practice prevents unauthorized network access. If the Disabled box is selected, the Account Expiration is not in effect. If the Disabled box is not selected, account expiration is in effect and may be changed by selecting the day, month, or year field and changing the value by clicking on the up or down button.

✔ **Allow User to Modify Account.** If this field is checked, users can change the password and disable the account after they log in. If the field is not checked, users must change the password and disable the account from the LANtastic Network Manager program.

The default setting for the Allow User to Modify Account option is checked for individual accounts and not checked for Wildcard Accounts. This is because normally you would want to allow an individual to change his or her password or disable his or her account, but you would not want to allow an individual using a wildcard account to do the same because it would then prevent others from using the same wildcard account.

✔ **Date Last Logged In.** LANtastic updates this each time a user logs in to the network. You cannot change the data in this field. This field currently displays none because this is a new account that has not yet been used.

✔ **Privileges.** This selection enables you to specify special access privileges for this account. Any privilege specified here overrides any resource access controls that have been set. To assign a privilege, click on this button and then select the privileges desired by clicking on the selection box next to each privilege.

These privileges are for special types of access; therefore, you should consider carefully before assigning any of these privileges to an account. An account does not have to have any of these account privileges assigned to it to access and use shared resources on the network.

✔ **Password.** Use this selection to specify password options including setting a password, disabling a password, setting a password expiration date, and setting a password renewal period in days.

✔ **Login Hours.** Use this selection to specify when the user is allowed to log in to the server. You can set specific limits on the days and specific times of day that a user can log in to the server with this selection.

The following sections walk you through specifying Privileges, Password options, and Login Hours. Although these features add flexibility and control to your LANtastic network, remember that you do not have to change any of the settings from their default values unless security concerns require it.

Selecting Privileges

To select privileges for an account, select Privileges from the Account Parameters dialog box. The Account Privileges dialog box appears with a list of the privileges that may be selected (see fig. 7.8). Select the privileges you want by clicking in the box next to the desired privilege, or use the hot key listed next to the privilege to select it. To set all the privileges, select the Set All button. To clear all the privileges, select the Clear All button.

Figure 7.8
The Account Privileges dialog box.

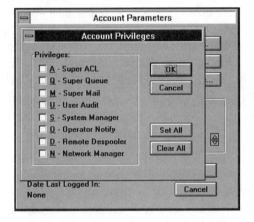

In this example, you set up the network administrator's account. You typically would not set these particular privileges for all users. You might want to consider giving one or two specific users the Q privilege to help manage the print queue for you.

The choices for setting account privileges are as follows:

✔ **A - Super ACL.** This privilege gives the user unlimited access to every shared resource on this server. You should reserve this assignment for the network administrator and alternate administrator accounts.

✔ **Q - Super Queue.** This privilege enables the user to exercise control over the print queue. The user can view all print jobs in the queue, start and stop selected jobs, delete selected jobs, and start and stop the print spooler. Do not grant this privilege to all users; reserve it for those users who need to control the print queue functions. Without this privilege, you can only view and control your own print jobs in the print queue.

✔ **M - Super Mail.** This privilege functions in much the same way as the Super Queue privilege except that it relates to the electronic mail functions of LANtastic. With the privilege enabled, a user can control all mail in the mail queue; without it a user can only view and control his or her own mail.

✔ **U - User Audit.** This privilege works in conjunction with the audit trail function of LANtastic. If you enable the audit trail function, this privilege enables a user to issue NET AUDIT commands and record entries in the server's audit log. Although this capability may be useful in some instances, its importance is left to the network manager. You normally do not assign this privilege to every user account.

✔ **S - System Manager.** This privilege should be assigned only to the network administrator and the alternate administrator because it enables the user to perform the special network manager functions that control the network. By using this privilege, the user can execute commands to shut down the network remotely or to log out users from the server(s).

✔ **O - Operator Notify.** This privilege provides the user with messages that require operator intervention, such as a message from a printer indicating it is out of paper.

✔ **D - Remote Despooler.** This privilege allows the remote despooling program to despool jobs from the server's print queue to a local printer.

✔ **N - Network Manager.** This privilege enables the user to gather statistics kept by the server.

Selecting Password Options

To specify password options for an account, select Password from the Account Parameters dialog box. The Account Password dialog box appears for this account (see fig. 7.9).

The Password section of this dialog box enables you to keep your existing password (Keep Password), disable the requirement for a password (No Password), and change or set a password (Set Password). When you select the Set Password option, you can then enter a new password.

Figure 7.9
The Account
Password dialog
box.

The Password Expiration section of this dialog box enables you to specify a password expiration date or the interval in days that must elapse before a new password is required. If you select the Disabled option, the password expiration feature is disabled. With the Disabled option cleared, you can use two password expiration methods—Expires On and Renew every:

✔ **Expires On.** This is the password expiration date. Placing an entry in this field causes the password to expire on a specific date. An attempt to log in after the expiration date will be refused, except as described in the following Renew every option.

✔ **Renew every.** This field contains the interval—in days—that the account password must be changed. As the end of the cycle approaches, LANtastic presents a warning to the user that his or her password needs to be changed. If the current date is later than the Password Expiration Date, the user can log in once and change his password. After an interval has been entered in this field, the Password Expiration Date is automatically updated according to the number in this field.

Selecting Login Hours

To specify login hours for an account, select Login Hours from the Account Parameters dialog box. The Time of Day Logins dialog box appears (see fig. 7.10).

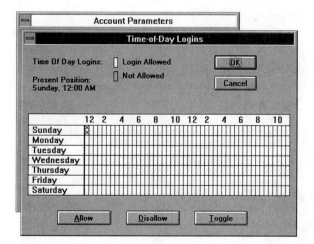

Figure 7.10
The Time of Day
Logins dialog
box.

With this option, you can control the specific time frames that a user can log in to the network. Each rectangular block represents a half-hour block of time. To select a block of time, click on the starting block and drag to the last block. To allow logins during the selected block of time select the **A**llow button. To prevent logins during the selected block of time select the **D**isallow button. Selecting the **T**oggle button will change the selected block of time to the opposite value.

You now have completed the setup for the NETMAN account. Repeat the preceding steps for each new user account that you want to establish. Omit the Privileges setup unless you want to grant a user some specific controls over one of LANtastic's functions.

Setting Up Wildcard Accounts

Wildcard accounts are accounts that can be used by more than one person at a time to access the server. Although individual accounts also can be used by more than one person, wildcard accounts enable you to set up a prefix for the account name; then the account will accept any characters for the rest of the account.

When LANtastic is installed, it normally sets up a wildcard account called *. This account does not require the user to enter a user name when logging in to a server; he or she is logged in automatically.

Wildcard accounts are set up almost the same way as individual accounts. To set up a wildcard account, first start the LANtastic Network Manager program located in the LANtastic program group by clicking on it and selecting **F**ile and then **O**pen from the Program Manager main menu. Select the Accounts option by clicking on it or selecting **M**anage and then **A**ccounts from the LANtastic Network Manager main menu. The Accounts dialog box appears (see fig. 7.11) with Individual Accounts and Wildcard Accounts under the Accounts heading. List the existing wildcard accounts by double-clicking on Wildcard Accounts. The * wildcard account created during installation appears on the list (see. fig. 7.12).

Figure 7.11
The Accounts dialog box.

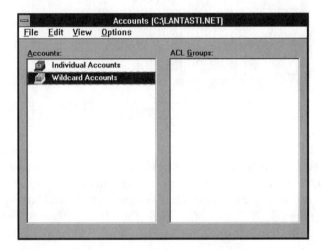

Figure 7.12
The Accounts dialog box showing the * Wildcard Accounts.

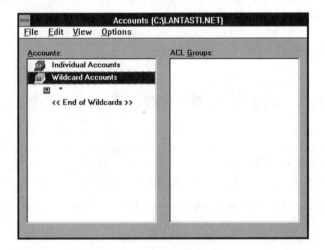

For this example, you will create a wildcard account called KS*. First, assume that you do not want the general wildcard account *. To delete an account, select the account name and press Del or select **D**elete from the **E**dit menu. Select Yes to delete the account and the wildcard account * is deleted.

To add a new wildcard account, select Wildcard Accounts by clicking on it and press Ins or select **A**dd from the **E**dit menu. The New Wildcard Account dialog box appears (see fig. 7.13).

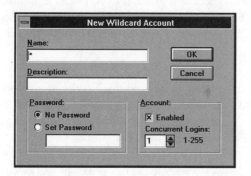

Figure 7.13
The New Wildcard Account dialog box.

Enter **KS*** in the Name field, followed by a description if desired in the Description field. Enter a password and the number of concurrent logins as you did when you set up individual accounts. Click on OK, and the wildcard account is created.

When creating new wildcard account names, you must include the asterisk (*) at the end. Unlike the DOS LANtastic Network Manager (NET_MGR) program, the Windows LANtastic Network Manager does not automatically append the * to the end of the name for you.

The number of concurrent logins defaults to 1 for wildcard accounts. Because wildcard accounts are typically created for more than one person to use concurrently, you should increase this number to allow for the number of users that will be accessing this account.

With this account, a user could log in to this server using any name that started with KS. The following account names are valid for this example: KS, KS123, KS-MIKE, KSMONICA, and so on.

When a user logs in to a server, LANtastic first searches the Individual Accounts list and then the Wildcard Accounts list for a match.

If you have defined multiple wildcard accounts with similar prefixes, the first match found will be the wildcard account used. If you have two wildcard accounts with the names SALE* and SALES* listed in order, and the user enters SALES-KEVIN, the wildcard account SALE* will be used.

When entering new accounts, the new account will be inserted above the current highlighted account. This enables you to control the order of your accounts list. For example, if you had the SALES1*, SALES*, and ENGR* wildcard accounts listed, and you want to insert the wildcard account SALES2* just before the SALES* account, highlight SALES* and press Ins to add a new account. SALES2* will be placed just before SALES*.

Highlight the KS* account by clicking on it and select the **M**odify option from the **E**dit menu. The Account Parameters dialog box appears showing the current settings for the account. Wildcard account parameters can be changed in a similar manner as previously described for individual accounts.

The default setting for the Allow User to Modify Account is disabled (not checked) for wildcard accounts. This is because normally you do not want to allow an individual to change his or her password or disable a wildcard account. To do so would prevent others from accessing the account unless they were notified of the changes.

After you have set up all your wildcard accounts, your Wildcard Accounts list may look similar to the one in figure 7.14.

Figure 7.14
A completed Wildcard Accounts list.

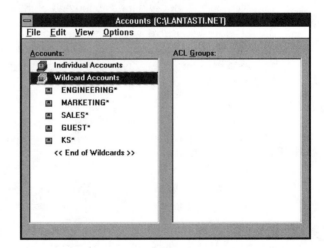

Setting Up ACL Groups

ACL groups are a powerful feature of LANtastic, enabling you to group different accounts according to the type or level of access they will have to your shared network resources. Using ACL groups also saves time when setting up new user accounts because you can define the new user as belonging to an ACL group that already exists. You do not have to add this new user to each shared resource ACL because the ACL group that the user belongs to already will be listed on the shared resource ACL.

To create an ACL group, select the **A**ccounts option by clicking on it or selecting **M**anage and then **A**ccounts from the LANtastic Network Manager main menu. The Accounts dialog box appears, displaying an Accounts field and an ACL Groups field. Expand the Individual Accounts and the Wildcard Accounts list by double-clicking on each, or by selecting each and pressing Enter (see fig. 7.15). The ACL Groups portion of the dialog box is empty because no ACL Groups have been defined yet.

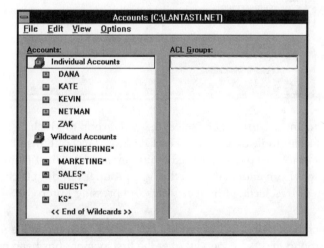

Figure 7.15
The Accounts dialog box showing the Accounts and ACL Groups fields.

To add a new ACL Group, click in the ACL Groups field. Select **A**dd from the **E**dit menu, and the ACL Group dialog appears. In this example, type the name **GEN-ERAL**, in the Name field and type **General ACL Group** in the Description field. Select the OK button, and GENERAL now appears as an ACL group (see fig. 7.16).

Figure 7.16
The ACL Group
dialog box.

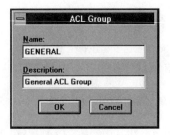

Figure 7.17
The Accounts
dialog box
showing the
General ACL
group.

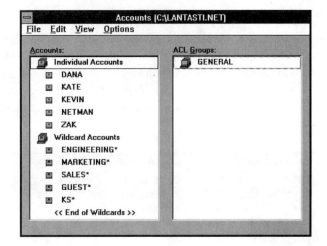

To add members to an ACL group, first select the ACL group to which you want to add members. Select an Individual Account or a Wildcard Account to add to the ACL group, and select Add To Group from the **E**dit menu. After the first member of the ACL group has been added, expand the ACL group list by double-clicking on the ACL group or by selecting the ACL group and pressing Enter.

The members of the ACL group will not appear as you add them unless you expand the ACL group list after the first member has been added. After the list has been expanded, additional members will appear under the ACL group as they are added.

In this example, you will select all the individual accounts and the GUEST* wildcard account to be members of the GENERAL ACL group. Select the GENERAL ACL group by clicking on it. Next select the Individual Accounts icon. Select Add To Group from the **E**dit menu to add all the Individual Accounts to the GENERAL ACL group list.

Selecting the Individual Accounts icon or the Wildcard Accounts icon chooses every account in the group.

Although all the Individual Accounts have been added to the GENERAL ACL group, they don't appear unless the GENERAL ACL group list is expanded. Expand the GENERAL ACL group by double-clicking on GENERAL or by selecting GENERAL and pressing Enter (see fig. 7.18). Add the GUEST* wildcard account as a member of the GENERAL ACL group by selecting the GENERAL ACL group then selecting the GUEST* wildcard account. Select Add To Group from the **E**dit menu and the GUEST* account is added to the GENERAL ACL group.

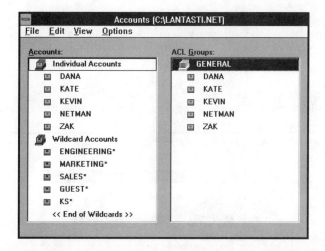

Figure 7.18
The GENERAL ACL group showing all the Individual Accounts as members.

You also can add or remove members from an ACL group by selecting Group Members from the **E**dit menu. The ACL Group Members dialog box appears (see fig. 7.19) enabling you to add and remove members from the list.

You can continue adding as many ACL groups as you like. Members can be added to or deleted from the groups at any time, and the groups themselves can be added or deleted at any time.

Figure 7.19
The ACL Group
Members dialog
box for the
GENERAL ACL
group.

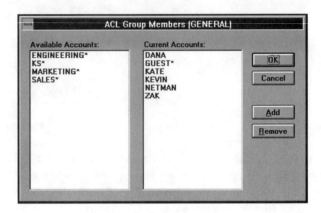

Setting Up Shared Resources

This section discusses the way to set up shared resources for use by all users on the network. A *resource* can be a device, such as a printer, a disk drive, or an application program; or it can be a capability, such as the capability to create and send mail messages to other network users. Shared resources are available to more than one user at a time.

From the LANtastic Network Manager program, select the **R**esources option by clicking on it, or selecting **M**anage and then **R**esources from the LANtastic Network Manager main menu. The Resources dialog box appears (see fig. 7.20).

Figure 7.20
The Resources
dialog box.

The Resources dialog box shows the default resources list that LANtastic created during the installation process. This list varies depending on the physical configuration of your computer(s). You can scroll through the list by clicking on the up or down arrow on the scroll bar.

The . resource represents the control directory for LANtastic that you specified during the installation process. The @MAIL, @KEYBD, @KEYBD.BIN, @PRINTER, @SCREEN, and @SCREEN.BIN resources also were added by LANtastic during the installation process. Leave these resources as they appear for now.

You can add and delete resources as you want. If you do not want to share your local floppy disk drives, you can delete them from the resource list. Select the resource to delete and select **D**elete from the **E**dit menu or press Del. Select Yes to confirm the deletion. Deleting resources from the resource list does not actually remove them from your system; they are removed from the access list that other computers can use.

To add a new resource, select **A**dd from the **E**dit menu or press Ins. The Add Resource dialog box appears (see fig. 7.21). When you add a new resource, LANtastic assumes you want to add a shared drive resource so the Shared Drive option is selected. To add a shared device resource such as a printer, select the Shared Device option instead. Adding shared devices is discussed in the next section, "Setting Up Shared Printer Resources." Also shown are Local Resource and Global Resource options. Local Resources exist on the local computer (the computer you are setting up), whereas Global Resources exist on another server. Only Local Resources are discussed in this chapter. Global Resources are discussed in Chapter 15, "Getting the Most out of LANtastic."

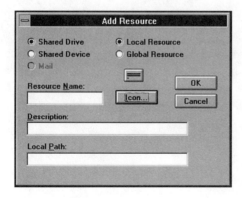

Figure 7.21
The Add Resource dialog box.

In this example, you will add a new resource called D-DRIVE. The D-DRIVE resource actually points to the physical D drive on the server. Type **D-DRIVE** as the name of the new resource in the Resource Name field. The Description field is not required and serves as additional information about the resource. In the Local Path field, type the physical drive that this resource name points to on the local computer. For this example, type **D:**. Figure 7.22 shows the Add Resource dialog box with the information required for the D-DRIVE resource. Select the OK button to create the D-DRIVE resource. The D-DRIVE resource appears on the Resources list (see fig 7.23).

Do not use the at (@) character as the first character in a drive resource name. This character is used when defining resources such as printers and mail. If you use the @ character as the first character in your resource name, LANtastic displays an error message.

Figure 7.22
The Add Resource dialog box for the new D-DRIVE resource.

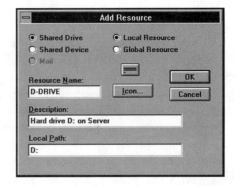

With the D-DRIVE resource selected, select AC**L** from the **E**dit menu to display the Access Control List dialog box for the D-DRIVE resource (see fig. 7.24).

The ACL determines the access that an account has to a shared resource. The ACL includes the account or the ACL group names, or both, and their associated rights. Before you make any changes to the Access Control List options, review table 7.1 to understand the meaning and function of each ACL right.

Figure 7.23
The Resources list showing the newly added D-DRIVE resource.

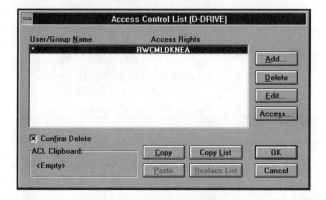

Figure 7.24
The Access Control List dialog box.

Table 7.1
Access Control List Options

Option	Function
R-Read Access	User can open files for reading
W-Write Access	User can write to files
C-Create File	User can create files
M-Make Directory	User can create a new subdirectory

continues

Table 7.1, Continued
Access Control List Options

Option	Function
L-Allow File Lookups	User can display or search through directories or subdirectories
D-Delete Files	User can delete files
K-Delete Directories	User can delete subdirectories
N-Rename Files	User can rename files
E-Execute Programs	User can execute programs
A-Change File Attributes	User can change the attributes of files in a shared directory
I-Indirect Files	User can create and use rect files within this shared directory
P-Physical Access	User can use a special subdirectory to connect directly to DOS devices without having to go through the server's spooler. Use this option with care because it can cause some delay in printer availability to network users

The Access Control List enables you to list any combination of accounts or ACL groups and the type of access each can have. When a resource is created, LANtastic gives full access to every account. The * listed in the Access Control List dialog box (see fig. 7.24) means every account has the full access rights listed to the shared resource. Buttons in the Access Control List dialog box enable you to **A**dd a new User/Group Name, **D**elete an existing User/Group Name, **E**dit a User/Group Name and its access rights, and change the Acce**s**s rights for a given User/Group Name. You can also copy an item in the list or the entire ACL to an ACL clipboard, which may be pasted into the ACL for a different resource.

To add a new ACL entry, select the **A**dd button. In the ACL Entry dialog box enter the User/Group Name. In this example, enter GENERAL as the User/Group Name (see fig. 7.25). To specify access rights, select **A**ccess to display the Access Control List Rights dialog box (see fig. 7.26). You can toggle the access rights on or off by clicking next to the desired access right. In addition, you can set the access

rights to the default values by selecting the Default button, set all the access rights by selecting the Set All button, or clear all the access rights by selecting the Clear All button.

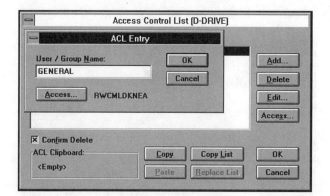

Figure 7.25
Entering GENERAL in the ACL Entry dialog box.

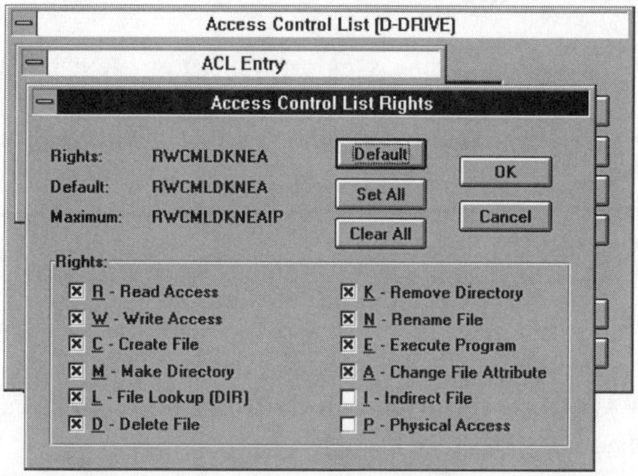

Figure 7.26
The Access Control List Rights dialog box.

For this example, clear all the access rights by selecting the Clear All button, and then set the read access right by selecting the R - Read Access right. Select OK to return to the ACL Entry dialog box, and then select OK again to return to the Access Control List dialog box, which now shows the * User/Group Name with full access and the GENERAL User/Group Name with only the Read access right (see fig. 7.27).

Once a User/Group Name has been defined, you may change the access rights in the Access Control List Rights dialog box by selecting the Access button.

Figure 7.27

The Access Control List dialog box with the GENERAL account added.

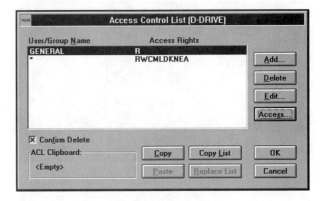

The list order of the User/Group Name is important because LANtastic starts at the top of the list and goes down to determine access rights for a particular user. Consider the following two accounts that could be listed in the Access Control List:

ACCT-DANA   RWCMLDKNEA—

ACCT-*   RWCML—NEA—

These entries allow the user ACCT-DANA to delete files and directories, but do not allow the rest of the users with the ACCT- prefix to do so. If ACCT-* had been listed before ACCT-DANA, after a user logged in using the ACCT-DANA account, LANtastic would see ACCT-* as the first match and would not allow files and directories to be deleted.

Wildcards also may be used when specifying entries. ACCT-* could be a wildcard account, or the * could represent any other characters appended to ACCT-. The account or ACL group does not have to be defined already.

The * account cannot be deleted from the Access Control List. If you do not want to allow all accounts access to this resource, clear all access rights for the * entry by selecting the Access button in the Access Control List dialog box and then selecting the Clear All button in the Access Control List Rights dialog box.

Figure 7.28 illustrates what could be a typical Access Control List. This example shows the GENERAL account as having full access to the resource. Someone who logs in using the GUEST account would have only read access to the files. Everyone else (*) would have no access to the resource.

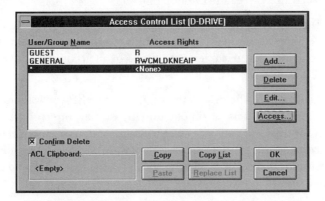

Figure 7.28
A typical Access Control List.

With the D-DRIVE resource selected, select **M**odify from the **E**dit menu to display the Resource Parameters dialog box for the D-DRIVE resource (see fig. 7.29).

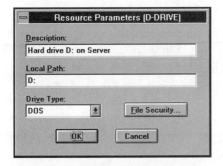

Figure 7.29
The Resource Parameters dialog box for the D-DRIVE resource.

The Resource Parameters dialog box contains the following information:

- ✔ **Description.** This description of the resource may be up to 64 characters long. The description is not required, but it helps give additional information when connecting to the resource using the LANtastic NET program.

- ✔ **Local Path.** This is the full path name of the resource as it is referenced locally from the server. The local path includes the drive letter and subdirectory (if applicable).

✔ **Drive Type.** This option is normally set to DOS. LANtastic also supports CD-ROM, WORM (Write Once Read Many), and other types of drives. Pressing Enter while in this field displays a list of drive types that you can select. The following drive types are listed: DOS, CD-ROM, WORM, NetWare, OS/2, and Other Non-DOS.

✔ **File Security.** This option enables you to control file-level security. By defining file templates, such as *.EXE, and associating them with access control lists, you can limit the access of an account to a resource at the file level.

The Local Path can be the drive letter on the server that you want to assign to the resource name, or it can be a combination drive letter/directory. After you assign a drive letter for the local path of a resource name and users access that resource, they are accessing the entire drive associated with the drive letter you assigned. The Access Control List and File Security sections for the resource establish the access limitations a user may have.

After creating a shared resource for a directory, a user will be able to access the shared directory and any subdirectories below it. The user will not be able to access any higher-level directories, such as the root directory.

Suppose that you create a shared resource called MYDOS, which has the local path C:\DOS. If users connect to the MYDOS resource using the drive letter K, for example, they will see the files in the C:\DOS directory of the server when they do a DIR of the K drive. Users cannot access the root directory on the server. From the users' standpoint, when they are at the K:\ prompt on their computer, they actually are at a root directory, even though they are at the C:\DOS directory on the server.

The Disk Drive Type you select will be DOS when sharing the standard hard drives or floppy disk drives on your computer. If you have a CD-ROM drive you want to share, select CD-ROM as the disk drive type. Be sure to specify the same drive letter for the local path that you use to access your CD-ROM drive from the local computer.

CD-ROM drives include device drivers and extension software (such as Microsoft's MSCDEX.EXE). The extension software assigns a DOS drive letter to access the CD-ROM drive. The CD-ROM extension software must be loaded after LANtastic's REDIR program but before LANtastic's SERVER program, as shown in the following example:

REDIR OFFICE1

MSCDEX.EXE /D:MSCD004 /L:D

SERVER

If you have a WORM drive, a device driver will have been loaded that assigns a drive letter to your WORM drive. Selecting WORM from the Disk Drive Type selection dialog box and choosing the appropriate local path drive letter enables you to share your WORM drive with the rest of the network.

The Other Non-DOS selection can be used to set up a drive resource that actually exists on another server. Suppose that the drive letter K on your computer is actually redirected to the C-DRIVE resource on another server. You could create a shared drive resource on the server you are sitting at that has a local path of K:. When users access this newly created drive resource on your computer, LANtastic will see that they really are accessing drive K, which is actually a shared resource on a different computer.

The technique just described is an excellent way to give a computer access to a drive it normally would not be able to access; such is the case when connecting a laptop computer to a computer on the network using LANtastic Z. Although you may have several computers in your network, LANtastic Z permits only the laptop computer to communicate with the computer to which it is physically connected. You might, however, set up a shared drive resource of the Other Non-DOS type that points to the drive letter being used to access the laptop computer from the computer to which it is physically connected. If you do so, other computers in the network may access that resource to use the shared drive on the laptop computer.

This technique is especially useful for backing up a laptop computer when the tape drive is located in a computer that is not physically connected to the laptop computer.

The **F**ile Security selection enables you to specify templates and associated ACLs to limit access to selected files or subdirectories or both.

To specify file-level security, select the **F**ile Security button and press Enter. The File Templates List dialog box appears (see fig. 7.30). To add a new file template, select the **A**dd button. The File Template dialog box appears. In the Template field, you can enter a template for files or subdirectories. \DOS*.EXE would be a valid template for specifying all files in the DOS directory with an EXE extension. For this example, you will restrict access to some specific subdirectories, so type **\ACCTG** in the Template field (see fig. 7.31).

When specifying file templates, the local path of the resource determines the actual location of the files. In this example, in which D: is the local path, a file template of \DOS*.EXE affects the files in D:\DOS*.EXE.

If the local path was D:\DOS, then to affect the same files, you would specify *.EXE as the file template. Putting the two together gives you D:\DOS*.EXE, which is what you want. If you specified \DOS*.EXE for the file template, you would be affecting the files in D:\DOS\DOS*.EXE, which probably does not exist.

Figure 7.30
The File Template List dialog box.

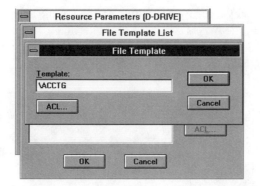

Figure 7.31
Entering a template in the File Template field.

To give everyone full access privileges, you can click on OK. In this example, you want to restrict access to the ACCTG directory, except for members of the accounting department (wildcard accounts ACCT*) and the network administrator (NETMAN account). To modify the ACL for this template, select the ACL button. The Access Control List dialog box appears showing full access for all accounts (*) (see fig 7.32).

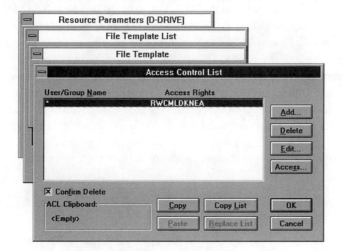

Figure 7.32
The Access Control List for the ACCTG directory.

With the * selected, click on the Access button to change the access rights. Select the Clear All button in the Access Control List Rights dialog box to clear the access rights (see fig. 7.33). Select OK and the * appears in the Access Control List dialog box with no access rights.

Figure 7.33

The Access Control List Rights dialog box with all access rights cleared.

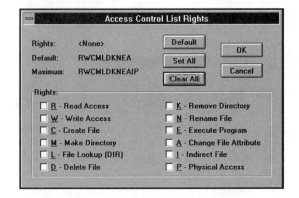

To add the NETMAN and ACCT* accounts to the Access Control List for the ACCTG file template select **A**dd. In the ACL Entry dialog box type **NETMAN** in the User/Group **N**ame field (see fig. 7.34). Select OK and the NETMAN account is added to the Access Control List. Repeat this same process to add the ACCT* account. When finished, the NETMAN and ACCT* User/Group Names have full access rights and all others have none (see fig. 7.35). Select OK to return to the File Template dialog box and then OK again to return to the File Template list. The ACCTG template now appears on the list (see fig 7.36). At this point, if you wanted to modify the access control list, you could select the AC**L** button. Select OK to return to the Resource Parameters for the D-DRIVE resource, and then select OK again to return to the Resources dialog box.

Figure 7.34

Entering the NETMAN account in the ACL Entry dialog box.

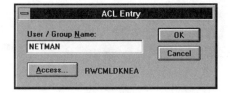

Figure 7.35
The Access
Control List for
the ACCTG file
template.

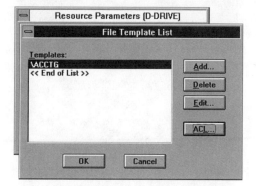

Figure 7.36
The ACCTG
template in the
File Template List
dialog box.

Setting Up Shared Printer Resources

Shared printer resources are set up in much the same way as other shared resources. One obvious difference, however, is that the names for printer resources begin with the @ character. This character tells LANtastic that this resource has a local path that is different from the drive letter/directory used for other drive resources.

In this example, you will set up a printer resource called @LASER, which points to an HP laser printer connected to port LPT1 on your computer. To set up a printer resource, select **A**dd from the **E**dit menu in the Resources dialog box. In the Add

Resource dialog box, select the Shared Device option. The dialog box changes to show the parameters required for a shared device instead of a shared drive (see fig. 7.37). Type @LASER in the Resource Name field. The device defaults to LPT1; however, if you want to select a different port such as LPT2, select the De**v**ice button which displays the Select Device Type dialog box (see fig. 7.38).

Figure 7.37

The Add Resource dialog box for entering a printer resource.

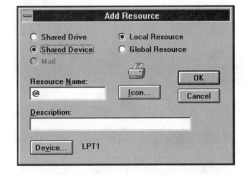

Select OK in the Add Resource dialog box and the @LASER resource is added and appears on the Resource list (see fig. 7.39). With the new printer resource selected, you could change the detailed resource parameters for this device by selecting **M**odify from the **E**dit menu. Additional configuration information for printers is discussed in Chapter 10, "Printing with LANtastic."

Figure 7.38

The Select Device Type dialog box.

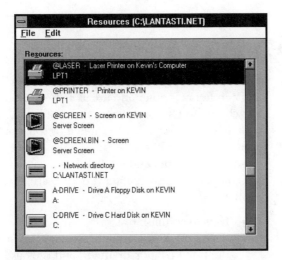

Figure 7.39
The @LASER
resource has
been added to
the Resource list.

Summary

This chapter led you through a detailed tour of the setup and configuration of individual accounts, wildcard accounts, ACL groups, and shared resources. You now have a strong working knowledge of ways in which accounts and shared resources are set up and configured with LANtastic.

The next chapter familiarizes you with the procedures and commands you must know to connect to and use disk drives and printers in your LANtastic network.

Chapter Snapshot

This chapter explores different ways you can connect to another computer and use its shared resources. Each method has advantages and disadvantages. The method you choose is determined by your specific requirements. Thus, more than one method might be useful for you, depending on the task you intend to accomplish. In this chapter you will learn about the following:

✔ How to establish disk drive and printer connections in DOS using the LANtastic NET program, the LANPUP pop-up utility, and LANtastic NET command line commands

✔ How to automate disk drive and printer connections in DOS

✔ How to establish disk drive and printer connections in Windows with the LANtastic Net Connections program

✔ How to save and automatically restore disk drive and printer connections in Windows

This chapter contains separate sections that describe the LANtastic programs and features available to you for making network connections to disk drives and printers in both DOS and Windows.

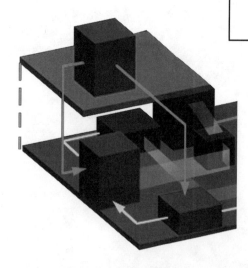

CHAPTER

8

Using Disk Drives and Printers

The preceding chapters showed you how to set up accounts and shared resources on your LANtastic servers. After you configure each server the way you want it, you are ready to begin using your network and accessing the shared resources available to you.

After each computer loads the LANtastic software, it is able to operate in your LANtastic network. Computers configured as LANtastic servers can share the resources you specified earlier with others on the network. The computers configured as LANtastic workstations (or servers) can access and use the shared resources of other computers.

Using LANtastic with DOS

LANtastic includes programs and features that enable you to make network connections in DOS and in Windows. The following sections describe methods available to establish network connections in DOS. Making network connections in Windows is covered later in this chapter.

Understanding Network Connections

Daily functions you perform in LANtastic usually include logging into servers, connecting to and using shared directories/drives and printers, sending and receiving electronic mail, sharing programs and data, and performing related tasks.

To run a program from DOS on your computer, specify the drive and directory, and then use the appropriate command to launch the program. Suppose you want to run Microsoft Word, which is located on your physical D drive in the WORD5 directory. The file name of the program is WORD.EXE. You would type the following DOS commands at the DOS prompt:

```
C:\>D:
D:\>CD \WORD5
D:\WORD5>WORD
```

Your prompt displays the current drive and directory as shown in the preceding lines, if the following command is part of your AUTOEXEC.BAT file or typed at the DOS prompt:

```
PROMPT $P$G
```

Now suppose you do not have Microsoft Word on your computer, but it is installed on another computer in the network. To access Word on another computer's hard drive and run it on your computer, you need to establish a network connection with that particular server.

To establish a network connection to a shared resource on another computer, choose a drive letter on your computer, which is then redirected to the shared resource you want to use on another computer. For example, if you choose to access the C-DRIVE resource on server KSOFFICE by redirecting your K drive to point to \\KSOFFICE\C-DRIVE, accessing your K drive is the same thing as accessing the C drive on server KSOFFICE. To run MS Word from the K drive, you type the following commands at the C:\> prompt:

```
C:\>K:
K:\>CD \WORD5
K:\WORD5>WORD
```

To connect to a shared printer resource on another computer, follow the same process of redirecting one of your printer devices (such as LPT1) to point to the shared printer resource (such as @PRINTER) on another computer.

You can establish a network connection to a shared resource on another computer in DOS in one of three ways: by using the LANtastic NET program, by using the LANtastic LANPUP pop-up utility, or by typing a LANtastic NET command at the DOS prompt or from within a batch file.

Understanding the NET Program

The LANtastic NET program was installed with LANtastic. NET enables you to perform daily network operations, which include logging in and out of servers, establishing network drive and printer connections, managing your user account, and sending and receiving electronic mail.

To run the NET program, type **NET** at the DOS prompt and press Enter. The NET program main menu appears and displays the following options (see fig. 8.1):

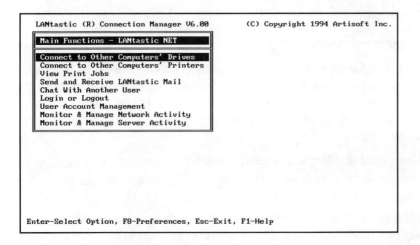

Figure 8.1
The NET program main menu.

✔ **Connect to Other Computers' Drives.** This selection enables you to establish network connections to disk drives on other computers. To do this, choose a drive letter (such as K:) to point to a shared drive resource on another computer, and specify the server name and associated drive resource name on the server to which you want to connect.

✔ **Connect to Other Computers' Printers.** This selection enables you to establish network connections to printers on other computers. To do this, choose a device name (such as LPT1:) to point to a shared printer resource on another computer and specify the server name and associated printer resource name on the server to which you want to connect.

✔ **View Print Jobs.** This selection is used to control and manage print jobs in the queue. You can add, delete, hold, and change the priority of print jobs. If you have the Q privilege, you can control any print job in the queue; otherwise you can only control your own print jobs. The Q privilege also enables you to start and stop printing to specific devices (LPT1, LPT2, and so on) or printer streams (@LASER, @PRINTER, and so on). Chapter 10, "Printing with LANtastic," discusses this selection in detail.

✔ **Send and Receive LANtastic Mail.** This selection is used to send or receive mail. If you have an Artisoft Sounding Board installed in your computer, you can send and receive voice mail. If you have the M privilege, you can control any mail item in the queue. Otherwise, you can only control mail sent to or by you.

✔ **Chat With Another User.** This selection enables you to carry on a text dialogue with another user on the network. If you have the Artisoft Sounding Board installed in both computers, you can carry on a voice chat with another user.

✔ **Login or Logout.** This selection enables you to log in to or log out from servers on the network. When you establish network connections using the Connect to Other Computers' Drives or Connect to Other Computers' Printers selections, you also can log in to or log out of the server at the same time.

✔ **User Account Management.** This selection enables you to change your password, disable your account, or check on the status of your account on the server.

✔ **Monitor & Manage Network Activity.** This selection enables you to view the activity of a specified group of computers in the network. You can, in addition, synchronize the clocks for a selected group of servers.

✔ **Monitor & Manage Server Activity.** This selection enables you to see which users are currently using the server and the actions they are performing. You can also view another server's screen and issue commands to that server with your keyboard. This selection also enables you to schedule server shutdowns if you have the S privilege.

Understanding the LANPUP Utility

LANPUP, a TSR (terminate-and-stay-resident) program, is the pop-up version of the LANtastic NET program. After you load LANPUP into RAM, you can use it as you work in another program. Unlike the LANtastic NET program or a NET command, LANPUP enables you to establish network connections to printers and disk drives while you are in another application. Suppose, for example, that you are working in a spreadsheet program and you need to print, but you have not established a connection to a printer . You can use LANPUP from within the program to connect to a printer and not lose your work or need to exit.

To load LANPUP into memory, type **LANPUP** at the DOS prompt and press Enter. After it is loaded, press Ctrl+Alt+L to activate it.

To run LANPUP without leaving it resident in memory, type **LANPUP STAND_ALONE** at the DOS prompt.

Figure 8.2 shows the LANPUP main menu. To select an item on the menu, use the arrow keys to highlight the selection and press Enter, or type the letter shown in uppercase and press Enter. Following is a description of the menu selections on the LANPUP main menu:

- ✔ **Servers.** This selection is used to log in or log out of a server.

- ✔ **Disks.** This selection is used to establish a network disk drive connection to a shared drive/directory resource on a server.

- ✔ **Printers.** This selection is used to establish a printer connection to a shared printer resource on a server.

- ✔ **Queues.** This selection enables you to control and manage the printer and mail queues.

- ✔ **Mail.** This selection enables you to read, delete, and send mail.

- ✔ **dEspooler.** This selection enables you to control the print spooler on a server. Valid selections are Halt, Stop, Pause, single, start, and Restart.

- ✔ **seNd.** This selection enables you to send a one-line (up to 64 characters) message to any network computer.

Figure 8.2
The LANPUP
main menu.

```
C:\>
Servers  Disks  Printers  Queues  Mail  dEspooler  seNd
```

Understanding NET Commands

NET commands are commands you can type at a DOS prompt or include in a batch file to perform various network functions, such as connecting to network drives and printers. You can create batch files that enable all your programs to connect to required drive resources and use the required network printers.

NET commands consist of the word NET followed by another command which describes the desired network action. If you want to log in to a server, for example, you begin by typing **NET LOGIN**. After NET LOGIN, you specify the server you want to log in to, as well as a user name and password if required. Most of the functions available in the NET program are also available through NET commands.

The following commands, included in a batch file, connects to the C-DRIVE resource on server KATIE, then runs MS Word:

```
NET LOGIN \\KATIE KEVIN ZAK
NET USE K: \\KATIE\C-DRIVE
K:
CD\WORD5
WORD
C:
NET LOGOUT \\KATIE
```

The first NET command logs you in to server KATIE as user KEVIN with password ZAK. The second NET command redirects your K drive to the C-DRIVE resource on server KATIE. Next, you make K your active drive and change to the WORD5 directory on the K drive. WORD is the command used to launch MS Word. After you exit MS Word, processing of the batch file continues. C becomes the active drive again and the last NET command logs you out from server KATIE: an action that disconnects your network connection K:. Chapter 14, "Using Net Command Line Commands," provides a detailed description of available NET commands.

Logging In to the Server

To establish network connections to shared drives/directories or printers on other computers, you must log in to servers containing resources you want to use. You can log in to a server by using the LANtastic NET program, the LANPUP utility, or a NET command.

If separate user accounts aren't set up and you are using the install program's default * wildcard account, you do not have to log in to the server that contains your intended resource. If you attempt to connect to the resource, you are automatically logged in.

Using the NET Program To Log In

You can log in to a LANtastic server through the NET program by following these steps:

1. Make sure that your LANtastic software is loaded and actively running on the computers you use.

2. To launch the NET program, type **NET** at the DOS prompt and press Enter. The NET program main menu appears, as shown in figure 8.1.

3. Select the Login or Logout option and press Enter.

   A list of server connections appears (see fig. 8.3). Connections available for login are surrounded by parentheses (). If they are already logged into, \\ is displayed before their names.

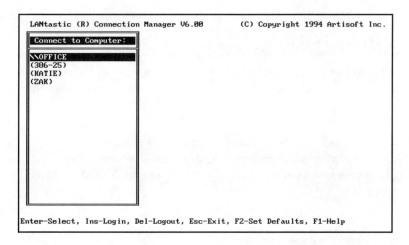

```
LANtastic (R) Connection Manager V6.00       (C) Copyright 1994 Artisoft Inc.
┌─Connect to Computer:─┐
│ \\OFFICE             │
│ (386-25)             │
│ (KATIE)              │
│ (ZAK)                │
│                      │
│                      │
│                      │
│                      │
│                      │
│                      │
│                      │
│                      │
│                      │
│                      │
│                      │
└──────────────────────┘
Enter-Select, Ins-Login, Del-Logout, Esc-Exit, F2-Set Defaults, F1-Help
```

Figure 8.3
The NET program Server Connections list.

4. Select the server to which you want to log in and press Enter.

5. Type your user name in the box that appears and press Enter.

6. Enter your password in the next box that appears and press Enter.

You are asked if you want to set your computer's clock to match the server's. Select No unless your computer does not have a clock that maintains the proper time. If you select Yes, the time and date on your computer is set to match the time and date of the computer you are logging in to. To accept the default No response, press Enter; otherwise, type Yes and press Enter.

If the * wildcard account exists without a password and autologin has not been disabled, you are automatically logged in as soon as you select the server; you are not asked for your user name and password.

If you need to use a specific user name to log in, select the Switch to New Username from the User Account Management option in the NET main menu.

You can disable automatic logins by typing **NET USER/DISABLE** at the DOS prompt. With automatic logins disabled, you are always prompted for a user name and password when you log in to a server.

7. Press Esc to return to the main menu.

You now are logged in and can use the other options on the menu.

Using the LANPUP Utility To Log In

To load LANPUP into memory, type **LANPUP** at the DOS prompt and press Enter. A message notifies you after the utility is finished loading. After LANPUP is loaded, you can call it up by using the keystroke combination Ctrl+Alt+L.

The LANPUP utility occupies approximately 6 KB of memory. Although 6 KB is a relatively small amount of RAM, it can slow down your machine's performance if you do not have more than 512 KB of RAM installed.

You may need to experiment with the order in which you load LANPUP and any other TSRs you are running on your system. If you cannot resolve conflicts with other TSRs, load LANPUP as a stand-alone program by entering the following at the DOS prompt:

LANPUP/STAND-ALONE

You can abbreviate this command by typing **LANPUP/STAN**.

To use LANPUP to log in to a server, perform the following steps:

1. Press Ctrl+Alt+L to bring up the LANPUP main menu (see fig. 8.2).

2. Highlight the Servers choice and press Enter.

   If you are not logged in to any servers, the block below the menu choices is blank.

3. Press Ins, and you are prompted to enter the name of the server to which you want to log in. Type the name of the server and press Enter (see fig. 8.4).

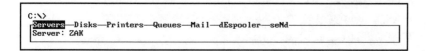

Figure 8.4
LANPUP prompt to enter server name.

4. Type your user account name and press Enter (see fig. 8.5).

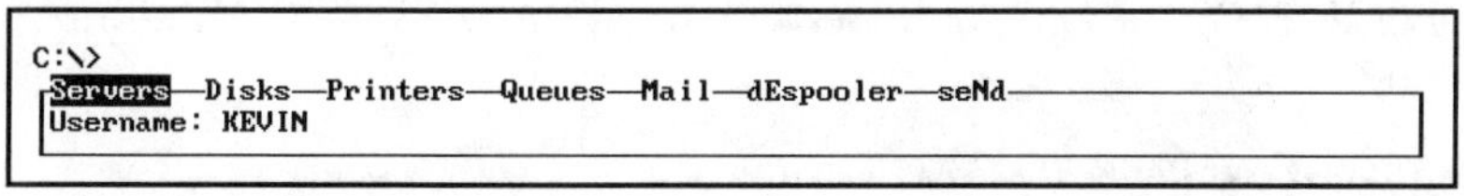

Figure 8.5
LANPUP prompt to enter user name.

5. Type your password and press Enter (see fig. 8.6).

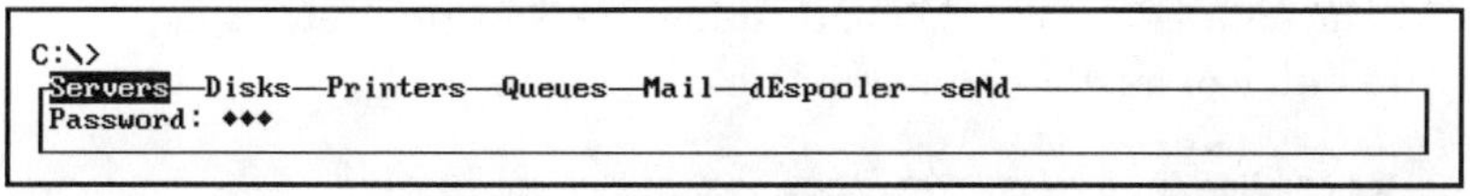

Figure 8.6
LANPUP prompt to enter password.

The block now displays the name of the server to which you are logged in. \\ appears before its name (see fig. 8.7).

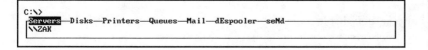

Figure 8.7
LANPUP server selection shown.

You can press Ins and log in to another server at this time. If you do, only the name of the last server logged in to appears in the LANPUP menu block. Use the up- and down-arrow keys to display the other servers you are logged in to. You are now ready to use the other LANPUP menu choices for network resources.

Using NET Commands To Log In

The NET LOGIN command is used to log in to a server. It can be typed at a DOS prompt or included in a batch file. The basic syntax of the NET LOGIN command is as follows:

```
NET LOGIN \\server-name user-name password
```

In place of *server-name,* enter the name of the server to which you want to log in. In place of *user-name,* enter the name of the account on that server, and in place of *password,* enter the account password.

If the server you want to log in to has the wildcard account * set up, you are not required to include a user name or password.

You can still log in using a user name and password if you want to, however. In fact, you may prefer this because you can choose to permit a higher level of access privileges for an individual user than a general wildcard account (*).

The following example logs you in to the server named DANA as user ZAK with password KATIE:

```
NET LOGIN \\DANA ZAK KATIE
```

Connecting to Disk Drives and Printers

Establishing a connection to a server's shared drive or printer resource is a fairly simple process. The connection may be made using the NET program, the LANPUP pop-up utility or a NET command-line command.

Connecting Using the NET Program

The following steps show how to use the LANtastic NET program to establish a network connection to a server's shared drive resource:

1. From the NET program main menu, highlight the Connect to Other Computers' Drives option.

   Your screen displays a list of the available drives (see fig. 8.8). If a connection is already made, it appears in the second column.

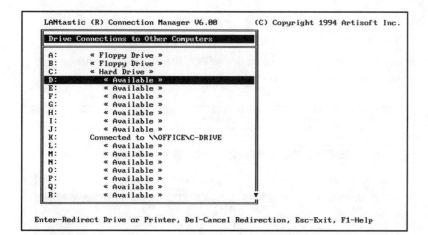

Figure 8.8
The Drive
Connections to
Other
Computers list.

To delete any connection, highlight the connection and press Del. Press
Enter to delete the connection. The drive letter is now available for use
in another network connection.

2. Highlight the drive letter that you want to use to connect to the
    server's drive and press Enter. Your screen displays a list of available
    servers, as shown in figure 8.9.

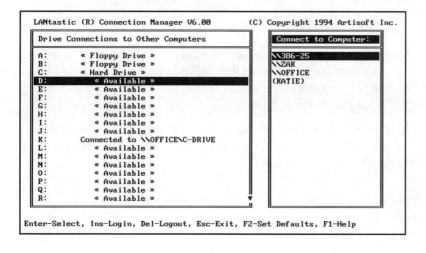

Figure 8.9
NET Server
Connections list.

3. Highlight the server you want to connect to and press Enter. If the server is not displayed, press Ins and type the server's name.

   After you connect to the server, the screen shows a list of shared directory/drive resources available for connection (see fig 8.10).

Figure 8.10
Shared resources available for connection.

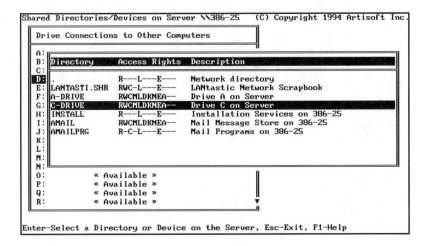

```
Shared Directories/Devices on Server \\386-25    (C) Copyright 1994 Artisoft Inc.
┌─────────────────────────────────────────────────────────────────────────────┐
│  Drive Connections to Other Computers                                         │
│                                                                               │
 A:│
 B:│Directory        Access Rights   Description                                │
 C:│
 D:│.                R---L---E---    Network directory                          │
 E:│LANTASTI.SHR     RWC-L---E---    LANtastic Network Scrapbook                 │
 F:│A-DRIVE          RWCMLDKNEA--    Drive A on Server                           │
 G:│C-DRIVE          RWCMLDKNEA--    Drive C on Server                          │
 H:│INSTALL          R---L---E---    Installation Services on 386-25             │
 I:│AMAIL            RWCMLDKNEA--    Mail Message Store on 386-25                │
 J:│AMAILPRG         R-C-L---E---    Mail Programs on 386-25                     │
 K:│
 L:│
 M:│
 N:│
 O:│        « Available »                                                        │
 P:│        « Available »                                                        │
 Q:│        « Available »                                                        │
 R:│        « Available »                                                      ▼ │
└─────────────────────────────────────────────────────────────────────────────┘
Enter-Select a Directory or Device on the Server, Esc-Exit, F1-Help
```

If you are not already logged in to the server, you are logged in automatically when you select it (if the * wildcard account exists), or you are asked for your user name and password.

The number of servers displayed in the Server Connections list is limited to the number you specify after the LOGINS= option on the REDIR line in your STARTNET.BAT file, or after the LOGINS= option under the [REDIR] section in the STARTNET.CFG if used.

To have all the available servers show up on your Server Connections list, make sure that you set LOGINS= to a number at least as high as the number of servers available.

4. Highlight the shared resource you want to use and press Enter. You are returned to the Drive Connections to Other Computers list with your new choice displayed (see fig. 8.11).

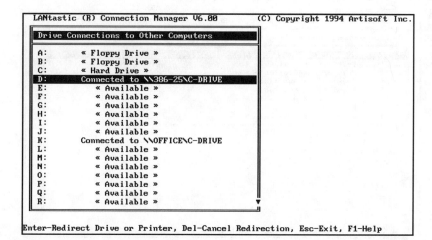

Figure 8.11
The Drive
Connections to
Other
Computers list
showing the new
connection.

The method used to connect to shared printer resources is similar to that used to connect to shared drive resources. Use the following steps to connect to a shared printer resource:

1. Select the Connect to Other Computers' Printers option from the NET program main menu. The Printer Connections to Other Computers list appears, showing the available devices as well as the existing connections (see fig. 8.12).

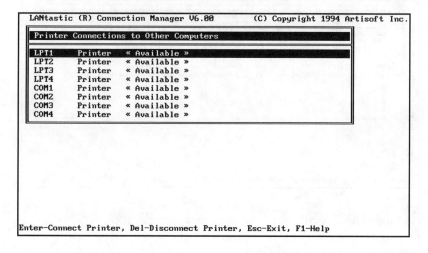

Figure 8.12
The Printer
Connections to
Other
Computers list.

2. Highlight the device you want to use (such as LPT1) and press Enter. Your screen displays a list of available servers, as shown in figure 8.13.

Figure 8.13
The list of available servers.

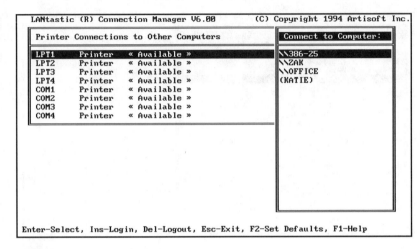

```
LANtastic (R) Connection Manager V6.00        (C) Copyright 1994 Artisoft Inc.
┌ Printer Connections to Other Computers ──────┐ ┌ Connect to Computer: ┐
│ LPT1     Printer    « Available »            │ │ \\386-25            │
│ LPT2     Printer    « Available »            │ │ \\ZAK               │
│ LPT3     Printer    « Available »            │ │ \\OFFICE            │
│ LPT4     Printer    « Available »            │ │ (KATIE)             │
│ COM1     Printer    « Available »            │ │                     │
│ COM2     Printer    « Available »            │ │                     │
│ COM3     Printer    « Available »            │ │                     │
│ COM4     Printer    « Available »            │ │                     │
│                                              │ │                     │
│                                              │ │                     │
│                                              │ │                     │
│                                              │ │                     │
│                                              │ └─────────────────────┘
│                                              │
└──────────────────────────────────────────────┘
 Enter-Select, Ins-Login, Del-Logout, Esc-Exit, F2-Set Defaults, F1-Help
```

3. Highlight the server you want to connect to and press Enter. If the server is not displayed, press Ins and type the server's name.

   After you connect to the server, the screen shows a list of shared devices available for connection (see fig. 8.14).

Figure 8.14
Shared devices available for connection.

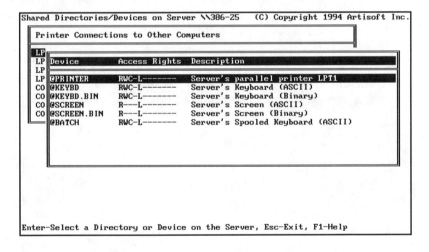

```
Shared Directories/Devices on Server \\386-25    (C) Copyright 1994 Artisoft Inc.
┌ Printer Connections to Other Computers ──────────────────┐
│ LP ┌──────────────────────────────────────────────────────┐
│ LP │ Device        Access Rights  Description             │
│ LP │                                                      │
│ LP │ @PRINTER      RWC-L-------   Server's parallel printer LPT1│
│ CO │ @KEYBD        RWC-L-------   Server's Keyboard (ASCII)│
│ CO │ @KEYBD.BIN    RWC-L-------   Server's Keyboard (Binary)│
│ CO │ @SCREEN       R---L-------   Server's Screen (ASCII) │
│ CO │ @SCREEN.BIN   R---L-------   Server's Screen (Binary)│
│    │ @BATCH        RWC-L-------   Server's Spooled Keyboard (ASCII)│
│    │                                                      │
│    └──────────────────────────────────────────────────────┘
│                                                          │
└──────────────────────────────────────────────────────────┘
 Enter-Select a Directory or Device on the Server, Esc-Exit, F1-Help
```

4. Highlight the shared device you want to use and press Enter. You are returned to the Printer Connections to Other Computers list with your new choice displayed (see fig. 8.15).

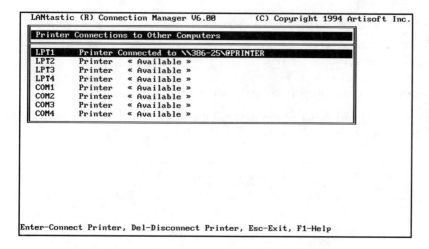

Figure 8.15
The Printer
Connections to
Other
Computers list
with the new
printer
connection
displayed.

Connecting Using the LANPUP Utility

The following steps show how to use the LANPUP utility to connect to a server's
disk drives or printers:

1. Press Ctrl+Alt+L to launch LANPUP.

2. Highlight the Disks option (see fig. 8.16) and press Enter.

Figure 8.16
LANPUP menu
with Disks option
highlighted.

3. Drive A is displayed in the block. Use the down arrow to
   change the display until the drive you want to use for the
   connection (D: for this example) appears in the window
   (see fig. 8.17).

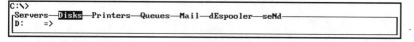

Figure 8.17
Selecting drive
letter D: to use.

4. Press Enter to see the server display.

5. Use the up and down arrows to scroll until the desired
   server appears in the window (see fig. 8.18).

Figure 8.18
Selecting server
386-25.

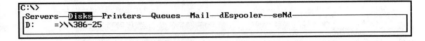

```
C:\>
 Servers─Disks─Printers─Queues─Mail─dEspooler─seNd──────
 D:    =>\\386-25
```

6. Press Enter to display the available drive/directory resources.

7. Use the up and down arrows to scroll the display until you see the shared resource you want to use (see fig. 8.19).

Figure 8.19
Selecting the
C-DRIVE
resource on
server 386-25.

```
C:\>
 Servers─Disks─Printers─Queues─Mail─dEspooler─seNd──────
 D:    =>\\386-25\C-DRIVE    Drive C on Server
```

8. Press Enter to select the shared resource. You return to the display that has D: in the window showing your new connection.

9. Select another drive or press Esc to clear the block.

If you want to connect to a shared printer, follow the preceding steps, but use the printer option. If you already have a printer redirected, you may get a warning message that your choice is a duplicate. Press Esc to clear the block and return to the LANPUP menu. You may want to delete the current printer connection and then reconnect it for practice.

Connecting Using NET Commands

The NET USE command is used to connect to a shared resource on a server. You can type NET USE at a DOS prompt or include it in a batch file. The basic syntax of the NET USE command is as follows:

```
NET USE drive-device: \\server-name\resource
```

Drive-device is the drive letter (such as K:) or device name (such as LPT1:) you want to use to access the resource on the server. *Server-name* is the name of the server that has the resource you want to use. *Resource* is the name of the shared drive/directory or printer resource you want to use.

If the server that has the resource you want to use has the * wildcard account set up, you do not have to log in to it before you issue the NET USE command.

The following example redirects the J drive to access the C-DRIVE resource on server KEVIN:

```
NET USE J: \\KEVIN\C-DRIVE
```

Using LANtastic with Windows

LANtastic includes several programs for use in Windows. The LANtastic NET program enables you to connect to the shared resources on other computers from within Windows. The following sections discuss making network connections in Windows.

Understanding Network Connections

The daily functions you perform in LANtastic usually include logging into servers, connecting to and using shared directories/drives and printers, sending and receiving electronic mail, sharing programs and data, and performing related tasks.

To run a program in Windows, you have several options. You can set up an Icon that, when activated, will run a program; you can select **R**un from the Program Manager **F**ile menu and enter the command line to execute the program; or you can select the program to run from within File Manager. All these options have two things in common: you specify the location of the program (the drive and directory) and you specify the name of the file you want to run. Once the program is running, you typically will access a data file, which also has a name and is stored in a specified location (drive and directory).

You may, for example, have Microsoft Works for Windows installed on your computer. To run Works, double-click on the Microsoft Works for Windows Icon. If you select the icon by clicking on it once and then select the **P**roperties item from the Program Manager **F**ile menu, the Program Item Properties dialog box appears (see fig. 8.20).

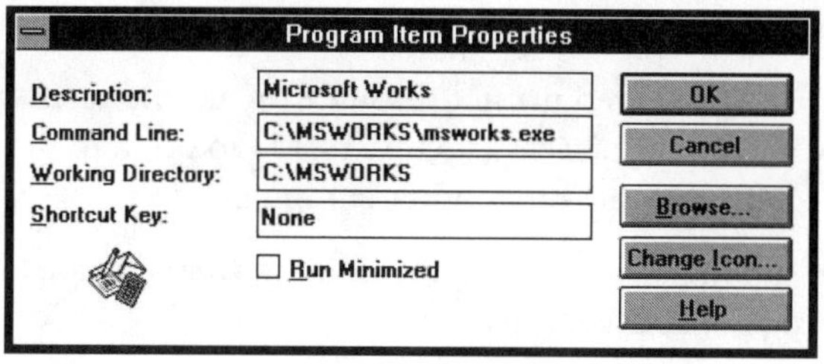

Figure 8.20
The Program Item Properties dialog box for MS Works for Windows.

The Command Line field contains the command C:\MSWORKS\MSWORKS.EXE, which tells Windows the location and name of the file to run. The program file is MSWORKS.EXE, and it is located in the MSWORKS directory on the C: drive. As soon as you run Works, you might open a document you created by specifying the location and name of the file such as C:\DATA\MYDOC in which MYDOC is the name of the file which is located on the C: drive in the DATA directory.

Now suppose you do not have Microsoft Works for Windows on your computer, but it is installed on another computer in the network. To access Works on another computer's hard drive and run it on your computer, you need to establish a network connection to the server you want to access.

Most Windows programs require some type of installation before they can be accessed across the network. For the programs to operate correctly, they usually need to update your Windows system files, an operation which is performed when the program is installed.

By redirecting a drive letter on your computer to point to a shared drive resource on another computer, you can install a Windows program that stores its program files on another computer.

Many programs also allow a network installation in which you can access and run the installation program from another computer. Once installed using the network installation, the main program files remain on the other computer where they enable you to access and run the program on your computer.

To establish a network connection to a shared resource on another computer, choose a drive letter on your computer that is redirected to the desired shared resource on another computer. For example, if you choose to access the C-DRIVE resource on server KSOFFICE by redirecting your K drive to point to \\KSOFFICE\C-DRIVE, accessing your K drive is the same thing as accessing the C drive on server KSOFFICE. To run MS Works from the K drive, your command line is K:\MSWORKS\MSWORKS.EXE. The working directory in this example is K:\MSWORKS, although you could choose a working directory that is not on the network, such as C:\MYDATA.

In order to connect to a shared printer resource on another computer, you must redirect one of your printer devices (such as LPT1) to point to the shared printer resource (such as @PRINTER) on another computer.

In Windows, you can make network connections to shared resources on other computers by using the LANtastic Net program.

Understanding the Net Program

The Windows LANtastic NET program is installed with LANtastic, and enables you to perform daily network operations, including logging in and out of servers, establishing network drive and printer connections, managing your user account, and sending and receiving electronic mail.

To run the LANtastic NET program, double-click on the LANtastic NET Connections icon (see fig. 8.21) in the LANtastic program group, or, with the LANtastic Net Connections icon selected, choose **O**pen from the Program Manager **E**dit menu. The LANtastic NET program appears, displaying the following selections (see fig. 8.22):

✔ **Drives.** This selection enables you to establish a network connection to a disk drive on another computer. Choose a drive letter (such as K:) to point to a shared drive resource on another computer, and specify the server name and associated drive resource name on the server to which you want to connect.

✔ **Printers.** This selection enables you to establish a network connection to a printer on another computer. To do this, choose a device name (such as LPT1:) to point to a shared printer resource on another computer, and specify the server name and associated printer resource name on the server to which you want to connect.

✔ **Mail.** This selection is used to send or receive mail. If you have an Artisoft Sounding Board installed in your computer, you can send and receive voice mail. If you have the M privilege, you can control any mail item in the queue. Otherwise, you can only control mail sent to or by you.

✔ **Cha_t.** This selection enables you to carry on a text dialogue with another user on the network. If you have the Artisoft Sounding Board installed in both computers, you can carry on a voice chat with another user.

✔ **Jobs.** This selection is used to control and manage print jobs in the queue. You can add, delete, hold, and change the priority of print jobs. If you have the Q privilege, you can control any print job in the queue. Otherwise you can only control your own print jobs. Moreover, the Q privilege lets you start and stop printing to specific devices (LPT1, LPT2, and so on) or printer streams (@LASER, @PRINTER, and so on). Chapter 10, "Printing with LANtastic," discusses this selection in detail.

✔ **Computers.** This selection enables you to log in to or log out from servers on the network. When you establish network connections using

the Drives or Printers selections, you also can log in to or log out of the
server at the same time.

✔ **Account.** This selection enables you to change your password, disable
your account, or check on the status of your account on the server.

✔ **Manage.** This selection enables you to see which users are currently
using the server and the actions they are performing. You can, moreover,
view another server's screen and issue commands to that server with your
keyboard. If you have the S privilege, you can also schedule server
shutdowns.

Figure 8.21
Selecting the
LANtastic Net
Connections
icon.

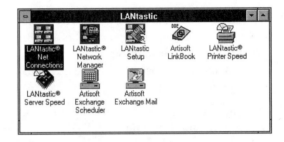

Figure 8.22
The Windows
LANtastic Net
program.

The previously described selections are also available from the **N**et
menu (see fig. 8.23). Several of the selections may also be accessed
from the **LA**Ntastic menu in the Windows File Manager program which
appears after LANtastic has been installed (see fig. 8.24).

Figure 8.23
The LANtastic
NET program
NET menu.

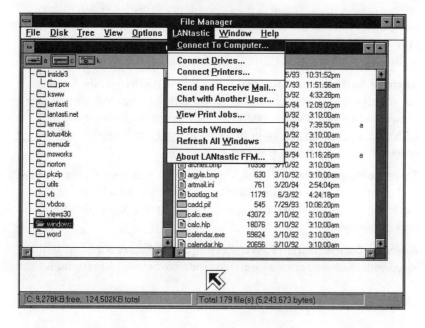

Figure 8.24
The LANtastic
menu in File
Manager.

Saving and Restoring Network Connections

The LANtastic NET program offers great flexibility and ease of use when making
network connections. Often, however, you want to automatically establish some
drive and printer connections to other computers each time you run Windows.
The LANtastic NET program can perform this function and also has the capability
to reestablish any disk drive and printer connections you saved.

If you have saved network connections that you logged in to with a specific user name and password, LANtastic NET will prompt you to enter the password when it tries to reestablish your connections at the start of Windows. LANtastic NET does not save password information.

The Windows LANtastic NET program will not have to prompt you for a password if you set a default user name and password using the NET USER command prior to entering Windows.

The LANtastic Net program **O**ptions menu enables you to specify when to save and when to restore saved network connections. The following is a description of the related items on the **O**ptions menu that pertain to saving and restoring network connections (see fig. 8.25):

✔ **Save Settings on Exit.** If this option is selected, all your drive and printer connections, as well as the computers you are logged in to, are saved when you exit the LANtastic NET program (or when you exit Windows). If you have any open LANtastic dialog boxes, that information is also saved.

✔ **Restore Settings on Startup.** If this option is selected, any settings saved with the Save Settings on Exit or the Save Settings Now options are restored when you start the LANtastic NET program. Because the LANtastic NET program is automatically activated when you start Windows, the settings are also restored at that time.

✔ **Save Settings Now.** Selecting this option saves all your current drive and printer connections as well as the computers on which you are logged in. If any LANtastic dialog boxes are currently open, that information is also saved.

✔ **Restore Connections Now.** Selecting this option restores any settings saved with the Save Settings on Exit or the Save Settings Now options

Figure 8.25
The LANtastic
NET Options
menu showing
the network
connections
save and restore
features.

Logging In to a Server

To establish a network connection to a shared drive/directory or printer on another computer, you must log in to the server that contains the resource you want to use. You have several options that enable you to log in to another computer while using Windows. You may log in prior to starting Windows or you may log in using the Windows LANtastic NET program. The Windows File Manager also has an option in the LANtastic menu, which calls the LANtastic NET program to enable you to log in.

If separate user accounts aren't set up and you are using the default * wildcard account established by the install program, you do not have to log in to the server that contains the resource you want to use. If you attempt to connect to the resource, you are automatically logged in.

Using the LANtastic NET Program To Log In

To use the LANtastic NET program to log in to a LANtastic server, do the following steps:

1. Make sure that your LANtastic software is loaded and actively running on the computers you use.

2. To run the NET program, double-click on the LANtastic Net Connections icon in the LANtastic program group, or select **O**pen from the Program Manager **F**ile menu with the LANtastic Net Connections icon selected. The NET program main menu appears, as shown in figure 8.22.

The LANtastic NET program starts when you run Windows. Other ways to make LANtastic NET the active window include pressing the Alt+Tab until you have attained your objective, or pressing Ctrl+Esc and selecting LANtastic Net from the Task List dialog box.

3. Select the **C**omputers icon or select **C**omputer Connections from the **N**et menu. The Computer Connections dialog box appears, showing the computers to which you are currently connected (logged in to), as well as those available for connection (see fig. 8.26).

Figure 8.26
The Computer
Connections
dialog box.

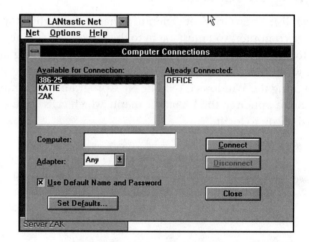

4. Select the server you want to connect to and press the **C**onnect button.

If the Use Default Name and Password option is selected and the default name and password is a valid account, you will be connected to the other computer. Otherwise, the Connect to Computer dialog box will appear, asking you to enter your user name and password.

You can log out of a computer by going to the Already Connected list and selecting the computer from which you want to disconnect; then select the **D**isconnect button

If the * wildcard account exists without a password on the computer to which you want to connect, and the Use Default Name and Password option is selected, you automatically are logged in as soon as you select **C**onnect. You are not asked for your user name and password.

If you need to use a specific user name to log in, select the Set De**f**aults button and enter the default user name and password you want to use. You also can deselect the **U**se Default Name and Password option; you will then be prompted for your user name and password.

5. Select Close, and you are returned to the LANtastic NET program main menu.

You now are logged in and can use the other options on the menu.

Logging In Prior to Windows

You can log in to another computer and use its shared drive and printer resources prior to starting Windows. Any network connections you established prior to starting Windows are recognized by and available for use within Windows, just as if you had made the connection using the LANtastic NET program in Windows.

Although the Windows LANtastic NET program provides features that automatically reestablish previously saved network connections, sometimes you may prefer to include NET commands in a DOS batch file to establish desired network connections prior to starting Windows. For example, you might have a DOS batch file called GOWIN.BAT that uses a drive resource on another computer for data storage, and includes the following commands to connect to a printer on another computer:

```
NET LOGIN \\DANA KEVIN ZAK
NET USE LPT1: \\DANA\@PRINTER
NET LOGIN \\KATIE KEVIN ZAK
NET USE K: \\KATIE\DATA
WIN
```

The GOWIN.BAT file first logs in to server DANA with the user name KEVIN and password ZAK. The LPT1 device is redirected to point to the @PRINTER printer resource that exists on server DANA. Next, the server named KATIE is logged in to with user name KEVIN and password ZAK. Drive K is redirected to point to the DATA resource on server KATIE. Finally WIN starts Microsoft Windows.

Connecting to Disk Drives and Printers

Several options exist for connecting to disk drives and printers. You can establish the connections prior to entering Windows using the methods described previously. Once you are in Windows, however, you can use the LANtastic Net program, the Windows File Manager, and the Windows Control panel to establish network connections.

Connecting Using the LANtastic NET Program

The following steps show how to use the LANtastic NET program to establish a network connection to a server's shared drive resource:

1. From the LANtastic NET program main menu, select the **D**rives icon or select Connect to **D**rives from the **N**et menu.

   The Drive Connections dialog box appears (see fig. 8.27), showing the available shared resources on other computers to which you can connect in the Available for Connection field. The My Connections field shows the drives currently used and the drive letters available to connect to shared drive resources on other computers. If a connection is already made, it appears next to the drive letter.

Figure 8.27
The Drive Connections dialog box.

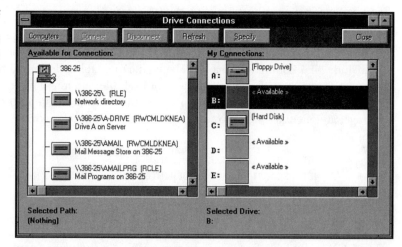

2. Select the drive letter you want to use from the list in the My Connec-
    tions field and the shared drive resource you want to use from the list
    in the Available for Connection field (see fig. 8.28). If you are not
    currently connected to the computer that has the drive resource you
    want to use, you may connect to the computer by selecting the Com-
    puters button.

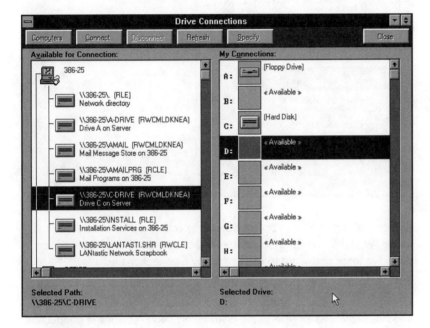

Figure 8.28
Selecting the
drive resource
to connect to
and the drive
letter to use for
the connection.

To show more of the list on the screen, maximize the Drive Connections
dialog box by clicking on the up icon in the upper righthand corner of
the window.

3. Select the Connect button. The connection is made and displayed in
    the My Connections list next to the selected drive letter (see fig. 8.29).

Figure 8.29
The Drive
Connections
dialog box
showing the new
connection using
drive letter D.

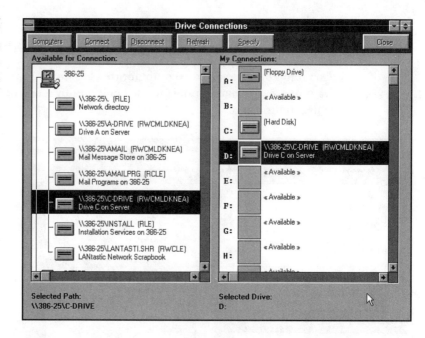

You can also establish a connection by selecting a drive resource icon
in the Available for Connection list, and dragging and dropping it on
the drive letter you want to use in the My Connections list.

If you prefer to type the parameters required for the connection rather
than selecting it as described previously, select the **S**pecify button, and
you are prompted to type in the parameters required for the connection
(see fig. 8.30).

Figure 8.30
The Establish
Drive
Connection
dialog box.

To delete any connection, select the connection you want to delete and select the **D**isconnect button. The drive letter is now available for use in another network connection.

The method used to connect to shared printer resources is similar to the way you connected to shared drive resources. To connect to a shared printer resource, perform the following steps:

1. From the LANtastic NET program main menu, select the **P**rinters icon or select Connect to **P**rinters from the **N**et menu.

   The Printer Connections dialog box appears (see fig. 8.31), showing the available shared resources on other computers you may connect to in the Available for Connection field. The My Connections field shows the devices currently used and the devices available to be used to connect to shared printer resources on other computers. If a connection is already made, it appears next to the device name.

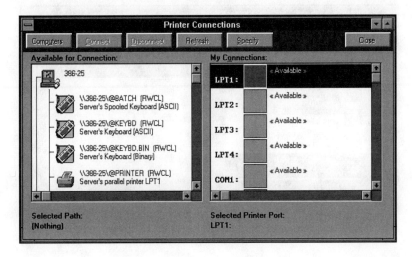

Figure 8.31
The Printer Connections dialog box.

2. Select the device name you want to use (such as LPT1) from the list in the My Connections field, and the shared printer resource you want to connect to from the list in the Available for Connection field (see fig. 8.32). If you are not currently connected to the computer that has the printer resource you want to use, you may connect to the computer by selecting the Comp**u**ters button.

Figure 8.32
Selecting the printer resource to connect to and the device name to use.

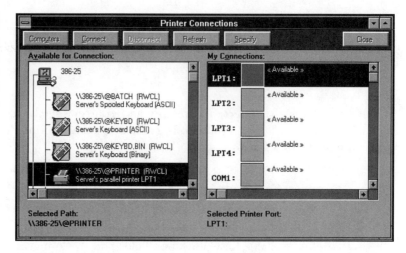

3. Select the **C**onnect button. The connection is made and displayed in the My Connections list next to the select device name (see fig. 8.33).

Figure 8.33
The Printer Connections dialog box showing the new connection using device LPT1.

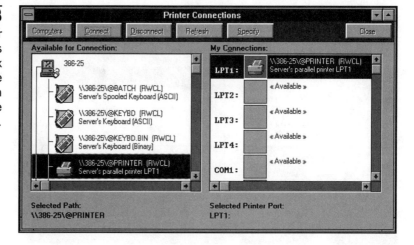

As with drive connections, you can drag and drop icons to establish printer connections, or specify the parameters necessary for the connection by using the **S**pecify button.

To delete any connection, choose the connection you want to delete and select the **D**isconnect button. The device name is now available for use in another network connection.

Connecting to Disk Drives Using File Manager

File Manager is a Windows program that helps manage directories and files. You can access File Manager by clicking on the File Manager icon in the Main program group. File Manager provides the capability to copy, move, and delete files and subdirectories, as well as an intuitive way of viewing directories and files.

When LANtastic is installed for Windows, the File Manager menu is modified to include a LANtastic selection (see fig. 8.34). When an option is selected from the **LA**Ntastic menu, such as the Connect **D**rives selection, the corresponding LANtastic NET program routine is performed, as described previously. In addition to providing the capability to connect to shared drive resources, the LANtastic menu also includes several other selections, such as the ability to connect (log in) to other computers and shared printer resources on other computers.

Figure 8.34
The LANtastic menu in File Manager.

File Manager also enables you to connect to and use network disk drives without using the LANtastic menu selections. To connect to a network drive in File Manager, select the **D**isk menu and then the **N**etwork Connections option (see fig. 8.35). From here, you can select the drive letter to be used for the connection in the Network Connection dialog box. In the Network Path field, you need to enter the resource name to which you want to connect, such as \\386-25\C-DRIVE.

Figure 8.35
Connecting to a
network drive
using File
Manager.

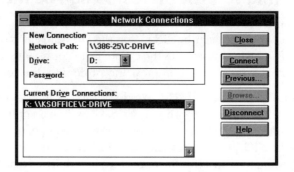

If user names and passwords are assigned to the server that contains the resources to which you are connecting, you must be logged in to that server before using the **N**etwork Connections option to connect. The reason why you must already be logged in is because File Manager does not enable you to enter a user name and password to log in to a network server with LANtastic. As long as you are already logged in to the server that you want to use, the resources on that server are available for connection.

File Manager saves the drive connection information and tries to reestablish the connection when Windows is started again.

Do not use the **N**etwork Connections option in File Manager to establish network connections; instead, use the LANtastic NET program or the LANtastic menu option in File Manager. Because File Manager will reestablish network connections created with the **N**etwork connections option independently of any connections that LANtastic NET is trying to reestablish, you could have a situation in which the network connections you expected are different than those obtained.

Connecting to Printers Using Control Panel

Windows provides you with the capability to connect to network printers independently of the LANtastic NET program. You can connect to and configure network printers by selecting Control Panel in Program Manager. By double-clicking on the Printers icon, you display the Printers dialog box. Click on the **C**onnect option, then choose the **N**etwork option. The Printers - Network Connections dialog box appears (see fig. 8.36).

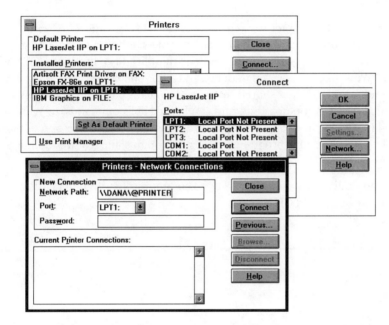

Figure 8.36
Connecting to network printers using Control Panel.

In the Printers - Network Connection dialog box, you can select the device name you want to redirect, such as LPT1. In the Network Path field, enter the shared resource name to which you want to connect, such as \\DANA\@PRINTER. If you assign user names and passwords to the server that contains the printer resources to which you are connecting, you must be logged in to that server before trying to connect to the printer. As long as you are logged in to the server, the printer resources on that server are available.

Establish printer connections in Windows by means of the LANtastic NET program. The NET program will help you avoid possible confusion caused by the Control Panel's attempts to reestablish printer connections when Windows is started.

Summary

The information in this chapter showed you ways to actively employ LANtastic to use the shared resources on other computers. Various methods of connecting to and using shared resources on other servers, which utilized LANtastic in DOS and LANtastic in Windows, was covered in detail. In DOS, you learned how to log in to other computers and use their shared resources by means of the LANtastic NET program, the LANPUP pop-up utility, and LANtastic NET commands. In Windows, you learned how to log in to other computers and use their shared resources by means of the LANtastic NET program, as well as through some features built into Windows programs.

The next chapter discusses using LANtastic to communicate with others using features such as E-Mail and CHAT.

Chapter Snapshot

This chapter explores different ways you can use
LANtastic to communicate with others. In this chapter
you will learn the following:

✔ How to send and receive LANtastic Mail in both
  DOS and Windows.

✔ How to use Chat to carry on an interactive
  conversation with another user in both DOS and
  Windows.

✔ How to incorporate voice mail and Chat into your
  LANtastic network using the Artisoft Sounding
  Board.

✔ The LANtastic features available to help you
  manage your user account in both DOS and
  Windows.

✔ How to shut down a server and the features
  available to notify others that the server is shutting
  down.

This chapter contains separate independent DOS and
Windows sections describing LANtastic programs and
features available to you for communicating with
others.

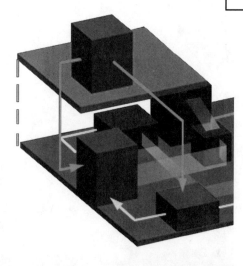

9

CHAPTER

Using LANtastic To Communicate with Others and Manage Your Account

One common reason why companies install a network is to increase the communications capability of the work force. Phone message sheets often get lost or buried. LANtastic provides several features that enhance the communications capability of your office, including electronic Mail, Chat, and even voice mail and voice Chat with the optional Artisoft Sounding Board. LANtastic also provides features to enable you to view the status of your LANtastic account, as well as options to manage your account—such as changing your password and disabling your account while you are gone.

Using LANtastic with DOS

LANtastic includes programs and features that enable you to communicate with others and manage your LANtastic account using LANtastic Mail and Chat in DOS and in Windows. The following sections describe LANtastic features available through DOS. The features available in Windows are covered later in this chapter.

Using the MAIL Function

LANtastic Mail enables you to communicate with others by sending and receiving messages. You can compose a message and send it to a specified user over the network. The user for which the message is meant is notified that a message has been sent. Messages can be read, saved to files, forwarded to other users, or deleted. The Artisoft Sounding Board enhances the features available with Mail by providing Voice Mail capability.

Sending and Receiving Mail Using the LANtastic Net Program

In order to send Mail using the LANtastic NET program, start LANtastic NET by typing NET at the DOS prompt and performing the following steps:

1. From the NET main menu, select Send and Receive LANtastic Mail (see fig. 9.1) and press Enter. The Connect to Computer window appears (see fig. 9.2).

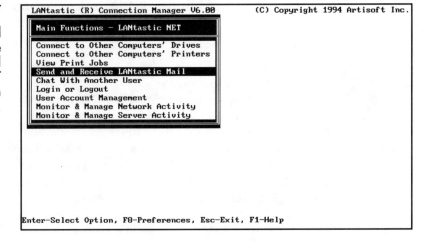

Figure 9.1
Selecting Send and Receive LANtastic Mail from the NET program main menu.

```
LANtastic (R) Connection Manager V6.00          (C) Copyright 1994 Artisoft Inc.

 Main Functions - LANtastic NET
┌─────────────────────────────────────┐
│ Connect to Other Computers' Drives   │
│ Connect to Other Computers' Printers │
│ View Print Jobs                      │
│ Send and Receive LANtastic Mail      │
│ Chat With Another User               │
│ Login or Logout                      │
│ User Account Management              │
│ Monitor & Manage Network Activity    │
│ Monitor & Manage Server Activity     │
└─────────────────────────────────────┘




Enter-Select Option, F8-Preferences, Esc-Exit, F1-Help
```

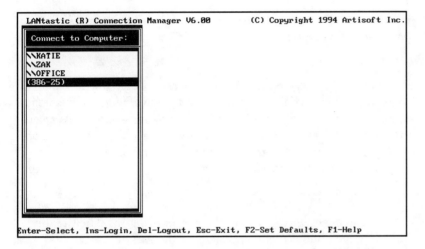

Figure 9.2
Selecting the computer to use for LANtastic mail.

2. Choose the server you want to use and press Enter. If you are not logged in to the server you want to use, you can log in to the server now. A screen similar to the one in figure 9.3 appears, which shows the INcoming Mail and OUTgoing mail for your account on the server you specified (386-25 in this example).

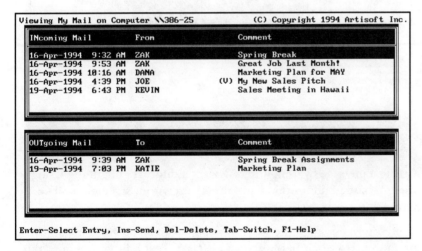

Figure 9.3
Viewing mail screen showing INcoming and OUTgoing mail.

Each server set up with an @MAIL resource contains a mail queue in which messages are stored. Only messages sent to the specified server for your account are shown on the screen. If you want to see messages you have on another server, choose that server after you select the Send and Receive LANtastic Mail option from the NET main menu.

continues

In order to avoid confusion, designate a single server as the LANtastic Mail server that everyone uses to send and receive mail.

If you are not already logged in to a server, LANtastic will attempt to log you in using the default username and password (unless automatic logins have been disabled) when you select the server and press Enter. If the account does not exist on the sever you are logging in to, you are prompted to enter your username and password. You can set the default username and password by pressing F2 - Set Defaults (see fig. 9.2).

3. You can send a message to another user by pressing Ins. The Creating a Mail Message options menu appears (see fig. 9.4).

Figure 9.4
The Creating a Mail Message options list.

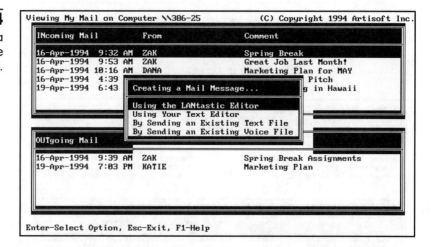

```
Viewing My Mail on Computer \\386-25          (C) Copyright 1994 Artisoft Inc.

INcoming Mail           From              Comment

16-Apr-1994  9:32 AM    ZAK               Spring Break
16-Apr-1994  9:53 AM    ZAK               Great Job Last Month!
16-Apr-1994 10:16 AM    DANA              Marketing Plan for MAY
16-Apr-1994  4:39                                              Pitch
19-Apr-1994  6:43       Creating a Mail Message...         g in Hawaii

                        Using the LANtastic Editor
                        Using Your Text Editor
                        By Sending an Existing Text File
                        By Sending an Existing Voice File

OUTgoing Mail

16-Apr-1994  9:39 AM    ZAK               Spring Break Assignments
19-Apr-1994  7:03 PM    KATIE             Marketing Plan




Enter-Select Option, Esc-Exit, F1-Help
```

4. Create a message by using the LANtastic Editor. Highlight the Using the LANtastic Editor option and press Enter. Your screen looks like figure 9.5.

5. Type your message in the same way you would if you are using a word processor. However, because the LANtastic Text Editor does not wrap words at the ends of lines, you must insert carriage returns.

6. After you finish your message, press F2 to send it. In the window that pops up, enter the name of the user to whom you are sending mail (see fig. 9.6), and press Enter.

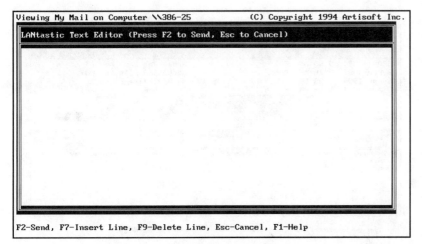

Figure 9.5

The LANtastic Text Editor.

If you want to list the users on the server, press F10, highlight the recipient of the mail, and press Enter.

You can send a message to multiple users using wildcards. To send a message to everyone, specify * for the user. In order to send the message to the users with SALES as the first part of their username, specify SALES* as the username.

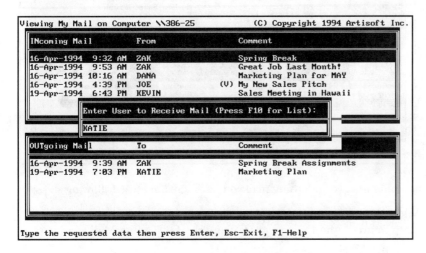

Figure 9.6

Selecting the user to receive mail.

7. Enter a comment to go with the mail message (see fig. 9.7). The comment you enter is the title that shows on the Viewing My Mail screen after you send the message.

Figure 9.7

Entering a comment to accompany mail.

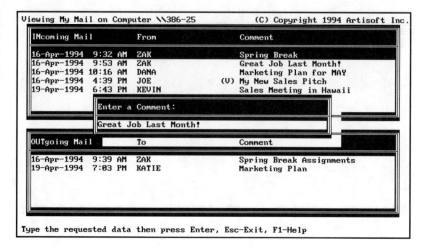

```
Viewing My Mail on Computer \\386-25          (C) Copyright 1994 Artisoft Inc.

 INcoming Mail              From              Comment

 16-Apr-1994  9:32 AM  ZAK                    Spring Break
 16-Apr-1994  9:53 AM  ZAK                    Great Job Last Month!
 16-Apr-1994 10:16 AM  DANA                   Marketing Plan for MAY
 16-Apr-1994  4:39 PM  JOE              (V)   My New Sales Pitch
 19-Apr-1994  6:43 PM  KEVIN                  Sales Meeting in Hawaii

                      Enter a Comment:

                      Great Job Last Month!

 OUTgoing Mail             To                Comment

 16-Apr-1994  9:39 AM  ZAK                    Spring Break Assignments
 19-Apr-1994  7:03 PM  KATIE                  Marketing Plan



 Type the requested data then press Enter, Esc-Exit, F1-Help
```

8. Press Enter to send the mail message and return to the Viewing My Mail screen, which shows the message you just sent in the OUTgoing Mail portion of the screen (see fig. 9.8).

Figure 9.8

The message just sent in the OUTgoing Mail section.

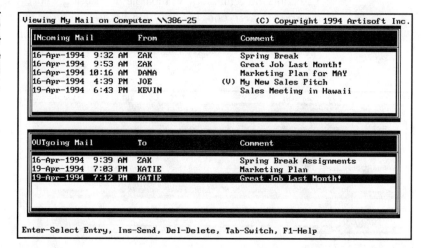

```
Viewing My Mail on Computer \\386-25          (C) Copyright 1994 Artisoft Inc.

 INcoming Mail              From              Comment

 16-Apr-1994  9:32 AM  ZAK                    Spring Break
 16-Apr-1994  9:53 AM  ZAK                    Great Job Last Month!
 16-Apr-1994 10:16 AM  DANA                   Marketing Plan for MAY
 16-Apr-1994  4:39 PM  JOE              (V)   My New Sales Pitch
 19-Apr-1994  6:43 PM  KEVIN                  Sales Meeting in Hawaii



 OUTgoing Mail             To                Comment

 16-Apr-1994  9:39 AM  ZAK                    Spring Break Assignments
 19-Apr-1994  7:03 PM  KATIE                  Marketing Plan
 19-Apr-1994  7:12 PM  KATIE                  Great Job Last Month!



 Enter-Select Entry, Ins-Send, Del-Delete, Tab-Switch, F1-Help
```

To read incoming mail (or outgoing mail you have sent), use the following steps:

1. Select the entry you want to read by using the arrow keys. Press Tab to jump between the INcoming Mail and the OUTgoing Mail windows.

2. Press Enter. The Mail Options menu appears (see fig. 9.9).

3. Select Read Mail and press Enter. The message you select to read is displayed on-screen (see fig. 9.10).

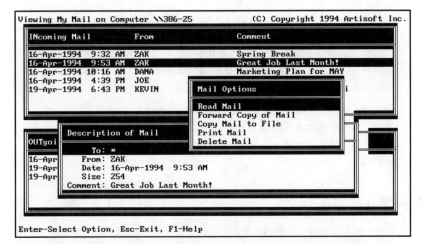

Figure 9.9
The Mail Options menu.

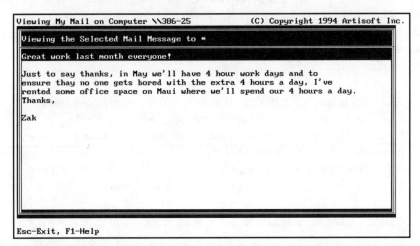

Figure 9.10
Reading a selected Mail message.

To delete a message you send, select it from the OUTgoing Mail window and select the Delete Mail option from the Mail Options menu. Press Enter at the next screen prompt to delete the message.

Using the LANPUP Utility MAIL Function

The memory-resident pop-up utility (LANPUP) also has a MAIL function. Press Ctrl+Alt+L to call up the LANPUP menu. Highlight the MAIL option and press Enter. The procedures are similar to what you use for the NET program. Practice sending, reading, and deleting mail.

LANPUP does not include an editor for composing messages. You are prompted to enter the name of a file to be sent. You can compose a message by selecting CON for the file name. You will be able to type one line at a time. When you are finished, press Esc to send your message.

If you specify CON for the file name when you read mail, you can display the message on the screen one line at a time. Specifying a name for the file name will save your message to a file with the name specified.

Managing Your Mail

Your responsibility to manage your mail is an important aspect of being a user on a network shared by others. If you do not remove mail messages that accumulate, you use up valuable disk space. More importantly, by allowing messages to accumulate in the mail queue, you slow down the NET utility so that it is forced to search through all the messages in the mail queue area to select and display the mail for a specific account.

Your mail queue is not difficult to manage. You already have been introduced to most of the required functions. What you need is personal dedication to do your part. Set a regular schedule to review messages in your INcoming Mail and OUTgoing Mail queues. Ideally, you should read your mail regularly, and then delete it or copy it to a file on disk. You also can print your mail for safekeeping.

LANtastic offers the following two ways to delete mail in your mail queue:

✔ Activate the NET program, select the Send and Receive LANtastic Mail option, and press Enter. Select the server that has the mail queue you want to use and press Enter. After the Viewing My Mail screen appears, scroll in the INcoming Mail window (as shown in the upper window in figure 9.11) and highlight the desired mail item. Press Del, and press Enter to confirm your deletion.

✔ You also can press Enter to select the mail item and to bring up the Mail Options menu (see fig. 9.12). Scroll down to select the Delete Mail option and press Enter. A confirmation message appears. Press Enter to confirm your deletion.

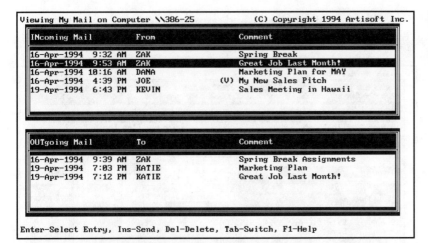

Figure 9.11
The messages in the mail queue.

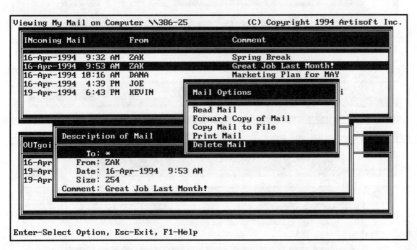

Figure 9.12
Deleting a mail entry using the Mail Options menu.

If you want to print a copy of the mail item (Print Mail), forward a copy to another user (Forward Copy of Mail), or save a copy of it to another file (Copy Mail to File), you can do all these things from the Mail Options menu.

To print a copy of your mail item, highlight the mail entry and press Enter. Select Print Mail from the Mail Options menu and press Enter. Select the name of the printer device to which you want to send the mail and press Enter (see fig. 9.13).

If you want to forward a copy of your mail to another user, highlight the mail entry and press Enter. Select Forward Copy of Mail from the Mail Options menu and press Enter. Enter the name of the user you want to receive the mail (see fig. 9.14), or press F10 to select a user from the list, and press Enter. Add a comment, press Enter, and the mail item is forwarded.

Figure 9.13
Printing a mail item.

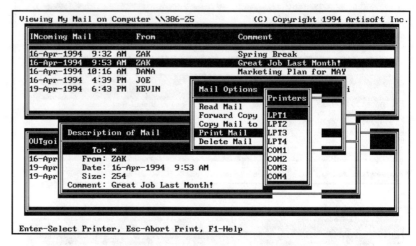

Figure 9.14
Forwarding a mail item to another user.

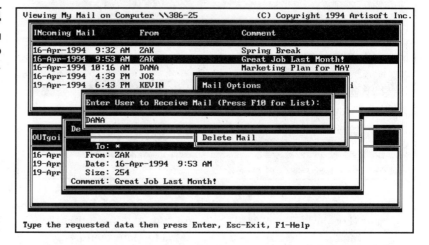

If you want to save your mail to a file, select Copy Mail to File, which brings up a prompt for you to enter the path name of the file to which you want to save your mail item (see fig. 9.15). Type the path, give the file a new name, and press Enter.

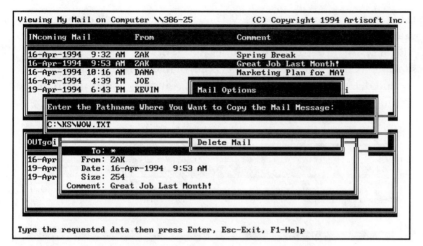

Figure 9.15
Copying a mail item to a file.

The figure shows a screen:

```
Viewing My Mail on Computer \\386-25          (C) Copyright 1994 Artisoft Inc.
INcoming Mail          From              Comment
16-Apr-1994  9:32 AM  ZAK               Spring Break
16-Apr-1994  9:53 AM  ZAK               Great Job Last Month!
16-Apr-1994 10:16 AM  DANA              Marketing Plan for MAY
16-Apr-1994  4:39 PM  JOE
19-Apr-1994  6:43 PM  KEVIN        Mail Options                        i
      Enter the Pathname Where You Want to Copy the Mail Message:
      C:\KS\WOW.TXT

OUTgoi                          Delete Mail
16-Apr     To: *
19-Apr   From: ZAK
19-Apr   Date: 16-Apr-1994   9:53 AM
         Size: 254
      Comment: Great Job Last Month!

Type the requested data then press Enter, Esc-Exit, F1-Help
```

Using the Super Mail Privilege

The network administrator can use the Super Mail (also called the M) privilege to manage the entire mail queue. This feature is important in large networks that have many users who generate a large volume of daily mail messages. The privilege enables a network administrator to read and delete all old mail from the queue. The intent is to free up storage space and restore speed to the NET mail search utility.

Because the administrator can read other people's mail, the administrator needs to be sensitive to users' feelings about their mail items. Do not give this privilege to anyone else.

Provide all users with a detailed policy that states the way the administrator manages the mail queue and what access rights users have. A policy statement helps prevent future misunderstandings between the administrator and the users.

Make it clear to your users that the administrator deletes only mail items that are several days old. The user is responsible for keeping saved mail items to a minimum. If users want to retain copies, they should print them out or copy them to their own hard disk.

A user with the Super Mail privilege has the additional option of F8 - View All listed at the bottom of the Viewing My Mail screen (see fig. 9.16). Pressing F8 causes the Viewing All Mail screen to be displayed, which shows all the mail contained in the mail queue for a particular server (see fig. 9.17). Highlighting a mail entry and pressing Enter displays the Mail Options menu (see fig. 9.18), which enables you to read mail (Read Mail), forward mail to another user (Forward Copy of Mail), copy mail items to a file (Copy Mail to File), print copies of mail items on a printer (Print Mail), and delete mail items (Delete Mail). Pressing F8 enables you to toggle from the Viewing All Mail view to the Viewing My Mail view.

Figure 9.16

The Viewing My Mail screen for a user with the Super Mail privilege.

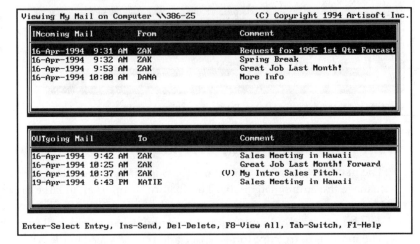

```
Viewing My Mail on Computer \\386-25              (C) Copyright 1994 Artisoft Inc.

 INcoming Mail           From              Comment

16-Apr-1994  9:31 AM  ZAK               Request for 1995 1st Qtr Forcast
16-Apr-1994  9:32 AM  ZAK               Spring Break
16-Apr-1994  9:53 AM  ZAK               Great Job Last Month!
16-Apr-1994 10:00 AM  DANA              More Info


 OUTgoing Mail          To                Comment

16-Apr-1994  9:42 AM  ZAK               Sales Meeting in Hawaii
16-Apr-1994 10:25 AM  ZAK               Great Job Last Month! Forward
16-Apr-1994 10:37 AM  ZAK          (V)  My Intro Sales Pitch.
19-Apr-1994  6:43 PM  KATIE             Sales Meeting in Hawaii


Enter-Select Entry, Ins-Send, Del-Delete, F8-View All, Tab-Switch, F1-Help
```

Figure 9.17

The Viewing All Mail screen.

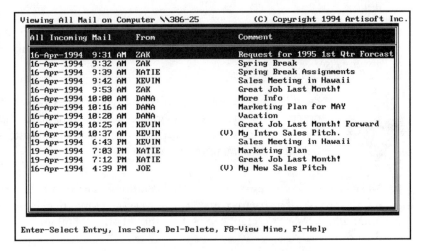

```
Viewing All Mail on Computer \\386-25             (C) Copyright 1994 Artisoft Inc.

 All Incoming Mail       From              Comment

16-Apr-1994  9:31 AM  ZAK               Request for 1995 1st Qtr Forcast
16-Apr-1994  9:32 AM  ZAK               Spring Break
16-Apr-1994  9:39 AM  KATIE             Spring Break Assignments
16-Apr-1994  9:42 AM  KEVIN             Sales Meeting in Hawaii
16-Apr-1994  9:53 AM  ZAK               Great Job Last Month!
16-Apr-1994 10:00 AM  DANA              More Info
16-Apr-1994 10:16 AM  DANA              Marketing Plan for MAY
16-Apr-1994 10:20 AM  DANA              Vacation
16-Apr-1994 10:25 AM  KEVIN             Great Job Last Month! Forward
16-Apr-1994 10:37 AM  KEVIN        (V)  My Intro Sales Pitch.
19-Apr-1994  6:43 PM  KEVIN             Sales Meeting in Hawaii
19-Apr-1994  7:03 PM  KATIE             Marketing Plan
19-Apr-1994  7:12 PM  KATIE             Great Job Last Month!
16-Apr-1994  4:39 PM  JOE          (V)  My New Sales Pitch


Enter-Select Entry, Ins-Send, Del-Delete, F8-View Mine, F1-Help
```

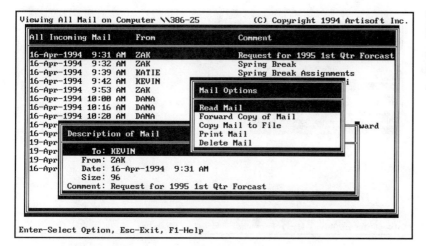

Figure 9.18
The Mail
Options menu
for the Viewing
All Mail view.

Using the Chat Function

LANtastic provides features that enable you to Chat with another user by typing
information in a window. Each user has two windows on the screen; one to type in
and the other to view what is being typed by the other person. If you have an
Artisoft Sounding Board, you can also carry on a voice Chat session with another
user.

Chat is available from the NET menu or, if you use NET commands, from the DOS
prompt.

Using the NET Program Chat Function

Perform the following steps to use the NET program Chat function:

1. Start the LANtastic NET program by typing NET at the DOS prompt.
    The LANtastic NET program main menu appears.

2. Highlight the Chat With Another User option (see fig. 9.19) and press
    Enter. Your screen changes to the Chat Connection Manager screen
    (see fig. 9.20).

3. Press Ins to initiate a call to the machine with which you want to Chat.

Unlike LANtastic Mail in which you send a message to another user,
LANtastic Chat requires you to enter the name of the computer where
the person with whom you want to Chat is located. For this reason, you
might want to name your machines after the primary users.

Figure 9.19
The Chat With Another User option on the LANtastic NET program main menu.

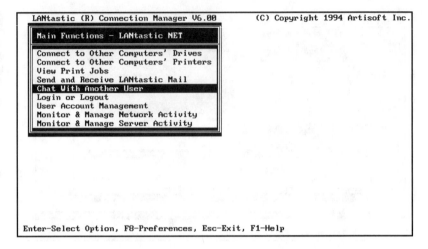

Figure 9.20
The CHAT Connection Manager screen.

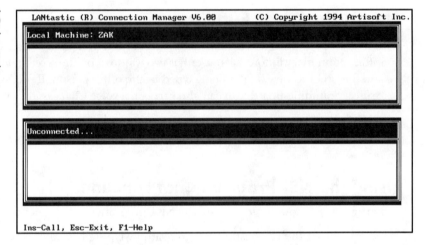

4. Type the name of the machine to be called, such as KATIE (see fig. 9.21), and press Enter.

   The computer you call displays a pop-up message on its screen that notifies the user that a Chat is being requested. The other user can type **NET Chat** from DOS or select Chat from Windows to establish the connection.

5. Type your message in the upper (Local Machine) box. Your message is displayed immediately on the remote machine's screen as you type. The message typed by the user on the other computer appears in the Remote Machine box on your computer. You can hold an interactive conversation this way (see fig. 9.22).

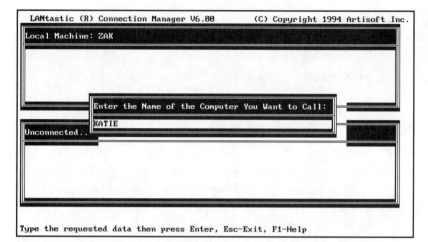

Figure 9.21
Entering a machine name to call.

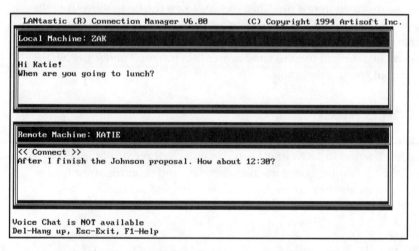

Figure 9.22
A sample Chat session.

6.   After you finish, press Del to hang up and return to the NET menu.

Using Chat from LANPUP and the DOS Command Line

The LANPUP menu does not have a Chat selection on the menu bar, but you can send a message to another machine by selecting the seNd option on the menu. In a box that appears below the menu, you are prompted to enter the name of the machine to which you are sending your message. After you type your message in the block, press Enter, and your message is sent to the selected recipient. After the recipient answers your note (using the seNd option on his or her LANPUP menu), a second block appears on-screen directly below the first block. This block shows the reply. Press Esc twice to exit the LANPUP utility. This feature is limited and is designed to enable you to send and receive short notes as you work in an application. You are limited to 70 characters in the message block, so use it to send messages such as the following:

```
You have a phone call on line 2.
```

or

```
You have a visitor at the front desk.
```

You can enter up to 112 characters in your message, but this forces the line to wrap to the next line and overwrites a portion of the message block outline.

If you want a full-screen interactive Chat session, access the Chat utility from the DOS prompt by typing **NET Chat** and pressing Enter. Your screen is identical to the one that appears when you use Chat With Another User from the NET program main menu. You can use the same procedures you used under the NET program to hold your conversation.

Using Voice Mail

The Artisoft Sounding Board enables you to send and receive voice mail and use the voice Chat features in LANtastic. Each computer that records or listens to voice mail must have a sounding board installed. Sending and receiving voice mail in LANtastic is almost identical to sending and receiving regular mail.

Sounding board installation is covered later in this chapter.

If you want to send a voice mail message, start the LANtastic NET program and select the Send and Receive LANtastic Mail option from the main menu. At the Viewing My Mail screen, press INS to send mail. When the Creating a Mail Message menu appears, select the By Recording a Voice Mail Message option (see fig. 9.23).

Type in the name of the user to receive the voice mail message, or press F10 to select a name from a list of accounts on the server and press Enter. Add a comment if you want, and then press Enter. Your screen will display a Voice Message

Recorder block (see fig. 9.24). Pick up the handset and press the space bar to begin recording your message. To pause the recording, press the space bar again. You can pause and continue recording as often as necessary by pressing the space bar. The screen shows the message length in bytes, minutes, and seconds. After you finish recording your message, press Enter and your voice mail is saved and sent to the recipient.

Figure 9.23

The Creating a Mail Message menu.

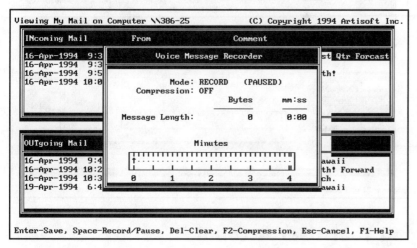

Figure 9.24

The Voice Message Recorder screen.

You can listen to a voice mail message by selecting Send and Receive LANtastic Mail from the NET menu. Next, select the voice mail message (preceded by a V indicator on the screen) in the INcoming Mail list and press Enter. Select the Listen to Mail option from the Mail Options menu (see fig. 9.25) to display the

Voice Message Recorder (see fig. 9.26) in Play mode. Pressing Space enables the listener to hear the message by using the telephone handset (or external speaker, if installed).

Figure 9.25
The Mail Options menu showing the Listen to Mail option.

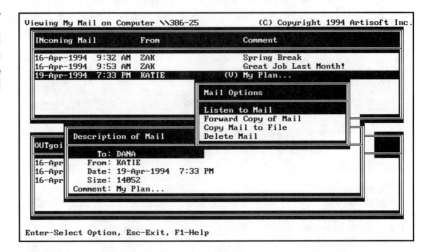

Figure 9.26
Listening to a voice mail message.

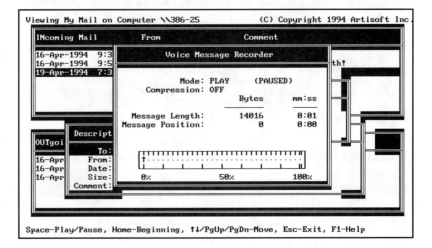

Managing Your User Account

The NET program provides users with limited control of their network accounts. The User Account Management option enables you to check the status of your account, change your account password, and disable your account. Users should become familiar with the three functions that are accessed through the User

Account Management option. To proceed with your account management functions, perform the following steps:

1. From the NET program main menu, select User Account Management and press Enter.

2. Select the server on which you want to manage your account. If you are not logged in to the server, you are required to do so at this time.

3. If you are logged in to the server using a different account name than the account you want to manage, select Switch to New Username from the User Account Management menu, and press Enter (see fig. 9.27). Enter your user name and then your password at the prompts.

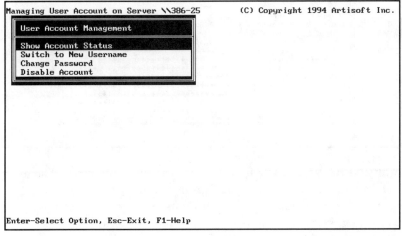

```
Managing User Account on Server \\386-25     (C) Copyright 1994 Artisoft Inc.
┌─────────────────────────────────────────────┐
│ User Account Management                       │
├─────────────────────────────────────────────┤
│ Show Account Status                           │
│ Switch to New Username                        │
│ Change Password                               │
│ Disable Account                               │
└─────────────────────────────────────────────┘




Enter-Select Option, Esc-Exit, F1-Help
```

Figure 9.27
The User Account Management menu.

> **Note**
> After you switch to a different user name on a server into which you are logged, any drive or printer redirections you had before are still maintained. The access rights to the network drives and printers may change, depending on the ACL rights assigned to the user account into which you are now logged.

The User Account Management menu displays three user account management functions available to you: Show Account Status, Change Password, and Disable Account:

✔ **Show Account Status.** This function displays information about your account, such as date of last login, account expiration date, password expiration date, privileges, number of concurrent logins, and time of day set aside for logins. You cannot change this information. Only the network administrator has access to these items. You can, however, note what is contained in your account status and request the administrator to make changes as necessary.

Figure 9.28 is an example of a User Account Status screen when the Show Account Status option is selected from the User Account Management menu.

Figure 9.28
The User Account Status screen.

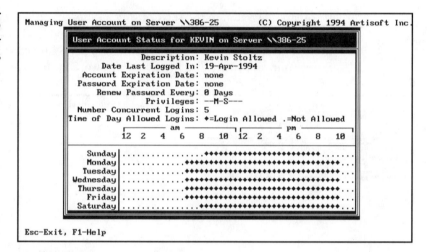

```
Managing User Account on Server \\386-25        (C) Copyright 1994 Artisoft Inc.
┌────────────────────────────────────────────────────────────────────────────┐
│ User Account Status for KEVIN on Server \\386-25                             │
│                              Description: Kevin Stoltz                        │
│                     Date Last Logged In: 19-Apr-1994                         │
│                  Account Expiration Date: none                               │
│                 Password Expiration Date: none                               │
│                     Renew Password Every: 0 Days                             │
│                              Privileges: --M-S---                            │
│                 Number Concurrent Logins: 5                                  │
│         Time of Day Allowed Logins: *=Login Allowed .=Not Allowed            │
│                  ┌─────── am ────────┐┌──────── pm ────────┐                 │
│                  12  2   4   6   8   10 12  2   4   6   8   10                │
│                                                                              │
│      Sunday    ...............*****************.......                       │
│      Monday    ...............*********************...                       │
│      Tuesday   ...............*********************...                       │
│      Wednesday ...............*********************...                       │
│      Thursday  ...............*********************...                       │
│      Friday    ...............*********************...                       │
│      Saturday  ...............*********************...                       │
└────────────────────────────────────────────────────────────────────────────┘
 Esc-Exit, F1-Help
```

✔ **Change Password.** This function enables you to completely change the password for your account. NET prompts you to enter your old password. After it validates your access rights to the account, NET asks you to enter the new password; it then prompts you to type your new password again to confirm that you know what it is before the new password is saved.

✔ **Disable Account.** This function enables you to make your account inactive. As a user, you might want to disable your account to prevent access by another network user when you are absent.

After you successfully disable your account and log off the network, you must get the network administrator to re-enable your account before you can log in again.

Shutting Down a Server

After you finish using your computer and network, shutdown is easy. If your computer is configured as a LANtastic server, press Ctrl+Alt+Del, just like you do to reboot your computer. A screen appears on the server that shows if any other users are logged in, and if any files are open. If no logins or open files appear on the screen, select the S option. This action sends a message to the other machines that the server is shutting down. If your computer is configured as a LANtastic workstation and not a server, other computers do not access your computer. You can, therefore, turn off your computer as you normally do without having to worry about affecting others.

You can view which users are currently logged in to your server and what activities they are performing, by selecting the Monitor & Manage Server Activity option from the NET program main menu.

Whether your computer is configured as a server or a workstation, always log out of any other network servers you are using before you turn off your computer. If you don't, there is a chance that the server might not allow you to log in later—in which case, you might have to restart the server.

Perhaps a better way to announce a server/network shutdown is to use the LANtastic command NET SEND and include a message that the server is shutting down in 15 minutes, or some reasonable time frame. This gives the other users time to close and save their work before you actually complete the shutdown.

If you have the S privilege, you can schedule an automatic server shutdown. From the LANtastic NET program main menu, select Monitor & Manage Server Activity. Choose the server you want to shut down and then press F2 + Control. From the Server Control Options menu, select Schedule Server Shutdown (see fig. 9.29). Specify the number of minutes until shutdown and press F2 + Execute to carry out the procedure.

The following is an example of a message that you might send across the network:

```
NET SEND * "Server KSOFFICE shutting down in 15 minutes!"
```

The NET SEND command sends a pop-up message to every user on the network that the KSOFFICE server shuts down in 15 minutes.

When you are finally ready to shut down, confirm that others are finished using your computer by pressing Ctrl+Alt+Del once to see if any logins or open files exist. If not, shut your computer off.

Figure 9.29
The Server
Control Options
menu.

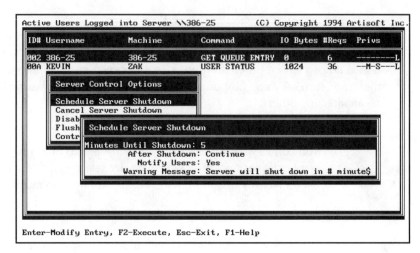

```
Active Users Logged into Server \\386-25        (C) Copyright 1994 Artisoft Inc.

 ID# Username          Machine          Command          IO Bytes #Reqs  Privs

 002 386-25            386-25           GET QUEUE ENTRY  0          6    --------L
 00A KEVIN             ZAK              USER STATUS      1024      36    --M-S---L
        ┌──────────────────────────────────┐
        │ Server Control Options           │
        ├──────────────────────────────────┤
        │ Schedule Server Shutdown         │
        │ Cancel Server Shutdown           │
        │ Disab┌─────────────────────────────────────────────────┐
        │ Flush│ Schedule Server Shutdown                        │
        │ Contr├─────────────────────────────────────────────────┤
        └──────│Minutes Until Shutdown: 5                        │
               │         After Shutdown: Continue                │
               │           Notify Users: Yes                     │
               │         Warning Message: Server will shut down in # minute$│
               └─────────────────────────────────────────────────┘


 Enter-Modify Entry, F2-Execute, Esc-Exit, F1-Help
```

Shutting off a server with open files can result in lost data or damaged files. Always make sure that no one is accessing programs or data on your computer before turning it off.

Using LANtastic with Windows

LANtastic provides several communications features in Windows. By using the Windows LANtastic NET program you can send and receive electronic mail and carry on an interactive Chat session with another user. LANtastic also includes a sophisticated electronic mail and scheduling program called Artisoft Exchange, which is described in Chapter 13, "Using Artisoft Exchange." The following sections describe the LANtastic Mail and Chat features available from the LANtastic NET program in Windows, as well as the features available for managing your LANtastic account.

Using the Mail Function

LANtastic Mail enables you to communicate with others by sending and receiving messages. You can compose and send a message to another user. The user for which the message is meant is then notified that a message has been sent. Messages are read, saved to a file, forwarded to another user, or deleted. The Artisoft Sounding board enhances the features available with Mail by providing Voice Mail capability.

Sending and Receiving Mail Using the LANtastic Net Program

To send mail using the LANtastic NET program, perform the following steps:

1. Start LANtastic NET by double-clicking on the LANtastic NET Connections icon in the LANtastic program group; or, with the LANtastic Net Connections icon selected, select **O**pen from the Program Manager's **F**ile menu. The LANtastic Net program's main menu appears (see fig. 9.30).

The LANtastic NET program starts when you run Windows. Another way, therefore, to make LANtastic NET the active window is by pressing the Alt+Tab or by pressing Ctrl+Esc and selecting LANtastic Net from the Task List dialog box.

Figure 9.30
The LANtastic NET program main menu.

2. From the LANtastic NET program main menu, select the **M**ail icon or select Send and Receive **M**ail from the **N**et menu.

Check the **O**ptions menu and make sure the Use Artisoft Exchange **M**ail option is not selected (see fig. 9.31). Artisoft Exchange is a sophisticated mail and scheduling program new to LANtastic 6.0 and is discussed in Chapter 13, "Using Artisoft Exchange." This chapter discusses the LANtastic Mail features that are always available from LANtastic and operate in both DOS and Windows.

Figure 9.31
The LANtastic
NET program
Options menu
without the Use
Artisoft
Exchange Mail
option enabled.

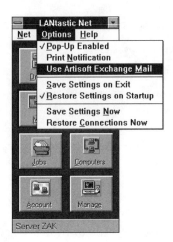

3. Select the computer that you use to store the mail messages from the Select Computer dialog box (see fig. 9.32). The computers to which you are currently logged in are shown in the Current Connections list. You can connect (log in) to other computers not shown on the list by selecting the **C**onnections button.

Figure 9.32
The Select
Computer
dialog box.

The My Mail dialog box appears showing Incoming Mail and Outgoing Mail (see fig. 9.33).

Each server set up with an @MAIL resource can contain a mail queue in which messages are stored. Only the messages on the server selected are shown on this screen. If you want to see messages you have on another server, select Computers or choose the Select **C**omputer option from the **M**ail menu.

To avoid confusion, a single server should be designated as the LANtastic Mail server that everyone uses to send and receive mail.

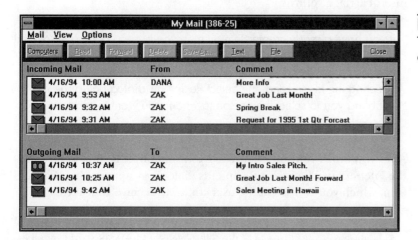

Figure 9.33
The My Mail dialog box.

Tip

To show more of the list on the screen, maximize the My Mail dialog box by clicking on the up icon in the upper right-hand corner of the window.

4. To create a mail message, select the **T**ext button or from the **M**ail menu select S**e**nd and then Use **E**ditor. The Mail Message window appears (see fig. 9.34).

Figure 9.34
The Mail Message window.

5. Type your message as if you are using a word processor; however, the LANtastic editor does not wrap words at the ends of lines, so you must insert carriage returns.

If you have already created a mail message to send and have saved it as a file, or wish to send a file to someone, select the **F**ile button. You can also select S**e**nd from the **M**ail menu and then Send a **F**ile. After selecting the file to send, the Select Recipients dialog box appears, enabling you to select the person to whom you want to send the file. Proceed as described below.

6. After you finish your message, send your mail by selecting **S**end from the **F**ile menu. The Select Recipients dialog box appears (see fig. 9.35) from which you can select the users that will receive your message.

Selecting Account Names in the Fill Recipient **L**ist With field lists all the user accounts on the selected server. Selecting Connected Users only shows those users who are currently logged in to the selected server.

Figure 9.35
The Select
Recipients
dialog box.

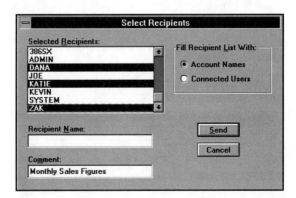

7. Choose the recipients for your message by selecting users from the Selected Recipients list or by typing a name into the Recipient Name field. Type a comment in the Comment field if desired and press **S**end to send the message. The Comment you enter is the title that appears next to the mail item after it is sent.

The mail you send now appears in the Outgoing Mail list in the My Mail dialog box (see fig. 9.36). In the example shown, DANA, ZAK, and KATIE were selected to receive the mail; therefore, an outgoing mail item appears for each of these three users. Activities are listed in ascending order, with the most recent activity listed at the top.

You can send mail to multiple users by selecting more than one user from the Selected Recipients list, or by using a wildcard in the Recipient Name field.

If you want to select more than one user in the Selected Recipients list, hold down Ctrl while selecting. In order to select the whole list or a portion of the list, click on the first user and then—while holding down Shift—click on the last user in the selected range. This method selects all the names listed between the first and last user.

If you want to send a message to everyone using wildcards, specify * in the Recipient Name field. In order to send the message to the users with SALES as the first part of their name, specify SALES* in the Recipient Name field.

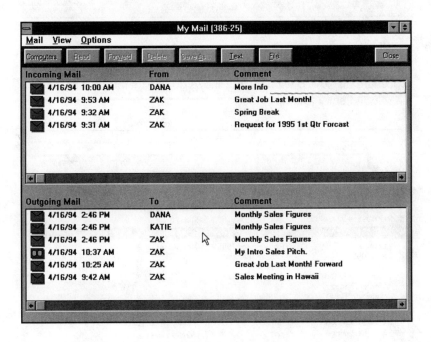

Figure 9.36
The message just sent is shown in the Outgoing Mail section for three users, in the bottom half of the screen.

To read incoming mail (or the outgoing mail you have sent), select the mail item to read from the Incoming Mail list and click on the **R**ead button. The Read Mail Message window displays the message (see fig. 9.37).

Figure 9.37
Reading a mail
message.

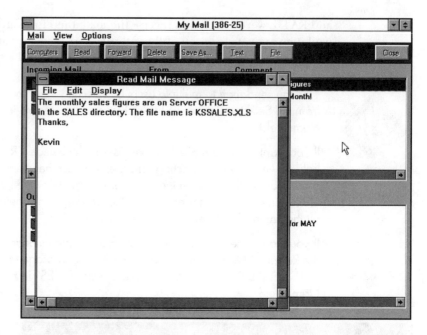

In order to display additional information about a selected mail item, with the mail item selected, choose De_tail from the **M**ail menu. This procedure displays a window that shows additional information about the selected entry (see fig. 9.38).

Figure 9.38
Detailed
information
about a selected
mail item.

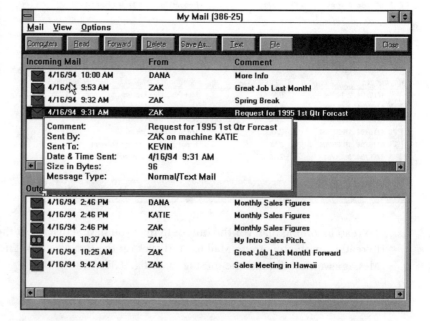

To delete a mail item you have sent, select the item to be deleted from the Outgoing Mail list, then click on the **D**elete button or choose **D**elete from the **M**ail menu.

Managing Your Mail

An important aspect of being a user on a network shared by others is your responsibility to manage your mail. If you do not remove mail messages that accumulate, you use up valuable disk space. More importantly, if you allow messages to accumulate in the mail queue, you slow down the NET utility by forcing it to search through all the messages in the mail queue area to select and display the mail for a specific account.

> Your mail queue is not difficult to manage. You already have been introduced to most of the required functions. What you need is the dedication to do your part of the job. Set a regular schedule to review messages in your Incoming Mail and Outgoing Mail lists. Ideally, you should read your mail regularly and then delete it or copy it to a file on disk.

Features available for managing LANtastic Mail include deleting mail, forwarding mail to another user, and saving mail as files.

To delete mail items from your Incoming Mail or Outgoing mail lists, select the mail item to be deleted and select the **D**elete button or choose **D**elete from the **M**ail menu.

To forward a mail item to another user, select the mail item to be forwarded and then select the For**w**ard button, or choose **F**orward from the **M**ail menu. The Select Participants dialog box appears. This box enables you to select the users to whom you want to forward the mail item. The process works the same way as the method for selecting users to receive mail you create.

To save a mail item as a file, select the mail item to be saved and then select the Save **A**s button or choose Save **A**s from the **M**ail menu. The Save As dialog box appears, which enables you to save the selected mail item by any name and to any location you choose (see fig. 9.39).

> Unlike the DOS LANtastic Mail utility, the Windows LANtastic Mail utility does not include an option to print a mail item. If you want to print a selected mail item to your printer, you must save the mail item as a file and then use one of the Windows utility programs such as File Manager or Notepad to print the file.

Figure 9.39
Saving a mail
item as a file.

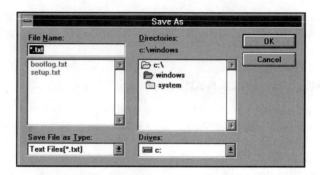

Using the Super Mail Privilege

The network administrator can use the Super Mail (also called the M) privilege to
manage the entire mail queue. This feature is important in a large network that
has many users who generate a large volume of daily mail messages. The privilege
enables a network administrator to read and delete all users' old mail from the
queue. The intent is to free up storage space and restore speed to the NET mail
search utility.

Because the administrator can read other people's mail, the administrator needs to
be sensitive to users' feelings about their mail items. Do not give this privilege to
anyone else.

Provide all users with a detailed policy that states the way the
administrator manages the mail queue and what access rights users
have. A policy helps prevent future misunderstandings between the
administrator and the users.

Make it clear to your users that the administrator deletes only mail items that are
several days old. The user is responsible for keeping saved mail items to a minimum. If users want to retain copies, they should print them out or save them as
files to their own hard disk.

A user with the Super Mail privilege is able to select the All Mail option from the
View menu, which displays the All Mail dialog box that lists all the mail items (see
fig. 9.40). The icons to the left of the mail item give additional information about
the mail, such as the speaker icon that represents voice mail. You can manage mail
items on the list using the features previously described.

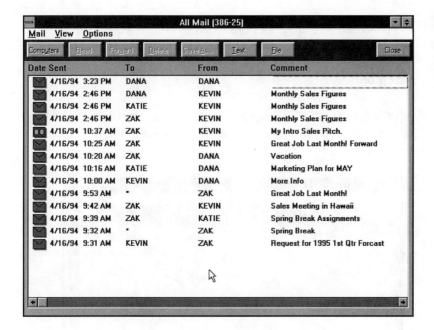

Figure 9.40
All the mail
items for server
386-25.

Using the Chat Function

LANtastic provides features that enable you to Chat with another user by typing information in a window. Each user has two windows on his or her screen: one to type in and the other to view what is being typed by the other person. If you have an Artisoft Sounding Board, you can also carry on a voice Chat session with another user.

In Windows, Chat is available as an option in the NET program.

Using the NET Program Chat Function

You can use the LANtastic Chat feature to carry on an interactive Chat session with another user by performing the following steps:

1. Start LANtastic NET by double-clicking on the LANtastic NET Connections icon in the LANtastic program group, or, with the LANtastic Net Connections icon selected, select **O**pen from the Program Manager's **F**ile menu.

The LANtastic NET program starts when you run Windows. Another way to make LANtastic NET the active window is by pressing Alt+Tab, or by pressing Ctrl+Esc and selecting LANtastic Net from the Task List dialog box.

2. From the LANtastic NET program main menu, select Cha̲t or select Ch̲at with Someone from the N̲et menu. The Chat dialog box appears (see fig. 9.41).

Figure 9.41
The Chat dialog
box.

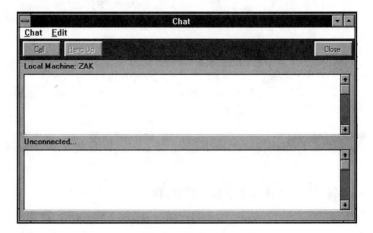

3. To initiate a call to another computer, select the Ca̲ll button or select C̲all from the C̲hat menu. The Call dialog box appears (see fig. 9.42).

Unlike LANtastic Mail, in which you send a message to another user, LANtastic Chat requires you to enter the name of the computer where the person with whom you want to Chat is logged in. This is why you might want to name your machines after the primary users.

4. Type the name of the computer to be called, such as KATIE (see fig. 9.42), and press Enter.

The computer you call displays a pop-up message on its screen, notifying the user that a Chat is being requested. The other user can type **NET Chat** from DOS or select Chat from Windows to establish the connection.

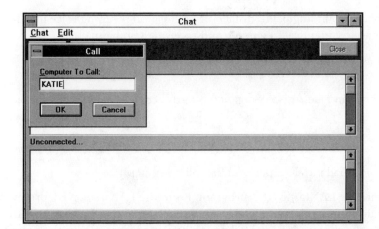

Figure 9.42
The Call dialog box.

5. Type your message in the upper (Local Machine) box. Your message is displayed immediately on the remote machine's screen as you type. The message typed by the user on the other computer appears in the Remote Machine box on your computer. You can hold an interactive conversation this way (see fig. 9.43).

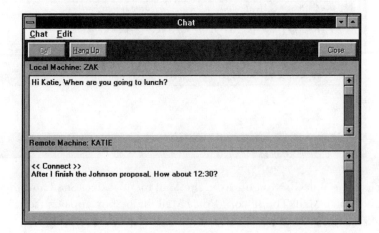

Figure 9.43
A sample Chat session.

6. After you finish, end the Chat session by selecting the **H**ang Up button or select **H**ang Up from the **C**hat menu.

Using Voice Mail

The Artisoft Sounding Board enables you to send and receive voice mail and use voice Chat features in LANtastic. Each computer that is to record or listen to voice mail must have a sounding board installed. Sending and receiving voice mail in LANtastic is almost identical to sending and receiving regular mail.

Installing the Artisoft Sounding Board is covered later in this chapter.

To send a voice mail message, perform the following steps:

1. Start the LANtastic NET program. From the LANtastic NET program main menu, select the **M**ail icon or select Send and Receive **M**ail from the **N**et menu. The My Mail dialog box appears and, with the Sounding Board installed, also has a Voic**e** button (see fig. 9.44).

Figure 9.44
The My Mail dialog box with the additional Voice button.

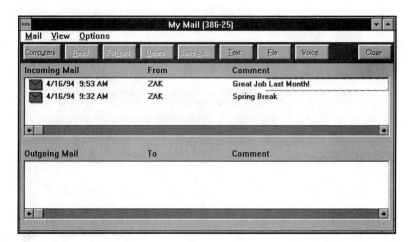

2. Select the Voic**e** button or, from the **M**ail menu, select S**e**nd and then Send **V**oice Mail. The Record Voice Mail dialog box appears (see fig. 9.45).

3. To start recording your message, select the **R**ecord button. When you finish recording, select the **S**top button. You can review your message by selecting the **P**lay button.

4. Select Send to continue. The Select Recipients dialog box appears (see fig. 9.46). Select the users you want to receive your voice mail message in the same way you select recipients for normal mail.

5. Select the **S**end button and your voice mail is sent to the selected recipients.

Figure 9.45
The Record Voice Mail dialog box.

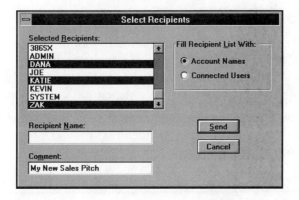

Figure 9.46
Selecting the recipients for voice mail.

The recipient can listen to voice mail messages by first selecting the voice mail item (indicated by a speaker icon) and then selecting the **P**lay button (see fig. 9.47). The recipient listens to the voice mail message by selecting the **P**lay button in the Play Voice Mail dialog box (see fig. 9.48).

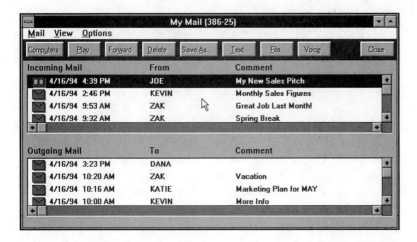

Figure 9.47
The My Mail dialog box listing a voice mail item and the associated Play button.

Figure 9.48
Listening to a
voice mail
message.

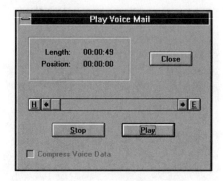

Managing Your User Account

The NET program provides you with limited control of your network account. The
Account option enables you to check the status of your account, change your
account password, and disable your account. You should become familiar with the
three account management functions. To proceed, perform the following steps:

1. From the NET program main menu, select **A**ccount or select View
    Account Information from the **N**et menu. The Select Computer dialog
    box appears (see fig. 9.49).

Figure 9.49
Selecting the
computer on
which to view
your account
information.

2. Select the server on which you want to manage your account. If you
    are not logged in to the server, you may do so at this time by selecting
    the **C**onnections button. After you select the computer on which you
    want to view your account information, the Account Management
    dialog box appears (see fig. 9.50).

The Account Management dialog box displays information about your account, such as date of last login, account expiration date, password expiration date, privileges, number of concurrent logins, and time of day set aside for logins. You cannot change this information. Only the network administrator has access to these items. You can, however, note what is contained in your account status and request the administrator to make changes as necessary.

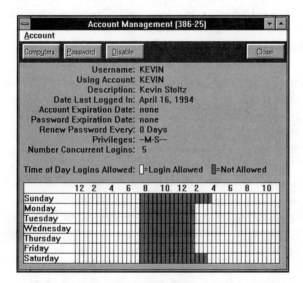

Figure 9.50
The Account Management dialog box.

In addition to viewing your current account information, you can change your password or disable your account.

To change your password, select the **P**assword button or select Change **P**assword from the **A**ccount menu. The Change Password dialog box appears, prompting you for your old password and the new password. Entering the appropriate passwords and then selecting OK changes your password.

To disable your account, select the **D**isable button or select **D**isable Account from the **A**ccount menu. The Disable Account dialog box appears, asking you to enter your password to confirm. Type your password and select OK to disable your account.

After you successfully disable your account and log out of the network, you must get the network administrator to re-enable your account before you can log in again.

Shutting Down a Server

After you finish using your computer and network, shutdown is easy. Exit Windows to return to a DOS prompt. If your computer is configured as a LANtastic server, press Ctrl+Alt+Del, just like you do to reboot your computer. A screen appears on the server, showing if any other users are logged in to the server and if any files are open. If no logins or open files appear on the screen, select the S option. This sends a message to the other machines that the server is shutting down. If your computer is configured as a LANtastic workstation and not a server, then other computers do not access your computer, so you can turn your computer off as you normally do without having to worry about affecting other users.

You can see which users are currently logged in to your server and what activities they are performing by selecting the Manag**e** icon from the NET program main menu or by selecting Ma**n**age Other Computers from the **N**et menu.

Whether your computer is configured as a server or a workstation, always log out of any other network servers you are using before you turn off your computer. If you don't, there is a chance that the server might not allow you to log in later, in which case, you might have to restart the server.

Perhaps a better way to announce a server shutdown is to send a LANtastic pop-up message to users that states that the server is shutting down in 15 minutes, or some other reasonable time frame. This gives the users time to close and save their work before you actually complete the shutdown.

If you have the S privilege, you can schedule an automatic server shutdown. From the LANtastic NET program main menu, select the Manag**e** icon or select Ma**n**age Other Computers from the **N**et menu. From the **M**anage menu in the User Statistics dialog box, select **S**hutdown (see fig. 9.51). The Computer Shutdown dialog box appears (see fig. 9.52), and in it you may specify the number of minutes until shutdown as well as the message to notify users of the shutdown. After entering the number of minutes until shutdown, select OK to initiate the shutdown procedure and then Yes to confirm the shutdown request.

The computer that you are shutting down should not be running Windows at the time the shutdown occurs. Attempting to shut down a computer while it is running Windows may lead to unstable behavior on the computer being shut down.

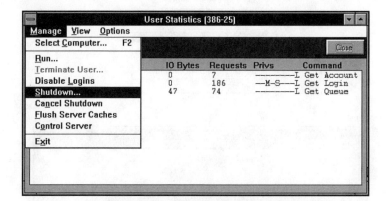

Figure 9.51
Selecting the Shutdown option.

Figure 9.52
The Computer Shutdown dialog box.

If you want to send a pop-up message to other LANtastic users, activate the LANtastic NET program and select Send Pop-Up Message from the Net menu (see fig. 9.53). The Pop-Up Messages dialog box appears (see fig. 9.54). If you want to send the message to everyone, type * in the Send To field. In the Message field, type the message you want to send, such as "Server KSOFFICE is shutting down in 15 minutes!" Select the Send button to send the pop-up message to all computers in the network.

When you are finally ready to shut down, confirm that others are finished using your computer by pressing Ctrl+Alt+Del once to see if any logins or open files exist. If not, shut your computer off.

Figure 9.53
Selecting Send Pop-Up message from the Net menu.

Figure 9.54
Sending a Pop-Up message.

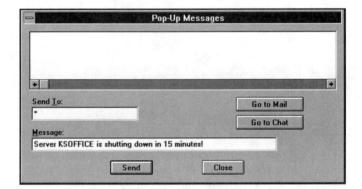

Shutting off a server with open files can result in lost data or damaged files. Always make sure that no one is accessing programs or data on your computer before turning it off.

The Artisoft Sounding Board

The Artisoft Sounding Board is a hardware/software product that, among other things, provides digitized voice-mail capability for the LANtastic Chat and MAIL functions. Every computer that uses the voice-mail option must have a Sounding Board and its supporting software installed. Digitized sound requires 8 KB of disk space per second of recorded sound (or 4 KB per second with compression turned on). An average voice message of 25 seconds requires 200 KB (100 KB with compression on) of disk space.

The LANtastic Voice Mail feature takes its required storage space from the server's spool area. Users must be diligent about maintaining voice-mail queues and delete mail often to free up space.

Artisoft provides the capability for compressed-mode sound recording. This mode reduces storage-space requirements by half, but some degradation occurs in the sound reproduction quality.

The Sounding Board also supports the LANtastic Chat feature. If two users have the board and software installed, they can carry on a Chat session that is much like a phone conversation. This type of communication does not require any storage space. During times of heavy network traffic, you may experience some delay in voice Chat transmissions.

The following are some of the features of the Sounding Board:

- ✔ Windows 3.1-compatible

- ✔ Full duplex operation, enabling simultaneous play and record

- ✔ PCM play and record at 8, 11, and 22 KHz

- ✔ Line-level audio in for external connection of CD player, cassette recorder, or radio

- ✔ Line-level audio out for external connection of a speaker or an amplifier (playback is mono only)

- ✔ Standard telephone handset connection (handset is included)

- ✔ Two strappable DMA (Direct Memory Access) channels

Installing the Sounding Board

You install the Sounding Board adapter in a similar manner as network adapters. Before you install the Sounding Board, make sure that the default jumper settings are set correctly to provide you with full duplex sound capability. Jumpers J1 and J2 should be set in such a way that the black plastic jumper covers pins 2 and 3.

Disable one of the jumpers (J1 or J2) only if one of your DMA channels is unavailable. If you disable one of the channels, you cannot perform full duplex (simultaneous) recording and playback operations.

After you verify the jumper settings, perform the following steps to install your Sounding Board:

1. Turn off your computer and all peripherals attached to it.

2. Remove the screws from the back of the computer and open its case.

3. Find an empty bus interface slot and remove the back panel cover plate and screw.

4. Grasp the Sounding Board carefully and place it into the empty slot.

The Sounding Board is sensitive to static electricity. Be sure to ground yourself by touching the power unit inside your computer before touching the Sounding Board.

5. Press down firmly on the back of the board until it seats fully in the slot.

6. Fasten the adapter's mounting bracket to the back plate with the screw you removed in step 3.

7. Replace the computer's case and fastening screws.

8. Connect the headset cord to the phone plug jack in the back of the Sounding Board.

9. You can attach other devices as desired—use the jack labeled IN for input and the jack labeled OUT for output connections.

The Micro Channel Sounding Board installation is similar, except you do not have any manual jumper settings to perform. The Micro Channel version has special installation software to configure the DMA channel settings.

Installing the Sounding Board Software

Use the following steps to install the Artisoft Sounding Board software. The first set of installation procedures is for a DOS installation, and the next set is for a Windows installation.

To install the device-driver program in DOS, perform the following steps:

1. Put the Artisoft Distribution Disk in drive A.

2. Type **A:** and press Enter.

3. Type **PCSETUP C:\LANTASTI** and press Enter.

If you do not have LANtastic installed in a directory called LANTASTI, you must enter the correct directory name in step 3.

If you are installing the Micro Channel version of the Artisoft Sounding Board, you need to type **MCASETUP** in step 3.

The Artisoft Sounding Board software is copied into the same directory on your hard disk as LANtastic. Before you can use the Sounding Board to record voice messages (or other sounds), you must load and run the device driver. Change to the LANTASTI directory on the C drive (type **C:**, then **CD\LANTASTI**, and press Enter). Type **SOUNDBD** and press Enter (this is the DOS command-line entry to load the device driver).

If you want to verify that the device driver is loading and more than the confirmation message is displayed on your monitor, add /VERBOSE to the end of the SOUNDBD statement, as in the following command:

SOUNDBD /VERBOSE

To install the Sounding Board driver and the ArtiSound Recorder program in Windows, run the Install program as follows:

1. Launch Windows.

2. Insert the Sounding Board distribution disk in drive A.

3. Select **R**un from the **F**ile menu in the Program Manager window.

4. After the Run dialog box appears, type **A:INSTALL** in the Command Line box, and press Enter or select OK.

   The ArtiSound Installation dialog box appears (see fig. 9.55). You can choose the installation directory and whether or not you want to install the Sounding Board driver. Accept the default C:\WINDOWS directory and make sure that the Install Driver box is selected.

5. Click on the **I**nstall button to begin the installation.

Figure 9.55
The ArtiSound
Installation
program.

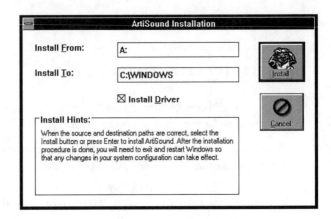

Figure 9.55
The ArtiSound
Installation
program.

6. The Install program installs the Sounding Board driver, copies the required files into the C:\WINDOWS directory, and creates the ArtiSound program group, which contains the ArtiSound Recorder program icon.

7. The Artisoft Sounding Board dialog box appears, enabling you to select the DMA channels you want to use (see fig. 9.56). Unless your computer does not support the Sounding Board using both DMA channels, leave both selected and click on OK to continue the installation.

Figure 9.56
Artisoft
Sounding Board
DMA channel
selection with the
newly created
ArtiSound
program group
in the
background.

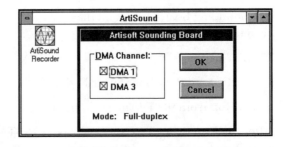

8. After the installation is finished, the Installation Complete dialog box appears (see fig. 9.57). Before the changes take effect, you must restart Windows. Click on the Restart Windows button.

The Windows drivers are installed and the Sounding Board is ready to use. In addition to the voice features LANtastic supports by using the Sounding Board, the ArtiSound Recorder program enables you to use

the Sounding Board for many other purposes, such as recording from CDs, mixing sound data, and creating special sound effects.

Figure 9.57

Installation of the Windows Sounding Board software complete.

Summary

In this chapter, you learned how to use LANtastic to communicate with others. You learned how to use the LANtastic Mail and Chat features in both DOS and Windows. In addition, you discovered ways to use voice mail with the Artisoft Sounding Board. You also learned how to manage your user account and how to shut down your server at the end of the day.

The next chapter discusses printing with LANtastic and the features available when you print with LANtastic.

Chapter Snapshot

This chapter covers all facets of network printing using LANtastic. The LANtastic network printing features discussed in this chapter include the following:

✔ The difference between a file server and print server

✔ How printing on a network differs from local printing

✔ How to configure printers for network use with LANtastic in both DOS and Windows environments

✔ How to connect to and use shared network printers in both DOS and Windows environments

✔ How to manage print jobs in the LANtastic print queue in both DOS and Windows environments

This chapter includes separate sections covering LANtastic printing features in both DOS and Windows.

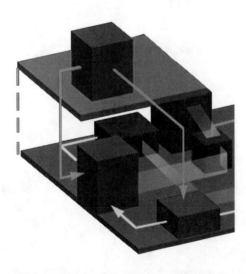

Printing with LANtastic

This chapter discusses printing with LANtastic. You learn how network printing differs from local printing. You also learn the terminology you must know to operate in a network printing environment.

After you become acquainted with the terminology, you are ready to learn the nuts and bolts of setting up your network printing. First, you learn to define printer resources, and then you learn the basic procedures you must follow to print on the network.

Understanding Network Printing

If this is your first exposure to network printing, you may find the process quite different from that of local printing, in which you have direct access and control of the printer. Another difference is that you share the printer resource(s) with other users. To use a printer resource in a network environment, you first must establish a connection to the specific printer you want to use.

When you send a print job to a printer in a LANtastic network, the file does not go directly to the printer. The file is temporarily stored in a special area on the server's hard disk called the *spool area*. Files are stored in the order in which they are received. When the printer is free, the first print job sent gets printed first, then the next job, and so on. The specifics of connecting to and using a network printer are covered in depth in the "Network Printing" section of this chapter.

One advantage of network printing is that you have access to all printers that are connected to servers on the network. You can use a laser printer for one job, a plotter for another, and a dot-matrix printer for yet a third job. You also can do all of this simultaneously!

With LANtastic's *Remote Printer Server* (RPS) program, you can even use printers that are connected to workstations. You set up the printer resource on a server, and it can be despooled to a remote printer on another workstation (or server).

Although you need to know only the name of the printer resource you want to use to print with LANtastic, you should understand the "how" of network printing to prevent interference with another user's printing job. The discussions that follow help you to understand the printing process so you can make better use of LANtastic's capabilities.

As with any technology, networking employs a specific language. Although the terminology you must know to use LANtastic is fairly limited, you will benefit from understanding the basic terms.

The following list contains definitions of some terms you see fairly often in your use of LANtastic:

✔ A *print job* is the output from an application program that is destined for a printer. The print job is transferred across the network and stored as a file before being sent to the printer.

✔ The *print spool area* is a location or directory on the server in which LANtastic stores the print files before sending them to the printer. The spool area also is referred to as the *print queue*.

✔ *Despooling* refers to the actual transmittal of the print data to the printer from the print spool area.

✔ *Logical printer streams* refer to different configurations for a printer, much like a resource name.

Suppose, for example, that you send printer-control codes to a dot-matrix printer to run in several modes. Each configuration can have a *logical name* assigned to it. After you select the logical name from the printer list, the following correct printer codes are downloaded for that configuration:

@DRAFT is for draft-mode printing

@LETTER is for letter-quality printing

@GRAPH is for graphics printing

@CONDNSD is for condensed printing

Distinguishing File Server Versus Print Server Setups

When you set up a LANtastic server, it is capable of sharing both its file resources and printer resources with others on the network. Although a LANtastic server is capable of sharing both files and printers concurrently, servers often are categorized according to their primary function of sharing files or sharing printers. The following section details both types of servers so you can understand their functions.

File Server

The LANtastic network operating system enables you to set up any computer on your network that is equipped with a hard disk as a *server*. A server's function is to provide support to other users, and it can be configured to share all its resources with other machines on the network, including its attached printer(s). Often, this type of server is referred to as a *file server*.

For more information on setting up shared network resources, see Chapters 6 and 7, "Setting Up User Accounts and Shared Resources in DOS" and "Setting Up User Accounts and Shared Resources in Windows."

By sharing its application, file, and disk resources with others, the server usually must give up a tremendous amount of hard disk storage space. Sharing resources also means that the network print queue is located on the server's hard disk, and that portions of the server's processing power are dedicated to performing print functions, as well as disk- and file-access functions.

If you have a 386- or 486-based CPU and a good amount of hard disk storage space, this mode of operation may not affect you. In a large network, however, you may find that your server's disk space is limited, or that your server is handling so many file operations that the print functions slow down. If you find yourself in this circumstance, you may want to move the print-management functions to another server.

Print Server

Because you can set up all computers with hard disks as servers in a LANtastic network, all users can access the printers attached to those servers. This setup, however, may not make the best use of your computer assets. You may not find it feasible to attach a printer to a server that also provides application and file access to other network users. In such cases, move the print-management functions to one of the other servers on the network so this server deals only with the network print functions. This setup offloads the processing requirements from the file server and helps to improve the overall efficiency of your network.

Another option you can use to offload the print functions from a server is to set up a global printer resource on the server. When a user establishes a connection to a global printer resource, LANtastic actually sets up a connection to the printer resource pointed to by the global printer resource, thereby offloading the printing responsibility to another server.

A *global resource* is a resource created on a server that points to another resource on a different server. Normally you would create a printer resource called @PRINTER, for example, which is defined as the printer connected to your LPT1 printer port. If you created a global printer resource, you could create a printer resource with a name such as @KSPRNTR, which is defined as the @LASER printer resource on the server named KSOFFICE. The following examples show a local printer resource and a global printer resource:

@PRINTER => LPT1: (@PRINTER points to LPT1: port)

@KSPRNTR => \\KSOFFICE\@LASER (@KSPRNTR points to @LASER resource on server KSOFFICE)

Remember that printers must be set up as a shared network resource before others on the network can use them.

Unlike the considerations for faster CPUs associated with the file server installation, a print server can be any computer on your network. Most printers accept data more slowly than the LANtastic despooler can provide; therefore, the despoolers end up waiting for the printer to catch up, even on slower computers. Hard disk storage, however, is a factor you must consider. You should have enough excess disk storage space so you can store multiple print jobs while you wait for the printer(s) to finish despooling the current print job .

In addition to the text contained in the file to be printed, other information may be attached to a print file by LANtastic and by your application software. LANtastic may attach some control information to print files, whereas applications may attach printer control information or PostScript header information to print files. This information requires additional, although limited, storage space.

You should allot several megabytes of free storage for the network print queue. LANtastic stores print files in the queue to await printing, which frees the sending CPU to do other things. This temporary storage for print files becomes extremely important should the printer run out of paper. Print files are stored safely as you reload the printer and bring it back online. If LANtastic runs out of disk space to store print files, you usually will see an error message displayed on your screen. Unfortunately, the error messages displayed by DOS, Windows, and your application programs often do not give you a clear indication that you have run out of disk storage space for your print files. One common error message you will see if this happens is Error Reading Drive C:.

Do not use a RAM disk for the print queue. In the event that the server is shut down or rebooted, all the information in a RAM disk area is lost. Do not take this chance with your network print files.

Using LANtastic with DOS

The following sections discuss how to define printer resources, configure printer resources, and connect to and use printer resources in the DOS environment. The same information as it applies in the Windows environment is covered later in this chapter. Also covered in the DOS section is the use of the Remote Printer Server (RPS) program, which allows any computer in your network to access the print spooler on a server to despool print jobs to its printer.

Defining Printer Resources

Before you can select and use a printer as a resource on your network, you first must define the resource so that LANtastic can recognize it. This section leads you through this process. You may remember that some of these steps were covered in Chapter 6, "Setting Up User Accounts and Shared Resources in DOS."

Printers on a network actually have two names: the DOS device name and the network resource name that the network manager assigns to them. The *DOS device name* is used by DOS and most application programs to refer to a printer, which actually is the name for the output port to which the printer attaches, such as LPT1, LPT2, COM1, or COM2. The *network resource name*, on the other hand, can be any name you choose, as long as it begins with the character @ and follows the same rules as DOS file names (eight characters maximum with a maximum three character extension). You may define multiple printer resource names for the same printer.

You can set up different print-output configurations for a single printer and give the printer more than one resource name, as discussed earlier in the terminology section of this chapter.

Perform the following steps to define a printer resource for your network:

1. Run the NET_MGR program from the DOS prompt. Type **NET_MGR** and press Enter.

   The NET_MGR menu appears.

2. Press the down-arrow key to scroll down and highlight Shared Resources Management. Then press Enter to select it.

3. Press Ins after the Resource Name list screen appears (see fig. 10.1).

4. Type the name you want to assign to this printer resource. Make sure that you precede the name by the @ sign.

   The @ sign tells LANtastic that the name is that of a printer resource. This way LANtastic will prompt you to enter an output device, such as LPT1, instead of a path name. Figure 10.2 uses @LASER as the resource name.

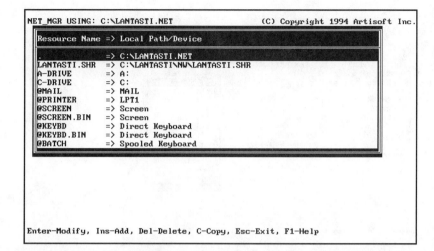

Figure 10.1
The Resource
Name list screen.

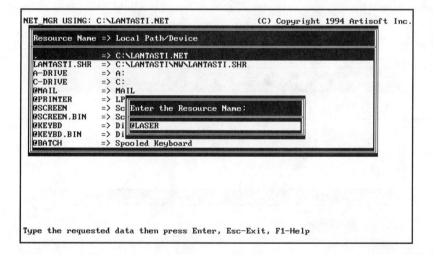

Figure 10.2
Entering a
printer resource
name.

5. From the pop-up menu, highlight the name of the output device and
   press Enter (see fig. 10.3).

The output device is the name of the port (such as LPT1) to which the
printer you want to share is physically connected. In this example, the
laser printer to be shared (with the @LASER resource name) is actually
connected to the LPT1 port on the server.

Figure 10.3

Selecting an output device port.

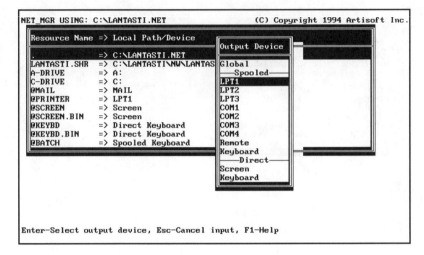

```
NET_MGR USING: C:\LANTASTI.NET          (C) Copyright 1994 Artisoft Inc.
┌─────────────────────────────────────┐┌────────────────┐
│ Resource Name => Local Path/Device   ││ Output Device  │
├─────────────────────────────────────┤├────────────────┤
│ .              => C:\LANTASTI.NET    ││Global          │
│ LANTASTI.SHR   => C:\LANTASTI\NW\LANTAS││─────Spooled────│
│ A-DRIVE        => A:                 ││LPT1            │
│ C-DRIVE        => C:                 ││LPT2            │
│ @MAIL          => MAIL               ││LPT3            │
│ @PRINTER       => LPT1               ││COM1            │
│ @SCREEN        => Screen             ││COM2            │
│ @SCREEN.BIN    => Screen             ││COM3            │
│ @KEYBD         => Direct Keyboard    ││COM4            │
│ @KEYBD.BIN     => Direct Keyboard    ││Remote          │
│ @BATCH         => Spooled Keyboard   ││Keyboard        │
│                                      ││────Direct──────│
│                                      ││Screen          │
│                                      ││Keyboard        │
│                                      │└────────────────┘
│                                      │
│ Enter-Select output device, Esc-Cancel input, F1-Help
└─────────────────────────────────────┘
```

After you complete these steps, your new printer resource is added to the Resource Name list (see fig. 10.4).

Figure 10.4

Resource Name list showing the addition of the @LASER printer resource.

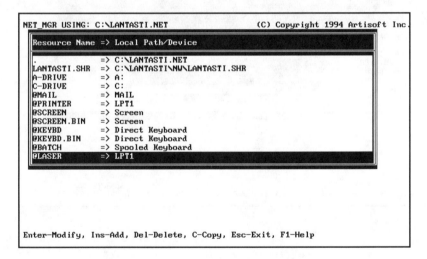

```
NET_MGR USING: C:\LANTASTI.NET          (C) Copyright 1994 Artisoft Inc.
┌─────────────────────────────────────────────────────────┐
│ Resource Name => Local Path/Device                        │
├─────────────────────────────────────────────────────────┤
│ .              => C:\LANTASTI.NET                         │
│ LANTASTI.SHR   => C:\LANTASTI\NW\LANTASTI.SHR             │
│ A-DRIVE        => A:                                      │
│ C-DRIVE        => C:                                      │
│ @MAIL          => MAIL                                    │
│ @PRINTER       => LPT1                                    │
│ @SCREEN        => Screen                                  │
│ @SCREEN.BIN    => Screen                                  │
│ @KEYBD         => Direct Keyboard                         │
│ @KEYBD.BIN     => Direct Keyboard                         │
│ @BATCH         => Spooled Keyboard                        │
│ @LASER         => LPT1                                    │
│                                                           │
│ Enter-Modify, Ins-Add, Del-Delete, C-Copy, Esc-Exit, F1-Help
└─────────────────────────────────────────────────────────┘
```

Now that you have entered the name for the resource and established the physical output port connection, you can set up the actual configuration of the printer control file within LANtastic.

Configuring Printer Resources

Naming the printer resource and assigning the physical output port to which the printer is connected are the only steps required to actually set up a printer resource. LANtastic provides many options for configuring your shared printer resources. Figure 10.5 shows the Detailed Information screen for the @LASER printer resource setup.

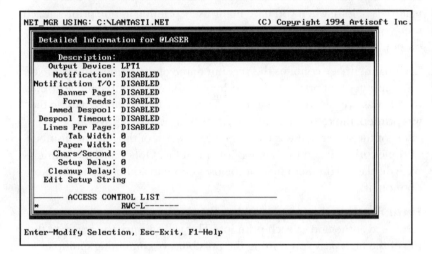

```
NET_MGR USING: C:\LANTASTI.NET                (C) Copyright 1994 Artisoft Inc.
  Detailed Information for @LASER
      Description:
    Output Device: LPT1
     Notification: DISABLED
 Notification T/O: DISABLED
      Banner Page: DISABLED
       Form Feeds: DISABLED
     Immed Despool: DISABLED
   Despool Timeout: DISABLED
    Lines Per Page: DISABLED
        Tab Width: 0
      Paper Width: 0
     Chars/Second: 0
      Setup Delay: 0
    Cleanup Delay: 0
    Edit Setup String

       ACCESS CONTROL LIST
 *            RWC-L--------

 Enter-Modify Selection, Esc-Exit, F1-Help
```

Figure 10.5
The Printer resource Detailed Information screen.

The Detailed Information screen contains the following fields:

✔ **Description.** In this field, you enter a description of your printer resource. You can use up to 64 characters.

✔ **Output Device.** In this field, you assign the physical printer connection port on the server. The port may be either a serial or a parallel port. The port listed is the one you chose when you defined the printer resource.

Parallel and *serial* ports are connectors on the back of your computer to which printers and other devices may be connected. Printers are usually connected to a parallel port while plotters are usually connected to a serial port.

✔ **Notification.** If this field is enabled, any user logged in to the server who has the operator privilege (O) will be notified of a situation that needs user intervention, such as when a printer is out of paper. The default value for this field is disabled.

✔ **Notification T/O.** If notification is enabled, the value in this field is the number of seconds that must elapse before the operator is notified of an event that requires operator intervention. If the condition is corrected before the notification is sent, the notification is canceled. The default value for this field is disabled.

✔ **Banner Page.** You can turn the two settings on or off by pressing Enter. The display changes from DISABLED to ENABLED. If you enable this feature, LANtastic prints a banner page before each print job. This feature is helpful when you have many users printing to one printer. Each user's output is easily identifiable by the banner page attached to the output. The default value for this field is disabled.

Each banner page contains the account name of the sender; the name of the computer that originated the print job; the day, month, and year that the file was printed; the time in hours, minutes, and seconds that the file was printed; the resource name of the printer used; the physical port name of the server that was used; the paper width of the file; the number of copies printed; and the name of the print file. Optionally, the banner page displays a comment field, if the user chose to add one, and the tab position, if any.

✔ **Form Feeds.** If this field is enabled, the printer is instructed to put a form feed at the end of each print job. This will advance the paper to the top of the next page, preventing the possibility of combining multiple print jobs on the same page. The default value for this field is disabled.

✔ **Immed Despool.** If you enable this field, data is sent from the spool area to a printer before all of the data is received from the originating machine. Because LANtastic does not cause the printer to wait for all of the data to be written to the spool area first, this feature speeds printing tasks. If the Immed Despool field is enabled, the Despool Timeout field automatically is set to the default value of 30 seconds. The default value for the Immed Despool field is disabled.

For immediate despooling to work for a device, confirm that the Immediate Despooling option in the Printers section of the Server Startup Parameters screen is enabled. From the main menu, select Server Startup Parameters. Select the Printers option and press Enter. Select the Immediate Despooling option and press Enter to toggle the selection between DISABLED and ENABLED.

✔ **Despool Timeout.** This field works in conjunction with the Immed Despool field. If the printer sits idle for a period of time longer than that which is set in this field, the server stops that print job and starts the next job in the queue. The aborted print job is resequenced to follow this new print job. This feature prevents an effective lockup of your printing capabilities if a file experiences difficulty as it is sent to the printer spool area. Setting the value in this field to 0 disables this function and gives the despooling print job exclusive use of the printer. This field accepts values between 0 and 3600. The default value for this field is 30 seconds.

✔ **Lines Per Page.** This field is useful only for formatting ASCII text files for printing. The value in this field is the number of lines printed before a form feed is inserted. This feature should be disabled when you print graphics or PostScript files. This field accepts values between 0 and 255. Entering a 0 will disable this field. The default value for this field is disabled.

✔ **Tab Width.** This field works only with ASCII text files. You can instruct the printer to insert a tab of a stated width at each location in which a tab is found in the text file. This field accepts values between 0 and 255. The default value is 0.

If you enable this feature and print files from word processing or graphics programs, the tab expansion feature causes printing errors. Make sure that you disable this feature before attempting to print these kinds of files.

✔ **Paper Width.** This field enables you to set the width of the paper size used for the banner page. If you are using standard 8 1/2 x 11 inch paper, you do not need to set this field.

✔ **Chars/Second.** This field enables you to set the minimum number of characters per second at which the despooler sends data to the printer. The range for this field is from 0 to 32,767 characters per second. Specifying any setting higher than 0 causes the server to give higher priority to the print task in an effort to print at the rate you specified. If you set a value that is higher than either the printer or the computer can achieve, the job prints at the highest possible speed.

Some application programs make heavy use of the CPU, resulting in very slow network printing from that server. If you notice a decrease in printing speed when running certain applications on the server to which the printer is connected, change this field to a higher value, such as 9,600, to improve printing performance.

✔ **Setup Delay.** This field enables you to set the delay in seconds that the despooler waits between sending the setup string to the printer and sending the actual data to the printer. The printer initializes to the setup

string before it begins receiving data. The range for this field is from 0 to
3,600 seconds. You do not need to use this field unless you are sending a
setup string to the printer.

✔ **Cleanup Delay.** This field enables you to set the delay in seconds that
the print spooler waits after it receives the cleanup string to reinitialize
the printer, and before it begins printing a new job. You do not need to
use this field unless you use a cleanup string for this printer. The range
for this field is from 0 to 3,600 seconds.

✔ **Edit Setup String.** This field enables you to edit the setup string that is
sent to the printer at the start of a print job. You do not need to enter a
setup string if you are using the default parameters of your printer or if
you need to send setups that your application software can handle. See
the examples in the configuration steps that follow.

The following steps illustrate how to configure a printer resource. In most situations, you do not have to change any of the settings from their default value; just
setting up the resource name and the physical port it points to is sufficient.

1. Scroll to and highlight the new printer resource you just added
   to the resource list. Press Enter to select the printer resource for
   modification.

   The Detailed Information screen appears (see fig. 10.5). In this
   example, you input the correct information for the @LASER printer
   resource.

2. Highlight the Description field and press Enter.

3. Type the description you want to use for this resource (see fig. 10.6),
   which can contain up to 64 characters.

4. You can skip the Output Device port setting field. You set this field
   when you defined the printer resource.

5. Highlight the Banner Page field, and press Enter to turn on the
   Enabled mode.

6. Highlight the Form Feeds field, and press Enter to turn on the Enabled mode.

7. Highlight the Immed Despool field, and press Enter to turn on the
   Enabled mode. Notice that this field automatically sets the Despool
   Timeout field to 30 seconds.

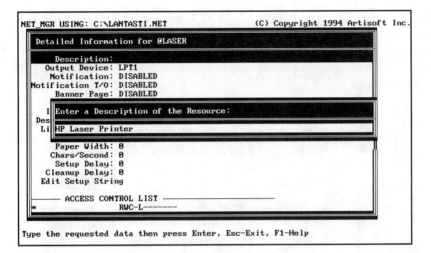

Figure 10.6
Entering a description of a resource.

8. Leave the next six options unchanged, and go to the Edit Setup String field. Press Enter to select it.

9. After the Setup String/File Menu dialog box appears, highlight Setup String and press Enter (see fig. 10.7).

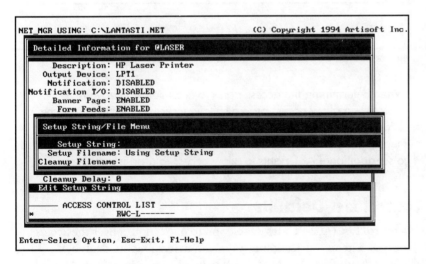

Figure 10.7
The Setup String/File Menu dialog box.

10. After the printer Setup String dialog box appears, press Ins to bring up a box for entering two-digit hexadecimal numbers or single setup-string characters (see fig. 10.8). Refer to your printer manual for the codes that correspond to the codes that you need to enter.

If you enter the hexadecimal codes, NET_MGR calculates the corresponding ASCII character, and if you enter individual ASCII characters, NET_MGR calculates the corresponding hexadecimal codes. Both the HEX code and the character are displayed in the printer Setup String field.

Figure 10.8
Entering the
setup string.

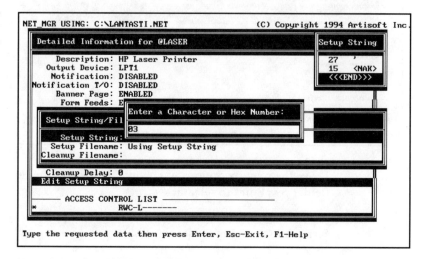

```
NET_MGR USING: C:\LANTASTI.NET                (C) Copyright 1994 Artisoft Inc.
┌─────────────────────────────────────────────────────┬───────────────────┐
│ Detailed Information for @LASER                       │ Setup String       │
│                                                       │                    │
│        Description: HP Laser Printer                  │   27        '      │
│      Output Device: LPT1                              │   15     <NAK>     │
│       Notification: DISABLED                          │   <<<END>>>        │
│   Notification T/O: DISABLED                          │                    │
│        Banner Page: ENABLED                           │                    │
│         Form Feeds: E┌─────────────────────────────────────┐              │
│ ┌──────────────────┐ │ Enter a Character or Hex Number:    │              │
│ │ Setup String/Fil │ │ 03                                  │              │
│ │                  │ └─────────────────────────────────────┘              │
│ │   Setup String:                                                          │
│ │  Setup Filename: Using Setup String                                      │
│ │ Cleanup Filename:                                                        │
│ │                                                                          │
│      Cleanup Delay: 0                                                      │
│  Edit Setup String                                                         │
│                                                                            │
│         ──── ACCESS CONTROL LIST ────                                      │
│ *                   RWC-L--------                                          │
└────────────────────────────────────────────────────────────────────────────┘
  Type the requested data then press Enter, Esc-Exit, F1-Help
```

11. Now scroll to the Access Control List area.

    The codes that appear as defaults are sufficient for most cases.

When determining the access rights to a printer, you have two choices—to allow access or to disallow access. Printer resources by default include the * account with the ACL rights of RWC-L----, which means that all accounts have full access to the printer. You do not need to set additional ACL rights to allow access to a printer resource.

Access Control List Defaults

The Access Control List (ACL) codes enable you to have control over the access to network resources. The network administrator can determine the degree of control by setting the different ACLs for each network resource. Printer ACLs can be set for each account, either to allow access to a printer or to disallow access.

In figure 10.8, the line that appears below the Access Control List heading has an asterisk in the left-hand column. This asterisk indicates that all users are granted access to the Read, Write, Create, and File Lookup functions. These ACL rights do not make as much sense for a printer resource as they do for a drive/file resource.

For the following example, suppose that you want give everyone in your office access to your laser printer, but you do not want to allow guests to use it. In this situation, you have set up an ACL group called GENERAL, of which everyone in your office is a member. The GUEST account will have no access to your laser printer. To set up your printer resource with these access controls, perform the following steps:

1. Scroll to and highlight the * ACL line. Press the F4 key to clear all access rights (see fig. 10.9). Because all accounts are included when you specify *, as it stands now, no accounts have access to the printer resource @LASER.

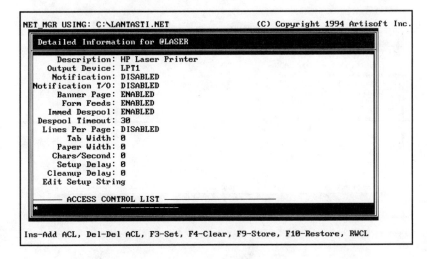

```
NET_MGR USING: C:\LANTASTI.NET            (C) Copyright 1994 Artisoft Inc.
┌──────────────────────────────────────────────────────────────┐
│  Detailed Information for @LASER                               │
│ ┌────────────────────────────────────────────────────────┐   │
│ │      Description: HP Laser Printer                       │   │
│ │    Output Device: LPT1                                   │   │
│ │     Notification: DISABLED                               │   │
│ │ Notification T/O: DISABLED                               │   │
│ │      Banner Page: ENABLED                                │   │
│ │       Form Feeds: ENABLED                                │   │
│ │    Immed Despool: ENABLED                                │   │
│ │  Despool Timeout: 30                                     │   │
│ │   Lines Per Page: DISABLED                               │   │
│ │        Tab Width: 0                                      │   │
│ │      Paper Width: 0                                      │   │
│ │     Chars/Second: 0                                      │   │
│ │      Setup Delay: 0                                      │   │
│ │    Cleanup Delay: 0                                      │   │
│ │  Edit Setup String                                       │   │
│ │                                                          │   │
│ │  ──── ACCESS CONTROL LIST ─────────                      │   │
│ │*      ─────────────                                      │   │
│ └────────────────────────────────────────────────────────┘   │
│ Ins-Add ACL, Del-Del ACL, F3-Set, F4-Clear, F9-Store, F10-Restore, RWCL │
└──────────────────────────────────────────────────────────────┘
```

Figure 10.9
Clearing the ACL rights for all accounts.

2. With the highlight bar on the * line, press Ins and type the name of the user account you want to add to the ACL.

   For this example, type **GENERAL** and press Enter (see fig. 10.10). The new GENERAL account appears on the list above the default * account (see fig. 10.11). Notice that when entering a new account to the Access Control List, the necessary ACL rights (RWC-L----) are set automatically to allow full access to the printer resource.

Figure 10.10
Adding the GENERAL account to the Access Control List.

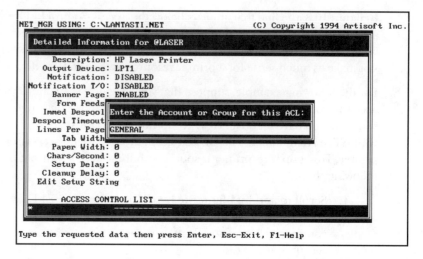

Figure 10.11
The GENERAL account added to the ACL.

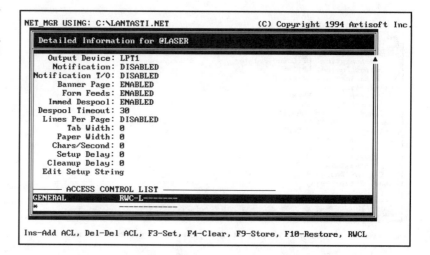

3. Press the Ins key and add the account GUEST when prompted in the Enter the Account or Group for this ACL dialog box. Press Enter and the GUEST account is added to the ACL (see fig. 10.12).

   The GUEST account has been added, but it has full access rights. To clear the access rights for the GUEST account, press the F4 key (see fig. 10.13). Now a user who has logged in using the GUEST account will not be able to use your laser printer.

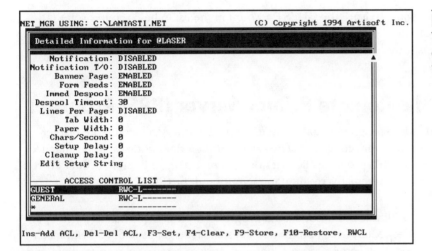

Figure 10.12
The GUEST account added to the ACL.

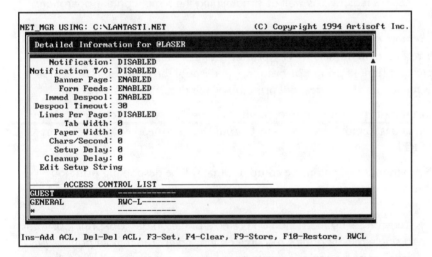

Figure 10.13
The GUEST account with the ACL rights cleared.

After you press Ins, LANtastic places the new account immediately before the account you had highlighted at the time. To enter accounts, a good sequence to use is one that goes from accounts with the fewest access rights to those with the most access rights.

Looking at the Access Control List you created for the @LASER printer resource, you may have noticed something interesting. Because the only users you want to be able to access your laser printer are members of the GENERAL ACL Group, just specifying full access rights for GENERAL and no access rights for all other user accounts (*) would suffice; you do not have to specify the GUEST account separately.

You may choose to leave the GUEST account in the list to help remind you that you specifically did not want guests to be able to use your laser printer. This might be especially useful later if you decide to allow additional users access to your laser printer.

Using the Remote Printer Server (RPS) Program

LANtastic's RPS program enables you to despool a print job to a remote printer located on a different computer. The remote printer does not have to be attached to a server; the RPS program allows a workstation to act as a Remote Printer Server. The RPS program remains resident in memory and uses 9K of memory.

LANtastic 5.0 introduced a program called RPD (Remote Printer Despooler) which performed the same function as RPS. RPS is a much more powerful program that incorporates additional management and control features, as well as streamlining the remote printer operations.

To use a remote printer, the user logs in to a server and establishes a connection to a printer resource on the server. The printer resource defined on the server is configured so a remote printer or printers can despool the print job. The remote printer is made available to despool print jobs when the RPS program is run.

To set up a remote printer resource, you first choose a server and create a printer resource that has Remote selected as its Output Device instead of an actual port (such as LPT1).

The RPS program is loaded on the computer that will be despooling print jobs from the server to its printer.

You can set up more than one remote printer to despool print jobs from a single remote printer resource on the server. The remote printers pull jobs out of the server's queue on a first-come, first-served basis. If you are in a high-volume printing environment, having multiple remote printers available allows more efficient network printing—instead of waiting for one printer, any available remote printer is used.

RPS also includes features which allow a single remote printer to despool print jobs on more than one server. In addition, RPS will support more than one printer on a workstation.

In the next two sections, you will learn how to create a remote printer resource on a server and how to run the RPS program to despool print jobs from the remote printer resource to a local printer on a workstation or server. The example used to help illustrate the RPS program assumes that you will create a remote printer resource called @LASER2 on the server named 386-25. The name of the remote despooler workstation's printer will be RPS-ZAK.

The following is a summary of the steps required to set up and use the RPS program. On a LANtastic server you will perform the following:

✔ Set up a shared printer resource that has Remote as it's output device name. This is the shared printer resource that users will connect to.

✔ In the Server Startup Parameters printing options, enable the RPS support selection; normally it is disabled.

✔ Change the Account privileges used by the remote workstation, which will be despooling the printer jobs from the server, to have the D-Despooler privilege.

On the workstation that will be despooling the remote printer resource, the following will be performed:

✔ Load the RPS program and specify the username and password to log in to the server with the remote printer resource.

✔ Specify the RPS workstation's printer name and the port that will be used.

✔ Establish the RPS program connection to the server with the remote printer resource to be despooled.

Creating a Remote Printer Resource

The process used to create a remote printer resource is almost identical to that used to create a regular shared printer resource. The only difference is that you select Remote as the Output Device instead of actually selecting a port (such as LPT1).

To create a remote printer resource on the server, select Shared Resources Management from the NET_MGR program main menu. From the Resource Name list screen, press the Ins key to add a new resource. Type the name of the remote printer resource to be added in the Enter Resource Name window. For this example, type **@LASER2** and press Enter (see fig. 10.14). Select Remote as the Output Device and press Enter (see fig. 10.15). The remote printer resource @LASER2 is created and appears on the Resource Name list (see fig. 10.16).

You can change an existing shared printer resource to a remote shared printer resource by selecting the shared printer resource to be changed and changing its Output Device to Remote.

Figure 10.14
Entering the name for a remote printer resource.

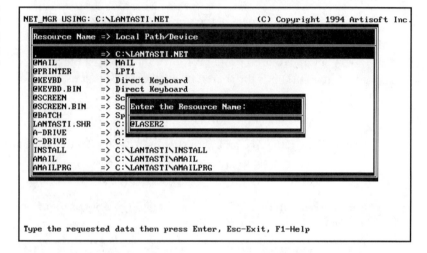

```
NET_MGR USING: C:\LANTASTI.NET                    (C) Copyright 1994 Artisoft Inc.

Resource Name => Local Path/Device
                    => C:\LANTASTI.NET
@MAIL            => MAIL
@PRINTER         => LPT1
@KEYBD           => Direct Keyboard
@KEYBD.BIN       => Direct Keyboard
@SCREEN          => Sc┌──────────────────────────────────┐
@SCREEN.BIN      => Sc│ Enter the Resource Name:         │
@BATCH           => Sp│                                  │
LANTASTI.SHR     => C:│ @LASER2                          │
A-DRIVE          => A:└──────────────────────────────────┘
C-DRIVE          => C:
INSTALL          => C:\LANTASTI\INSTALL
AMAIL            => C:\LANTASTI\AMAIL
AMAILPRG         => C:\LANTASTI\AMAILPRG



Type the requested data then press Enter, Esc-Exit, F1-Help
```

Figure 10.15
Selecting Remote as the Output Device.

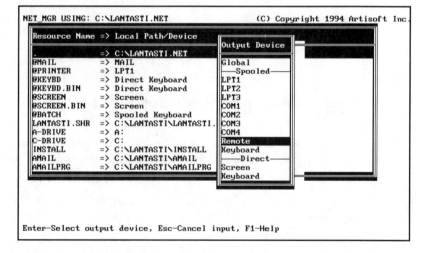

```
NET_MGR USING: C:\LANTASTI.NET                    (C) Copyright 1994 Artisoft Inc.

Resource Name => Local Path/Device         ┌─Output Device─┐
                    => C:\LANTASTI.NET      │Global         │
@MAIL            => MAIL                     │──Spooled──    │
@PRINTER         => LPT1                     │LPT1           │
@KEYBD           => Direct Keyboard          │LPT2           │
@KEYBD.BIN       => Direct Keyboard          │LPT3           │
@SCREEN          => Screen                   │COM1           │
@SCREEN.BIN      => Screen                   │COM2           │
@BATCH           => Spooled Keyboard         │COM3           │
LANTASTI.SHR     => C:\LANTASTI\LANTASTI.    │COM4           │
A-DRIVE          => A:                       │Remote         │
C-DRIVE          => C:                       │Keyboard       │
INSTALL          => C:\LANTASTI\INSTALL      │──Direct──     │
AMAIL            => C:\LANTASTI\AMAIL        │Screen         │
AMAILPRG         => C:\LANTASTI\AMAILPRG     │Keyboard       │
                                             └───────────────┘

Enter-Select output device, Esc-Cancel input, F1-Help
```

After the remote printer resource has been created, you can highlight it and press Enter to edit the detailed information for this resource.

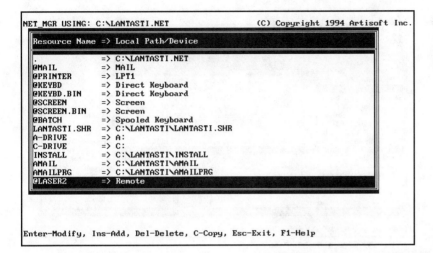

```
NET_MGR USING: C:\LANTASTI.NET          (C) Copyright 1994 Artisoft Inc.
┌──────────────────────────────────────────────────────────────────────┐
│ Resource Name => Local Path/Device                                     │
│ ┌──────────────────────────────────────────────────────────────────┐ │
│ │ .              => C:\LANTASTI.NET                                   │ │
│ │ @MAIL          => MAIL                                             │ │
│ │ @PRINTER       => LPT1                                             │ │
│ │ @KEYBD         => Direct Keyboard                                  │ │
│ │ @KEYBD.BIN     => Direct Keyboard                                  │ │
│ │ @SCREEN        => Screen                                           │ │
│ │ @SCREEN.BIN    => Screen                                           │ │
│ │ @BATCH         => Spooled Keyboard                                 │ │
│ │ LANTASTI.SHR   => C:\LANTASTI\LANTASTI.SHR                         │ │
│ │ A-DRIVE        => A:                                               │ │
│ │ C-DRIVE        => C:                                               │ │
│ │ INSTALL        => C:\LANTASTI\INSTALL                              │ │
│ │ AMAIL          => C:\LANTASTI\AMAIL                                │ │
│ │ AMAILPRG       => C:\LANTASTI\AMAILPRG                             │ │
│ │ @LASER2        => Remote                                           │ │
│ └──────────────────────────────────────────────────────────────────┘ │
│                                                                        │
│ Enter-Modify, Ins-Add, Del-Delete, C-Copy, Esc-Exit, F1-Help          │
└──────────────────────────────────────────────────────────────────────┘
```

Figure 10.16
The Resource Name list with the @LASER2 remote printer resource added.

Note

The operator notification (Notification) and immediate despooling (Immed Despool) features on the Detailed Information screen are not supported when using remote despooling.

If you specify setup and cleanup files in the Edit Setup String option of the Detailed Information screen for the shared remote printer resource, the path you specify must be the network path and not the DOS path. For example, \C-DRIVE\SETUP.TXT is the network path, whereas C:\SETUP.TXT is the DOS path.

To enable RPS support on the server, select Server Startup Parameters from the main menu. Press Enter to accept the current server, then select the Printing: Select to Manage option from the Server Startup Parameters screen. Select the RPS Support option from the Printer Configuration options box and press Enter to toggle the RPS Support option to Enable (see fig. 10.17).

The final task to perform on the server which contains the remote printer resource is to add the D-Despooler privilege for the account that will be used by the remote printer workstation to log in to the server. Select either the Individual Account Management or Wildcard Account Management from the main menu, and then the account which will be used by the workstation to log in to the server. In this example, assume the wildcard account * is used. With the Privileges section of the Account Information screen highlighted, press the D key to toggle on the despooler privilege (see fig. 10.18).

Figure 10.17
Enabling the RPS
Support option in
the Server
Startup
Parameters.

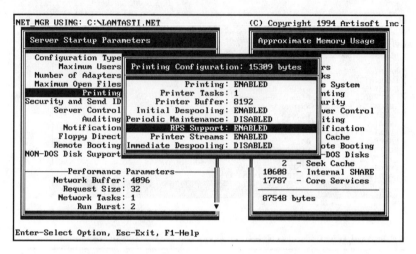

Although the RPS program may be run on a computer configured as a
server, it makes more sense to set up a Global printer resource on
another server to point to the printer on a different server than to use
the RPS program. The exception to this statement would be if RPS is
being used to enable more than one printer to despool a single printer
resource.

Figure 10.18
Specifying the
Despooler
privilege for
the wildcard
account *.

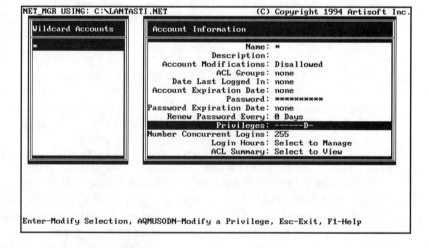

Running the RPS Program

The LANtastic Remote Printer Server (RPS) program must be running to enable a
printer on a workstation (or server) to remotely despool a remote printer resource
on a server.

The D (Despooler) privilege must be set for the account that will be used to log in to the server containing the remote printer resource.

You run the RPS program from the DOS command line, where its operating parameters also are specified. No separate configuration program exists for specifying the RPS settings other than specifying the options on the command line. You will actually have three RPS command line statements; the first to load the RPS program, the second to configure the RPS workstation printer port, and the third to establish the connection to the server.

To install the RPS program, use the following format:

RPS USERNAME=*username switches*

in which *username* is the name used to log in to the server that contains the remote printer resources. The following additional switches are available:

✔ **PASSWORD=.** This is the password, if one exists, for the username specified.

✔ **PRINTERS=.** This specifies the number of printers attached to the workstation that will be used for network printing. The default is 1.

✔ **RESOURCES=.** This specifies the number of remote printer resources the workstation will connect to and despool. The default is 1.

✔ **BUFFER_SIZE=.** This option specifies the buffer size for each printer task. The larger the buffer, the faster the network printing speed at the expense of available memory. The default size is 512 with valid options of 512, 1K, 2K, 3K, 4K, 5K, 6K, 8K, 10K, 12K, 14K, 16K, 18K, 20K, 24K, 28K, and 32K.

 If running RPS on a workstation, it should be loaded after the LANtastic redirector program, REDIR. If running RPS on a server, it should be loaded after the LANtastic redirector program but before the server program, SERVER.

To configure the RPS workstation's printer port, use the following format:

RPS DEVICE_NAME=*name* PORT=*port switches*

in which *name* is the name you give to the RPS workstation's printer, and *port* is the physical port which will be used for network printing. The name can be up to eight characters in length and must be unique on the network. The port can be LPT1, LPT2, LPT3, COM1, COM2, COM3, or COM4. The following additional switches are available:

✔ **BAUD_RATE=.** This is the baud rate for the RPS workstation printer if the printer is a serial printer (connected to a COM port). The default is the value set up for the remote printer resource on the server. Values may range from 110 to 115200.

✔ **CLEAR_PORT=.** This removes the connection from a port and cancels any connection parameters you have set. The default is LPT1 and valid settings are LPT1, LPT2, LPT3, COM1, COM2, COM3, AND COM4.

✔ **DATA_WIDTH=.** This is the word size for a serial port. The default is the value setup for the remote printer resource on the server. Values may be either 7 or 8. Eight is the value used in most cases.

✔ **FLOW_CONTROL=.** This is the flow control used for the serial port. The default is the value setup for the remote printer resource on the server. Valid settings are NONE, HARDWARE, or XON/XOFF. Most serial ports use Hardware flow control.

✔ **PARITY=.** This is the parity used for the serial port. The default is the value setup for the remote printer resource on the server. Valid settings are NONE, ODD, EVEN, or MARK.

✔ **STOP_BITS=.** This is the number of stop bits used when using a serial printer. The default is the value setup for the remote printer resource on the server. Valid settings are 1 or 2.

To attach to the remote server resource on the server and begin despooling print jobs, use the following format:

RPS ATTACH *port:\\servername\resource*

in which *port* is the workstation port to be used (LPT1, LPT2, LPT3, COM1, COM2, COM3, or COM4), *servername* is the name of the server with the remote printer resource, and *resource* is the name of the remote printer resource on the server.

For the example described earlier, you want to use the printer on your workstation to despool the @LASER2 resource on the 386-25 server. Assuming that your workstation's printer name is RPS-ZAK and the printer is connected to your LPT1 port, the following RPS commands would be used:

RPS USERNAME=ZAK PASSWORD=ZZZ

RPS DEVICE_NAME=RPS-ZAK PORT=LPT1

RPS ATTACH LPT1:\\386-25\@LASER2

The command RPS USERNAME=ZAK PASSWORD=ZZZ installs the RPS program with ZAK as the username and ZZZ as the password. The second RPS command defines the RPS workstation's printer name as RPS-ZAK, and specifies LPT1 as the port to which the printer is connected. Figure 10.19 shows your screen after successfully installing and configuring the RPS program.

The Remote Printer Server was NOT installed now message that appears after all RPS statements, except the first one, does not indicate an error; it simply means that the RPS command performed some action rather than installing the RPS program in memory, such as configuring the RPS workstation's port.

The third RPS command actually establishes the connection between the RPS workstation and the @LASER2 remote printer resource on server 386-25 for the LPT1 port on the RPS workstation.

Do not put a space between the port and the servername when using the RPS ATTACH command. You will get an error message and the desired RPS connection will not be made.

Figure 10.20 shows your screen after improperly putting a space between the port name and the server connection, and then your screen after successfully establishing the connection between the RPS workstation and the server with the remote printer resource.

The RPS workstation will now despool print jobs sent to the remote printer resource @LASER2 on server 386-25. You could also set up your RPS workstation to despool to another printer, such as LPT2:, and to despool other remote printer resources which exist on the same or even different servers. For example, the following RPS statements would set up RPS connections to despool the @LASER2 remote printer resource on server 386-25 and the @TILASER remote printer resource on server KATIE to the RPS workstation's LPT1 port. The @DOT-MAT remote printer resource on server 386-25 would despool to the RPS workstation's LPT2 port:

RPS USERNAME=ZAK PASSWORD=ZZZ RESOURCES=3 PRINTERS=2

RPS DEVICE_NAME=RPS-ZAK1 PORT=LPT1

RPS DEVICE_NAME=RPS-ZAK2 PORT=LPT2

RPS ATTACH LPT1:\\386-25\@LASER2

RPS ATTACH LPT2:\\386-25\@DOT-MAT

RPS ATTACH LPT1:\\KATIE\@TILASER

Figure 10.19
The RPS program installed and configured.

```
C:\>RPS USERNAME=ZAK PASSWORD=ZZZ
Remote Print Server V1.00 - (C) Copyright 1994 ARTISOFT Inc.

        ---- Remote Print Server installed ----

C:\>RPS DEVICE_NAME=RPS-ZAK PORT=LPT1
Remote Print Server V1.00 - (C) Copyright 1994 ARTISOFT Inc.

CONFIGURATION COMMAND...


        Printer port LPT1 assigned to RPS-ZAK
        Printer tasks allocated: 1
        Printer tasks available: 0
        Resources allocated: 1
        Resources available: 1

        ---- Remote Print Server was NOT installed now ----

C:\>
```

Figure 10.20
The result of a syntax error using the RPS command and then the RPS workstation connected to the remote printer resource on the server.

```
C:\>RPS ATTACH LPT1: \\386-25\@LASER2
Remote Print Server V1.00 - (C) Copyright 1994 ARTISOFT Inc.

GENERAL COMMAND...

ERROR: Illegal switch - ATTACH

        ---- Remote Print Server was NOT installed now ----

C:\>RPS ATTACH LPT1:\\386-25\@LASER2
Remote Print Server V1.00 - (C) Copyright 1994 ARTISOFT Inc.

ATTACH/DETACH COMMAND...


        \\386-25\@LASER2 has been ATTACHED to LPT1

        Printer tasks allocated: 1
        Printer tasks available: 0
        Resources allocated: 1
        Resources available: 0

        ---- Remote Print Server was NOT installed now ----

C:\>
```

After you have set up and configured your RPS workstation the way you want it, use the RPS BATCH statement to save your settings to a batch file which may be used later to establish the RPS connections. You will have to edit the batch file to remove some of the comments and insert a password if required. The command RPS BATCH>KSRPS.BAT will save the current RPS configuration to the DOS batch file with the name KSRPS.BAT

Additional RPS commands that may be used are described as follows:

- ✔ **BATCH.** This displays the RPS statements required for the current RPS connections. The output may be directed to a batch file using the > operator.

- ✔ **CONFIGURATION.** This displays the name of your workstation, your RPS username, the current printer port assignments, and the number of printer tasks and resources allocated and available.

- ✔ **CPS=.** This specifies the number of Characters Per Second that will be printed on the RPS workstation. The value specified here overrides the setting on the server for the remote printer resource.

- ✔ **CPS_OFF.** This cancels the CPS= setting and reverts back to the setting specified on the server for the remote printer resource.

- ✔ **MORE.** This displays the RPS HELP output a single screen at a time.

- ✔ **STATUS.** This displays the current jobs being printed by the workstation.

Network Printing

This section discusses the specifics of printing across the network under LANtastic control. The first thing you must do to use a printer is to establish a connection to the desired printer. You can do so by using the LANPUP or the NET utility program. You also can establish a connection using a NET command, which can be typed at the DOS prompt or included in a DOS batch file.

Recall that the LANtastic NET program enables you to log in to servers and establish network connections, including connections to printer resources. LANPUP is the *terminate-and-stay resident* (TSR) version of the LANtastic NET program. It enables you to establish network connections and perform network functions without exiting the application you are currently using.

After you have established a network printer connection and you print to the port (LPT1, LPT2, and so on) that is redirected to a network printer, the print job is sent over the network and despooled to the selected network printer. When printing, the print job is stored in the print queue (a special location on the server's hard disk) on the server to which the printer is connected. After your application program finishes sending the print job, LANtastic despools the print job to the printer.

If you have enabled the Immed Despool field in the Detailed Information screen for the resource, LANtastic begins despooling the print job as soon as your application begins sending it. LANtastic does not wait to receive the entire print job before it begins despooling.

Some application programs do not properly close a print file being sent to a network printer. If this is the case, you will notice that your print job does not start printing until after you have exited your application program. To resolve this problem, you can press the Ctrl+Alt+* keys simultaneously to close the print job and initiate printing.

Including the NET LPT TIMEOUT statement in your network startup batch file also closes a print job so it is released for printing. LANtastic automatically puts the following statement in your STARTNET.BAT file:

NET LPT TIMEOUT 10

This statement has the following meaning: if at least 10 seconds have elapsed since the last information was sent from the application for the current print job, close the print job and release it for printing.

Using LANPUP

LANPUP may be used to establish network printer connections if the LANPUP utility has been loaded into memory. To load LANPUP into memory, type **LANPUP** at the DOS prompt.

To establish a network printer connection using LANPUP, follow these steps:

1. Activate the LANPUP pop-up utility by pressing Ctrl+Alt+L (see fig. 10.21). If you are not already logged in to the server that has the printer resource you want to use, log in to it now.

To log in to a server, highlight Server by using your arrow keys and
press Enter. Press Ins and type the name of the server you wish to log
in to when prompted. Enter your user account name and associated
password when prompted, and you will be logged in.

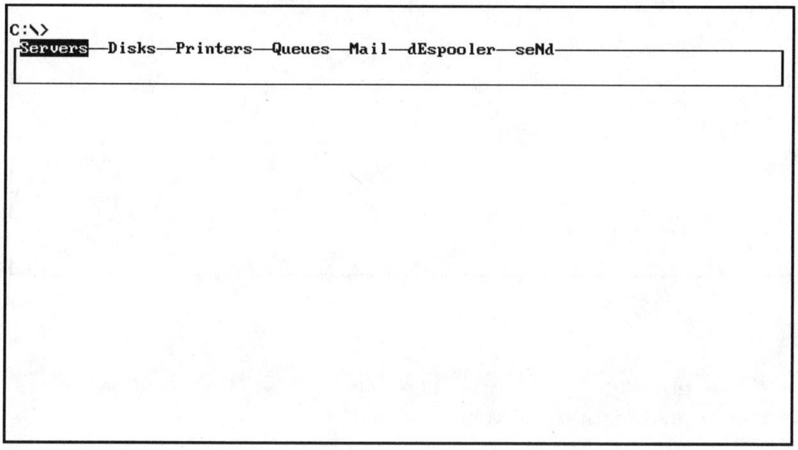

```
C:\>
┌Servers─Disks─Printers─Queues─Mail─dEspooler─seNd───────────────────────┐
│                                                                        │
└────────────────────────────────────────────────────────────────────────┘
```

Figure 10.21
The LANPUP
pop-up utility.

2. Highlight the Printers option and press Enter.

3. Scroll up or down to see the available printer ports. Select the printer
    port you want to use to connect to a network printer resource and
    press Enter.

4. Scroll up or down to see the servers you currently are logged in to.
    Select the server that has the printer resource you want to use and
    press Enter.

5. Scroll up or down to see the printer resources available on the server
    you have selected. Select the desired printer resource, and press Enter
    to establish the connection.

    Figure 10.22 shows an example of a connection established in
    LANPUP. In this example, when you send a print job to your LPT1
    port, it is redirected to the @PRINTER resource on the OFFICE server.

6. Press Esc to get back to the LANPUP menu, and then press Esc again
    to exit the LANPUP utility.

Figure 10.22

Connecting to a network printer resource using LANPUP.

Using NET

The LANtastic NET program can be used to establish network connections to printer resources located on other servers.

To use NET to establish a printer connection, follow these steps:

1. Start the NET program by typing **NET**, and then press Enter at the DOS prompt.

2. Select the Connect to Other Computers' Printers option from the menu (see fig. 10.23).

3. Select the printer port you want to use from the list by highlighting it and pressing Enter.

Figure 10.23

Selecting Connect to Other Computers' Printers from the NET program main menu.

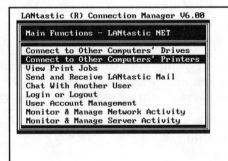

4. In the Connect to Computer window, highlight the server that contains the printer resource you want to use and press Enter. If you are not already logged in to the server, enter your user account name and associated password, and press Enter.

5. Highlight the printer resource you want to use and press Enter.

6. The printer connection is established and is shown in the Printer Connections to Other Computers window (see fig. 10.24).

Now you have made the printer connection. You can print a file from within an application, and the file prints on the selected printer.

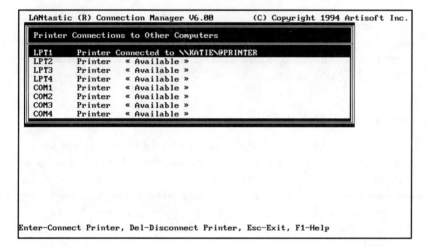

```
LANtastic (R) Connection Manager V6.00        (C) Copyright 1994 Artisoft Inc.
┌─────────────────────────────────────────────────────────────┐
│  Printer Connections to Other Computers                       │
├─────────────────────────────────────────────────────────────┤
│ LPT1     Printer  Connected  to  \\KATIE\@PRINTER             │
│ LPT2     Printer  « Available »                               │
│ LPT3     Printer  « Available »                               │
│ LPT4     Printer  « Available »                               │
│ COM1     Printer  « Available »                               │
│ COM2     Printer  « Available »                               │
│ COM3     Printer  « Available »                               │
│ COM4     Printer  « Available »                               │
└─────────────────────────────────────────────────────────────┘


Enter-Connect Printer, Del-Disconnect Printer, Esc-Exit, F1-Help
```

Figure 10.24
An established network printer connection in NET.

After you send a file to the printer, the job does not go directly to the printer. Instead, it is sent to the *printer spool area,* which is the area in which all print jobs are managed.

You can control the print jobs by using the View Print Jobs option on the NET main menu. Figure 10.25 shows the NET screen for the print queue.

Using the NET Command Line

To establish a network printer connection, you can use a NET command from the DOS prompt or in a batch file. The NET USE command is used to redirect a printer port on your computer to a printer resource on another server. The syntax of the NET USE command for printers is as follows:

NET USE *local-device**server-name*\@*resource-name*

Local-device is the port on your computer that will be redirected (LPT1, LPT2, LPT3, COM1, COM2, COM3, and COM4).

Server-name is the name of the server in which the printer resource you want to use is defined.

@resource-name is the name of the printer resource you want to use.

If you want to redirect your LPT2 port to use the @LASER printer resource on server DANAS-PC, for example, the following NET USE command would make the connection:

NET USE LPT2: \\DANAS-PC\@LASER

Before you can use a resource on another server, you first must be logged in to that server. If the server has the wildcard account * without a password, you will be logged in to the server automatically when you issue the NET USE command.

Understanding the Print Queue

All print files are sent to LANtastic's print spool area, which also is called the *print queue*. The files are stored in the order in which they are received, and they are printed in sequence as the printer becomes free for the next job. As a user, you can control files in the print queue, but only those files that you sent to the printer. A user with the Q privilege, however, can control all print jobs in the queue. The procedures that a user with the Q privilege uses are the same as those discussed in the following section.

When you select the View Print Jobs option, you must select the server that is attached to the printer you want to access before you can access the Viewing My Jobs screen (see fig. 10.25).

The Viewing My Jobs screen contains information about each print job—the sequence number, the destination printer, the current status of the job, the user who sent the file for printing, and a displayed comment if attached by the sender.

The status items can be one of the following:

✔ **PRINTING.** This print job is being sent to the printer.

✔ **IMMEDIATE.** This device has immediate despooling enabled, and the job has begun to print even though all of the data have not been spooled to the server's hard disk.

✔ **WAITING.** This print job is waiting in the queue ready to be despooled to the printer.

✔ **HELD.** A user has stopped despooling of this entry. A held entry can be deleted or restarted.

✔ **DELETING.** A user is deleting the marked entry. An entry is marked as deleted only if it is in the process of printing. The print job will remain in a deleted status until *CANCELED* has been printed.

✔ ***RUSH*.** This entry has been moved to the front of the print order. You must have the Super Q privilege to rush a print job.

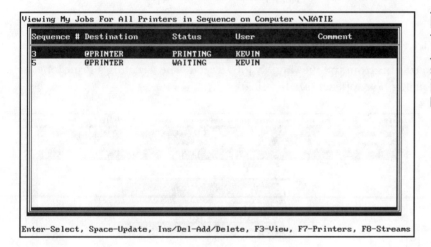

```
Viewing My Jobs For All Printers in Sequence on Computer \\KATIE
┌────────────────────────────────────────────────────────────────┐
│Sequence # Destination     Status      User          Comment      │
│3           @PRINTER        PRINTING    KEVIN                      │
│5           @PRINTER        WAITING     KEVIN                      │
│                                                                  │
│                                                                  │
│                                                                  │
│                                                                  │
│                                                                  │
│                                                                  │
│                                                                  │
│                                                                  │
│                                                                  │
│                                                                  │
│                                                                  │
└────────────────────────────────────────────────────────────────┘
Enter-Select, Space-Update, Ins/Del-Add/Delete, F3-View, F7-Printers, F8-Streams
```

Figure 10.25
The Viewing My Jobs screen showing the print jobs to be printed.

Pressing the F3-View key displays the Print Job View options menu. A user with the Q privilege may toggle the Show Jobs option between Mine, which only displays print jobs you sent, and All, which will display all the print jobs currently in the queue.

Pressing F8-Streams displays the Logical Streams dialog box for this server. You may recall that *printer streams* are logical references to different printer configurations. If you previously defined printer streams for the server's ports that you are using, they appear in this dialog box.

Pressing F7-Printers displays a dialog box showing the devices for this server, the current status of each, the characters per second at which the device is printing (if any), and the number of copies that the printer is making of the file being printed.

Adding Files to the Print Queue

Files usually are placed in the print queue from within an application program. After the print job has been sent from your application program, you can exit your program and use the Print Queue window to control the print job. You also can add print jobs to the print queue from within the queue window. These jobs, however, can only be ASCII text files or batch program files that are in text format.

If you place a file in the queue that you created with an application program, the file will not print correctly. To print correctly, such files need their originating applications to send the job.

To place a text file in the print queue, follow these steps:

1. Press Ins from the Viewing My Jobs screen. The Creating a Print Job dialog box appears (see fig. 10.26).

Figure 10.26

The Creating a Print Job dialog box.

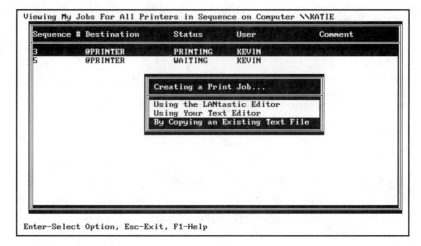

```
Viewing My Jobs For All Printers in Sequence on Computer \\KATIE

Sequence # Destination        Status         User           Comment

3            @PRINTER         PRINTING       KEVIN
5            @PRINTER         WAITING        KEVIN

                    ┌──────────────────────────────────────┐
                    │   Creating a Print Job...            │
                    ├──────────────────────────────────────┤
                    │ Using the LANtastic Editor           │
                    │ Using Your Text Editor               │
                    │ By Copying an Existing Text File     │
                    └──────────────────────────────────────┘




Enter-Select Option, Esc-Exit, F1-Help
```

2. Select the By Copying an Existing Text File option and press Enter.

3. The next dialog box prompts you to select the printer device that you want to use (see fig. 10.27).

   In this example, the @PRINTER device is selected.

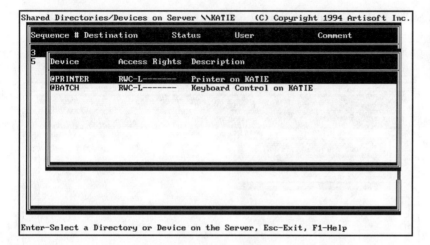

Figure 10.27
Selecting the
shared printer
device.

4. Type the path and name of the file you want to place in the queue, and press Enter (see fig. 10.28).

In this example, the path and file names are as follows:

C:\LANTASTI\STARTNET.BAT.

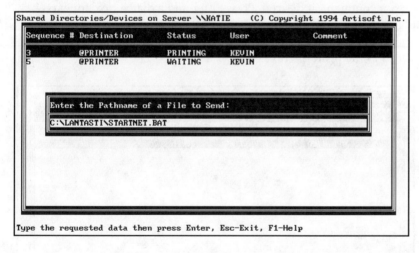

Figure 10.28
Entering the path
and file name of
the file to add to
the queue.

5. The Start Time for Printing dialog box appears with the current date and time (see fig. 10.29). To begin printing immediately, press Enter. If you want to specify the time or date (or both) when printing will begin, highlight the parameter you want to change (either date or time); press the Tab key to increment the value shown, or press the

Shift+Tab keys to decrement the value shown. You also can manually type the desired time or date by highlighting the parameter and pressing E-Edit.

Figure 10.29
Specifying the start time for printing.

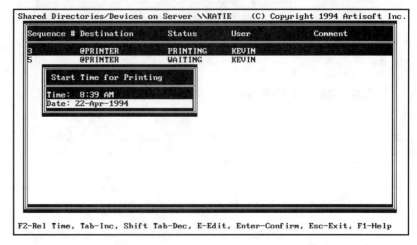

```
Shared Directories/Devices on Server \\KATIE    (C) Copyright 1994 Artisoft Inc.

Sequence # Destination        Status      User        Comment
3          @PRINTER           PRINTING    KEVIN
5          @PRINTER           WAITING     KEVIN

    Start Time for Printing

    Time:  8:39 AM
    Date: 22-Apr-1994

F2-Rel Time, Tab-Inc, Shift Tab-Dec, E-Edit, Enter-Confirm, Esc-Exit, F1-Help
```

6. The Enter a Comment for This Print Job dialog box appears. You may enter a comment, if desired. Press Enter and a dialog box appears asking for the number of copies you want printed. Type the number of copies to be printed (if different from 1), and press Enter. The file is placed in the print queue (see fig. 10.30).

Figure 10.30
The Viewing My Jobs screen with the newly added entry.

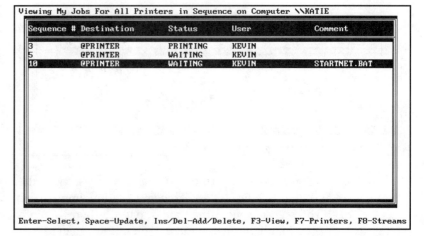

```
Viewing My Jobs For All Printers in Sequence on Computer \\KATIE

Sequence # Destination        Status      User        Comment
3          @PRINTER           PRINTING    KEVIN
5          @PRINTER           WAITING     KEVIN
10         @PRINTER           WAITING     KEVIN       STARTNET.BAT

Enter-Select, Space-Update, Ins/Del-Add/Delete, F3-View, F7-Printers, F8-Streams
```

7. You can control the actions of this file by highlighting the file and pressing Enter to display the Controlling the Selected Print Job menu (see fig. 10.31). The actions that these options perform are apparent from their descriptions on the menu.

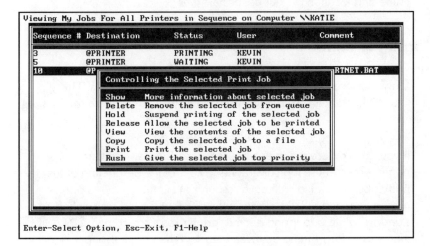

Figure 10.31

The Controlling the Selected Print Job menu.

You also can use the LANtastic editor to create a print job to be printed. Simply choose the Using the LANtastic Editor function in the Creating a Print Job menu (see fig. 10.26), and type your text file as desired (see fig. 10.32). Then press F2 to send the file to be printed.

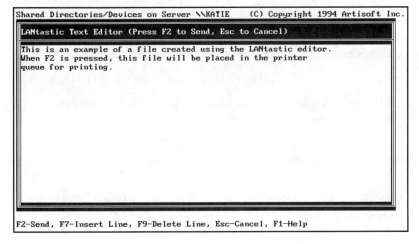

Figure 10.32

Creating a text file using the LANtastic editor.

If you have your own text editor that you would like to use, you can specify it by selecting Using Your Text Editor and entering the full path name, including the program name of the editor. LANtastic will ask if you want to save this configuration, so you do not have to specify the name and location of your editor next time.

Adding Logical Streams

Logical streams are used to control which printer resources are allowed to be despooled. Only users with the Q privilege may add or control streams. The Logical Streams dialog box is displayed by pressing F8-Streams while in the Viewing My Jobs screen.

If you have different printer resources associated with different types of paper, you can use logical streams to control the despooling of the print jobs associated with each resource. You might have a printer resource named @PRINTER, for example, that is used for printing on standard white paper and another printer resource named @INVOICE that is used for printing on invoice stock. When regular paper is in the printer, you could disable the logical stream @INVOICE until you put the invoice stock in the printer, at which time you would enable the logical stream @INVOICE and disable the logical stream @PRINTER.

In the Logical Streams dialog box, you see only the default stream @???????.??? displayed. You can add a new logical stream to the streams list by following these steps:

1. Press F8-Streams to display the Logical Streams dialog box .

2. Use the arrow keys to scroll to a blank position and press Enter.

3. Type the stream name in the Enter the Stream Mask dialog box that appears, and press Enter (see fig. 10.33).

The new logical stream name appears in the dialog box (see fig. 10.34). You can toggle the stream between enabled and disabled by pressing the F5 key.

LANtastic processes logical streams in the order they are listed in the Logical Streams list. The @???????.??? stream matches all possible logical streams, so if it is enabled and the first stream in the list, all streams will be sent to the printer even if the status of other streams listed after it is disabled.

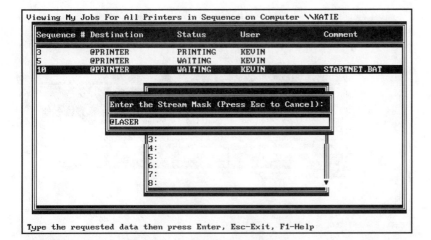

Figure 10.33
Entering a new logical stream.

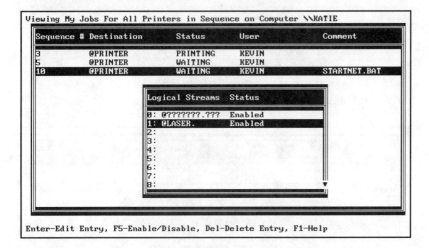

Figure 10.34
The Logical Streams dialog box with the @LASER stream added.

Controlling the Physical Printer Ports

In the same way that logical streams are used to control despooling of specific printer resources, LANtastic also enables you to control the individual physical printer ports on a server. To make changes in the physical printer ports, you must have the Q privilege for this server. To alter the physical printer ports, follow these steps:

1. Press F7-Printers to display the devices dialog box.

2. Scroll down and highlight the LPT1 option, and then press Enter.

   The Control For LPT1 dialog box appears (see fig. 10.35).

Figure 10.35
The Control For
LPT1 dialog box.

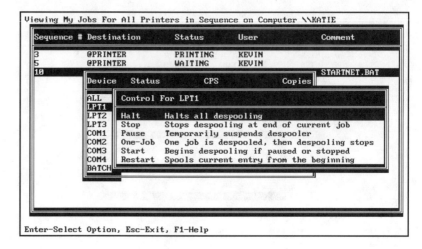

Figure 10.35
The Control For
LPT1 dialog box.

3. Highlight the action you want to take for this printer port, and press Enter to execute it. Descriptions of the choices appear next to each selection.

   In this example, you choose to select the Halt all despooling option. The LPT1 physical printer port is disabled, and the status next to LPT1 changes to DISABLED (see fig. 10.36).

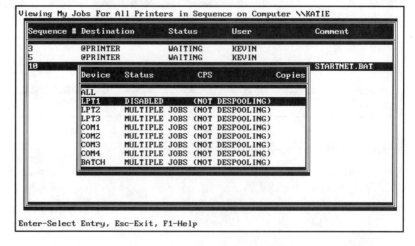

Figure 10.36
LPT1 device
disabled.

4. To restart the despooler, highlight the LPT1 selection and press Enter. The Control For LPT1 dialog box appears.

5. Now select the Start option to begin despooling the disabled printer device.

Using the DOS Command Line for Printing

You also can get printed results by entering a command line at the DOS prompt to print a file. If you want to print your CONFIG.SYS file to LPT1, which has been redirected to a network printer resource, enter the following command and then press Enter:

```
COPY C:\CONFIG.SYS LPT1
```

This method is suitable only for printing ASCII text files or your batch command files. Files created by a word processing package must have the application running in order to have the correct control codes and special characters for formatting to take effect (unless you saved the file as an ASCII text file).

If you are logged in to a server that has a printer resource to which you want to print a file, you could type the following command:

```
COPY C:\CONFIG.SYS \\KATES-PC\@PRINTER
```

This would print the CONFIG.SYS file on your C drive to the @PRINTER printer resource located on the server with the name KATES-PC.

To control the print queue from the DOS command line, you must have the Q privilege in your account. The most common use of this feature is to stop the printer in the event that a paper jam occurs or the paper runs out. You need to suspend printing while you correct the situation.

The following commands enable you to stop the despooling until you can fix the problem:

✔ Type **NET QUEUE STOP** *\\servername* and press Enter.

   This command stops the despooling for the server named. This command also stops all printers attached to the server named.

✔ Type **NET QUEUE HALT** *\\servername* and press Enter.

   This command immediately stops the printers. After the despooling is restarted, the jobs print from the beginning again.

✔ Type **NET QUEUE PAUSE** *\\servername* and press Enter.

   This command stops the printers, but after the despooling is restarted, the jobs resume from the point at which they left off.

The following commands enable you to restart the despooler:

✔ Type **NET QUEUE START** *\\servername* and press Enter.

   This command restarts the despooler for the server named.

✔ Type **NET QUEUE RESTART** *servername* and press Enter.

This command restarts the despooler and prints the current job from the beginning again.

Using LANtastic with Windows

The following sections discuss how to define printer resources, configure printer resources, and connect to and use printer resources in the Windows environment.

Defining Printer Resources

Before you can select and use a printer as a resource on your network, you first must define the resource so LANtastic can recognize it. This section leads you through this process. You may remember that some of these steps were covered in Chapter 7 , "Setting Up User Accounts and Shared Resources in Windows."

Printers on a network actually have two names: the DOS device name and the network resource name that the network manager assigns to them. The *DOS device name* is used by DOS and most application programs to refer to a printer, which actually is the name for the output port to which the printer attaches, such as LPT1, LPT2, COM1, or COM2. The *network resource name*, on the other hand, can be any name you choose, as long as it begins with the character @ and follows the same rules as DOS file names (eight characters maximum with a maximum three character extension). You may define multiple printer resource names for the same printer.

You can set up different print-output configurations for a single printer and give the printer more than one resource name, as discussed earlier in the terminology section of this chapter.

Perform the following steps to define a printer resource for your network:

1. Run the LANtastic Network Manager program by double-clicking on the LANtastic Network Manager icon in the LANtastic program group, or with the icon selected, choose **O**pen from the **F**ile menu.

   The LANtastic Network Manager menu appears.

2. Select the **R**esources icon, or choose **R**esources from the **M**anage menu.

3. Press Ins after the Resources dialog box appears (see fig 10.37) or select **A**dd from the **E**dit menu.

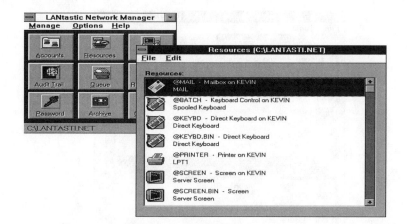

Figure 10.37
The Resources
dialog box.

4. Click on the Shared Device option and type the name you want to
   assign to this printer resource in the Resource Name field (see fig.
   10.38). Make sure that you precede the name with the @ sign.

   Figure 10.38 uses @LASER as the resource name which is connected to
   port LPT1:.

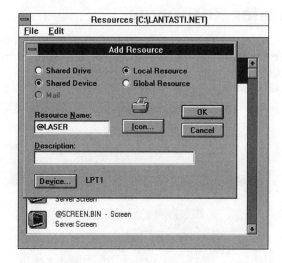

Figure 10.38
Entering a printer
resource name.

After you complete these steps, your new printer resource is added to the Resources list (see fig. 10.39).

Figure 10.39
Resources list
showing the
addition of the
@LASER printer
resource.

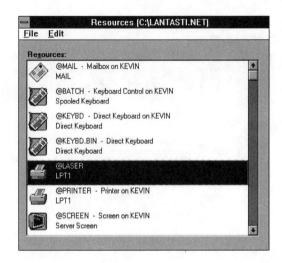

Figure 10.39
Resources list
showing the
addition of the
@LASER printer
resource.

Now that you have entered the name for the resource and specified the output device port (LPT1:), you can set up the actual configuration of the printer control file within LANtastic.

Configuring Printer Resources

Naming the printer resource and assigning the physical output port to which the printer is connected are the only steps required to actually set up a printer resource. LANtastic provides many options for configuring your shared printer resources. From the Resources dialog box, select **M**odify from the **E**dit menu to display the Resource Parameters dialog box (see fig. 10.40) for the @LASER printer resource.

Figure 10.40
The Resource
Parameters
dialog box.

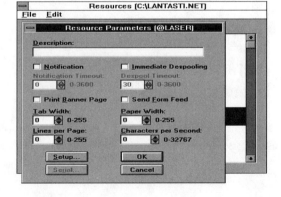

The Resource Parameters dialog box contains the following fields:

- ✔ **Description.** In this field, you enter a description of your printer resource. You can use up to 64 characters.

- ✔ **Notification** If this field is enabled, any user logged in to the server who has the operator privilege (O) will be notified of a situation that needs user intervention, such as when a printer is out of paper. The default value for this field is disabled.

- ✔ **Notification Timeout.** If notification is enabled, the value in this field is the number of seconds that must elapse before the operator is notified of an event that requires operator intervention. If the condition is corrected before the notification is sent, the notification is canceled. The default value for this field is disabled.

- ✔ **Immediate Despooling.** If you enable this field, data is sent from the spool area to a printer before all of the data is received from the originating machine. Because LANtastic does not cause the printer to wait for all of the data to be written to the spool area first, this feature speeds printing tasks. If the Immediate Despooling field is enabled, the Despool Timeout field automatically is set to the default value of 30 seconds. The default value for the Immediate Despooling field is disabled.

 For immediate despooling to work for a device, confirm that the Immediate Despooling of Print Jobs option in the Printing and Despooling section of the LANtastic Server Control Panel is Enabled. From the main menu select **S**erver, or select **S**erver Startup from the **M**anage menu. Select OK to accept the current **S**erver Directory. Scroll down the Configured Modules list and select the Printing and Despooling option. The LANtastic Server Configuration Printing Parameters Module dialog box appears (see fig. 10.41). Select or deselect Immediate Despooling of print jobs by clicking on the box next to the option.

- ✔ **Despool Timeout.** This field works in conjunction with the Immediate Despooling field. If the printer sits idle for a period of time longer than that which is set in this field, the server stops that print job and starts the next job in the queue. The aborted print job is resequenced to follow this new print job. This feature prevents an effective lockup of your printing capabilities if a file experiences difficulty as it is sent to the printer spool area. Setting the value in this field to 0 disables this function and gives the despooling print job exclusive use of the printer. This field accepts values between 0 and 3600. The default value for this field is 30 seconds.

Figure 10.41
The LANtastic
Server
Configuration
Printing
Parameters
Module dialog
box.

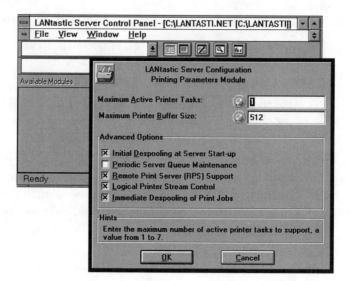

✔ **Print Banner Page.** If you enable this feature, LANtastic prints a banner page before each print job. This feature is helpful when you have many users printing to one printer. Each user's output is easily identifiable by the banner page attached to the output. The default value for this field is disabled.

Each banner page contains the account name of the sender; the name of the computer that originated the print job; the day, month, and year that the file was printed; the time in hours, minutes, and seconds that the file was printed; the resource name of the printer used; the physical port name of the server that was used; the paper width of the file; the number of copies printed; and the name of the print file. Optionally, the banner page displays a comment field, if the user chose to add one, and the tab position, if any.

✔ **Send Form Feed.** If this option is enabled, the printer is instructed to put a form feed at the end of each print job. This will advance the paper to the top of the next page, preventing the possibility of combining multiple print jobs on the same page. The default value for this field is disabled.

✔ **Tab Width.** This field works only with ASCII text files. You can instruct the printer to insert a tab of a stated width at each location in which a tab is found in the text file. This field accepts values between 0 and 255. The default value is 0.

If you enable this feature and print files from word processing or graphics programs, the tab expansion feature causes printing errors. Make sure that you disable this feature before attempting to print these kinds of files.

✔ **Paper Width.** This field enables you to set the width of the paper size used for the banner page. If you are using standard 8 1/2 x 11 inch paper, you do not need to set this field.

✔ **Lines per Page.** This field is useful only for formatting ASCII text files for printing. The value in this field is the number of lines printed before a form feed is inserted. This feature should be disabled when you print graphics or PostScript files. This field accepts values between 0 and 255. Entering a 0 will disable this field. The default value for this field is 0 (disabled).

✔ **Characters per Second.** This field enables you to set the minimum number of characters per second at which the despooler sends data to the printer. The range for this field is from 0 to 32,767 characters per second. Specifying any setting higher than 0 causes the server to give higher priority to the print task in an effort to print at the rate you specified. If you set a value that is higher than either the printer or the computer can achieve, the job prints at the highest possible speed.

Some application programs make heavy use of the CPU, resulting in very slow network printing from that server. If you notice a decrease in printing speed when running certain applications on the server to which the printer is connected, change this field to a higher value, such as 9,600, to improve printing performance.

✔ **Setup.** The **S**etup button enables you to specify the setup string that is sent to the printer at the start of a print job. You do not need to enter a setup string if you are using the default parameters of your printer or if you need to send setups that your application software can handle.

You can specify a setup string that you enter or specify a setup or cleanup file that contains the required printer information. In addition, you can specify a setup or cleanup delay in seconds.

The **S**etup Delay enables you to set the delay in seconds that the despooler waits between sending the setup string to the printer and sending the actual data to the printer. The printer initializes to the setup string before it begins receiving data. The range for this field is from 0 to 3,600 seconds. You do not need to use this field unless you are sending a setup string to the printer.

The **C**leanup Delay enables you to set the delay in seconds that the print spooler waits after it receives the cleanup string to reinitialize the printer and before it begins printing a new job. You do not need to use this field unless you use a cleanup string for this printer. The range for this field is from 0 to 3,600 seconds.

To change the port assigned to the shared printer resource, from the Resources dialog box, select Typ**e** from the **E**dit menu. The Resource Types dialog box appears (see fig. 10.42), and from this dialog box you can specify the port the printer is connected to as well as other types including Global, Screen, and Keyboard types.

Figure 10.42
The Resource Types dialog box.

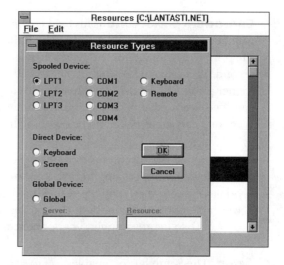

Parallel and *serial* ports are connectors on the back of your computer to which printers and other devices may be connected. LPT1, LPT2, and LPT3 refer to parallel ports, while COM1, COM2, COM3, and COM4 refer to serial ports. Printers are usually connected to a parallel port, while plotters are usually connected to a serial port.

The access control list (ACL) for a device is changed by selecting the AC**L** option from the **E**dit menu in the Resources dialog box.

The following steps illustrate how to configure a printer resource. In most situations, you do not have to change any of the settings from their default value; just setting up the resource name and the physical port it points to is sufficient.

1. Select the new printer resource you just added to the resource list by clicking on it. Select **M**odify from the **E**dit menu.

    The Resource Parameters dialog box appears (see fig. 10.43). In this example, you input the correct information for the @LASER printer resource.

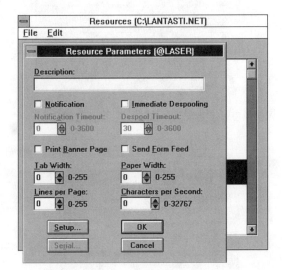

Figure 10.43

The Resource Parameters dialog box for the @LASER printer resource.

2. Type the description you want in the **D**escription field and press Enter.

3. Enable immediate despooling by selecting the Immediate Despooling option. Notice that this field automatically sets the Despool Timeout field to 30 seconds.

4. Change the Characters per Second field to 9600 by selecting the field and typing 9600 or by using the increment/decrement arrows next to the text box.

5. Select the **S**etup button. The Printer Setup dialog box appears (see fig. 10.44).

6. To type in a setup string, select the Use Setup String option in the Printer Setup field. The Printer Setup dialog box changes so that you can add setup codes (see fig. 10.45).

Printer setup strings are codes sent to your printer that cause the printer to perform a specified action, such as changing to a different font, ejecting blank lines or pages, or simply resetting itself.

Figure 10.44
The Printer Setup dialog box.

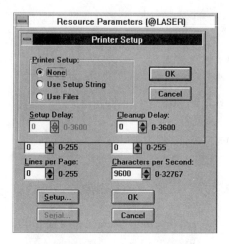

Figure 10.45
The Printer Setup dialog box after selecting the Use Setup String option.

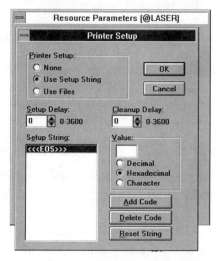

7. Enter the first setup code you want in the Value field. Select **A**dd Code to add the code to your setup string. Continue adding codes as described previously until you are finished and all the required codes for your printer show up in the Setup String list (see fig. 10.46). Refer to your printer manual for the codes that correspond to the codes you need to enter. Select OK to return to the Resource Parameters dialog box and then select OK again to return to the Resources list.

The code you enter is assumed to be hexadecimal. If entering a decimal number or a character, click on the appropriate option in the Value field.

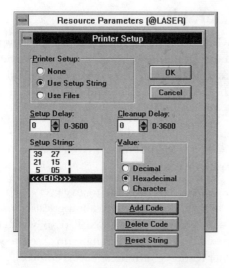

Figure 10.46
The Printer Setup dialog box after entering a printer setup string.

8. To change the access control list (ACL), select AC**L** from the **E**dit menu. The Access Control List dialog box appears (see fig. 10.47).

The codes that appear as defaults are sufficient for most cases.

When determining the access rights to a printer, you have two choices—to allow access or to disallow access. Printer resources by default include the * account with the ACL rights of RWCL, which means that all accounts have full access to the printer. You do not need to set additional ACL rights to allow access to a printer resource.

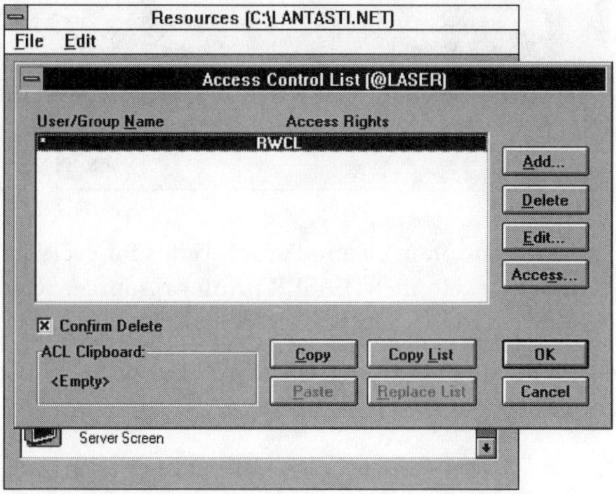

Figure 10.47
The Access Control List dialog box.

Access Control List Defaults

The Access Control List (ACL) codes enable you to have control over the access to network resources. The network administrator can determine the degree of control by setting the different ACLs for each network resource. Printer ACLs can be set for each account, either to allow access to a printer or to disallow access.

In figure 10.47, an asterisk appears in the User/Group Name column. This asterisk indicates that all users are granted access to the Read, Write, Create, and File Lookup functions. These ACL rights do not make as much sense for a printer resource as they do for a drive/file resource.

For the following example, suppose that you want to give everyone in your office access to your laser printer, but you do not want to allow guests to use it. In this situation, you have set up an ACL group called GENERAL, of which everyone in your office is a member. The GUEST account will have no access to your laser printer. To set up your printer resource with these access controls, perform the following steps:

1. With the * selected in the User/Group Name field, select the Access button. The Access Control List rights dialog box appears (see fig. 10.48).

Figure 10.48
The Access
Control List
dialog box.

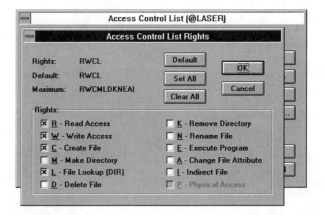

2. Select the Clear All button to clear all access rights for everyone. Now no accounts have access to the @LASER printer resource. Select OK and you are returned to the Access Control List dialog box.

3. To add the GENERAL account, select the **A**dd button. The ACL Entry dialog box appears.

4. Type **GENERAL** in the User/Group Name field (see fig. 10.49).
    Notice that when entering a new account to the Access Control List,
    the necessary ACL rights (RWCL) are set automatically to allow full
    access to the printer resource. Select OK and you are returned to the
    Access Control List dialog box, which now also displays the GENERAL
    account with full access to the printer (see fig. 10.50).

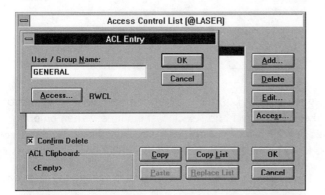

Figure 10.49
Entering the
GENERAL
account in the
ACL Entry dialog
box.

Figure 10.50
The Access
Control List
dialog box
showing the
newly added
GENERAL
account.

5. To add the GUEST account to the list, select the **A**dd button and when
    the ACL Entry dialog box appears, type **GUEST** in the User/Group
    Name field.

6. You want to restrict access for the GUEST account, so select the **A**ccess
    button. From the Access Control List Rights dialog box, select the
    Clear All button so the GUEST account has no access to the @LASER
    printer resource. Select OK to return to the ACL Entry dialog box and
    then OK again to return to the Access Control List dialog box, which
    now shows the GUEST account with no access (see fig. 10.51).

Figure 10.51

The Access
Control List
showing the
newly added
GUEST account
with no access
rights.

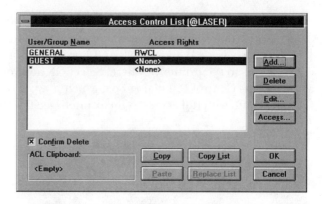

After you select **A**dd, LANtastic places the new account immediately before the account you had selected at the time. When entering accounts in your access control list (ACL), you should list the accounts with the fewest access rights first and those with the most access rights last.

Looking at the Access Control List you created for the @LASER printer resource, you may have noticed something interesting. Because the only users you want to be able to access your laser printer are members of the GENERAL ACL Group, just specifying full access rights for GENERAL and no access rights for all other user accounts (*) would suffice; you do not have to specify the GUEST account separately.

You may choose to leave the GUEST account in the list to help remind you that you specifically did not want guests to be able to use your laser printer. This might be especially useful later if you decide to allow additional users access to your laser printer.

Network Printing

This section discusses the specifics of printing across the network under LANtastic control. The first thing you must do to use a printer is to establish a connection to the desired printer. You can do so by using the LANtastic NET program.

Recall that the LANtastic NET program enables you to log in to servers and establish network connections, including connections to printer resources. You could also establish network connections prior to starting Windows using one of the methods described in the DOS section.

After you have established a network printer connection and you print to the port (LPT1, LPT2, and so on) that is redirected to a network printer, the print job is sent over the network and despooled to the selected network printer. When printing, the print job is stored in the print queue (a special location on the server's hard disk) on the server to which the printer is connected. After your application program finishes sending the print job, LANtastic sends the print job to the printer.

If you have enabled the Immediate Despooling option in the Resource Parameters dialog box for the resource, LANtastic begins despooling the print job as soon as your application begins sending it. LANtastic does not wait to receive the entire print job before it begins despooling.

Some application programs do not properly close a print file being sent to a network printer. If this is the case, you will notice that your print job does not start printing until after you have exited your application program. To resolve this problem, you can press the Ctrl+Alt+* keys simultaneously to close the print job and initiate printing.

Including the NET LPT TIMEOUT statement in your network startup batch file also closes a print job so that it is released for printing. LANtastic automatically puts the following statement in your STARTNET.BAT file:

NET LPT TIMEOUT 10

This statement has the following meaning: if at least ten seconds have elapsed since the last information was sent from the application for the current print job, close the print job and release it for printing.

Using NET

The LANtastic NET program can be used to establish network connections to printer resources located on other servers.

To use NET to establish a printer connection, follow these steps:

1. Start the NET program by double-clicking on the LANtastic Net Connection icon in the LANtastic program group or by selecting the icon and choosing **O**pen from the Program Manager's **F**ile menu.

2. Select the **P**rinters icon or select Connect to **P**rinters from the **N**et menu (see fig. 10.52). The Printer Connections dialog box appears (see fig. 10.53), showing the available shared resources on other computers you may connect to in the Available for Connection field. The My Connections field shows the devices currently used and the devices available to be used to connect to shared printer resources on other computers. If a connection is already made, it appears next to the device name.

Figure 10.52
The LANtastic
Net program
main menu.

Figure 10.53
The Printer
Connections
dialog box.

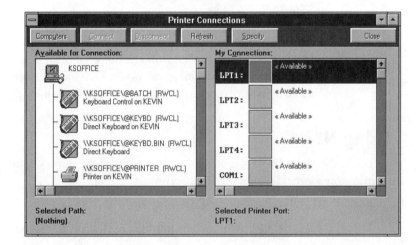

3. Select the device name you want to use (such as LPT1) from the list in the My Connections field, and the shared printer resource you want to connect to from the list in the Available for Connection field (see fig. 10.54). If you are not currently connected to the computer that has the printer resource you want to use, you may connect to the computer by selecting the Computers button.

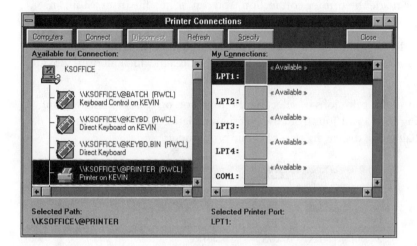

Figure 10.54
Selecting the printer resource to connect to.

4. Select the Connect button; the connection is made and displayed in the My Connections list next to the select device name (see fig 10.55).

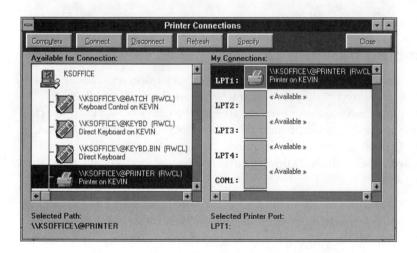

Figure 10.55
The Printer Connections dialog box showing the specified printer connection.

You can also make a printer connection by selecting the resource to connect to from the Available for Connection list and dragging it and dropping it on the device (such as LPT1) to be used for the connection. In addition, you can also make a connection by specifying the parameters necessary for the connection using the **S**pecify button.

Now you have made the printer connection. You can print a file from within an application, and the file prints on the selected printer.

After you send a file to the printer, the job does not go directly to the printer. Instead, it is sent to the *printer spool area,* which is the area in which all print jobs are managed.

You can control the print jobs by selecting the **J**obs icon on the NET main menu or by selecting View Print **J**obs from the **N**et menu. Figure 10.56 shows the My Print Jobs dialog box displaying items in your print queue.

Figure 10.56
The My Print
Jobs dialog box.

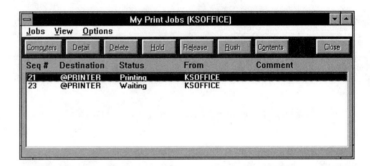

Understanding the Print Queue

All print files are sent to LANtastic's print spool area, which also is called the *print queue.* The files are stored in the order in which they are received, and they are printed in sequence as the printer becomes free for the next job. As a user, you can control files in the print queue, but only those files that you sent to the printer. A user with the Q privilege, however, can control all print jobs in the queue. The procedures that a user with the Q privilege uses are the same as those discussed in the following section.

 When you select the **J**obs icon, you must select the server that is attached to the printer you want to access before you can access the My Print Jobs dialog box (see fig. 10.56).

The My Print Jobs dialog box contains information about each print job—the sequence number, the destination printer, the current status of the job, the user who sent the file for printing, and a displayed comment if attached by the sender.

The status items can be one of the following:

- ✔ **PRINTING.** This print job is being sent to the printer.

- ✔ **WAITING.** This print job is waiting in the queue ready to be despooled to the printer.

- ✔ **HELD.** A user has stopped despooling of this entry. A held entry can be deleted or restarted.

- ✔ **UPDATING.** Another user is sending a print job.

- ✔ **DELETED.** This entry has been marked for deletion. An entry is marked as deleted only if it is in the process of printing. The print job will remain in a deleted status until *CANCELED* has been printed.

- ✔ **RUSH.** This entry has been moved to the front of the print order. You must have the Q privilege to rush a print job.

The **View** menu has the selection My Jobs and All Jobs. A user with the Q privilege may select the All Jobs option to display all the print jobs in the queue.

Selecting the Printer Stre**am**s option from the **J**obs menu displays the Logical Streams dialog box for this server. You may recall that *printer streams* are logical references to different printer configurations. If you previously defined printer streams for the server's ports that you are using, they appear in this dialog box.

Selecting the Control **P**rinters option from the **J**obs menu displays the printers dialog box showing the devices for this server, the current status of each, the characters per second at which the device is printing (if any), and the number of copies that the printer is making of the file being printed.

Adding Files to the Print Queue

Files usually are placed in the print queue from within an application program. After the print job has been sent from your application program, you can exit your program and use the Print Queue window (My Print Jobs) to control the print job. You also can add print jobs to the print queue from within the queue window.

These jobs, however, can only be ASCII text files or batch program files that are in text format.

If you place a file in the queue that you created with an application program, the file will not print correctly. To print correctly, such files need their originating applications to send the job.

To place a text file in the print queue, follow these steps:

1. From the Jobs menu in the My Print Jobs dialog box, select Send Job and then Send a File. The Open dialog box appears, from which you can select a file to be printed.

2. Specify the file you want to be printed (see fig. 10.57). Select OK to continue. Notice in this example that the file to be printed includes the complete path:

   C:\LANTASTI\STARTNET.BAT.

Figure 10.57
Specifying the
STARTNET.BAT
file to be printed.

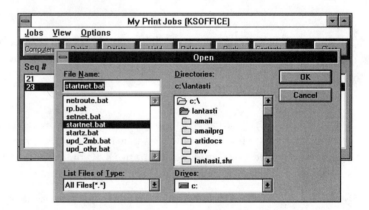

3. The Select Printer dialog box appears (see fig. 10.58). Select the printer you want the file sent to by typing in the resource name or selecting it from the Printer list drop-down selection box.

4. Enter an optional comment in the Comment field. The name of the file to be printed is automatically placed in the Comment field.

5. Select the Delayed Printing button. The Select Printer dialog box changes to show Print Delay options of No Delay, Print Time, and Delay Time (see fig. 10.59). Selecting the Print Time option enables

you to specify a date and time for the printing to begin. If you select
the Delay Time option, you can specify the delay in hours and minutes
until the printing begins.

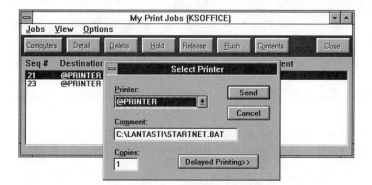

Figure 10.58
The Select Printer
dialog box.

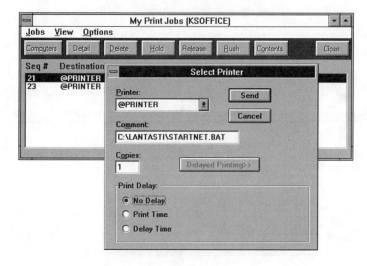

Figure 10.59
The Select Printer
dialog box
showing the Print
Delay options.

6. Select the Send button; the print job is sent to the print queue and
   appears on the My Print Jobs list (see fig. 10.60).

You can use the LANtastic editor to create a text file to be printed.
From the Jobs menu, select **S**end Job and then select Use **E**ditor. The
Job Entry dialog box appears, enabling you to type the information
you want to send to be printed. When finished, select **S**end from the
File menu and proceed as described previously.

Figure 10.60
The My Print Jobs
list with the new
entry added.

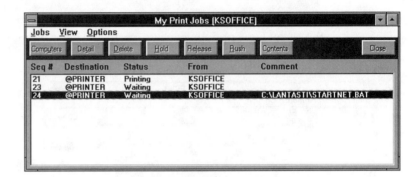

The following options are available as command buttons in the My Print Jobs
windows and as menu selections from the **J**obs menu:

✔ **Detail.** This option shows additional information for a selected entry
(see fig. 10.61), including the date and time sent, the delay time if any,
the size of the print job, and the number of copies to be printed.

Figure 10.61
The detail
information for
a print job in
the queue.

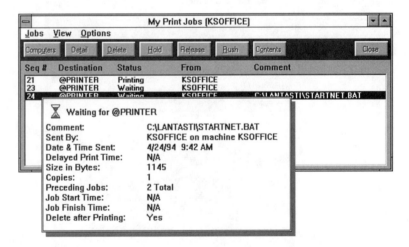

✔ **Delete.** This selection enables you to delete the selected print job.

✔ **Hold.** This selection holds the selected print job from printing.

✔ **Release.** This selection releases a held print job so it may be printed.

✔ **Rush.** This selection rushes the selected print job. It will be placed as the
next job to be printed. You must have the Q privilege to rush a print job.

✔ **Contents.** This selection displays the contents of the print job to be
printed.

Selecting Save **A**s from the **J**obs menu enables you to save a print job as a file to be printed at a later date or for another purpose.

Adding Logical Streams

Logical streams are used to control which printer resources are allowed to be despooled. Only users with the Q privilege may add or control streams. The Logical Streams dialog box is displayed by selecting Printer Strea**ms** from the **J**obs menu while in the My Print Jobs dialog box (see fig. 10.62).

If you have different printer resources associated with different types of paper, you can use logical streams to control the despooling of the print jobs associated with each resource. You might have a printer resource named @PRINTER, for example, that is used for printing on standard white paper, and another printer resource named @INVOICE that is used for printing on invoice stock. When regular paper is in the printer, you could disable the logical stream @INVOICE until you put the invoice stock in the printer, at which time you would enable the logical stream @INVOICE and disable the logical stream @PRINTER.

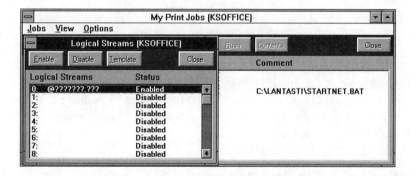

Figure 10.62
The Logical Streams dialog box.

In the Logical Streams list, you see only the default stream @???????.??? displayed. You can add a new logical stream to the streams list by following these steps:

1. Select the position in the list where you want to add a logical stream, and click on that position.

2. Select the **T**emplate button, and the Logical Stream dialog box appears (see fig. 10.63). Type the stream name in the Stream Template field and select OK.

Figure 10.63
Specifying a
Logical Stream
Template.

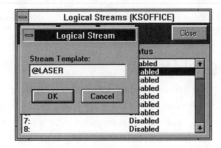

The new logical stream name appears on the list (see fig 10.64). To enable or disable any stream, select the stream and then select **E**nable to enable the stream or **D**isable to disable the stream.

Figure 10.64
The Logical
Streams list with
the @LASER
stream added.

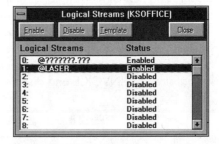

LANtastic processes logical streams in the order they are listed in the Logical Streams list. The @???????.??? stream matches all possible logical streams; if it is enabled and is the first stream in the list, all streams will be sent to the printer, even if the status of other streams listed after it is disabled.

Controlling the Physical Printer Ports

In the same way that logical streams are used to control despooling of specific printer resources, LANtastic also enables you to control the individual physical printer ports on a server. To make changes in the physical printer ports, you must have the Q privilege for this server. To alter the physical printer ports, follow these steps:

1. Select Control **P**rinters from the **J**obs menu. The Printers dialog box appears (see fig. 10.65).

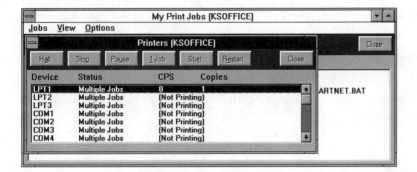

Figure 10.65
The Printers
dialog box.

2. Select the device you want to control by clicking on it. LPT1 is selected in figure 10.65.

3. Select the action you want to take for this printer port by selecting the appropriate button.

   In this example, you choose to select the Halt option, which halts all despooling for the selected port. The LPT1 physical printer port is disabled, and the status next to LPT1 changes to DISABLED (see fig. 10.66).

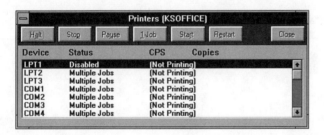

Figure 10.66
The Printers
dialog box
showing port
LPT1 as disabled.

4. To restart the despooler, with the LPT1 device selected, select the Start button.

The following is a list of the options available to control the physical devices:

✔ **Halt.** This stops all printing to the selected port.

✔ **Stop.** This stops printing to the selected port at the end of the current print job.

✔ **Pause.** This temporarily stops printing to the selected port.

✔ **1-Job.** This prints one print job to the selected port and then stops printing to that port.

✔ **Start.** This starts printing to the selected port from the point where the print job was stopped or paused.

✔ **Restart.** This restarts the print job that was being printed when printing was stopped.

Summary

This chapter explained the LANtastic printing features in detail. Differences between network printing and local printing were discussed, and common terms encountered in the network printing arena were defined.

You learned to define and configure printer resources in both DOS and Windows. You also learned the function of LANtastic's Remote Printer Server (RPS) program and how to despool print jobs from a server to a workstation or server by running the RPS program. You found out about the two LANtastic utilities that enable you to print in DOS: LANPUP and NET, and NET in Windows. Adding and managing print jobs in the queue were also covered.

Chapter Snapshot

This chapter will be of most interest to those who have the responsibility of network management. Both DOS and Windows versions of the LANtastic Network Manager programs are discussed, with emphasis placed on the following topics:

✔ Managing individual and wildcard accounts

✔ Managing ACL group accounts

✔ Managing shared resources

✔ Changing network operation using server startup parameters

✔ Managing the printer and mail queues as well as the LANtastic audit trail

✔ Managing the LANtastic control directory and specifying a password for the control directory

✔ Using the LANtastic remote boot capability

✔ The NET_MGR DOS command line options

The chapter also discusses the System Manager Privileges and concludes with a look at the Network Management Commands that enable you to control the overall network.

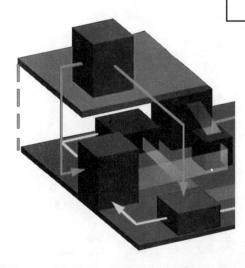

11

CHAPTER

Managing Your Network Using the LANtastic Network Manager

In Chapters 6 and 7, you used the LANtastic Network Manager program to set up your initial user accounts and shared resources. This chapter expands on that basic introduction to provide a more detailed look at the DOS LANtastic Network Manager program, NET_MGR, and the Windows LANtastic Network Manager program.

LANtastic management functions available from the DOS and Windows LANtastic Network Manager programs are similar in function but have very different user interfaces. The DOS and Windows programs are discussed in separate sections independent of each other, so you can read the section that best covers your individual needs.

Using LANtastic with DOS

The following sections cover the features available to manage your LANtastic network in DOS. The same information, as it applies to LANtastic in Windows, is covered later in the chapter.

Understanding NET_MGR Functions

The LANtastic Network Manager program, NET_MGR, enables you to configure your network, set up user accounts, define shared resources, create printer queues, and modify your server parameters as required. NET_MGR is a powerful program, and as a network administrator you should become familiar with its operation. In order to give you a sound foundation and understanding of the program, this section looks at each of the functions that appear on the NET_MGR menu.

You run NET_MGR from the DOS command line by typing the following command and pressing Enter:

```
NET_MGR
```

If you want to manage a control directory that is different from the default LANtastic control directory you specified during installation, you must let NET_MGR know this at the startup by including the new control directory path name in the command line, as in the following example:

```
NET_MGR CONTROL=C:\CNTRLDIR.NET
```

You might have different configurations for LANtastic that you want to run from time to time. You can store the alternate configurations in a separate control directory, which can be accessed by typing a command line similar to the preceding example.

By specifying the LAN_DIR environment variable, you can change the default location where NET_MGR and the SERVER program look for the control directory. To change the default location of the control directory to C:\LANOTHER, for example, type the following line from a DOS prompt or include it in a batch file:

```
SET LAN_DIR=C:\LANOTHER
```

NET_MGR runs in the full-screen mode. LANtastic does not enable you to compress its windows or move them on-screen. Figure 11.1 shows the NET_MGR main menu display.

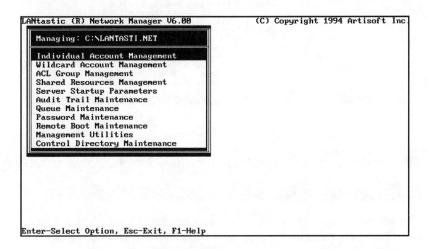

```
LANtastic (R) Network Manager V6.00          (C) Copyright 1994 Artisoft Inc
 ┌──────────────────────────────────────┐
 │ Managing: C:\LANTASTI.NET             │
 │┌──────────────────────────────────────┐
 ││Individual Account Management          │
 ││Wildcard Account Management            │
 ││ACL Group Management                   │
 ││Shared Resources Management            │
 ││Server Startup Parameters              │
 ││Audit Trail Maintenance                │
 ││Queue Maintenance                      │
 ││Password Maintenance                   │
 ││Remote Boot Maintenance                │
 ││Management Utilities                   │
 ││Control Directory Maintenance          │
 │└──────────────────────────────────────┘


Enter-Select Option, Esc-Exit, F1-Help
```

Figure 11.1
The LANtastic
NET_MGR main
menu.

The following sections discuss the functions of each option on the main menu.

Using the Individual Account Management Function

You can use the Individual Account Management function to set up or edit your network users' accounts. By using this option, you can assign a user a login account name, give a brief description of who the user is, give the account a password, and assign the login and access privileges for the account.

You used this option to add new users in Chapter 6, "Setting Up User Accounts and Shared Resources in DOS." To add additional users, do the following:

1. Select the Individual Account Management option by highlighting it and pressing Enter.

2. When the Individual Accounts dialog box appears, press Ins.

3. Enter the account name, password, description, and number of concurrent logins when prompted in the appropriate dialog boxes, and press Enter after entering each item.

4. Next, highlight the new user account name and press Enter to edit the account information in the Account Information dialog box (see fig. 11.2).

Figure 11.2
The Account
Information
dialog box.

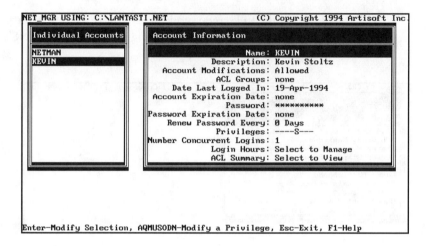

```
NET_MGR USING: C:\LANTASTI.NET                    (C) Copyright 1994 Artisoft Inc
┌─Individual Accounts─┐ ┌─Account Information──────────────────────────────┐
│ NETMAN              │ │                        Name: KEVIN               │
│ KEVIN               │ │                 Description: Kevin Stoltz         │
│                     │ │        Account Modifications: Allowed             │
│                     │ │                  ACL Groups: none                 │
│                     │ │           Date Last Logged In: 19-Apr-1994        │
│                     │ │      Account Expiration Date: none                │
│                     │ │                    Password: **********           │
│                     │ │     Password Expiration Date: none                │
│                     │ │         Renew Password Every: 0 Days              │
│                     │ │                   Privileges: ----S---            │
│                     │ │     Number Concurrent Logins: 1                   │
│                     │ │                  Login Hours: Select to Manage    │
│                     │ │                  ACL Summary: Select to View      │
│                     │ │                                                   │
└─────────────────────┘ └───────────────────────────────────────────────────┘

Enter-Modify Selection, AQMUSODN-Modify a Privilege, Esc-Exit, F1-Help
```

The following discusses each of the account information items:

✔ **Name.** The Name item is the network login name that you assign to the individual user. You should keep the name as short as possible, because the user has to type it each time he or she logs in to the network.

✔ **Description.** The Description item is a short descriptive title for the account. You may want to put the user's real name in this field for clarity. You can use up to 32 characters in this field, but LANtastic displays only 24 on the Account Information screen.

✔ **Account Modifications.** This item may be toggled between Allowed or Disallowed. If Allowed, users may change their passwords or disable their accounts after they log in.

The default setting for the Account Modifications field is Allowed for individual accounts and Disallowed for wildcard accounts. This is because normally you want individuals to be able to change their passwords or disable their accounts. You do not, however, want someone using a wildcard account to do the same, because that action would then prevent others from using the same wildcard account.

✔ **ACL Groups.** This selection enables you to select and modify the Access Control List Groups to which an account belongs. An account does not have to belong to any ACL Group.

✔ **Date Last Logged In.** This field is updated by LANtastic each time the user logs in to the network. You cannot make any changes in this field.

✔ **Account Expiration Date.** This field enables you to set a date at which time the account is no longer active. You can use this item to set up accounts for users who may need access to your network only for a limited period of time. After the expiration date, the user cannot use the account anymore. Account expiration dates can help you maintain control of your network.

✔ **Password.** The system manager can make changes directly in the Password field. The manager makes the changes when initially setting up the account, but after that, the user normally makes his or her own changes by using the NET utility functions as part of his or her account-management responsibilities. The actual password does not appear on-screen; instead, a string of asterisks is displayed to mask the password.

✔ **Password Expiration Date.** As the network manager, you can use this field to force a user to change his or her password on a specific date. An attempt to log in after the Password Expiration Date is refused, except as summarized in the Renew Password Every description below. A good security practice is to have users change their passwords at regular intervals to prevent unauthorized people from discovering a password and using it to access the information on your network.

✔ **Renew Password Every.** This field contains the time interval in which the account password must be changed. This interval is expressed in days. As the end of the cycle approaches, LANtastic presents a warning to the user that his password needs to be changed. If the current date is later than the Password Expiration Date, the user is allowed to log in once and change his password. After an interval has been entered in this field, the Password Expiration Date automatically updates according to the number in this field. This is a good choice for forcing regular password changes. Pick a cycle of days that is not a burden to your users, but is effective in preventing password compromise. Thirty days is a good number.

✔ **Privileges.** Use the Privilege field to assign special access privileges for the user account. The user account access privileges you assign override any access-control levels you assign to shared resources. To assign privileges, highlight the field and type the letters that represent the privileges.

These privileges are for special types of access, and you should consider them with care before giving them to a user. A user account with no assigned privileges still can access shared resources on the network, but is controlled by the specific ACLs assigned to that shared resource. The assignment of ACLs to network resources is covered in Chapter 6.

The following sections discuss the privileges that you can assign:

A. - Super ACL. Called the Super ACL Privilege, the A privilege gives users access to every resource on the network. If a user has this privilege, the ACL list for a resource is not checked when he or she uses a resource.

Q. - Super Queue. Called the Super Queue Privilege, the Q privilege enables users to view and manipulate all the jobs in the print queue, not just their own jobs. A user with this privilege can control the server's despooler and cause it to start and stop, as well as delete items from the queue. You should give this privilege only to users who need this level of control, such as your assistant network administrator and a few select others who are knowledgeable about network printing operations.

M. - Super Mail. Called the Super Mail Privilege, the M privilege enables the user to read and manipulate all of the mail items in the server's mail queue, not just his or her own. Because of the sensitive nature of users' mail, you might not want to give this privilege to anyone except the network administrator.

U. - User Auditing. Called the User Auditing Privilege, the U privilege enables a user to create audit entries in the server's audit log and to issue NET AUDIT commands. You should not give this privilege to many users. If a large number of audit entries are being created and stored on the server's hard disk, you could run out of usable hard disk storage space. You should keep this privilege for yourself and your assistant.

S. - System Manager. This privilege, called the System Manager privilege, should only be assigned to the network administrator and the alternate administrator. It enables the user to perform special network manager functions that control the network. With this privilege, the user can execute commands to remotely shut down the network or log users out of the server(s).

O. - Operator. This privilege, called the Operator privilege, provides the user with messages that might require operator intervention, such as a message from a printer indicating it is out of paper.

D. - Despooler. This privilege, called the Despooler privilege, enables the remote despooling program to despool jobs from the server's print queue to a local printer.

N. - Network Manager. This privilege, called the Network Manager privilege, enables the user to view the status information and performance statistics of a server.

✔ **Number Concurrent Logins.** This field enables you to set the number of concurrent logins that a user account can make to the server. If, for example, you set the number of concurrent logins to 3, there can be three different computers at a time logged in to the server using this account name. If you log in to the server at which you are sitting with this account name, it counts as one of the three allowed. Having more than one concurrent login is useful if you have a single account that multiple users use (such as a GUEST account) or if you log in to the server from more than one computer at the same time. To disable an account, set the Number of Concurrent Logins to 0.

Each server must have a set of user accounts set up for the users that access that machine. If you have multiple servers on your network, you should set up identical accounts for all of the users on each server. This way, your users can log in to each server by using the same password and access rights and not have to remember a series of different passwords and user names. LANtastic enables you to copy user accounts to other servers, saving you the time and trouble of typing them all again. In addition, you can specify account servers that contain the user accounts for other servers to access.

✔ **Login Hours.** This option defines the time of day when the user account is allowed to log in to this server. If you have sensitive information on your network and you do not want all your users to have access to the network at all times, set up specific limits by using this function. When you select this option, the Time of Day Allowed Logins window appears (see fig. 11.3). The diamonds represent the half-hour periods in which the user can log in to the server. Initially, all half hours of access are enabled. To change the times of authorized access, move the cursor to the time slots that you want to change and press Del. If you disable a time slot by mistake, move to that slot and press Ins to enable access for that time. Press Enter to save your new definition.

✔ **ACL Summary.** Selecting this item displays a summary of the ACL (Access Control List) for an account, as determined by the ACL for each shared resource on a computer. This summary is extremely useful because it verifies that the ACLs have been set up the way you want them. For each shared resource listed on the ACL Summary list, there are three columns of information: ACLs, Accounts, and Groups (see fig. 11.4). The ACLs column is the sum of the Accounts column and the Groups column, and represents all the ACL rights for the account. The Accounts column shows the ACL rights for a specific account. The Groups column shows the ACL rights for the group or groups for which the account is a member.

Figure 11.3
The Login Hours screen.

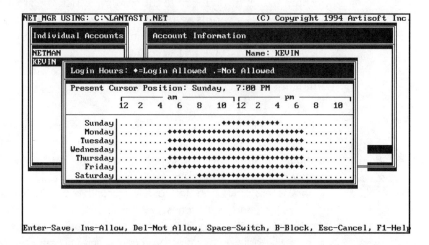

```
NET_MGR USING: C:\LANTASTI.NET                (C) Copyright 1994 Artisoft Inc.
 Individual Accounts      Account Information
NETMAN                                        Name: KEVIN
KEVIN
         Login Hours: +=Login Allowed  .=Not Allowed

         Present Cursor Position: Sunday,  7:00 PM
                           am                    pm
                  12  2   4   6   8  10  12  2   4   6   8  10

          Sunday  ...........................++++++++++++.........
          Monday  .........+++++++++++++++++++++++++++++++.........
         Tuesday  .........+++++++++++++++++++++++++++++++++.......
       Wednesday  .........+++++++++++++++++++++++++++++++.........
        Thursday  .........+++++++++++++++++++++++++++++++.........
          Friday  .........+++++++++++++++++++++++++++++...........
        Saturday  ...........................++++++++++++++........

Enter-Save, Ins-Allow, Del-Not Allow, Space-Switch, B-Block, Esc-Cancel, F1-Help
```

Figure 11.4
The ACL Summary list for an account.

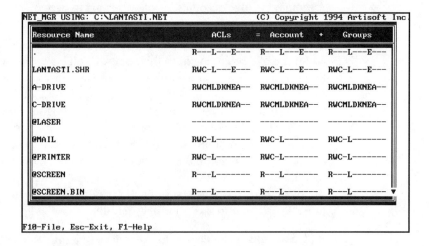

```
NET_MGR USING: C:\LANTASTI.NET                (C) Copyright 1994 Artisoft Inc.
Resource Name                      ACLs     =  Account   +    Groups

.                               R---L---E---   R---L---E---   R---L---E---

LANTASTI.SHR                    RWC-L---E---   RWC-L---E---   RWC-L---E---

A-DRIVE                         RWCMLDKNEA--   RWCMLDKNEA--   RWCMLDKNEA--

C-DRIVE                         RWCMLDKNEA--   RWCMLDKNEA--   RWCMLDKNEA--

@LASER                          ------------   ------------   ------------

@MAIL                           RWC-L-------   RWC-L-------   RWC-L-------

@PRINTER                        RWC-L-------   RWC-L-------   RWC-L-------

@SCREEN                         R---L-------   R---L-------   R---L-------

@SCREEN.BIN                     R---L-------   R---L-------   R---L------- ▼

F10-File, Esc-Exit, F1-Help
```

Using the Wildcard Account Management Function

The Wildcard Account Management menu option is used to set up or edit an account that can be used by more than one person at a time to access a server. Wildcard accounts provide an easy and manageable way to set up group accounts for people with similar work needs, hours, and duties. You can set up accounts for users who are all in one workgroup, give them the same access privileges, and not require separate individual user accounts for each.

LANtastic sets up one universal group account as part of its installation process. On the Wildcard Accounts display, you can see an account with only the * displayed. This account enables anybody who logs in to have access to the server. You should delete this account after you establish your own user and system manager accounts.

In figure 11.5, several wildcard accounts are shown. The OPS account, for example, is set up to be used by any users in the operations department. Members of this group can log in by using the name OPS, followed by their own initials or name, or they can type the OPS login name (they do not have to include the asterisk (*)).

 For network control purposes, it is better if users are required to add their name or initials to the login name, especially if you are using audit trails and tracking user activity on the network. You establish the policy on the way you want to use such controls.

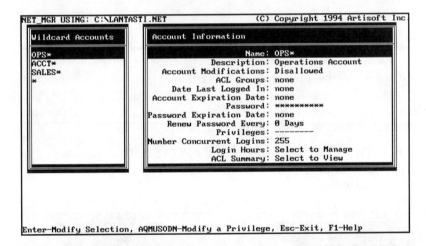

Figure 11.5
The Wildcard Account Information screen.

Using the ACL Group Management Option

The ACL Group option is a powerful feature of LANtastic that enables you to group different accounts according to the type or level of access they have to your shared network resources. You can save time by using ACL Groups—especially when setting up new user accounts, because you can define the new user as belonging to an ACL group that already exists. You do not have to add this new user to each shared resource ACL, because the ACL group to which the user already belongs is listed on the shared resource ACL.

When you select this option, a window appears showing the defined ACL Groups and the number of members that belong to each group (see fig. 11.6). You can add a new ACL group by pressing Ins. To delete an ACL group, press Del. To add or delete members from an ACL group, highlight the ACL group and press Enter.

Figure 11.6
The defined ACL
group list.

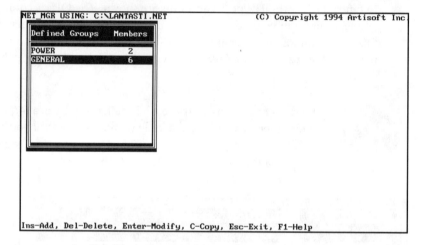

You enter the name and description of the ACL group when creating a new ACL group. After the new ACL group is created, it shows up on the ACL group list. A new ACL group has no members, so highlighting the new ACL group and pressing Enter enables you to select members for the ACL group.

Figure 11.7 shows the selection of members for the POWER ACL group. As members are selected for the group, their account names appear in the ACL Group Information window.

Figure 11.7
Selecting
members for the
POWER ACL
group.

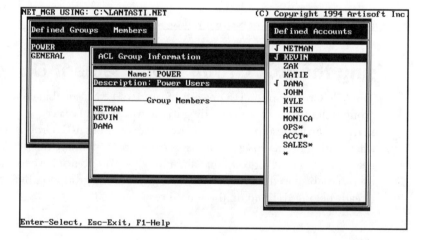

Chapter 6, "Setting Up User Accounts and Shared Resources in DOS," includes detailed information and examples for setting up ACL groups.

Using the Shared Resources Management Option

As was discussed in Chapter 6, the Shared Resources Management option sets up shared network resources for the users on a server. If you have multiple servers, you must set up shared resources for each server. Network resources can be disk drives, files, application programs, printers, and other devices, such as CD-ROM drives.

When you select this option, the Resource Name list appears (see fig. 11.8). If this is the first time you have looked at this file since you installed LANtastic, you see the default settings that the INSTALL process set up. INSTALL gets this information by scanning your server's configuration and from the information you enter during the installation process.

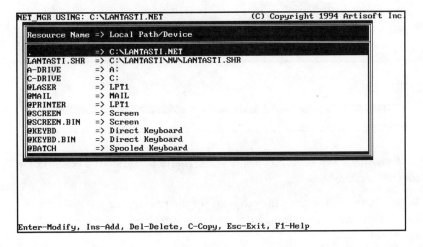

Figure 11.8
Shared Resource Name list.

The printer and mail resources are preceded by the @ character. Shared screen and keyboard resources also are preceded by the @ character. Do not use this character with a file resource because LANtastic thinks it is a printer and you cannot configure it as a shared file resource.

Shared screen and keyboard resources enable you to access the screen and keyboard on a server from a different computer in the network. The Monitor & Manage Server Activity option in LANtastic's NET program makes it possible for you to use a server's screen and keyboard remotely.

Because shared drive resources and shared printer resources are different, the Detailed Information screen for each type of resource differs accordingly.

The Detailed Information Screen for a Drive Resource

You can modify the following five parameters on the Detailed Information screen for a shared drive resource (see fig. 11.9):

Figure 11.9
Shared
Resource
Detailed
Information list.

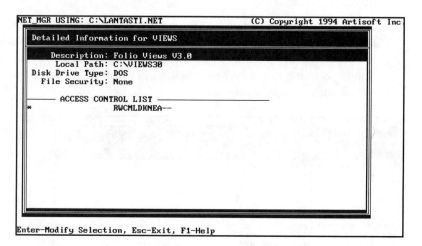

```
NET_MGR USING: C:\LANTASTI.NET                    (C) Copyright 1994 Artisoft Inc.
┌─ Detailed Information for VIEWS ──────────────────────────────────┐
│        Description: Folio Views V3.0                               │
│         Local Path: C:\VIEWS30                                     │
│    Disk Drive Type: DOS                                            │
│      File Security: None                                           │
│                                                                    │
│        ─── ACCESS CONTROL LIST ──────────────────────────         │
│     *              RWCMLDKNEA--                                    │
│                                                                    │
│                                                                    │
└────────────────────────────────────────────────────────────────┘
Enter-Modify Selection, Esc-Exit, F1-Help
```

✔ **Description.** You can enter a short description of the shared resource for easy recognition.

✔ **Local Path.** This is the full path name of the resource as it is referenced locally from the server. It includes the drive letter and subdirectory (if applicable).

✔ **Disk Drive Type.** This is normally set to DOS. LANtastic also supports CD-ROM drives, WORM (Write Once Read Many) drives, and other drive types. Pressing Enter while in this field displays a list of drive types that you can select. The following drive types are listed: DOS, CD-ROM, WORM, NetWare, OS/2, and Other.

✔ **File Security.** This option allows you to enable file level security. By defining file templates, such as *.EXE, and associating them with access control lists, you can limit the access of an account to a resource at the file level. If the resource you are sharing includes multiple directories, this option also enables you to restrict access to chosen directories.

✔ **Access Control List.** The Access Control List option enables you to assign access to this resource on a selective basis. It specifies the access that an account has to a shared resource. The ACL includes the account and/or ACL group names and their associated rights.

To enter a new ACL, do the following:

1. Highlight the * line below the ACL list title, and press Ins.

2. Type the individual user account, wildcard account, ACL group, or a wildcard for which you want to create an ACL, and press Enter.

3. Press F4 to clear the ACL rights for the new account.

4. Press the letter representing each access right that you want to give users for this resource. You can choose from the following access rights:

R-Read Access	User can open files for reading
W-Write Access	User can write to files
C-Create File	User can create files
M-Make Directory	User can create a new subdirectory
L-Allow File Lookups	User can display or search through directories or subdirectories
D-Delete Files	User can delete files
K-Delete Directories	User can delete subdirectories
N-Rename Files	User can rename files
E-Execute Programs	User can execute programs

A-Change File Attributes	User can change the attributes of files in a shared directory
I-Indirect Files	User can create and use indirect files within this shared directory
P-Physical Access	User can connect to devices directly without having to go through the server's spooler. Use this option with care because it can cause some delay in printer availability to network users.

Chapter 6 includes detailed instructions and examples for setting up shared drive resources.

The Detailed Information Screen for a Printer Resource

You can modify the following parameters on the Detailed Information screen for a shared printer resource (see fig. 11.10):

Figure 11.10
Detailed Information screen for @LASER printer resource.

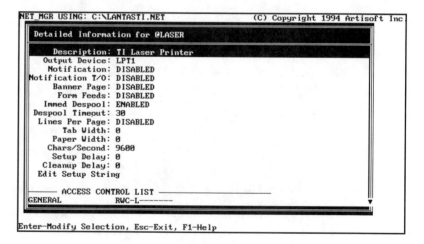

```
NET_MGR USING: C:\LANTASTI.NET                (C) Copyright 1994 Artisoft Inc
┌─ Detailed Information for @LASER ──────────────────────────────────────┐
│       Description: TI Laser Printer                                     │
│     Output Device: LPT1                                                 │
│      Notification: DISABLED                                             │
│  Notification T/O: DISABLED                                             │
│       Banner Page: DISABLED                                             │
│        Form Feeds: DISABLED                                             │
│     Immed Despool: ENABLED                                              │
│    Despool Timeout: 30                                                  │
│    Lines Per Page: DISABLED                                             │
│         Tab Width: 0                                                    │
│       Paper Width: 0                                                    │
│      Chars/Second: 9600                                                 │
│       Setup Delay: 0                                                    │
│     Cleanup Delay: 0                                                    │
│  Edit Setup String                                                      │
│                                                                         │
│  ─────── ACCESS CONTROL LIST ───────────────────────────                │
│GENERAL              RWC-L-------                                      ▼ │
└─────────────────────────────────────────────────────────────────────────┘
Enter-Modify Selection, Esc-Exit, F1-Help
```

✔ Description

✔ Output Device

✔ Notification

✔ Notification T/O

✔ Banner Page

✔ Form Feeds

✔ Immed Despool

✔ Despool Timeout

✔ Lines Per Page

✔ Tab Width

✔ Paper Width

✔ Chars/Second

✔ Setup Delay

✔ Cleanup Delay

✔ Edit Setup String

See Chapter 10, "Printing with LANtastic," for detailed instructions and examples for setting up shared printer resources.

Using the Server Startup Parameters Option

You control the Server program's operation by using the Server Startup Parameters option (see figs. 11.11 and 11.12). You can modify these parameters to optimize your server's performance, set up audit trails, and make general changes to your network configuration. The following discussions cover each of the parameters and show the LANtastic defaults, as set by Artisoft (refer to Chapter 15, "Getting the Most Out of LANtastic," for possible improvements to the default settings).

Figure 11.11
Server Startup
Parameters
screen (upper
portion).

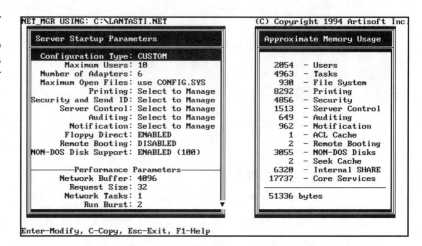

```
NET_MGR USING: C:\LANTASTI.NET                  (C) Copyright 1994 Artisoft Inc.
┌─Server Startup Parameters──────┐          ┌─Approximate Memory Usage──────┐
│  Configuration Type: CUSTOM    │          │                               │
│     Maximum Users: 10          │          │  2054  - Users                │
│ Number of Adapters: 6          │          │  4963  - Tasks                │
│ Maximum Open Files: use CONFIG.SYS│       │   930  - File System          │
│          Printing: Select to Manage│      │  8292  - Printing             │
│Security and Send ID: Select to Manage│    │  4856  - Security             │
│     Server Control: Select to Manage│     │  1513  - Server Control       │
│          Auditing: Select to Manage│      │   649  - Auditing             │
│      Notification: Select to Manage│      │   962  - Notification         │
│     Floppy Direct: ENABLED     │          │     1  - ACL Cache            │
│    Remote Booting: DISABLED    │          │     2  - Remote Booting       │
│NON-DOS Disk Support: ENABLED (100)│       │  3055  - NON-DOS Disks        │
│                                │          │     2  - Seek Cache           │
│      ──Performance Parameters──│          │  6320  - Internal SHARE       │
│    Network Buffer: 4096        │          │ 17737  - Core Services        │
│      Request Size: 32          │          │                               │
│     Network Tasks: 1           │          │ 51336 bytes                   │
│         Run Burst: 2         ▼ │          │                               │
└────────────────────────────────┘          └───────────────────────────────┘
Enter-Modify, C-Copy, Esc-Exit, F1-Help
```

Figure 11.12
Server Startup
Parameters
screen (lower
portion).

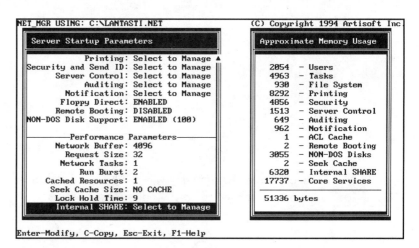

```
NET_MGR USING: C:\LANTASTI.NET                  (C) Copyright 1994 Artisoft Inc.
┌─Server Startup Parameters──────┐          ┌─Approximate Memory Usage──────┐
│          Printing: Select to Manage ▲│    │                               │
│Security and Send ID: Select to Manage│    │  2054  - Users                │
│     Server Control: Select to Manage│     │  4963  - Tasks                │
│          Auditing: Select to Manage│      │   930  - File System          │
│      Notification: Select to Manage│      │  8292  - Printing             │
│     Floppy Direct: ENABLED     │          │  4856  - Security             │
│    Remote Booting: DISABLED    │          │  1513  - Server Control       │
│NON-DOS Disk Support: ENABLED (100)│       │   649  - Auditing             │
│                                │          │   962  - Notification         │
│      ──Performance Parameters──│          │     1  - ACL Cache            │
│    Network Buffer: 4096        │          │     2  - Remote Booting       │
│      Request Size: 32          │          │  3055  - NON-DOS Disks        │
│     Network Tasks: 1           │          │     2  - Seek Cache           │
│         Run Burst: 2           │          │  6320  - Internal SHARE       │
│   Cached Resources: 1          │          │ 17737  - Core Services        │
│    Seek Cache Size: NO CACHE   │          │                               │
│      Lock Hold Time: 9         │          │ 51336 bytes                   │
│    Internal SHARE: Select to Manage│      │                               │
└────────────────────────────────┘          └───────────────────────────────┘
Enter-Modify, C-Copy, Esc-Exit, F1-Help
```

As you change the Server Startup Parameter settings, LANtastic displays the approximate amount of memory usage associated with the change. This new feature enables you to immediately see the effect your changes have on memory usage, and enables you to make the required adjustments.

✔ **Configuration Type.** This field may contain several different server configurations which are optimized for different types of server usage. As a starting point, you can select the server configuration that best suits your needs, and then proceed to make additional changes to meet your requirements. Press Enter to select a pre-defined server configuration (see fig. 11.13). The following list describes the available configurations you can select:

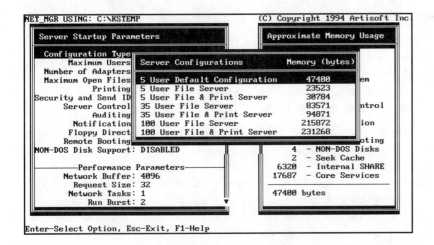

Figure 11.13
The Server Configurations window.

5 User Default Configuration. This is the default configuration from when you first installed LANtastic. The Server program with this configuration uses approximately 47,400 bytes of memory.

5 User File Server. Because this configuration uses the minimum amount of memory, it is for sharing files and not printers. The Server program with this configuration uses approximately 23,523 bytes of memory.

5 User File & Printer Server. This configuration uses the minimum amount of memory for sharing files and printers. The Server program with this configuration uses approximately 30,784 bytes of memory.

35 User File Server. This configuration takes advantage of some of LANtastic's basic security and performance improvement features, and is used for sharing files but not printers. The Server program with this configuration uses approximately 83,571 bytes of memory.

35 User File & Printer Server. This configuration takes advantage of some of LANtastic's basic security and performance improvement features, and is used for sharing files and printers. The Server program with this configuration uses approximately 94,871 bytes of memory.

100 User File Server. This configuration takes full advantage of LANtastic's security and performance improvement features, and is used for sharing files but not printers. The Server program with this configuration uses approximately 215,872 bytes of memory.

100 User File & Printer Server. This configuration takes full advantage of LANtastic's security and performance improvement features and is used for sharing files and printers. The Server program with this configuration uses approximately 231,268 bytes of memory.

✔ **Maximum Users.** This field sets the maximum number of users that can log in to the server. The range for this field is 2 to 500. LANtastic has a default setting of 5. If you have more than five users that log in to this server at the same time, increase the number in this field to equal the number of users that can log in.

✔ **Number of Adapters.** This field sets the number of network adapters that are installed in the server. The range for this field is from 1 to 6. The default setting is 6. Normally, a server only has one network adapter installed. If you have a LANtastic network that is using the LANtastic 2 Mbps adapters and another LANtastic network that is using Ethernet adapters, you could put one of each kind of adapter in this server. Each network can then access this common server.

✔ **Maximum Open Files.** You can set the number of files that users can have open simultaneously by using the Max Files Open option. Normally, you would let the DOS CONFIG.SYS file control this function. The range for this field is from 50 to 5,100. The default value is use CONFIG.SYS (specified by selecting 0) and means that the FILES= statement in CONFIG.SYS will be used to determine the maximum number of files that may be open. DOS has a maximum open files limit of 255; therefore, if you need more open files, setting a number higher than this causes the server to use its own separate files to handle network functions. The value specified in CONFIG.SYS is then used for the local file functions.

✔ **Printing.** This option will either display Select to Manage if printing is ENABLED, or DISABLED if printing functions are disabled. Selecting this option will display a menu with the following printing configuration options (see fig. 11.14).

Printing. Press Enter to toggle this field between ENABLED and DISABLED. If disabled, this server may not be used for network printing functions. This feature must be enabled to use LANtastic Mail. The default for this field is ENABLED.

Printer Tasks. This setting enables the server to despool to multiple printers at one time. Set this field to equal the number of printers that are physically attached to this server. The range for this field is from 0 to 7, and the default is 1.

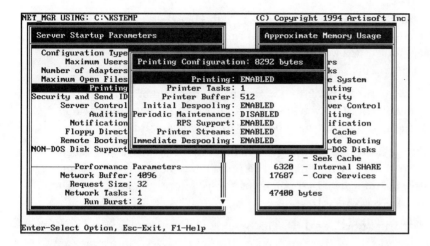

Figure 11.14
The Printing
Configuration
menu.

If you are running Microsoft Windows and you experience slow printing, set the number of Printer Tasks to 1, even if you have more than one printer attached to the server. Setting Printer Tasks to a number other than 1 may result in extremely slow network printing when the server is running Windows.

Printer Buffer. The Printer Buffer option sets the size of the print buffer. By increasing the size of the print buffer, you can enhance print performance by reducing the number of disk accesses required to read the data from the spool area. The range for this field is from 512 to 32,768 bytes. The default is 512 bytes.

Initial Despooling. You can set this field to ENABLED or DISABLED by highlighting this option and pressing Enter. The default setting is enabled. With this setting, all print jobs automatically despool to the network printer(s) serviced by the server. If you set this option to DISABLED, you need to issue the NET QUEUE START or NET QUEUE SINGLE commands to begin despooling to a printer.

Periodic Maintenance. Press Enter to toggle this field between ENABLED and DISABLED. Enabling this option causes the printer control file to be rebuilt periodically to optimize printing speed. Normally this is done each time the server is started, so unless you leave your computer on all the time you do not need to enable this feature. The default is DISABLED.

RPS Support. Press Enter to toggle this field between ENABLED and DISABLED. If you have remote printer resources on this server that are despooled by a workstation running the Remote Printer Server (RPS) program, this feature must be enabled. The default is ENABLED.

Printer Streams. Press Enter to toggle this field between ENABLED and DISABLED. If you intend to control your printers using printer streams, this feature must be enabled. The default is ENABLED.

Immediate Despooling. Press Enter to toggle this field between ENABLED and DISABLED. This option must be enabled if you intend to specify Immediate Despooling for any of your printer resources. The default is ENABLED.

✔ **Security and Send ID.** This option will either display Select to Manage if security features are enabled, or DISABLED if security features are disabled. Selecting this option will display a menu with the following security configuration options (see fig. 11.15):

Figure 11.15
The Security Configuration options menu.

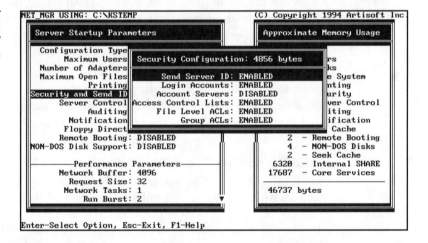

```
NET_MGR USING: C:\KSTEMP                      (C) Copyright 1994 Artisoft Inc
┌─Server Startup Parameters─────┐      ┌─Approximate Memory Usage──┐
│   Configuration Type          │      │                           │
│      Maximum Users ┌─Security Configuration: 4856 bytes─┐rs      │
│   Number of Adapters│                                    │ks      │
│   Maximum Open Files│    Send Server ID: ENABLED         │e System│
│          Printing   │    Login Accounts: ENABLED         │nting   │
│ Security and Send ID│  Account Servers: DISABLED         │urity   │
│    Server Control Access Control Lists: ENABLED          │ver Control│
│          Auditing   │    File Level ACLs: ENABLED        │iting   │
│       Notification  │      Group ACLs: ENABLED           │ification│
│     Floppy Direct   └────────────────────────────────────┘ Cache  │
│    Remote Booting: DISABLED                  2  - Remote Booting  │
│NON-DOS Disk Support: DISABLED                4  - NON-DOS Disks   │
│                                              2  - Seek Cache      │
│     ──Performance Parameters──            6320  - Internal SHARE  │
│    Network Buffer: 4096                   17687  - Core Services  │
│     Request Size: 32                                             │
│     Network Tasks: 1                      46737 bytes            │
│        Run Burst: 2            ▼                                 │
└───────────────────────────────┘      └───────────────────────────┘
Enter-Select Option, Esc-Exit, F1-Help
```

Send Server ID. Press Enter to toggle this field between ENABLED and DISABLED. If enabled, the server sends its ID, which is displayed in the list of servers when using the NET program or when issuing the NET SHOW command. The default is ENABLED.

Login Accounts. Press Enter to toggle this field between ENABLED and DISABLED. If enabled, a user must use a valid individual or wildcard account to log in to the server. If disabled, any user can log in to the server without using an account name. The default is ENABLED.

Account Servers. This option enables you to choose one or more LANtastic servers from which account files will be used. The default setting for this field is DISABLED. By highlighting this field and pressing Enter, you can select the servers to scan for accounts. The accounts from the first server found on the list are used for this server. Enabling the Account Servers feature disables the accounts defined on the server you are configuring. Pressing Ins enables you to add a server name to the Account Servers list. With an account server highlighted, press Del to remove the server from the list.

When you use the NET program to log in to a server that is using an account list from another server, if autologin is enabled and a valid account does not exist, LANtastic does not give you the option to enter a name and password as it normally does when not using an account from another server. In this situation, you need to disable the autologin feature by typing the following NET command at the DOS prompt:

```
NET USER/DISABLE
```

Access Control Lists. Press Enter to toggle this field between EN-ABLED and DISABLED. When enabled, the ACL for each shared resource is checked before a user is given access. When disabled, the ACLs are ignored and full access to shared resources is given to everyone. The default is ENABLED.

File Level ACLs. Press Enter to toggle this field between ENABLED and DISABLED. When enabled, the file level ACL is checked before access is allowed. When disabled, the file level ACLs are ignored and everyone can have full access. Access Control Lists must be enabled if you want to use this option. The default is ENABLED.

Group ACLs. Press Enter to toggle this field between ENABLED and DISABLED. When enabled, users can gain access through group ACLs. Access Control Lists must be enabled to use this option. The default is ENABLED.

✔ **Server Control.** This option will either display Select to Manage if server control features are enabled, or DISABLED if server control features are disabled. Selecting this option will display a menu with the following two options (see fig. 11.16):

Figure 11.16
The Server
Control options
menu.

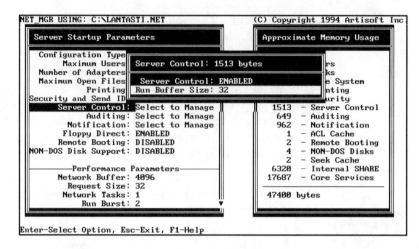

```
NET_MGR USING: C:\LANTASTI.NET              (C) Copyright 1994 Artisoft Inc.
┌ Server Startup Parameters ──────────┐    ┌ Approximate Memory Usage ──────┐
  Configuration Type┌ Server Control: 1513 bytes ┐rs
      Maximum Users │                            │ks
  Number of Adapters│  Server Control: ENABLED   │e System
  Maximum Open Files│  Run Buffer Size: 32       │nting
          Printing  └────────────────────────────┘urity
Security and Send ID
      Server Control: Select to Manage      1513  - Server Control
          Auditing: Select to Manage         649  - Auditing
      Notification: Select to Manage         962  - Notification
     Floppy Direct: ENABLED                    1  - ACL Cache
    Remote Booting: DISABLED                   2  - Remote Booting
NON-DOS Disk Support: DISABLED                 4  - NON-DOS Disks
                                               2  - Seek Cache
    ────Performance Parameters────          6320  - Internal SHARE
    Network Buffer: 4096                    17687 - Core Services
      Request Size: 32
     Network Tasks: 1                       47400 bytes
         Run Burst: 2                  ▼
Enter-Select Option, Esc-Exit, F1-Help
```

Server Control. Press Enter to toggle this field between ENABLED and DISABLED. When enabled, this option allows others to remotely control this server. Control options include enabling others to shut down the server, flush the server's caches, log users off the server, enable and disable logins, and control the server's keyboard and screen. The default is ENABLED.

Run Buffer Size. This is the size of the buffer used for NET RUN commands. Values may range from 32 to 1,024 with the default value of 32. Server Control must be enabled to use the NET RUN commands.

✔ **Auditing.** This option will either display Select to Manage if auditing features are enabled, or DISABLED if auditing features are disabled. The AUDITING features work with the NET_MGR Audit Trail Maintenance functions. When an auditing feature is enabled, entries are automatically made to the audit trail file when certain events occur. Many of the auditing features also notify a user of an event if that user has the operator privilege enabled for his account. Selecting this option will display a menu with the following options (see fig. 11.17):

Auditing. Press Enter to toggle this field between ENABLED and DISABLED. If enabled, an audit trail file is created, containing entries for the following options. The default is ENABLED.

Server Up. Press Enter to toggle this field between To File and DISABLED. If enabled, an audit trail entry is made each time the server is started or shut down. The default is DISABLED.

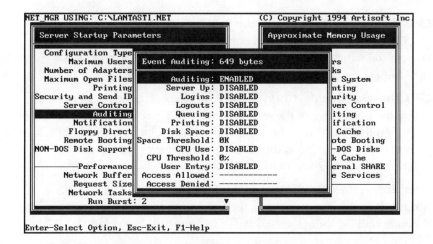

Figure 11.17
The Event
Auditing options.

Logins. Press Enter to toggle this field between To File and DISABLED. If enabled, an audit trail entry is made each time a user logs in to the server. The default is DISABLED.

Logouts. Press Enter to toggle this field between To File and DIS-ABLED. If enabled, an audit trail entry is made each time a user logs out of the server. The default is DISABLED.

Queuing. Press Enter to toggle this field between To File and DIS-ABLED. If enabled, an audit trail entry is made each time a print job or mail item is sent to the queue. The default is DISABLED.

Printing. Press Enter to toggle this field between To File and DIS-ABLED. If enabled, an audit trail entry is made each time a print job finishes printing. The default is DISABLED.

Disk Space. Press Enter to toggle this field between To File and DISABLED. If enabled, an audit trail entry is made each time the available disk space on the server falls below the value specified in the Space Threshold field. The default is DISABLED.

Space Threshold. If the Disk Space option is enabled, the value in this field is the minimum available disk space (in kilobytes) that must exist on the hard drive before an audit trail entry is made. Once the available disk space falls below the Space Threshold value, an audit trail entry is made. The default is 0 KB.

CPU Use. Press Enter to toggle this field between To File and DIS-ABLED. If enabled, an audit trail entry is made each time the CPU usage exceeds the value specified in the CPU Threshold field. The default is DISABLED.

CPU Threshold. If the CPU Use option is enabled, the value in this field is the percentage of the server's maximum capacity at which point an entry will be made to the audit trail file. If the value specified is 75 percent, for example, an audit trail entry is made each time the server's usage exceeds 75 percent of its maximum capacity. The default is 0.

User Entry. Press Enter to toggle this field between To File and DIS-ABLED. If enabled, any user with the U privilege may make an entry to the audit trail file using the NET AUDIT command. The default is DISABLED.

Access Allowed and **Access Denied.** You can enable these two features by typing the letter that corresponds to the ACL that you want to be audited. If you want to track all Read and Write accesses that are allowed, for example, highlight the Access Allowed option and type **R** and **W**. These access types appear on the dashed line to the right of the option. You can do the same for the Access Denied option. The following is a list of the access types:

R - Read

W - Write

C - Create

M - Make Directory

L - Lookups (DIR)

D - Delete files

K - Delete directories

N - Rename a file

E - Execute a program

A - Change file attributes

I - Indirect file access

P - Physical access to a file

✔ **Notification.** This option will either display Select to Manage, if operator notification features are enabled, or DISABLED, if operator notification features are disabled. Selecting this option will display a menu with the following options (see fig. 11.18):

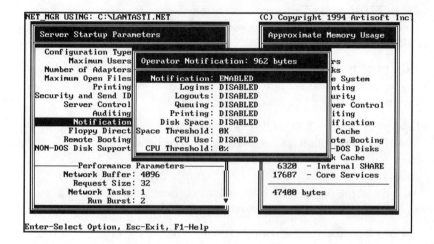

Figure 11.18
The Operator Notification options.

Notification. Press Enter to toggle this field between ENABLED and DISABLED. If enabled, users with the O-Operator privilege are notified when any of the selected events below occur. The default is ENABLED.

Logins. Press Enter to toggle this field between To Operator and DISABLED. If enabled, operators are notified when anyone logs in to the server. The default is DISABLED.

Logouts. Press Enter to toggle this field between To Operator and DISABLED. If enabled, operators are notified when anyone logs out of the server. The default is DISABLED.

Queuing. Press Enter to toggle this field between To Operator and DISABLED. If enabled, operators are notified when a mail message or print job is sent to the queue. The default is DISABLED.

Printing. Press Enter to toggle this field between To Operator and DISABLED. If enabled, operators are notified each time a print job finishes printing. The default is DISABLED.

Disk Space. Press Enter to toggle this field between To Operator and DISABLED. If enabled, operators are notified each time the available disk space on this server falls below the value specified in the Space Threshold field. The default is DISABLED.

Space Threshold. Press Enter to enter the minimum amount of disk space (in kilobytes) that must be available. If the amount of available disk space falls below the value specified here, operators are notified.

CPU Use. Press Enter to toggle this field between To Operator and DISABLED. If enabled, operators are notified each time the server usage exceeds the percentage specified in the CPU Threshold field. The default is DISABLED.

CPU Threshold. Press Enter to specify how heavily this server may be used before operators are notified. Specify the CPU Threshold as a percentage of the server's maximum capacity.

✔ **Floppy Direct.** You can set this field to ENABLED or DISABLED by highlighting the option and pressing Enter. The default setting is enabled. This enables a user to issue the DOS FORMAT and CHKDSK commands to floppy disks in the server's floppy drives. If this field is enabled and the floppy drive is shared with others on the network, a network user can format a floppy disk in the drive; therefore, use caution.

✔ **Remote Booting.** You can set this field to DISABLED or ENABLED by highlighting the option and pressing Enter. The default setting is disabled. If you are using diskless workstations on your network, enabling this option gives the server the ability to remotely boot those workstations, provided they have a network adapter installed that is equipped with a remote boot ROM chip. If you do use remote booting, you must create a boot image on the server by using the Remote Boot Maintenance option in NET_MGR, as discussed later in this chapter.

✔ **NON-DOS Disk Support.** This option may be toggled between ENABLED and DISABLED by pressing the Enter key. To enable NON-DOS Disk Support (CD-ROM drives, WORM—Write Once Read Many—drives, etc.) enter the number of non-DOS disk drive entries to be supported by the server. If the entire list does not appear when performing a directory listing (DIR) of the non-DOS disk, you will need to increase this value. Valid entries for this field range from 0 to 2,400.

The remaining options on the Server Startup Parameters screen are listed under the Performance Parameters section. Changing these items affects how the server performs in the network.

✔ **Network Buffers.** This field sets the size of the network buffers used for network communication and disk operations. The range for this setting is from 2,048 to 57,344 bytes, and the LANtastic default is set at 4,096 bytes. A larger buffer setting enables the server to transfer more

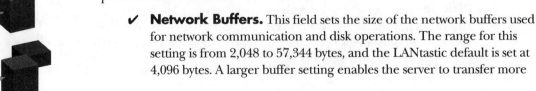

data at one time and increase network performance. This larger buffer setting, however, requires more memory to accomplish. A buffer setting of between 12,000 to 18,000 bytes (8 KB-12 KB) should provide good performance for a network of 5-6 users, and does not use up a large amount of memory. If you have only two or three users, you can start with the default and increase it later if needed.

✔ **Request Size.** Your server uses a small buffer to listen for user requests, such as directory lookups or file-find operations. The range for this field is from 32 to 65,535 bytes, with a default of 32. Increasing the size of the Request Size buffer improves performance for these types of operations, but it uses up additional server memory. For each Maximum Users value you set, LANtastic allocates a request buffer. If you have Maximum Users set to 15 and allocate 20 bytes per request buffer, the server uses a total of 300 bytes of memory for request buffers.

✔ **Network Tasks.** The Network Tasks option sets the number of concurrent user requests that the server can process at one time. The range for this field is from 1 to 32, and the default setting is 1. If you have multiple adapters installed in the server, you should have one task set per adapter installed. Artisoft suggests that you calculate the number of network tasks to set by dividing the number of network users who access this server by 4 and then add 1. Each network task requires a network buffer; therefore, increasing this number increases the amount of memory the server uses.

Increase the number of network tasks you specified by one if you will be using LANtastic's internal SHARE.

✔ **Run Burst.** This field sets the maximum number of ticks that the server takes to process network requests in 1/18 of a second increments. The range for this field is from 1 to 255 and the default setting is 2. When you set this to a large number, network response time improves but the performance of local workstation tasks is slower. Artisoft recommends that if the server is used as a local machine, keep this number at or near 2. If the server is dedicated to network support, set the Run Burst to around 200 for better performance.

✔ **Cached Resources.** This option enables you to set the number of network resources that have user requests cached. User access controls are stored in server memory, enabling the server to respond more quickly to directory lookups and file openings. By increasing this setting, you improve server performance. Artisoft recommends that you set this number to the maximum number of server resources that are used simultaneously. The range for this field is from 1 to 50 and the default is 1.

✔ **Seek Cache Size.** This sets the size of the cache used for random access file locations. The range for this field is from 0 to 64 KB, and the default is NO CACHE. If you increase the setting in this field, the server can find files more quickly, improving network performance. Artisoft recommends using a setting of 64 KB if you have a large database application.

✔ **Lock Hold Time.** This option enables the server to hold a request for the given number of ticks if a record is already in use (locked) by another user. After the file is free, the stored request is acted on and the file is locked for the delayed user. This feature increases server performance because the server does not have to devote CPU cycles to constantly retrying the lock, thus allowing other processing to occur. The range for this field is from 2 to 182 and the default is 9. The default setting is adequate for most applications, but if you have a lot of user requests in a database, you might want to increase this number.

✔ **Internal SHARE** This option will either display Select to Manage if LANtastic's internal SHARE features are enabled or DISABLED if the features are disabled. LANtastic's internal SHARE performs the same file-sharing and record-locking functions as the DOS SHARE command, but is more efficient. With this option highlighted, pressing Enter displays the following options (see fig. 11.19).

The DOS SHARE command provides file and record-locking features that are used by most multiuser applications to prevent users from accessing the same files or records at the same time, which could result in one user overwriting the work of another.

Internal Share. Press Enter to toggle this field between ENABLED and DISABLED. If enabled, the internal SHARE will be used. The default is ENABLED.

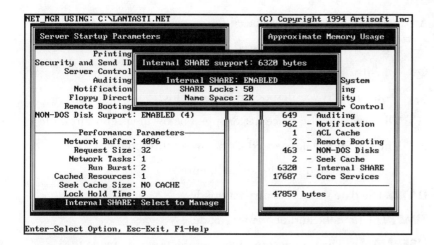

Figure 11.19
The options for LANtastic's internal SHARE.

If the DOS SHARE command is loaded before LANtastic's Server program, LANtastic's internal SHARE will not be used.

SHARE Locks. Press Enter to specify the number of simultaneous locks you want LANtastic's internal SHARE to support. The default is 50.

Name Space. Press Enter to specify the space required for storing file sharing name information. The default is 2 KB.

Audit Trail Maintenance Option

If you have enabled audit functions, as discussed in the previous sections, you can use the Audit Trail Maintenance option to view your audit trail entries, to copy them to a separate file, or to delete the audit trail file (see fig. 11.20). If you view an audit trail file, you see a window similar to the one shown in figure 11.21.

The Audit Trail screen contains the following fields:

✔ **TYPE.** The type of entry logged. The following are the different types of entries:

* - Server Started

! - Server Shutdown

I - A user successfully logged in to a server

O - A user logged out of the server or the server connection was broken

A - Access was allowed to a shared resource

D - Access was denied to a shared resource

Q - An entry was placed in the queue

S - A queue entry was despooled to the printer

H - The available disk space has dropped below the preset threshold

B - The CPU usage has exceeded the preset threshold

U - A user requested to write an audit entry

✔ **DATE.** The date the audit entry was made.

✔ **TIME.** The time the audit entry was made.

✔ **USERNAME.** The user account name of the user who made the request.

✔ **MACHINE.** The network name of the computer from which the request was made.

✔ **REASON.** The reason the entry was made.

✔ **VARIABLE.** This field contains information that varies with the type of audit entry.

Figure 11.20
The Audit Trail
Maintenance
screen.

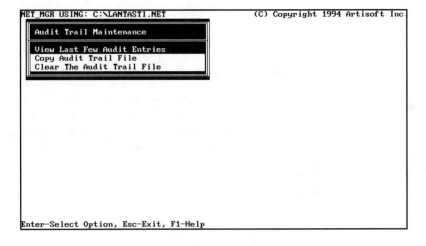

```
NET_MGR USING: C:\LANTASTI.NET              (C) Copyright 1994 Artisoft Inc
View last few entries of audit file.
A 94.04.26 07:44:18 KSOFFICE      KSOFFICE      L
\C-DRIVE
A 94.04.26 07:44:22 KSOFFICE      KSOFFICE      L
\C-DRIVE\????????.???
A 94.04.26 07:44:22 KSOFFICE      KSOFFICE      L
\C-DRIVE\????????
A 94.04.26 07:44:22 KSOFFICE      KSOFFICE      L
\C-DRIVE\????????.???
A 94.04.26 07:44:23 KSOFFICE      KSOFFICE      L
\C-DRIVE\
A 94.04.26 07:44:31 KSOFFICE      KSOFFICE      R
\C-DRIVE\AUTOEXEC.BAT
O 94.04.26 07:45:41 KSOFFICE      KSOFFICE      SHUTDOWN
1 29
! 94.04.26 07:45:42
Server is shutting down.
! 94.04.26 07:47:12
Server is shutting down.

↑/Home/PgUp-Go up, ↓/End/PgDn-Go down, Esc-Exit, F1-Help
```

Figure 11.21
The View last few entries of audit file screen.

Using the Queue Maintenance Option

The Queue Maintenance option (see fig. 11.22) enables you to change the location of the spool area to a different physical disk location or to a RAM disk on the server. You also can use the option to clear print jobs, mail messages, or both from the queue. You can access this function only when the server program is not running.

Clearing a queue area also compacts the queue control file for improved performance.

```
NET_MGR USING: C:\LANTASTI.NET              (C) Copyright 1994 Artisoft Inc
Queue Maintenance

Change the Queue Location
Clear Print Jobs From the Queue
Clear Mail Messages From the Queue
Clear All Entries From the Queue
```

Figure 11.22
The Queue Maintenance screen.

```
Enter-Select Option, Esc-Exit, F1-Help
```

Password Maintenance Option

The Password Maintenance option enables you to set up password protection for the current control directory being accessed with the NET_MGR program.

If you have not set a password for the LANtastic control directory using NET_MGR, you can set one by pressing Enter with the Enable Password Access For NET_MGR selection highlighted (see fig. 11.23). You then enter the password you wish to use and confirm your selection.

If a password has been enabled, the password maintenance screen changes to allow you to either disable or change the password for NET_MGR (see fig. 11.24).

Figure 11.23
The Password Maintenance screen to enable password.

```
NET_MGR USING: C:\LANTASTI.NET              (C) Copyright 1994 Artisoft Inc
┌─────────────────────────────────────────┐
│ Password Maintenance                     │
│ Enable Password Access For NET_MGR       │
│                                          │
└─────────────────────────────────────────┘




Enter-Select Option, Esc-Exit, F1-Help
```

Figure 11.24
The Password Maintenance screen to disable or change password.

```
NET_MGR USING: C:\LANTASTI.NET              (C) Copyright 1994 Artisoft Inc
┌─────────────────────────────────────────┐
│ Password Maintenance                     │
│ Disable Password Access For NET_MGR      │
│ Change Password                          │
└─────────────────────────────────────────┘




Enter-Select Option, Esc-Exit, F1-Help
```

The password is actually on the LANtastic control directory and not the NET_MGR program. A password, therefore, is required when you access the network control directory, even if the NET_MGR program on another computer is used to access this control directory.

Using the Remote Boot Maintenance Option

The Remote Boot Maintenance option enables you to build a remote boot-image disk on the server for a diskless workstation. This function copies the image of a bootable floppy disk that you have prepared to the server in the form of a remote boot image file. For a workstation to be able to boot from this server, you must enable the Remote Booting option on the Server Startup Parameters screen. A diskless workstation with a network adapter that has a remote boot ROM installed can now boot from this server. The Remote Boot Maintenance feature can be accessed only when the Server program is not running.

Management Utilities

Management Utilities enables you to import or export individual accounts, wildcard accounts, and ACL groups in three different formats. You can use these utilities if you manage your account information by means of another application. Selecting this option displays the Management Utilities menu (see fig. 11.25), enabling you to either Read Accounts from File or Write Accounts to File. After selecting either of these options, the Conversion Format Options menu appears (see fig. 11.26), enabling you to specify the format of the file.

```
LANtastic (R) Network Manager V6.00          (C) Copyright 1994 Artisoft Inc
┌─────────────────────────────────────┐
│ Management Utilities                 │
├─────────────────────────────────────┤
│ Read Accounts From File              │
│ Write Accounts To File               │
└─────────────────────────────────────┘




Enter-Select Option, Esc-Exit, F1-Help
```

Figure 11.25
The Management Utilities menu.

Figure 11.26
The Conversion
Format Options
menu.

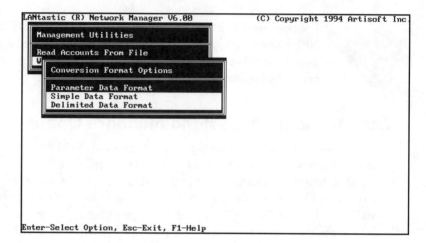

The three format options are:

✔ **Parameter Data Format.** This format places each field on a separate line. The field name is included and is followed by a colon. The associated data for that field is next to the field name.

✔ **Simple Data Format.** This format places each record on a separate line, but the fields contained in each record are placed in columns next to each other.

✔ **Delimited Data Format.** This format uses the standard delimited format, which separates fields by commas and encloses each field in quotation marks. Each record is contained in a single line.

Control Directory Maintenance Option

If you want to have several configurations of LANtastic set up for different processing tasks, you can create multiple control directories (see fig. 11.27). Use this function to change the control directory used, to back up the control directory, to restore a deleted control directory, to delete a control directory, or to create a new control directory. Because most backup programs do not correctly back up network control directories, use the Backup Control Directory option to back up the control directory to a DOS file on your hard drive or a floppy. Later, you can restore the network control directory from the file on your hard drive or floppy.

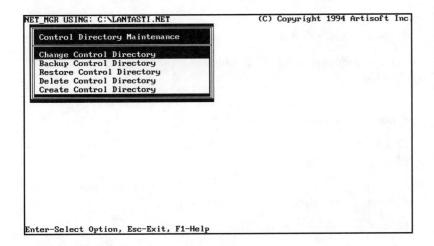

Figure 11.27
The Control
Directory
Maintenance
screen.

NET_MGR Commands

Several of the NET_MGR's commands can be run from the DOS prompt. By using these commands, you can back up the control directory or copy, create, edit, and delete accounts without running NET_MGR from its menu interface.

✔ **BACKUP.** The BACKUP command enables you to back up the server's control directory to a specified file. The syntax is as follows:

```
NET_MGR BACKUP {/P=password} path target-file
```

password is the password of the control directory if a password has been set up.

path is the control directory that you want to back up.

target-file is the name of the file to which you want to back up.

In the following example, LANTASTI.NET is the control directory and LANTASTI.BAK is the file to which you want to back up:

```
NET_MGR BACKUP LANTASTI.NET LANTASTI.BAK
```

✔ **COPY.** This command enables you to copy existing individual accounts, wildcard accounts, ACL groups, resources, or server startup parameters to another account with a different account name or to another control directory. The syntax is as follows:

```
NET_MGR {/C=path1}{/P=pw1}{/DC=path2}{/DP=pw2} COPY (ACLGROUP
INDIVIDUAL RESOURCE STARTUP WILDCARD) {source} {destination}
```

path1 is the control directory from which to copy. The default is \LANTASTI.NET.

pw1 is the password of the control directory from which to copy (if a password has been defined).

path2 is the destination control directory. The default is the same as path1.

pw2 is the password of the destination control directory (if a password has been defined). The default is the same as pw1.

ACLGROUP specifies that an ACL group is to be copied.

INDIVIDUAL specifies that an individual account is to be copied.

RESOURCE specifies that a shared resource is to be copied.

STARTUP specifies that the server startup parameter settings are to be copied.

WILDCARD specifies that a wildcard account is to be copied.

source is the name of the individual account, wildcard account, ACL group, or resource you want to copy.

destination is the destination name of the item copied. The default is the same as the source.

In the following example, JOHN is name of the user account to copy and RAY is the account to which you are copying the file:

```
NET_MGR COPY INDIVIDUAL JOHN RAY
```

✔ **CREATE.** This option enables you to create a new individual or wildcard account that has LANtastic's default parameters. The following is the syntax:

```
NET_MGR {/C=path}{/P=pw} CREATE (INDIVIDUAL WILDCARD) name
```

path is the control directory where the new account will be created. The default is \LANTASTI.NET.

pw is the password of the control directory (if a password has been defined).

INDIVIDUAL specifies an individual account.

WILDCARD specifies a wildcard account.

name is the name of the account to be created.

In the following example, JOE is the new account name:

```
NET_MGR CREATE INDIVIDUAL JOE
```

✔ **DELETE.** The DELETE option enables you to delete an individual or wildcard account. The syntax is as follows:

```
NET_MGR {/C=path}{/P=pw} DELETE (INDIVIDUAL WILDCARD) name
```

path is the control directory with the account to delete. The default is \LANTASTI.NET.

pw is the password of the control directory (if a password has been defined).

INDIVIDUAL specifies that an individual account is to be deleted.

WILDCARD specifies that a wildcard account is to be deleted.

name is the name of the account to be deleted.

In the following example, JOE is the individual account name that you want to delete:

```
NET_MGR DELETE INDIVIDUAL JOE
```

In the following example, *OPS** is the wildcard account name that you want to delete:

```
NET_MGR DELETE WILDCARD OPS*
```

✔ **RESTORE.** The RESTORE option enables you to restore a control directory from a backed-up copy. The syntax is as follows:

```
NET_MGR {/P=pw} RESTORE backup-file path
```

pw is the password of the control directory to be restored to (if a password has been defined).

backup-file is the name of the backed up control directory.

path is the name of the control directory to be restored.

In the following example, LANTASTI.BAK is the backup file and LANTASTI.NET is the control directory:

```
NET_MGR RESTORE LANTASTI.BAK LANTASTI.NET
```

✔ **SET.** The SET option enables you to set attributes for an individual or wildcard account. The syntax is as follows:

```
NET_MGR{/C=path}{/P=pw} SET (INDIVIDUAL WILDCARD) name
{attribute=value}
```

path is the control directory in which the account exists. The default is \LANTASTI.NET.

pw is the password of the control directory (if a password has been defined).

INDIVIDUAL specifies an individual account.

WILDCARD specifies a wildcard account.

The following are the attributes from which you can choose:

USERNAME	Specifies the account name (up to 16 characters)
PASSWORD	Specifies the account password
LOGINS	Specifies the number of concurrent logins allowed
PRIVILEGES	Specifies the account privileges (AQMUSOD)
ACCT_EXP	Specifies the account expiration date
PW_EXP	Specifies the account password expiration date

The following is an example of using this command:

```
NET_MGR SET INDIVIDUAL JOE USERNAME=JOE_K LOGINS=2
PRIVILEGES=AQMUSOD
```

✔ **SHOW.** The SHOW option enables you to view the account status of an individual or wildcard account. The syntax is as follows:

```
NET_MGR {/C=path}{/P=pw} SHOW (INDIVIDUAL WILDCARD) name
```

path is the name of the control directory in which the account exists. The default is \LANTASTI.NET.

pw is the password of the control directory (if a password has been defined).

INDIVIDUAL specifies an individual account.

WILDCARD specifies a wildcard account.

name is the name of the account to view.

The following are examples of using this command:

```
NET_MGR SHOW INDIVIDUAL JOE
```

or

```
NET_MGR SHOW WILDCARD OPS*
```

Examining System Manager Privileges

LANtastic also provides the system manager with the capability to perform certain functions to control the network. If you have the S privilege in your account, you can log a user out of a server, disable logins to a server, schedule server shutdowns, and cancel the scheduled server shutdown. The following sections examine each of these privileges and how they work.

Possession of the S privilege is necessary in order to log users out of servers, disable logins, schedule shutdowns, and cancel scheduled shutdowns. Another step, however, is also required. You must enable the Ser**v**er Control option, located in the Server Setup Parameters. This module can be accessed from the NET_MGR program. If you do not enable the Ser**v**er Control option, the selections described in the following sections will not be available to you.

Logging a User Out of a Server

You can access the Logging a User Out of a Server feature by using the NET Main Functions menu, as shown in the following steps:

1. Select the Monitor & Manage Server Activity option, and press Enter.

2. Select the server where the user is logged in, and press Enter.

3. Select the user that you want to log out from the displayed list, and press Del.

4. A screen pops up, prompting you for the time in minutes that you want to wait before logging the user out of the server. Type the number or accept the default of 0. If you accept the default of 0 and press Enter, the user is immediately logged out.

Disabling Server Logins

The Disabling Server Logins function enables you to prevent users from logging in to the server. It has no effect on current sessions, but when the users log out, they will not be able to log back in. This function is accessed by using the NET Main Functions menu, as shown in the following steps:

1. Select the Monitor & Manage Server Activity option, and press Enter.

2. Select the server for which you want to disable logins, and press Enter.

3. Press F2. A menu appears, showing the Server Control Functions screen (see fig. 11.28).

4. Select the Disable Server Logins option and press Enter. You can switch between Disable Server Logins and Enable Server Logins by pressing Enter.

When you select the Disable Server Logins option, you prevent new logins to this server from occurring. Only a user with the S privilege can reenable logins.

Figure 11.28
The Server Control Functions menu.

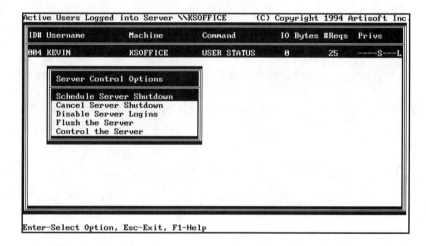

```
Active Users Logged into Server \\KSOFFICE        (C) Copyright 1994 Artisoft Inc
 ID# Username          Machine          Command       IO Bytes #Reqs  Privs
 004 KEVIN             KSOFFICE         USER STATUS      0        25   ----S---L

         ┌─ Server Control Options ──────────┐
         │                                   │
         │  Schedule Server Shutdown         │
         │  Cancel Server Shutdown           │
         │  Disable Server Logins            │
         │  Flush the Server                 │
         │  Control the Server               │
         └───────────────────────────────────┘




 Enter-Select Option, Esc-Exit, F1-Help
```

Scheduling Server Shutdown

The Schedule Server Shutdown function enables the system manager to schedule a server shutdown. This function is accessed by using the NET Main Functions menu, as shown in the following steps:

1. Select the Monitor & Manage Server Activity option, and press Enter.

2. Select the server that you want to shut down, and press Enter.

3. Press F2. A menu appears, showing the Server Control Functions (see fig. 11.28).

4. Select the Schedule Server Shutdown option, and press Enter. Another screen appears (see fig. 11.29), in which you can set the following parameters:

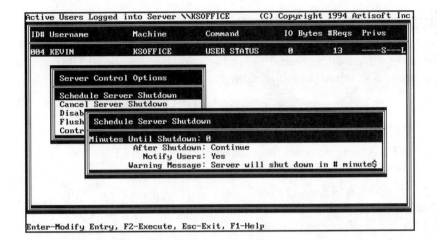

Figure 11.29
The Schedule Server Shutdown screen.

✔ **Minutes Until Shutdown.** This setting sets the number of minutes before the server shuts down.

✔ **After Shutdown.** This setting tells the server what to do after you shut down the server. In this field, you can switch between one of the following options by pressing Enter:

  ✔ **Continue.** The Continue option sets up the server to continue functioning, but as a workstation.

  ✔ **Halt.** This option halts all server processing. You have to reboot to use the computer again.

  ✔ **Reboot.** This option reboots the server machine after the Server program is removed from memory.

  ✔ **Notify Users.** If you enable the Notify Users option, users logged in to the server are notified that the server is shutting down. They are sent the message contained in the Warning Message line. In the Notify Users option, you can switch between Yes and No by pressing Enter. The Yes option sends warnings to your users. The Yes option is the default.

  ✔ **Warning Message.** The Warning Message is sent to users when you enable the Notify Users option. The default message is Server will shut down in # minute$, in which # displays the number of minutes you enter in the first option and $ changes to s if more than one minute remains before shutdown.

5. Press F2 to execute the shutdown. When the time expires, the server will close all open network files and remove the Server program from memory.

Cancelling a Server Shutdown

The Cancel Server Shutdown function enables the system manager to cancel a scheduled server shutdown. You can access this function by using the NET Main Functions menu, as shown in the following steps:

1. Select the Monitor & Manage Server Activity option, and press Enter.

2. Select the server that you want to shut down, and press Enter.

3. Press F2. A menu appears, showing the Server Control Functions (see fig. 11.28).

4. Select the Cancel Server Shutdown option, and press Enter. You are prompted to confirm the shutdown cancellation by pressing Enter. After you confirm the cancellation, the screen looks like figure 11.30.

5. Press Enter to continue.

Figure 11.30
The Server shutdown cancellation confirmation.

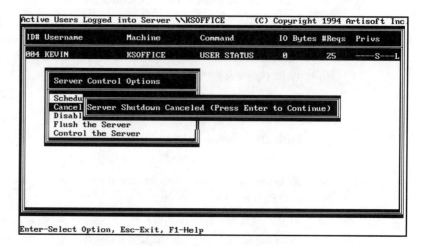

```
Active Users Logged into Server \\KSOFFICE        (C) Copyright 1994 Artisoft Inc

 ID# Username        Machine        Command        IO Bytes #Reqs  Privs

 004 KEVIN           KSOFFICE       USER STATUS        0      25    ----S---L

        ┌─────────────────────────────┐
        │  Server Control Options     │
        │ ┌──────┐                    │
        │ │Schedu│ ┌──────────────────────────────────────────────────┐
        │ │Cancel│ │Server Shutdown Canceled (Press Enter to Continue)│
        │ │Disabl│ └──────────────────────────────────────────────────┘
        │ │Flush the Server          │
        │ │Control the Server        │
        └─────────────────────────────┘




Enter-Select Option, Esc-Exit, F1-Help
```

Using LANtastic with Windows

The following sections cover the features available to manage your LANtastic network in Windows. Although the features available in the Windows LANtastic Network Manager program are almost identical to the features in the DOS LANtastic Network Manager program, the Windows interface implements the features in a strikingly different format.

Understanding the Network Manager Program Functions

The LANtastic Network Manager program enables you to configure your network, set up user accounts, define shared resources, create printer queues, and modify your server parameters, as required. The LANtastic Network Manager is a very powerful program, and as a network administrator you should become familiar with its functions. This section looks at each of the functions that appear on the LANtastic Network Manager menu to give you a sound foundation and understanding of the program.

You run the LANtastic Network Manager by double-clicking on the LANtastic Network Manager icon in the LANtastic program group, or by selecting the icon and choosing **O**pen from the Program Manager's **F**ile menu. The LANtastic Network Manager program appears (see fig. 11.31).

Figure 11.31
The LANtastic Network Manager program.

By specifying the LAN_DIR environment variable, you can change the default location where NET_MGR and the SERVER program look for the control directory. To change the default location of the control directory to C:\LANOTHER, for example, type the following line from a DOS prompt or include it in a batch file:

```
SET LAN_DIR=C:\LANOTHER
```

The following sections discuss the functions of each option on the LANtastic Network Manager program menu.

Using the Accounts Management Function

You use the <u>A</u>ccounts management function to set up or edit your network users' accounts. By using this option, you can assign a user a login account name, give a brief description of who the user is, give the account a password, and assign the login and access privileges for the account.

Two types of accounts can be set up: individual accounts and wildcard accounts. Individual accounts are usually for use by one person, whereas wildcard accounts usually are used by more than one person at a time.

Wildcard accounts can be used to set up group accounts. This is an easy and manageable way to set up accounts for people with similar work needs, hours, and duties. You can set up accounts for users who are all in one workgroup, give them the same access privileges, and not require separate individual user accounts for each. The wildcard account OPS*, for example, may be set up to be used by any users in the operations department. Members of this group can log in by using the name OPS followed by their own initials or name, or they can type the OPS login name (they do not have to include the asterisk (*)).

LANtastic sets up one universal wildcard account(called *)as part of its installation process. This account enables anybody who logs in to have access to the server. You may want to delete this account after you establish your own user and system manager accounts.

To manage individual accounts, wildcard accounts, and ACL groups, select the Accounts option by selecting the <u>A</u>ccounts icon or select <u>A</u>ccounts from the <u>M</u>anage menu. The Accounts dialog box appears (see fig. 11.32), showing an Individual Accounts and Wildcard Accounts icon listed in the Accounts field. The ACL Groups field shows the ACL groups that have been defined.

Figure 11.32
The Accounts dialog box.

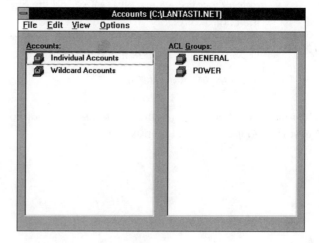

To expand the list to show all the individual accounts that have been defined, double-click on the Individual Accounts icon. Similarly to show the wildcard accounts, double-click on the Wildcard Accounts Icon. You can view the members of an ACL group by double-clicking on the ACL group name. Figure 11.33 shows all the individual accounts, wildcard accounts, and members of the ACL groups.

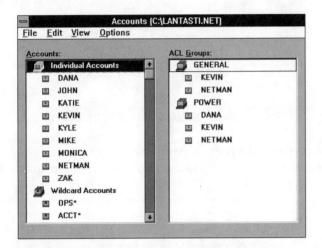

Figure 11.33
The Accounts dialog box showing the expanded list of individual accounts, wildcard accounts, and ACL groups.

You used the **A**ccounts option to add new users in Chapter 7, "Setting Up User Accounts and Shared Resources in Windows." To add additional users, do the following:

1. Select the icon representing the type of account you want to add (either individual or wildcard), and choose **A**dd from the **E**dit menu. The New Individual Account dialog box appears (see fig. 11.34) when you add individual accounts, or the New Wildcard Account dialog box appears when you add wildcard accounts. The fields in the dialog box are the same for both individual and wildcard accounts.

2. Enter the account name in the Name field and an optional description in the Description field.

3. To enter a password for the account, select the Set Password option in the Password field and type in the password you want for the account.

4. To allow more than one user to access this account at a time, increase the value in the Concurrent Logins field.

5. Select OK and the account is added.

Figure 11.34
The New
Individual
Account
dialog box.

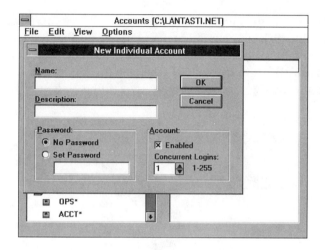

To modify an account once it has been created, select the account to edit, and choose **M**odify from the **E**dit menu. The Account Parameters dialog box appears (see fig. 11.35).

Figure 11.35
The Account
Parameters
dialog box.

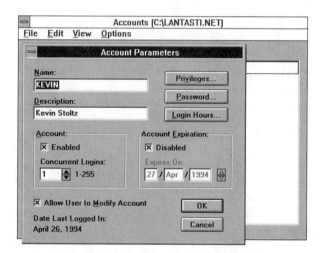

The following discusses each of the account information items:

✔ **Name.** The Name item is the network login name that you assign to the individual user. You should keep the name as short as possible, because the user has to type it in each time she logs in to the network. The account name may contain up to 15 characters.

✔ **Description.** The Description item is a short descriptive title for the account. You might want to put the user's real name in this field for clarity. You can use up to 32 characters in this field.

✔ **Account.** This section has two selections, Enabled and Concurrent Logins. If the Enabled box is not selected, the account is disabled and no one may access the server using this account. If the Enabled box is selected, the value in the Concurrent Logins field represents the number of concurrent logins a user account can make to the server. If, for example, you set the number of concurrent logins to 3, there can be three different computers at a time logged in to the server using this account name. If you log in to the server you are sitting at with this account name, it counts as one of the three allowed. Having more than one concurrent login is useful if you have a single account that multiple users use (such as a GUEST account), or if you log in to the server from more than one computer at the same time.

✔ **Account Expiration.** This section enables you to set a date at which time the account is no longer active. If the Disabled box is selected, then the account expiration date feature is disabled and will not be used. If the Disabled box is not selected, then the date in the Expires On field is the date the account will no longer be active. You can use this item to set up accounts for users who may need access to your network only for a limited period of time. After the expiration date, the user cannot use the account any more. This can help you maintain control of your network.

✔ **Allow User to Modify Account.** If this option is selected, users may change their password or disable their account after they log in.

The default setting for the Account Modifications field is Allowed for individual accounts and Disallowed for wildcard accounts. Under normal circumstances, you want an individual to be able to change his or her password or disable his or her account. You would not, however, want an individual using a wildcard account to be able to do the same since it would then prevent others from using the same wildcard account.

✔ **Date Last Logged In.** This field is updated by LANtastic each time the user logs in to the network. You cannot make any changes in this field.

✔ **Privileges.** Selecting the Privileges button displays the Account Privileges dialog box (see fig. 11.36) where you can assign special access privileges for the user account. The access privileges you assign in a user account override any access-control levels that you assign to a shared resource. To assign a privilege, type the letter for the privilege that you want to assign or select the box next to the privilege you want for the account. Selecting the Set All button will select all the privileges and selecting the Clear All button will deselect all the privileges.

Figure 11.36
The Account Privileges dialog box.

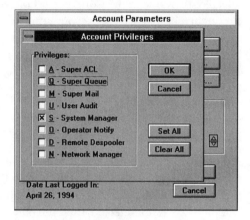

These privileges are for special types of access, and you should consider them with care before giving them to a user. A user account with no privileges assigned still can access shared resources on the network, but is controlled by the specific ACLs assigned to that shared resource. The assignment of ACLs to network resources is covered in Chapter 7, "Setting Up User Accounts and Shared Resources in Windows."

The following sections discuss the privileges that you can assign:

A - Super ACL. The Super ACL privilege gives users access to every resource on the network. If a user has this privilege, the ACL list for a resource is not checked when he or she uses a resource.

Q - Super Queue. The Super Queue privilege enables users to view and manipulate all of the jobs in the print queue, not just their own jobs. A user who has this privilege can control the server's despooler and cause it to start and stop, as well as delete items from the queue. You should give this privilege only to users who need this level of control, such as your assistant network administrator and a few select others who are knowledgeable about network printing operations.

M - Super Mail. The Super Mail privilege enables the user to read and manipulate all of the mail items in the server's mail queue, not just his or

her own. Because of the sensitive nature of individual user's mail, you may not want to give this privilege to anyone but the network administrator.

U - User Audit. The User Audit privilege enables a user to create audit entries in the server's audit log and to issue NET AUDIT commands. You should not give this privilege to many users. If a large number of audit entries are being created and stored on the server's hard disk, you could run out of usable hard disk storage space. You should keep this privilege for yourself and your assistant.

S - System Manager. The System Manager privilege should only be assigned to the network administrator and the alternate administrator. It enables the user to perform the special network manager functions that control the network. With the privilege, the user can execute the commands to remotely shut down the network or log users out of the server(s).

O - Operator Notify. The Operator privilege provides the user with messages that might require operator intervention, such as a message from a printer indicating it is out of paper.

D - Remote Despooler. The Despooler privilege enables the remote despooling program to despool jobs from the servers print queue to a local printer.

N - Network Manager. The Network Manager privilege enables the user to view the status information and performance statistics of a server.

✔ **Password.** Selecting the **P**assword button displays the Account Password dialog box (see fig. 11.37). The **P**assword section enables you to keep your existing password (Keep Password), disable the requirement for a password (No Password), and change or set a password (Set Password). When you select the Set Password option, you can enter a new password.

The Password Expiration section enables you to specify a password expiration date or interval in days that may elapse before a new password is required. If you select the Disabled option, the password expiration feature is disabled. With the Disabled option cleared, there are two password expiration methods used: Expires On and Renew Every, which are described as follows:

Figure 11.37
The Account
Password
dialog box.

✔ **Expires On.** This is the password expiration date. Placing an entry in this field causes the password to expire on a specific date. Attempts to log in after the expiration date will be refused, except as described in the following Renew Password Every description.

✔ **Renew Every.** This field contains the interval, in days, that the account password must be changed. As the end of the cycle approaches, LANtastic presents a warning to the user that his or her password needs to be changed. If the current date is later than the Password Expiration Date, the user can log in once and change his password. After an interval has been entered in this field, the Password Expiration Date will automatically be updated according to the number in this field.

✔ **Login Hours.** Selecting this button displays the Time-of-Day Logins dialog box (see fig. 11.38), which defines when the user account is allowed to log in to this server. If you have sensitive information on your network and do not want all your users to have access to the network at all times, set up specific limits by using this function.

Each rectangular block represents a half-hour block of time. To select a block of time, click on the starting block and drag to the last block. To allow logins during the selected block of time select the **A**llow button. To prevent logins during the selected block of time select the **D**isallow button. Selecting the **T**oggle button will change the selected block of time to the opposite value.

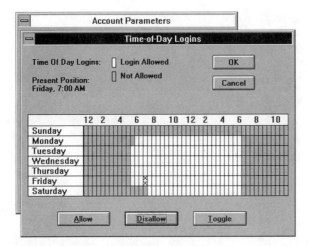

Figure 11.38
The Time-of-Day Logins dialog box.

ACL groups are a powerful feature of LANtastic, and enable you to group different accounts according to the type or level of access they have to your shared network resources. Using ACL groups also saves time when setting up new user accounts because you can define the new user as belonging to an ACL group that already exists. You do not have to add this new user to each shared resource ACL because the ACL group that the user belongs to already will be listed on the shared resource ACL.

To add a new ACL group, click in the ACL Groups field. Select **A**dd from the **E**dit menu selection and the ACL Group dialog box appears (see fig 11.39). Type the name for the ACL group in the Name field and type an optional description in the Description field. Select OK to create the ACL group name.

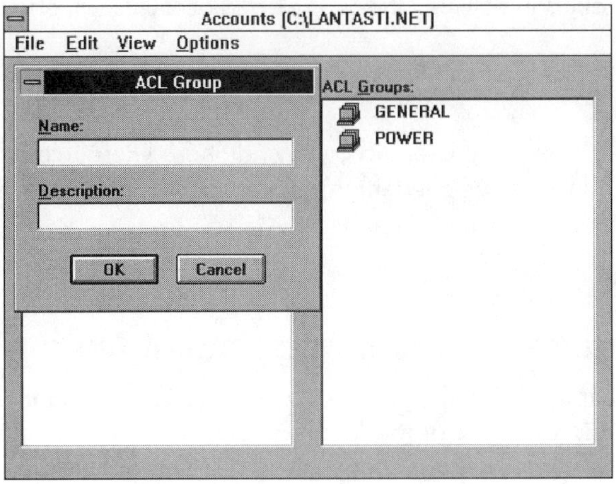

Figure 11.39
The ACL Group dialog box.

To add members to an ACL group, first select the ACL group to add members to. Select Group Members from the **E**dit menu. The ACL Group Members dialog box appears (see fig. 11.40).

Figure 11.40
The ACL Group Members dialog box for the POWER group.

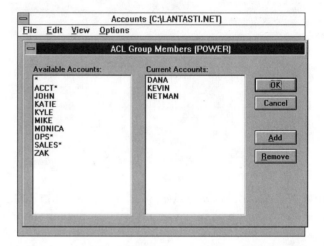

To add members to the group, choose the account or accounts to add from the Available Accounts list and click on the **A**dd button. To remove members from the group, select the account or accounts to remove from the Current Accounts list and click on the **R**emove button.

To choose multiple accounts on the list, hold down the Ctrl key while selecting the accounts. To choose a range of accounts, select the first account and hold down the Shift key while selecting the last account. All the accounts in between the two selected accounts will also be selected.

Chapter 7, "Setting Up User Accounts and Shared Resources in Windows," includes detailed information and examples for setting up ACL groups.

Using the Shared Resources Management Option

As was discussed in Chapter 7, the Shared Resources Management option is used to set up shared network resources for the users on a server. If you have multiple servers, you must set up shared resources for each server. Network resources can be disk drives, files, application programs, printers, and other devices, such as CD-ROM drives.

From the LANtastic Network Manager program, select the **R**esources option or select **R**esources from **M**anage menu. The Resources dialog box appears (see fig. 11.41).

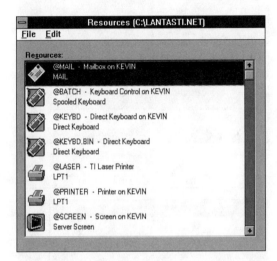

Figure 11.41

The Resources dialog box.

The printer, and mail resources are preceded by the @ character. Shared screen and keyboard resources also are preceded by the @ character. Do not use this character with a file resource.

Shared screen and keyboard resources enable a user to access the screen and keyboard on a server from a different computer in the network. Using a server's screen and keyboard remotely is accomplished from the Manage option in LANtastic's NET program.

To add a new resource, select **A**dd from the **E**dit menu or press the Ins key. The Add Resource dialog box appears (see fig. 11.42). When you add a new resource, LANtastic assumes you want to add a Shared Drive resource, and selects the Shared Drive option. To add a Shared Device resource such as a printer, select the Shared Device option and the Add Resource dialog box changes (as shown in figure 11.43).

Figure 11.42
The Add Resource dialog box for a shared drive resource where a local path is specified.

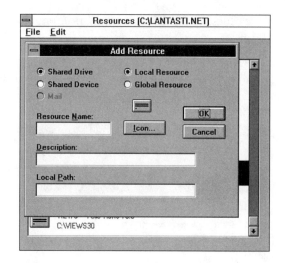

Figure 11.43
The Add Resource dialog box for a shared device resource where a device is specified and the resource name is preceded by a @.

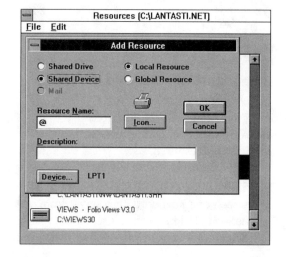

Modifying Drive Resources

To modify the parameters of a selected drive resource, select the resource from the Resources list, and choose **M**odify from the **E**dit menu to display the Resource Parameters dialog box (see fig. 11.44).

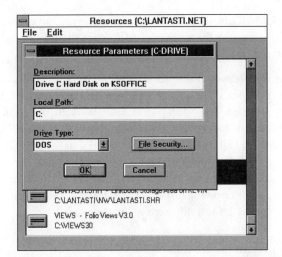

Figure 11.44
The Resource Parameters dialog box for the C-DRIVE resource.

The Resource Parameters dialog box contains the following information:

✔ **Description.** This is the description of the resource. It may be up to 64 characters long. The description is not required, but it provides additional information when you connect to the resource by means of the LANtastic NET program.

✔ **Local Path.** This is the full path name of the resource as it is referenced locally from the server. The local path includes the drive letter and subdirectory (if applicable).

✔ **Drive Type.** This option is normally set to DOS. LANtastic also supports CD-ROM, WORM (Write Once Read Many), and other types of drives. By pressing Enter while in this field, you can display a list of drive types from which you can select. The following drive types are listed: DOS, CD-ROM, WORM, NetWare, OS/2, and Other Non-DOS.

✔ **File Security.** This option enables you to enable file-level security. By defining file templates, such as *.EXE, and associating them with access control lists, you can limit the access of an account to a resource at the file level.

To change the Access Control List (ACL) for a shared drive resource, select the drive resource from the Resources list and select AC**L** from the **E**dit menu to display the Access Control List dialog box (see fig. 11.45).

The Access Control List enables you to list any combination of accounts or ACL groups and the type of access each can have. When a resource is created, LANtastic gives full access to every account. The * listed in the Access Control List dialog box means every account has the full access rights listed to the shared resource. The buttons in the Access Control List dialog box include **A**dd a new User/Group Name, **D**elete an existing User/Group Name, **E**dit a User/Group Name and its access rights, and change the Acce**s**s rights for a given User/Group Name. You can also copy an item in the list, or copy the entire ACL to an ACL clipboard, which can then be pasted into the ACL for a different resource.

Figure 11.45

The Access
Control List
dialog box.

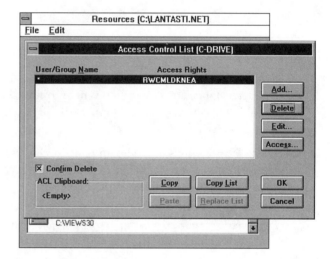

To add a new ACL entry, select the **A**dd button. In the ACL Entry dialog box, enter the user/group name (see fig. 11.46). To specify access rights, select **A**ccess to display the Access Control List Rights dialog box (see fig. 11.47). You can toggle the access rights on or off by clicking next to the desired access right. In addition, you can set the access rights to the default values by selecting the Default button, set all the access rights by selecting the Set All button, or clear all the access rights by selecting the Clear All button.

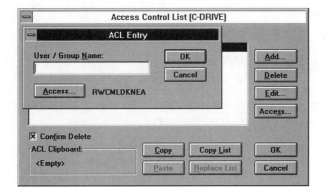

Figure 11.46
The ACL Entry
dialog box.

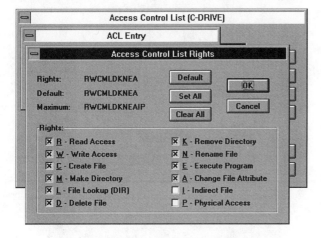

Figure 11.47
The Access
Control List Rights
dialog box.

The following is a description of the available ACL rights:

Access Rights	Description
R-Read Access	User can open files for reading.
W-Write Access	User can write to files.
C-Create File	User can create files.
M-Make Directory	User can create a new subdirectory.
L-Allow File Lookups	User can display or search through directories or subdirectories.
D-Delete Files	User can delete files.
K-Delete Directories	User can delete subdirectories.

N-Rename Files	User can rename files.
E-Execute Programs	User can execute programs.
A-Change File Attributes	User can change the attributes of files in a shared directory.
I-Indirect Files	User can create and use rect files within this shared directory.
P-Physical Access	User can use a special subdirectory to connect directly to DOS devices without having to go through the server's spooler. Use this option with care because it can cause some delay in printer availability to network users.

To change the type of resource select Typ**e** from the **E**dit menu. The Resource Types dialog box appears (see fig. 11.48).

Figure 11.48

The Resource Types dialog box for a local resource.

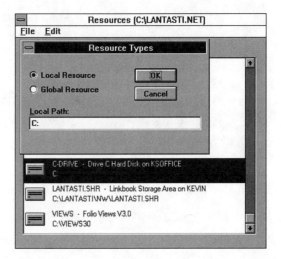

The Local Resource check box indicates that the drive resource exists on the server you are working on. The Local Path field specifies the actual drive or path to which the resource name points on the server.

Selecting the Global Resource check box causes the Resource Types dialog box to change, as shown in figure 11.49. Now, instead of the Local Path field, two other fields exist, as described in the following:

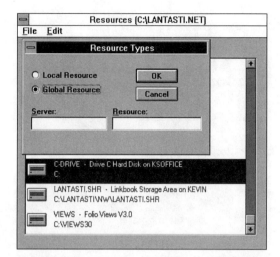

Figure 11.49
The Resource Types dialog box for a global resource.

✔ **Server.** This field contains the name of the server where the actual drive resource exists.

✔ **Resource.** This field contains the name of the actual drive resource on the server that the global drive resource name points to.

A global resource is a resource which actually exists on another computer. The user connects to the computer where the global resource is defined and, in turn, LANtastic establishes a direct connection between the user and the resource on another server to which the global resource points.

Chapter 7, "Setting Up User Accounts and Shared Resources in Windows," includes detailed instructions and examples for setting up shared resources.

Modifying Printer Resources

To modify the parameters of a selected printer resource, select the printer resource from Resources list and select **M**odify from the **E**dit menu to display the Resource Parameters dialog box (see fig. 11.50).

Figure 11.50
The Resource Parameters dialog box for the @PRINTER resource.

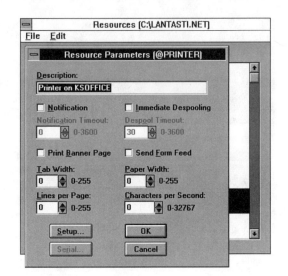

The Resource Parameters dialog box contains the following information:

✔ **D**escription

✔ **N**otification

✔ **I**mmediate Despooling

✔ Notific**a**tion Timeout

✔ Desp**o**ol Timeout

✔ Print **B**anner Page

✔ Send **F**orm Feed

✔ **T**ab Width

✔ **P**aper Width

✔ **L**ines per Page

✔ **C**haracters per Second

See Chapter 10, "Printing with LANtastic," for detailed instructions and examples for setting up shared printer resources.

The Access Control List (ACL) for a shared printer resource is changed the same way it is for a shared drive resource as described above.

To change the type of resource, select Typ**e** from the **E**dit menu. The Resource Types dialog box appears (see fig. 11.51).

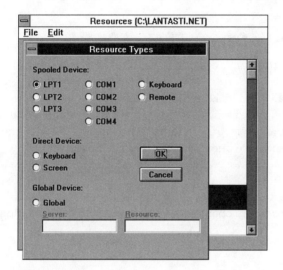

Figure 11.51
The Resource Types dialog box.

Three categories of resource types are shown: Spooled Device, Direct Device, and Global Device.

The Spooled Device types include parallel (LPT1, LPT2, LPT3) and serial ports (COM1, COM2, COM3, COM4) that are used primarily for printers. Other Spooled Device types include the Keyboard and Remote types. The Keyboard type of Spooled Device is used for spooling keystrokes to another servers keyboard, and the Remote type is used for remote printers that utilize the RPS (Remote Printer Server) program. Direct Devices include the Keyboard and Screen types which are used for remotely controlling another server. Selecting the Global Device option allows the shared device resource to actually point to a shared device resource on another computer.

If Global is selected as the device type, the Server and Resource fields must be completed with the information described below:

✔ **Server.** This field contains the name of the server where the actual drive resource exists.

✔ **Resource.** This field contains the name of the actual drive resource on the server that the global drive resource name points to.

A global resource is a resource which actually exists on another computer. The user connects to the computer where the global resource is defined and, in turn, LANtastic establishes a direct connection between the user and the resource on the other server to which the global resource points.

Using the LANtastic Server Control Panel

You control the Server program's operation by using the Server Control Panel. You make changes in LANtastic's server parameters to optimize your server's performance, set up audit trails, and make general modifications to your network server configuration. The following discussions cover each of the parameters and show the LANtastic defaults, as set by Artisoft. Refer to Chapter 15, "Getting the Most Out of LANtastic," for possible improvements to the default settings.

The DOS equivalent of the LANtastic Server Control Panel is the Server Startup Parameters option in the LANtastic DOS Network Manager program.

From the LANtastic Network Manager program, select the **S**erver option, or select **S**erver from the **M**anage menu. The Select Loadable Server dialog box appears, and enables you to specify a Server Directory. Select the desired directory and choose OK. The LANtastic Server Control Panel dialog box appears (see fig. 11.52).

Figure 11.52
The LANtastic
Server Control
Panel
dialog box.

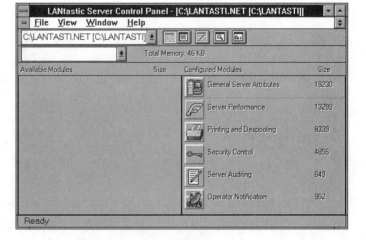

As you change the Server's settings, LANtastic displays the approximate amount of memory usage associated with the change. This new feature enables you to immediately see the effect your changes have on memory usage and, thus, make the required adjustments.

The LANtastic Server Control Panel has an Available Modules list, which consists of the LANtastic server modules which are disabled, and a Configured Modules list, which consists of the enabled and configured modules.

The Server Control Panel enables you to open multiple server configuration windows, and copy module configurations between the different server configurations by dragging modules between the windows.

The first drop-down options box is the Control Directories List. This list shows the control directory you are currently working on, as well as recent previous control directories.

The second drop-down options box is the Server Personalities List (see fig. 11.53). These are preset server configurations optimized for different types of server usage. As a starting point, you can select the server configuration that best suits your needs, and then proceed to make additional changes to meet your requirements.

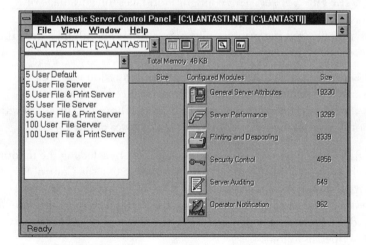

Figure 11.53
The LANtastic Server Control Panel showing the drop-down Server Personalities List.

Following is a description of the available configurations you may select:

✔ **5 User Default Configuration.** This is the default configuration from when you first installed LANtastic. The Server program with this configuration uses approximately 47,400 bytes of memory.

✔ **5 User File Server.** This configuration uses the minimum amount of memory, and is for sharing files but not printers. The Server program with this configuration uses approximately 23,523 bytes of memory.

✔ **5 User File & Printer Server.** This configuration uses the minimum amount of memory for sharing files and printers. The Server program with this configuration uses approximately 30,784 bytes of memory.

✔ **35 User File Server.** This configuration takes advantage of LANtastic's basic security features and some of the performance improvement features, and is used for sharing files but not printers. The Server program with this configuration uses approximately 83,571 bytes of memory.

✔ **35 User File & Printer Server.** This configuration takes advantage of LANtastic's basic security features and some of the performance improvement features, and is used for sharing files and printers. The Server program with this configuration uses approximately 94,871 bytes of memory.

✔ **100 User File Server.** This configuration takes full advantage of LANtastic's security and performance improvement features, and is used for sharing files but not printers. The Server program with this configuration uses approximately 215,872 bytes of memory.

✔ **100 User File & Printer Server.** This configuration takes full advantage of LANtastic's security and performance improvement features, and is used for sharing files and printers. The Server program with this configuration uses approximately 231,268 bytes of memory.

Each of the six LANtastic Server modules can be modified by selecting the module icon and then choosing **M**odule Configuration from the LANtastic Control Panel **V**iew menu. A module can be enabled or disabled by selecting the module and dragging it to either the Available Modules list to disabled the module or to the Configured Modules list to enable the module. The following six LANtastic Server Modules are described as follows:

✔ **General Server Attributes.** This is the General Parameters Module. This module is always enabled and contains the general operating parameters for the LANtastic server program.

✔ **Server Performance.** This is the Performance Parameters Module. This module is always enabled and contains the parameters that affect server performance.

✔ **Printing and Despooling.** This is the Printing Parameters Module and is used for specifying parameters related to network printing and despooling.

✔ **Security Control.** This is the Security Parameters Module and is used for specifying network security options including the use of user accounts.

✔ **Server Auditing.** This is the Auditing Parameters Module and is used for specifying the auditing parameters to be tracked.

✔ **Operator Notification.** This is the Operator Notification Parameters Module and is used for specifying the events that will cause an operator to be notified that the event has occurred.

General Server Attributes

The General Parameters Module (see fig. 11.54) includes the following configuration options:

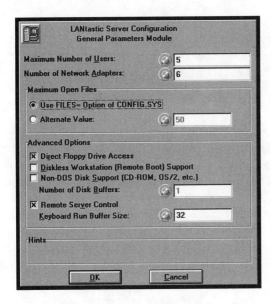

Figure 11.54
The General Parameters Module.

✔ **Maximum Number of Users.** This field sets the maximum number of users that can log in to the server. The range for this field is 2 to 500. LANtastic has a default setting of 5. If you have more than five users that log in to this server at the same time, increase the number in this field to equal the number of users that can log in.

✔ **Number of Network Adapters.** This field sets the number of network adapters that are installed in the server. The range for this field is from 1 to 6. The default setting is 6. Normally, a server only has one network adapter installed. If you had a LANtastic network that was using the LANtastic 2 Mbps adapters and another LANtastic network that was using Ethernet adapters, you could put one of each kind of adapter in this server. Each network can then access this common server.

✔ **Maximum Open Files.** You can set the number of files that users can have open simultaneously by using the Maximum Open Files option. Normally, you would let the DOS CONFIG.SYS file control this function. The range for this field is from 50 to 5,100. The default value is Use FILES=Option of CONFIG.SYS, which means that the FILES= statement in CONFIG.SYS will be used to determine the maximum number of files that may be open. DOS has a maximum open files limit of 255; therefore, if you need more open files, setting an Alternate Value number higher than this causes the server to use its own separate files to handle network functions. The value in CONFIG.SYS is then used for the local file functions.

✔ **Direct Floppy Drive Access.** Selecting this option enables a user to issue the DOS FORMAT and CHKDSK commands to floppy disks in the server's floppy drives. If this option is selected, and the floppy drive is shared with others on the network, a network user can format a floppy disk in the drive. Because of this possibility, use caution. The default setting is enabled.

✔ **Diskless Workstation (Remote Boot) Support.** Selecting this option enables support for remote booting of diskless workstations. The default setting is disabled. If you are using diskless workstations on your network, enabling this option allows the server to remotely boot those workstations provided that have a network adapter installed that is equipped with a remote boot ROM chip. If you do use remote booting, then you must create a boot image on the server by using the Remote Boot option in the LANtastic Network Manager, as discussed later in this chapter.

✔ **Non-DOS Disk Support (CD-ROM, OS/2, etc.).** Selecting this option enables support for non-DOS drives such as CD-ROM drives, WORM (Write Once Read Many) drives, and so forth. If the option is enabled, you can enter the number of non-DOS disk drive entries to be

supported by this server in the Number of Disk Buffers field. If the entire
list does not appear when performing a directory listing (DIR) of the
non-DOS disk, you will need to increase this value. Valid entries for this
field range from 0 to 2400.

✔ **Remote Server Control.** Select this option so that others can remotely
control this server which includes allowing others to shut down the server,
flush the server's caches, log users off the server, enable and disable
logins, and control the server's keyboard and screen. The default is
enabled. If this option is enabled, you can enter the size of the buffer
used for the NET RUN commands in the Keyboard Run Buffer Size field.
Values may range from 32 to 1,024 with the default value of 32.

Server Performance

The Performance Parameters Module (see fig. 11.55) includes the following
configuration options:

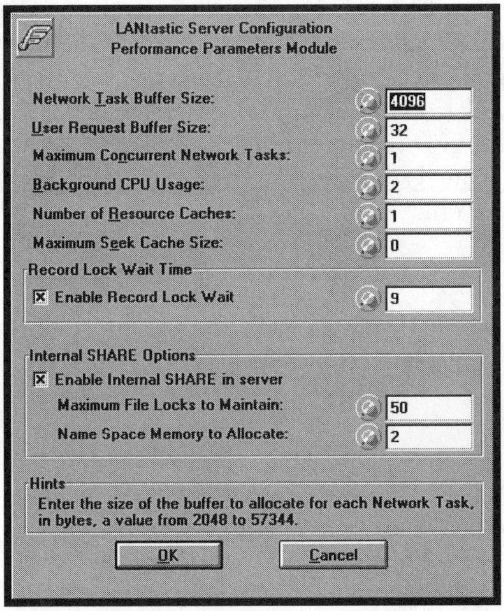

Figure 11.55
The Performance
Parameters
Module.

✔ **Network Task Buffer Size.** This field sets the size of the network
buffers used for network communication and disk operations. The range
for this setting is from 2,048 to 57,344 bytes, and the LANtastic default is
set at 4,096 bytes. A larger buffer setting enables the server to transfer

more data at one time and increase network performance. This larger buffer setting, however, requires more memory to accomplish. A buffer setting of between 12,000 to 18,000 bytes (8 KB-12 KB) should provide good performance for a network of 5-6 users, and does not use up a large amount of memory. If you have only two or three users, you can start with the default and increase it later if needed.

✔ **User Request Buffer Size.** Your server uses a small buffer to listen for user requests, such as directory lookups or file-find operations. The range for this field is from 32 to 65,535 bytes with a default of 32. Increasing the size of the Request Size buffer improves performance for these types of operations, but it uses up additional server memory. For each Maximum Users value you set, LANtastic allocates a request buffer. If you have Maximum Users set to 15 and allocate 20 bytes per request buffer, the server uses a total of 300 bytes of memory for request buffers.

✔ **Maximum Concurrent Network Tasks.** This option sets the number of concurrent user requests that the server can process at one time. The range for this field is from 1 to 32, and the default setting is 1. If you have multiple adapters installed in the server, you should have one task set per adapter installed. Artisoft suggests that you calculate the number of network tasks to set by dividing the number of network users who access this server by 4 and then add 1. Each network task requires a network buffer, so increasing this number increases the amount of memory the server uses.

Increase the number of network tasks you specified by one if you will be using LANtastic's internal SHARE.

✔ **Background CPU Usage.** This field sets the maximum number of ticks that the server takes to process network requests in 1/18 of a second increments. The range for this field is from 1 to 255 and the default setting is 2. When you set this to a large number, network response time improves but the performance of local workstation tasks is slower. Artisoft recommends that if the server is used as a local machine, keep this number at or near 2. If the server is dedicated to network support, set the Run Burst to around 200 for better performance.

✔ **Number of Resource Caches.** This option enables you to set the number of network resources that have user-requests cached. User access controls are stored in server memory, enabling the server to respond more quickly to directory lookups and file openings. By increasing this setting, you improve server performance. Artisoft recommends that you set this number to the maximum number of server resources that are used simultaneously. The range for this field is from 1 to 50 and the default is 1.

✔ **Maximum Seek Cache Size.** This sets the size of the cache used for random access file locations. The range for this field is from 0 to 64 KB and the default is 0. If you increase the setting in this field, the server can find files more quickly, improving network performance. Artisoft recommends using a setting of 64 KB if you have a large database application.

✔ **Record Lock Wait Time.** If you enable this option by selecting the Enable Record Lock Wait box, the server is able to hold a request for the specified number of ticks if a record is already in use (locked) by another user. After the file is free, the stored request is acted on and the file is locked for the delayed user. This feature increases server performance because the server does not have to devote CPU cycles to constantly retrying the lock, thus allowing other processing to occur. The range for this field is from 2 to 182 and the default is 9. The default setting is adequate for most applications, but if you have a lot of user requests in a database, you might want to increase this number.

✔ **Internal SHARE Options.** Enable this option by selecting the Enable Internal SHARE in Server box. LANtastic's internal SHARE performs the same file-sharing and record-locking functions as the DOS SHARE command but is more efficient. If enabled, specify the following parameters:

The DOS SHARE command provides file and record-locking features that are used by most multiuser applications to prevent users from accessing the same files or records at the same time which could result in one user overwriting the work of another.

If the DOS SHARE command is loaded before LANtastic's Server program, LANtastic's internal SHARE will not be used.

Maximum File Locks to Maintain. In this field, specify the number of simultaneous locks you want LANtastic's internal SHARE to support. The default is 50.

Name Space Memory to Allocate. Press Enter to specify the space required for storing file sharing name information. The default is 2 KB.

Printing and Despooling

The Printing Parameters Module (see fig. 11.56) includes the following configuration options:

Figure 11.56
The Printing
Parameters
Module.

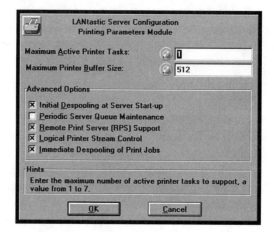

✔ **Maximum Active Printer Tasks.** This setting enables the server to despool to multiple printers at one time. Set this field to equal the number of printers that are physically attached to this server. The range for this field is from 0 to 7, and the default is 1.

If when running Microsoft Windows you experience slow printing, set the number of Printer Tasks to 1, even if you have more than one printer attached to the server. Setting Printer Tasks to a number other than 1 may result in extremely slow network printing when the server is running windows.

✔ **Maximum Printer Buffer Size.** This option sets the size of the print buffer. By increasing the size of the print buffer, you can enhance print performance by reducing the number of disk accesses required to read the data from the spool area. The range for this field is from 512 to 32,768 bytes. The default is 512 bytes.

Using LANtastic with Windows **445**

✔ **Initial Despooling at Server Start-up.** If enabled, all print jobs automatically despool to the network printer(s) serviced by the server. If this option is disabled, you need to issue the NET QUEUE START or NET QUEUE SINGLE commands to begin despooling to a printer. The default setting is enabled.

✔ **Periodic Server Queue Maintenance.** Enabling this option will cause the printer control file to periodically be rebuilt to optimize printing speed. Normally this is done each time the server is started, so unless you leave your computer on all the time you do not need to enable this feature. The default is disabled.

✔ **Remote Print Server (RPS) Support.** If you have remote printer resources on this server that will be despooled by a workstation running the RPS (Remote Printer Server) program, then this feature must be enabled. The default is enabled.

✔ **Logical Printer Stream Control.** If you will be controlling your printers using printer streams, this feature must be enabled. The default is enabled.

✔ **Immediate Despooling of Print Jobs.** This option must be enabled if you will specify Immediate Despooling for any of your printer re- sources. The default is enabled.

Security Control

The Security Parameters Module (see fig. 11.57) includes the following configura- tion options:

✔ **Broadcast Send Server ID to all Network Users.** If enabled, this server will send it's name ID which will be displayed in the list of servers when using the NET program or when issuing the NET SHOW com- mand. The default is enabled.

✔ **Individual and Wildcard Accounts.** If enabled, a user must use a valid individual or wildcard account to log in to the server. If disabled, any user may log in to this server without using account names. The default is enabled.

✔ **Remote.** Selecting the remote button displays the Edit Remote Account Servers dialog box (see fig. 11.58). This option enables you to choose one or more LANtastic servers from which account files will be used for this server. Add servers to the Remote Account Servers list by entering a server in the Server Name field and selecting the **A**dd Server button. Similarly a server may be removed from the list by selecting the server to remove and then selecting the **R**emove button. The accounts from the first server found on the list are used for this server. Enabling this feature disables the accounts defined on this server.

Figure 11.57
The Security
Parameters
Module.

Figure 11.58
The Edit Remote
Account Servers
dialog box.

✔ **Access Control Lists.** Select the **E**nable Resource-Level Access Control Checking box for each shared resource to be checked before a user is given access. When disabled, the ACLs are ignored and full access to shared resources is given to everyone. The default is enabled. When enabled, the following options are available:

File-Level Access Control Checking. When enabled, the file level ACL is checked before access if allowed. When disabled, the file level ACLs are ignored and full access is allowed to everyone. The default is enabled.

Group-Level Access Control Checking. When enabled, a user may gain access through a group ACL. The default is enabled.

Server Auditing

When an auditing feature is enabled, entries are automatically made to the audit trail file when certain events occur. Many of the auditing features also notify users of an event if they have the operator privilege enabled for their accounts.

The Auditing Parameters Module (see fig. 11.59) includes the following configuration options:

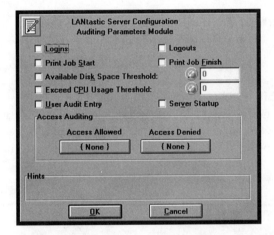

Figure 11.59
The Auditing Parameters Module.

✔ **Logins.** If enabled, an audit trail entry is made each time a user logs in to the server. The default is disabled.

✔ **Logouts.** If enabled, an audit trail entry is made each time a user logs out of the server. The default is disabled.

✔ **Print Job Start.** If enabled, an audit trail entry is made each time a print job or mail item is sent to the printer. The default is disabled.

✔ **Print Job Finish.** If enabled, an audit trail entry is made each time a print job finishes printing. The default is disabled.

✔ **Available Disk Space Threshold.** If enabled, an audit trail entry is made each time the available disk space on the server falls below the value specified (in kilobytes). The default is disabled.

✔ **Exceed CPU Usage Threshold.** If enabled, an audit trail entry is made each time the CPU usage exceeds the value specified. The default is disabled.

The value in this field is the percentage of the server's maximum capacity at which point an entry will be made to the audit trail file. If the value specified is 75 percent, for example, an audit trail entry is made each time the server's usage exceeds 75 percent of its maximum capacity.

✔ **User Audit Entry.** If enabled, any user with the U privilege may make an entry to the audit trail file using the NET AUDIT command. The default is disabled.

✔ **Server Startup.** If enabled, an audit trail entry is made each time the server starts or is shut down. The default is disabled.

✔ **Access Allowed and Access Denied.** Selecting either of these buttons displays the Access Control Auditing Rights dialog box (see fig. 11.60), thus enabling you to specify which access rights you want to be audited when access is allowed or denied. If you want to track all Read and Write accesses that are allowed, for example, select the Access Allowed button and then the **R-Read** and **W-Write** access rights.

Figure 11.60

The Access Control Auditing Rights dialog box.

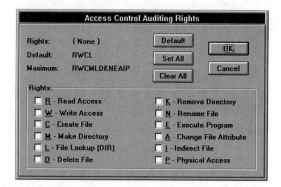

Operator Notification

The Operator Notification Module enables users with the O-Operator privilege to be notified when specified events occur. The Operator Notification Parameters Module (see fig. 11.61) includes the following configuration options:

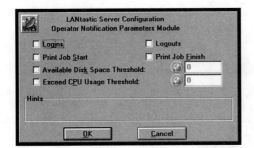

Figure 11.61
The Operator
Notification
Parameters
Module.

✔ **Logins.** If enabled, operators are notified when anyone logs in to the server. The default is DISABLED.

✔ **Logouts.** If enabled, operators are notified when anyone logs out of the server. The default is DISABLED.

✔ **Print Job Start.** If enabled, operators are notified when a print job is sent to the printer. The default is DISABLED.

✔ **Print Job Finish.** If enabled, operators are notified each time a print job finishes printing. The default is DISABLED.

✔ **Available Disk Space Threshold.** If enabled, operators are notified each time the available disk space on the server falls below the value specified (in Kilobytes). The default is DISABLED.

✔ **Exceed CPU Usage Threshold.** If enabled, operators are notified each time the CPU usage exceeds the value specified. The default is DISABLED.

After configuring each module, you can display a detailed breakdown of the server's memory usage or a chart illustrating the server's memory usage. Select Detailed Memory from the Server Control Panel View menu to display the Detailed Memory Breakdown list (see fig. 11.62). Select Chart Memory from the Server Control Panel View menu to display the View Memory Usage Chart (see fig. 11.63).

Figure 11.62
The Detailed Memory Breakdown List.

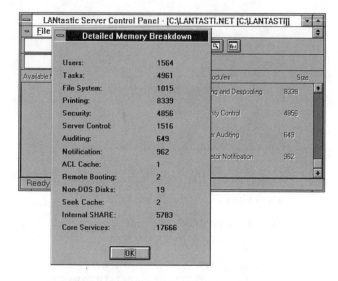

Figure 11.63
The View Memory Usage Chart.

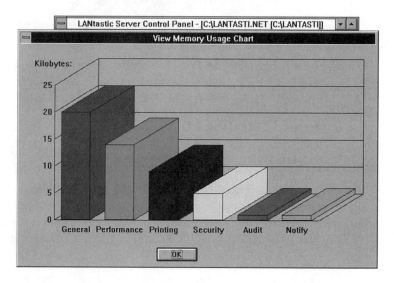

Audit Trail Maintenance Option

If you have enabled audit functions, as discussed in the previous sections, you can use the Audit Trail option to view your audit trail entries, to copy them to a separate file, or to delete the audit trail file. From the LANtastic Network Manager, select the Audit **T**rail icon, or choose Audit **T**rail from the **M**anage menu. The Audit Trail window appears (see fig. 11.64), which displays the audit trail.

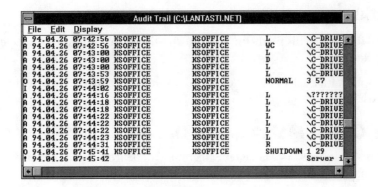

Figure 11.64
The Audit Trail
window.

The Audit Trail screen contains the following fields:

✔ **TYPE.** The type of entry logged. The different types of entries follow:

* - Server Started

! - Server Shut down

I - A user successfully logged in to a server

O - A user logged out of the server or the server connection was broken

A - Access was allowed to a shared resource

D - Access was denied to a shared resource

Q - An entry was placed in the queue

S - A queue entry was despooled to the printer

H - The available disk space has dropped below the preset threshold

B - The CPU usage has exceeded the preset threshold

U - A user requested to write an audit entry

✔ **DATE.** The date the audit entry was made.

✔ **TIME.** The time the audit entry was made.

✔ **USERNAME.** The user account name of the user who made the request.

✔ **MACHINE.** The network name of the computer from which the request was made.

✔ **REASON.** The reason the entry was made.

✔ **VARIABLE.** This field contains information that varies with the type of audit entry.

To clear the audit trail, select **C**lear Audit Trail from the **F**ile menu. To save the audit trail to a file, select **S**ave as file from the **F**ile menu.

Using the Queue Maintenance Option

From the LANtastic Network Manager, Select the **Q**ueue icon or choose **Q**ueue from the **M**anage menu. The Queue Maintenance dialog box appears (see fig. 11.65).

The Queue Maintenance option enables you to change the location of the spool area to a different physical disk location, or to a RAM disk on the server. You also can use the option to clear the spool area. You can access this function only when the server program is not running.

Figure 11.65
The Queue
Maintenance
dialog box.

Clearing a queue area also compacts the queue control file for improved performance.

Using the Remote Boot Maintenance Option

You can access the Remote Boot Maintenance option by selecting the Remote **B**oot icon or choosing Remote **B**oot from the **M**anage menu.

The Remote Boot Maintenance option enables you to build a remote boot-image disk on the server for a diskless workstation. This function copies the image of a bootable floppy disk that you have prepared to the server in the form of a remote boot-image file. For a workstation to be able to boot from this server, you must enable the **D**iskless Workstation (Remote Boot) Support in the LANtastic Server Configuration General Parameters Module. A diskless workstation with a network adapter that has a remote boot ROM installed can now boot from this server. The Remote Boot maintenance feature can be accessed only when the Server program is not running.

Password Maintenance Option

The Password Maintenance option enables you to set up password protection for the LANtastic control directory you are accessing using the LANtastic Network Manager program.

From the LANtastic Network Manager, select the **P**assword icon or choose **P**assword from the **M**anage menu. The Control Directory Password dialog box appears (see fig. 11.66).

Figure 11.66
The Control Directory Password dialog box.

If you have not set a password for the LANtastic control directory, select Enable and you are prompted to enter a password. Select Disable to disable the existing password, or select Change to change the password.

The password exists on the LANtastic control directory being accessed and not the LANtastic Network Manager program. For this reason, a password is required when you access the network control directory, even if you are using the LANtastic Network Manager program on another computer to access the control directory.

Control Directory Archive Option

The Control Directory Archive option enables you to backup or restore your network control directory. From the LANtastic Network Manager, select the Archi**v**e icon or select Archi**v**e from the **M**anage menu. The Control Directory Archive dialog box appears (see fig. 11.67).

Figure 11.67
The Control
Directory
Archive dialog
box.

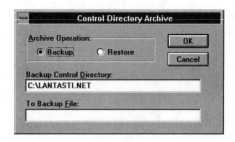

To back up the control directory, select Backup. Specify the name of the Backup Control Directory to back up, and the directory and file name in the To Backup File field, for the backed up file. To restore the control directory, select Restore. Specify the backup file name in the From Backup File field, and the directory to be restored to in the To Directory Path field. Select OK to carry out the operation.

Because most backup programs do not correctly back up network control directories, use the Backup option to back up the control directory to a DOS file on your hard drive or a floppy. Later you can restore the network control directory from the file on your hard drive or the floppy.

Control Directory Maintenance Option

If you want to have several configurations of LANtastic set up for different processing tasks, you can create multiple control directories. Use this function to specify a control directory to use, to delete a control directory, or to create a new control directory.

From the LANtastic Network Manager, select the **C**ontrol Dir icon or choose **C**ontrol Directory from the **M**anage menu. The Select Control Directory dialog box appears (see fig. 11.68).

To specify a control directory to use, type its name in the Directory Path field, or choose the control directory from the Di**r**ectories list and select OK. To create a new control directory, type the control directory's name in the Directory Path field and select the **C**reate button. To delete a control directory, type the name of the control directory to be deleted in the Directory Path field, or choose the Control directory from the Directories list and choose the **D**elete button.

Examining System Manager Privileges

LANtastic provides the system manager with the capability to perform certain functions to control the network. If you have the S privilege in your account, you can log a user out of a server, disable logins to a server, schedule server shutdowns, and cancel scheduled server shutdowns. The following sections examine each of these privileges and the ways in which they work.

Figure 11.68
The Select
Control Directory
dialog box.

Possession of the S privilege is necessary to log users out of servers, disable logins, schedule shutdowns, and cancel scheduled shutdowns. Another step, however, is also required. You must enable the Remote Ser**v**er Control option, located in the LANtastic Server Configuration General Parameters module. This module can be accessed from Server in the LANtastic Network Manager program. If you do not enable the Remote Ser**v**er Control option, the selections described in the following sections will not be available to you.

Logging a User Out of a Server

You can log a user out of a server by means of the LANtastic NET program, as shown in the following steps:

1. Select the Manag**e** icon from the LANtastic NET program or choose Ma**n**age Other Computers from the **N**et menu.

2. At the Select Computer dialog box, choose the computer where the user is logged in, and choose OK. The User Statistics dialog box appears (see fig. 11.69).

3. Choose the user whom you want to log out from the displayed list, and select **T**erminate User from the **M**anage menu.

4. The Terminate user dialog box appears, prompting you for the time in minutes that you want to wait before logging the user out. Type the number or accept the default of 0. If you accept the default of 0 and select OK, the user is immediately logged out.

Figure 11.69
The User
Statistics dialog
box.

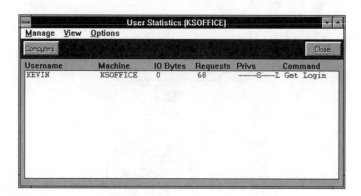

Username	**Machine**	**IO Bytes**	**Requests**	**Privs**	**Command**	
KEVIN	KSOFFICE	0	68	----S---L	Get Login	

Disabling Server Logins

You can disable logins for a server and thus prevent users from being able to log in. This action has no effect on current sessions, but when the user logs out, he or she will not be able to log back in. You can access this function through the LANtastic NET program, as shown in the following steps:

1. Select the Manage icon from the LANtastic NET program or choose Manage Other Computers from the Net menu.

2. In the Select Computer dialog box, choose the computer you want to disable logins on, and choose OK. The User Statistics dialog box appears (see fig. 11.69).

3. Choose Disable Logins from the Manage menu.

Future logins to this server are now disabled. You can reenable logins by selecting Enable Logins. Only a user with the S privilege can reenable logins.

Scheduling a Server Shutdown

You can schedule a server shutdown using the LANtastic NET program, as shown in the following steps:

1. Select the Manage icon from the LANtastic NET program, or choose Manage Other Computers from the Net menu.

2. In the Select Computer dialog box, choose the computer you want to schedule to shut down, and choose OK. The User Statistics dialog box appears (see fig. 11.69).

3. Choose Shutdown from the Manage menu. The Computer Shutdown dialog box appears (see fig. 11.70) with the following options:

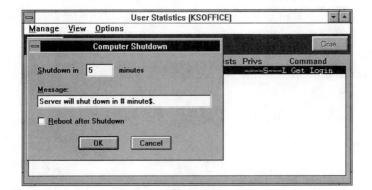

Figure 11.70
The Computer
Shutdown dialog
box.

✔ **Shutdown in ... Minutes.** This setting sets the number of minutes that must pass before the server shuts down.

✔ **Message.** The message is sent to users notifying them of the shutdown. The default message is Server will shut down in # minute$, in which # displays the number of minutes you enter in the first option and $ changes to s if more than one minute remains before shutdown.

✔ **Reboot after Shutdown.** If this option is selected, the server will reboot after shutdown.

4. Select OK to initiate the server shutdown.

The computer scheduled for shutdown should not be running Windows at the time the shutdown takes place. Attempts to shut down a computer while it is running Windows can lead to unstable behavior on the computer being shut down.

Canceling a Server Shutdown

You can cancel a scheduled server shutdown using the LANtastic NET program, as shown in the following steps:

1. Select the Manage icon from the LANtastic NET program, or select Manage Other Computers from the Net menu.

2. At the Select Computer dialog box, choose the computer for which you want to cancel the scheduled shutdown, then choose OK. The User Statistics dialog box appears (see fig. 11.69).

3. Select Ca<u>n</u>cel Shutdown from the <u>M</u>anage menu. The scheduled shutdown is canceled.

Summary

This chapter discussed the System Manager Privileges, and features of the LANtastic Network Manager program. The DOS and Windows LANtastic Network Manager programs were also discussed in detail. You are now prepared to manage your LANtastic network. The next chapter covers installing and configuring LANtastic with Windows.

Chapter Snapshot

This chapter discusses what to consider and how to install Microsoft Windows on an existing LANtastic network. In addition, the Windows-specific LANtastic features are also covered. Essentially, in this chapter you learn about the following topics:

✔ Installing and configuring Microsoft Windows after LANtastic is already installed

✔ Installing and configuring Microsoft Windows to run over a LANtastic network

✔ Special configuration issues to consider when running Windows and LANtastic

✔ The LANtastic Linkbook feature for network DDE (Dynamic Data Exchange)

✔ The LANtastic Windows Server Speed and Printer Speed utilities

By the end of this chapter, you will understand the unique features available to you when using LANtastic with Windows, as well as the configuration requirements to optimize your use of LANtastic and Windows together.

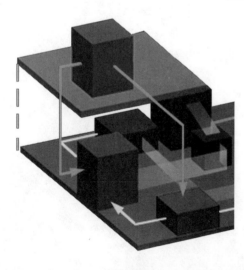

CHAPTER

12

Installing and Configuring LANtastic with Windows

Microsoft Windows provides the user with an easy-to-use graphical interface to perform various tasks. You run different programs in Windows, which you can size, move, and organize. Windows also enables you to run various programs in different windows. To switch between programs (called *changing the focus*), you click the mouse on the window in which you want to work.

You have many advantages when you choose to use Windows with LANtastic. LANtastic and Windows work very well together, creating a system that you can use to substantially improve your productivity.

When you run Windows with LANtastic, for example, you can configure and easily select the printers with which you want to print. LANtastic also gives Windows the capability to use printers that are connected to different computers. This same capability also is available for disk drives. LANtastic enables Windows to use different disk drives on different computers. You can, for example, run two separate programs in two different windows, with one program stored on your local hard drive and the other program stored on another PC's hard drive.

The flexibility and options available with the peer-to-peer features of LANtastic and the multitasking capabilities of Windows are almost limitless.

The LANtastic Windows programs consist of a group of separate programs providing the same features available with LANtastic DOS NET and NET_MGR in an easy-to-use Windows style interface. LANtastic for Windows also includes additional Windows network utility programs to make the joint use of LANtastic and Windows even more beneficial.

This chapter discusses the requirements for installing Microsoft Windows 3.1 after a LANtastic network is already up and running. Chapter 5, "Installing a LANtastic Network," discusses the procedure to follow when installing LANtastic on a computer that already has Windows installed.

Installing and Configuring Windows with LANtastic

Microsoft Windows was developed with networks such as LANtastic in mind; it therefore expects certain parameters to be configured if you are going to use it on a network. The Windows Setup program enables you to select the type of network and network drivers you want to load so Windows can access the features of the selected network. When you install LANtastic, the LANtastic installation program searches for Windows and, if found, installs the LANtastic Windows network drivers and LANtastic Windows programs, as well as making changes to the Windows configuration files. To take advantage of the many features LANtastic provides for Windows, you will have to reinstall LANtastic after you install Windows.

The LANtastic Windows drivers allow Windows to run in all modes, including 386-enhanced mode on a LANtastic server. If you want to run Windows in 386-enhanced mode without the LANtastic Windows drivers, you have to configure your computer as a workstation, not as a server. This means other users cannot access the resources on your computer.

Windows 386-enhanced mode enables you to perform "true" multitasking, which includes running more than one DOS application at the same time. True multitasking, for example, enables you to download a file from an electronic bulletin board while at the same time you are writing a document with your word processing program. 386-enhanced mode also gives you the capability to use virtual memory. *Virtual memory* is the process of using available space on your hard disk as RAM (random-access memory) when your application has used all the other available RAM.

Installing Windows on LANtastic Networks

You can use two methods to install Microsoft Windows 3.1 in a networked environment. Both methods have advantages and disadvantages, and the time you spend initially to determine which method best suits your situation is well worth it. You can combine the two methods to take advantage of the capabilities and features of individual computers.

The first method installs Windows 3.1 on a local hard drive. This method of installation is similar to installing Windows 3.1 on a stand-alone (or non-networked) computer. All the Windows files are stored in a directory on your local hard drive. When you run Windows from this setup, all primary program files are run from your local hard drive. With this type of installation, you still can run programs and access information that is stored on other computers. Printers connected to other LANtastic servers can also be used.

The second method you can use to install Windows 3.1 on a LANtastic network actually stores all the Windows files in a common location on a single computer. You can store the Windows files on any computer that you have configured as a LANtastic server. All computers on the network can then access the common Windows files from the LANtastic server's hard drive. After all Windows files are installed on the server, a second part of the installation is performed that installs specific Windows files for each user. These files contain configuration information for each user and typically are installed in a separate directory for each user. These files can be located on the local hard drive of the user's computer, the network hard drive of the computer that contains the Windows files, or any other available network hard drive. Because these files contain configuration information for each user, you need to make sure that these files are located in a different directory, separate from the common Windows files.

You need to make sure that each user's Windows configuration files are located apart from the common Windows files. This is especially important if you have different types of monitors on different computers. Users who access the wrong configuration information and video drivers most likely will have problems starting Windows.

Advantages and Disadvantages of Installation Methods

As you just learned, when you run Windows on a LANtastic network, you can share disk drives and printers that are on other computers. This capability is independent of whether Windows is being run from a local hard drive or from a network hard drive. The real determining factor as to which type of Windows installation is best for a given situation is really just a question of available hard disk space and performance. Also, you need to install Windows on a network hard drive if the workstations on your LANtastic network do not have hard disks installed in them.

Windows runs faster and performs better when you run it from a local hard drive than when you run it from a network hard drive. This is true for all programs, not just Windows. With Windows, however, the performance degradation is greatly exaggerated because of the heavy use of system resources, such as memory and hard drives, that Windows requires. The amount of hard disk space Windows occupies when installed on a network hard drive is approximately 16 MB, whereas it occupies only about 10 MB when you install it on a local hard drive. This is because you must install all the Windows files (including all the drivers) in the Windows subdirectory on the network drive. When installed on a local drive, Windows is configured for that computer and copies only the drivers necessary for that particular configuration.

Because Windows performance is so poor when run from a server over a network, you should install Windows on your local hard drive, if possible.

Installing Windows on a Local Hard Disk

Before you start installing Windows on your local hard drive, make sure that LANtastic is up and running. You can install Windows by using the Windows Setup program. Generally, this is performed by inserting the Windows Setup disk in the floppy drive (usually drive A or B), changing to that drive, and entering **Setup**. The Setup program gives you instructions concerning any input it requires.

When setting up Windows 3.1, choose the Custom Setup option rather than the Express Setup option (see fig. 12.1). Custom Setup gives you the option of selecting the type of network that you want to use. If LANtastic is detected by Setup during Windows installation, the Network section of the System Information screen shows Artisoft LANtastic (version 4.x). If Setup does not detect the correct network type, select LANtastic, and press Enter to continue the installation. Windows Setup prompts you to insert the required Windows disks until the setup is complete.

```
Windows Setup

   Setup has determined that your system includes the following hardware
   and software components. If your computer or network appears on the
   Hardware Compatibility List with an asterisk, press F1 for Help.

       Computer:          MS-DOS System
       Display:           VGA with Monochrome display
       Mouse:             Microsoft, or IBM PS/2
       Keyboard:          All AT type keyboards (84 - 86 keys)
       Keyboard Layout:   US
       Language:          English (American)
       Network:           Artisoft LANtastic (versions 4.X)

       No Changes:        The above list matches my computer.

   If all the items in the list are correct, press ENTER to indicate
   "No Changes." If you want to change any item in the list, press the
   UP or DOWN ARROW key to move the highlight to the item you want to
   change. Then press ENTER to see alternatives for that item.

 ENTER=Continue  F1=Help  F3=Exit
```

Figure 12.1
The Windows Setup System Information screen.

Express Setup asks fewer questions than the Custom Setup option and automatically chooses certain default parameters, making it quicker and easier to use. Express will not let you review the Network Type under the System Information screen.

To run LANtastic 6.0 with Windows, you must have Windows 3.1 and at least 2 MB of RAM installed.

When installing printers in Windows, be sure to choose all the printers that you want to use, including network printers. You also can install and configure printers after you set up Windows if you are not sure which printers you will use or how they are configured.

After you have installed Windows 3.1, reboot your computer and reinstall LANtastic as described in the "Upgrading a Previous Version of LANtastic" section in Chapter 5. The LANtastic installation program will recognize Windows on your system and install the appropriate LANtastic Windows network drivers and LANtastic applications in Windows.

When reinstalling LANtastic, you can keep your existing LANtastic settings. Only the new Windows-related information needs to be added.

Installing Windows on a LANtastic Server

To install Windows on a network drive for multiuser access, you must perform two steps. The first is the actual installation of the common Windows files on the server. The second, which is performed for each user (or workstation) on the network, involves installing user-specific Windows files in separate user directories. When Windows starts, it uses the configuration setup for the user's directory from which Windows was started.

Installing Windows Files on the Server

When you install Windows 3.1 files on the server, Windows performs an administrative setup that copies all the Windows files to the specified directory on a network server. To do this, insert the Windows Setup disk in the floppy drive at the server and type the following command:

A:\SETUP /A

The /A parameter in the preceding command tells Windows 3.1 to perform the Administrative Setup. The Windows Setup program asks you to specify which network directory to which you want to copy the Windows files. This can be any network drive or directory you specify (such as the WINADMIN directory). Windows Setup copies all the Windows files to the specified location and changes the DOS file attributes to Read Only to enable multiple users to access the networked Windows.

If you install Windows 3.1 files on a LANtastic Server using the Administrative Setup option, you can install Windows on other computers on the LANtastic network by accessing the Windows files over the network rather than using the disks. If you have a number of computers on which to install Windows, using the Windows files installed on the LANtastic Server rather than the floppy disks speeds up the Windows installation process significantly.

If you selected the Install Services option when you installed LANtastic 6.0, you can also take advantage of reinstalling LANtastic over the network. As with the Windows installation, this speeds up the process of reinstalling your network software.

Installing Windows Files on LANtastic Workstations

After you copy the Windows 3.1 files to the Windows directory on the LANtastic server you specified in Windows Setup (in this case, the WINADMIN directory), you need to set up each workstation. You can do this in two ways.

The first way is just like installing Windows from floppy disks, except that you install Windows from the network server rather than from the floppy disks. Windows installed in this manner does not require the network to be active for the workstation to run Windows after you install it. To install Windows this way, first redirect the network drive letter you want to use to connect to the LANtastic Server containing the Windows files. Then run the Windows Setup program, and follow the directions on-screen. The following example shows how this process can be performed:

C:\> NET USE W: \\SERVER1\C-DRIVE

C:\> W:

W:\> CD \WINADMIN

W:\WINADMIN> SETUP

In the preceding example, the first line creates a redirected drive W, which actually is drive C on the network server, named SERVER1. In this example, the Windows files are located on this server. The second line changes to the network drive W. The third line changes the current directory to WINADMIN. The last line runs the Windows SETUP program to begin the installation process.

You can have your DOS prompt appear as it does on the last line of the preceding example by including the following statement in your AUTOEXEC.BAT file:

PROMPT=PG

The second method of installing Windows on a LANtastic workstation involves running SETUP so Windows actually is run from the network server. This is called the *network setup*. Each workstation accesses the common Windows files from one place. A separate directory is created for each workstation that contains configuration information specific to that workstation. Windows installs just a few configuration files in the workstations directory (about 300 KB).

To install Windows this way, first connect to the network server that contains the Windows files. Perform the same steps as described in the first method, except use the network switch on the SETUP command at the DOS prompt, as follows:

W:\WINADMIN> SETUP /N

Windows SETUP adds the redirected drive and path (W:\WINADMIN in this example) of the common Windows program files to the PATH statement in your AUTOEXEC.BAT file.

After you have installed Windows 3.1, reboot your computer and reinstall LANtastic as described in the "Upgrading a Previous Version of LANtastic" section in Chapter 5. The LANtastic installation program will recognize Windows on your system and install the appropriate LANtastic Windows network drivers and LANtastic applications in Windows.

When reinstalling LANtastic, you can keep your existing LANtastic settings. Only the new Windows-related information needs to be added.

Examining Windows Configuration Procedures and Issues

Windows 3.1 and LANtastic work together to create a powerful and flexible operating environment. Because Windows 3.1 and LANtastic both add a number of features and benefits to the way most users work on their PCs, you should be aware of issues and configuration parameters that may affect the way LANtastic and Windows work together.

Using SMARTDrive and LANcache

When you install Windows 3.1 on your local hard drive, Windows adds the disk-caching program SMARTDrive to your AUTOEXEC.BAT file. LANtastic also comes with a disk-caching program called LANcache, which performs the same task as SMARTDrive, but is optimized for use with LANtastic. Unlike SMARTDrive, however, LANcache does not install automatically when you install LANtastic. Because both programs perform the same disk-caching function, you cannot use SMARTDrive and LANcache at the same time. If you do, your system might experience conflicts, resulting in data corruption or data loss.

SMARTDrive and LANcache both are disk-caching programs. Disk-caching programs use the computer's RAM to temporarily hold information being transferred to and from the computer's hard drive. With a disk-caching program, each time the hard drive is read, the information also is read into the cache (an area in your RAM). The next time information is needed from the hard drive, the disk-caching program first checks to see if it is located in the cache; if it is, the program reads it from there instead of the hard disk. Reading information from RAM (the cache) is much faster than reading from the hard disk. Because a disk-caching program contains algorithms to maximize the efficiency of transferring this data, Windows performance and general system performance are greatly improved by using one.

A disk-caching program helps the performance of the hard drives on the computer on which the disk cache is loaded. This means that if you have a disk cache on your computer, but the computer that you are accessing does not, you will not see any improvement. If, however, you access your own hard drive or another user on the network accesses your hard drive, both you and the other user will see an increase in hard drive performance.

To verify that SMARTDrive and LANcache are not being run at the same time, look in your AUTOEXEC.BAT, CONFIG.SYS, and any batch files that start the network, such as STARTNET.BAT. Make sure that you do not see more than one occurrence of either the program SMARTDRV or LANCACHE. If more than one of these programs are listed in any combination of the preceding files, remove one of them.

If you have DOS 5.0 or later, you can view the contents of memory by typing the following at a DOS prompt:

MEM /C|MORE

If you see both LANcache and SMARTDrive, you need to remove one of them from your AUTOEXEC.BAT or CONFIG.SYS file.

Whether you use LANcache or SMARTDrive, the program should be placed in your AUTOEXEC.BAT file prior to starting the network.

Prior to LANtastic 5.0, you had to load LANcache after the LANtastic REDIR program but before SERVER. This is no longer necessary, due to changes in the LANcache program.

Configuring Printers

After you install Windows on your LANtastic network, you need to configure the printers and their operating characteristics. You do this by using the LANtastic Network Manager program. The configuration performed in Windows automatically installs the appropriate printer drivers for the applications being used in Windows, setting some performance and operating parameters, and configuring to which ports (which actually may be redirected through LANtastic) to send the information. When you reinstall LANtastic, additional changes are made to the Windows printer configuration. When you run the LANtastic Network Manager to configure your printers, you need to specify the names of the printer resources that you use, the actual operating characteristics of the ports to which they are connected, and the rate at which network printing is accomplished.

Because LANtastic includes a print spooler, you do not need to use the Windows print spooler, Print Manager. You can disable Print Manager by selecting Control Panel (usually located in the Main Program Group) and choosing the Printers icon (see fig. 12.2). If the **U**se Print Manager box is selected, click on the box to turn it off. The LANtastic installation program normally disables the Print Manager selection.

Next, click on **C**onnect, and verify that the **F**ast Printing Direct to Port option is not selected (see fig. 12.2). The LANtastic installation program disables this selection. Also, change the Device Not Selected value to 900 and the Transmission Retry value to 950.

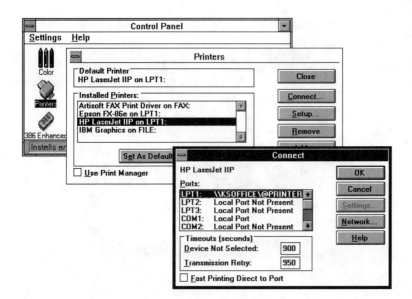

Figure 12.2
The Windows Printers and Connect dialog boxes.

Using the LANtastic Network Manager

Windows makes heavy use of the processor, even when it appears to be sitting idle. Often when Windows is running on a computer configured as a LANtastic server, any print jobs that you send to a printer that is physically connected to that computer can be extremely slow. The following printer configuration changes made using the LANtastic Network Manager program will help speed up printing (see fig. 12.3).

Run the LANtastic Network Manager program by double-clicking on the LANtastic Network Manager icon in the LANtastic program group, or with the icon selected, choose **O**pen from the **F**ile menu. Select the **R**esources icon or choose **R**esources from the **M**anage menu. The Resources dialog box appears (see fig. 12.4).

Figure 12.3
The LANtastic Network Manager.

Figure 12.4
The Resources
dialog box.

Figure 12.4
The Resources
dialog box.

Select the printer resource you want to configure, and then select **M**odify from the **E**dit menu. The Resource Parameters dialog box appears (see fig. 12.5). Change the Characters per Second field to 9600.

This field specifies the minimum characters per second that LANtastic attempts to send to the printer port.

Figure 12.5
Changing the
Characters per
Second field in
the Resource
Parameters
dialog box.

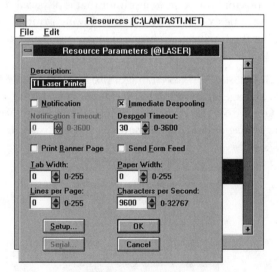

If you experience slow printing from a printer connected to a server running Windows, change the Maximum Active Printer Tasks to 1 in the LANtastic Server Configuration Printing Parameters Module. This module may be accessed by selecting the **S**erver icon in the LANtastic Network Manager program, and then selecting the Printing and Despooling icon.

Creating a Windows Swap File

A Windows swap file takes advantage of the 80386 and 80486 capability to use virtual memory. When Windows uses the existing RAM on your system, it uses space on the hard drive as virtual memory if you create a swap file. Windows 3.1 must be running in 386-enhanced mode to create and use a Windows swap file. When installing Windows, SETUP attempts to automatically create a Windows swap file. Setup cannot create a swap file if the LANtastic Server program is running. If your system is a 386-class machine or higher with over 2 MB of RAM and you want to enable Windows Setup to create a permanent swap file, you must remove the LANtastic Server program from memory before running Windows SETUP. You can remove SERVER by typing the following command at the DOS prompt:

SERVER /REMOVE

You also can create a permanent Windows swap file from within Windows, as long as the LANtastic Server program is not running or has been removed from memory before you start Windows.

The LANtastic Server program must not be running when you try to create a Windows permanent swap file. After the swap file is created, however, the LANtastic Server program may be running.

You can create a permanent Windows swap file by selecting Control Panel, choosing the 386-enhanced program (see fig. 12.6), and using the following steps:

1. In the 386 Enhanced dialog box, click on the **V**irtual Memory option.

2. In the Virtual Memory dialog box (see fig. 12.6), select the **C**hange button to display a second Virtual Memory dialog box (see fig. 12.7).

Figure 12.6

Creating a Windows permanent swap file.

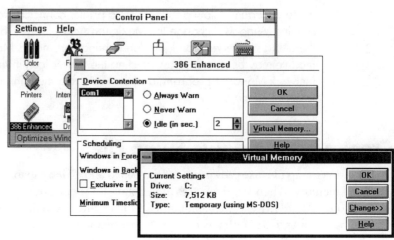

Figure 12.7

The Virtual Memory dialog box.

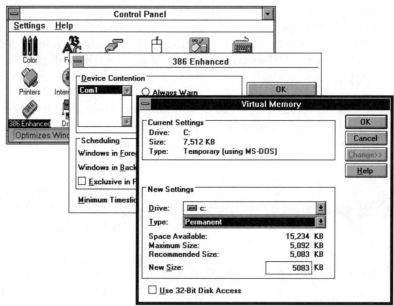

3. Windows displays the Current Settings and New Settings fields. In the New Settings field, Windows provides the space available, the maximum swap file size, and a recommended swap file size. If a swap file does not exist or you want to change its size, you can do so at this point by typing the new size in the New **S**ize field (see fig. 12.7).

4. Choose the type of swap file desired (either temporary or permanent) in the **T**ype field, and click on OK to create the swap file. A permanent swap file is faster, but takes up hard disk space even when Windows is not running. A temporary swap file is deleted when Windows is not running, but is not as fast as a permanent swap file.

If the LANtastic Server program is running, Windows does not display the option of a permanent swap file and may display an error message.

Configuring DOS and SETVER

If you have DOS 5 or later installed, and the SETVER command is installed in CONFIG.SYS, you may experience printing problems from Windows. You can eliminate this problem by removing SETVER from the CONFIG.SYS file or removing the REDIR.EXE and NET.EXE files from the SETVER table. This can be done by typing the following commands at the DOS prompt:

C:\> SETVER REDIR.EXE /D

C:\> SETVER NET.EXE /D

Changing the Windows SYSTEM.INI Files

When the LANtastic network drivers are installed by the LANtastic installation program, several changes are made automatically to the SYSTEM.INI file.

Under the [BOOT] section of the SYSTEM.INI file, the network.drv option is changed to:

network.drv=C:\LANTASTI\LANTNET.DRV

Under the [386Enh] section, changes are made as shown to the following options:

Network=*VNETBIOS,C:\LANTASTI\LANTASTI.386

NetAsynchFallback=TRUE

NetAsynchTimeout=5.0

NetHeapSize=64

PerVMFiles=0

The following line is added to the [boot.description] section:

network.drv=LANtastic for Windows Version 6.00

The LANtastic installation program also creates the [LANtastic] section and adds the following line:

Network_IRQ=15

in which 15 is the IRQ number used by the network interface card. If you have more than one network interface card in your computer, you need to add a separate line for each card.

In addition, if you are using an Artisoft 2 Mbps adapter or a remote boot ROM, you should add the following line to the [386Enh] section of the SYSTEM.INI file:

EMMExclude=D800-DFFF

The EMMExclude statement is required to avoid the possibility of a RAMBASE (or address) conflict (in which more than one application is trying to use the same part of upper memory). If the network adapter RAMBASE is not the default D800-DFFF address setting, then the EMMExclude statement should be changed so the actual RAMBASE used by the adapter matches that in the EMMExclude statement. Artisoft's Ethernet adapter cards do not use a RAMBASE, so the EMMExclude statement is not required.

The RAMBASE is a 32 KB area of memory between the 640 KB and the 1024 KB address space. This 32 KB area is used by the Artisoft 2 Mbps network adapter cards. Many hardware adapters, including video adapters, use other areas of the address space between 640 KB and 1024 KB.

The LANtastic installation program changes the WIN.INI to include the following line in the [Windows] section to automatically run the LANtastic NET program when Windows is started:

LOAD=C:\LANTASTI\WNET.EXE

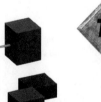

If you get an informative message when starting Windows regarding NetHeapSize, change the NetHeapSize=64 statement in the [Standard] section of the SYSTEM.INI file to NetHeapSize=63.

If you have upgraded from LANtastic version 2.x or 3.x, remove the following lines from the SYSTEM.INI file if they exist:

InDOSPolling=TRUE

ReflectDOSInt2a=TRUE

UniqueDOSPSP=TRUE

Redirecting Network Drives

If you have Windows set up to run from a network drive, the only way to access it is by first making a network connection to that drive, and then by starting Windows. You can create the connection in the batch file when LANtastic is first started or in a batch file that starts Windows. The following is a typical batch file for starting Windows. This batch file first connects to the network drive containing the Windows program files:

NET LOGIN \\WIN_SERV KEVIN ZAK

NET USE W: \\WIN_SERV\C-DRIVE

C:

CD\MYWIN

WIN

NET LOGOUT \\WIN_SERV

In the preceding batch file, the first line logs in to the server WIN_SERV as user KEVIN with password ZAK. WIN_SERV is the LANtastic server that contains the common Windows files. The second line makes the network drive connection W, which is redirected to the C-DRIVE resource on the server named WIN_SERV. Next, the batch file changes to the MYWIN directory on the local drive C from where Windows is run (specified by the WIN command). The MYWIN directory contains the unique Windows files for each user/workstation. The preceding batch file assumes that W:\WINADMIN is in the path statement—when Windows starts from the MYWIN directory, the batch file is going to look in the PATH for the location of the other common Windows files it needs to run. Also remember that the drive letter that shows up in the path statement must be the same letter used in the NET USE command.

In the preceding example, the C-DRIVE resource you connect to is actually the C:\ drive/directory on the server. You just as easily could have connected to a different resource, such as WINFILE, which may be pointing to the C:\WINADMIN directory on the server. If this was the case, the PATH statement would have to be W:\ instead of W:\WINADMIN.

With LANtastic version 4.1 and later, you do not need to log in to a server first if you do not have users/passwords setup. You can go straight to the NET USE line, which automatically logs you in. For this to be true, the wildcard account * must exist or the Individual and Wildcard **A**ccounts option in the LANtastic Server Configuration Security Parameters Module must be disabled.

If you are running Windows from a diskless workstation, your private windows directory is located on another computer. The preceding batch file still works if you have redirected drive C on your computer to point to a shared resource on another computer that contains your personal Windows files. If your computer is a diskless workstation (that is, you do not have a hard drive), when your computer boots up, for example, your AUTOEXEC.BAT file may contain the following lines:

NET LOGIN \\SERVER1 KEVIN ZAK

NET USE C: \\SERVER1\MYSTUFF

C:

The preceding commands log you in to SERVER1 and then redirect drive C to point to the MYSTUFF resource on SERVER1. The MYSTUFF resource contains all your files; when you access C, it operates as if you had a physical hard drive C in your computer.

Even if you will not be running Windows over the network, you may want to make some network connections before starting Windows. For organization and security purposes, you might want to keep data files in a common location on the network so no confusion arises when trying to locate a file you may need from a co-worker. Also, you may want to connect to a printer located somewhere else in the network. In this type of situation, your batch file to start Windows may look like the following:

NET LOGIN \\SERVER1 KEVIN ZAK

NET USE K: \\SERVER1\WIN_DATA

NET LOGIN \\SERVER2 KEVIN ZAK

NET USE LPT2: \\SERVER2\@LASER

C:

CD\WINDOWS

WIN

NET LOGOUT \\SERVER1

NET LOGOUT \\SERVER2

The preceding batch file creates drive K, redirected to the WIN_DATA resource on server SERVER1. In this example, WIN_DATA is a directory that stores the Windows data files (such as documents and spreadsheets). The batch file also redirects the printer port LPT2: to the @LASER resource on server SERVER2. @LASER is a laser printer on which users can print from Windows.

Using SUBST for Redirecting Local Drives

Sometimes you need to create a drive that actually is redirected to a local physical drive. This happens if the common Windows files for the network are installed on your computer. When you start Windows from your local drive, Windows looks to the path statement for the location of the common Windows files. The path statement in the previous example reads W:\WINADMIN. If a drive letter (W in this case) is redirected to a local physical drive, Windows typically locks up when going in or when accessing a redirected disk drive. If you need to create a drive that actually is redirected to a local physical drive, you should use the DOS SUBST command and not go through the network. The following is the format for the SUBST command for this example:

SUBST W: C:\

Examining the LANtastic Windows Programs

When LANtastic is installed for Windows, the LANtastic installation program creates the LANtastic program group which contains six icons, each representing different LANtastic utility programs (see fig. 12.8).

Figure 12.8
The LANtastic
Program group.

The LANtastic Net Connections icon represents the LANtastic NET program, which is used for establishing network drive and printer connections and performing other network related tasks, as described in previous chapters.

The LANtastic Network Manager icon represents the LANtastic Network Manager program, which is used for all network management functions including configuring and managing shared resources and accounts. The LANtastic Network Manager program is discussed in previous chapters.

The LANtastic Setup icon displays the Artisoft Install Setup Menu (see fig. 12.9). Options on this menu enable you to install the default resources normally installed with the LANtastic installation program, erase and create a new control directory without any resources or accounts, view configuration information about your computer, read LANtastic's online documentation, and disable LANtastic or the LANtastic server program the next time the computer boots.

Figure 12.9
The Artisoft
Install Setup
Menu.

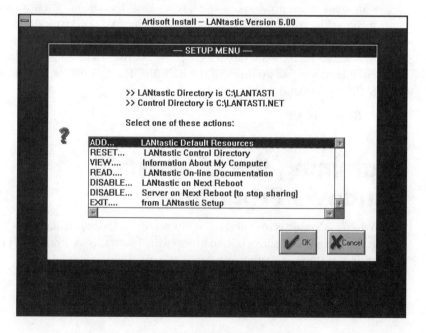

If you choose to keep your existing configuration when you install LANtastic 6.0, your STARTNET.BAT file will not be in the new format and some of the options listed previously will not be available.

The Artisoft Linkbook enables you to save and read items from your Windows Clipboard in a network accessible linkbook. In addition to sharing clipboard information across the network, the Artisoft Linkbook also supports network DDE (Dynamic Data Exchange).

The LANtastic Printer Speed program enables you to specify how many characters per second will be despooled to your printer while you are running Windows.

The LANtastic Server Speed program enables you to specify the amount of your CPU's capability that will be spent on processing network requests, as compared to the amount of your CPU's capability spent on local non-network operations.

The Artisoft Exchange Mail and Scheduler programs are sophisticated electronic mail and scheduling programs with built-in fax and paging capability. Artisoft Exchange is covered in detail in Chapter 13, "Using Artisoft Exchange."

Examining Artisoft Linkbook

The Artisoft Linkbook expands on the capabilities provided by the Windows Clipboard. While the Windows Clipboard holds a single item temporarily and can be accessed only by the local computer, the linkbook can contain multiple items permanently and be accessed by other network users.

In addition to providing clipboard features, the linkbook supports network DDE (Dynamic Data Exchange), enabling you to share "live" data between different computers for those Windows applications that support it. For example, if you were creating a chart with a spreadsheet program, you could copy the chart to your clipboard. With the Artisoft Linkbook, you could make the chart available to others over the network. A user on another computer could be creating a document and could paste the chart into his or her document. As you update the chart, the changes would appear in the other user's document.

The Artisoft Linkbook replaces the Scrapbook feature that came with LANtastic for Windows 5.0. When you upgrade to LANtastic 6.0, the information previously in your scrapbook is automatically transferred to the Artisoft Linkbook. Users who are running LANtastic 5.0 can use their scrapbook features to share files with a LANtastic 6.0 linkbook.

Like the Windows Clipboard, the Artisoft Linkbook can be used to store items such as text, graphics, and sound files.

To have a linkbook, the LANTASTI.SHR resource must exist on your computer. The LANTASTI.SHR resource is created when you install LANtastic, and points to the C:\LANTASTI\LANTASTI.SHR directory.

To open the Artisoft Linkbook, double-click on the Artisoft Linkbook icon in the LANtastic program group. The Artisoft Linkbook window appears, containing the Clipboard and Local Linkbook icons (see fig. 12.10). Double-click on the Clipboard icon to view the contents of the Windows Clipboard and double-click on the Local Linkbook icon to view the contents of the Local linkbook.

Figure 12.10
The Artisoft
Linkbook
window.

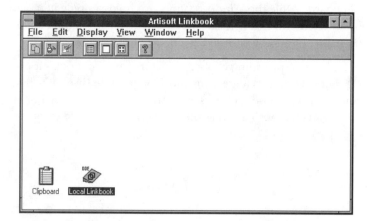

The Artisoft Linkbook has the following pull-down menu options:

✔ **F**ile

✔ **E**dit

✔ **D**isplay

✔ **V**iew

✔ **W**indow

✔ **H**elp

File

The File selection has menu options to enable you to Create a **N**ew Linkbook or a New **P**age, to **R**efresh the display, or to **V**iew Active DDE Links.

The Artisoft Linkbook enables you to have other linkbooks in addition to your Local Linkbook. To create a new linkbook, select **N**ew Linkbook. Type the description of the new linkbook and select the server to contain the linkbook (see fig. 12.11).

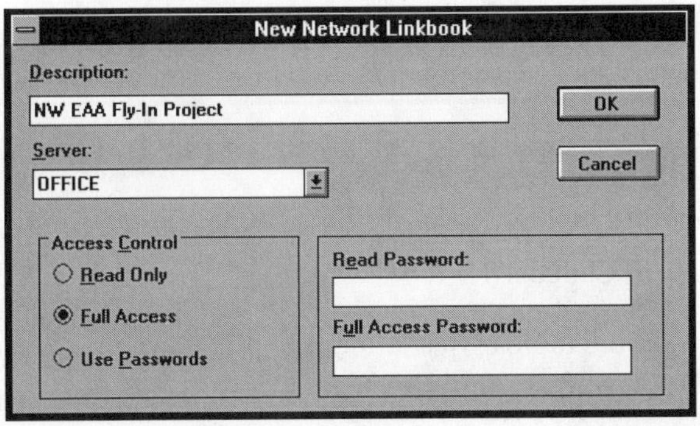

Figure 12.11
The New Network Linkbook dialog box.

In the Access Control dialog box, you can select the type of access other network users can have to this linkbook. Selecting **R**ead Only access enables other users to look at and copy entries from the linkbook, but they will not be able to change or write to the linkbook entries. Selecting **F**ull Access enables users to view, read, and write to the linkbook. The Use **P**asswords selection enables read only access or full access, depending on the password entered.

Each linkbook can have multiple pages. Each time you paste an item to the Windows Clipboard, you can save that item as a separate page in one of your network linkbooks. If you want to create a new page in your linkbook, select New **P**age from the **F**ile menu. From the New Linkbook Page window, enter the description of your page and specify whether other users will have Read Only or Full Access to the page (see fig. 12.12). Click on OK, and the new page is created.

Figure 12.12
Creating a New
Linkbook Page.

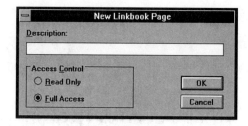

Edit

The **E**dit pull-down menu selection contains the following:

- ✔ **C**opy
- ✔ **P**aste
- ✔ **D**elete
- ✔ Change Name/**S**ecurity
- ✔ **L**ink to Clipboard
- ✔ C**a**ncel Link to Clipboard

The first three icons on the toolbar (just under the pull-down menu selections) are the equivalent of the **C**opy, **P**aste, and **D**elete selections.

The **C**opy selection copies the contents of the selected linkbook page to the Windows Clipboard.

The **P**aste selection pastes the contents of the Windows Clipboard to the selected linkbook page.

The **D**elete selection deletes an item depending on which items are selected. If the Windows Clipboard currently is selected, **D**elete deletes the contents of the Windows Clipboard. If a linkbook page is selected, **D**elete deletes the linkbook page. If a linkbook icon is selected, **D**elete deletes the entire linkbook.

The Change Name/$\underline{S}$ecurity selection enables you to change the name and access control of an existing linkbook or linkbook page. If a linkbook page is selected, you are enabled to edit the name and access control for the linkbook page. If a linkbook is selected, this selection enables you to edit the name and access control for the linkbook.

The $\underline{L}$ink to Clipboard selection enables you to create a link between the Windows Clipboard and a page in your network linkbook. When you set up a link to Clipboard, you can specify $\underline{R}$ead, $\underline{W}$rite, or $\underline{B}$oth. If you specify $\underline{R}$ead, when you update the linkbook page, the Windows Clipboard automatically is updated with the same change. If you specify $\underline{W}$rite, the linkbook page automatically is updated when the Windows Clipboard is updated. If you specify $\underline{B}$oth, the linkbook page is updated when the Windows Clipboard is updated, and when you update the linkbook page, the Windows Clipboard is updated.

The Cancel Link selection cancels an existing Network Linkbook to Windows Clipboard link.

Display

The $\underline{D}$isplay option enables you to specify $\underline{A}$uto and other display formats. The other display formats listed will vary depending on the type of item currently in the Clipboard. Choosing $\underline{A}$uto causes Network Linkbook to try to pick the best format to display the item.

View

The $\underline{V}$iew option enables you to specify $\underline{L}$ist, $\underline{S}$ingle Page, or $\underline{T}$humbnail. Selecting $\underline{L}$ist displays a list of available pages in the linkbook. Selecting $\underline{S}$ingle Page displays the currently selected page. Selecting $\underline{T}$humbnail displays the linkbook as a set of miniature images.

Window

The $\underline{W}$indow option enables you to specify which window to make the active window and how to organize the windows. You can select $\underline{C}$ascade or $\underline{T}$ile as an organizational method for the windows. The Arrange $\underline{I}$cons option will organize the placement of the icons on the screen.

LANtastic Printer Speed

The LANtastic Printer Speed program enables you to specify the minimum characters per second that will be sent to the printer while you are in Windows.

Start the LANtastic Printer Speed program by double-clicking on the LANtastic Printer Speed icon. The LANtastic Printer Speed program appears (see fig. 12.13), enabling you to specify the CPS that will be sent to the printer by sliding the adjustment knob from the left to the right. The maximum value is 32767 CPS. While the LANtastic Printer Speed program is running, the values specified override the CPS setup configuration for the printer resource using the LANtastic Network Manager program.

Figure 12.13
The LANtastic
Printer Speed
program.

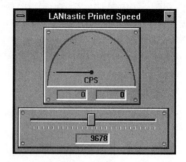

LANtastic Server Speed

The LANtastic Server Speed program enables you to specify the Run Burst to be used on your computer while running Windows. The higher the Run Burst, the more CPU time allotted to processing network tasks.

Start the LANtastic Server Speed program by double-clicking on the LANtastic Server Speed icon. The LANtastic Server Speed program appears (see fig. 12.14), enabling you to specify the Run Burst setting by sliding the adjustment knob from the left to the right. The maximum value is 255. While the LANtastic Server Speed program is running, the values for Run Burst in Server Speed override the values specified in the LANtastic Server Configuration Performance Parameters Module for the **B**ackground CPU Usage (Run Burst).

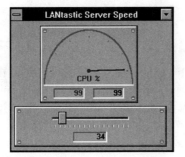

Figure 12.14
The LANtastic
Server Speed
program.

Summary

The combination of LANtastic and Windows creates a very powerful and flexible operating environment. Windows provides an intuitive graphical operating environment; LANtastic enables the resources of any other computers on the network to be used from within Windows. Windows 3.1 recognizes and provides features for network operation. After Windows has been installed and configured for use with LANtastic, all the features of LANtastic are available from within Windows.

LANtastic for Windows goes one step further by providing a Windows interface for the features found in the NET and NET_MGR programs—it even adds a few. LANtastic for Windows is an excellent LANtastic interface and makes network use within Windows almost effortless.

Chapter Snapshot

This chapter discusses all facets of the powerful new
Artisoft Exchange mail and scheduling programs
included with LANtastic 6.0. Specifically, this chapter
covers the following topics:

- ✔ Installing Artisoft Exchange

- ✔ Setting up accounts for Exchange Users

- ✔ Configuring Exchange Mail as client-based or
  server-based

- ✔ Setting up using the Fax Gateway, LANtastic Mail
  Gateway, and the Pager Gateways

- ✔ Managing Exchange Mail

- ✔ Setting up and using public and private address
  books and mailing lists, as well as addresses to
  access the gateways

- ✔ Creating, sending, and receiving Exchange Mail

- ✔ Using Exchange Scheduler

After reading this chapter, you will understand the
many features available in Artisoft Exchange and will be
able to set up, configure, and use Artisoft Exchange
confidently.

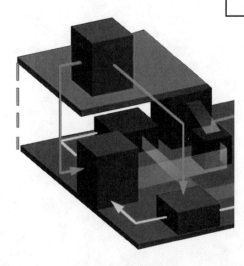

Using Artisoft Exchange

Artisoft Exchange is a sophisticated mail and scheduling program included with LANtastic 6.0 that runs under Microsoft Windows. A DOS version of Artisoft Exchange is expected to be released with a later version of LANtastic. Artisoft Exchange consists of two separate programs, Exchange Mail and Exchange Scheduler, which are tightly integrated. Exchange not only provides sophisticated mail and scheduling features for users on your network, it also includes Gateways so that you can communicate with fax machines, pagers, and users who utilize LANtastic Mail instead of Exchange Mail. Exchange Mail enables you to attach files to your outgoing messages. You can also request a return receipt through Exchange Mail, which informs you that the intended recipient has read your message, or enables you to mark your message as a priority.

Artisoft Exchange uses an object-oriented user interface, which means that you perform your tasks by modifying objects. Each object is represented by an icon. A *folder*, for example, is a type of object that might contain other objects such as user account or message objects. You may have a folder named In Basket that contains message objects (messages) that have been sent to you. Objects also have attributes that are characteristics of the object, such as the icon associated with the object, the name of the object, or even how much information contained in an object is actually shown.

You can create new objects using the templates packaged with Exchange. Several types of templates are included. You can create an object by copying a template and specifying the required information for your specific object. You can also create new objects that prompt you to type required information when the object is used. An example of this type of object would be a fax address object. When you send a fax and specify this template object, you are prompted to type in the fax telephone number.

Artisoft Exchange Mail enables you to have shadow objects. A *shadow object* enables you to access the same item from different locations. If you change a shadow object, the changes are also made to the original and any other shadows of the original. Shadow objects however, have their own attributes so you can change the name of a shadow object without changing the name of the original. This feature enables you to set up aliases for the original object by using a shadow object. Shadow objects are easily identified because they are displayed in italics.

Artisoft Exchange Mail has other features built into it as well. If you place your mouse over an object and press the right mouse button, you can display information about the object. Using this feature, you can even get an explanation of what the toolbar icons do.

Because you can organize objects and move them to any location you prefer, Exchange Mail enables you to search for objects by object type and name. You can also use wildcards in searches.

Installing Artisoft Exchange

You can install Artisoft Exchange when you install LANtastic 6.0 (see fig. 13.1) if you have Microsoft Windows 3.1 on your computer. If your computer doesn't have Windows, you can configure it as an Exchange post office, but you cannot use the Artisoft Exchange Mail and Schedule program.

After selecting the option to install Artisoft Exchange, you are given three options for installation: Artisoft Exchange – Mail Client, Artisoft Exchange – Network Mail Client, and Artisoft Exchange – Mail Post Office (see fig. 13.2). One computer in your network must be set up as the Artisoft Exchange Post Office. The *Post Office* is the location where the mail is stored for the entire network.

The act of selecting the Artisoft Exchange – Mail Client option copies all the Artisoft Exchange program files to your computer. Upon activation, the Exchange program runs from your hard disk and the mail files are accessed from the post office computer. If you activate the Artisoft Exchange – Network Mail Client option, the Artisoft Exchange programs can be accessed over the network from the post office computer. Although this option saves disk space on your computer, it causes Artisoft Exchange to run slower because the program is running across the network.

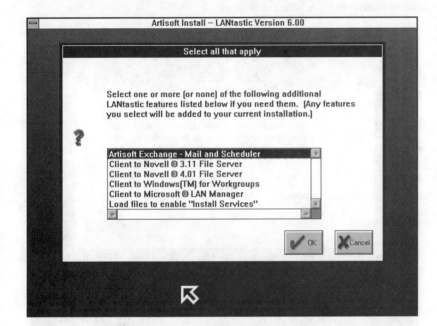

Figure 13.1
Selecting the Artisoft Exchange option during installation.

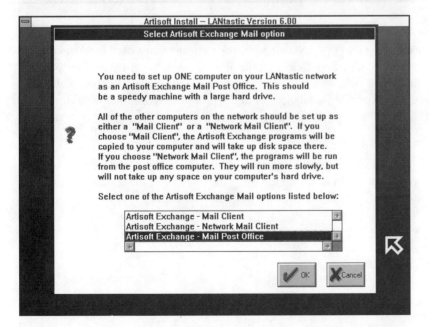

Figure 13.2
Selecting the type of Artisoft Exchange installation.

If you select the Artisoft Exchange–Mail Post Office option, you can configure your computer as the post office for Artisoft Exchange mail. First you are asked to give the post office on your computer a name (see fig. 13.3). The name does not have to be the same as your computer's network name.

Figure 13.3

Naming an Artisoft Exchange Post Office.

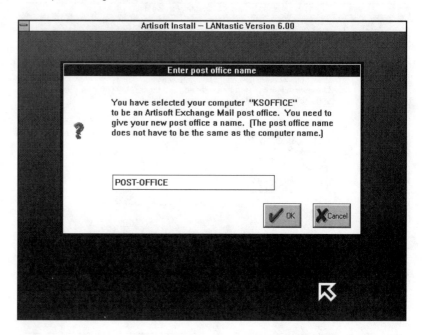

The Same Accounts for LANtastic or Mail? dialog box lets you specify whether you want the accounts set up in LANtastic to be the same accounts used for Artisoft Exchange Mail (see fig. 13.4). Selecting the Yes–Use same accounts option spares you from the necessity to set up accounts for both LANtastic and Exchange. If you select this option, you must be logged in to the post office computer with your individual account.

If you select to use the same accounts for LANtastic and Exchange, you may not log in to Exchange using the * wildcard account. Attempting to do so will cause an error message from Exchange.

If you select the No - Use separate accounts option, your LANtastic accounts and Exchange accounts are different. You must set up an account in Exchange for each user that utilizes Exchange. The advantage of using separate accounts is that you can be logged in to the post office computer with any account name, including the * Wildcard account. After you start Exchange you are asked for a username and password which have been set up in Exchange. The separate account option is especially useful if you have more than one person that uses the same computer; you can configure the system to log in to other servers and use the server's shared resources without having to worry about setting up individual accounts in LANtastic for each user. When Artisoft Exchange starts, it prompts the user for a username and password. Upon receiving the correct response, Exchange proceeds and notifies the user if any mail exists for him or her.

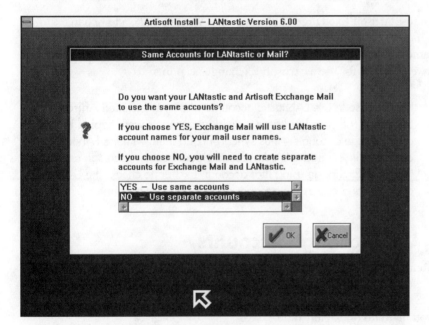

Figure 13.4
Specifying whether to use the same accounts for LANtastic and Exchange.

After LANtastic 6.0 is installed with the Artisoft Exchange programs, the LANtastic program group is created—which includes icons representing Artisoft Exchange Mail and Artisoft Exchange Scheduler (see fig. 13.5) in addition to icons for the LANtastic 6.0 Windows programs. If the computer at which you are sitting is the post office computer, you also have an Artisoft Exchange Post Office icon.

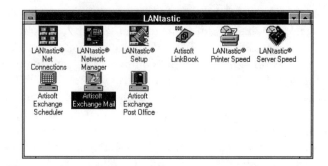

Figure 13.5
The LANtastic program group showing icons for Exchange Mail and Scheduler.

Configuring Artisoft Exchange Mail

Before you use Artisoft Exchange Mail, you might want to make a few changes to the default configuration to suit your needs. If, during installation, you chose to use the same accounts for LANtastic and Artisoft Exchange, your LANtastic user accounts were copied for use as Artisoft Exchange accounts.

If you chose to use LANtastic accounts when you installed Artisoft Exchange, all your LANtastic individual accounts were copied for use as Exchange accounts—thus synchronizing them with the LANtastic accounts. If you add a LANtastic individual account, as soon as you try to access Exchange using that account, Exchange checks the LANtastic accounts and copies the account as an Exchange account.

Setting Up Exchange Accounts

When you install Artisoft Exchange, an account with the name SYSTEM is created. To add, delete, or modify accounts in Exchange, you must log in to Exchange Mail using the SYSTEM account. Initially SYSTEM does not contain a password, although you may add one at any time.

If you chose to use LANtastic accounts when you installed Artisoft Exchange, you must log in to the post office computer using the SYSTEM account; Exchange does not prompt you for a username and password.

If you chose to use separate accounts for LANtastic and Exchange, Exchange prompts you to enter a username and password, at which point you can type in SYSTEM for the username. You must already be logged in to the post office computer with any account (including the * wildcard account) to use Exchange.

If your LANtastic and Exchange accounts are synchronized, you can add a new Exchange account using the LANtastic Network Manager program, as described in previous chapters. If you are logged in to the post office computer with the newly created account, when you start Exchange the new account will automatically be copied as an Exchange account

If your LANtastic and Exchange accounts are not synchronized, add a new Exchange account using the following steps:

1. Start Artisoft Exchange Mail by double-clicking on the Artisoft Exchange icon in the LANtastic program group, or, with the icon selected, choose **O**pen from the Program Manager **F**ile menu.

2. When prompted for a **U**sername and **P**assword, enter SYSTEM as the username and do not enter a password (see fig. 13.6). Select OK and the Artisoft Exchange Mail dialog box appears (see fig. 13.7).

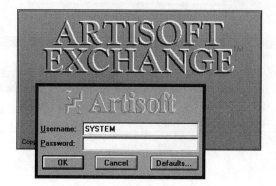

Figure 13.6
Starting
Exchange Mail
using the
SYSTEM
account.

3. Double-click on the User Accounts folder, or, with the folder selected, choose **O**pen from the **O**bjects menu. The User Accounts dialog box appears (see fig. 13.8).

The User Accounts folder only appears if you are logged in using the SYSTEM account.

4. To create a new user account object, select **N**ew Account from the **A**dministration menu. The Create New Account dialog box appears (see fig. 13.9).

Figure 13.7
The Artisoft
Exchange Mail
dialog box.

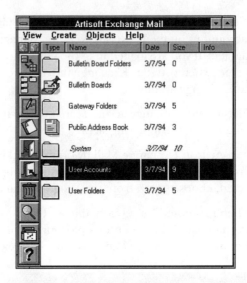

Figure 13.8
The User
Accounts
dialog box.

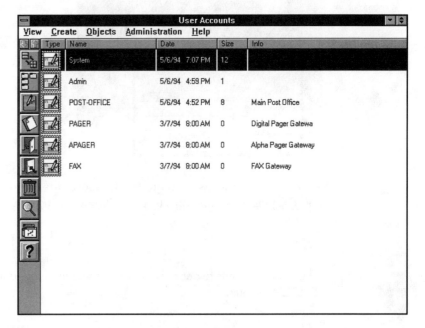

5. Leave the Account **T**ype as User and type the name for the user you
    are adding in the **U**ser Name field. The user name may be up to 30
    characters and—unlike a LANtastic account name—may contain
    spaces. Fill in any additional information for this user. The other fields
    are described as follows:

✔ The Post**o**ffice field displays the name of your post office and cannot be changed when adding an account.

✔ The **E**mail Address field contains the post office name appended by the user name and cannot be changed when you add an account.

The Post**o**ffice field and the **E**mail Address field may be changed later by selecting the account object to be changed and then choosing **O**pen from the **Ob**jects menu.

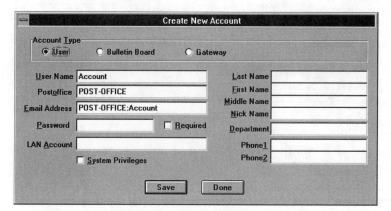

Figure 13.9
Creating a new Exchange account.

✔ The **P**assword field is the password that is associated with the user name. If the **R**equired field is selected you cannot continue without entering a password for this account.

✔ The LAN **A**ccount field can contain the name of the LANtastic account for this user. This field is optional and is for informational purposes only; the value in this field is not used by Artisoft Exchange.

✔ Selecting the **S**ystem Privileges option enables the user to create and delete system level folders such as the Public Address Book.

A user with **S**ystem Privileges cannot add or delete users. User accounts can only be added or deleted by logging in using the SYSTEM account.

✔ All the other fields are for informational use only and can contain any information you want to put in them. The information in these fields can be viewed but not changed by other users.

Figure 13.10 shows an example of a completed Exchange account.

Figure 13.10

A completed Create New Account dialog box.

```
┌─────────────────────────────────────────────────────────────────┐
│ ─                       Create New Account                        │
├───────────────────────────────────────────────────────────────────┤
│  ┌─Account Type────────────────────────────────────────────────┐  │
│  │  ● User        ○ Bulletin Board      ○ Gateway              │  │
│  └─────────────────────────────────────────────────────────────┘  │
│                                                                     │
│    User Name  Kevin Stoltz              Last Name  Stoltz          │
│    Postoffice POST-OFFICE               First Name Kevin           │
│                                         Middle Name J              │
│  Email Address POST-OFFICE:Kevin Stoltz Nick Name                  │
│    Password   ZAK          ☒ Required   Department                 │
│                                                                     │
│  LAN Account  Kevin                     Phone1  206-353-9623       │
│               ☒ System Privileges       Phone2                     │
│                                                                     │
│                    ┌──────┐   ┌──────┐                             │
│                    │ Save │   │ Done │                             │
│                    └──────┘   └──────┘                             │
└─────────────────────────────────────────────────────────────────┘
```

6. Select the Save button to create the new account. The new account is created and the Create New Account dialog box is cleared, enabling you to enter another new account. Continue adding as many new accounts as you want. When finished, select the Done button and you return to the User Accounts window displaying the new Exchange accounts. To delete an account, select the account to be deleted in the User Accounts window and then choose **D**elete Account from the **A**dministration window, or select the trash can icon from the tool bar on the left side of the screen.

To modify the information in an existing account, double-click on the account to be changed (shown in the User Accounts window) or select **O**pen from the **O**bjects menu. The dialog box for the selected account appears, enabling you to change the desired information (see fig. 13.11). While modifying accounts, you can change the Post**o**ffice and **E**mail Address fields, which cannot be changed when adding a new account. After you finish making your changes, select Sa**v**e from the A**c**count menu. This selection saves your changes and returns you to the User Accounts window.

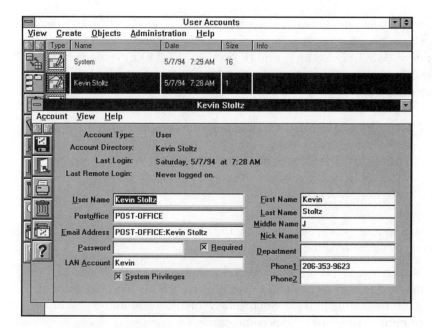

Figure 13.11
Modifying an Exchange Mail account.

Configuring Exchange Mail as Client-Based or Server-Based

When Artisoft Exchange is installed, it is set up by default as a client-based system. In *client-based systems*, each (client) computer sends its own mail, using the post office computer as the central storage location for messages. A *server-based system* relies on the post office (server) computer to send the messages to others. To use any Gateway features, such as the fax and pager gateways, your Exchange system must be set up in the Server mode.

The post office computer must have at least a 386 coprocessor to operate in server-based mode. You will find it advantageous if you dedicate the server to processing mail tasks and nothing else. If you can't dedicate the server, you should increase each Gateway's interval (described as follows) to 60 seconds or more.

After you set up your post office computer to operate in server mode, your Artisoft Exchange Post Office Server program provides mail server and gateway functions. Both Windows (WMTAEXEC.EXE) and DOS (MTAEXEC.EXE) versions of the Artisoft Exchange Post Office Server program exist, providing the Exchange server functions.

Because the DOS MTAEXEC.EXE program does not run in the background, you cannot use your computer as anything else but a post office server. Therefore, if at all possible, run the Windows version of MTAEXEC so you can run other programs in other Windows to perform various operations.

If you want to be able to use gateways, configure your Exchange system in the Server mode by performing the following steps:

1. If Exchange is configured to use LANtastic accounts (synchronized mode) log in to the post office computer using the SYSTEM account. If it is not configured for synchronized mode, log in to the post office computer using any valid account name.

2. Start Artisoft Exchange Mail by double-clicking on the Artisoft Exchange Mail icon in the LANtastic program group, or, with the icon selected, choose **O**pen from the Program Manager **F**ile menu. If you are not using synchronized mode, you are asked for a user name and password. Enter SYSTEM as the user name and leave the password blank (unless you have specified a password for the SYSTEM account in Exchange).

3. Double-click on the User Accounts folder or, with the folder selected, choose **O**pen from the **O**bjects menu. The User Accounts dialog box appears (see fig. 13.8).

The User Accounts folder only appears if you are logged in using the SYSTEM account.

4. From the **A**dministration menu select **P**ostoffice Mode and the Server/ Client dialog box appears (see fig. 13.12).

Figure 13.12
Specifying the
Server mode for
Artisoft Exchange
mail.

5. Select the **S**erver option and choose OK. The post office computer is
now configured to operate in the Server mode for Exchange.

For the post office computer to operate in Server mode, it must be running the
Artisoft Exchange Post Office Server program. To run the Artisoft Exchange Post
Office Server program from DOS, change to the \LANTASTI\AMAILPRG directory
and type MTAEXEC from the DOS prompt. To run the Windows version of the
Artisoft Exchange Post Office Server program, double-click on the Artisoft Ex-
change Post Office icon or, with the icon selected, choose **O**pen from the Program
Manager's **F**ile menu.

The Artisoft Exchange Post Office Server program must be running for
the Artisoft Exchange server features to operate. If you are running the
DOS program, include the MTAEXEC command in the network startup
batch file STARTNET.BAT. To start the Windows version of MTAEXEC,
drag the Artisoft Exchange Post Office icon to the STARTUP program
group. Now when Windows starts, WMTAEXEC also starts.

When you start the Artisoft Exchange Post Office Server program, it
prompts you for the post office name and password, a message store
directory, and a temporary working directory. Selecting the Save as
Default option in the Windows version of the Post Office Server
program saves the current settings as the default the next time the
program is run, although you still have to select OK to start the
program (see fig. 13.13).

If you want to change from a server-based to a client-based configuration, repeat
the above steps and specify the **C**lient option instead of the **S**erver option in the
Server/Client dialog box.

Figure 13.13
The Post Office
Initialization
dialog box.

```
┌─────────────── Artisoft Exchange Post Office Server ──────────────────┐▼
│ Pr ┌──────────────── Post Office Initialization ───────────────┐   wn │
│ Ev │                                                           │     t │
│ Ev │  Enter the main post office name:    POST-OFFICE          │      │
│ Sta│                                                           │      │
│    │  Enter the main post office password:                     │      │
│    │                                                           │      │
│    │  Main post office message store directory  Main post office temporary work directory │
│    │  \\KSOFFICE\AMAIL            C:\LANTASTI\TEMP             │      │
│ Las│              ☐ Save as default                            │      │
│    │              [   Ok   ]   [  Cancel  ]                    │      │
│    └───────────────────────────────────────────────────────────┘      │
│ Last Error Time:              Time Started:                            │
│ Error Count:   0              MTAs Started:        MTAs Active:         │
└────────────────────────────────────────────────────────────────────────┘
```

Setting Up Gateways

Gateways provide a means for you to communicate with other devices and communication resources, such as fax machines, pagers, and LANtastic Mail. For a gateway to be operational, Exchange must be configured in the Server mode and not the Client mode.

Included with LANtastic 6.0 are the following Artisoft Exchange gateways:

- ✔ **Fax Gateway.** The Fax Gateway enables you to send and receive faxes using the fax card on the Exchange Mail server.

- ✔ **Digital Pager Gateway.** The Digital Pager Gateway enables you to send a number to a digital pager.

- ✔ **Text Pager Gateway.** The Text Pager Gateway lets you send up to 255 alpha-numeric characters to a text pager.

- ✔ **LANtastic Mail Gateway.** The LANtastic Mail Gateway lets you exchange messages between LANtastic Mail and Exchange Mail.

- ✔ **LANtastic Queue Gateway.** The LANtastic Queue Gateway enables you to send a print job to a LANtastic printer queue.

Several other gateways are available from Artisoft including the following:

- ✔ **MCI Mail Gateway.** The MCI Mail Gateway lets you exchange messages with users accessing the MCI Mail service via telephone.

- ✔ **MHS Gateway.** The MHS Gateway enables you to exchange messages with other MHS compatible mail systems on your network or connected via modems and telephone lines.

✔ **Network PO to PO Gateway.** The Network PO to PO Gateway lets you exchange messages between different post offices on the same network.

✔ **Remote PO to PO Gateway.** The Remote PO to PO Gateway enables you to exchange messages with a remote user via synchronous devices such as modems.

To set up an operational gateway, follow these steps:

1. Set up your post office computer in the Server mode as previously described.

2. Set up an account in the User Accounts folder for each gateway. When setting up a new Gateway account, proceed as previously described, but select Gateway as the Account **T**ype. When you install Artisoft Exchange, Gateway accounts are automatically created for the Fax, Digital Pager, Text Pager, and LANtastic Mail gateways.

3. Set up a Gateway event in the Exchange Mail Servers folder located in the Gateway Folders folder. When you set up Gateway events, you specify how often Gateway events are processed.

4. Run the Windows or DOS version of the Artisoft Exchange Post Office Server program (WMTAEXEC.EXE or MTAEXEC.EXE) to manage the mail server and Gateway functions.

At the time you set up your post office in Server mode, steps 1 and 4 of the above were performed. A Gateway account was created during the installation of Artisoft Exchange; therefore, if you are intending to set up one of the gateways included with Exchange, all that is necessary is to activate the gateway.

To activate a gateway, perform the following steps:

1. Start Artisoft Exchange Mail by double-clicking on the Artisoft Exchange Mail icon in the LANtastic program group, or, with the icon selected, choose **O**pen from the Program Manager **F**ile menu. If you are not using synchronized accounts, you are asked for a user name and password. Enter SYSTEM as the user name and leave the password blank (unless you have specified a password for the SYSTEM account in Exchange). If you are using synchronized accounts, you must be logged in to the server using the SYSTEM account name.

2. When the Artisoft Exchange Mail dialog box appears, double-click on the Gateway Folders icon or, with the icon selected, choose **O**pen from the **O**bjects menu (see fig. 13.14).

Figure 13.14
Selecting the
Gateway Folders
icon.

3. When the Gateway Folders dialog box appears, open the folder with the same name as the Post Office (POST-OFFICE in this example) by double-clicking on the folder or with the folder selected, choosing **O**pen from the **O**bjects menu (see fig. 13.15).

Figure 13.15
Opening the
POST-OFFICE
folder.

4. Open the MTA Events folder by double-clicking on it, or by selecting it and choosing **O**pen from the **O**bjects menu (see fig. 13.16).

Figure 13.16
Opening the
MTA Events
folder.

5. Select the MTA Event you want to activate by double-clicking on the desired MTA Event, or by selecting the MTA Event and choosing **O**pen from the **O**bjects menu (see fig. 13.17).

Figure 13.17
Selecting the
desired MTA
Event to activate.

6. The MTA dialog box for the selected MTA Event appears (see fig. 13.18). To activate the gateway, enter a number in the **I**nterval (seconds) field. The value entered is the number of seconds the Artisoft Exchange Post Office Server program waits between processing events for the gateway. Leaving the value blank disables the gateway.

In Post Office Server mode, the MTA Server event is automatically enabled with an Interval of 60 seconds. All other MTA Server events must be manually enabled by entering a value in the Interval field.

Figure 13.18
Activating a gateway by specifying an Interval in seconds.

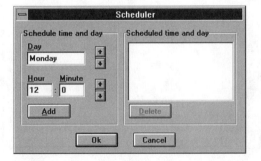

7. To specify days and times when the gateway sends messages, click on the **S**chedule button to display the Scheduler dialog box (see fig. 13.19). Select the desired days and times and click on the **A**dd button to add the selections to the Scheduled time and day list. To delete a Scheduled time and day entry, select the entry to delete and click on the **D**elete button. When you are finished, select OK.

Figure 13.19
The Scheduler dialog box.

Clicking on the **O**ptions button displays a different dialog box for each type of gateway, as described below:

✔ MTA Server displays the option for the post office to be server-based or client-based (see fig. 13.20).

✔ MTA CAS Fax displays the Fax Gateway Information dialog box (see fig. 13.21). The account listed in the **A**dministrator's account field is the account to which the incoming faxes are sent. The **D**ial Prefix field contains the number to dial to reach an outside line. If you do not have to dial a special number for an outside line, ignore this field.

✔ MTA Digital Pager or MTA Alpha Pager displays the Pager Administration dialog box (see fig. 13.22). To select a **M**odem initialization string, click on the Modem **I**nit button and select the modem you have installed. You do not need to specify information in the **B**aud Rate, **P**arity, **D**ata Bits, or **S**top Bits fields for a digital pager, but you do for a text pager. Most text pager services use 1200 baud, 7 data bits, 1 stop bit, and even parity. The Dial P**r**efix field contains the number to dial to reach an outside line. If you do not have to dial a special number for an outside line, leave this field blank. Use the **C**onnector field to specify the COM port your modem uses.

✔ MTA LANtastic Mail does not have an enabled **O**ptions button; you must configure the LANtastic Queue object in the MTA Events folder from the LANMail Gateway folder as described in the "Setting Up the LANtastic Mail Gateway" section.

Figure 13.20

The server-based or client-based post office option.

Figure 13.21
The Fax
Gateway
Information
dialog box.

Fax Gateway Information
Administrator's account: [Admin]
Dial prefix: [ ]
[OK] [Cancel]

Figure 13.22
The Pager
Administration
dialog box.

Pager Administration

Modem initialization string: [ ]

Baud Rate: [1200]
300
600
1200
2400
4800

Connector: [COM2]
COM1
COM2
COM3
COM4
COM5

[Modem Init]
[OK]
[Cancel]

Dial Prefix: [ ]

Parity
○ None
○ Odd
● Even

Data Bits
○ 5 ○ 6 ● 7 ○ 8

Stop Bits
● 1 ○ 2

After the MTA Event has been activated for the desired gateway, select Save from the MTA menu to save the changes.

Once you perform the preceding steps to activate the gateway, the following sections describe additional steps required for specific gateways.

Setting Up the Fax Gateway

The Fax Gateway requires a Communicating Application Specification (CAS) 1.2 or higher compatible fax modem. CAS compatibility is provided for all Class 1, Class 2, and Sendfax modems that use the CAS manager TSR software included with Artisoft Exchange.

To install the CAS manager software, place the WordPerfect FaxDirect for Artisoft Exchange disk in your floppy drive and type **A:INSTALL** (or **B:INSTALL**) at the DOS prompt. Follow the directions on screen for loading the software. Your AUTOEXEC.BAT file will be changed to load the FaxDirect software when you start your computer.

Do not change your AUTOEXEC.BAT file to load the FaxDirect software into upper memory; it will not operate properly.

If the post office computer is running both Windows and the WordPerfect FaxDirect CAS manager that ships with LANtastic 6.0, perform the following steps:

1. Copy the Windows drivers from the CAS manager installation disk to the Windows system directory by typing the following commands at the DOS prompt:

   ```
   COPY A:\EXPCOMM.DRV C:\WINDOWS\SYSTEM\*.*
   ```

   ```
   COPY A:\EXPVCD.386 C:\WINDOWS\SYSTEM\*.*
   ```

   A: is the floppy drive containing the installation disk and C:\WINDOWS is the location of the Windows program files.

2. Using a text editor such as DOS Edit or Windows Notepad, edit your SYSTEM.INI file (located in the Windows directory) as follows:

   In the [386ENH] section add the line

   ```
   TimerCriticalSection=500
   ```

   and replace the DEVICE=*VCD line with

   ```
   DEVICE=EXPVCD.386
   ```

If you experience lockup problems during the operation of the Fax Gateway, or while using the Fax printer driver, increase the TimerCriticalSection value to **1000**.

In the [BOOT] section replace the COMM.DRV= line with the following (or add it if it doesn't exist):

```
COMM.DRV=EXPCOMM.DRV
```

3. Change the Fastest Fax Speed field in the FaxDirect CAS manager from the Use Fastest setting to 9600 or lower by performing the following steps:

   a. At the DOS prompt, start the WordPerfect FaxDirect CAS manager configuration program by typing the following:

      ```
      CD \FAXDIRECT

      SETUP
      ```

   b. Select the 5 Miscellaneous Setup menu selection.

   c. Press the down arrow key until the Highest Fax Speed field is selected.

   d. Toggle through the selections by pressing the spacebar until 9600 or lower is displayed in the field.

   e. Press the F10 key twice to Exit/Save your new configuration

Failure to perform these configuration steps results in system lockups and file corruption in most situations when using the Artisoft Windows Fax Printer Driver or the Fax Gateway.

If the Artisoft Exchange Post Office Server program discontinues the Fax Gateway MTA event because of problems opening data files, you will have to delete all the files in the \LANTASTI\AMAIL directory and reinstall Artisoft Exchange.

Setting Up the LANtastic Mail Gateway

To set up the LANtastic Mail Gateway, you must configure a few additional items for the Gateway to operate correctly.

The Q privilege must be set for the Exchange Post Office Server computer's LANtastic account to log in to itself. For example, if the computer that has the Exchange post office is named KSOFFICE and it logs in to the * Wildcard account as user KSOFFICE when it boots, the * Wildcard account must have the Q privilege set. You can set privileges for an account by means of the LANtastic Network Manager program.

You must also configure the MTA events in the LANMail Gateway folder, as described in the following steps:

1. From the Gateway Folders dialog box, open the LANMail folder by double-clicking on it, or by selecting it and choosing **O**pen from the **O**bjects menu (see fig. 13.23).

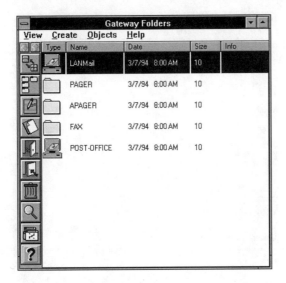

Figure 13.23
Opening the
LANMail folder.

2. From the LANMail dialog box, open the MTA Events folder by double-clicking on it or by selecting it and choosing **O**pen from the **O**bjects menu (see fig. 13.24).

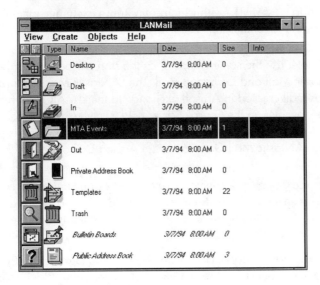

Figure 13.24
The LANMail
dialog box.

3. From the MTA Events dialog box, open the LANtastic Queue object by double-clicking on it or by selecting it and choosing **O**pen from the **O**bjects menu (see fig. 13.25)

Figure 13.25
The MTA Events
dialog box.

4. The LANtastic Queue Object dialog box contains several fields (see fig. 13.26), including the following required fields:

    ✔ **S**ource Server is the name of the server that has the LANtastic Mail resource (@MAIL) with which you want to exchange mail. Use the format *servername* for this field.

If possible, use the same computer as the storage location for both LANtastic Mail and Exchange Mail. The LANtastic Mail Gateway passes mail created in Artisoft Exchange to the @MAIL resource on the server specified in the Source Server field. Only LANtastic mail sent to the @MAIL resource on the Exchange Mail server, however, is passed by the LANtastic Mail Gateway as an Artisoft Exchange mail message.

    ✔ Source **R**esource is the name of the LANtastic Mail resource on the server specified in the **S**ource server field. The format for this field is \@MAIL, assuming the @MAIL resource is the name of the LANtastic Mail resource.

    ✔ Destination **A**ddress, **D**estination Server, and D**e**stination Resource are fields that should be left blank when you set up the LANtastic Mail Gateway.

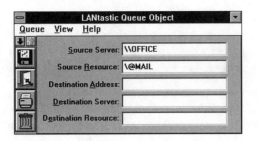

Figure 13.26
The LANtastic
Queue Object
dialog box.

5. Select Sa**v**e from the **Q**ueue menu to save your changes.

If your LANtastic and Exchange accounts are not synchronized and
you have users that do not have the same account names in LANtastic
and Exchange, you need to set up aliases for these users so the
Exchange LANtastic Mail Gateway knows which Exchange account
should receive LANtastic mail. The Exchange LANtastic Mail Gateway
looks in its own Private Address Book for aliases when transferring mail
from LANtastic Mail to Exchange Mail format. To set up account
aliases, perform the following steps:

1. Start Exchange Mail and log in with the SYSTEM account.

2. Open the Gateway Folders folder by double-clicking on it, or,
   with it selected, choose **O**pen from the **O**bjects menu.

3. Open the FAX folder by double-clicking on it, or, with it
   selected, choose **O**pen from the **O**bjects menu.

4. Open the Private Address Book and Public Address Book
   folders and position them next to each other.

5. You can create shadows of the accounts in the Private Address
   Book from the Public Address Book. Select the account in the
   Public Address Book and drag it to the Private Address Book
   while holding down the Shift key.

6. Select the account in the Private Address Book for which you
   want to create an alias, and double-click your right mouse
   button or select **A**ttributes from the **O**bjects menu.

7. In the Object Attributes dialog box, enter the alias name for the
   account in the **N**ame field. Press the Change button to save
   your changes and press Close to exit. The name of the shadow
   account changes in the Private Address Book but the actual
   account name remains the same.

Your Artisoft Exchange gateways are now configured and ready for operation. Before actually sending information through the gateway, information specific to each user accessing the gateway needs to be entered, as described in the appropriate section of Using Exchange Mail.

To start the Artisoft Exchange gateway operations, run the Artisoft Exchange Post Office Server program. If you want to run the DOS version, change to the \LANTASTI\AMAILPRG directory and type MTAEXEC from the DOS prompt. To run the Windows version, double-click on the Artisoft Exchange Post Office icon, or, with the icon selected, choose **O**pen from the Program Manager's **F**ile menu. Figure 13.27 shows the Windows Artisoft Exchange Post Office Server program running.

Before you start the Artisoft Exchange Post Office Server program for the first time, you should back up the \LANTASTI\AMAIL directory. This directory contains configuration information for Artisoft Exchange. In the event a file becomes corrupted (which is very likely if everything isn't configured exactly right when you start the Post Office Server program), you have to delete the \LANTASTI\AMAIL directory and reinstall Artisoft Exchange. The following command typed at the DOS prompt backs up the \LANTASTI\AMAIL directory to a directory called AMAIL_BU in the \LANTASTI directory:

```
XCOPY C:\LANTASTI\AMAIL\*.* C:\LANTASTI\AMAIL_BU\*.* /S /E
```

If you need to restore the \LANTASTI\AMAIL directory from the backup you created, type the following command at the DOS prompt:

```
XCOPY C:\LANTASTI\AMAIL_BU\*.* C:\LANTASTI\AMAIL\*.* /S
```

Figure 13.27
The Windows Artisoft Exchange Post Office Server program in operation.

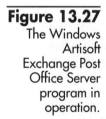

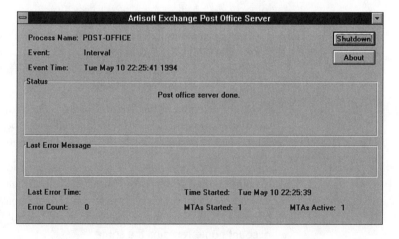

Managing Exchange Mail

After you have Artisoft Exchange Mail set up and configured, there are additional management tasks you might want to perform, such as adding users to the Public Address Book, setting up mailing lists, distributing incoming faxes, and even setting up BBSs (Bulletin Boards) for users to post messages that can be read by all other users.

You must log in to Exchange Mail using the SYSTEM account to add or delete Exchange accounts. An Exchange account that is given System Privileges may perform other functions including creating system-level folders, such as the Public Address book or mailing lists.

When you install Artisoft Exchange, the ADMIN account is created (in addition to the SYSTEM account). By default, all incoming faxes and special error messages are sent to the ADMIN account.

There are also management tasks that individuals should perform, which include organizing their mail and routinely changing their passwords.

Artisoft Exchange uses folders to help you organize your information and messages.

Using Folders

Artisoft Exchange enables you to organize your information using folders. Folders may contain objects such as mailing lists, shadowed objects from other folders, or even other folders themselves. Folders are given names so you can easily identify the contents of the folder.

Figure 13.28 is an example of a typical Artisoft Exchange Mail dialog box that appears when a user starts Exchange Mail. Suppose you want to create a To Do folder that is used to store the messages on which you are working.

To create a new folder, first select **F**older from the **C**reate menu. In the New Folder dialog box, type in the name for the new folder in the **N**ame field, and an optional description in the **D**escription field (see fig. 13.29). The new folder is created and now appears as an object on your screen (see fig. 13.30).

To create a new folder in an existing folder, all you need to do is open the folder that will contain the new folder and then create the new folder as described previously. For example, to create a folder named DO NOW in your newly created TO DO folder, open your TO DO folder by double-clicking on it; or, with it selected, choose **O**pen from the **O**bject menu. The TO DO folder dialog box appears with no items in it (see fig. 13.31). Notice that the same menu and toolbar appear that were in the previous dialog box; you have the same features available to you independent of the folder in which you are currently working. Now create a new folder as described above. The new folder appears in the current folder's dialog box.

Figure 13.28
A typical Artisoft
Exchange Mail
dialog box.

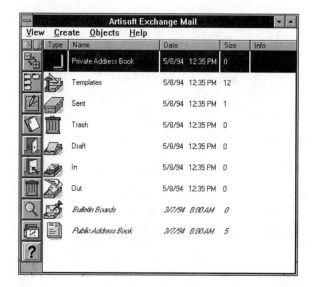

Figure 13.29
Specifying a
name and
description for
the new folder.

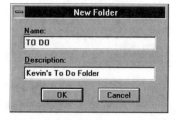

Another way to create a new folder is by selecting **O**bject from the **C**reate menu, or by selecting the New Object tool (see fig. 13.32). From the New Object dialog box (see fig. 13.33), select Folder. A new folder is created with the name Folder. To change the name and description of the folder, double-click the right mouse button, or select **A**ttributes from the **O**bjects menu. Change the **N**ame and **D**escription fields as desired and select the Change button to save the changes (see fig. 13.34). Select Close when finished and you return to your folder's dialog box.

Figure 13.30
The new TO DO folder.

Figure 13.31
The TO DO folder's dialog box.

Pointing to an object and pressing the right mouse button displays information about that object as shown in figure 13.32.

Figure 13.32
The New
Object tool.

Figure 13.33
Selecting Folder
from the
New Object
dialog box.

Figure 13.34
The Object
Attributes
dialog box.

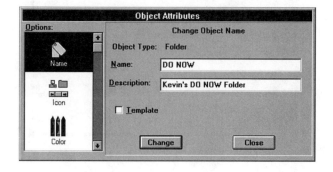

Changing Your Password

To prevent unauthorized use of your Exchange account, you should develop the habit of routinely changing your account password. To change your password, perform the following steps:

1. Start Artisoft Exchange Mail and log in using the password you want to change.

2. Select **A**ttributes from the **V**iew menu. The Object Attributes dialog box appears (see fig. 13.35).

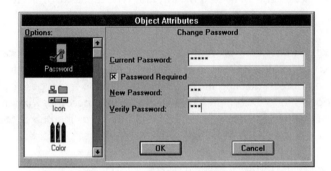

Figure 13.35
Changing your password.

3. Type in your **C**urrent Password followed by your **N**ew Password, and then type your new password again in the **V**erify Password field. Passwords display as asterisks when typed. Select the OK button and your password changes.

   To delete an existing password, type your current password in the **C**urrent Password field and deselect the Password Required option. Select OK and you no longer need a password for this account. This action is highly discouraged.

Setting Up a BBS

You can create a BBS, or Bulletin Board System, to which Exchange Mail users can send messages. Several BBSs can be set up for different categories or topics. After a BBS is set up, individuals can send messages to selected BBSs by specifying BBS addresses when sending messages. Once a message is sent, only the system administrator or users with the System Privilege can delete messages.

You set up a BBS as you would a new user account. To set up a BBS, perform the following steps:

1. Start Artisoft Exchange Mail and log in as the System account.

2. Open the User Account folder by double-clicking on it, or by selecting **O**pen from the **O**bjects menu.

3. Select **N**ew Account from the **A**dministration menu in the User Accounts dialog box.

4. Select Bulletin Board as the Account **T**ype in the Create New Account dialog box (see fig. 13.36). Type in the name for your Bulletin Board account in the **B**ulletin Board field. If you want a password for this account, select the **R**equired option and type a password in the **P**assword field.

> Entering a **P**assword prevents an unauthorized person from logging in to Exchange Mail by means of the BBS account name and, after gaining access, deleting messages. To delete BBS messages you must be logged in to Exchange Mail with the System account, with an account with System Privileges, or be logged in as the BBS account name.

5. Select the Save button to save this account. The new BBS account is saved and you may enter another account. When finished, select the Done button to exit the Create New Account dialog box.

Figure 13.36

Creating a Bulletin Board account.

Create New Account
Account Type: ○ User ● Bulletin Board ○ Gateway
Bulletin Board: General Bulletin Board
Postoffice: POST-OFFICE
Email Address: POST-OFFICE:General Bulletin Boar
Password: ☐ Required
LAN Account:
☐ System Privileges
Last Name:
First Name:
Middle Name:
Nick Name:
Department:
Phone1:
Phone2:
Save   Done

Distributing Faxes

Incoming faxes are automatically sent to the ADMIN account unless you specify a different account when you enable the Fax Gateway. To distribute faxes to their intended recipients, log in to Exchange Mail using the ADMIN account (or the account you specify when setting up the Fax Gateway) and open the In folder. When you open the fax, you can read its contents using the built-in fax viewer. The viewer lets you read the header information on the fax and determine the intended recipient. From the **M**essage menu select **F**orward to forward the fax to the intended recipient.

Detailed instructions for forwarding messages are discussed later in this chapter.

Adding to the Public Address Book

When an account is created, it is automatically added to the Public Address Book so you do not have to perform any additional steps to add a newly created account. To make changes to the Public Address Book, you must have the System Privilege. The System Privilege lets you add, modify, and delete objects in the Public Address Book. The objects in the Public Address Book are available for use by all Exchange accounts, and any changes that are made appear in the Public Address Book for all accounts.

Because accounts in the Public Address Book are shadows of the original account (shadows are indicated by italics) if your account has the System Privilege, you can modify the actual account by double-clicking on the account, or by selecting **O**pen from the **O**bject menu. If your account has the System Privilege, you can also delete the shadow account. This deletes the shadow account from the Public Address Book but does not delete the actual account. If you want to add a deleted account to the Public Address Book, you need to log in to Exchange Mail as the System account and copy a shadow of the account from the User Accounts folder to the Public Address Book folder.

You can also copy objects such as fax addresses to the Public Address Book. Suppose, for example, that you have an office across town to which you and others in your group send several faxes a day. You could set up a fax address for your other office so that documents can be sent out through your LANtastic Exchange Fax Gateway to the fax machine in your other office.

The process for creating fax addresses is discussed later in this chapter.

The following example assumes that a fax address for a Seattle office has been created and is located in the System folder's Private Address Book. As the system administrator, you will want to copy the fax address from the SYSTEM account's Private Address Book (which isn't available to other users) to the Public Address Book so that everyone has access to it. The following steps show how to add the Fax Address object to the Public Address Book:

1. Start Exchange Mail and log in as the SYSTEM account.

2. Open the System folder by double-clicking on it or by selecting **O**pen from the **O**bjects menu.

3. Open the Public Address Book and the Private Address Book by double-clicking on each one.

4. Position the Public Address Book dialog box next to the Private Address Book dialog box (see fig. 13.37).

Figure 13.37
The Public Address book next to the Private Address Book.

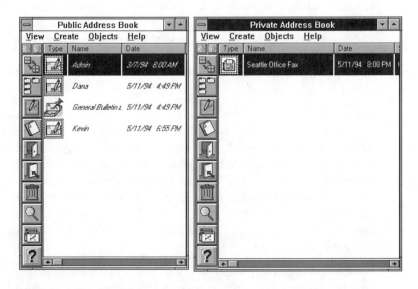

5. Create a shadow of the Seattle Office Fax object by selecting the Seattle Office Fax object in the Private Address Book. While holding

your Shift key down, drag a shadow to the Public Address Book. Now a shadow of the Seattle Office Fax object appears in the Public Address book (see fig. 13.38).

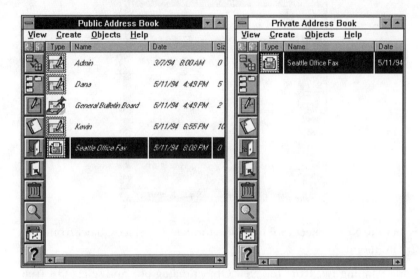

Figure 13.38
The Seattle Office Fax object in the Public Address Book.

Setting Up Mailing Lists

Mailing lists help you to send information to a group of people. Instead of choosing the recipients one at a time from the Address Book, you can organize your mailing lists to contain a list of recipients. By selecting a Mailing List object as the recipient, you can send your message to everyone in the list.

You can set up mailing lists for an individual in the individual's Private Address Book, and for all users in the Public Address Book (discussed in this section). An example of a powerful use of mailing lists is a situation in which you need to send information to many customers. You can create mailing lists for different types of customers that contain the fax addresses for each customer. Using the Fax Gateway, you can then send group faxes to everyone on a mailing list by selecting the mailing list that contains the customers to which you want to send the fax You can even select multiple mailing lists.

To set up a mailing list in the Public Address Book, perform the following steps:

1. Start Artisoft Exchange Mail and log in using the System account.

2. Open the Public Address Book by double-clicking on it, or selecting the object and choosing **O**pen from the **O**bject menu. The Public Address Book dialog box appears (see fig. 13.39).

Figure 13.39
The Public
Address Book.

3. Select the New Object tool from the toolbar, or select **O**bject from the **C**reate menu.

4. Select Mailing List from the New Object dialog box and select OK (see fig. 13.40). A Mailing List object is created and appears in the Public Address Book dialog box (see fig. 13.41).

Figure 13.40
Selecting a
Mailing List
object type.

5. Open the Mailing List object by double-clicking on it, or by selecting **O**pen from the **O**bjects menu.

An alternative way to set up a mailing list is to drag a Mailing List object from the Templates folder to the Public Address Book folder.

Figure 13.41
The newly created Mailing List object in the Public Address Book.

6. Move the Mailing List dialog box next to the Public Address Book dialog box (see fig. 13.42).

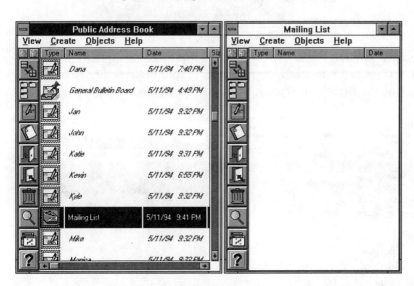

Figure 13.42
The Public Address Book dialog box next to the Mailing List dialog box.

7. Copy the names you want in the mailing list from the Public Address Book. You accomplish this task by selecting each name and dragging it to the Mailing List dialog box while holding down the Shift key.

You are actually copying a shadow of the original object to your mailing list. If you don't hold down the Shift key, you actually move the shadow object in the Public Address Book to the Mailing List.

8. To change the name of the Mailing List Object, select **A**ttributes from the **V**iew menu. In the Object Attributes dialog box, type in the **N**ame and **D**escription fields for the mailing list (see fig. 13.43). Select the Save button to save the changes and then select Close when finished.

Figure 13.43
Changing the name and description of the mailing list.

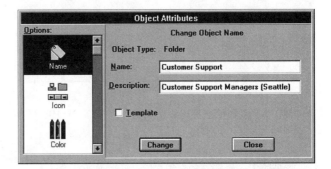

In this example, you have created a Customer Support mailing list that contains the names of the six customer support managers in your Seattle office (see fig. 13.44). Because this list is in the Public Address Book, all Exchange Mail users can access it.

Figure 13.44
The Customer Support mailing list.

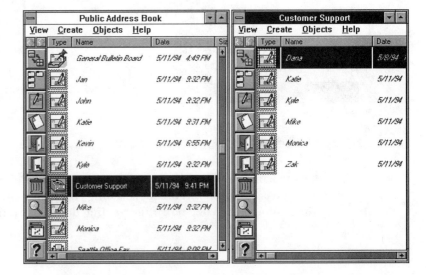

Using Exchange Mail

With Artisoft Exchange Mail set up and configured the way you want it, you are ready to start using it for your daily communication tasks. Exchange Mail is a very powerful and flexible program that enables you to organize folders and the objects in those folders to fit the way you work and are most productive. As a user of Exchange Mail, you probably want to set up your own set of folders to organize your information. In this section, you will customize your Private Address Book by copying names from the Public Address book and adding new addresses. Using filters, you can specify what actions to take when messages are sent to specific folders.

Adding to the Private Address Book

The information in the Public Address Book includes a list of all the Exchange accounts. This information cannot be changed by users unless they are given System Privileges when their account is set up. Each user has a Private Address Book that can be used and modified as each individual user desires. Names from the Public Address Book can be copied to the Private Address Book; new names can be added as well. The Private Address Book can also contain mailing lists and gateway addresses.

Copying from the Public Address Book

Because the Public Address Book likely contains names that you rarely use, you probably want to copy the names you use frequently to your Private Address Book. This way, you have fewer entries to sort through when selecting names to which to send your mail.

To copy names from the Public Address Book to your Private Address Book, perform the following steps:

1. Start Exchange Mail and log in using your Exchange account name.

2. Open the Public Address Book by double-clicking on it, or, with the object selected, choose **O**pen from the **O**bjects menu.

3. Copy the desired names from the Public Address Book to your Private Address Book by selecting the object and dragging it from the Public Address Book and dropping it on the Private Address Book icon (see fig. 13.45).

To see the contents of your Private Address Book as you add names to it, you can open the Private Address Book and add names as you did previously in the Public Address Book.

Figure 13.45
Copying names from the Public Address Book to the Private Address Book.

Creating Mailing Lists

Mailing lists can be set up and used in your Private Address Book in the same way they are set up and used in the Public Address Book. A mailing list in a Private Address Book is controlled entirely by the user; entries may be added, modified, or deleted.

To set up a mailing list in the Private Address Book, perform the following steps:

1. Start Artisoft Exchange Mail and log in using your Exchange account name.

2. Open the Private Address Book by double-clicking on it, or selecting the object and choosing **O**pen from the **O**bject menu.

3. Select the New Object tool from the toolbar, or select **O**bject from the **C**reate menu.

4. Select Mailing List from the New Object dialog box and select OK. A Mailing List object is created and appears in the Private Address Book dialog box.

5. Open the Mailing List object by double-clicking on it or selecting **O**pen from the **O**bjects menu.

6. You can create your mailing list from names in the Public Address Book or your Private Address Book, or a combination of the two. If you intend to include names from the Public Address Book in your mailing list, open the Public Address Book and position it next to your Mailing List dialog box (see fig. 13.46).

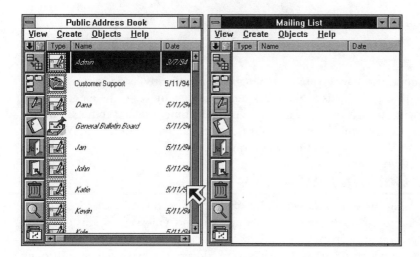

Figure 13.46
The Public Address Book dialog box next to the Mailing List dialog box.

7. Copy the names you want in the mailing list from the Public Address Book by selecting each name and dragging it to the Mailing List dialog box. A shadow object will appear in your Mailing List dialog box.

If you are copying from your Private Address Book to the Mailing List, hold down the Shift key as you copy. Otherwise, you will move the object from the Private Address Book to the Mailing List instead of copying it. You also need to hold down the Shift key when copying from the Public Address Book if your account has System Privileges. As in the case of copying from the Private Address Book, if you don't hold it down you actually move the shadow object in the Public Address Book to the Mailing List.

8. To change the name of the Mailing List Object, select **A**ttributes from the **V**iew menu. In the Object Attributes dialog box, type in the **N**ame and **D**escription for the mailing list (see fig. 13.47). Select the Save button to save the changes and then select Close when finished.

Figure 13.47
Changing the name and description of the mailing list.

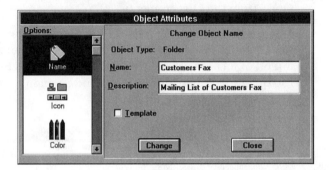

In this example you have created a mailing list that contains fax addresses for your customers. If you select this mailing list when sending a message, the message would be sent through the Fax Gateway to each customer's fax machine. Because this mailing list is in your Private Address Book, it is available only to you. You can add and remove names from the list as required.

Creating Gateway Addresses

If you are using gateways with Artisoft Exchange, you need to create addresses in order to send messages through the gateways. To send a message to a fax machine, for example, you must create a fax address that includes the phone number of the fax machine you are calling. Because it is a fax address, the message is sent through the Fax Gateway to the fax machine at the specified number.

The following sections discuss how to set up Gateway addresses for the LANtastic Mail Gateway, the Fax Gateway, the Pager Gateway, and the Text (Alpha) Pager Gateway.

Creating a Fax Address

You can create a fax address for every fax machine you call. When you send a message and select a fax address object, your message is sent through the Fax Gateway to the fax number specified in your fax address object. You can also create a fax address template that prompts you for a telephone number when you send the message to the fax machine.

To create a fax address in your Private Address Book perform the following steps:

1. Start Artisoft Exchange Mail and log in using your Exchange account name.

2. Open your Private Address Book by double-clicking on it, or by selecting the object and choosing **O**pen from the **O**bjects menu.

3. Select the New Object tool or select **O**bjects from the **C**reate menu.

4. From the New Object dialog box, select Fax Address and select OK (see fig. 13.48). The fax address object is added to your Private Address Book.

Figure 13.48
Selecting a Fax
Address object.

5. Open the Fax Address object by double-clicking on it or by selecting **O**pen from the **O**bjects menu. The Fax Address dialog box appears (see fig. 13.49).

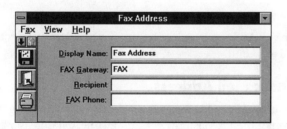

Figure 13.49
The Fax Address
dialog box.

6. Fill in the following information in the Fax Address dialog box:

    ✔ The **D**isplay Name is the name of the Fax Address object as it will be displayed on your screen.

    ✔ The FAX **G**ateway is the name of the Fax Gateway used for sending the fax. Unless the name of the Fax Gateway has been changed from its default value, leave this field as it is.

✔ The **R**ecipient is the name of the person or company the fax is addressed to. This field is optional.

✔ The **F**AX Phone is the phone number where the fax machine you are calling is located.

If you want to be prompted for the recipient and fax phone number, leave the Recipient and FAX Phone number fields empty and perform the following steps to make this fax address a template:

1. Select **A**ttributes from the **V**iew menu. The Object Attributes dialog box appears (see fig. 13.50).

2. Select the **T**emplate option.

3. Select the Change button to save your changes, then select the Close button to return to the Fax Address dialog box.

Figure 13.50
The Object
Attributes dialog
box.

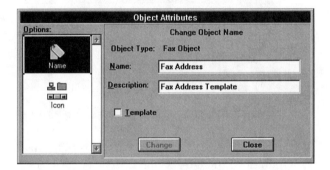

4. Save your Fax Address by selecting the Save tool or by selecting Sa**v**e from the F**a**x menu.

Creating a LANtastic Mail Address

You can create LANtastic Mail addresses to use when you send messages from Exchange Mail through the LANtastic Mail Gateway to LANtastic users who are using LANtastic Mail instead of Exchange Mail. LANtastic Mail is used on machines that are running DOS or LANtastic 5.0.

To create a LANtastic Mail address in your Private Address Book perform the following steps:

1. Start Artisoft Exchange Mail and log in using your Exchange account name.

2. Open your Private Address Book by double-clicking on it, or by selecting the object and choosing **O**pen from the **O**bjects menu.

3. Select the New Object tool or select **O**bjects from the **C**reate menu.

4. From the New Object dialog box, select LANtastic Mail Address and click on OK (see fig. 13.51). The LANtastic Mail Address object is added to your Private Address Book.

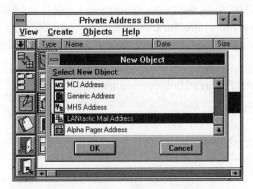

Figure 13.51
Selecting a
LANtastic Mail
Address object.

5. Open the LANtastic Mail Address object by double-clicking on it or by selecting **O**pen from the **O**bjects menu. The LANtastic Mail Address dialog box appears (see fig. 13.52).

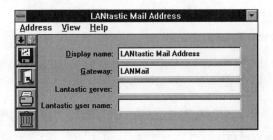

Figure 13.52
The LANtastic
Mail Address
dialog box.

6. Fill in the following information in the LANtastic Mail Address dialog box:

✔ The **D**isplay Name is the name of the LANtastic Mail Address object as it will be displayed on your screen. Normally you will specify the intended mail recipient in this field.

✔ **G**ateway is the name of the LANtastic Mail Gateway used for sending the message. Unless the name of the LANtastic Mail Gateway has been changed from its default value, leave this field as it is.

✔ The LANtastic **s**erver is the name of the LANtastic server that holds the LANtastic Mail. You should store your LANtastic mail on the same computer that your Exchange Post Office is on.

You MUST include the \\ in front of the server name (i.e. \\KSOFFICE). Also, the LANtastic account that is used to log in to the LANtastic server where the LANtastic mail messages are stored must have the Q privilege (set in the LANtastic Network Manger program).

If the above two requirements are not met, the Artisoft Exchange Post Office Server Program will not be able to process the LANtastic mail information and the gateway will shut down.

✔ The LANtastic **u**ser name is the LANtastic account name of the person who is to receive the LANtastic mail specified with this LANtastic Mail Address object.

If you want to be prompted for the LANtastic user recipient for your message, leave the LANtastic user name field empty and perform the following steps to make this LANtastic Mail Address a template:

a. Select **A**ttributes from the **V**iew menu. The Object Attributes dialog box appears (see fig. 13.53).

b. Select the **T**emplate option.

c. Select the Change button to save your changes, then select the Close button to return to the LANtastic Mail Address dialog box.

Figure 13.53
The Object
Attributes
dialog box.

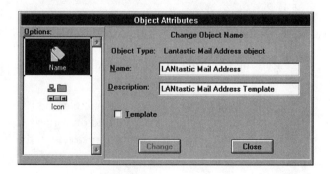

7. Save your LANtastic Mail Address by selecting the Save tool, or by selecting Save from the **A**ddress menu.

Creating a Pager Address

You can create a Pager Address to send a number to a digital pager by means of the Digital Pager Gateway. The Pager Address lets you page someone if you need to talk with them or if they have a message.

To create a Pager Address in your Private Address Book perform the following steps:

1. Start Artisoft Exchange Mail and log in using your Exchange account name.

2. Open your Private Address Book by double-clicking on it, or by selecting the object and choosing **O**pen from the **O**bjects menu.

3. Select the New Object tool or select **O**bjects from the **C**reate menu.

4. From the New Object dialog box, select Pager Address and select OK (see fig. 13.54). The Pager Address object is added to your Private Address Book.

Figure 13.54
Selecting a Pager Address object.

5. Open the Pager Address object by double-clicking on it or by selecting **O**pen from the **O**bjects menu. The Pager Address dialog box appears (see fig. 13.55).

Figure 13.55

The Pager
Address
dialog box.

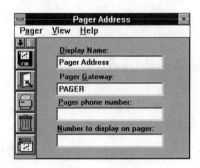

6. Fill in the following information in the Pager Address dialog box:

✔ The **D**isplay Name is the name of the Pager Address object as it is displayed on your screen. Normally you specify the name of the person to be paged in this field.

✔ The Pager **G**ateway is the name of the Pager Gateway used for sending the message. Unless the name of the Pager Gateway has been changed from its default value, leave this field as it is.

✔ The **P**ager phone number is the phone number to be dialed to reach the pager.

✔ The **N**umber to display on pager is the number you want to be sent to the pager. Usually this is your phone number if you want the person being paged to call you back.

✔ If you want to be prompted for the **P**ager phone number and the **N**umber to display on pager, leave these two fields empty and select the **T**emplate option in the Object Attributes dialog box. You can access this box by selecting **A**ttributes from the **V**iew menu.

7. Save your Pager Address by selecting the Save tool or by selecting Sa**v**e from the P**a**ger menu.

Creating an Alpha Pager Address

You can create an Alpha Pager Address, which you can use to send a message to a text pager by means of the Alpha Pager Gateway. Text pagers can usually display up to 256 characters of information which the Alpha Pager Gateway will send to them.

To create an Alpha Pager Address in your Private Address Book perform the following steps:

1. Start Artisoft Exchange Mail and log in using your Exchange account name.

2. Open your Private Address Book by double-clicking on it, or by selecting the object and choosing **O**pen from the **O**bjects menu.

3. Select the New Object tool or select **O**bject from the **C**reate menu.

4. From the New Object dialog box, select Alpha Pager Address and select OK (see fig. 13.56). The Alpha Pager Address object is added to your Private Address Book.

Figure 13.56
Selecting an Alpha Pager Address object.

5. Open the Alpha Pager Address object by double-clicking on it, or by selecting **O**pen from the **O**bjects menu. The Alpha Pager Address dialog box appears (see fig. 13.57).

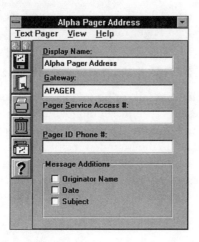

Figure 13.57
The Alpha Pager Address dialog box.

6. Fill in the following information in the Alpha Pager Address dialog box:

    ✔ The **D**isplay Name is the name of the Alpha Pager Address object as it is displayed on your screen. Normally you specify the name of the person to be paged in this field.

    ✔ The **G**ateway is the name of the Alpha Pager Gateway used for sending the message. Unless the name of the Alpha Pager Gateway has been changed from its default value, leave this field as it is.

    ✔ The Pager **S**ervice Access # is the phone number of the pager service.

    ✔ The **P**ager ID Phone # is the ID phone number for the person you want to page.

    ✔ Message Additions enable you to add the following specified information to your message sent to the Alpha Pager:

    The Originator Name displays your account name at the end of the message sent to the pager.

    The Date option displays the date at the end of the message sent to the pager.

    The Subject option displays the subject for the message sent to the pager.

    If you want to be prompted for the Pager **S**ervice Access # or the **P**ager ID Phone #, leave these two fields empty and select the **T**emplate option in the Object Attributes dialog box. You can access this box by selecting **A**ttributes from the **V**iew menu.

7. Save your Alpha Pager Address by selecting the Save tool or by selecting Sa**v**e from the **T**ext Pager menu.

Creating and Sending Exchange Mail

Now that you have your Exchange Mail configured exactly as you want it, you are ready to use its many features for creating, sending, and receiving mail. When you send messages or other information to a gateway address, Artisoft Exchange automatically makes sure it goes to the intended recipient, whether it's another Exchange Mail user, a fax machine, or even a pager device. You can attach files (including faxes) to mail messages, forward mail to others, and even request a return receipt after your mail has been received by the intended recipient.

To create a message, you must first start Artisoft Exchange Mail. If you are using separate LANtastic accounts and Exchange accounts, you are prompted to enter your Exchange account name and password.

The first step is to create the message you want to send. From the Artisoft Exchange Mail Dialog box, select the Compose tool (see fig. 13.58), or from the **C**reate menu select **M**essage.

You can display information about any object by pointing to the object and pressing the right mouse button.

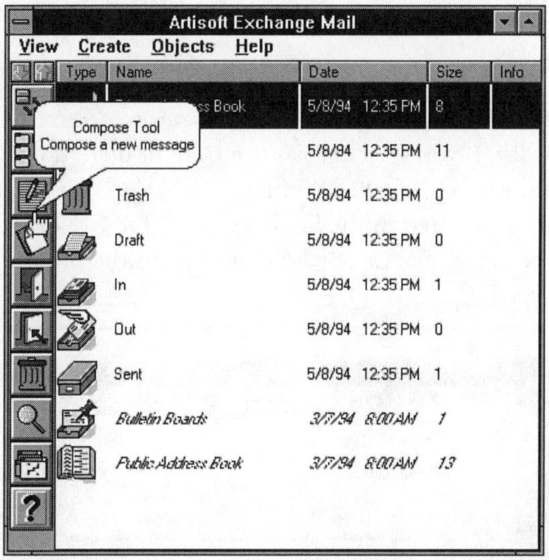

Figure 13.58

The Artisoft Exchange Mail dialog box showing the Compose tool.

The Address Dialog box appears, enabling you to specify the intended recipients of your message (see fig. 13.59). Information from the Public Address Book, your Private Address Book, and all the mailing lists, templates, and BBSs are available.

Figure 13.59
The Address
dialog box.

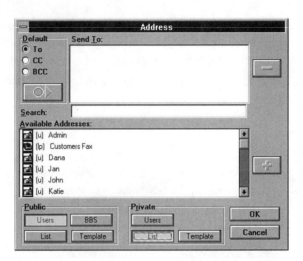

The **D**efault field specifies if the address names you select are To, CC, or BCC. For example, if the To option is selected, your message is addressed to the names you select from the address list. If you select CC as the **D**efault field, the additional names you select appear with CC next to them instead of To (see fig. 13.60). You may change whether a name listed in the Send **T**o list is To, CC, or BCC. Select the name to change, choose either To, CC, or BCC, and press the button at the bottom of the **D**efault section.

Figure 13.60
The Address
dialog box with
recipients
selected.

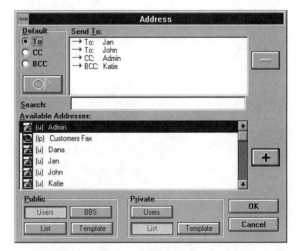

The **S**earch field enables you to search for a name in the list of **A**vailable Addresses. As you type each letter, the closest match in the **A**vailable Addresses list is displayed. You can add the name to the Send **T**o list by pressing enter or selecting the + button.

The **A**vailable Addresses list shows all the addresses to which you may send your message. To add names to the Send **T**o list, select each name and press Enter, or select the + button. To remove a name from the Send **T**o list, select the name in the Send **T**o list to be removed and then select the - button to remove the name.

The address names that appear in the **A**vailable Addresses list are determined by the buttons that are selected in the **P**ublic and **P**rivate fields. The **P**ublic field represents the address names in the Public Address Book, which includes the following selections:

✔ The Users button displays all the user accounts in the Public Address Book.

✔ The List button displays all the mailing lists in the Public Address Book.

✔ The BBS button displays all the bulletin boards in the Public Address Book.

✔ The Template button displays all the templates in the Public Address Book.

The address names shown in the **A**vailable Addresses list (see fig. 15.60) are preceded by letters in parentheses that indicate the type of address, as in the following list:

(u) User in Public Address Book

(l) Mailing list in Public Address Book

(b) Bulletin Board in Public Address Book

(t) Template in Public Address Book

(up) User in Private Address Book

(lp) Mailing list in Private Address Book

(tp) Template in Private Address Book

The Private field represents the address names in the Private Address Book, and includes the following selections:

✔ The Users button displays all the user accounts in the Private Address Book.

✔ The List button displays all the mailing lists in the Private Address Book.

✔ The Template button displays all the templates in the Private Address Book.

When a template address is selected, a dialog box appears requesting you to complete the address by filling in the required information in the template. Figure 13.61 is an example of a Fax Address template that appears when the Fax Address name is selected.

After you finish specifying the recipients for your message, select OK and the Message Dialog box appears (see fig. 13.62).

Figure 13.61
The Fax Address
template.

FAX Mail
Display Name: Fax Address
FAX Gateway: FAX
Recipient:
FAX Phone:
OK   Cancel

The upper part of the Message dialog box displays your account name in the From field, and the current date and time in the Date field. You can type a subject for your message in the Subject field. The subject you type becomes the name of your message as it is displayed. The address names listed in the To field are those that you chose earlier from the address list. If you want to change the address names shown in the To field, you can go back to the Address dialog box by selecting the Address tool, or by selecting **A**ddress from the **O**ptions menu.

You can type your message in the large Edit box. The Exchange message editor includes several features, some of which allow you to change the font, the color of the font, implement cut and paste options, and even use a spell checker. These features are available from the **E**dit menu.

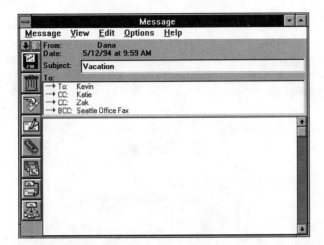

Figure 13.62
The Message
Dialog box.

In the following scenario, assume you are having problems with your computer.
You decide to send a copy of your AUTOEXEC.BAT and CONFIG.SYS files to the
local experts in your company to see if they can figure out the problem. You have
addressed your message to the system administrator, with CCs to two other knowledgeable people. In addition, you are sending a copy of your message to the
Seattle office using the Fax Gateway.

Figure 13.63 shows the message that you created. You need to attach your
AUTOEXEC.BAT and CONFIG.SYS files to your message. To create attachments
to your message, select the Attachments tool (paperclip) or select Attachments
from the **O**ptions menu.

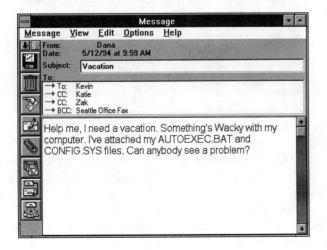

Figure 13.63
Creating a
message with
attachments.

To specify the files that you want to attach to your message, type the file name in the **F**iles field and select the + button to add it to your **A**ttachments list (see fig. 13.64). You can also select files using the Find button if you do not want to have to type in the file names. After you are finished adding attachments, select OK to return to your Message dialog box.

Figure 13.64
Adding attachments to a message.

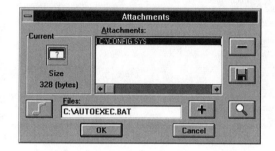

An **A**ttachments list appears, showing that you have two attachments in your file (see fig. 13.65). You can include any type of file you want as an attachment.

Figure 13.65
The Message dialog box showing attachments.

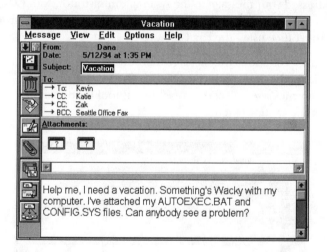

To set the priority of your message or to request a return receipt, select the Delivery tool or select **D**elivery from the **O**ptions menu. The Delivery dialog box (see fig. 13.66) enables you to specify a **P**riority of Low, Normal, or Urgent. Messages with Low and Normal priority appear as green in the In folder. Messages with Urgent priority appear as red. Selecting the **R**eturn Receipt option sends you a message when your message has been opened by the recipient. If you select the Pri**v**ate Mail option, your mail cannot be forwarded.

Figure 13.66
The Delivery
Dialog box.

When you finish composing your message you can save it or send it immediately. To save a message, select the Save tool (the icon that looks like a disk), or select Save from the **M**essage menu. To send your message, select the Send tool (the icon that looks like a flying letter) or select **S**end from the **M**essage menu. When you send a message, it is transferred to your Sent folder.

Reading Exchange Mail

When you log in to Exchange Mail, you are notified if you have any new mail. Mail that has been sent to you appears in your In folder. Mail that is sent to you with the Urgent priority option selected appears red in your In folder.

To open your mail, double-click on the message you want to read; or with the object selected, choose **O**pen from the **O**bjects menu. The message opens and can be read (see fig. 13.67). Messages may have attachments that can be any type of a file, such as a fax, a text file, a program file, or even data files (spreadsheets, databases, and so on). Depending on the type of attachments you have, you may be able to view the attachments directly or you may have to export them to a file to use. The attachments in figure 13.67 need to be exported to a file. You can export attachments to files by selecting the Attachments tool, or by selecting A**t**tachments from the **O**ptions menu. After the Attachments dialog box appears, select the file to export and then choose the Export tool (the icon that looks like a disk). You are prompted to enter the filename for the file; after you have done so, the file is exported.

You can reply to a message by selecting the Reply tool, or by selecting **R**eply from the **M**essage menu. The Reply Options dialog box appears (see fig. 13.68). If you select the Reply to **A**ll option, everyone to whom the message was addressed—in addition the sender—will receive your reply. By selecting the **I**nclude Original Message, you include a copy of the original message in your reply. The other steps required to reply to a message are just like the steps required to send a message (see fig 13.69).

Figure 13.67
Reading a
mail message.

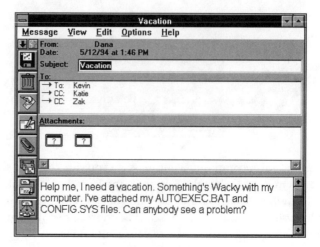

Figure 13.68
The Reply
Options
dialog box.

Figure 13.69
Replying to a
message.

If you want to forward a message to another person or group of people, select the Forward tool, or select **F**orward from the **M**essage menu. The Forward Options dialog box appears (see fig. 13.70). If you want to forward the message with attachments, select the option and choose OK. Select the recipients for the forwarded mail from the Address dialog box by selecting the Address tool, or by selecting **A**ddress from the **O**ptions menu. The edit box is blank when you forward a message (see fig. 13.71). Any information you type appears before the original message when the forwarded message is sent. When you are finished, send the message by selecting the Send tool, or by selecting **S**end from the **M**essage menu.

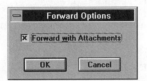

Figure 13.70
The Forward
Options
dialog box.

Figure 13.71
Forwarding a
message.

If you want to delete mail, select the mail object you want to delete. Then choose the Delete tool or select **D**elete from the **O**bjects menu.

Using Filters

Filters enable you to perform simple tasks automatically, or when certain criteria are met. You can use filters to perform operations such as moving messages, sending responses to messages, forwarding messages, making shadows of messages, and making copies of messages.

You can place a filter on any folder. After a message enters the folder, the action specified by the filter is performed. For example, if you are going to be out of the office, you can put a filter on your In folder that automatically notifies senders that you will be out of the office until a specified day.

You can also set up a filter that only responds to certain types of files. You can specify the following criteria:

✔ The source address of the message

✔ The date or time the message was created

✔ Whether the message has been read or not

✔ If the message has a certain subject

✔ The priority of the message

First you create a filter. Next you define the filter, and finally you place the filter on a folder.

To create a filter, select **O**bject from the **C**reate menu. When the New Object dialog box appears, select Message Filter and select OK (see fig. 13.72). A message filter is created and appears in your current folder.

You can also create a message filter by dragging a filter object from the Templates folder to the desired folder.

Figure 13.72
Selecting a Message Filter-type object from the New Object dialog box.

To define the filter, open it by double-clicking on it, or select **O**pen from the **O**bjects menu. The Message Filter dialog box appears (see fig. 13.73).

Figure 13.73
The Message
Filter dialog box.

The following is a description of the fields in the Message Filter dialog box.

✔ The **T**rigger filter when field specifies when the filter is to be triggered. Currently the only option available is When a message enters a folder.

✔ The Activate filter on/Deactivate filter on fields enable you to specify when the filter is or is not activated.

To specify the activation date, select the Activation Date tool or select Activation Date from the **S**earch Criteria menu. The Filter Activation Date/Time dialog box appears (see fig. 13.74), enabling you to specify the activation and deactivation date. The default selections of **I**mmediate in the Filter activated section and **N**ever in the Filter **d**eactivated section cause the filter to be active as soon as it is created.

✔ The Message Criteria section enables you to specify the messages on which the filter will act, as described in the following list:

The Status field enables you to control the filter so that it acts only on messages that have been read, unread, or both, by selecting a combination of the **R**ead and Unrea**d** options.

The Priority field enables the filter to act only on messages that have a priority of **L**ow, **N**ormal, **U**rgent, or any combination, by selecting the appropriate combination of these options.

Figure 13.74
The Filter
Activation Date/
Time dialog box.

The **S**ubject field enables the filter to act only on messages with a specified subject, which you type into this field.

The **F**rom field enables you to make the filter act only on messages from specific people.

To add or change the addresses in the **F**rom field, select the Message Sender tool or select Message **S**ender from the **S**earch Criteria menu. The Originator address dialog box appears (see fig. 13.75). To add selected addresses to the list, you can type addresses and click on the **A**dd button, or you can open an address book, select addresses, and then click on the **A**dd button. When you select the **O**pen/Close button, all the addresses contained in the selected folder are listed below the folder. To remove addresses from the list, select the **D**elete button. When finished, select OK.

Figure 13.75
The Originator
address
dialog box.

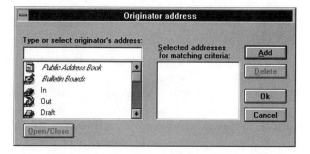

✔ The Created on or before/Created on or after fields are a summary of the dates that messages must have for the filter to act on them.

To change the message dates on which the filter will act, select the Message Date tool or select Message **D**ate from the **S**earch Criteria menu. The Message Creation Time/Date dialog box appears (see fig. 13.76), enabling you to specify the message time and date range on which the filter will act. The default selections—Any **T**ime/Date in the Messages created on or **a**fter section and Any Time/**D**ate in the Messages created on or **b**efore—cause the filter to act on messages that have any message date.

Figure 13.76
The Message Creation Time/ Date dialog box.

✔ The Filter Action field specifies the action performed by the filter after a specified criterion is met.

To change the filter action, select the Action tool or select the **A**ctions! menu selection. The Filter Action Selection dialog box appears (see fig. 13.77), allowing you to select one of the following actions:

To have more than a single filter action performed, you must set up additional message filters for each action.

✔ The Clear action clears any previous action.

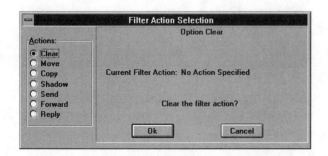

Figure 13.77
The Filter Action Selection dialog box with the Clear action selected.

✔ The Move action moves a filtered message into the folder you specify. By selecting this action, you can display a list of folders from which to choose (see fig. 13.78). You can open a folder to display its contents by selecting the folder and clicking on the **O**pen/Close button. Select the folder to which you want a message moved, and click on the OK button.

Figure 13.78

Selecting the folder in the Filter Action Selection dialog box.

✔ The Copy action is similar to the Move action except it copies the message to the folder you specify.

✔ The Shadow action makes a shadow of the filtered messages and puts the shadow in the specified folder.

✔ The Send action sends a specified message (prepared in advance) when a message meeting the filter criteria enters the folder. You specify the message (see fig. 13.79) by selecting it from the list shown. To select a message in a folder, select the folder with the message you want to use and click on the **O**pen/Close button. The messages appear under the folder name, enabling you to select the desired message.

Figure 13.79

Selecting the message in the Filter Action Selection dialog box.

✔ The Forward action sends a received message as an attachment to a message you create earlier. You select the message from a list similar to the one shown in figure 13.79.

✔ The Reply action sends a message you prepared earlier as a reply to a message. You select the reply message from a list similar to the one shown in figure 13.79.

After selecting the desired filter action, select OK to save your selection.

When you have finished defining your filter, select Sa**v**e from the F**i**lter menu.

To change the name of your filter, select your filter object and choose **A**ttributes from **O**bjects menu. Enter the new name in the **N**ame field. You can also enter a description for the filter in the **D**escription field (see fig. 13.80). Click on the Change button to save the new information and then click on the Close button when finished.

Do not change the name of your filter using the **A**ttributes option in the **V**iew menu. The new name initially appears, but then reverts back to the previous name.

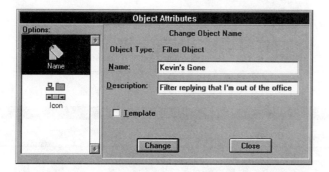

Figure 13.80
Entering a name and description for a filter.

To place a filter on a folder, select a folder and then select **A**ttributes from the **O**bjects menu. When the Object Attributes dialog box appears, select Filter from the **O**ptions list and then select the filter from the Available **F**ilters list (see fig. 13.81). Select OK and the filter is placed on the selected folder.

Figure 13.81
Placing a filter on a folder.

Using Exchange Scheduler

Artisoft Exchange Scheduler enables you to schedule and keep track of your personal and group appointments. The Exchange Scheduler uses the Exchange account names created in Exchange Mail.

To start Artisoft Exchange Scheduler, double-click on the Artisoft Exchange Scheduler in the Artisoft Program Group (see fig. 13.82), or select the icon and choose **O**pen from Program Manager's **F**ile menu.

Figure 13.82
The LANtastic program group.

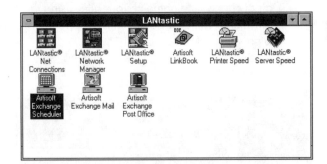

Figure 13.83
The Artisoft Exchange Scheduler dialog box.

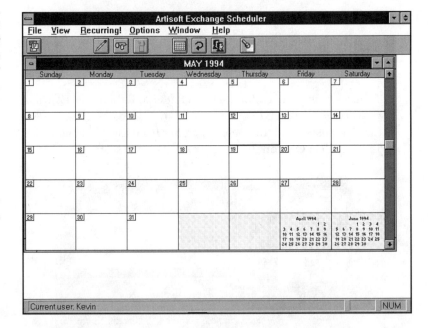

If you have specified separate (not synchronized) LANtastic and Exchange accounts, you will be prompted to enter your <u>U</u>sername and <u>P</u>assword.

The Artisoft Exchange Scheduler dialog box appears (see fig. 13.83), displaying the current months calendar.

Configuring Exchange Scheduler

The configuration requirements for Exchange Scheduler are minimal, because the accounts and mailing lists set up in Exchange Mail are used in Exchange Scheduler.

To set the configuration options in Exchange Scheduler, select <u>C</u>onfigure from the <u>F</u>ile menu. The Scheduler Configuration dialog box appears (see fig. 13.84). The following list describes the configuration options available:

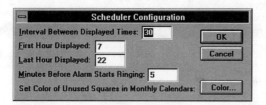

Figure 13.84
The Schedule Configuration dialog box.

✔ The <u>I</u>nterval Between Displayed Times field enables you to specify the number of minutes between the appointment times displayed. The default value is 30, however you can choose a different interval such as 15 or 60 minutes.

✔ The <u>F</u>irst Hour displayed/<u>L</u>ast Hour displayed fields enable you to specify the earliest and latest times displayed on your schedule. You must specify the hours in 24-hour time, which means that to specify a time between noon and midnight you have to add 12 to the time. For example, to specify 6:00 pm as the <u>L</u>ast Hour displayed, you would specify 18 (6+12) in this field.

✔ <u>M</u>inutes Before Alarm Starts Ringing field specifies the number of minutes in advance you will be notified of your scheduled appointment, if you have selected the Alarm option for the appointment.

Creating Appointments

You can create personal or group appointments. There are two types of calendars that can be active: your personal calendar and the group calendar. You can open a group calendar by selecting the Group tool or by selecting **G**roup from the **V**iew menu. Each time you select either **G**roup or **M**onthly from the **V**iew menu, you open up another view of either your monthly or a group monthly calendar. To close a calendar view, double-click in the upper left corner of the window. You can toggle between the active calendar views by selecting the desired window from the **W**indow menu.

To create a personal appointment, perform the following steps:

1. With your monthly calendar active, double-click on the day of the appointment you want to schedule; or select **O**pen from the **F**ile menu. The daily appointment list appears (see fig. 13.85).

Figure 13.85
The daily appointment list.

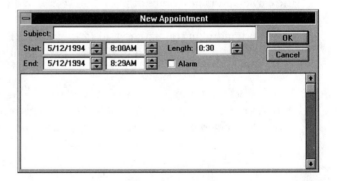

Figure 13.86
The New Appointment dialog box.

2. Double-click on the time for which you want to schedule the appointment, or select **O**pen from the **F**ile menu. The New Appointment dialog box appears (see fig. 13.86).

You can go immediately to the New Appointment dialog box by selecting the New tool, or by selecting **New** from the File menu. Although this method initially saves a step, you lose that savings when you have to specify the start time for the appointment.

3. Type the subject of the appointment in the Subject field. You can type additional information about the appointment in the Notes field.

4. Specify the Start, End, and Length of the appointment as necessary. If you change the Length, the End time is automatically adjusted, and vice versa. Using the increment/decrement buttons next to each field, you can adjust the appointment times in the displayed time increments specified during configuration (such as 30-minute increments). If your appointment time does not conform to the displayed increments, such as a 30-minute time interval, you can type any value you want in each field.

5. If you want to set the alarm to notify you of the appointment, select the Alarm option.

6. Select OK to save your appointment. Your appointment appears on your daily appointment list (see fig. 13.87).

Thursday May 12, 1994	
7:00AM	
7:30AM	
8:00AM– 8:59AM	Breakfast Meeting with Zak
8:30AM	
9:00AM	
9:30AM	
10:00AM	
10:30AM	
11:00AM	
11:30AM	
12:00PM	
12:30PM	
1:00PM	
1:30PM	
2:00PM	
2:30PM	

Figure 13.87
The daily appointment list with the new appointment listed.

To close your daily appointment list view, double-click in the upper left corner of the list. Your appointments appear on your monthly calendar.

To create a group appointment, perform the following steps:

1. With the group monthly calendar active, select the day for which you want to schedule the group appointment, then select the New tool or select **N**ew from the **F**ile menu. The New Group Appointment Dialog box appears (see fig. 13.88).

Figure 13.88
The New Group
Appointment
dialog box.

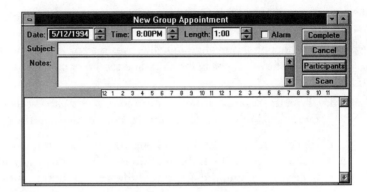

2. Specify the Date, Time, and Length of the appointment. You also can select the Alarm option if you want to be notified of the appointment.

3. Type in the subject of the appointment in the Subject field, and any additional notes in the Notes field.

4. Select the Participants button to specify who you want to attend. The Participants dialog box appears (see fig. 13.89).

Figure 13.89
The Participants
dialog box
showing some
selected
participants.

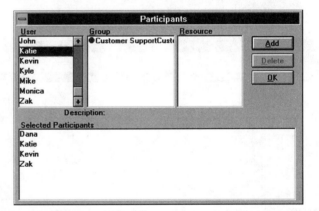

5. Select the members you want to attend the meeting by double-clicking on each person, or by selecting the participants and clicking on the **A**dd button. To specify more than one person at a time, hold down the Ctrl key while selecting. The selected participants appear in the Selected Participants list (see fig. 13.89).

6. Select **O**K when finished. This action returns you to the New Group Appointment dialog box (see fig. 13.90). The light gray bar indicates the time of the scheduled appointment. The black squares indicate a previous commitment for a user.

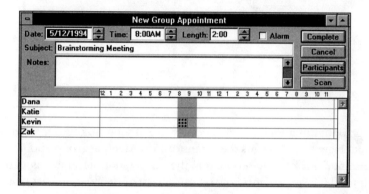

Figure 13.90
The New Group Appointment dialog box showing the selected participants.

7. If any participant is not available at the specified time, click on the Scan button to find the first available time slot when everyone is available.

8. Select the Complete button to schedule the group appointment. The Processing Group Appointment dialog box appears, indicating the status of the group appointment for each participant (see fig. 13.91). Select OK to continue.

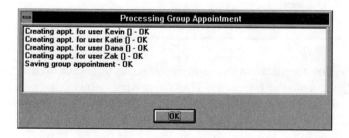

Figure 13.91
The Processing Group Appointment dialog box.

9. The group appointment appears in the Group Appointment list (see fig. 13.92). Double-click in the upper left corner of the Group Appointment List to close the list.

Figure 13.92
The Group Appointment list showing the new group appointment.

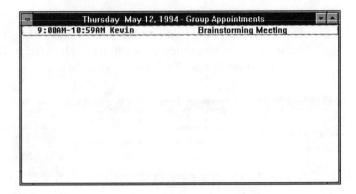

Once a group appointment has been scheduled, it will show up on your schedule if you are invited. Figure 13.93 shows the Brainstorming Meeting group appointment. The question mark in the box next to the subject indicates that it is a group appointment to which you are invited. You can accept or decline the invitation.

Figure 13.93
The daily appointment list showing the group appointment.

To accept or decline an invitation to a group meeting, double-click on the meeting, or select **O**pen from the **F**ile menu. The Group Appointment dialog box appears (see fig. 13.94). Select the Accept button to accept the group appointment, or select the Decline button to decline it. If you accept the appointment, a check mark appears in the box next to the appointment (see fig. 13.95). If you decline the group appointment, an X appears in the box next to the appointment.

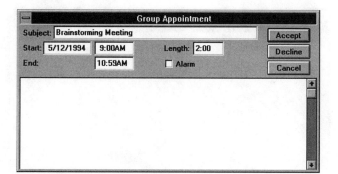

Figure 13.94
Accepting or
declining an
invitation to a
group
appointment.

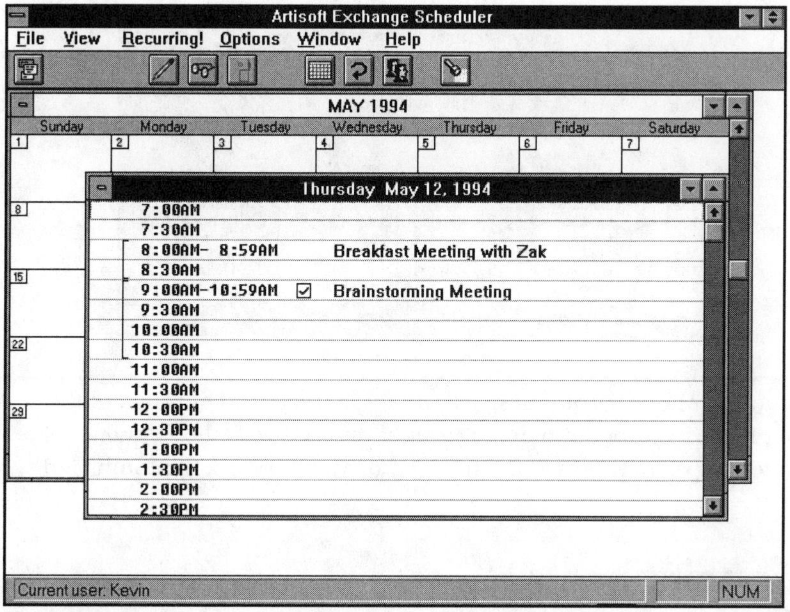

Figure 13.95
The daily
appointment list
showing an
accepted group
appointment.

You can create recurring appointments in your schedule. Select the Recurring tool
or the **R**ecurring menu selection. The Recurring Appointments dialog box
appears (see fig. 13.96). Now, when you add a new appointment, the New Recurring Appointment dialog box appears (see fig. 13.97).

Figure 13.96
The Recurring
Appointments
dialog box.

Figure 13.97
The New
Recurring
Appointment
dialog box.

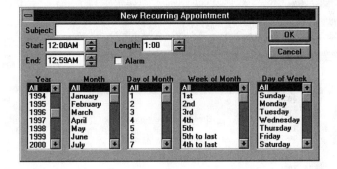

As with other appointments, you can specify a subject, time, and duration of the appointment. Recurring appointments also allow you to specify the frequency of the appointment by specifying Year, Month, Day of Month, Week of Month, and Day of Week.

Editing Appointments

After you have created an appointment, your plans may change requiring you to edit or change your appointments.

To change a personal appointment, double-click on the appointment from your daily appointment list or select **O**pen from the **F**ile menu. The Edit Appointment dialog box appears with the same information as when you created the appointment. Change the information as required and select OK to change the appointment.

To change a group appointment, display the Group Appointment calendar. Double-click on the day that has the group appointment you want to change; or, with the day selected, choose **O**pen from the **F**ile menu. The Group Appointments dialog box appears (see fig. 13.98). Open the group appointment you want to

change by double-clicking on the appointment; or, with the group appointment selected, choose **O**pen from the **F**ile menu. The Edit Group Appointment menu appears allowing you to change the same information as when you created the appointment.

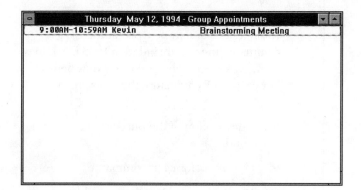

Figure 13.98
The Group
Appointments
dialog box.

To delete an appointment, choose the appointment on either your daily appointment list or the group appointment list, then select the Delete tool or choose **D**elete from the **F**ile menu.

Printing Your Schedule

You can print out your schedules in several different formats. Printing options include daily, weekly, monthly, or combination schedules. The combination schedule has three columns and includes your daily schedule, 10 mini-calendars, and a place for notes.

To print your schedule, select **P**rint from the **F**ile menu. Choose the **D**aily, **W**eekly, **M**onthly, or **C**ombination option. Make any desired adjustments to your Report dialog box and select OK to print the desired schedule.

Summary

In this chapter you learned about Artisoft Exchange, the sophisticated mail and scheduling program included with LANtastic 6.0. You learned about Artisoft Exchange's setup requirements, and the many features that it makes available to you. You discovered how to install Exchange, and add user accounts, address books, and other management options. You also became familiar with setting up and using the Fax, LANtastic Mail, and Pager Gateways. After learning how to set up and change Exchange's configuration, you discovered ways to use Exchange for your daily mail and scheduling requirements.

Chapter Snapshot

This chapter discusses the 37 LANtastic NET commands that may be typed at the DOS command line and included in DOS batch files to automate accessing and using your network. For each NET command, the following is discussed:

✔ A description of the purpose of each command.

✔ The syntax for each command

✔ Any options and switches available for each command

✔ Specific Rules and Considerations which you should be aware of when using each command

✔ Examples of the usage of each command

After reading through this chapter, you will have a good understanding of the LANtastic NET command line commands available, their functions, and how each one is used.

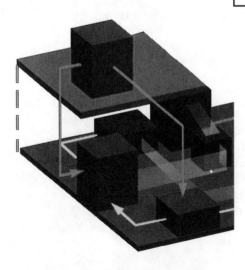

14

CHAPTER

Using NET Command Line Commands

U ntil now, you have used NET as a menu-driven program, and menus
frequently are the most convenient way to control LANtastic features. You
might encounter instances, however, when it is easier to simply type a
command from the DOS command line. This can save a bit of time because you
don't have to start and stop NET. The chief advantage, however, is that line
commands can be put into batch files while menu commands cannot.

You can get a feel for NET commands by examining the STARTNET.BAT file that
was created when LANtastic was installed. Here are some examples of NET
command lines:

```
C:\LANTASTI\NET LOGIN/WAIT \\ACCT JOE
C:\LANTASTI\NET USE G: \\ACCT\C-DRIVE
C:\LANTASTI\NET USE H: \\ACCT\D-DRIVE
C:\LANTASTI\NET USE LPT1: \\ACCT\@PRINTER
C:\LANTASTI\NET LPT TIMEOUT 10
```

When these commands are put in a batch file and the batch file is executed, user JOE is automatically logged in to the server named ACCT. JOE is then set up to use the C and D drives on ACCT. Finally, JOE starts to use @PRINTER on ACCT. As a result, JOE doesn't need to manually start NET, log in, and use the server's drives or printer.

You will find many of the NET commands to be familiar because they relate closely to NET menu options. As you become familiar with LANtastic, you will probably find that you are performing sets of network tasks repeatedly. Consider putting the required commands into batch files to reduce repetition and to streamline your network usage.

The commands in this chapter all start with the command word NET followed by a subcommand such as LOGIN or USE. In turn, the subcommands may accept optional or required information.

It is common to present computer commands in the form of syntax diagrams that include all the possible information that might be included. In grammar, the word syntax describes the way sentences are constructed; a *command syntax diagram* is a formal definition of the structure of the commands.

The description of the NET commands follows fairly closely the syntax diagrams from the LANtastic manuals, so you will have no trouble moving between this book and your product references:

✔ UPPERCASE TEXT is required and does not vary.

✔ lowercase text shows variable information that you add to the required command text.

✔ (Parentheses) surround optional items. These items may be included or not, depending on the desired effect.

✔ [Square brackets] surround choice lists. One item only from the choices in the brackets may be entered with the command.

The following example shows how this works:

```
NET STREAM [/ENABLE /DISABLE] \\server_name ((stream-index)
(stream-value))
```

NET STREAM is a required part of the command and appears in upper-case.

[/ENABLE /DISABLE] indicates that you must enter either \ENABLE or \DISABLE, but not both. Because these items are not surrounded by parentheses, they are not optional and exactly one must be supplied.

server_name appears in lowercase, indicating that you enter variable text, not the phrase "\\server_name." Here you might enter \\ACCT, for example.

(*stream-index*) and (*stream-value*) are enclosed by parentheses showing that these items are optional.

In addition to the syntax diagrams, each command description will include some actual command examples, along with explanations for what the examples accomplish.

Five global switches may be used with the NET command line options. The syntax used is NET(/switch) command, such as NET/HELP SHOW.

The following is a brief description of each global switch:

✔ **/HELP.** Displays a list of help items, including global switches, help commands, and general help topics.

✔ **/?.** Also displays a list of help items including global switches, help commands, and general help topics.

✔ **/MONO.** Invokes the NET menu interface in monochrome mode.

✔ **/NOERROR.** Executes a NET command but does not display any error text if an error occurs. You can test for an error by checking the NET_ERROR environment variable. This variable will be set to an error number or 0 if no error occurred.

✔ **/SCREEN_SAVER.** Enables the screen saver in the LANtastic NET program. If no keyboard activity occurs after two minutes, the screen will blank until a key is pressed.

NET ATTACH

Purpose: This command redirects all available drives to every shared resource on a server. This command is the equivalent of issuing a NET USE command for each of the server's shared resources.

Syntax: `NET ATTACH(/VERBOSE) \\`*server_name*

Option:

server_name Name of server to which you redirect drives.

Switch:

/VERBOSE   Displays drives and their redirections.

Rules and Considerations: *Server_name* must be the name of an active server on the network.

You must be logged in to the *server_name* computer before you can issue NET ATTACH, or autologin must be enabled and the default username and password must exist on the server.

Example: In this example, the next available drive letter is F, but drive letter G is already being used by another shared resource; the server named TECH has four shared resources: A-DRIVE, B-DRIVE, C-DRIVE, and WORD.

```
NET ATTACH/VERBOSE \\TECH
```

After you issue this command, the following lines are displayed:

```
Attaching
     F: to \\TECH\A-DRIVE
     H: to \\TECH\B-DRIVE
     I: to \\TECH\C-DRIVE
     J: to \\TECH\WORD
```

Notes: If you issue the same NET ATTACH command a second time, it assigns the shared resources starting at the next available drive letter. The same resource is assigned to two drive letters.

NET ATTACH does not attach to printer or mail resources.

In some cases, it is better to use specific NET USE commands rather than NET ATTACH—because NET ATTACH assigns all shared resources in the named server to the next available drive letters, which can cause confusion if a shared resource is added to or removed from a server. All drive letters from the point at which the change occurred are different. You may not find applications on the same network drive that you previously assigned them.

See Also: NET DETACH, NET USE, NET LOGIN, NET USER

NET AUDIT

Purpose: This command creates an audit entry in the server's audit file.

Syntax: `NET AUDIT \\server_name reason "audit-text"`

Options:

> *\\server_name* Name of server to which you redirect drives
>
> *reason* A string of up to eight characters that provides the reason for the audit entry
>
> *audit-text* A string of up to 64 characters that gives detailed information about the audit. If the string includes blanks and commas, it must be enclosed in quotation marks

Rules and Considerations: *Server_name* must be the name of an active server on the network.

You must be logged in to the *server_name* computer, or autologin must be enabled and the default username and password must exist on the server, before you can create an audit entry in the server's audit file. You must use the LANtastic Network Manager program Server Startup Parameters to enable user auditing. In addition, you must have the U (User Auditing) privileges on that server, and the text must be placed inside of quotation marks.

Example:

```
NET AUDIT TECH test: "This is a test."
```

After you issue this command, the server named TECH will contain an entry in its audit logs showing the current time and date, the user name of the person who recorded the entry, the name of the workstation from which it was sent, the reason for the entry, and the text of the message.

Notes: If you do not have the U privilege on the server, the command does not work and no error message is displayed.

Using NET AUDIT is a good way to briefly document network problems. You also will find it useful in documenting the time for certain long-running tasks. Suppose, for example, that a batch job can be set up that writes a start time record in the audit file, runs the long job, and then, on completion of that job, writes a finish time record in the audit file.

See Also: NET_MGR

NET CHANGEPW

Purpose: This command enables you to change your password on a server.

Syntax: `NET CHANGEPW \\server_name old-password new-password`

Options:

> *server_name* Name of the server on which the password will be changed.
>
> *old-password* The password you used to log in to the server.
>
> *new-password* The new password.

Rules and Considerations: *Server_name* must be the name of a server to which you have already logged in, or autologin must be enabled and the default username and password must exist on the server.

The *new-password* can be a string of up to 16 letters, numbers, or characters with no embedded blanks. You also cannot use some special characters such as \ and /.

Example:

```
NET CHANGEPW \\TECH TINY RAM
```

After you issue this command, your password on server \\TECH is changed from TINY to RAM.

Notes: If you forget your password, your network administrator can delete the user name by using Individual Account Management in NET_MGR. The administrator then can re-create your login with a new password.

Select a password that you can remember but that an intruder cannot guess. Don't ever write your password on anything.

See Also: NET_MGR, NET LOGIN, NET LOGOUT

NET CHAT

Purpose: This command starts up the interactive Chat mode.

Syntax: NET CHAT

Rules and Considerations: Entering this command is equivalent to entering the NET Main Functions menu and selecting the Chat With Another User option.

After the Chat screen is displayed, follow its on-screen directions.

Example:

    NET CHAT

After you issue this command, the Chat screen appears. You then follow its on-screen instructions to page and chat with the user over the network.

See Also: NET

NET CLOCK

Purpose: This command sets the date and time on your workstation from the server's clock.

Syntax: NET CLOCK *server_name*

Option:

> *server_name* Name of server from which you want to get time information.

Rules and Considerations: *Server_name* must be the name of a server to which you are logged in, or autologin must be enabled and the default username and password must exist on the server.

Example:

    NET CLOCK \\TECH

After you issue this command, the time and date on the computer from which the command is issued changes to match that of server \\TECH.

Establish one server on your network as the master clock server. Use NET CLOCK to synchronize the time in all computers on the network with the time in this master server.

NET COPY

Purpose: This command performs file copies from one location on a server's hard disk(s) to another location on the same server's hard disk(s). The copy takes place directly on a server, bypassing network data transfers.

Syntax: `NET COPY(/VERBOSE)` *from-path to-path*

Options:

from-path	The path name of source files. You can use wildcard characters.
to-path	The path name of destination files or directory.

Switch:

/VERBOSE Displays the from-path before it is copied.

Rules and Considerations: If drive letters are used as part of the path name, they must be redirected drive letters (such as K); physical drive letters (such as C) are not valid.

The from-path and to-path may include redirected drive letters, such as K:\JUNK.TXT, or the full network path name, such as \\SERVER\C-DRIVE\JUNK.TXT.

Example:

```
NET COPY/VERBOSE h:\base\*.bat i:\work
```

This command copies all BAT files in the subdirectory \base on the redirected network drive H on a server, to a subdirectory named \work on the redirected network drive I on the same server. The copy takes place entirely within that server; no network traffic is generated.

If the H drive is redirected to \\OFFICE\C-DRIVE, the preceding example could be written as:

```
NET COPY/VERBOSE \\OFFICE\C-DRIVE\base\*.bat i:\work
```

The /VERBOSE switch causes the names of all copied files to be listed.

Notes: Network performance improves if you use NET COPY rather than COPY or XCOPY whenever possible.

DOS wildcard characters can be used with NET COPY.

NET DETACH

Purpose: This command breaks all disk redirections with a server and is equivalent to issuing a NET UNUSE command for each redirection already made.

Syntax: `NET DETACH \\server_name`

Option:

   server_name Names the server for which you want to break all disk
                   redirections.

Rules and Considerations: *Server_name* must be the name of an active server on the network.

Example: In this example, redirected drive letters E, F, and H are assigned to shared resources on server \\TECH.

    NET DETACH \\TECH

After you issue this command, drive letters E, F, and G no longer are assigned to network resources.

Notes: NET DETACH has no effect on printer or mail resource assignments.

NET DETACH does not log you out of the server.

See Also: NET ATTACH, NET USE, NET UNUSE

NET DIR

Purpose: This command displays directory and file information. Unlike the DOS DIR command, NET DIR works on network paths, such as paths that start with the name of a server.

Syntax: `NET DIR(/ALL) (pathname)`

Option:

   pathname   The path or file name for which you want directory informa-
                    tion. May be a network path (such as \\SERVER\C-DRIVE).

Switch:

   /ALL   Display all files, including system and hidden files. Do not
                    leave space between the R in DIR and the /. May be substi-
                    tuted as /A.

Rules and Considerations: NET DIR works basically the same as DOS DIR except that it recognizes network server and shared resource names, and also displays more information.

Directory information is displayed in the following format:

FILENAME   Name of the file

ATTRIBUTES   File's attributes

     I—Indirect file   A—Archive flag

     D—Directory flag   V—Volume label

     S—System file   H—Hidden file

     R—Read-only file

SIZE   Size of the file in bytes

DATE   File's creation date

TIME   File's creation time

Example: Assume that E is redirected (by NET USE) to network resource \\TECH\C-DRIVE. In this case, NET DIR e:\base*.BAK produces a display in the following format:

```
Directory of \\TECH\C-DRIVE\BASE\

NETWORK.BAK    -A——      618     8-Jun-1994    16:29:20
P.BAK          -A——       62    28-May-1994    15:52:36
11.BAK         -A——      208    16-Apr-1994    11:10:12
```

Some software programs, such as WordPerfect, require that you use the DOS ATTRIB command to make many of their files read-only so that they can be shared on the network. Running NET DIR is a useful way of checking whether files on a directory have been set to read-only.

See Also: NET ATTACH, NET DETACH, NET USE

NET DISABLEA

Purpose: This command disables your account from further log ins. This command only operates if the account has concurrent log ins set to 1.

Syntax: `NET DISABLEA \\server_name password`

Options:

> *server_name* Name of server on which the account will be disabled.
>
> *password*   The password of your account.

Rules and Considerations: *Server_name* must be the name of a server that you have already logged in to, or autologin must be enabled and the default username and password must exist on the server.

Password is the password of the account with which you are currently logged in to the server.

This command will work only if account modifications are enabled.

Example:

```
NET DISABLEA \\TECH RAM
```

After you issue this command, your account on server \\TECH will be disabled if your account password is RAM.

Notes: NET_MGR must be used to reestablish an account after it has been disabled with NET DISABLEA.

It is good security practice to disable your accounts on all servers before leaving for an extended period, such as going on vacation.

See Also: NET_MGR, NET USER, NET LOGIN

NET ECHO

Purpose: This command displays a string of characters and is similar to the DOS ECHO command, except that it enables you to use special strings.

Syntax: `NET ECHO string`

Option:

> *string*   The string of characters or special characters to be displayed.

Rules and Considerations: See NET STRING and NET MACRO for information about special characters that can be used with NET ECHO.

Example:

```
NET ECHO "This is machine" !"machineid"
This is machine JOHN
```

Notes: You can type **NET HELP STRING** and **NET HELP MACRO** to find out which special strings you can use.

See Also: NET STRING, NET MACRO

NET EXPAND

Purpose: This command expands a path name to its full resolution. It enables you to find the physical or network path to any file. NET EXPAND is particularly useful in working with indirect files.

Syntax: NET EXPAND(/PHYSICAL)(/RECURSE) *pathname*

Option:

pathname   The name of the path name that you want to expand.

Switches:

/PHYSICAL Expand to the server's physical path for this path name.

/RECURSE Expand to show the full network path to the final referenced indirect file.

Rules and Considerations: You can abbreviate /PHYSICAL to /P and /RECURSE to /R.

No path name is needed for this command to work. For example, you have a server named \\TECH with a shared resource named C-DRIVE. This server contains a directory named \BASE, but BASE does not contain a file named NOTHERE.FIL. If you enter **NET EXPAND/R \BASE\NOTHERE.FIL**, LANtastic displays \\TECH\C-DRIVE\BASE\NOTHERE.FIL.

Do not place a space between the D in EXPAND and the / in /R or /D. If you do, the switch will be viewed by LANtastic as the path name and LANtastic will ignore the actual path name.

Example: Because NET EXPAND is primarily useful in relationship to indirect files, the following example uses indirect files (see NET INDIRECT for more information on this command).

```
NET INDIRECT level2.bat original.bat
NET INDIRECT level3.bat level2.bat
```

The preceding statements create two layers of indirect files. Assuming these files are created on a redirected drive which points to \\KSOFFICE\C-DRIVE, if you type:

NET EXPAND level3.bat

the following is displayed:

```
\\KSOFFICE\C-DRIVE\LEVEL3.BAT
```

If you type:

NET EXPAND/R level3.bat

the following is displayed:

```
\\KSOFFICE\C-DRIVE\ORIGINAL.BAT
```

If you type:

NET EXPAND/P

the following is displayed:

```
C:\ORIGINAL.BAT
```

See Also: NET INDIRECT

NET FLUSH

Purpose: This command flushes the resource cache, the random-access cache, and LANCACHE on the specified server.

Syntax: NET FLUSH *server_name*

Option:

server_name The name of the server to flush.

Rules and Considerations: To perform a NET FLUSH on a server, you must log in to that system under a user name that has the SYSTEM MANAGER privilege in NET_MGR.

Example:

```
NET FLUSH \\TECH
```

Notes: This command is useful if you modified a resource with NET_MGR and want to force the update to take effect.

See Also: NET_MGR, LANCACHE

NET HELP

Purpose: This command displays reference information about a command. This command is the same as NET ?.

Syntax: NET HELP *(command)*

Option:

> *command*   Name of the command that you want information about.

Rules and Considerations: You can use NET HELP to display information about NET's 37 commands, its five global switches (/HELP, /?, /MONO, /NOERROR, /SCREEN_SAVER), and three related topics (MACROS, ERRORS, and SYNTAX).

Entering **NET HELP** without any command specified displays the complete list of help topics.

Example: If you need help on the proper syntax for the login command, enter **NET HELP LOGIN**.

This message is displayed:

```
NET LOGIN(/WAIT /DEFERRED) \\server_name (username) (password)
(adapter#)
```

Logs you in to a server, thus enabling you to redirect your drives and printers to the server.

> /WAIT   Wait for server to come online.
>
> /DEFERRED   Retries a failed login attempt later when a user attempts to use the connection.
>
> *server-name*   Name of server to log in to. The wildcard character (*) is accepted as the last character, in which case all matching servers in the server list are logged into. If you are already logged into the server, changes your user name without detaching drives or closing files.

username	User name to use for log in. If not specified, the default user name, password, and adapter number specified with NET USER will be used.
password	Password to gain access to server.
adapter#	Optional adapter number to log in through.

Note: You can use NET ? in place of NET HELP.

See Also: NET ?

NET INDIRECT

Purpose: This command enables you to indirectly access a file by referencing a file whose contents are the path of the file to be accessed.

Syntax: NET INDIRECT *pathname actual-name*

Options:

pathname	The name of the indirect file to create. This option must be a network path. The path name uses the form of \\server\resource\directory\ind_name. If ind_name is in the current directory, you can omit the \\server\resource\directory part of this parameter.
actual-name	The name of the actual file name to which the indirect file refers. This file must be on the same server. The actual name uses the form \resource\directory\act_name. Note that the server name cannot be included here. This operation only works on the same server and that server name is assumed.

Rules and Considerations: Although indirect files are useful in some cases, enabling the I (Indirect File) access right has a significant adverse effect on network performance because the server must consider the attributes of a file before it attempts to open the file. If indirect files are being used, it must then go through one or more additional file reads to complete the operation. In addition to reduced performance, using indirect files has the further disadvantage of complicating network management.

If you erase, rename, or change the ATTRIB setting of an indirect file, the indirect file, rather than the actual file being referenced by the indirect file, is affected. Operations on indirect files, such as TYPE and COPY, affect the actual file being referenced by the indirect file, not the indirect file.

The indirect file must be on a server (the same server on which the actual file is located).

Example: Suppose that H is redirected to a server resource named C-DRIVE and that the I ACL was set for this resource. A batch job contains the following:

```
H:
NET INDIRECT IND.BAT \C-DRIVE\MYJOB.BAT
IND
```

When this batch job is executed, MYJOB.BAT executes.

Notes: Use NET EXPAND to see how the network will interpret NET INDIRECT commands.

Use NET DIR to see whether the INDIRECT attribute has been set for a file. Note that the expansion of the indirect file is shown where the creation date would normally be shown in the directory listing. LANtastic does this to distinguish indirect files from normal files.

Don't use NET INDIRECT unless you have an unusual requirement and know exactly what you are doing.

See Also: NET EXPAND, NET DIR

NET LOGIN

Purpose: This command logs you in to a server, enabling you to access those shared resources on that server that your username and password authorizes you to access.

Syntax: NET LOGIN(/WAIT /DEFERRED) *server_name (username) (password)* *(adapter#)*

Options:

\\server_name The name of the server to which you want to log in. The wildcard character (*) is accepted as the last character, in which case all matching servers in the server list are logged in to. If you already are logged in to the server, your user

name is changed without detaching drives or closing files. LANtastic performs the LOGOUT for you before it logs you in under the new user name.

username	The name you use for login purposes. If not specified, the default user name, password, and adapter number specified with NET USER are used.
password	The password to gain access to the server.
adapter#	Optional adapter number through which to log in.

Switches:

/WAIT	Waits for the server to come online. You can abbreviate /WAIT to /W. Pressing Esc terminates the wait and exits without accomplishing the login.
/DEFERRED	Retries a failed login attempt later when the user attempts to use a connection associated with this server. You can abbreviate /DEFERRED to /D.

Rules and Considerations: *Server_name* must be the name of an active server on the network.

The *username* and *password* must be valid on that server.

Example:

```
NET LOGIN \\TECH MANAGER MAN
```

This command waits for server TECH to come online, and then logs you in under user name MANAGER and password MAN.

Notes: You can concurrently log in to as many servers as exist, up to the limit that is specified by the LOGINS= parameter in the REDIR line. The default value for LOGINS=2.

LANtastic special strings can be used in conjunction with NET LOGIN statements in a batch job to prompt the user for his user name and password. For example, NET LOGIN \\TECH ? "Enter user name" ^ "Enter password" prompts the user for a username and password. The characters in the username appear as they are typed. The characters in the password do not appear. See NET STRING for more information on this feature.

See Also: NET ATTACH, NET LOGOUT, NET STRING, NET USER

NET LOGOUT

Purpose: This command logs you out of a server and cancels all drive and printer redirections.

Syntax: NET LOGOUT *server_name*

Option:

> *server_name* The name of the server from which you want to log out. The wildcard character (*) may be used for the last character, in which case you are logged out of multiple servers.

Rules and Considerations: *Server_name* must be the name of server that you previously logged in to.

Example:

    NET LOGOUT \\TECH

This command logs you out of \\TECH.

Notes: As long as you do not exceed your LOGINS= parameter in the REDIR line, you do not have to log out of one server to log in to another.

See Also: NET ATTACH, NET LOGIN, NET UNUSED

NET LPT

Purpose: This command enables you to perform specified printer functions to control printing produced within a batch job.

NET LPT COMBINE enables you to combine printed output from separate print jobs into a single print job with no breaks.

NET LPT FLUSH is used after NET LPT COMBINE to flush the printer output out of the printer.

NET LPT NOTIFY notifies a user when the print job they have sent is completed.

NET LPT SEPARATE is used after NET LPT COMBINE to disable the COMBINE feature and return to separated print jobs.

NET LPT TIMEOUT specifies the length of time in seconds that LANtastic will wait before it assumes the print job is finished.

Syntax:

```
NET LPT COMBINE
NET LPT FLUSH
NET LPT (/ENABLE)(/DISABLE) NOTIFY
NET LPT SEPARATE
NET LPT TIMEOUT TIME-OUT
```

Option:

time-out   Time out in seconds.

Switches:

/ENABLE   Enables Notification.

/DISABLE   Disables Notification.

Rules and Considerations: COMBINE, FLUSH, and SEPARATE only apply to printout produced with a batch job.

NET LPT COMBINE becomes effective as soon as it is issued in a batch file, and is disabled as soon as the batch file is completed, at which time your printer output file will be closed.

A *time-out* value of 0 has the effect of disabling the automatic time-out feature. The maximum *time-out* that can be set is 3,600 seconds. The LANtastic install program includes a NET LPT TIMEOUT statement in STARTNET.BAT with a default value of 10.

Examples:

The following batch job prints four one-line reports. The first two would be combined and immediately flushed to the printer. The third and fourth would be separated and flushed after the batch job is completed.

```
NET LPT COMBINE
ECHO This is the first report > LPT1:
ECHO This is the second report > LPT1:
NET LPT FLUSH
NET LPT SEPARATE
ECHO This is the third report > LPT1:
ECHO This is the fourth report > LPT1
```

The following is an example of a time-out setting:

```
NET LPT TIMEOUT 10
```

For most situations, you should use a TIMEOUT value of 10. Setting a time-out value too low can actually slow down printing. Faster printing can be obtained with the LANtastic Network Manager program SHARED RESOURCE parameters of IMMEDIATE DESPOOLING and CPS. If your printed data is being separated, you probably need to increase your time-out value.

See Also: NET USE

NET MAIL

Purpose: This command sends a mail file to a user on a server.

Syntax: NET MAIL(/VERBOSE)(/VOICE) *filename* *server_name recipient (comment)*

Options:

filename	The path name of file to send.
server_name	The name of the server whose mail queue is to receive the file.
recipient	The name of the user who is to receive mail. Wildcard characters are permitted.
comment	Comment text that is associated with mail.

Switches:

/VERBOSE	Displays the file name as it is sent.
/VOICE	Indicates that the file contains voice information (not text).

Rules and Considerations: If NET MAIL is typed with no options, the NET program will be run where you can select a server's mail queue to view.

The *filename* must be a valid path name of an existing file.

The *server_name* must be the name of an active server on the network.

The *recipient* can be a person who is not currently logged in, or a person who does not have a current valid username. Wildcards are allowed. You can send the mail to all users by using * as the username.

A *comment* is any text comment. If the comment text is not enclosed in quotation marks, LANtastic truncates the message after the first 24 characters.

Example: In this example, a network user sends the system manager a copy of his CONFIG.SYS file:

```
NET MAIL/VERBOSE CONFIG.SYS \\TECH manager "This is my CONFIG.SYS"
```

Notes: Text files sent by the NET MAIL command can be read within MAIL in the NET menu system. That system enables you to copy the file to another file name. Program files, therefore, can be sent; after they are copied to a file ending in EXE or COM, they can be used by the recipient.

If you have a LANtastic Voice Adapter, you can play and hear voice messages.

Specifying CON as the file name enables you to type the file contents from the keyboard. Pressing Ctrl+Z terminates the file.

See Also: NET, NET SEND, NET MESSAGE

NET MESSAGE

Purpose: This command determines whether pop-up messages appear on your workstation's screen. You can use the BEEP argument to enable or disable the sound that accompanies pop-up messages; use the POP argument to enable or disable the messages themselves.

Syntax: NET MESSAGE(/ENABLE)(/DISABLE) (BEEP)(POP)(SPEAK)(ALL)

Options:

BEEP　　　　When BEEP is enabled, messages beep when they are received at the workstation. When BEEP is disabled, messages do not beep.

POP　　　　When POP is enabled, messages pop up when they are received at the workstation. When POP is disabled, messages do not pop up.

SPEAK　　　When SPEAK is enabled, voice error messages will be active. When SPEAK is disabled, voice error messages will not be used.

ALL   Enables or disables all three options at once (BEEP, POP, SPEAK).

Switches:

/ENABLE   Enables the specified options.

/DISABLE   Disables the specified options.

Rules and Considerations: The default is that ALL message notification features are enabled.

Do not put a space between the word MESSAGE and the slash (/) in the /EN-ABLE or /DISABLE switch. You can use /E or /D in place of /ENABLE or /DISABLE.

Example: NET MESSAGE/D POP

After you issue this command, the workstation beeps when it receives messages, but the messages do not pop up.

Notes: LANtastic will not attempt to display a pop-up message if your screen is set to a graphics mode. By default, messages pop up when they arrive at the workstation, and the workstation beeps.

 If you do not want to be disturbed by pop-up messages appearing on-screen, you should disable the workstation's pop-up facility. You may want to leave the beep active so you at least can be alerted that a message is waiting for you.

See Also: NET, NET SEND, NET MAIL

NET PAUSE

Purpose: This command will halt batch file processing for a specified number of seconds or until the user presses a key. If desired, a message to be displayed may be entered.

Syntax: NET PAUSE(/NEWLINE) *(message) (time)*

Options:

message   The message to be displayed. The message is not newline-terminated unless the /NEWLINE switch is present.

time	The time in seconds (0 to 999) to delay while displaying the message. If the specified time is 0, the message is displayed indefinitely until the user presses a key.

Switches:

/NEWLINE	Generates a new line at the end of the message.

Rules and Considerations: Do not put a space between the word PAUSE and the slash (/) in the /NEWLINE switch.

Example:

```
NET PAUSE/newline "Wait 30 seconds." 30
```

This statement displays the message "Wait 30 seconds," moves the cursor to the next line, and halts processing for 30 seconds. At the end of 30 seconds or when a key is pressed, processing continues.

NET PING

Purpose: You can use this command to view information about the computers in your network. This command will list the Machine Name, Adapter number, LANtastic NOS version being run, and whether or not each computer is a server.

Syntax: NET PING *(machine)*

Option:

machine	The name of the computer or computers you want to view information about. Wildcards may be used to specify all computers or groups of computers.

Rules and Considerations: It takes one tick (1/18th second) to process each name, so 'pinging' a larger network may take a considerable amount of time.

The * wildcard may be used to specify all computers in the network. Wildcards such as A* may be used to specify groups of computers in a network.

Example: NET PING *

This command would display the following information for a sample five-station network:

Machine Name	Adapter	Version	Server
386-25	0	6.0	X
ZAK	0	6.0	X
KATIE	0	6.0	X
DANA	0	6.0	
KSOFFICE	0	6.0	X

See Also: NET SHOW

NET POSTBOX

Purpose: You can use this command to see if you have mail waiting on any server into which you are logged.

Syntax: NET POSTBOX (\\server_name)

Option:

\\server_name   The name of the server that you want to scan for waiting
                 mail. If you do not supply a server name, LANtastic scans all
                 the servers you are logged in to.

Rules and Considerations: The server_name must be the name of an active server on the network.

Example:

```
NET POSTBOX
You have 4 mail messages on server \\TECH
You have 2 mail messages on server \\DEMO
```

See Also: NET, NET SEND, NET MESSAGE

NET PRINT

Purpose: This command prints a file through the network.

Syntax: NET PRINT(/BINARY)(/DELETE)(/DIRECT)(/(NO)NOTIFY) (/DATE=)(/
TIME=)(/DELAY=)(/VERBOSE) filename device ("comment") (copies)

Options:

filename	The path name of file that is to be printed. Wildcard characters are accepted.
device	The name of the device on which the file will be printed. You can specify a DOS device name (such as PRN or LPT1) that has been redirected to a network printer. You also can use the shared resource name, such as \\DEMO\@PRINTER.
comment	The comment text that is associated with the print job. If you leave out this text, the file name is used.
copies	The number of copies to be printed. If you do not specify a number, LANtastic prints only one copy.

Switches:

/BINARY	Prints the file in binary mode. /B may also be used.
/DELETE	Deletes the file after printing. This switch works only with the /DIRECT switch.
/DIRECT	Tells LANtastic not to copy the file to a queue area; instead, the file is used directly on the server.
/NOTIFY	Notifies the user when the print job is complete. This switch overrides NET LPT/DISABLE NOTIFY.
/NONOTIFY	Tells LANtastic not to notify the user when the print job is complete. This switch overrides NET LPT/ENABLE NOTIFY.
/DATE=	Sets the despool date. The default is the current date. The date format is month-day-year, such as 6-8-1993, or day-month-year, such as 8-JUN-1993.
/TIME=	Sets the despool time. The default is the current time. The time format is hour:minute(AM/PM), such as 19:30 or 7:30PM.
/DELAY=	Sets a despool delay. The default is no delay. The delay format is hours:minutes, such as 1:20, which would be 1 hour and 20 minutes. The maximum delay is 96 hours.
/VERBOSE	Displays the file names as they are queued.

Rules and Considerations: When specifying the device, do not include the colon (:) in the device name. For example, NET PRINT \config.sys LPT1 is valid, but NET PRINT \config.sys LPT1: will result in an error message.

If you want to use the /DIRECT switch, make sure that the file is on a server that is connected to the network printer that you want to use.

Example:

```
NET PRINT/DIRECT/DELETE/BINARY FILE1 \\DEMO\@PRINTER 2
```

This command prints two copies of the binary file FILE1, which is located in the current directory on the server named \\DEMO. The file is printed to the @PRINTER device on \\DEMO. LANtastic prints the file without first copying it to the print queue. When the print job is done, file1 is deleted.

Notes: You must specify the options in the order shown earlier, in the description of this command's syntax.

The NET PRINT/DIRECT/BINARY command offers a faster way to print graphics files on the server. If you need multiple copies of a file, the copies option provides additional performance benefits.

See Also: NET, NET QUEUE, NET LPT

NET QUEUE

Purpose: This command provides physical printer queue control from the command line. NET QUEUE provides most of the queue-control functions that are available within the NET menu system. If you want to issue NET QUEUE commands, your user name must be assigned the Q privilege on the printer server.

Syntax: NET QUEUE options *server_name* *([LPTn COMn despooler-name ALL])*

Options:

START	Starts despooling if stopped, halted, or paused.
STOP	Stops despooling at the end of the current job.
HALT	Halts despooling immediately. The current print job is placed back in the queue and restarted when despooling is reenabled.

PAUSE	Pauses despooling immediately. The current print job is not closed and resumes when despooling is restarted.
SINGLE	Despools a single print job and then stops despooling.
RESTART	Restarts the current print job from its beginning.
STATUS	Displays the status of the physical printer on the server.
server_name	The name of server on which to perform the despooling operation.
LPT*n*	The parallel printer to control (LPT1, LPT2, or LPT3).
COM*n*	The serial printer to control (COM1, COM2, COM3, or COM4).
despooler-name	Name of the remote print server (RPS).
ALL	Controls all printers (this is the default).

Rules and Considerations: NET QUEUE is somewhat similar to NET STREAM. The difference is that NET QUEUE works on physical printer queues (such as LPT1 or COM1), and NET STREAM works on logical printer streams (such as @LASER or @DOT).

You must have Q (Super Queue) privileges to use this command.

Examples:

```
NET QUEUE START \\DEMO ALL
NET QUEUE STOP \\DEMO LPT1
NET QUEUE HALT \\DEMO COM1
NET QUEUE PAUSE \\DEMO ALL
NET QUEUE RESTART \\DEMO ALL
NET QUEUE STATUS \\DEMO LPT1
```

Notes: STOP, HALT, and PAUSE all stop the queue, but in different ways. Use STOP if you want the current job to finish before the queue is stopped. Suppose, for example, that the printing is getting light because of a worn-out printer ribbon. You want to change the ribbon, but don't mind if the report currently being printed comes out a little light. If you want despooling to stop immediately so you can change the ribbon and at least have the rest of that report darker, use PAUSE. If you want to stop despooling to change the ribbon, and then you want the current report to be reprinted from the beginning, use HALT.

See Also: NET, NET STREAM

When you enable despooling within LANtastic Network Manager SERVER STARTUP PARAMETERS, the effect is the same as issuing the NET QUEUE START \\SERVER_NAME command in your STARTNET.BAT file.

NET RECEIVE

Purpose: This command displays the last unsolicited message received.

Syntax: NET RECEIVE *(position delay)*

Options:

position	The line number on which the pop-up message appears. Line numbers range from 0 to 23.
delay	Length of time in seconds that a message appears before it is removed.

Rules and Considerations: Only the last unsolicited message is displayed.

Example: NET RECEIVE 18 3

In this example, the last message is displayed on line 18 for three seconds. All subsequent messages are displayed on that specific line/duration.

Notes: The "unsolicited" messages can be truly unsolicited as in the case of a NET SEND message from another user, or they can be the result of turning on NOTIFY in various commands, such as NET LPT/ENABLE NOTIFY. In this case, after a print job finishes, you would receive an "unsolicited" message.

Add NET RECEIVE 6 5 to your STARTNET.BAT to reduce the time that pop-up messages display from ten seconds to five seconds. In most cases, five seconds is enough time to read a one-line message.

See Also: NET, NET MESSAGE, NET LPT, NET SEND

NET RUN

Purpose: This command sends a command string to the server to be processed as if it had been entered from the server's keyboard.

Syntax: NET RUN(/NOCR) *server_name* "*command*"

Options:

server_name   The name of the server on which you want to run the command.

command   Command to run on server.

Switch:

/NOCR   Do not append a carriage return to the command string.

Rules and Considerations: The RUN_BUFFER_SIZE as set up in the LANtastic Network Manager SERVER STARTUP PARAMETERS must be large enough to hold the command.

If a local program is being run on the server when the NET RUN request is submitted, the results are unpredictable. In some cases, the keystrokes contained in *command* suddenly appear on the screen within the application. For example, a person working locally on the server in WordPerfect may see a command such as NET STREAM/ENABLE \\TECH 1 @envelope suddenly appear within the current document. In this case, the person sending the RUN request is not notified that the request could not be run because the computer is busy. In other cases, sending a NET RUN request to a server that is running something locally can cause that server to lock up. If a NET RUN request is sent to a server while that server is running the ALONE command, for example, the server locks up.

Examples:

```
NET RUN \\TECH "PRINTJOB.BAT"
```

In this case, the user wants to run a long print job on the server computer instead of from his workstation. He set up a batch job named PRINTJOB.BAT that contains the commands needed to run the print job.

```
NET RUN/NOCR \\TECH "DON'T Touch the keyboard... Network Manager"
```

In this case, the network manager sends a message asking that the server not be used locally. The message remains displayed on the server's screen as long as no user presses the Enter key. If Enter is pressed, a bad command or filename message appears.

Notes: Because NET RUN does not notify the person sending the command that the command has been run successfully, it is best to create batch jobs that contain the commands you want to run, as well as the NET SEND command to inform you of the success of your request.

NET RUN can be a beneficial command, but its use should be tightly controlled. Do not issue a NET RUN command unless you are certain that no one is working locally on the server computer and that it is not running the ALONE program.

See Also: NET, NET SEND

NET SEND

Purpose: This command sends an unsolicited message.

Syntax: `NET SEND machine-name "message" (server_name (username))`

Options:

machine-name	Name of the machine to which you want to send the message. The wildcard * can be used to represent all machines.
message	Message to send.
server_name	The optional name of the server on which the user must be logged in to receive the message. The wildcard * can be used to represent any server, rather than one particular server.
username	Optional name of user to receive message. You must specify a server name to use this option. The wildcard * can be used to send the message to all users logged in to the specified server.

Rules and Considerations: You cannot specify the optional user name parameter unless you specify a server_name to which the user name applies. The wildcard * can be used to represent all.

Examples:

```
NET SEND * "Happy Birthday, Mary!" * Mary
```

This example sends a message to Mary on any server that she logs in to.

```
NET SEND \\MARY "Happy Birthday, Mary!"
```

This example sends a message to Mary at machine \\MARY.

```
NET SEND * "We close at 4 PM today"
```

This example sends a message to everyone.

Use NET SEND to inform users whenever a network printer must be taken offline so they can redirect their data to another network printer.

See Also: NET, NET MESSAGE, NET RECEIVE, NET SHUTDOWN

NET SHOW

Purpose: This command displays information about your workstations' network status and the state of the network.

Syntax: NET SHOW(/BATCH)

Switch:

/BATCH   Displays information suitable for use in a batch file.

Rules and Considerations: REDIR must be loaded for this (or any other) NET command to work.

Example:

    NET SHOW

This command displays the following information:

    LANtastic (R) Connection Manager V6.00 - (C) Copyright 1994
    ARTISOFT Inc.
    Machine 386-25 is being used as a Redirector and a Server
    File and record locking is currently ENABLED
    Unsolicited messages will BEEP, POP-UP, and SPEAK
    LPT notification is DISABLED
    LPT timeout in seconds: 10
    Autologin is ENABLED with username KEVIN
    Logged into \\386-25 as 386-25 on adapter 0
    Logged into \\OFFICE as KEVIN on adapter 0
    Logged into \\KATIE as KEVIN on adapter 0
    Disk G: is connected to \\KATIE\C-DRIVE
    Disk K: is connected to \\OFFICE\C-DRIVE
    Printer LPT1 is connected to \\KATIE\@PRINTER
    Printer LPT2 is connected to \\OFFICE\@PRINTER
    Server \\ZAK is available on adapter sft
    NET SHOW/BATCH

In this format, the command displays the following information:

```
NET MESSAGE/ENABLE BEEP
NET MESSAGE/ENABLE POP
NET MESSAGE/ENABLE SPEAK
NET LPT/DISABLE NOTIFY
NET LPT TIMEOUT 10
NET USER KEVIN ^"Enter default password for user KEVIN: "
NET LOGIN \\386-25 386-25 ^"Enter password for 386-25 on
                          \\386-25: " 0
NET LOGIN \\OFFICE
NET LOGIN \\KATIE
NET USE G: \\KATIE\C-DRIVE
NET USE K: \\OFFICE\C-DRIVE
NET USE LPT1 \\KATIE\@PRINTER
NET USE LPT2 \\OFFICE\@PRINTER
```

> The information in NET SHOW/BATCH can be captured to a file named FILE1 by entering NET SHOW/BATCH > FILE1. The contents of FILE1 can then be merged into your STARTNET.BAT file by using the DOS EDIT command or most other text editors.

See Also: NET, NET QUEUE

NET SHUTDOWN

Purpose: This command shuts down a server.

Syntax: NET SHUTDOWN(/REBOOT)(/CANCEL)(/HALT)(/SILENT) *server_name* ((*minutes*) "*message*")

Options:

server_name The name of the server you want to shut down.

minutes   Number of minutes before actual shutdown (default=0).

message   Message to send to logged in users to warn them of the coming shutdown. You can include a '#' in the message; it will be expanded to the number of minutes remaining. A '$' will expand to the letter 's' if the minutes remaining is not equal to 1.

Switches:

/REBOOT   Reboot the server after shutting down.

/HALT   Halts processing on the server after it shuts down. The keyboard on the server is locked. Rebooting is required to reactivate that machine.

/SILENT   Do not notify logged in users of impending shutdown.

/CANCEL   Cancel a pending shutdown for the server.

Rules and Considerations: You must have S privileges to execute this command.

Example:

```
NET SHUTDOWN/REBOOT \\TECH 1 "TECH will shutdown in 1 minute"
```

This command shuts down and reboots server TECH in one minute.

 Make sure that users have no open files on the server before you shut it down. Ask everyone to log out, and then check the server activity within the NET program before issuing the NET SHUTDOWN command.

See Also: NET, NET TERMINATE, NET SLOGINS

NET SLOGINS

Purpose: This command globally enables or disables logins to the specified server. If logins are disabled, no new users can connect to the server. Users already logged in are not affected. You must have the S (System Manager) privilege to use this command.

Syntax: NET SLOGINS[/ENABLE][/DISABLE] *server_name*

Option:

server_name Name of server on which logins are enabled/disabled.

Switches:

/ENABLE   Enable logins on the server (default).

/DISABLE Disable logins on the server.

Rules and Considerations: *Server_name* must be the name of an active server on the network.

If you disable logins and then all users with the S privilege log out, logins cannot be reenabled without restarting the server.

Example:

```
NET SLOGINS/DISABLE \\TECH
```

In this example, additional logins are disabled for server TECH. Existing logins are not affected.

 If you are planning a server shutdown, you may want to first disable logins so that no one logs in to the server during the shutdown process. Then issue NET TERMINATE to log out all existing users.

See Also: NET, NET SHUTDOWN, NET TERMINATE

NET STREAM

Purpose: This command gets or sets a logical printer stream on a server so you can enable or disable individual printer streams instead of disabling the server's printer. Logical streams are used to control different types of printing that can be done on one printer (such as draft, letter quality, and envelopes).

Syntax: NET STREAM[/ENABLE /DISABLE] *server_name ((stream-index)* *(stream-value))*

Options:

    server_name The server whose printer stream you want to get or set.

    stream-index Optional stream index number for which you want to set or get stream information.

    stream-value Printer resource name to assign to stream-index.

Switches:

    /ENABLE   Enables the printer stream.

    /DISABLE   Disables the printer stream.

Rules and Considerations: Your user name must be assigned Q privileges on this server to issue commands, such as NET STREAM, that affect the management of the print queues.

Logical streams are numbered and named. The *stream-index* is the number. It is an integer in the range of 0 to 19. The *stream-value* is the name assigned to the stream. *Stream-names* must start with an @ sign. Examples of *stream-names* are @LASER, @DOT, and @LANDSCP.

Examples:

```
NET STREAM/ENABLE \\TECH 0 @LASER
NET STREAM/ENABLE \\TECH 1 @DRAFT
NET STREAM/DISABLE \\TECH 2 @LETTER
NET STREAM/DISABLE \\TECH 3 @ENVELOPE
```

In this example, the server controls two physical printers: a laser printer and a dot-matrix printer. The dot-matrix printer can be used in three different ways: as a draft printer (fast, but with poor print quality), as a letter-quality printer (slow, but with attractive print quality), or as an envelope printer. At the moment, it is set up to handle draft print streams. Printed data intended for letter-quality or envelopes would wait in the queue until the stream that runs that type of printing is enabled.

```
NET STREAM \\KSOFFICE
```

This example lists all the logical streams for server KSOFFICE.

```
NET STREAM \\KSOFFICE 1 @LASER
```

This example creates the logical stream named @LASER in index 1 location on server KSOFFICE.

Notes: When the server boots up, the only entry in the logical streams table is the default @???????.??? entry in the 0 position of the table. If you want to use logical streams in your standard setup, you must load them in your STARTNET.BAT job. To eliminate the risk of a print job starting before the NET STREAM commands in STARTNET.BAT are run, disable DESPOOLING in the LANtastic Network Manager SERVER STARTUP PARAMETERS and then add a NET QUEUE START SERVER_NAME command after the NET STREAM commands in STARTUP.BAT.

If you use logical streams, it is best to turn off DESPOOLING in the LANtastic Network Manager program SERVER STARTUP PARAMETERS and to control printer startup with a NET QUEUE START command.

See Also: NET, NET QUEUE

NET STRING

Purpose: This command assigns a string of characters to a preexisting environment variable that is either typed by the user or extracted from one of LANtastic's (R) special string macros. Type NET HELP MACROS for more information on string macros. If two strings are specified, they are first linked together (concatenated) before any characters are extracted.

Syntax: `NET STRING(/LEFT=n)(/RIGHT=n) variable (string1 (string2))`

Options:

variable	Preexisting environment variable to receive string.
string1	String to assign to environment variable.
string2	Optional second string to concatenate after string1.

Switches:

/LEFT=*n*	Counting from the left, the number of the character to begin extraction.
/RIGHT=*n*	Counting from the left, the number of the character to end extraction.

Rules and Considerations: The variable must previously exist for this command to work. NET STRING cannot create it. If the existing environment variable does not have sufficient space for the result of the NET STRING command, characters are truncated.

LANtastic's special strings are identified by three special prefix characters: ?, ^, and !. The ? and ^ are used in prompts and signify whether the response that is keyed in is to be displayed on-screen. The ! identifies what follows as being a LANtastic special string.

The following is a list of LANtastic's prompts and special strings:

?"prompt"	Prompts for input with echo. Expands to typed input.
^"prompt"	Prompts for input with no echo. Expands to typed input.
!"DATE"	Expands to the current date.
!"DAY"	Expands to the current day of the week.
!"DIRECTORY"	Expands to current disk and directory.
!"ETEXT=n"	Expands to error text associated with error number n.

!"FILE=pathname"	Expands to the first line contained in the file.
!"INSTALLED"	Expands to characters corresponding to installed programs. N=NETBIOS R=REDIR S=SERVER P=LANPUP -=Not installed
!"LOGIN=server"	Expands to TRUE if logged in to server; otherwise it expands to FALSE.
!"NODEID"	Expands to the current 12-digit NETBIOS node number.
!"MACHINEID"	Expands to the machine name.
!"PROGRAM"	Expands to the full path of the NET program.
!"TIME"	Expands to the current time.
!"USER"	Expands to the default autologin user name.
!"USERID=server"	Expands to the current user name on the server. Expands to FALSE if not logged in to the server. Expands to TRUE if logged in to the server, but unable to get account information.

See Also: NET

NET TERMINATE

Purpose: This command terminates (logs out) specified users from a server. You must have the S (System Manager) privilege to use this command. The user may log back in, subject to the restrictions of his account and the NET SLOGINS state for the server.

Syntax: NET TERMINATE *server_name username (machinename) (minutes)*

Options:

server_name	Name of server to log user(s) out from.
username	Name of user(s) to terminate. You can end this in an asterisk (*) to match multiple users.
machinename	Optional name of machine to terminate. You can end this in an asterisk (*) to match multiple machines. Both username and machine-name must match for a user to be terminated. Defaults to * (any machine).

minutes	Number of minutes advance warning to give the user before logging him out. Defaults to 0 (immediately).

Rules and Considerations: You must have S privileges on the specified server to use this command.

You cannot terminate your own login with this command. Use NET LOGOUT instead.

Example:

```
NET TERMINATE \\TECH * * 2
```

The preceding line terminates all logins on server TECH in two minutes.

Issue a NET SLOGINS command to disable new logins before issuing a NET TERMINATE command. This command prevents users from logging back in after you terminate their current session.

See Also: NET, NET LOGIN, NET SLOGINS

NET UNLINK

Purpose: This command is used to disconnect a redirected drive from a boot server. It is used in cases in which a workstation with local floppy drives is booted by using a BOOT ROM chip on the network card. This boot process uses a redirection of the boot floppy drive to a floppy disk image on a server. Once the workstation is active on the network, NET UNLINK can be used to cancel the redirection, thereby allowing use of the physical floppy drives.

Syntax: NET UNLINK

Rules and Considerations: You cannot unlink a drive that you currently are using. You must redirect a drive with the NET USE command and change to that drive before running NET UNLINK.

Example: NET UNLINK

See Also: NET, NET UNUSE

NET UNUSE

Purpose: This command cancels a disk or device redirection.

Syntax: NET UNUSE [D: LPT*n* COM*n*]

Options:

D:	The disk drive designator (A-Z) used to access the redirected shared resource.
LPT*n*	Parallel printer/plotter to cancel redirection for (LPT1, LPT2, or LPT3).
COM*n*	Serial printer/plotter to cancel redirection for (COM1, COM2, COM3, or COM4).

Rules and Considerations: After a resource is unused, it reverts to its state prior to loading the network. Suppose, for example, that a local printer was attached to the first physical parallel printer port on the workstation. Before any network redirection takes place, any print lines sent to LPT1 would print on that local printer. LPT1 might then be redirected to a printer on a network server with the statement NET USE LPT1 \\server_name\@PRINTER. A NET UNUSE LPT1 statement would reestablish the local printer's assignment of print lines going to LPT1.

Examples:

```
NET UNUSE LPT1
NET UNUSE C:
```

See Also: NET, NET USE

NET USE

Purpose: This command redirects a disk or a printer.

Syntax: NET USE(/DEFERRED) *D:* *server_name(\path...)*

NET USE(/DEFERRED) [LPT*n* COM*n*] *server_name*\ @*device*

Options:

D:	The disk drive designator (A-Z) used to access the redirected shared resource.
LPT*n*	Printer device to redirect (LPT1, LPT2, or LPT3).

COM*n*	Printer device to redirect (COM1, COM2, COM3, or COM4).
server_name	Server where the shared disk or printer resource resides.
path	The name of the shared drive resource on the server (such as C-DRIVE or WORDPERF) that you want to use; or, the full network path to the file to which a printer device will be redirected.
@device	The name of the shared printer resource on the server (such as @PRINTER) that you want to use.

Rules and Considerations: There is a special form of NET USE available for redirecting printer output to a file. For example,

```
NET USE LPT1 \\OFFICE\C-DRIVE\BASE\PRINTFIL.TXT
```

redirects any print data to a file named PRINTFIL.TXT in sub-directory \BASE on the C-DRIVE resource of server TECH. For this command to work, the file must already exist.

Examples:

```
NET USE G: \\TECH\C-DRIVE
```

This command redirects drive G on the workstation to the shared resource named C-DRIVE on server TECH.

```
NET USE LPT1 \\TECH\@PRINTER
```

This command redirects the LPT1 printer device to the network printer resource named @PRINTER on server TECH.

```
NET USE LPT2 \\KSOFFICE\WINDOWS\JUNK.TXT
```

This command redirects the LPT2 printer device to a file named JUNK.TXT located on the WINDOWS resource of server KSOFFICE.

Notes: The disk drive designator of a physical drive on the workstation can be used by a network resource. The physical drive is then not available until the disk drive designator is unused. It is not necessary to unuse a physical drive before redirecting its drive letter. When you want the drive letter to revert to its physical drive condition, run NET UNUSE D:, in which D is the letter of the physical drive.

Sometimes drive designations are hard-coded into programs or are established in tables at the time a program is installed on the server's hard disk. If the program was installed on the server's C drive, users at workstations with local C drives may not successfully operate the program from the server because it only runs when C is the current directory. One way around this problem is to execute the program from a batch job that includes a NET USE C: statement at the beginning to redirect the C drive designator to the server's C drive, and a NET UNUSE C: statement at the end of the batch job to reestablish C as the workstation's physical C drive. Make sure that the batch job is not located on the physical C drive. You will not be able to run it past the step that reassigns C to the network resource.

See Also: NET, NET UNUSE, NET ATTACH, NET DETACH

NET USER

Purpose: This command sets the default user name, password, and adapter number to be used for automatic logins to servers.

Syntax: NET USER(/DISABLE) *username (password) (adapter#)*

Options:

username	User name to use for autologins.
password	Password to use for autologins.
adapter#	Optional adapter number to log in through. If not specified, all adapters will be attempted.

Switch:

/DISABLE	Do not set a default user; instead, prevent autologins from being attempted.

Rules and Considerations: To accomplish an autologin to all servers, you must use the same user name and password on each server on the network.

Example:

```
NET USER manager man
```

After issuing this command, NET LOGIN * logs you in to all servers that have manager as a valid user name and man as the password, provided that the maximum allowable logins are not exceeded.

Notes: The default is autologin enabled.

Recording passwords within a batch file can be a security risk because anyone who reads the batch file sees the password. You can use NET USER to enter the user name only, and then require that the password be entered when the login is taking place.

See Also: NET, NET LOGIN, NET ATTACH, NET USE

NET ?

Purpose: This command displays reference information about a command. This command is the same as NET HELP.

Syntax: NET ? *(command)*

Option:

   command   Name of the command that you want information about.

Rules and Considerations: NET ? can be used to display information about NET's 37 commands, its five global switches (/HELP, /?, /MONO, /NOERROR, and SCREEN_SAVER), and three related topics (MACROS, ERRORS and SYNTAX).

Entering NET ? without any command specified displays the complete list of help topics.

Example:

If you need help on the proper syntax for the login command, enter **NET ? ATTACH**.

This command results in the following message:

```
NET ATTACH(/VERBOSE) \\server-name
```

Redirects all available drives to every shared resource on a server. This command is the equivalent of issuing a NET USE command for each of the server's shared resources.

   /VERBOSE Displays drives and their redirections.

   server_name Name of server to which you redirect drives.

Notes: NET ? can be used in place of NET HELP.

See Also: NET HELP

Chapter Snapshot

This chapter covers some of the advanced features of
LANtastic and explains how to get the most out of your
network by combining features of LANtastic with other
hardware and software configurations: a kind of tips
and tricks tutorial. This chapter covers the following
topics:

✔ Optimizing LANtastic for the greatest flexibility
and performance

✔ Using Global Resources to simplify network
administration and use

✔ Accomplishing more with your LANtastic network
by using tips and tricks

✔ Operating your computer remotely from a
different computer in the network or by using a
modem

✔ Connecting LANtastic networks by installing more
than one network adapter card in a computer

✔ Creating a low-cost WAN to connect two LANtastic
networks using standard telephone lines and
modems.

After reading this chapter, you will have a good
understanding of some of the advanced features
available to you, as well as how to use LANtastic with
other hardware and software to maximize the effective-
ness of your LANtastic network.

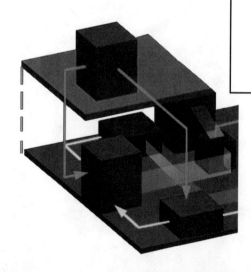

15

CHAPTER

Getting the Most Out of LANtastic

By now you have a good understanding of the way to install LANtastic, set up user accounts, set up shared resources, use LANtastic, and manage your LANtastic network.

LANtastic has features that enable you to accomplish more in less time. Tips and tricks used by network professionals can enable you to get even more flexibility and performance out of your LANtastic network. Optimizing and fine tuning your network lets you successfully equip your network with various software and hardware configurations. You may encounter situations that require you to connect two or more separate LANtastic networks to share a common server, or you may need to connect LANtastic networks located in physically separate locations.

Optimizing LANtastic

Several factors affect network performance and the way other programs operate in a network environment. This section explains the way you can reclaim some of the memory used by LANtastic when it is running and how you can optimize the performance of your LANtastic network.

Saving Conventional Memory by Loading LANtastic High

After you start LANtastic, the network operating system is loaded into your computer's memory along with any other software, such as DOS or a mouse driver. DOS application programs typically use the first 640 KB of memory (referred to as conventional memory). Even if you have 4 MB (4096 KB) of memory on your computer, most programs can only use the memory area between 0 KB and 640 KB.

Conventional memory is the memory from 0 KB to 640 KB. Most DOS applications use this memory. Software drivers and TSRs also are loaded into conventional memory.

The memory area between 640 KB and 1024 KB (1 MB) is reserved for display adapters and other hardware devices, including some network adapter cards. This memory is referred to as *upper memory*.

Memory above 1024 KB (1 MB) is called *extended (XMS) memory*. Most DOS applications cannot use this memory area. Microsoft Windows and disk caching programs, such as SMARTDRIVE and LANCACHE, use extended memory.

After you start your computer, part of the available 640 KB of memory is used by DOS. If you have other devices, such as a mouse, the devices typically load device drivers, which also take up part of the 640 KB of memory. Finally, after you start your network, additional memory is used by LANtastic when the LANtastic software is loaded into memory.

Some application programs require 512 KB or more of available memory to operate. Chances are, if you had 512 KB available before loading your network software, after loading you will not have the 512 KB required to run the program (especially if your computer is configured as a LANtastic server).

A computer with an Artisoft Ethernet adapter configured as a LANtastic workstation typically uses 43 KB of conventional memory. If configured as a LANtastic server, the same computer typically uses an additional 46 KB, for a total of 89 KB.

A computer with an Artisoft 2 Mbps adapter configured as a LANtastic workstation typically uses 20 KB of conventional memory. If the same computer is configured as a LANtastic server, it typically uses an additional 46 KB, for a total of 66 KB.

MS-DOS versions 5.0 and later enables you to load DOS into extended memory if you have an 80286 computer or higher and at least 1 MB of RAM (with 384 KB of it configured as extended memory). Loading DOS into extended memory frees up a good portion of the conventional memory previously occupied by DOS. To load DOS into extended memory, include the following two lines in your CONFIG.SYS file:

    DEVICE=C:\DOS\HIMEM.SYS

    DOS=HIGH

HIMEM.SYS is the device driver that makes your extended memory available to load DOS high (the first 64 KB of extended memory). The DOS=HIGH statement actually specifies to DOS that it is to be loaded into the high memory area.

If you have an 80386 computer or higher, you can load some programs and device drivers into the unused portion of upper memory (640 KB-1024 KB). Programs, such as QEMM 386 and 386 MAX, are expanded memory manager programs (also called upper memory managers), which enable you to load and run some programs and device drivers in your computer's upper memory area. MS-DOS versions 5.0 and later also includes an upper memory manager that enables you to load some programs and device drivers into upper memory (the name of DOS's upper memory manager is EMM386.EXE). To create the capability to load programs and device drivers into the area of upper memory not used by hardware devices, include the following lines in your CONFIG.SYS file:

    DEVICE=C:\DOS\HIMEM.SYS

    DEVICE=C:\DOS\EMM386.EXE NOEMS

If you use an Artisoft 2 Mbps adapter, you must tell EMM386 the address range used by the network adapter so it doesn't try to load other software into that area of upper memory. The default address range used by the 2 Mbps adapter is D800-DFFF. To prevent this address range from being used by EMM386, include the X= switch, as follows:

DEVICE=C:\DOS\EMM386.EXE NOEMS X=D800-DFFF

The Artisoft Ethernet adapters do not use part of upper memory.

If you also load DOS into extended memory, replace the DOS=HIGH statement with DOS=HIGH, UMB. The following statements, if you include them in your CONFIG.SYS file, load DOS into extended memory and make the unused portion of upper memory available to load programs and device drivers:

DEVICE=C:\DOS\HIMEM.SYS

DOS=HIGH,UMB

DEVICE=C:\DOS\EMM386.EXE NOEMS

Now you can load LANtastic and other device drivers into upper memory. To load a program into upper memory, you must type **LH** (Load High) before the command that normally loads the program. If, for example, your AUTOEXEC.BAT file contains the following statement to load your mouse driver:

MOUSE.COM

you can load it high by changing it to the following:

LH MOUSE.COM

The MEM command shows you the amount of used and available memory in your system. Specifying MEM with the /C switch shows you which programs are loaded in memory and whether they use conventional or upper memory.

Loading DOS and LANtastic High

To load DOS into extended memory and LANtastic into upper memory, type **MEM/C** at the DOS prompt to see your current memory configuration (see fig. 15.1).

Typing **MEM/C|MORE** causes the display to pause after each screen.

The following output shows the results of typing **MEM/C** on a computer with MS-DOS 6.0 before DOS or LANtastic is loaded high. Here, DOS and the LANtastic software are loaded into conventional memory, leaving only 443 KB free for use by other applications; an application that requires 512 KB of conventional memory does not have enough available memory.

```
Modules using memory below 1 MB:

    Name        Total       =  Conventional  +  Upper Memory
    ____      _____       _____       _____

    MSDOS     74509   (73K)    74509   (73K)        0   (0K)
    HIMEM      3792    (4K)     3792    (4K)        0   (0K)
    COMMAND    4992    (5K)     4992    (5K)        0   (0K)
    SMARTDRV  26784   (26K)    26784   (26K)        0   (0K)
    NR         3488    (3K)     3488    (3K)        0   (0K)
    AILANBIO  22144   (22K)    22144   (22K)        0   (0K)
    REDIR     18480   (18K)    18480   (18K)        0   (0K)
    SERVER    47168   (46K)    47168   (46K)        0   (0K)
    Free     453824  (443K)   453824  (443K)        0   (0K)

Memory Summary:

Type of Memory      Total      =     Used      +     Free
_____         _____       _____       _____

Conventional      655360  (640K)    201536  (197K)    453824  (443K)
Upper                  0    (0K)         0    (0K)         0    (0K)
Adapter RAM/ROM    65536   (64K)     65536   (64K)         0    (0K)
Extended (XMS)   1376256 (1344K)   1114112 (1088K)    262144  (256K)
_____         _____       _____       _____

Total memory     2097152 (2048K)   1381184 (1349K)    715968  (699K)

Total under 1 MB  655360  (640K)    201536  (197K)    453824  (443K)

Largest executable program size       453520  (443K)
Largest free upper memory block            0    (0K)
The high memory area is available.
```

Now change your CONFIG.SYS file to load DOS high and make upper memory available for loading programs by adding the following to the beginning of your CONFIG.SYS file in MS-DOS Editor:

DEVICE=C:\DOS\HIMEM.SYS

DOS=HIGH,UMB

DEVICE=C:\DOS\EMM386.EXE NOEMS

You can invoke the MS-DOS Editor by typing **EDIT** at the DOS prompt, followed by the file name you want to edit. To edit CONFIG.SYS, type **EDIT C:\CONFIG.SYS**.

After the changes are made, save them and reboot your computer so that the changes take effect. Type **MEM/C** again, and a slightly different memory configuration appears:

```
Modules using memory below 1 MB:

    Name          Total     =    Conventional   +    Upper Memory
    ————      ————————        ————————           ————————
    MSDOS        21405    (21K)     21405    (21K)         0     (0K)
    HIMEM         1168     (1K)      1168     (1K)         0     (0K)
    EMM386        3120     (3K)      3120     (3K)         0     (0K)
    COMMAND       2912     (3K)      2912     (3K)         0     (0K)
    NR            3488     (3K)      3488     (3K)         0     (0K)
    AILANBIO     22144    (22K)     22144    (22K)         0     (0K)
    REDIR        18480    (18K)     18480    (18K)         0     (0K)
    SERVER       47168    (46K)     47168    (46K)         0     (0K)
    SMARTDRV     26704    (26K)         0     (0K)     26704    (26K)
    Free        667408   (652K)    535296   (523K)    132112   (129K)
```

```
Memory Summary:

Type of Memory        Total      =      Used      +      Free
_____   _____        _____        _____

Conventional        655360  (640K)    120064  (117K)    535296  (523K)
Upper               158816  (155K)     26704   (26K)    132112  (129K)
Adapter RAM/ROM      65536   (64K)     65536   (64K)         0    (0K)
Extended (XMS)     1217440 (1189K)   1213344 (1185K)      4096    (4K)
                   _____        _____        _____

Total memory       2097152 (2048K)   1425648 (1392K)    671504  (656K)

Total under 1 MB    814176  (795K)    146768  (143K)    667408  (652K)

Largest executable program size       535088  (523K)
Largest free upper memory block       132064  (129K)
MS-DOS is resident in the high memory area.
```

Now most of DOS is loaded into high memory and uses only 21 KB of conventional memory. Note that the disk cache program SMARTDRIVE has automatically loaded itself into upper memory now that it is available. This simple change increases available conventional memory from 443 KB to 523 KB—an improvement of 80 KB!

You haven't loaded the LANtastic software high, so it still is using conventional memory. Figure 15.1 shows the relevant part of the STARTNET.BAT file before you specify any programs to be loaded high. Use the MS-DOS Editor to reconfigure STARTNET.BAT to load NR, AILANBIO, REDIR, and SERVER high by using the LH command before every statement (see fig. 15.2).

You might not have enough available upper memory to load all the LANtastic programs high for your specific configuration. Some of the LANtastic programs also require more upper memory when loading than they use once loaded, so you may not be able to load some of the programs into upper memory that seem like they should fit. Experiment by loading different combinations of programs into upper memory until you find the combination that frees up the most conventional memory.

Figure 15.1
The STARTNET.BAT file before loading LANtastic high.

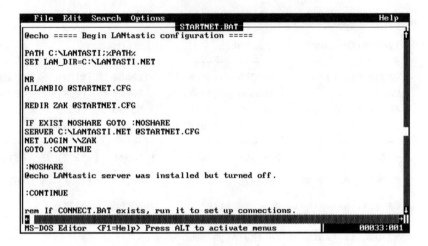

```
 File  Edit  Search  Options                                    Help
                        STARTNET.BAT
@echo ===== Begin LANtastic configuration =====

PATH C:\LANTASTI;%PATH%
SET LAN_DIR=C:\LANTASTI.NET

NR
AILANBIO @STARTNET.CFG

REDIR ZAK @STARTNET.CFG

IF EXIST NOSHARE GOTO :NOSHARE
SERVER C:\LANTASTI.NET @STARTNET.CFG
NET LOGIN \\ZAK
GOTO :CONTINUE

:NOSHARE
@echo LANtastic server was installed but turned off.

:CONTINUE

rem If CONNECT.BAT exists, run it to set up connections.

MS-DOS Editor  <F1=Help> Press ALT to activate menus     00033:001
```

Figure 15.2
The STARTNET.BAT file after loading LANtastic high.

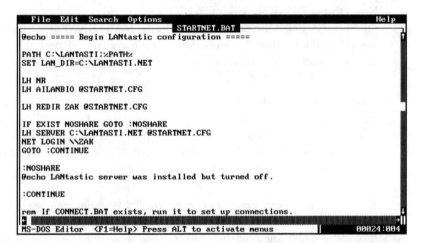

```
 File  Edit  Search  Options                                    Help
                        STARTNET.BAT
@echo ===== Begin LANtastic configuration =====

PATH C:\LANTASTI;%PATH%
SET LAN_DIR=C:\LANTASTI.NET

LH NR
LH AILANBIO @STARTNET.CFG

LH REDIR ZAK @STARTNET.CFG

IF EXIST NOSHARE GOTO :NOSHARE
LH SERVER C:\LANTASTI.NET @STARTNET.CFG
NET LOGIN \\ZAK
GOTO :CONTINUE

:NOSHARE
@echo LANtastic server was installed but turned off.

:CONTINUE

rem If CONNECT.BAT exists, run it to set up connections.

MS-DOS Editor  <F1=Help> Press ALT to activate menus     00024:004
```

After modifying the STARTNET.BAT file and saving the changes, reboot your computer for the changes to take effect. Typing **MEM/C** now shows you the results of loading LANtastic high. Available conventional memory increases to 612 KB—an additional 89 KB! The combination of loading DOS and LANtastic high has yielded a net increase of 169 KB of available conventional memory.

```
Modules using memory below 1 MB:

    Name        Total       =   Conventional    +   Upper Memory
    ____      _____        _____          _____

    MSDOS       21405  (21K)      21405  (21K)             0   (0K)
    HIMEM        1168   (1K)       1168   (1K)             0   (0K)
    EMM386       3120   (3K)       3120   (3K)             0   (0K)
    COMMAND      2912   (3K)       2912   (3K)             0   (0K)
    SMARTDRV    26704  (26K)          0   (0K)         26704  (26K)
    NR           3488   (3K)          0   (0K)          3488   (3K)
    AILANBIO    22144  (22K)          0   (0K)         22144  (22K)
    REDIR       18480  (18K)          0   (0K)         18480  (18K)
    SERVER      47168  (46K)          0   (0K)         47168  (46K)
    Free       667408 (652K)     626576 (612K)         40832  (40K)
```

```
Memory Summary:

Type of Memory      Total       =      Used       +      Free
_____      _____        _____         _____

Conventional        655360  (640K)     28784   (28K)     626576  (612K)
Upper               158816  (155K)    117984  (115K)      40832   (40K)
Adapter RAM/ROM      65536   (64K)     65536   (64K)          0    (0K)
Extended (XMS)     1217440 (1189K)   1213344 (1185K)       4096    (4K)
                  _____        _____         _____

Total memory      2097152 (2048K)   1425648 (1392K)     671504  (656K)

Total under 1 MB   814176  (795K)    146768  (143K)     667408  (652K)

Largest executable program size         626480  (612K)
Largest free upper memory block          40592   (40K)
MS-DOS is resident in the high memory area.
```

ALONE

A *dedicated server* is one that is not used as a workstation; its only purpose is to process and service network requests. If you run your server as a dedicated server, you can significantly increase its performance by running the ALONE program on the server. This program temporarily disables the local computer capabilities of the unit so it can handle only network tasks, resulting in higher network performance.

Do NOT run the disk caching program SMARTDRIVE if you are running ALONE. SMARTDRIVE will cause your dedicated server to lock up. Use LANcache instead.

To run ALONE, perform the following steps:

1. Run your network software, including the SERVER program.

Do not try to run ALONE with any TSR programs, including LANPUP. ALONE ignores these programs and does not process their local requests.

2. At the DOS prompt, type **ALONE** and press Enter.

   ALONE runs and displays a status screen on the server that includes the following information for every user logged in:

   ✔ **ID#.** The session number of each user logged in to the server.

   ✔ **Username.** The account name of the user logged in to the server.

   ✔ **Machine.** The name of the computer from which the user is logged in.

   ✔ **Command.** The last command entered.

   ✔ **IOBytes.** The amount of data the server has processed for the user.

   ✔ **Requests.** The number of requests performed since the user logged in.

   ✔ **Privs.** The account privileges the user has (AQUMSODL).

Pressing the F2 key will display a second line for each entry showing the path of the file most recently accessed.

If you always run a computer as a dedicated server, edit the STARTNET.BAT file to include ALONE after the SERVER command. If you include STARTNET.BAT in your AUTOEXEC.BAT file, the network automatically runs; the ALONE program is implemented when you turn on your computer.

Selecting an entry on-screen and pressing Enter displays the Detailed User Information screen. This screen displays the file-access (Read-only, Write-only, or Read/Write) and file-sharing modes (Compatibility, Deny-Read, Deny-Write, and Deny-None). The current position of the file, the size of the file, and the position of a record lock in the file also are displayed.

> You can prevent users from exiting the ALONE program by password-protecting it. Password-protecting the ALONE program prevents users from using the computer in the local mode. Press F3 while the ALONE program is running to enable or disable the password-protection feature.

Performance Considerations

Usually, the default setups LANtastic installs provide acceptable performance for average-size networks (up to five nodes without highly intensive data transfer requirements). As your network grows in data file usage (as in heavy database application use) and physical size, you might need to reconfigure to maintain an acceptable level of performance.

A number of factors contribute to how well your network performs. Some factors you cannot control; others you can. The following is a short list of the major elements that individually, and in combination, affect network performance:

- ✔ The CPU type (8088, 8086, 80286, 80386, 80486, Pentium)
- ✔ The clock speed of the CPU (10 MHz, 20 MHz, 33 MHz, 66 MHz)
- ✔ The access speed of your hard disk (8 ms, 16 ms, 64 ms)
- ✔ The hard disk interleave setting (1:1, 2:1, 3:1)
- ✔ The amount of RAM installed (512 KB, 640 KB, 1 MB, 2 MB, 4 MB, 8 MB) and available for disk-caching, resource-caching, and random-access caching
- ✔ The configuration of your DOS software
- ✔ The configuration of your LANtastic software
- ✔ The speed of your network interface cards (2 Mbps or 10 Mbps)
- ✔ The configuration of your network drivers

The factors you actually control depend on where you are in the acquisition process. If you are beginning from scratch—buying your computer equipment at the same time you are buying your LANtastic network—you can control all of these factors. If you buy the better performance factors in the hardware, your overall network performance is better.

Unfortunately, most users are stuck with the computers they already have. If this is your situation, the first four factors are out of your control. You can improve your network performance, however, by modifying the remaining factors on the preceding list. This section discusses the factors that are more easily adjusted. Surprisingly, the same factors also net significant performance improvements when modified.

Establishing a Baseline

Before you begin to optimize your network's performance, you must establish a baseline from which to adjust. If you do not establish a baseline, you'll spend a lot of time in trial and error attempting to get a "perceived" performance improvement. Unless you have a measure against which you can test improvements, you cannot tell if your efforts are effective.

The easiest and fastest way to establish a baseline is to pick the most data-intensive program you have, run this program through some file manipulations, and clock the time it takes to complete the task. Try to choose operations that are typical for your network.

Optimizing your network for one particular type of activity or program can slow down the network performance of more important programs on your network. Make sure that the programs and tests you perform reflect typical network activity for your situation.

Be sure to choose a series of tests that take long enough to perform so you can determine any performance improvements made. Record the specific file manipulations that you perform and the time it takes to complete the task. Put this information in a binder or folder with your other network information.

When you run your tests, be sure to run them on the server that is being accessed, and from a different computer that accesses the server across the network. This enables you to measure the effect of modifying the server's configuration as it relates to the server and the workstations accessing it.

Optimizing the Network

What should you change first? The more RAM you can dedicate to network-related operations, the better.

Unless your computer is used as a dedicated server, carefully monitor the amount of memory you allocate to network-related activity. Increasing network tasks and buffer sizes, for example, takes away from the conventional memory available to other applications on your computer. If you're not careful, you can get stuck with a super-performing network server that can't run any applications locally.

Implementing a disk-caching program, such as LANCACHE or SMARTDRIVE, is a change that probably nets the most dramatic increase in network performance. A disk-caching program uses extended memory; generally, the more you can allocate to the cache, the better.

Disk-caching programs use RAM to temporarily hold information being transferred to and from the computer's hard drive. By using a disk-caching program, every time the hard drive is read, the information also is read into the cache (an area in your RAM). The next time information is needed from the hard drive, the disk-caching program checks whether it's in the cache; if it is, it reads it from the cache, rather than from the hard disk. Reading information from RAM (the cache) is much faster than reading from the hard disk—a disk-caching program contains algorithms to maximize the efficiency of transferring data.

A disk-caching program helps the performance of the hard drives on the computer on which the disk cache is loaded. If you have a disk cache on your computer, but the computer you access does not have a disk cache, you won't see any improvement. If, however, you access your own hard drive or another user on the network accesses your hard drive, both you and the other user see an increase in hard drive performance.

DOS buffers work in conjunction with disk caching. Because disk caching controls the management of disk buffering, you must reduce the number of buffers assigned in DOS to eliminate duplication of effort. Artisoft recommends a DOS buffers setting of 8 for the best performance with a disk-caching program. Change the BUFFERS= line in your CONFIG.SYS file to BUFFERS=8.

The LANtastic installation program will set your buffers statement to BUFFERS=30. This value is fine if you don't use a disk cache program such as LANCACHE or SMARTDRIVE.

Place the DOS FASTOPEN command in your server's AUTOEXEC.BAT to improve performance. DOS FASTOPEN stores information about files that have been opened and closed. If your applications try to reopen a file, DOS locates it immediately and avoids the normal disk scan required. The time required to open and use files is therefore reduced.

If you have DOS 4.0 or higher, you can place the FASTOPEN function in expanded memory to conserve conventional memory (below 640 KB) for application use.

Next, adjust the startup parameters for your server(s). Use the LANtastic Network Manager program to make changes to the performance parameters in the server startup parameters. Figure 15.3 shows the performance parameters section of the server startup parameters in the DOS LANtastic Network Manager (NET_MGR) program. Figure 15.4 shows the LANtastic Server Configuration Performance Parameters Module section of the Windows LANtastic Network Manager program.

Several predefined server configurations exist; they may be used as a starting point for your own optimization tasks. These configurations are selected from the server section in the LANtastic Network Manager program. Chapter 11, "Managing Your Network Using the LANtastic Network Manager" includes detailed instructions for accessing a predefined server configuration.

LANtastic's Installation program sets the server's Network Buffer to 4 KB. This setting is fine for most networks—up to five machines—that do not perform many data-intensive activities. If your server hosts a database application that is used regularly, consider doubling (or even tripling) the Network Buffer size.

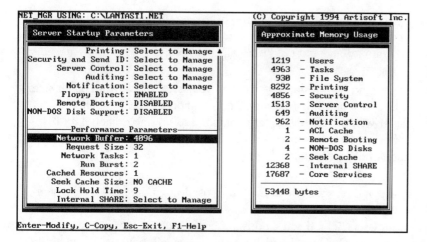

Figure 15.3
The DOS LANtastic Network Manager Server Startup Parameters dialog box.

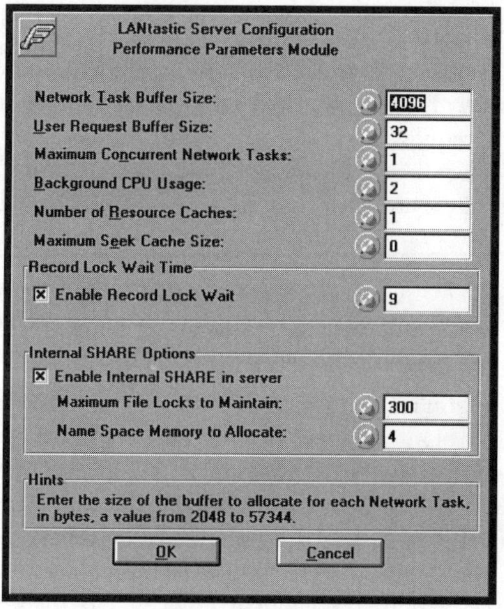

Figure 15.4
The Windows LANtastic Network Manager Server Configuration Performance Parameters Module dialog box.

Another way to improve network performance is to adjust the number of Network Tasks permitted in the server startup parameters. If you increase the number of tasks, LANtastic can service multiple-user requests more efficiently. Each network task requires additional memory to serve as its data buffer. You don't want to add too many because they decrease the conventional memory available to run your application programs. If your server is constantly subjected to simultaneous user requests, increase the number of tasks to two or three. The incremental improvement produced with the addition of each network task becomes smaller and smaller. Setting more than eight tasks is usually not helpful.

Depending on how large you set up your server's Network Buffer size to be, each network task sets up an additional matching buffer. A server with a 4 KB buffer, for example, sets up an additional 4 KB buffer per task. If you have a 16 KB buffer, each task sets up an additional 16 KB buffer.

The Request Size option is the size of the buffer used when the network is "listening" for user requests. One Request Size buffer is allocated for each user specified in the Maximum Users field. If you set this buffer to 50 or more, you improve performance for operations such as file lookups, and small requests to write to the disk. Setting a value of 500 or more enables the buffer to handle user read and write requests.

The Run Burst setting (the Background CPU Usage field in Windows) is the number of ticks (1/18 second) the server dedicates to processing network requests before it processes a local request. Increasing this value improves network response performance, but slows down the performance of local tasks. Normally, keep this setting around 2 for a locally used server, but increase it to 255 for a dedicated server.

Increasing the Seek Cache Size allows the server to find random positions in files faster when it performs data-intensive operations, such as using a database application. If you use a large database, a 64 KB Seek Cache Size is the most useful.

The Cached Resources option is the number of resources cached in memory. This function stores access control information for each network resource in the server's memory. The server reads the access-control information from RAM, and approves or denies access to a requester much faster than it can by performing a standard disk-retrieve operation. Enable this function by entering the number of resources to be cached. Setting this number to the maximum number of server drive and printer resources that are used concurrently enables the server to respond more quickly to directory lookups and file opens—access information is read from memory rather than from the server's drive.

The Lock Hold Time setting in the server startup parameters specifies the amount of time a server holds a lock request for a record when the record is already locked by another user. Normally, the default value of 9 is fine. If, however, you have several simultaneous database users, you may want to increase this setting. Try experimenting to find the optimum value.

Several options are available to improve printing performance. Figure 15.5 shows
the Printing Configuration section of the server startup parameters in the DOS
LANtastic Network Manager (NET_MGR) program. Figure 15.6 shows the
LANtastic Server Configuration Printing Parameters Module section of the
Windows LANtastic Network Manager program.

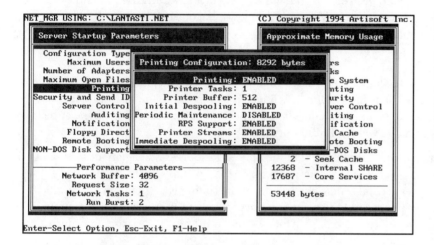

Figure 15.5
The DOS
LANtastic
Network
Manager Server
Startup
Parameters
Printing
Configuration.

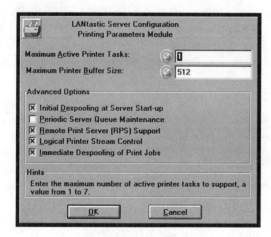

Figure 15.6
The Windows
LANtastic
Network
Manager Server
Configuration
Printing
Parameters
Module.

The Printer Buffer setting in the server startup parameters specifies the size of the
print buffer. Increasing the size of the buffer reduces the number of disk accesses
required to spool data to the printer.

If you have more than one printer, increasing the number of Printer Tasks in the server startup parameters enables the server to simultaneously despool to more than one printer.

Setting this value higher than 1 may actually decrease printing performance in Microsoft Windows, because of the way Windows interacts with other programs.

The Immediate Despooling feature enables you to specify that a print job begin despooling to the printer before it is finished being sent to the LANtastic spooler. This results in less time between when the print job is first started from the application program and when it finishes printing.

The Characters per Second field in the Shared Resources Management section of the LANtastic Network Manager program enables you to specify the minimum characters per second sent to the printer. If the setting is higher than the number of characters per second the printer can accept, the printer is sent the maximum it can accept. If you run Microsoft Windows on a print server, increase this value to 9,600.

You also can reconfigure your redirector (workstation). The REDIR.EXE controls workstation parameters the same way the LANtastic Network Manager program controls the server's performance parameters. Like the server parameters, the more efficient you make the redirector configuration, the better the network performs.

If you increase the data-buffer size in the redirector program, the workstation handles whole file and printer operations more efficiently. If your workstation is not used to process printer output or perform large file-copying tasks (as in file/disk backup operations), then you probably don't need to change this parameter. Increasing the number of buffers improves programs that sequentially read and write small blocks of information at a time.

The command to modify a REDIR parameter looks like the following:

REDIR machine-name /SIZE=*nnnn* /BUFFERS=*n*

The default SIZE is 1024 and the default BUFFERS is 1.

If you still need better performance from your server, you can try to dedicate a computer as your network server. A computer is more efficient if it does not share its time by handling both local and network tasks. If you use a computer as a dedicated server, run the ALONE program to improve network efficiency even more. The trade-off is that you lose the capability to use the machine in its local mode unless you exit the ALONE program.

Hopefully, one or more of these ideas can significantly improve your network performance. Other tricks are possible, but not as easy to implement. If you need more technical optimization, dial in to the Artisoft BBS and read the various technical notes that users and technicians post for others.

Understanding Global Resources

A *global resource* is a resource created on a server that points to another resource on a different server. For example, normally you create a printer resource called @PRINTER, which you define as the printer connected to your LPT1: printer port. If you create a global printer resource, you can create a printer resource with a name such as @KSPRNTR, defined as the @LASER printer resource on the server named KSOFFICE. The following is an example that illustrates the difference between a local printer resource and a global printer resource:

> @PRINTER => LPT1: (@PRINTER points to LPT1: port)

> @KSPRNTR => \\KSOFFICE\@LASER (@KSPRNTR points to @LASER resource on server KSOFFICE)

You can create global resources for both drive/directory resources and printer resources. Global resources enable users to log in to a single server and use the resources on multiple servers. To users, it seems like all the resources exist on the computer to which they are logged in. When a connection to a global resource is made, LANtastic sets up a direct link between the user and the resource to which the global resource points. This way, using global resources does not adversely affect performance.

Creating a Global Resource in DOS

To create a global resource, select Shared Resources Management from the LANtastic Network Manager (NET_MGR) program main menu (see fig. 15.7). From the resource list screen, press Ins and type the name of the global resource to be added. For this example, type **BIG-C** as the resource name and press Enter (see fig. 15.8). Type the path, which in this case consists of the server and resource to which this global resource points, and press Enter. For this example, type **\\OFFICE\C-DRIVE** (see fig. 15.9). Press Enter and the global resource is created (see fig. 15.10).

Figure 15.7
The LANtastic
Network
Manager,
NET_MGR
main menu.

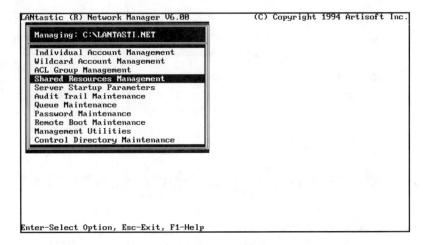

Figure 15.8
Entering a
global resource
name.

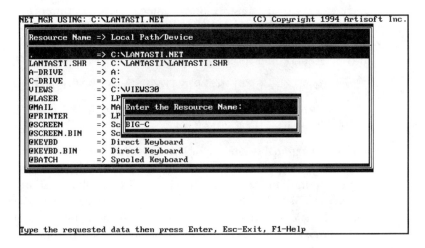

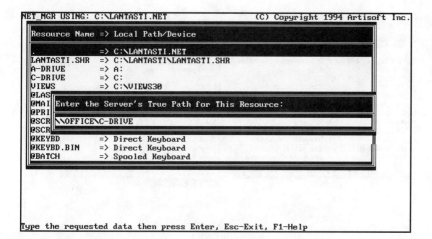

Figure 15.9
Entering the path for the global resource.

```
NET_MGR USING: C:\LANTASTI.NET              (C) Copyright 1994 Artisoft Inc.
┌──────────────────────────────────────────────────────────────────────────┐
│ Resource Name => Local Path/Device                                         │
│ ┌────────────────────────────────────────────────────────────────────────┤
│ .               => C:\LANTASTI.NET                                         │
│ LANTASTI.SHR    => C:\LANTASTI\LANTASTI.SHR                                │
│ A-DRIVE         => A:                                                      │
│ C-DRIVE         => C:                                                      │
│ VIEWS           => C:\VIEWS30                                              │
│ @LAS┌──────────────────────────────────────────────────────────┐          │
│ @MAI│ Enter the Server's True Path for This Resource:          │          │
│ @PRI│                                                          │          │
│ @SCR│ \\OFFICE\C-DRIVE                                         │          │
│ @SCR└──────────────────────────────────────────────────────────┘          │
│ @KEYBD          => Direct Keyboard                                         │
│ @KEYBD.BIN      => Direct Keyboard                                         │
│ @BATCH          => Spooled Keyboard                                        │
│                                                                            │
└────────────────────────────────────────────────────────────────────────────┘
Type the requested data then press Enter, Esc-Exit, F1-Help
```

Figure 15.10
The Shared Resources screen with the global resource BIG-C added.

```
NET_MGR USING: C:\LANTASTI.NET              (C) Copyright 1994 Artisoft Inc.
┌──────────────────────────────────────────────────────────────────────────┐
│ Resource Name => Local Path/Device                                         │
│ ┌────────────────────────────────────────────────────────────────────────┤
│ .               => C:\LANTASTI.NET                                         │
│ LANTASTI.SHR    => C:\LANTASTI\LANTASTI.SHR                                │
│ A-DRIVE         => A:                                                      │
│ C-DRIVE         => C:                                                      │
│ VIEWS           => C:\VIEWS30                                              │
│ @LASER          => LPT1                                                    │
│ @MAIL           => MAIL                                                    │
│ @PRINTER        => LPT1                                                    │
│ @SCREEN         => Screen                                                  │
│ @SCREEN.BIN     => Screen                                                  │
│ @KEYBD          => Direct Keyboard                                         │
│ @KEYBD.BIN      => Direct Keyboard                                         │
│ @BATCH          => Spooled Keyboard                                        │
│ BIG-C           => \\OFFICE\C-DRIVE                                        │
└────────────────────────────────────────────────────────────────────────────┘
Enter-Modify, Ins-Add, Del-Delete, C-Copy, Esc-Exit, F1-Help
```

Creating a global printer resource is almost identical to creating a global shared-drive resource. When you create a global printer resource, specify Global as the Output Device (see fig. 15.11) instead of an actual device name (such as LPT1). When prompted, enter the path to the global resource (such as \\OFFICE\@PRINTER).

Figure 15.11
Specifying a
global printer
resource.

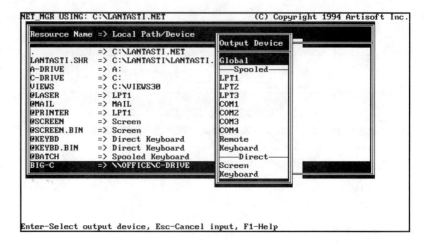

To restrict access to the global resource, highlight the resource and press Enter.
The Detailed Information screen for the global resource appears (see fig. 15.12).
From this screen, specify a description of the global resource, change the path, and
specify your ACL list.

Figure 15.12
The Detailed
Information
screen for a
global resource.

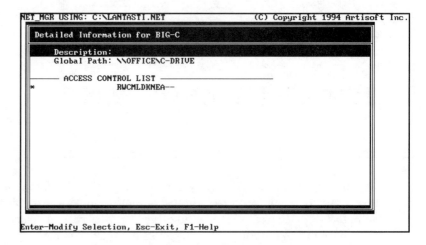

Creating a Global Resource in Windows

To create a global resource in Windows, select the **R**esources icon from the
LANtastic Network Manager program or select **R**esources from the **M**anage menu

(see fig. 15.13). Select **A**dd from the **E**dit menu when the Resources dialog box appears. The Add Resource dialog box appears (see fig. 15.14). Select the Global Resource option and the Local Path field changes to a Server and a Resource field (see fig. 15.15). For this example, enter BIG-C as the resource name. The BIG-C resource will point to the C-DRIVE on server OFFICE; type **OFFICE** in the Server field, and **C-DRIVE** in the Resource field. Select OK—the Global resource is created and appears on the Resources list (see fig. 15.16).

Figure 15.13
The LANtastic Network Manager, NET_MGR main menu.

Figure 15.14
The Add Resource dialog box.

Figure 15.15
Entering a global
drive resource.

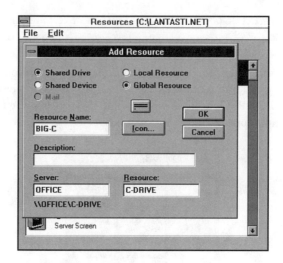

Figure 15.16
The Resources
dialog box
showing the
global resource
BIG-C.

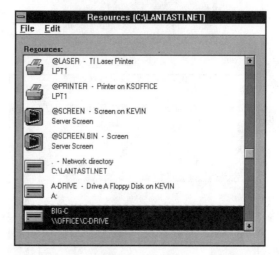

Creating a global printer resource is almost identical to creating a global shared-drive resource. At the Add Resource dialog box, select the Shared Device option instead of the default Shared Drive option, with the Global Resource option selected (see fig. 15.17). Enter the name of the Global printer resource in the Resource Name field. Enter the name of the server and the resource that the global resource points to in the Server and Resource fields.

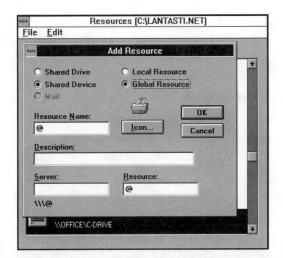

Figure 15.17
Specifying a global printer resource.

LANtastic Tips and Tricks

LANtastic includes many features that simplify the use of your existing hardware and software in a network environment. Each program you run on your computer is different, and the requirements for the application when operating with LANtastic determine what adjustments may need to be made to the system.

This section discusses some of the tips and tricks you can use to enable your software applications and LANtastic to coexist and work to meet your requirements.

Redirecting Drive C

Typically, when you install a software application, you specify the drive on which to install it. Ordinarily you specify drive C because that is the designation for the physical hard drive. If you run the program, specify drive C, and everything should work fine.

Suppose that you want to run the program over the network, and that the program and data exist on the LANtastic server named ZAK. If you want to access the program from another computer, you need to choose a drive letter to redirect, so that when you use that letter, you are actually accessing the physical drive C on server ZAK. You might redirect your E drive to point to \\ZAK\C-DRIVE. Because your E drive points to the C-DRIVE resource on server ZAK, when you access drive E, you are actually accessing the physical drive C on server ZAK.

Next, you change to drive E and proceed to run the program. This approach normally works fine because most applications look for program information and data on the current drive (E in this example). Some applications don't work if you access them over the network—they look for their program and data on drive C.

Following are two common reasons a program may look to drive C for its program and data:

✔ When the program is installed, drive C is identified as the drive to which you install the program; the program records this information to use when accessing information later.

✔ The application is written with drive C "hard coded" into the program; it can't be changed.

Many programs enable you to change the location where the program looks for data. This is usually changed in the configuration section of the program. If your program is like this, you can change the location of the data files from drive C to another drive (E in this example). If you access the program from more than one computer, after you change the configuration information to a different drive letter, make sure everyone redirects the same drive letter when accessing this particular program. Otherwise, every time the program is run, the users have to reconfigure to reflect the drive letter they choose to redirect to access this program. If the program exists on your computer, but the configuration has been changed to look for the data on a different drive letter (such as E), you need to redirect drive E to point to the C-DRIVE resource on your own computer. You also can use the E-drive letter to access your C drive by using the DOS SUBST command, shown as follows:

SUBST E: C:\

The preceding command substitutes drive C for drive E. Whenever an attempt is made to access drive E, that request is directed to drive C.

Sometimes you can't change the configuration of the program to use a different drive letter. If the program you are using requires you to use drive C to access the program and its data, and you want to access the program over the network , you have to redirect your drive C to point to the C drive on the computer you are trying to access. LANtastic makes this easy enough; just redirect your C drive like any other drive. The problem is that when you redirect your C drive to another drive/directory resource on the network, you no longer have access to the physical C drive on your computer. The following are items to consider if you redirect your C drive:

1. If you run a batch file from your C drive to run the program, as soon as you redirect drive C, the batch file no longer exists on C (because drive C is redirected to another computer's shared drive/directory).

    The solution is to redirect another drive letter to your physical C drive or use the DOS SUBST command to do the same before you redirect your C drive. If you run the batch file, run it from the redirected (or substituted) drive letter.

2. If your PATH statement includes references to the programs and directories on your C drive, and you need access to any of those programs, redirect another drive to your C drive and then change the PATH statement to include the redirected drive. Don't forget that the DOS and LANTASTI directories are on your physical C drive (the hard drive installed in your computer). You need access to the LANTASTI directory to USE and UNUSE any network C-drive connections. If you don't have access to the LANTASTI directory for the NET command, you can't remove the network redirection of your C drive and access your physical C drive without rebooting your computer.

Making Program Files Read-Only

Often, if more than one user tries to access and run the same program simultaneously, DOS registers a Sharing Violation error. Sometimes this even happens when running the network version of the application program. To eliminate this problem, set the DOS attribute for the program files to read-only by using the DOS ATTRIB command. To make a file read-only, use the following form of the ATTRIB command:

> ATTRIB +R *filename*

in which *filename* is the name of the files you want to make read-only, including wildcards. If you want to delete or overwrite those files later, first remove the read-only attribute with the -R switch on the command, as shown in the following:

> ATTRIB -R *filename*

If your program needs to write information to a file, make sure that you don't make that file read-only. The program can't write required information to read-only files, and might not be able to continue because it encounters an error when trying to write a file.

Making a program read-only enables multiple users to access the program at the same time, even if the program is not the network version. Generally, more than one user should not try to access the same data at the same time unless the system has a network version of the program. A sharing violation usually occurs if more than one person tries to access the same data.

Backing Up Your Computer

LANtastic can make the process of backing up the hard drive easier and more enjoyable. Without a network, you typically have two ways to back up your hard drive: floppy disks or, if you're lucky, a backup tape drive. If you use the LANtastic network, you can back up to a different computer's hard drive or use a single tape drive on one computer to back up all the other computers in the network.

Backing Up to a Different Drive

One of the most beneficial aspects of having a network is the capability to access disk drives on other computers. If you have available space on a hard drive on one of your network computers, you can use that space to back up valuable data from your hard drive. Suppose, for example, that you want to back up the data in your \DBASE\DATA directory to the \KSBACKUP directory, which is located on the C drive of server KATIE. Assuming the resource name of the C drive on KATIE is C-DRIVE and you don't need to specify a user name or password to access the C-DRIVE resource, the following DOS batch file named BACK.BAT performs your backup:

> NET USE K: \\KATIE\C-DRIVE
>
> XCOPY C:\DBASE\DATA*.* K:\KSBACKUP*.* /S
>
> NET UNUSE K:

This DOS batch file is executed when you type **BACK** from the DOS prompt. It redirects drive K to use the C-DRIVE resource on server KATIE. By using the XCOPY command, all data in your C:\DBASE\DATA directory is copied to the \KSBACKUP directory on the redirected drive K (which actually points to drive C on server KATIE). The /S option on the XCOPY command also copies the information in any subdirectories that exist under \DBASE\DATA.

By using this simple batch file, all you have to do to back up your data is type **BACK**.

The same principle applies to initiating larger scale backups of other valuable data on your network. You can incorporate a file compression program into the batch file so data also is compressed while it is backed up. This way, the storage requirements on the backup drive are minimized.

Backing Up to a Tape Drive

LANtastic enables you to use a tape backup on one computer to back up other computers on the network. Because tape backup drives are not assigned a drive letter as disk drives are, the tape drive cannot be a shared resource. When you perform a tape backup, you must perform the back up at the computer that has the tape backup drive installed. To back up another computer, you first redirect a drive on the computer with the tape backup to point to the drive on the server you want to back up. Then you perform the tape backup just like you back up a physical drive, but instead of specifying drive C, you specify the drive you redirected, such as K.

Remote Operations

A *remote operation* or function is the process of controlling a computer at which you are not physically sitting from a *remote computer* (a computer located somewhere else). This is valuable in many situations, such as executing programs on another computer or assisting users with problems on their computers while you are at a remote computer.

The NET RUN command enables you to send commands to servers on the network. LANtastic permits you to view another server's screen and to control its keyboard. Other third-party programs enable you to access and control a computer on the network remotely across a phone line by using a modem.

Using NET RUN

NET RUN enables you to send a command to a remote server on the network. NET RUN sends the commands to the remote server as if you sat down at its keyboard and typed the commands. To issue a NET RUN command, you must be logged in to the server to which you issue the command and have the S (System Manager) privilege. The syntax of the NET RUN command is as follows:

NET RUN(/NOCR) *server* "*command*"

Server is the name of the server to which you want to send the command and "*command*" is the command to be typed at the server's keyboard. If you specify NOCR, a carriage return is not sent at the end of the command.

NET RUN is useful for many tasks that need to run remotely, such as a batch file that performs a tape backup on all your network computers.

Before issuing a NET RUN command, make sure someone else isn't using the server to which you want to issue the command. If someone is, the command might interfere with their work and probably won't perform the action you intend. Suppose, for example, that you send a NET RUN command called BACK which, when executed at the DOS prompt, backs up your computer to the tape drive. If a user is using that server for word processing when you issue the NET RUN command, the word BACK is typed in the document on which the user is working.

Controlling Another Computer

LANtastic includes a feature that enables you to control a server's screen and keyboard from a remote computer on the network. This feature only works if the server you want to control is operating in text mode and is not running a graphics application.

To issue keyboard commands on a server remotely, you must have write access to the server's keyboard resource. To view the screen on a server remotely, you must have read access to the server's screen resource. These ACLs are changed in the LANtastic Network Manager program the same way as other shared resources.

Controlling Another Computer from DOS

To control a remote server, run NET and select Monitor & Manage Server Activity from the main menu (see fig. 15.18). Next, select the server you want to control from the list of servers (see fig. 15.19). If you are not logged in to the server, you can log in now. For this example, choose server OFFICE.

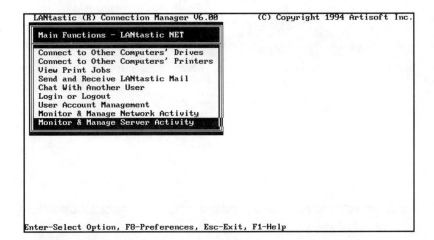

Figure 15.18
Selecting Monitor & Manage Server Activity from NET.

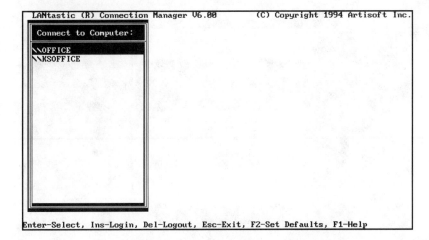

Figure 15.19
Selecting the server to control from the Server Connections list.

The activity screen for the server you choose appears (see fig. 15.20). To control the server press the F2 key. The display now changes to show the screen on the server OFFICE which you are currently controlling (see fig 15.21). In this example, the server you are controlling is running a Folio Infobase application, as shown on your screen. Any commands you type at this point are actually being typed on the server's keyboard that you control (OFFICE). The display you see on your screen is actually the display of server OFFICE.

Figure 15.20
Server Activity
screen for
server OFFICE.

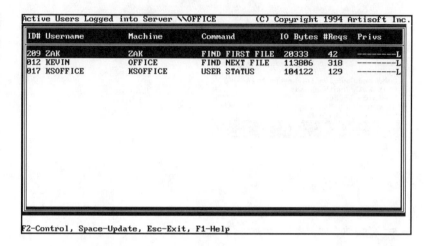

```
Active Users Logged into Server \\OFFICE        (C) Copyright 1994 Artisoft Inc.

ID# Username          Machine        Command         IO Bytes #Reqs  Privs

209 ZAK               ZAK            FIND FIRST FILE  20333    42     --------L
012 KEVIN             OFFICE         FIND NEXT FILE   113806   318    --------L
017 KSOFFICE          KSOFFICE       USER STATUS      104122   129    --------L




F2-Control, Space-Update, Esc-Exit, F1-Help
```

Figure 15.21
Controlling
server OFFICE.

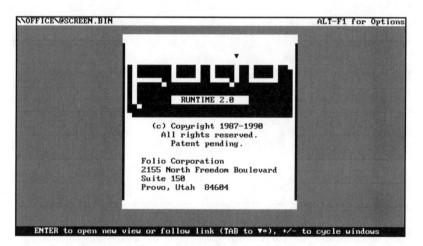

```
\\OFFICE\@SCREEN.BIN                                      ALT-F1 for Options




                        RUNTIME 2.0

                   (c) Copyright 1987-1990
                      All rights reserved.
                      Patent pending.

                   Folio Corporation
                   2155 North Freedom Boulevard
                   Suite 150
                   Provo, Utah  84604


ENTER to open new view or follow link (TAB to ▼+), +/- to cycle windows
```

The first line of the display shows the computer you control (OFFICE in this example), and also displays Alt+F1 for Options. Press Alt+F1, and the options menu appears (see fig. 15.22). To stop controlling the server, select Exit Control and press Enter.

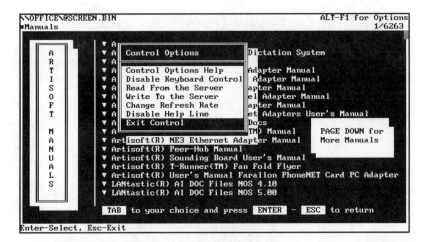

Figure 15.22
The Control
Options menu.

The other options available to control a remote server are described in the following list:

- ✔ **Control Options Help.** Displays help for the menu items.

- ✔ **Enable/Disable Keyboard Control.** Enables you to activate or deactivate your keyboard control of the server.

- ✔ **Read From the Server.** Enables you to choose the shared screen resource used to view the server's screen. Also enables you to copy the information displayed on-screen to a file or print it to a printer.

- ✔ **Write To the Server.** Enables you to send information from a file or from the built-in screen editor to the remote server's screen as if it was typed in with the keyboard.

- ✔ **Change Refresh Rate.** Enables you to specify the frequency at which the screen is updated (in ticks—1/18 second intervals). Setting a faster refresh rate increases network traffic because screen update information is sent across the network more often.

- ✔ **Enable/Disable Help Line.** Enables or disables the help line displayed at the top of the screen.

- ✔ **Exit Control.** Exits the remote control function and returns you to the server activity screen.

Controlling Another Computer from Windows

To control a remote server from Windows, start NET and select the Manage icon, or select Manage Other Computers from the Net menu (see fig. 15.23). Next, select the server you want to control from the list of servers (see fig. 15.24). If you are not logged in to the server, you can log in now by selecting the Connections button. For this example, choose server OFFICE.

Figure 15.23

Selecting Manage from the LANtastic NET program menu.

Figure 15.24

Selecting the server to control.

The User Statistics dialog box appears (see fig. 15.25). To control the server, select Control Server from the Manage menu. The Control Server windows appear, showing the screen on the server OFFICE which you are now controlling (see fig. 15.26). In this example, the server you are controlling is running a Folio

Infobase application, as shown on your screen. Any commands you type at this point are actually being typed on the server's keyboard you are controlling (OFFICE).

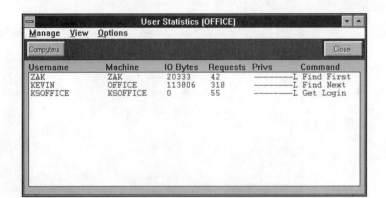

Figure 15.25
The User Statistics dialog box.

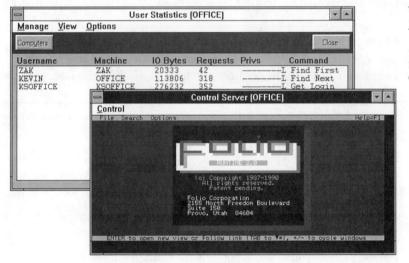

Figure 15.26
The Control Server windows for server OFFICE.

To stop controlling the server, select E**x**it from the **C**ontrol menu (see fig. 15.27).

Figure 15.27
The Control
menu.

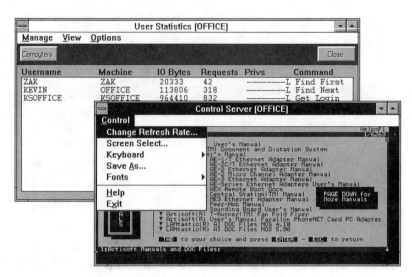

The other options available to control a remote server are described in the following list:

- ✔ **Change Refresh Rate.** Enables you to specify the rate at which the screen is updated (in tenths of a second). Setting a faster refresh rate increases network traffic because screen update information is sent across the network more often.

- ✔ **Screen Select.** Selects which server screen resource to use if more than one resource is set up.

- ✔ **Keyboard.** Enables you to activate or deactivate your keyboard control of the server. If the server has more than one keyboard resource set up, this selection also enables you to choose which keyboard resource to use.

- ✔ **Save As.** Enables you to save the current screen image to a text file. Use an ASCII screen resource type when copying screen images to files.

- ✔ **Fonts.** Enables you to specify the font to be used for displaying the screen image.

- ✔ **Help.** Provides help information for using the **C**ontrol menu.

- ✔ **Exit.** Exits the remote control function and returns you to the User Statistics dialog box.

Remote Control Using a Modem

Often you need to access the network from a remote location. Because of the volume of data that transfers over a network and the limited speed of standard phone lines, it is not possible to provide a temporary link to the network that provides acceptable performance without very sophisticated and expensive equipment. Regardless, the need for remote access still exists.

The best solution to remote network access is probably to use a remote control program, such as pcANYWHERE or Carbon Copy Plus. A remote control program enables you to call up another computer and take control of it. The computer you take control of (often called the *host*) transmits its display information to your screen. When you type on your keyboard, that information is sent to the host as if you were typing on the host's keyboard. You can think of a *remote control program* as a program that makes it seem as though you are working at one computer (the host) when you are actually working at another computer (the remote).

By using a remote control program, all actual processing is still performed on the host. Only the display and keyboard information is transferred between the host computer and the remote computer.

If the remote computer was configured to act as a remote node (a computer that is part of the network, but exists at a remote location) in the network, the processing would be performed on the remote computer. Instead of display and keyboard information passing back and forth between the host and the remote (as is the case with a remote control program), actual program and data information is transferred back and forth. This results in much slower operation because of the relatively large amount of information that must be transferred, compared to just the screen and keyboard information transferred by the remote control program.

Because the remote control program makes it appear as if you were sitting in front of the host computer, you can still perform network operations and other functions as if you were sitting in front of the host.

The speed of the modems used between the host and remote computer have a direct impact on the speed of the operation. A 2,400 baud modem with error correction gives you acceptable performance if you work with text-based applications, but a 9,600 baud modem is the minimum speed required if you work with graphics-based applications, such as Windows.

For a remote control program to operate, software is loaded on the host computer, which enables the host to wait for a phone call from a remote computer. The remote control software on the host computer remains resident while it is active and waiting for a phone call. The remote computer also has special software that enables it to act as the remote and call the host. After the call to the host is made, a password is typically required. After the password is entered, the remote has control of the host.

With an understanding of how remote control programs operate and their capabilities for use as a network computer configured as a host, a summary list of advantages and disadvantages to using a remote control program for operating a network computer follows:

Advantages:

✔ Remote access using inexpensive standard modems.

✔ You usually have features that enable the transfer of files between the host and the remote, and the capability to use the remote computer's printer rather than the host.

✔ In addition to giving you access to the network, you can troubleshoot problems encountered by users and train users remotely.

Disadvantages:

✔ Typically requires a large amount of memory on the host computer to run resident. This can result in not enough conventional memory for the applications you want to run on the host from the remote computer.

✔ Because you are taking control of the host, another user cannot work at the host when you are logged in remotely.

Connecting LANtastic Networks Using Multiple Adapters

LANtastic permits you to install as many as six network adapter cards in one computer. Usually you need only one network adapter card per computer. You have times, however, when you need to install more than a single adapter, such as when you connect an Ethernet LANtastic network to a 2 Mbps LANtastic network.

Suppose that you have a six-station LANtastic network using 2 Mbps network adapter cards, and you want to add two more computers. Because the new computers you add are for accounting and because they access and share large amounts of data, you decide to connect them by using Ethernet adapters. The accounting program and data, however, is on one of your computers that is part of the 2 Mbps LANtastic network. Because Ethernet and 2 Mbps use different cabling and cannot be connected together, you have a dilemma—you need the performance of Ethernet and don't want to install 2 Mbps adapters in the new computers, but you cannot afford to buy six new Ethernet adapters for the rest of the network. The solution is to install an Ethernet adapter in the computer on the 2 Mbps network that contains the accounting program and data. This server communicates with the 2 Mbps LANtastic network by using the 2 Mbps adapter, and communicates with the Ethernet LANtastic network by using the Ethernet adapter. The server with two installed network adapter cards is common to both networks and can be considered part of both networks.

A LANtastic server with multiple network adapter cards installed is common to all networks and can access any other server on any other network. Other servers, however, can only access servers that are part of their own network.

Suppose that computers A, B, and C are part of a LANtastic 2 Mbps network, and computers D, E, and F are part of a separate LANtastic Ethernet network. If you put an Ethernet adapter in computer A in addition to the 2 Mbps adapter, computer A can access every other computer, and every other computer can access computer A (see fig. 15.28). Now computers A, B, and C can access each other and computers A, D, E, and F can access each other. Computers B and C cannot access computers D, E, or F because they exist on different types of networks.

Artisoft Interchange is a software product which may be purchased separately to enable you to bridge two LANtastic networks so all stations may communicate with the others. Artisoft Interchange is installed on the computer with the two network adapters installed to allow network traffic to pass between the two network segments.

Figure 15.28
Connecting two
LANtastic
networks to a
common server
using multiple
adapters.

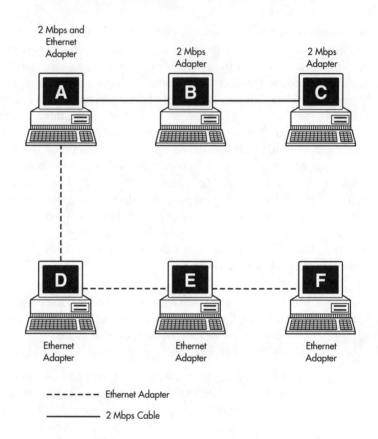

If you install multiple network adapter cards in a single computer, certain hardware parameters must be unique for each network adapter:

1. Each network adapter card must be assigned its own unique hardware interrupt (IRQ).

2. Each network adapter card must be assigned its own I/O port address.

3. If used, each card must be assigned its own RAMBASE address (this is the case for 2 Mbps network adapter cards).

Before you install multiple network adapter cards, you must consider the following software parameters:

1. A separate low-level driver and NETBIOS must be installed for each adapter. (Examples of low-level drivers are NR, NODERUN, AEX, and NE3. An example of NETBIOS is AILANBIO.)

The low-level drivers for LANtastic 2 Mbps network adapter cards include the NETBIOS, so a separate NETBIOS driver doesn't have to be loaded like it does for the Ethernet adapters. The low-level drivers for LANtastic 2 Mbps network adapter cards are LANBIOS, LANBIOS2, and LANBIOS3, depending on which version of the 2 Mbps adapter you have.

2. You only need to load a single occurrence of the REDIR and SERVER programs, regardless of the number of network adapter cards.

3. Specify a different adapter (ADAPTER=) number for each card.

4. Specify a different multiplex (MPX=) number for each card.

The LANtastic 2 Mbps network adapter cards do not use multiplex numbers, so you can't specify an MPX number for the 2 Mbps network adapter cards.

Figure 15.29 shows a typical STARTNET.BAT file for a LANtastic server using 2 Mbps network adapter cards. Figure 15.30 shows the same STARTNET.BAT file for a LANtastic server using the NodeRunner/SI Ethernet adapter cards.

The STARTNET.BAT files created by the LANtastic 6.0 installation program include several configuration options and variable information so the file may be modified later by the installation program. For clarity, the STARTNET.BAT files shown in this section do not have this additional information in them, although they do have everything required for the network to be fully functional if executed.

The low-level driver and NETBIOS are contained in LANBIOS3 for the STARTNET.BAT file shown in figure 15.29. In figure 15.30, the low-level driver is NR and the NETBIOS is AILANBIO.

Figure 15.29
The STARTNET.BAT file for a LANtastic 2Mbps network adapter.

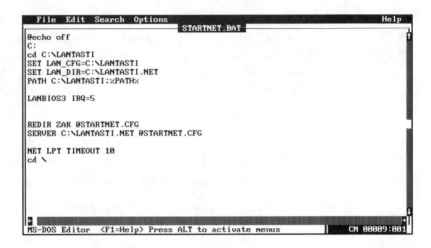

```
   File  Edit  Search  Options                              Help
                          STARTNET.BAT
@echo off
C:
cd C:\LANTASTI
SET LAN_CFG=C:\LANTASTI
SET LAN_DIR=C:\LANTASTI.NET
PATH C:\LANTASTI;%PATH%

LANBIOS3 IRQ=5


REDIR ZAK @STARTNET.CFG
SERVER C:\LANTASTI.NET @STARTNET.CFG

NET LPT TIMEOUT 10
cd \



MS-DOS Editor  <F1=Help> Press ALT to activate menus      CN 00009:001
```

Figure 15.30
The STARTNET.BAT file for a LANtastic NodeRunner/SI Ethernet network adapter.

```
   File  Edit  Search  Options                              Help
                          STARTNET.BAT
@echo off
C:
cd C:\LANTASTI
SET LAN_CFG=C:\LANTASTI
SET LAN_DIR=C:\LANTASTI.NET
PATH C:\LANTASTI;%PATH%

NR
AILANBIO

REDIR ZAK @STARTNET.CFG
SERVER C:\LANTASTI.NET @STARTNET.CFG

NET LPT TIMEOUT 10
cd \



MS-DOS Editor  <F1=Help> Press ALT to activate menus       N 00009:010
```

Figure 15.31 shows the STARTNET.BAT file that enables both the 2 Mbps network adapter card and a NodeRunner Ethernet adapter card to operate in the same computer.

Network software drivers must be loaded low-level driver first, then the NETBIOS, and then REDIR followed by SERVER (if configured as a SERVER). Because the low-level driver and the NETBIOS are included in one driver for LANtastic 2 Mbps network adapter cards, you must load the 2 Mbps drivers after the low-level drivers and NETBIOS for the other adapter(s).

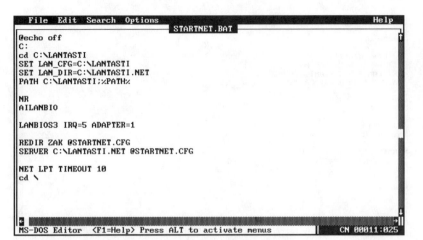

```
 File  Edit  Search  Options                              Help
┌──────────────────────── STARTNET.BAT ─────────────────────────┐
│@echo off                                                      ↑│
│C:                                                              │
│cd C:\LANTASTI                                                  │
│SET LAN_CFG=C:\LANTASTI                                         │
│SET LAN_DIR=C:\LANTASTI.NET                                     │
│PATH C:\LANTASTI;%PATH%                                         │
│                                                                │
│NR                                                              │
│AILANBIO                                                        │
│                                                                │
│LANBIOS3 IRQ=5 ADAPTER=1                                        │
│                                                                │
│REDIR ZAK @STARTNET.CFG                                         │
│SERVER C:\LANTASTI.NET @STARTNET.CFG                            │
│                                                                │
│NET LPT TIMEOUT 10                                              │
│cd \                                                            │
│                                                                │
│                                                                │
│                                                               ↓│
│█▒▒▒▒▒▒▒▒▒▒▒▒▒▒▒▒▒▒▒▒▒▒▒▒▒▒▒▒▒▒▒▒▒▒▒▒▒→║│
└────────────────────────────────────────────────────────────────┘
 MS-DOS Editor   <F1=Help> Press ALT to activate menus    CN 00011:025
```

Figure 15.31
The STARTNET.BAT file for a computer with both 2 Mbps and NodeRunner network adapter cards installed.

In this example, the NodeRunner adapter uses a default IRQ of 15, and the 2 Mbps card specifies an IRQ of 5, so there is no conflict. The default adapter number is 0, which is used by the NodeRunner card. The LANBIOS3 line specifies adapter number 1 to be used for the 2 Mbps card. The 2 Mbps cards do not use MPX numbers.

> Normally, you do not have to change any options on the command line for the drivers associated with the first network adapter cards, because the first card uses the default values that are usually available. When the drivers for additional network adapter cards are installed, however, the default values are typically already used by the first adapter; you need to specify new values (for IRQ, ADAPTER number, and so on).

The next example shows the way to install LANtastic Z by using the Parallel port driver on a computer that has a NodeRunner Ethernet adapter installed. Figure 15.32 shows the STARTNET.BAT file for this configuration. NR is the low-level driver for the NodeRunner Ethernet adapter card and PPORT is the low-level driver for the parallel port used for LANtastic Z. NR uses the default IRQ 15 and MPX number C7. PPORT uses the parallel port in the computer that uses IRQ 7, and an MPX number of D7 is specified. The first implementation of AILANBIO is for the NR driver, using the default MPX number C7, and is for Adapter number 0. The second implementation of AILANBIO is for PPORT, specifying an Adapter number of 1 and the MPX value of D7, which is associated with PPORT.

Figure 15.32

The
STARTNET.BAT
file for a
computer with a
NodeRunner
Ethernet adapter
installed and
running the
LANtastic Z
parallel port
driver.

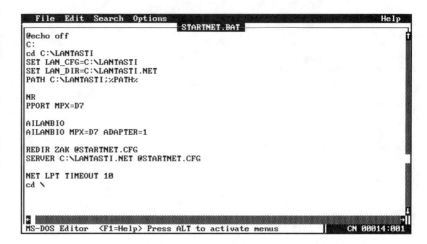

```
  File  Edit  Search  Options                              Help
                          STARTNET.BAT
@echo off
C:
cd C:\LANTASTI
SET LAN_CFG=C:\LANTASTI
SET LAN_DIR=C:\LANTASTI.NET
PATH C:\LANTASTI;%PATH%

NR
PPORT MPX=D7

AILANBIO
AILANBIO MPX=D7 ADAPTER=1

REDIR ZAK @STARTNET.CFG
SERVER C:\LANTASTI.NET @STARTNET.CFG

NET LPT TIMEOUT 10
cd \



MS-DOS Editor  <F1=Help> Press ALT to activate menus        CN 00014:001
```

Note

The versions of REDIR and SERVER that come with LANtastic Z only support two computers in the network, because LANtastic Z can only be used between two computers. If you install LANtastic Z after your other LANtastic network software (such as the Ethernet) on your common server, the REDIR and SERVER programs are replaced by the LANtastic Z versions. To access all your computers in the network from this computer, you need to copy the REDIR and SERVER program from another computer in the network to this one.

The computer using LANtastic Z, with its only connection to the network through the parallel port, can only access the computer to which it is physically connected; it cannot access the other computers in the network.

LANtastic Interchange is available separately which will enable a computer using LANtastic Z to communicate with all other servers in the network.

The final example in figure 15.33 shows the STARTNET.BAT file for a computer that has a NodeRunner Ethernet adapter, a 2 Mbps adapter, and the PPORT LANtastic Z driver installed. This example is the equivalent of having three adapters installed in one computer. The following is a quick rundown of the parameters used by each adapter:

LANtastic NodeRunner Ethernet adapter

(NR, AILANBIO)

IRQ=15 (Default)

MPX=C7 (Default)

ADAPTER=0 (Default)

LANtastic Z parallel port driver

(PPORT MPX=D7, AILANBIO MPX=D7 ADAPTER=1)

IRQ=7 (Default for printer port)

MPX=D7 (Specified since default of C7 already used by NodeRunner)

ADAPTER=1 (Specified since default of 0 already used)

LANtastic 2 Mbps adapter

(LANBIOS3 IRQ=5 ADAPTER=2)

IRQ=5 (Specified since default of 3 already used)

MPX (Does not apply)

ADAPTER=2 (Specified since 0 and 1 already assigned)

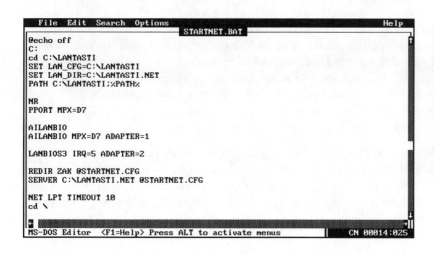

Figure 15.33
The STARTNET.BAT file for a NodeRunner Ethernet adapter and a 2 Mbps adapter installed and running the LANtastic Z parallel port.

Creating a Wide Area Network (WAN)

The process of connecting two or more physically separate networks using communications mediums, such as phone lines, infrared devices, microwave, or other techniques, creates a WAN. The most common method of connecting networks is using special telephone lines, referred to as leased line, dial-up, and T1; these all typically cost several thousand dollars for the equipment, in addition to the charges incurred from the phone company.

It is not uncommon for a business to have two or more separate locations, each with a network. It is often desirable to have the two networks communicate with each other; however, the cost to implement a WAN is prohibitive. Often the next best thing is to use a remote control program for a remote station to access a computer in the other network.

LANtastic Z and LANtastic Interchange

With the combination of LANtastic Interchange and the modem features provided with LANtastic Z, you now can connect two physically separated LANtastic networks using standard telephone lines and modems to form an inexpensive WAN. Even with high speed modems, such as 14.4 KB modems with data compression and error correction (V.42bis), a WAN created with LANtastic Z and LANtastic Interchange is relatively slow and by no means fast enough to allow programs to be run across the phone lines. It does, however, provide an inexpensive way to give all the servers in one LANtastic network access to data on all the other servers in the other LANtastic network.

LANtastic Z enables you to create a 2-station LANtastic network using the parallel port, serial port, or modem on each computer. Implementing the modem feature allows one computer that is part of one LANtastic network to communicate with one computer that is part of another LANtastic network. The computer in each network that is running LANtastic Z effectively has two network adapters installed, as discussed in the previous section; the modem (or serial port to which the modem is connected) is one adapter and the network adapter card, which connects the computer with the rest of the network, is the other adapter.

LANtastic Interchange bridges the two adapters in a single computer so the network accessed from each adapter is able to communicate with the other. By installing LANtastic Interchange on the computer in each network that has LANtastic Z and the modem installed, every network node may access any server in both networks.

Summary

This chapter built upon the knowledge you gained from previous chapters by discussing some of the additional benefits you can gain from a LANtastic network. You learned how to optimize your network, and what tips and tricks to use to enable your LANtastic network and software to work together to perform the tasks you require. Also discussed were topics of a more advanced nature, including global resources, remote operation, and connecting LANtastic networks together using multiple network adapters in a single computer.

Chapter Snapshot

In a perfect world, nothing goes wrong. The world isn't perfect, however, and Murphy's Law (anything that can go wrong will go wrong) is unfortunately alive and well. When your network is not operating correctly, to resolve the problem, you need to identify the cause and then implement a solution. This chapter covers troubleshooting problems that may occur with your network. Specifically, the following topics are covered:

✔ Components of a troubleshooting toolkit

✔ The general troubleshooting procedures to use to isolate a problem

✔ Steps to take to determine the cause of a problem

✔ How to resolve various types of problems ranging from hardware to software to configuration problems

✔ Printer-related problems

When finished with this chapter, you will have a good understanding of the problems that might occur with your computer's hardware and software, and configurations that cause your network to operate incorrectly. As soon as the cause of the problem is identified, you will then be able to easily correct the problem.

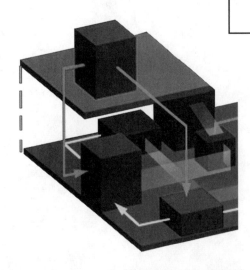

CHAPTER

Troubleshooting Your Network

Part of your responsibility as a network manager includes hand-holding and problem-solving; you frequently have to answer requests for help from your network users. Their requests can range from simple questions, such as "How do I...?" to the more complex "I was trying to print this 50-page spreadsheet, and I couldn't get my header to fit on the page, so I kept sending print jobs and resetting the print feature, and that's when the @#*&%^ locked up on me. Can you fix it?" or "I was just typing my report when the whole thing locked up—I couldn't move my cursor or anything. What's wrong?"

It would be a blessing if both computers and their users functioned without problems. Nevertheless, computers are mechanical devices and people make mistakes—at some point, you will experience problems with your computer or your network.

A way to prepare for network problems is to carefully document the configuration of your network and any changes you make. When you encounter a network problem, it is important to ask, "Did this ever work before?" If you are fixing a component that once functioned properly but has since failed, your next question is, "What has changed?" Proper network documentation enables you to isolate changes more easily.

This chapter lists the tools you need for a handy network toolkit. It then introduces you to troubleshooting flow chart to help you isolate problem areas. At each decision point on the flow chart, you are directed to a section in this chapter that diagnoses the cause of your network failure.

Assembling a Troubleshooting Toolkit

The first law of network management is DO NOT PANIC! Most problems have a simple explanation. The best way to handle such situations is to examine the most likely causes. The first question to ask if something that previously worked doesn't anymore is: What has changed? Most problems that suddenly appear on previously functioning systems may be traced to either a hardware or software configuration change. For new installations, *always* suspect a hardware problem before you try to determine if you have a software problem. This simple, systematic approach to problem-solving saves hours of wasted time and irritation.

To prepare yourself for successful network problem-solving, put together a troubleshooter's toolkit to have handy when problems arise. Your kit should include the following items:

✔ Medium flathead screwdriver

✔ Small flathead screwdriver

✔ Medium Phillips-head screwdriver

✔ Small Phillips-head screwdriver

✔ Torx screwdrivers, if you have Compaqs or other computers with Torx screws

✔ Needlenose pliers

✔ A simple electrical power tester

✔ Emergency boot disk

✔ Tested and certified workstation network cable (preferably factory-made)

✔ One spare network card for each type of card on your network

These items help you troubleshoot and fix many types of problems.

Your emergency boot disk should have the minimum configuration necessary to get a LANtastic workstation running. Place a copy of LANtastic configured as a workstation on the disk. You also might want to include your favorite DOS text editor and a copy of LANCHECK. You can add programs gradually as you gain troubleshooting experience. Nevertheless, keep the configuration simple—do not load unnecessary TSRs (terminate-and-stay resident programs).

One way to simplify your troubleshooting is to keep variables to a minimum. Virtually every PC runs DOS 5.0 or higher—do not keep older versions on any machines. Standardize on a single model of network card, if possible. Do not buy the cheapest card available every time you need to add a PC to the network. Keep things consistent and simple.

You also can benefit from creating a new binder for trouble reports. You can create a form for these reports or use blank paper. Whatever type of form you choose, be sure to keep a detailed written record of reported problems and the way they are resolved. This type of documentation helps you find repeated problems and avoid "reinventing the wheel" every time you encounter another network malfunction. Vendor technical support personnel use trouble reports, which is why they can fix problems quickly. Artisoft's technical support group tracks each call made to them using a program called Folio Views, which enables them to access and search for information in several information databases (called infobases).

Initial Troubleshooting Procedures

Now that you are prepared to take on the problems of your users, what do you do first? Begin by educating your users about what to do when a problem occurs. If you decide to create a special form for trouble reports, such as the sample form in figure 16.1, give your users a copy and show them how to fill it out. Ask them to copy everything that appears on-screen and give a detailed description of what they were trying to do when problems occurred. It is unimportant whether users understand what they view on-screen; just have them write down what they see.

Make sure that you tell your users to leave their computers on and find you immediately when a problem occurs. If they turn off their computers, the information on-screen disappears.

When a user reports a problem, ask him to describe what he was doing when the problem occurred. Review the trouble report, and fill in any blanks by asking the user probing questions—get as many details as possible. Listen for improper procedures or omissions of procedures; for instance, the user may have forgotten a step or used an improper step. Ask other users if they have had similar problems, and if so, what they were doing or trying to do. Ask each user if they were able to overcome the problem, and if so, the way they did. Use the information to review and revise your procedure guides.

Armed with a good description of what happened, you can begin the solution process. Begin this phase with a review of your network management notes. Look for a record of any recent changes to the problem machine's hardware or software. Write down these changes so you have a record when you begin working at the computer.

Figure 16.1
A sample Trouble Report form.

Trouble Report

User submitting report: _____

Date submitted: _____

Problem computer name: _____

Problem computer location: _____

Problem description: _____
_____
_____
_____
_____
_____

Troubleshooting action taken: _____
_____
_____
_____
_____

Disposition: _____
_____
_____

Date action closed: _____ By whom: _____

Report assignment number: _____

Isolating the Problem Area

When you diagnose a problem, it is helpful to have a standard set of procedures. If the procedures are systematic, you quickly eliminate some areas from consideration and zero in on the specific component that is causing the problem. To assist you in systematically isolating a network problem or failure, work through the network troubleshooting flow chart in figure 16.2.

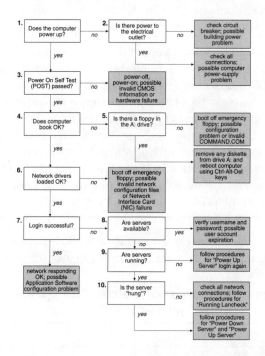

Figure 16.2
Network troubleshooting flow chart.

As you respond to questions in the flow chart, you encounter boxes that describe procedures. Many of these boxes direct you to a troubleshooting task in the next section of this chapter. Go to the appropriate task heading and follow the detailed steps.

Decision One: Does the Computer Power Up?

Answer	Response
NO	Go to Decision Two
YES	Go to Decision Three

Although this concern may seem obvious, some computer peripherals require their own power supplies.

Decision Two: Is There Power to the Electrical Outlet?

Answer	Response
NO	Your building may have a power problem. Check the workstation's surge protector and the building's circuit breakers before you call an electrician.
YES	Check all the power connections and then try the procedures in "Task Six: Troubleshooting Hardware Problems" in "Troubleshooting Tasks" later in this chapter. The problem may be a failed power supply or simply a bad power cord. Other PC problems resemble the effects of a failed power supply, such as when a failed computer component shorts out and shuts down the power supply, but does not destroy it. If you have checked all connections, and the steps described in Task Six do not help you correct the problem, have the PC repaired.

Use your electrical power tester (you can get one from Radio Shack or most hardware stores) to determine whether you have power to the outlet.

Decision Three: Does the PC Pass the Power On Self-Test (POST)?

Answer	Response
NO	If the Power On Self-Test (POST) fails, check the system configuration according to your operating manual, run the system-diagnostic routines, and then try the procedures in "Task Six: Troubleshooting Hardware Problems." If you reconfigure the system and the problem persists, the machine needs service. If the steps in Task Six do not help you correct the problem, have the PC repaired.
YES	Go to Decision Four.

Whenever a PC boots, it executes a self-test (POST) that checks memory and major components.

Decision Four: Does the PC Boot Successfully?

Answer	Response
NO	Go to Decision Five. The boot failure is unlikely to be caused by a computer malfunction, although it is possible that the boot disk drive has failed.
YES	Go to Decision Six.

If the PC boots correctly, you see DOS commands. At the end of the boot sequence, a DOS prompt appears (unless the AUTOEXEC.BAT file includes commands to start a program such as Microsoft Windows).

Decision Five: Is There a Floppy Disk in the A Drive?

Answer	Response
NO	Try to boot from your emergency floppy disk or go to "Task Seven: Troubleshooting Program and Memory Problems." You may have a failed hard drive, but more than likely it's a file problem. Have any changes been made to the PC's boot files? Check the CONFIG.SYS and AUTOEXEC.BAT files—errors in these files can cause the system to hang up when it boots. In addition, consider any recent changes to the system. Some hardware failures can cause boot problems. If a hardware driver program is run after the related hardware has failed, the driver can hang. Task Seven has more suggestions.
YES	Remove the floppy disk and boot from the hard drive. If the computer does not boot, read the response to the NO answer in Decision Five.

If you are booting from a hard disk, you do not want a floppy disk in drive A. If you are booting from a floppy disk in drive A, the floppy may be bad.

Decision Six: Do the Network Drivers Load?

Answer	Response
NO	Boot from your emergency boot disk. Use the text editor on this disk to examine AUTOEXEC.BAT, STARTNET.BAT, and any other batch files. Look for

continues

Decision Six, continued

Answer	Response
	recent changes. If you see something suspicious, edit the line by adding REM to the beginning. The REM command turns the line into a remark so that it cannot execute. Double-check the settings in STARTNET.BAT to ensure that they match those on the network card. Check the interrupts and any other parameters your card requires.
YES	Go to Decision Seven.

Improperly configured network drivers can cause all sorts of problems. For example, if the I/O port specified when loading the low-level network driver conflicts with another adapter in your computer, you will receive an error message and the network drivers will not load. Trying to load a low-level network driver from a network adapter different than that installed in your computer will also register an error message and prevent the network drivers from loading.

Decision Seven: Is a Login Successful?

Answer	Response
NO	Go to Decision Eight.
YES	The network is working. Some application problems look like network problems. Applications can hang if the files are corrupted or if the memory setup on the PC is incorrect. If nothing has changed since the system was working properly, try reinstalling the application.

Decision Eight: Are Servers Available?

Answer	Response
NO	Go to Decision Nine.
YES	Verify the user name and password, then review "Task Three: Logging In and Logging Out."

Decision Nine: Are Servers Running?

Answer	Response
NO	Follow the procedures in "Task Two: Powering Up Servers."
YES	Go to Decision Ten.

Decision Ten: Is the Server "Hung?"

Answer	Response
NO	Follow the procedures in "Task Four: Running LANCHECK." If the PCs cannot pass the LANCHECK test, check the network cable connections and then go to "Task Seven: Troubleshooting Network Problems."
YES	Follow the procedures in "Task One: Powering Down Servers" and in "Task Two: Powering Up Servers."

You know the server is hung if it does not respond to any keystrokes.

Troubleshooting Tasks

The following sections show you how to perform some common network manager tasks for a LANtastic network. Each task is broken into steps that outline the exact operations you need to perform to complete the task.

Task One: Powering Down Servers

This task covers shutting down one or more servers on the network. This operation usually is performed for system maintenance or to recover from a server "crash." One or more computers on the network may be "bleeping." The bleep signals that a network connection has been broken or there is a delay in accessing the required information. As a rule, the computers that are bleeping are not the computers that are frozen. Often, you can "free" bleeping computers by powering down the server. To do so, follow these steps:

1. Tell all users who are logged in to the server to exit any applications they are running, and then to exit to a DOS prompt. If you are powering down a server because it has "hung" and users are unable to exit

their applications, have the users wait for the server to be rebooted (it might be possible to recover after the server has been rebooted).

2. Exit any applications being run on the server and exit to a DOS prompt. If you are unable to exit to a DOS prompt, you may lose changes made to the files being worked on since the last time the files were saved.

3. Press Ctrl+Alt+Del (all three at once). You hear a series of beeps, and a box appears that offers the following choices:

   PRESS:

   S   To shutdown and remove

   Ctrl+Alt+Del   To reboot immediately

   Other keys   To continue

   If users can exit their applications and exit to a DOS prompt, the screen should show the message 0 Open Network Files. Press S to shut down the server. You hear a series of beeps while the message SERVER SHUTDOWN flashes on-screen.

   If you press Ctrl+Alt+Del and the system beeps but the instruction box does not appear, continue to press S.

   If you do not hear a series of beeps when you press Ctrl+Alt+Del or the message does not display, the server probably is completely frozen and cannot shut down properly. Try pressing Ctrl+Alt+Del again. If you still do not hear a series of beeps or see the instruction box, go on to the next step.

4. Turn off the server.

Task Two: Powering Up Servers

This task covers the process of booting or powering up one or more servers. You usually boot up after system maintenance or after recovering from a server crash.

1. Check whether all peripheral devices attached to the servers are turned on. Peripherals include printers, external modems, and external CD-ROM drives.

2. Turn on the computer. As the computer boots, it goes through a series of self-tests.

3. Run STARTNET.BAT to launch LANtastic. This batch file usually is part of the AUTOEXEC.BAT file, which means you may not have to launch LANtastic manually.

4. If you are using the computer as a server and a workstation, make sure that all the servers are booted before you log in.

Task Three: Logging In and Logging Out

This task covers logging in and logging out of a server. The login performs several important functions:

✔ Logs out the previous network user

✔ Identifies and verifies you as a valid user on the server

✔ Enables you to access and use the shared resources on the server to which you are logged in

You can see the servers you are currently logged in to by typing the **NET SHOW** command at the DOS prompt. NET SHOW displays a list of available servers, the servers you are logged in to (along with the user name you are logged in as), and a list of resources you are connected to on the servers (see fig. 16.3).

```
C:\>NET SHOW
LANtastic (R) Connection Manager V6.00 - (C) Copyright 1994 ARTISOFT Inc.
Machine ZAK is being used as a Redirector and a Server
File and record locking is currently ENABLED
Unsolicited messages will BEEP, POP-UP and SPEAK
LPT notification is DISABLED
LPT timeout in seconds: 10
Autologin is ENABLED with username ZAK
Logged into \\ZAK as ZAK on adapter 0
Logged into \\OFFICE as ZAK on adapter 0
Logged into \\KATIE as KEVIN on adapter 0
Disk G: is connected to \\KATIE\C-DRIVE
Disk K: is connected to \\OFFICE\C-DRIVE
Printer LPT1 is connected to \\KATIE\@PRINTER
Printer LPT2 is connected to \\ZAK\@PRINTER

Server \\386-25          is available on adapter 0

C:\>
```

Figure 16.3
The results of the NET SHOW command.

To log in to a server, follow these steps:

1. Exit any application that might be running so the DOS prompt appears.

2. From the DOS prompt, type **NET LOGIN** *server-name user-name password* where *server name* is the name of the server you want to log in to, *user name* is the name of the user account you log in to the server as,

and *password* is the password associated with the account. Press Enter to log in to the server.

If your login is not successful, you receive an error message such as ERROR: Cannot locate network name, LOGIN has failed, or ERROR: Invalid username or password, LOGIN has failed. The only indication that your login is successful is that you do not receive an error message.

If your login fails, first check to make sure that the primary server(s) are available. Type **NET SHOW** at the DOS prompt, and press Enter. A list of available servers should be listed. If the servers appear to be available, try logging in again and double-check your user name and password.

To log out of a server, type **NET LOGOUT** *server-name* at the DOS prompt where *server-name* is the name of the server of which you want to log out.

If the computer at which you are sitting is already logged in to a particular server, you can log in to the same server using your user account with the NET LOGIN command. The previous user is then logged out and you are logged in to the server as the user account specified. Any network connections established by the previous user account are maintained.

If you log out of a server using the NET LOGOUT command, all network connections established to the server you are logging out of are canceled.

Task Four: Running LANcheck

This section shows you the benefits of running LANcheck, a utility that provides a wealth of information about the "physical health" of the network. LANcheck usually is run to help isolate cabling problems and failing Network Interface Cards (NICs). The longer a computer has been running with the network software loaded, the more useful LANcheck is. *LANcheck must be running on all computers on the network for it to be most effective.*

1. Make sure that the network software is loaded. To do this, type **NET SHOW** at the DOS prompt and press Enter. If the network software is loaded, you should see a display similar to that shown in figure 16.3. If you receive an error message such as ERROR: LANtastic (R)

Redirector (REDIR) must be installed, after typing NET SHOW, you can load the network software by typing the command **\LANTASTI\STARTNET** at the DOS prompt and pressing Enter.

2. After the network software is loaded, type **LANCHECK** and then press Enter.

    After a brief initialization period, you should see a display similar to the one in figure 16.4.

Stop Do not run LANcheck from within a Windows DOS box. Doing so will cause your computer to lock up.

```
 LANtastic (R) LANCHECK (R) Version 4.12 (C) Copyright 1992 Artisoft Inc.
┌──────────────────────────────────────────────────────────────────────────┐
│ A#  NAME          NODE NUMBER    MINUTES RUNNING    STATUS    ERROR-INDEX   │
│                                                                            │
│ 0   ZAK           00006E44D201          358        local     0%  (  0%)    │
│ 0   OFFICE        00006E23C9E7        20370        active    0%  (  0%)    │
│ 0   KATIE         00026705BA8F          358        active    0%  (  0%)    │
│ 0   386-25        00006E237BFF         4289        active    0%  (  0%)    │
│                                                                            │
│                                                                            │
│                                                                            │
│                                                                            │
│                                                                            │
│                                                                            │
│                                                                            │
│                                                                            │
│                                                                            │
│                                                                            │
│                                                                            │
│                                                                            │
└──────────────────────────────────────────────────────────────────────────┘
Enter-Select, Ins-Enter, Space-Update, R-Refresh, F10-File, Esc-Exit, F1-Help
```

Figure 16.4
Testing network connections with LANcheck.

If the computer freezes while loading LANcheck, the system possibly has a network hardware or software configuration problem. If LANcheck loads properly, the screen lists the computers running LANcheck, whether it's the local computer (LOCAL) or a remote computer (ACTIVE), and displays an error index. You may also occasionally see *waiting* in the Status field, which simply means the local computer is not currently receiving packets for other stations. If any of the computers running LANcheck do not appear on-screen, you probably have a cabling problem.

The Error Index is used to check the relative performance of the adapters on the network. A low error-index value is better than a high one. More importantly, values that are significantly higher or lower than other adapters can indicate a Network Interface Card (NIC) or cabling problem.

By highlighting a computer name and pressing Enter, more detailed information appears (see fig. 16.5).

CRC and Alignment Errors usually indicate a cabling or interference problem. A detailed explanation of the various statistics can be found in your LANtastic manual.

Figure 16.5
Detailed connection information in LANcheck.

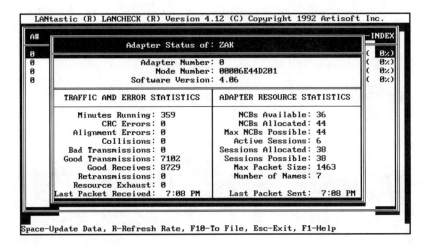

```
LANtastic (R) LANCHECK (R) Version 4.12 (C) Copyright 1992 Artisoft Inc.
A#                                                                  INDEX
0                    Adapter Status of: ZAK                      (  0%)
0                                                                (  0%)
0                     Adapter Number: 0                          (  0%)
0                        Node Number: 00006E44D201               (  0%)
0                   Software Version: 4.06

       TRAFFIC AND ERROR STATISTICS    │  ADAPTER RESOURCE STATISTICS

       Minutes Running: 359            │     NCBs Available: 36
            CRC Errors: 0              │     NCBs Allocated: 44
      Alignment Errors: 0              │  Max NCBs Possible: 44
            Collisions: 0              │    Active Sessions: 6
      Bad Transmissions: 0             │ Sessions Allocated: 38
     Good Transmissions: 7102          │  Sessions Possible: 38
         Good Receives: 8729           │    Max Packet Size: 1463
        Retransmissions: 0             │    Number of Names: 7
       Resource Exhaust: 0             │
   Last Packet Received:  7:08 PM      │   Last Packet Sent:  7:08 PM

Space-Update Data, R-Refresh Rate, F10-To File, Esc-Exit, F1-Help
```

Task Five: Checking Network Connections

This section covers checking the physical connections of the network. Typically, you check physical connections when you try to locate a cabling fault or determine if a Network Interface Card (NIC) has failed. If you turned to this section, one or more computers on your network probably do not see any available server(s), even if you checked the servers to make sure that their network software was loaded successfully.

Always check to make sure that the proper cable is being used in your installation. Cables that "look" correct but do not have the proper specifications result in serious network communications problems.

Twisted-Pair Cabling (10BASE-T)

If a computer is "missing" and your network uses twisted-pair cabling, you need to check the concentrators to make sure they have power. If the concentrators appear to have power, the next step is to check all the RJ-45 connections (telephone type connectors) to make sure they are seated firmly. When an RJ-45 connector is seated properly, you should hear or feel a click. There are generally just one or two cables with RJ-45 connectors on each end that you easily can check. The first cable to check runs from the NIC in the back of the computer to a wall jack or a port on a concentrator. The other cable, if it exists, runs from a punch-down block where all the cables come together to a single port on a concentrator. If a physical link exists between the computer and the concentrator, a Light Emitting Diode (LED) is lit, both on the NIC and the associated port on the concentrator (when both are turned on).

The easiest procedure for isolating the problem is to work backward from the concentrator. The following table serves as a guide to isolating the trouble:

Action	Result
Plug the end of the cable segment into a "known-good" port on the concentrator.	If this solves the problem, you probably have a bad port on the concentrator.
Note which port is bad and plug the end of the patch cable into another available port.	If there is not an extra available port, the concentrator should be serviced.
Replace the cable between the punch-down block and the concentrator with a "known-good" patch cable.	If this solves the problem, it is likely that the patch cable has failed.
Replace the patch cable with the original.	If this solves the problem, it is likely that the patch cable has failed.
Replace the cable between the NIC and the wall jack or concentrator with a "known-good" cable from another office.	If this solves the problem, the NIC probably has failed. Try swapping the original.

continues

Action	Result
Replace the patch cable with computers or NICs with "known-good" components.	If this does not solve the problem, there may be a cabling problem within the walls. Replace the NIC. Test the cable in the walls with a line tester.

Thinnet Cabling

The four physical components of a thin Ethernet network subject to failure are the following:

- ✔ 50-ohm terminators at the extreme within the walls of the cabling
- ✔ T-connectors that twist onto the NIC and provide for two coaxial cable connections
- ✔ The coaxial cable
- ✔ The NIC

If just one computer is having trouble "seeing" any available server(s), the problem might be the T-connector or NIC in that machine. More than likely, none of the computers see any available server(s). In this scenario, the best course of action is to keep halving the network by moving one terminator progressively closer to the other end of the network until you isolate the bad cable or T-connector. If halving the network does not isolate the problem, you can test the terminators with a MultiMeter by checking for 50-ohm resistance between the center pin and shell.

Task Six: Troubleshooting Hardware Problems

Go to the computer that is having problems. Feel the outside of the computer case to see if it is excessively hot. If it is, you may have an overheating problem. Turn off the computer and let it cool down for about an hour. In the meantime, check the physical location of the computer and see if it lacks proper air circulation. Allow for approximately four inches of space behind the computer and a couple of inches on either side for good air circulation. Check to make sure that the computer is not directly in line with a heat duct, and that the room is adequately ventilated. Check that the ventilation holes on the front and back of the computer are clear of obstructions. Clean off any visible dust and dirt using a vacuum cleaner and a small brush attachment.

A symptom of overheating is that when the computer is cool, the problem does not occur; after a period of use, however, the problem appears again.

Open the computer's case. Touch your hand to the power-supply housing (make sure that the power cord is plugged in to the wall) to draw off static electricity from you and the vacuum cleaner. Disconnect the power cord and vacuum out the inside. Be careful not to touch any internal cards or devices with the vacuum cleaner nozzle. Blow out any stubborn dust that you cannot reach with the nozzle. Regular cleaning of computer equipment should be part of your network maintenance plan.

While you have the case open, try pressing down on the interface cards to ensure that they are fully seated in their bus slots. Close the case after you finish, and reconnect the power cord.

After the computer has cooled sufficiently, turn it on again and try to duplicate the problem. If it does not occur right away (but does occur again once the computer warms up), suspect overheating. You can have an additional cooling fan added to the computer, or you can try removing any extra boards from the computer to reduce internal heat sources. If the problem never occurs again, suspect that dust caused the overheating and make cleaning a monthly chore. Be sure to clean all your computers regularly, not just the problem one.

If overheating is not the problem, but you have recently made a change to the computer's physical or software configuration, undo the change and rerun the network. See if you can duplicate the problem again. If you cannot duplicate the problem, the problem is due to your last change. Recheck the sequence you used to change the hardware or software to see if you performed it correctly.

If you have made no recent changes, or if the computer case does not feel excessively warm, turn off the computer and then turn it back on after a few minutes. Rerun the network software and try to duplicate the problem. It is possible that everything may work this time. Sometimes static electricity or stray voltage can cause a temporary problem, and resetting the computer can eliminate it. If you are unable to duplicate the problem, consider buying a surge protector for your computer's power line (if you do not already have one) and a static discharge mat that users can touch before touching their computer. Try to get enough surge protectors and static mats for every computer. If your budget does not cover the purchases all at once, buy what you need in weekly or monthly increments. A little prevention saves your hardware (and your nerves) in the long run.

If you are still having problems, turn off the computer and check the area around it. Verify that the electrical cord is plugged in to the computer and the wall socket, and that the monitor cable and the network cable connections are tight. You would be amazed at the problems a loose cable or electrical cord can cause. Users have been known to kick the power cords and cables loose with their feet. You might want to try a different power cord to eliminate a bad electrical cord as a possible cause.

If you suspect that your problem is due to a failure in one of the components in your computer, the easiest way to identify the source of the problem is to eliminate or replace components until the problem goes away. For example, if you suspect a faulty network interface card, first remove the card and see if the problem goes away. If the network interface card is a required component for the particular problem you're having, replace the card with a "known-good" one and see if the problem goes away. If it does, you have a faulty network adapter. If not, you have eliminated the network adapter as the cause, and should continue narrowing down the list of potential causes.

Task Seven: Troubleshooting Program and Memory Problems

By far the most common software problem that users encounter is a conflict between memory-resident programs, called TSRs (for terminate-and-stay resident programs), and their applications, network drivers, or both. The symptom is a sudden lockup of the computer without warning when attempting to use a TSR, or performing a task that conflicts with the TSR's use of memory. The only thing you can do in this situation is reboot the computer.

If you have any memory-resident programs running on your computers, and you are experiencing unexplained lockups of them, suspect the TSRs. Comment (remark) out their startup commands in the AUTOEXEC.BAT file by adding REM to the beginning of each command line. After you comment out the startup commands, reboot your computer and rerun the network software. If the problem goes away, you can begin reloading the TSRs from the keyboard, one at a time, to see if the problem returns. If it does recur, remove the last TSR that you installed and retry. If the problem is gone, you have isolated the culprit—do away with the offending TSR, try loading it in a different order, or do not load it while using the network. The last option is best because the fewer memory-using programs you have running with your network software, the better. In many cases, you may find that your LANtastic network drivers must be loaded last to prevent interference from TSRs.

Use a software utility such as CheckIt to check the memory-interrupts allocations. If you are using a memory manager, make sure that the address mapping used by the memory manager is not overlapping any of the memory addresses used by your Artisoft interface adapters in the 640 KB to 1 MB memory area. If you discover an overlap, use the EXCLUDE command with your memory manager to set aside the Artisoft adapter addresses (refer to your adapter manuals for specific addresses).

Only the Artisoft 2 Mbps adapters use an address window in the 640 KB to 1 MB memory area. The default used by Artisoft 2 Mbps adapters is D800-DFFF.

Another memory-related problem that you might encounter is not having enough main memory to run your application programs and the network software. (For this example, assume that you have no TSRs installed on your computer.) Your computer just locks up without warning and you can't do anything. This can be a serious problem, and may require multiple steps and take much time to resolve, just as the potential hardware problems did. Again, a systematic approach saves time in the long run.

Managing Printing Problems

This section covers the concept of network printing and how to resolve several printing issues you might encounter in the day-to-day use of the network. If you have turned to this section, it is possible your printer is spewing paper profusely and you cannot stop it—if so, skip to the section called "Stopping a Print Job."

A stand-alone printer is relatively easy to use. The printer is physically attached to one computer and when you print, the computer immediately sends information to that printer. A network printer differs in that it can receive jobs sent from any or all computers on the network. Without some mechanism to control the information sent to the printer, imagine the resulting chaos if everyone sends a job to the printer at the same time. The mechanism by which network printing is controlled is called a *print queue*. The process by which print jobs are placed on the queue and subsequently printed is called *spooling* and *despooling*. The following example helps illustrate the process.

Suppose that you just finished a letter, saved it, and want to print it. When you give your word processing program the command to print, a print job is opened in the print queue to receive the information from the word processor. After your word processing program finishes printing the letter, the print job is closed and the job waits in the queue to be despooled. If no other print jobs are ahead of it in the print queue, the letter begins to print. If other print jobs are ahead of your letter, the print job waits its turn to be despooled on a "first-in, first-out" basis.

The example in the previous paragraph describes a word processing program opening a print job, printing a letter, and closing the print job so that it can be despooled and printed. Although virtually all application programs open print jobs properly, not all applications close the print job. If a print job is not closed, it cannot be printed. There are two ways around this. The first is to set what is called an LPT time-out period. A typical LPT time-out period might be 10 seconds. An LPT time-out period specifies to the print queue the period of time the queue waits to receive information from an open print job. If no information is received after this period, the print job is closed. You hear a beep when the LPT time-out period expires.

The second way to close a print job is to press the key combination Ctrl+Alt+Print Screen (or Ctrl+Alt+*). Again, you hear a beep as the job is "closed."

The letter-printing example illustrates how the process of printing to a network printer differs from that of a stand-alone printer. These differences appear in the following ways:

1. Control typically is returned to your application more quickly after printing because the print queue can receive information faster than a printer.

2. For large jobs, the overall printing time can take longer on a network printer because the entire print job must be first sent to the print queue before it can begin printing.

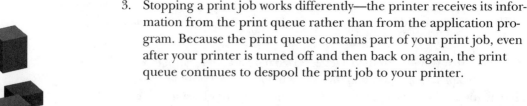

LANtastic allows for immediate despooling, which can speed up the printing process for large jobs. Printing can begin without having to wait for the whole print job to be sent to the print queue.

3. Stopping a print job works differently—the printer receives its information from the print queue rather than from the application program. Because the print queue contains part of your print job, even after your printer is turned off and then back on again, the print queue continues to despool the print job to your printer.

Stopping a Print Job

The following are the steps for stopping spooling to a printer, removing a print job, and then restarting the printer using the DOS LANtastic NET program. The same functions may be performed using the Windows LANtastic NET program.

1. Type **NET** at a DOS prompt and press Enter to display the NET Main Functions menu.

2. Highlight View Print Jobs and press Enter. You see a list of the available server connections.

3. Choose the server attached to the printer that you want to stop and press Enter. After you select a server, you should see a display similar to figure 16.6.

```
Viewing All Jobs For All Printers in Sequence on Computer \\KATIE
 ┌─────────────────────────────────────────────────────────────────┐
 │Sequence # Destination      Status       User         Comment      │
 ├───────────────────────────────────────────────────────────────────┤
 │7          @PRINTER         PRINTING     386-25                     │
 │10         @PRINTER         WAITING      KEVIN        STARTNET.BAT   │
 │12         @PRINTER         WAITING      KEVIN                       │
 │14         @PRINTER         WAITING      KEVIN                       │
 │16         @PRINTER         WAITING      KATIE                       │
 │18         @PRINTER         WAITING      ZAK                         │
 │                                                                     │
 │                                                                     │
 │                                                                     │
 │                                                                     │
 │                                                                     │
 │                                                                     │
 │                                                                     │
 └─────────────────────────────────────────────────────────────────┘
Enter-Select, Space-Update, Ins/Del-Add/Delete, F3-View, F7-Printers, F8-Streams
```

Figure 16.6
Manipulating the LANtastic printer queue.

4. Press F7-Printers to display the list of devices and their status (see fig. 16.7). Press Enter while Device LPT1 (or the device you need to stop) is highlighted. A menu shown in figure 16.8 pops up in the middle of the screen.

5. Highlight Halt and press Enter. This stops the LPT1: printer attached to the server. The print jobs listed should now have a status of WAITING. Press Esc and, using the UP or DOWN arrow keys, highlight the print job you want to delete and press DEL. You will be prompted for confirmation before the job is actually deleted.

Figure 16.7
The list of devices and their status.

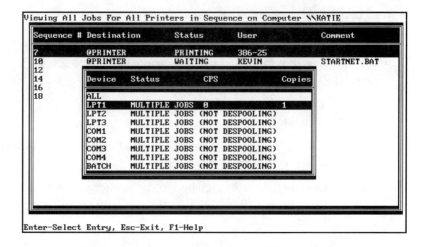

Figure 16.8
Controlling the LPT1 device.

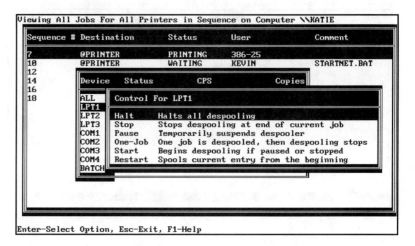

6. Press F7-Printers, and press Enter with the device you halted (LPT1 in this example) selected. A menu pops up in the middle of the screen.

   Highlight Start and press Enter. The print spooler is now started and the printer now begins processing print jobs in the queue.

   Press Esc until you return to the DOS prompt or to your menu program.

Summary

If, after following the procedures in this chapter, you still can't resolve your problem, call the technical support hotline at Artisoft and seek help from its staff of professionals. Because you have been careful to record all of the symptoms of the problem and the steps you have taken so far, they should be able to help you in short order. Artisoft's technical support number is (602) 670-7000.

The LANtastic Installation and Management Guide, a reference guide that comes with LANtastic, includes a helpful chapter on troubleshooting. Artisoft also has included an appendix that discusses the various error messages that you can encounter. Refer to your Artisoft manual for technical examples and explanations of LANtastic problems.

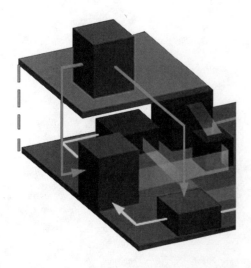

APPENDIX

A

Network Adapter Configuration

Your LANtastic network's communications between computers is controlled through a series of memory interrupts (IRQs) and input/output (I/O) port addresses. To operate properly in your LANtastic network, your network adapter must be configured properly so as not to interfere with other devices in your computer. In most situations, the default configuration of your network adapter will work properly in your computer. Situations, however, do occur in which you will need to change the default configuration of your network adapter for it to operate properly with your computer. For example, you might have a CD-ROM drive in your computer. It's possible that the adapter card for your CD-ROM drive uses the same I/O port address as your network adapter. In this situation, you would need to change the address of your network adapter (or the CD-ROM adapter) for it to operate properly in your computer.

This appendix lists the IRQs and I/O addresses available to you. You may find that you need to change the addresses and interrupts to meet your particular installation requirements.

If you have an Artisoft NodeRunner 2000 series or NodeRunner/SI 2000 series Ethernet adapter, you will run a setup program called NRSETUP to change the configuration of your adapter. This appendix also covers running the NRSETUP program to change the configuration of the NodeRunner adapter; there are no jumpers on the NodeRunner adapter to change. If you have an Artisoft AE Series Ethernet adapter, you change the adapter configuration by changing the position of jumpers on the network adapter. Refer to the manual that came with your interface card for settings you can use.

Hardware Interrupts

If your adapter interface needs the CPU to perform a particular function, it sends a signal through the interrupt line to your CPU. The CPU suspends processing and services the request. After it services the request, it returns to processing the task on which it was working. Table A.1 lists the memory interrupts assigned and available for XT and AT class computers. Refer to your user's manual for specific settings for your particular network interface card and installation.

Table A.1
Memory Interrupts List

IRQ	XT Computer	AT Computer
2	Available	Available
3	Second serial port (COM2) or a Bus mouse	Second serial port (COM2) or a Bus mouse
4	First serial port (COM1) or a Bus mouse	First serial port (COM1) or a Bus mouse
5	Hard disk controller	Second parallel port or a Bus mouse
6	Floppy disk controller	Floppy disk controller
7	Parallel port at LPT1	Parallel port at LPT1
10	Not available	Available
15	Not available	Available

Input/Output (I/O) Addresses

Your computer communicates with all of its associated hardware through I/O ports. Each I/O has its own unique address, and no two devices can share the same I/O address. If devices share the same address, conflicts occur and your computer may lock up or exhibit unpredictable behavior. The I/O addresses shown in table A.2 are provided for information only. Refer to your network interface card user's manual for available settings for your installation.

Table A.2
Input/Output (I/O) Addresses

Address	XT Computer	AT Computer
200-20F	Reserved	Available
220-22F	Reserved	Available
240-24F	Reserved	Available
260-26F	Unassigned	Available
280-28F	Unassigned	Available
2A0-2AF	Unassigned	Available
2C0-2CF	Unassigned	Available
2E0-2EF	Unassigned	Available
300-31F*	Prototype card	Prototype card
320-33F*	Hard disk controller	Available
340-35F*	Available	Available
360-37F*	LPT2 (or LPT1)	LPT2 (or LPT1)
380-38F	Unassigned	Available
3A0-3AF	Unassigned	Available
3C0-3CF	Reserved	Reserved
3E0-3EF	Unassigned	Available

* Options available for NodeRunner and NodeRunner /SI 2000 Series and AE Series adapters

Configuring Artisoft NodeRunner 2000 Series Adapters

The Artisoft NodeRunner 2000 and NodeRunner/SI 2000 series Ethernet adapters are configured using the NRSETUP program. The network adapter card has no jumpers.

The NRCONFIG program is for configuring only NodeRunner 2000 series adapters and not the NodeRunner/SI 2000 series adapters. NRSETUP is for configuring both the NodeRunner 2000 and NodeRunner/SI 2000 series adapters. NRSETUP is copied to your LANtastic directory when you install LANtastic 6.0.

If the configuration of your NodeRunner network adapter needs to be changed, run the setup program by typing **NRSETUP** at the DOS prompt from your LANTASTI directory. The NodeRunner Setup Utility Main Options menu appears (see fig. A.1).

To run the NRSETUP program, your network software must not be running. If NRSETUP still won't run, you may have an I/O base conflict with another device. Use the NRMOVE utility to temporarily move the I/O base address of your NodeRunner adapter by typing the following command at your DOS prompt from the LANTASTI directory:

NRMOVE

This command moves the I/O base address from the default 300 hex address to 320. You can specify the I/O base address with the IOBASE= switch using one of the following commands:

NRMOVE IOBASE=300

NRMOVE IOBASE=320

NRMOVE IOBASE=340

NRMOVE IOBASE=360

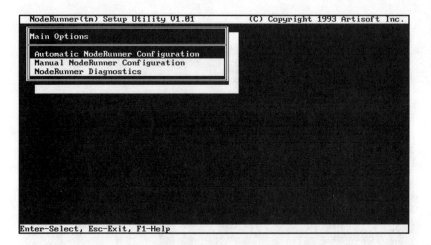

Figure A.1
The NodeRunner
Setup Utility
Main Options
menu.

The Automatic NodeRunner Configuration option will cause NRSETUP to automatically determine the best setting for your computer. If you want to manually specify the configuration of your NodeRunner adapter, select the Manual NodeRunner Configuration option and press Enter to display the configuration information screen for this adapter (see fig. A.2).

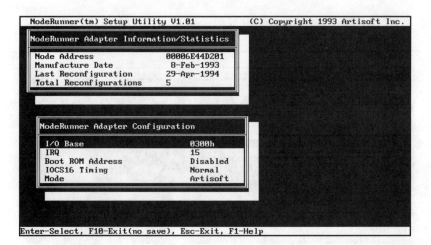

Figure A.2
The NodeRunner
adapter
information and
configuration
screen.

To change the I/O base address, highlight the I/O Base selection and press Enter. Select the I/O base address from the list of four options (see fig. A.3) and press Enter.

The options shown in the NodeRunner Adapter Configuration box in figure A.2 are the default configuration settings for the NodeRunner adapters (I/O Base—300h, IRQ—15, Boot ROM Address—Disabled, IOCS16 Timing—Normal, Mode—Artisoft).

Figure A.3
Selecting the
I/O base
address.

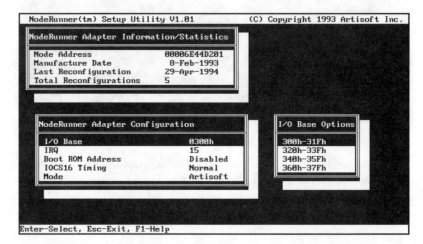

To change the IRQ setting, highlight the IRQ option and press Enter. Select the IRQ you want from the list and press Enter (see fig. A.4).

Figure A.4
Selecting an
IRQ for the
NodeRunner
adapter.

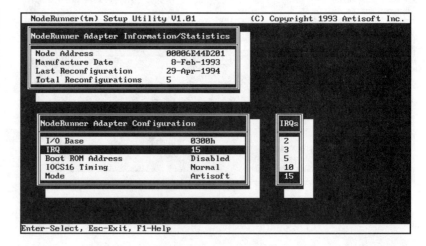

If you have a remote boot ROM on your NodeRunner adapter, you can specify the boot ROM address. The IOCS16 Timing option may be toggled between Normal and Early by pressing Enter. This changes the timing of the IOCS16 bus control term and may be required to eliminate intermittent disconnects encountered on some PCs.

The Mode option enables you to select the mode in which your NodeRunner adapter is running. In addition to the default Artisoft mode, you can specify Artisoft/8 if using your adapter in an 8-bit slot, or you can have it emulate a Novell NE-2000 or NE-1000 network adapter (see fig. A.5).

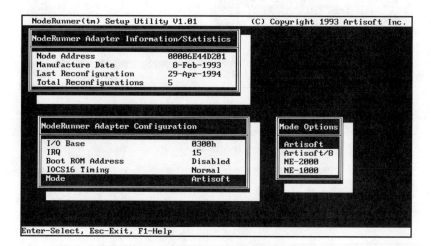

```
NodeRunner(tm) Setup Utility V1.01          (C) Copyright 1993 Artisoft Inc.
┌─NodeRunner Adapter Information/Statistics─┐
│                                           │
│  Node Address            00006E44D201     │
│  Manufacture Date          8-Feb-1993     │
│  Last Reconfiguration     29-Apr-1994     │
│  Total Reconfigurations   5               │
└───────────────────────────────────────────┘


┌─NodeRunner Adapter Configuration─┐   ┌─Mode Options──┐
│                                  │   │               │
│  I/O Base              0300h     │   │  Artisoft     │
│  IRQ                   15        │   │  Artisoft/8   │
│  Boot ROM Address      Disabled  │   │  NE-2000      │
│  IOCS16 Timing         Normal    │   │  NE-1000      │
│  Mode                  Artisoft  │   └───────────────┘
└──────────────────────────────────┘


Enter-Select, Esc-Exit, F1-Help
```

Figure A.5
Specifying the operating mode for the NodeRunner adapter.

When finished with your manual configuration, press Esc to exit; your changes are saved to the NodeRunner configuration. You can ignore the changes by pressing F10.

You can perform diagnostics on your NodeRunner adapter and check network communications between NodeRunner adapters by selecting the NodeRunner Diagnostics option from the Main Options menu (see fig. A.1). You are prompted to enter a unique station name, which is used to show your station on the screens of the other computers running the NRSETUP diagnostics option. Enter the desired name and press Enter to display the NodeRunner Statistics and Diagnostics Results screen (see fig. A.6).

Selecting the NodeRunner Diagnostics option is an easy way to check the basic network communication between the NodeRunner network adapters in your network without having to first start your network software on each computer.

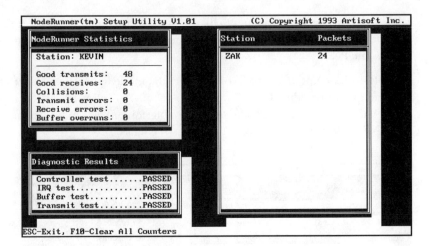

```
NodeRunner(tm) Setup Utility V1.01          (C) Copyright 1993 Artisoft Inc.
┌─NodeRunner Statistics─────────┐   ┌─Station          Packets────┐
│ Station: KEVIN                │   │ ZAK                24        │
│                               │   │                             │
│ Good transmits:    48         │   │                             │
│ Good receives:     24         │   │                             │
│ Collisions:        0          │   │                             │
│ Transmit errors:   0          │   │                             │
│ Receive errors:    0          │   │                             │
│ Buffer overruns:   0          │   │                             │
└───────────────────────────────┘   │                             │
                                     │                             │
┌─Diagnostic Results────────────┐   │                             │
│ Controller test.......PASSED  │   │                             │
│ IRQ test..............PASSED  │   │                             │
│ Buffer test...........PASSED  │   │                             │
│ Transmit test.........PASSED  │   │                             │
└───────────────────────────────┘   └─────────────────────────────┘
ESC-Exit, F10-Clear All Counters
```

The station name entered in this example is KEVIN and is displayed next to the Station field in the NodeRunner Statistics box. Other stations running the same diagnostics appear in the box to the right. In this example, station ZAK appears.

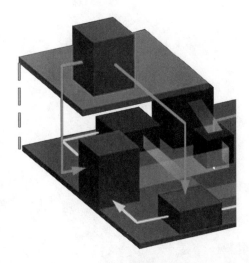

APPENDIX B

Glossary

A

Access Control List. In LANtastic, files that contain records of network resources that each user can access and the user's rights to them.

ACL. Acronym for Access Control List. *See* Access Control List.

analog. An energy form or mechanical device characterized by a continuously varying physical property. Sound is an example of analog energy, as are the electrical signals used to transmit sound information through telephone lines.

architecture. In computer engineering, the structure of a complete system that includes all hardware and software components required for proper operation.

ASCII character set. The American Standard Code for Information Interchange is the most common system for encoding character data on microcomputers and minicomputers. The standard ASCII character set uses 7 bits and can represent 128 characters. Characters 0 through 31 are control characters used in various protocols to control data communication, screen display, and other functions. Characters 32 through 127 represent displayable characters. An informal, extended-ASCII character set uses 8 bits to represent 256 characters. Characters 128 through 255 are used to represent additional printable characters for graphics, foreign languages, mathematics, and other functions.

asynchronous transmission. Any serial communication not controlled by a master timer. Asynchronous transmissions begin with a specific data pattern to indicate the beginning of a message, but depend on the transmitting device to send data at the same rate expected by the receiving device. Because sender and receiver are likely to drift apart slightly, asynchronous transmissions are limited to short messages, usually a character at a time. Modems to support asynchronous transmissions are inexpensive, but they make inefficient use of the available communication bandwidth.

attenuation. The loss of signal strength that results when a signal is transmitted through a medium. Because of attenuation, all data networks have a maximum operating range. If the signal is not degraded by other factors, such as noise or distortion, the operating range of a data network can be extended through the use of repeaters, which amplify the weakened signal.

B

bandwidth. The range of frequencies that can be transmitted through a medium. All media have a practical upper limit to the frequencies that can be transmitted. A typical voice telephone system has a bandwidth of 3000Hz, and accommodates frequencies ranging from 300Hz to 3000Hz.

batch file. A text file that contains MS-DOS commands. Batch file names always have the extension BAT. The file name can be entered as a command, causing the MS-DOS commands in the batch file to be executed in order. Batch files are used to store commands necessary for a multistep task so the command sequence can be executed easily with a single command.

baud. The number of signal changes that can be accommodated by a transmission medium. A voice-grade telephone line can support a maximum baud rate of 2,400. Baud is frequently misconstrued to represent the bit rate that can be transmitted by a given modem. The proper measure, however, is bits-per-second (bps). For data rates exceeding 2,400bps, multiple bits are encoded for each signal change by combining modulation techniques; a 9,600bps modem encodes four bits for each signal change by utilizing a combination of amplitude modulation and phase modulation.

bit. The smallest unit of computer data. A bit can have only two states, usually defined as 1 or 0, or ON or OFF, respectively.

BNC connector. A standard connector used with coaxial cable. BNC connectors lock together with a 90-degree bayonet attachment.

bridge. A networking device used to interconnect two different local area networks (LANs). The bridge acts as a "traffic cop," preventing messages on one network from entering the other network, unless it is necessary to deliver the message to its destination. Bridges are frequently used to subdivide large networks so traffic levels on any given network segment are not excessive.

bus. An electrical circuit configured so all components on the circuit receive all available signals. The expansion bus in an IBM-compatible microcomputer, for example, is a bus consisting of multiple lines for the transmission of electrical power, computer data, and control signals. A control system usually is incorporated into the bus design so that specific components react to specific sets of signals on the bus.

bus network. A network configured as an electrical bus. Ethernet, IEEE 802.3, and ARCnet are common examples of bus networks. Each node on a network segment receives and processes each message on a bus network. A unique address is assigned to each node on the segment so data transmissions intended for that node are identifiable.

byte. A unit of computer data that has eight bits. A byte is capable of representing 256 possible values.

C

cable. A configuration of wires in a common jacket. Examples are shielded and unshielded twisted-pair, coaxial, and fiber optical.

cache. A device that compensates for the differences in operating speeds between computer components. It is much faster to read and write data to computer memory, for example, than to a hard disk. If a program needs to write data to a disk file, a disk-caching program can be installed that intercepts data and stores it temporarily in the computer's memory. After the data is stored in memory, the program that wrote the data can resume processing. The disk-caching program then works in the background to transfer the data from memory to the hard disk; this technique is called a *write behind cache.* A disk-caching program also can store in memory the data that was most recently read from disk, on the theory that this data is most likely to be needed again. This process is called *read ahead buffering.* Disk file cache programs can significantly improve the responsiveness of a computer system. The LANtastic LANcache program is a sophisticated disk file cache program.

central processing unit. The device in a computer that controls the central computing function. In a personal computer, this device usually includes a microprocessor. *See* microprocessor.

coaxial cable. A cable design in which a central conductor is surrounded by a concentric shield. The conductor and shield are separated by an insulating layer, called a dielectric. This shield can be constructed of braided wire or metal foil, and it serves to isolate the conductor from the influences of external electromagnetic interference.

communication medium. Refers to the path over which data moves.

communication protocol. A formal set of rules that defines the way data is transmitted between devices. Common examples are the Open System Interconnect standards, *CSMA/CD*, *IPX*, and *RS-232C*.

communication server. A station on a LAN that shares communication facilities with other nodes. Communication servers can be used to share modems and to provide access to minicomputer and microcomputer systems.

concentrator. A device used primarily in a 10BASE-T network, which receives network signals from one network segment and retransmits them to the other segments connected to the concentrator.

CPU. Acronym for central processing unit. *See* central processing unit.

CSMA/CD. Carrier Sense Multiple Access/Collision Detection is the network access-control mechanism utilized by Ethernet and IEEE 802.3. This is a contention-based protocol, in which any station on the network can access the network and transmit information after determining that the network is idle (a carrier is sensed). If multiple transmissions occur simultaneously, a collision-detection mechanism goes into effect; the stations generate a jamming pulse to notify the network that a collision has occurred. Stations then wait a random amount of time before attempting to transmit again. Collisions are normal control mechanisms of CSMA/CD networks, and they do not become a problem except under high traffic levels.

D

D connector. A connector that has a D-shaped lip surrounding the pins. A 25-pin D connector is commonly used to implement RS-232C serial connections, although a 9-pin D connector is also commonly used.

data. In data processing, symbolic information that is transmitted, stored, or processed.

digital. In data processing, the technique of representing data symbolically in numeric format.

DOS. Acronym for Disk Operating System. In PCs, DOS is used to refer to Microsoft MS-DOS or IBM PC DOS.

E

Ethernet. A network standard, developed by Xerox in 1976, from which the IEEE 802.3 standard was derived. Ethernet uses a bus architecture and the CSMA/CD protocol to control media access. Ethernet supports a data rate of 10 Mbps. The Ethernet standard includes three types: 10BASE5, 10BASE2, and 10BASE-T. 10BASE5 is also known as thick Ethernet. 10BASE2, or thin Ethernet, uses coaxial cable. 10BASE-T, also known as UTP (unshielded twisted pair), uses the same type of cable used in most phone systems. Computers connected using 10BASE-T are connected to a central hub or concentrator.

H

Hayes compatible. A vendor-defined standard defining a command set that controls functions of asynchronous modems. This command set also is known as the AT command set because all control sequences begin with the characters "AT." The majority of modern commercial modems support the Hayes AT command set.

hertz (Hz). The measure of the frequency of a waveform in cycles per second. 2,500 Hz is 2,500 cycles-per-second.

hub. A module serving as a central connecting point for a star-wired network. Hubs are used in 10BASE-T, token ring, and ARCnet networks.

Hz. *See* hertz.

I

IEEE. Abbreviation for the Institute of Electrical and Electronics Engineers. The IEEE is a professional organization that has developed a wide variety of standards, including the 802 group of standards relating to local area networks.

IEEE 802.3. The IEEE standard that defines CSMA/CD networks derived from Ethernet. The 802.3 standard defines standards for broadband and baseband networks utilizing coaxial cable and unshielded twisted-pair cable.

IEEE 802.5. The IEEE standard, defining networks derived from IBM's token-ring technology.

impedance. The sum of opposition to the flow of alternating current in a conductor. The impedance of a cable summarizes a variety of factors, including the resistance of the conductors (also frequency, reactance, and capacitance). The impedance of a cable must match the impedance required by the attached electronic devices if the circuit is to function optimally.

interrupt request line. A hardware feature in a PC that enables peripheral devices to request the attention of the microprocessor. Network cards are configured to use an interrupt. Interrupts enable the computer to switch rapidly among a variety of tasks. Interrupt request lines are assigned to printers, communication ports, disk drives, and some peripheral cards (such as network cards). Each device must be assigned a unique interrupt so that the devices do not conflict.

IPX. Internetwork Packet Exchange protocol used in Novell NetWare networks.

IRQ. Acronym for Interrupt Request line.

ISO. Acronym for the International Standards Organization, an international organization that develops standards for communication and information interchange. The ISO is best known in data processing as the developer of the seven-layer OSI network model. *See* OSI model.

K

K. Abbreviation for kilo. *See* kilo-.

KB. Common abbreviation for kilobytes. *See* kilo-.

kilo-. Except in data processing, a prefix designating "thousand," as in kilometer (abbreviated km). In data processing, kilo ordinarily designates the quantity 1,024, which conforms more closely with computer data because powers of two are the most common measurements of computer memory capacity and other quantities. To distinguish the two usages, it is common to use lowercase *k* to designate 1,000 and uppercase *K* to designate 1,024. Thus, 1,024 bytes of memory is conventionally designated as 1K.

L

LAN. Acronym for local area network. *See* local area network.

local area network. A system for interconnecting two or more computers to support the sharing of data or physical devices. Local area networks usually operate at high speeds within a limited geographic area.

logical topology. The way data travels through a network. In a logical ring, such as a token ring, data is transmitted from station to station—each station receives data from the previous station and retransmits the data to the next station in the ring. At any given time, only one station in the ring can interact with the data. In a logical bus, signals are broadcast into the network; they propagate throughout the network so all stations on the network receive each data transmission more or less simultaneously.

M

Mbps. Abbreviation for million bits-per-second.

medium. In data communication, any substance used to transport data between devices. Typical media are cables, optical fibers, and radio transmissions.

mega-. Except in data processing, a prefix designating "one million." In data processing, mega ordinarily designates the quantity 1,048,576. The abbreviation used in data processing is ordinarily a capital letter M; for example, MB conventionally represents megabytes.

MHz. Abbreviation for one million hertz. *See* hertz.

microcomputer. Traditionally, a computer that incorporates a microprocessor as its central processing unit. As microprocessors have become more powerful, they have been incorporated into the designs of mini- and mainframe computers; a sharp distinction thus no longer exists between the categories.

microprocessor. An integrated circuit that incorporates the functionality of a complete central processing unit.

multitasking. The execution of several tasks simultaneously. In some computers, multitasking is accomplished by incorporating more than one central processing unit. Often, though, multitasking is a matter of sharing the central processing unit among several tasks, each of which takes a turn. This sharing process takes place rapidly enough that it is normally invisible to the end user.

N

NCP. Acronym for NetWare Core Protocols. *See* NetWare Core Protocol.

NDIS. Network Driver Interface Specification followed by most network vendors. The NDIS specification provides a set of rules used to enable the network hardware, such as network adapter cards and network operating systems like LANtastic, to communicate properly with each other.

NetBIOS. An application program interface that provides a consistent set of commands for requesting network services.

NetWare Core Protocol. A set of protocols used by servers in Novell's network operating systems to respond to network requests.

network. A configuration of devices and media that is used to transfer data between computer devices.

network interface card. A card installed in a PC that is used to connect the computer to a local area network. *See* NIC.

network operating system. A software product that manages a local area network server and data communications on the LAN. Commonly abbreviated as NOS, the network operating system is responsible for a wide variety of functions, including file services, security, internetwork routing, and network communications. Add-in modules can expand the server's roles, adding services such as database management and asynchronous modem communication. LANtastic is an example of a network operating system.

NIC. Acronym for network interface card. *See* network interface card.

node. In computer networks, any component on a network that is addressable as a unique entity. Workstations, file servers, and routers are examples of network nodes. Repeaters are not network nodes because they are not associated with network addresses.

noise. Any interference that degrades the integrity or clarity of a transmitted signal. Noise can be generated by natural or man-made sources. Designers of data networks take elaborate precautions to prevent noise from introducing errors into data.

NOS. Acronym for network operating system. *See* network operating system.

O

ohm. The standard unit of resistance to the flow of an electrical current. This unit is frequently used to indicate the impedance of coaxial cable. *See* impedance.

OSI model. A model consisting of seven layers used to define how networked computers communicate with each other. Each layer defines a different function from the physical connection in the network to the software application layer. The seven layers of the OSI model are Physical link, Data link, Network, Transport, Session, Presentation, and Application.

P

path. In DOS, a path is used to define a list of directories that DOS uses to search for programs to be executed. A path enables DOS to execute programs not located in the current default directory.

PC. Generally, an acronym for any type of personal computer. PC is frequently used to refer specifically to the class of personal computers that are based on the design of the original IBM PC.

personal computer. A computer of moderate capability designed to be dedicated to the use of a single individual.

phone connector. The familiar, standard, snap-in telephone connector used for connecting a variety of data networks cabled with unshielded twisted-pair cabling.

physical topology. The mechanical layout of a data network. Examples of physical topologies are star, bus, and token ring. The physical configuration of the wiring does not necessarily reflect the logic used to manage the data transmissions on the network—that is the function of the network logical topology.

protocol. In networks, a set of rules that enables devices to communicate without error.

Q

queue. A mechanism for holding tasks in order until they can be performed. The LANtastic print queues store print jobs in files until the requested printer becomes available. After the print job is stored in the queue, the printing program can return control to the user. The print job is printed in the background by LANtastic while the user performs other tasks.

R

RAM. Acronym for random-access memory. Data can be written to and read from RAM, and RAM is used to store data that must be accessed very quickly. Data in RAM is erased when the computer is turned off.

Repeater. A hardware device used to amplify and transmit the network signal. Repeaters enable a network cable segment to be extended past standard lengths.

ring network. A network topology that functions by passing data from one network node to the next. The most common examples are token ring and FDDI. Although these network standards have a ring logical topology, they are normally cabled with star topologies.

RJ-11. A phone connector that has four conductors. Most telephones use this type of connector, which is smaller than the RJ-45 connector used with UTP.

RJ-45. A phone connector that has eight conductors. This is the most popular connector for networks cabled with unshielded twisted-pair wiring.

RS-232C. An industry standard that describes serial-communication connections and protocols. This is the standard adhered to by most serial devices, such as modems. Originally intended only to interface terminals (data terminal equipment or DTEs) with modems (data communication equipment or DCEs), the standard has been stretched by manufacturers for interfacing many other device types, including printers, plotters, and mice.

S

serial communication. Data communication that transmits data one bit at a time. Serial communication can be done with one wire and a ground.

Server Message Block. A network communications protocol used by servers in Microsoft and IBM network operating systems to respond to network requests.

shield. A wire or conductive foil jacket that surrounds the conductors of a shielded cable. The shield protects signals on the conductors from interference, and prevents the radiation of signals into the environment.

SMB. Acronym for Server Message Block. *See* Server Message Block.

star network. A network physical topology in which each computer is networked by an individual cable connected to a central wiring hub. 10BASE-T, token ring, and ARCnet are examples of networks that use a star physical topology.

T

T connector. (Also called BNC T connector.) A connector used to connect a network interface card (NIC) to the network segment primarily in a 10BASE2 type of network (coax). The main segment is connected to the crossbar of the T; the network interface card is connected to the base of the T.

terminate-and-stay resident. A type of DOS program that is loaded and executed, and then returns control to DOS while remaining loaded in memory. Commonly referred to as TSRs, these programs enable more than one program to run at a given time. These programs must cooperate so they do not interfere with one another and so each program has access to the data and resources it requires. SHARE, LANBIOS, AILANBIO, and LANCACHE are examples of TSRs.

thick Ethernet. Ethernet based on a cable having a diameter of approximately .4 inch. The equivalent IEEE 802.3 standard is 10BASE5, a CSMA/CD network operating in baseband mode at a data rate of 10 megabits-per-second. The 5 designates a maximum segment length of approximately 500 meters. It also is referred to as standard Ethernet or thicknet. Because of its cost and the difficulty of working with the cable, thick Ethernet cable is used primarily for installations that must span more than 185 meters. *See* thin Ethernet.

thin Ethernet. Ethernet based on coaxial cable with a small diameter. The equivalent IEEE 802.3 standard is 10BASE2, a CSMA/CD network that operates in baseband mode at a data rate of 10 megabits-per-second. The 2 designates the maximum segment length of approximately 200 meters (actually, 185 meters). Also referred to as Thinnet or Cheapernet. *See* thick Ethernet.

tick. A measure of execution time in an IBM PC compatible microcomputer. A tick is equivalent to 1/18 of a second.

token passing. A media access control technology in which a station must be in possession of a token before being allowed to transmit data to the network. The token is a specific type of packet defined by the network protocol in use. Because only one station can possess the token at a time, contention cannot exist on a token-passing network. Also, because the token is passed from station to station according to a predetermined method, each station is guaranteed a regular opportunity to transmit. Token-passing networks are preferred in applications such as manufacturing process control, in which it is essential to guarantee all stations access to the network, regardless of the level of network traffic. Token ring, FDDI, and ARCnet use token passing to arbitrate network access.

token ring. A network standard developed by IBM that uses token passing to manage network access. Token rings have a ring logical topology and a star physical topology. Each station is cabled to a central concentrator designated as an MAU or MSAU, which consists of relays or electronic switches that connect or disconnect the station from the network ring. Two wire pairs connect each station with the MAU: one to receive data and one to transmit data. Packets are passed from station to station on the ring; each station receives and reamplifies the packet and then transmits the packet to the next station. When referring to IBM-specific products, the term is frequently capitalized: Token Ring.

topology. In networks, the network topology describes the arrangement of the network components. Coaxial Ethernet has a bus topology because each computer on the network is connected along a single piece of cable.

TSR. Acronym for terminate-and-stay resident. *See* terminate-and-stay resident.

twisted pair. Cabling that consists of two conductors that are twisted into a spiral. The spiral configuration reduces the tendency of the cable to transmit radio interference and reduces the effect of outside interference.

U

unshielded twisted pair (UTP). Twisted-pair cabling that is not surrounded by a shield. Because no shield is in place, unshielded twisted-pair wiring is somewhat more susceptible to interference than shielded twisted pair. *See* shield.

user account. A set of records that defines the characteristics of a LANtastic user, such as the username and password.

UTP. Acronym for unshielded twisted pair. *See* unshielded twisted pair.

W

WAN. Acronym for wide area network. *See* wide area network.

wide area network (WAN). A data network that connects computers over large geographic areas. Wide area networks are usually designed with relatively low performance due to the high cost of long-distance communications media such as leased telephone lines.

INDEX

Index

Symbols

INDEX

INDEX

INDEX

INDEX

INDEX

INDEX

INDEX

INDEX

INDEX

INDEX

INDEX

INDEX

INDEX

INDEX

INDEX

INDEX

INDEX

INDEX

INDEX

INDEX

INDEX

INDEX

INDEX

INDEX

INDEX

INDEX

INDEX

INDEX

INDEX

INDEX

INDEX

INDEX

INDEX

O

O (Operator) privilege, 169, 199, 315, 351, 380, 423, 448-449
Object Attributes dialog box, 519, 526, 530
Object command (Create menu), 516, 524, 548
Object menu commands
  Open, 515
object-oriented interfaces (Artisoft Exchange), 489-490
Objects menu commands
  Attributes, 516
  Delete, 547
  Open, 495
ohms (unit of resistance), 699
  see also impedance
omitting inventory items, 68
Open command (Edit menu), 243
Open command (File menu), 202, 248, 291, 348
Open command (Objects menu), 495, 515
Open Files (NET SHUTDOWN command), 597
opening Artisoft Linkbook, 482
Operator Notification Module (Server Control panel), 448-449
Operator Notify (O) privilege, 169, 199, 315, 351, 380, 423, 448-449
optimizing networks, 620-627
Options menu commands
  Address, 542, 547
  Attachments, 543, 545
  Delivery, 544
  Modify on Double-click, 195
Originator Address dialog box, 550
OSI model, 696
output devices (DOS printing), 313
Output Device dialog box, 187
Output Device field (Detailed Information screen), 315
overheated computers (hardware problems), 672

P

packets (data transmission), 42
Pager Address dialog box, 535
Pager Address option (New Object dialog box), 535
Pager Addresses (gateway addresses), 535-536
Pager Administration dialog box, 507
Pager Gateway option (Pager Address dialog box), 536
Pager ID Phone # option (Alpha Pager Address dialog box), 538
Pager menu commands
  Save, 536
Pager Service Access # option (Alpha Pager Address dialog box), 538
Paper Width field
  Resource Parameters dialog box (Windows), 353
  Detailed Information screen, 317
Parallel port driver (LANtastic Z installation), 651
parallel ports, 36, 315, 354
Parameter Data format (Management Utilities option), 408
parameters for server startup (network optimization), 622
parentheses in NET commands, 566
PARITY (RPS workstation configuration), 330
Participants dialog box, 558
Password command (Manage menu), 453
Password Expiration Date field
  Individual Account Management function (DOS), 379
  individual account setup, 163
Password field
  Account Parameters dialog box, 197
  Windows, 423
  Individual Account Management function (DOS), 379
  individual account setup, 163
  New Account dialog box, 497
Password icon, 453
Password Maintenance option
  DOS, 406-407
  Windows, 453

INDEX

INDEX

INDEX

INDEX

INDEX

INDEX

INDEX

INDEX

INDEX

INDEX

INDEX

INDEX

INDEX

INDEX

INDEX

INDEX

INDEX

Inside LANtastic 6.0
REGISTRATION CARD

Fill out this card to receive information about future networking books and other New Riders titles!

Name _____ **Title** _____

Company _____

Address _____

City/State/ZIP _____

I bought this book because: _____
_____

I purchased this book from:

☐ A bookstore (Name _____)

☐ A software or electronics store (Name _____)

☐ A mail order (Name of Catalog _____)

I purchase this many computer books each year:

☐ 1–5   ☐ 6 or more

I currently use these applications: _____
_____
_____
_____

I found these chapters to be the most informative: _____
_____

I found these chapters to be the least informative: _____
_____

Additional comments: _____
_____

☐ I would like to see my name in print! You may use my name and quote me in future New Riders products and promotions. My daytime phone number is: _____

New Riders Publishing 201 West 103rd Street • Indianapolis, Indiana 46290 USA

- -

Fold Here

New Riders Publishing
201 West 103rd Street
Indianapolis, Indiana 46290
USA

- -

Fold Here

PLACE
STAMP
HERE

New Riders Publishing
201 West 103rd Street
Indianapolis, Indiana 46290
USA

OPERATING SYSTEMS

INSIDE MS-DOS 6.2, 2E

NEW RIDERS PUBLISHING

A complete tutorial and reference!

MS-DOS 6.2
ISBN: 1-56205-289-6
$34.95 USA

DOS FOR NON-NERDS

MICHAEL GROH

Understanding this popular operating system is easy with this humorous, step-by-step tutorial.

Through DOS 6.0
ISBN: 1-56205-151-2
$18.95 USA

INSIDE SCO UNIX

STEVE GLINES, PETER SPICER,
BEN HUNSBERGER, & KAREN WHITE

Everything users need to know to use the UNIX operating system for everyday tasks.

**SCO Xenix 286, SCO Xenix 386,
SCO UNIX/System V 386**
ISBN: 1-56205-028-1
$29.95 USA

INSIDE SOLARIS SunOS

KARLA SAARI KITALONG,
STEVEN R. LEE, & PAUL MARZIN

Comprehensive tutorial and reference to SunOS!

**SunOS, Sun's version of UNIX for the
SPARC workstation, version 2.0**
ISBN: 1-56205-032-X
$29.95 USA

To Order, Call 1-800-428-5331

WINDOWS TITLES